HORSE TALES

HORSE TALES

Timeless and Compelling Stories of Horses and Their Riders

EDITED BY LAMAR UNDERWOOD

LYONS
PRESS

Essex, Connecticut

An imprint of Globe Pequot, the trade division of The Rowman & Littlefield Publishing Group, Inc.
4501 Forbes Blvd., Ste. 200
Lanham, MD 20706
www.rowman.com

Distributed NATIONAL BOOK NETWORK

British Library Cataloguing in Publication Information available

Library of Congress Cataloging-in-Publication Data

Names: Underwood, Lamar, editor.
Title: Horse tales : timeless and compelling stories of horses and their
  riders / edited by Lamar Underwood.
Description: Guilford, Connecticut : Lyons Press, [2022] | Summary: "A
  perfect gift for riders, writers, or literary buffs, Horse Tales is an
  essential collection of some of the most compelling stories ever written
  on the subject of horses"— Provided by publisher.
Identifiers: LCCN 2021060708 (print) | LCCN 2021060709 (ebook) | ISBN
  9781493065523 (cloth) | ISBN 9781493068210 (epub)
Subjects: LCSH: Horses. | Horsemanship. | Horses—Anecdotes. |
  Horsemanship—Anecdotes.
Classification: LCC SF301 .H675 2022 (print) | LCC SF301 (ebook) | DDC
  636.1—dc23/eng/20211221
LC record available at https://lccn.loc.gov/2021060708
LC ebook record available at https://lccn.loc.gov/2021060709

♾™ The paper used in this publication meets the minimum requirements of American National Standard for Information Sciences—Permanence of Paper for Printed Library Materials, ANSI/NISO Z39.48-1992.

When bestride him, I soar, I am a hawk: he trots the air; the earth sings when he touches it; the basest horn of his hoof is more musical than the pipe of Hermes.

—William Shakespeare, *Henry V*

CONTENTS

Introduction: The Horses in Print xi
    Lamar Underwood

1: Smoky the Cowhorse. 1
    Will James

2: Black Beauty's Early Home 15
    Anna Sewell

3: A Horse's Tale 22
    Mark Twain

4: White Horse Winter. 40
    Wilbur Daniel Steele

5: How Comanche Came into Camp. 55
    Elbridge Streeter Brooks

6: The Ben Hur Chariot Race. 65
    Lew Wallace

7: Wildfire 87
    Zane Grey

8: The Story of a Jockey. 103
    Richard Harding Davis

9: "Old Bill". 114
    Henry C. Wallace

10: World Record Is Set by Man o' War 120
    The New York Times

11: How I Bought and Trained Captain 124
    W. A. Sigsbee, His Owner

12: Sensations of a Cavalry Charge 137
    Winston Churchill

13: Philippa's Fox Hunt 145
    E. OE Somerville and Martin Ross

14: The Chimaera 162
    Nathaniel Hawthorne

15: Strider—The Story of a Horse 171
   Leo Tolstoy
16: Blue Murder 209
   Wilbur Daniel Steele
17: The Horse of Hurricane Reef 230
   Charles Tenney Jackson
18: The Round-Up 247
   Theodore Roosevelt
19: Esmé 261
   Saki (H. H. Munro)
20: The Story of the Pony Express 266
   Glenn D. Bradley
21: Mark Twain's Pony Express Adventure 284
   Mark Twain
22: The Pacing Mustang 287
   Ernest Thompson Seton
23: The Maltese Cat 306
   Rudyard Kipling
24: Jerry Strann and the Gift Horse 325
   Max Brand
25: How Blister Got His Name 336
   John Taintor Foote
26: The White Dandy Story 347
   Velma Caldwell Melville
27: The Great Match Race: Eclipse and Sir Henry 357
   An Old Turfman
28: Horses 367
   Stephen Crane
29: Memoirs of a Conquistador 380
   Bernal Di'Az Del Castillo
   Translated by John Ingram Lockhart (1844)
30: The Dun Horse 384
   George Bird Grinnell
31: His Love for His Old Gray Horse 390
   Laura Spencer Portor and Charles Marshall Graves

32: A Ride with a Mad Horse in a Freight-Car 398
    W. H. H. Murray
33: The Camp of the Wild Horse 416
    Washington Irving
34: The American Cavalry Horse 422
    Captain Wilmot E. Ellis
35: Anecdotes of American Horses 428
    Author Unknown
36: The Cumbersome Horse 433
    H. C. Bunner
37: Chu Chu 444
    Bret Harte
38: In Which True Becomes Justin Morgan 465
    Eleanor Waring Burnham
39: Memoirs of a Fox-Hunting Man 470
    Siegfried Sassoon
40: The Man Who Hunts and Doesn't Like It 481
    Anthony Trollope
41: Bones 487
    Helen Busher
42: Dark Clouds, Then Tall Grass 499
    Will James
Sources 513

INTRODUCTION

THE HORSES IN PRINT
By Lamar Underwood

As YOUR EDITOR FOR THIS COLLECTION OF HORSE STORIES, IT IS MY duty and privilege to describe the book you have in front of you. You might as well forget the old bromide "You can't tell a book by its cover." Of course you can! Our cover has already told you this is a book of horse stories, and the book's heft seems pleasing with the promise of extensive reading.

In my own way of urging you to give this collection a prominent spot beside your reading chair, I'm offering here the words of one of our authors, Will James. Among his many works on horses and horsemanship, his novel *Smoky the Cowhorse* is an enduring triumph. An excerpt from *Smoky* is our first chapter, and you'll soon see why the honest, straightforward prose of Will James is so appealing. His grammar was the type spoken by plainsmen and cowboy wranglers. In his preface to *Smoky*, Will James puts his love of horses into words that hit deep and hard.

To my way of thinking there's something wrong, or missing, with any person who hasn't got a soft spot in their heart for an animal of some kind. With most folks the dog stands highest as man's friend, then comes the horse, with others the cat is liked best as a pet, or a monkey is fussed over; but whatever kind of animal it is a person likes, it's all hunkydory so long as there's a place in the heart for one or a few of them.

I've never yet went wrong in sizing up a man by the kind of a horse he rode. A good horse always packs a good man, and I've always dodged the hombre what had no thought nor liking for his horse or other animals, for I figger that kind of gazabo is best to be left unacquainted with. No good would ever come of the meeting.

With me, my weakness lays towards the horse. My life, from the time I first squinted at daylight, has been with horses. I admire every step that creature makes. I know them and been thru so much with 'em that I've come to figger a big mistake was made when the horse was classed as an animal. To me, the horse is man's greatest, most useful, faithful, and powerful friend. He never whines when he's hungry or sore footed or tired, and he'll keep on a going for the human till he drops.

Since I have never owned a horse, my love of horse stories may need some explaining.

When I was much younger and lived adjacent to pastures and open spaces suitable for horses, I had no money. Later, when I had enough money for a horse, I had to make my living surrounded by city streets and concrete. With the absence of stables and horses, I missed all the chores of horse ownership—feeding, stables, exercise, and training. Such activities might have nurtured a horse story of my own, perhaps one for an anthology such as this.

For me, the horses in print have been a constant companion since my teenage years when I discovered that reading about horses was the best I could do to experience the skills of horsemanship and the love of trusted horses.

My only experiences of actually being in the saddle have come from the occasions when I rode to follow bird dogs in field trials. Rest assured, as I was when I first placed a foot in a stirrup, that the horses under me were not trained to run races or buck to throw me aside. No Bronco Billy feats for me.

The stories I have selected here were chosen for a diversity of characters and settings. They are not presented chronologically but are placed one story after another with the hope you will be struck by the appeal of each individual tale. Writers like Zane Grey, Anna Sewell of *Black Beauty* fame, Mark Twain, Leo Tolstoy, Max Brand, and many others will hold you hard with their prose, always with the comforting feeling that in a book of this size there will be many more dramas unfolding ahead.

Mostly, horses work for a living. That may seem a strange notion when your heart is about to burst with your affection for a familiar animal that hastens to your call or whistle, neighs to you from its stable, gallops across fields, and responds quickly to the commands of your reins or boot heels. Beyond any green pastures where they may graze in leisure, horses perform tasks from a long and diversified list. There are racehorse thoroughbreds, cart horses, show horses, broncs, trail horses, casual riding horses, and, once upon a time, plow horses.

There will come a time for all horses when they graze undisturbed in peaceful green pastures, no longer feisty and eager for work. Even then, they will listen for your call or whistle and appreciate troughs of food and water when weather and winter shut down life outdoors.

Some owners who have spent a lot of time in the saddle or caring for horses in pastures or stables have writing talent that enables them to share a great deal of their feelings about horses. Their prose leaps from the pages to become a "felt life" in your mind. You become part of the story. And as you will see in many of the stories here, the writers' talent and imagination put you into the minds of horses as they face challenges and interesting landscapes. From race tracks to mountain passes, such good prose makes the adventures ignite your affection for seeing a job well done.

Movies of great and beloved horses in action have been firmly locked in my affectionate memories since my long-ago preteen years. Whether seen in theaters or at home in front of DVD disks, the drama in memorable movies is hard hitting and emotionally gripping. Because this is not an introduction about horse movies, I'll not go into details. But I do want to mention a movie moment about horses related by the late Jack Palance on the Johnny Carson show.

Palance, playing the most evil (and evil looking) gunfighter ever, is first seen in the movie *Shane* as he rides into the lonely outpost that is the Grafton saloon. As related on Johnny Carson, Palance said the script called for him to come into view with the horse galloping. He fell off. Next they tried a slow trot. He almost fell off. Now director George Stevens told Palance to walk the horse into the scene. That worked fine and is the way you see gunfighter Jack Wilson for the first time in *Shane*.

As you will see again and again in the stories ahead, horses will do anything you want. But first you have to let them know exactly *what* you want. Sometimes that's not easy and creates drama—a good thing for storytellers.

—Lamar Underwood

(Editor's Note: The stories in this book were compiled from collections edited by Sharon B. Smith, Steven D. Price, Jessie Shiers, and Lamar Underwood.)

Smoky the Cowhorse

By Will James

As a Scribner's Publishing author, Will James (1892–1942) could claim a seat at the table with such literary giants as Ernest Hemingway, Thomas Wolfe, and F. Scott Fitzgerald. He was a superstar author despite being far from a "literary" type. When he wasn't writing and drawing pictures for his books, he was a real cowboy, a bronc-busting, cattle-driving, ranch hand cowboy. His many books began with Cowboys North and South *in 1924 and included such titles as* All in a Day's Riding *in 1933 and his masterpiece,* Smoky the Cowhorse, *published in 1926. His prose included grammatical errors and misspellings, among the many qualities that gave his works a pure straight-from-the-heart quality that endeared him to readers.*

THE HORSE IS NOT APPRECIATED AND NEVER WILL BE APPRECIATED enough—few humans, even them that works him, really know him, but then there's so much to know about him. I've wrote this book on only one horse and when I first started it I was afraid I'd run out of something to write, but I wasn't half thru when I begin to realize I had to do some squeezing to get the things in I wanted; and when I come to the last chapter was when I seen how if I spent my life writing on the horse alone and lived to be a hundred I'd only said maybe half of what I feel ought to be said.

The horse I wrote of in this book is not an exception, there's quite a few like him. He's not a fiction horse that's wrote about in a dream and made to do things that's against the nature of a horse to do. Smoky is just a horse, but all horse; and that I think is enough said.

As for Clint, the cowboy who "started" Smoky, he's no exception either. He's just a man who was able to see and bring out the good that was in the horse—and no matter how some writers describe the cowboy's handling of horses, I'm here to say that I can produce many a cowboy what can show feelings for a horse the same as Clint done.

But Smoky met other humans besides Clint, many others, and of all kinds, and that's where the story comes in. And now, my main ambition as I turn Smoky loose to making hisself acquainted is that the folks who will get to know him will see that horse as I seen him.

A RANGE COLT

It seemed like Mother Nature was sure agreeable that day when the little black colt came to the range world and tried to get a footing with his long wobbly legs on the brown prairie sod. Short stems of new green grass was trying to make their way up thru the last year's faded growth, and reaching for the sun's warm rays. Taking in all that could be seen, felt, and inhaled, there was no day, time, nor place that could beat that spring morning on the sunny side of the low prairie butte where Smoky the colt was foaled.

"Smoky" wouldn't have fitted the colt as a name just then on account he was jet black, but that name wasn't attached onto him till he was a four-year-old, which was when he first started being useful as a saddle horse. He didn't see the first light of day thru no box stall window, and there was no human around to make a fuss over him and try to steady him on his feet for them first few steps. Smoky was just a little range colt, and all the company he had that first morning of his life was his watchful mammy.

Smoky wasn't quite an hour old when he begin to take interest in things. The warm spring sun was doing its work and kept a pouring warmth all over that slick little black hide, and right on thru his little body, till pretty soon his head come up kinda shaky and he begin nosing around them long front legs that was stretched out in front of him. His mammy was close by him, and at the first move the colt made she rim her nose along his short neck and nickered. Smoky's head went up another two inches at the sound, and his first little answering nicker was heard. Of course a person would of had to listen mighty close to hear it, but then if you'd a watched his nostrils quivering you could tell that's just what he was trying to do.

That was the starting of Smoky. Pretty soon his ears begin to work back and forth towards the sound his mammy would make as she moved. He was trying to locate just where she was. Then something moved right in front of his nose about a foot; it'd been there quite a good spell but he'd never realized it before; besides his vision was a little dim yet and he wasn't interested much till that something moved again and planted itself still closer.

Being it was right close he took a sniff at it. That sniff recorded itself into his brain and as much as told him that all was well. It was one of his mammy's legs. His ears perked up and he tried nickering again with a heap better result than the first time.

One good thing called for another and natural like he made a sudden scramble to get up, but his legs wouldn't work right, and just about when he'd got his belly clear of the ground, and as he was resting there for another try at the rest of the way up, one of his front legs quivered and buckled at the elbow, and the whole works went down.

He layed there flat on his side and breathing hard. His mammy nickered encouragement, and it wasn't long when his head was up again and his legs spraddled out all around him the same as before. He was going to try again, but next time he was going to be more sure of his ground. He was studying it seemed like, and sniffing of his legs and then the earth, like he was trying to figger out how he was going to get one to stand up on the other. His mammy kept a circling around and a talking to him in horse language; she'd give him a shove with her nose then walk away and watch him.

The spring air, which I think is most for the benefit of all that's young, had a lot to do to keep Smoky from laying still for very long. His vision was getting clearer fast, and his strength was coming in just as fast. Not far away, but still too far for Smoky to see, was little calves, little white-faced fellers a playing and bucking around and letting out wall-eyed bellers at their mammies, running out a ways and then running back, tails up, at a speed that'd make a greyhound blush for shame.

There was other little colts too all a cavorting around and tearing up good sod, but with all them calves and colts that was with the bunches of cattle or horses scattered out on the range, the same experience of helplessness that Smoky was going thru had been theirs for a spell, and a few hadn't been as lucky as Smoky in their first squint at daylight. Them few had come to the range world when the ground was still covered with snow, or else cold spring rains was a pouring down to wet 'em to the bone.

Smoky's mother had sneaked out of the bunch a few days before Smoky came, and hid in a lonely spot where she'd be sure that no cattle nor horses or even riders would be around. In a few days, and when Smoky would be strong enough to lope out, she'd go back again; but in the meantime she wanted to be alone with her colt and put all her attention on him, without having to contend with chasing off big inquisitive geldings or jealous fillies.

She was of range blood, which means mostly mustang with strains of Steeldust or Coach throwed in. If hard winters come and the range was covered with heavy snows, she knowed of high ridges where the strong winds kept a few spots bare and where feed could be got. If droughts came to dry up the grass and water holes, she sniffed the air for moisture and drifted out acrost the plain which was her home range, to the high mountains where things was more normal. There was cougars and wolves in that high country, but her mustang instinct made her the "fittest." She circled around and never went under where the lion was perched a waiting for her, and the wolf never found her where she could be cornered.

Smoky had inherited that same instinct of his mammy's, but on that quiet spring morning he wasn't at all worried about enemies. His mammy was there, and besides he had a hard job ahead that was taking all of his mind to figger out: that was to stand on them long things which was fastened to his body and which kept a spraddling out in all directions.

The first thing to do was to gather 'em under him and try again. He did that easy enough, and then he waited and gathered up all the strength that was in him. He sniffed at the ground to make sure it was there and then his head went up, his front feet stretched out in front of him, and

with his hind legs all under him, he used all that strength he'd been stor-
ing up and pushed himself up on his front feet, his hind legs straightened
up to steady him; and as luck would have it there was just enough distance
between each leg to keep him up there. All be had to do was to keep them
legs stiff and from buckling up under him, which wasn't at all easy, cause
getting up to where he was had used up a lot of his strength, and them
long legs of his was doing a heap of shaking.

All would of been well maybe, only his mammy nickered "that's a good
boy," and that's what queered Smoky. His head went up proud as a peacock
and he forgot all about keeping his props stiff and under him. Down he
went the whole length of his legs, and there he layed the same as before.

But he didn't lay long this time. He either liked the sport of going
up and coming down or else he was getting peeved; he was up again,
mighty shaky, but he was up sure enough. His mammy came to him. She
sniffed at him and he sniffed back. Then nature played another hand and
he nursed, the first nourishment was took in, his tummy warmed up and
strength came fast. Smoky was an hour and a half old and up to stay.

The rest of that day was full of events for Smoky. He explored the
whole country, went up big mountains two feet high, wide valleys six
or eight feet acrost, and at one time was as far as twelve feet away from
his mammy all by himself. He shied at a rock once; it was a dangerous-
looking rock, and he kicked at it as he went past. All that action being put
on at once come pretty near being too much for him and he come close
to measuring his whole length on Mother Earth once again. But luck was
with him, and taking it all he had a mighty good time. When the sun
went to sinking over the blue ridges in the West, Smoky, he missed all the
beauty of the first sunset in his life—he was stretched out full length, of
his own accord this time, and sound asleep.

The night was a mighty good rival of what the day had been. All
the stars was out and showing off, and the braves was a chasing the buffalo plum around the Big Dipper, the water hole of The Happy Hunting
Grounds. But all that was lost to Smoky; he was still asleep and recuperating from his first day's adventures, and most likely he'd kept on sleeping
for a good long spell, only his mammy who was standing guard over him
happened to get a little too close and stepped on his tail.

Smoky must of been in the middle of some bad dream. His natural instinct might of pictured some enemy to his mind, and something that looked like a wolf or a bear must of had him cornered for sure. Anyway, when he felt his tail pinched that way he figgered that when a feller begins to feel it's sure time to act, and he did. He shot up right under his mammy's chin, let out a squeal, and stood there ready to fight. He took in the country for feet and feet around and looking for the enemy that'd nipped him, and finally in his scouting around that way he run acrost the shadow of his mammy. That meant but one thing, safety; and that accounted for and put away as past left room for a craving he'd never noticed in his excitement. He was hungry, and proceeded right then and there to take on a feed of his mammy's warm, rich milk.

The sky was beginning to get light in the East, the stars was fading away and the buffalo hunters had went to rest. A few hours had passed since Smoky had been woke up out of his bad dream and there he was, asleep again. He'd missed his first sunset and now he was sleeping thru his first sunrise, but he was going to be prepared for that new day's run, and the strength he was accumulating through them sleeps and between feeds would sure make him fit to cover a lot of territory.

There wasn't a move out of him till the sun was well up and beginning to throw a good heat. He stacked up on a lot of that heat, and pretty soon one of his ears moved, then the other. He took a long breath and stretched. Smoky was coming to life.—His mammy nickered, and that done the trick; Smoky raised his head, looked around, and proceeded to get up. After a little time that was done and bowing his neck he stretched again. Smoky was ready for another day.

The big day started right after Smoky had his feed; then his mother went to grazing and moving away straight to the direction of some trees a mile or so to the south. A clear spring was by them trees, and water is what Smoky's mammy wanted the most right then. She was craving for a drink of that cold water, but you'd never thought it by the way she traveled. She'd nose around at the grass and wait for spells, so as little Smoky could keep up with her and still find time to investigate everything what throwed a shadow.

A baby cottontail had jumped up once right under his nose, stood there a second too scared to move, and pretty soon made a high dive between the colt's long legs and hit for his hole; Smoky never seen the rabbit or even knowed he was there or he might of been running yet, cause that's what he'd been looking for, an excuse to run. But he finally made up an excuse, and a while later as he brushed past a long dry weed and it tickled his belly, he let out a squeal and went from there.

His long legs tangled and untangled themselves as he run, and he was sure making speed.

Around and around he went and finally lined out straight away from where his mammy was headed. She nickered for him and waited, all patience. He turned after a spell and headed for his mammy again the same as tho he'd run acrost another enemy at the other end; and as he got close to his mammy he let out a buck, a squeal, a snort, and stopped—he was sure some little wild horse.

It took a couple of hours for them two to make that mile to the spring. The mother drank a lot of that good water, a few long breaths and drank some more till the thirst was all gone. Smoky came over and nosed at the pool, but he didn't take on any of the fluid, it looked just like so much thin air to him, the same with the tender green grass that was beginning to grow in bunches everywhere; it was just growing for him to run on.

The rest of that day was pretty well used up around that one spot; adventures of all kinds was numerous for Smoky, and when he wasn't stretched out and asleep there was plenty of big stumps in the cotton-wood grove that could be depended on to give him the scare he'd be looking for.

But there was other things and more threatening than stumps which Smoky hadn't as yet spotted, like for instance—a big cayote had squatted and been watching him thru dead willow branches. He wasn't at all inter-ested in the action Smoky was putting into his play, and only wished the colt's mammy would move away a little further when he would then take a chance and try to get him down—colt meat was his favorite dish and he sure wasn't going to let no chance slip by even if it took a whole day's waiting for one to show itself.

A couple of chances had come his way but they was queered by Smoky's mammy being too close, and he knowed better than show himself and get run down by them hoofs of hers. Finally, and when he seen his appetite wouldn't win anything by sticking around that spot any longer, he took a last sniff and came out of his hiding place. Keeping the willows between him and the horses, he loped out till he was at a safe running distance and where he could see all around him, and there he squatted again, in plain sight this time. He hadn't quite made up his mind as yet whether to go or stick around a while longer.—Just about then Smoky spots him.

To him, the cayote was just another stump, but more interesting than the others he'd kicked at, on account that this stump moved, and that promised a lot of excitement. With a bowed neck and kinked tail Smoky trotted up towards the cayote. The cayote just set there and waited and when the colt got to within a few feet from him, he started away and just fast enough so as the colt's curiosity would make him follow. If he could only get the colt over the ridge and out of his mammy's sight.

It all was only a lot of fun to Smoky, and besides he was bound to find out what was that grey and yellow object that could move and run and didn't at all look like his mammy. His instinct was warning him steady as he went, but curiosity had the best of him, and it wasn't till he was over the hill before his instinct got above his curiosity and he seen that all wasn't well.

The cayote had turned and quicker than a flash made a jump for Smoky's throat.—The generations of mustang blood that'd fought the lobo and cougar, and which was the same blood that flowed in Smoky's veins, is all that saved the colt. That inherited instinct made him do the right thing at the right time, he whirled quicker than lightning and let fly with both hind feet with the result that the cayote's teeth just pinched the skin under his jaws. But even at that, he wasn't going to get rid of his enemy (it was a sure enough enemy this time) that easy, and as he kicked he felt the weight of the cayote, and then a sharp pain on his ham strings.

Smoky was scared, and he let out a squeal that sure made every living thing in that neighborhood set up and wonder; it was a plain and loud distress signal, and it was answered. His mammy shot up the hill, took in the goings-on at a glance, and ears back, teeth a shining, tore up the earth and lit into the battle like a ton of dynamite.

The battle was over in a second, and with hunks of yellow fur a flying all directions it wound up in a chase. The cayote was in the lead and he stayed in the lead till a second hill took him out of sight.

Smoky was glad to follow his mammy back to the spring and on to the other side a ways. He didn't shy at the stumps he passed on the way, and the twig that tickled his tummy didn't bring no play. He was hungry and tired, and when the first was tended to and his appetite called for no more he lost no time to picking out a place to rest his weary bones. A thin stream of blood was drying on one of his hind legs, but there was no pain, and when the sun set and the shadow of his mammy spread out over him he was sound asleep, and maybe dreaming of stumps, of stumps that moved.

When the sun came up the next morning, Smoky was up too, and eyes half closed was standing still as the big boulder next to him and sunned himself. A stiff hind leg was a reminder of what happened the day before, but the experience was forgotten far as dampening his spirits was concerned, even the stiffness wouldn't hold him back from whatever the new day would hold. He'd always remember the cayote, and from then on never mistake him for a stump, but that sure wasn't going to take any play out of him.

He was two days old now and strength had piled up fast, he felt there was no trail too long for him and when the sun was a couple of hours high that morning and his mother showed indications that she wanted to drift he sure wasn't dragging along behind. The stiffness gradually went out of his hind leg as he traveled, and by the afternoon of that day he was again shying at everything and sometimes even shying at nothing at all.

They kept a traveling and traveling, and it seemed like to Smoky that the trail was getting pretty long after all. They skirted the flat along the foot of the mountains, crossed one high ridge, and many creeks, and still his mother was drifting on. She wouldn't hardly even stop for him to nurse, and Smoky was getting cranky, and tired.

The pace kept up till the sun was well on its way down, when it slackened some and finally the mother went to grazing. A short while later Smoky was layed out full length and dead to the world.

Smoky didn't know and didn't care much just then, but his mammy was headed back to her home range, where there was lots of horses and other little colts for him to play with; and when late that night she lined out again traveling steady he wasn't in any too good a humor.

Finally it seemed like they'd got there, for his mammy after watering at a creek went to grazing at the edge of some big cottonwoods; she showed no indications of wanting to go any further. Right there Smoky was willing to take advantage of the chance and recuperate for all he was worth. The sun came up, but Smoky was in the shade of the cottonwoods what was beginning to leaf out. He slept on and a twitching ear once in long spells is all that showed he was still alive.

That day never seen much of him; once in a while he'd get up and nurse but right away after he'd disappear again and stretch out flat on the warm earth.

He kept that up till way in the middle of the next night, and it was well towards morning before he felt like he was all horse again.

He come out of it in fine shape though, and he was stronger than ever. His vision was taking more territory too, and he was getting so he could see near half as far as his mammy could. She was the first to see the bunch of range horses trailing in to water early that morning. Smoky heard her nicker as she recognized the bunch and it drawed a heap of interest as to what she was nickering about, for he was right there alongside of her and he couldn't see nothing for her to nicker at, but pretty soon he could hear the horses as they trailed towards him. His ears straightened towards the sound and a while later he could make out the shapes of 'em. Smoky just kind of quivered at the sight of so many that looked like his mammy. He was all interested, but at the same time, and even tho his instinct told him that all was well, he had no hankering to leave his mammy's side till he knowed for sure just what was up.

The mother watched the bunch coming closer with ears pointed straight ahead, but soon as some of the leaders discovered little Smoky there was a commotion and they all begin crowding in to get a look at and greet the newcomer, about which time the mother layed her ears back. It was a warning that none of 'em come too close.

Little Smoky's knees was a shaking under him at the sight of so many of his kind; he leaned against his mammy half afraid, but his head was up far as he could get it and facing 'em and showed by the shine in his eyes that he liked the whole proceeding mighty well at that. He rubbed nostrils with a strange gelding which was braver than the rest and dared come close, and when that gelding was nipped at by his mammy he had a mighty strong hankering to help her along just for fun, and nip him himself.

The preliminary introduction took a good hour, and the mother stood guard; not for fear that any of 'em would harm Smoky, but she wanted it understood from the start that he was her little colt and she had the say over him. It finally was understood, but it took all that day and part of the next for the bunch to get used in having the new little feller around and quit making a fuss over him.

They was all jealous of one another and fought amongst themselves to be the only one near him, and his mother, of course she'd declared herself from the start, and it was took for granted from all around that her place in Smoky's heart couldn't be considered, and all knowed better than try and chase her away from him. Fillies and old mares, young geldings and old ponies and all, had it out as to which was the most fit to tag along and play with Smoky and keep a watchful eye over him along with his mammy. All wanted the job, but a big buckskin saddle horse who all the time had been the boss of the herd took it to hand to show them that he would be the all around guardeen for Smoky, and second only to his mammy. He delivered a few swift kicks, pounded on some ribs, left teeth marks on shiny hides, and after taking one last look and making sure that all was persuaded, grazed out towards Smoky who by his mammy had watched the whole proceeding with a heap of interest.

There was three other little colts in the bunch besides Smoky, and each time one of them little fellers came the buckskin horse had to whip the bunch so as he'd have the say over the newest one. Now Smoky was the newest one, and the buckskin horse had first rights as an outsider once again. He was an old horse full of scars showing where he'd had many a scrap; there was saddle marks on his back and at one time he had been a mighty fine cowhorse. Now he was pensioned; he'd more than earned a rest and all he had to do for the rest of his life was to pick out good feed grounds for the winter, shady places and tenderest green grass for the summer, and his other interest in life was them little colts that came in spring time.

Smoky's mother was young, at least ten years younger than the buckskin horse, but the buckskin was like a colt compared to her when it come to be playful. She had the responsibility of Smoky and while she let him play with her, kick or bite at her, she never played with him and once in a while if he'd get too rough she'd let him know about it. She loved little Smoky with all her heart and would of died for him any time, and her main interest was to see that she kept in condition so that Smoky would never be stunted by lacking of rich milk. She had no time for play.

And that's where the old buckskin came in. Him and Smoky was soon acquainted, in a short while they was playing, Smoky would kick at him while the big buckskin nipped him easy and careful along the flank, then he'd run away from him, and the little colt had a lot of fun chasing that big hunk of horseflesh all over the country. The rest of the bunch would watch the two play and with no effort to hide how jealous they felt.

Smoky's mother kept her eye on the buckskin, but never interfered, she knowed, and it was only when Smoky came back to her, tired and hungry, that she put her ears back and warned him to keep away.

It took a few days before the buckskin would allow any of the other horses to get near Smoky, and then he had no say about it for he found that Smoky had his own ideas about things, and if he wanted to mingle in with the other horses that was his business, and all the buckskin could do then was to try and keep the other horses away. That was quite a job, specially if Smoky wanted to be with them. So the buckskin finally had to give it up and do the best he could which was to see that none of 'em done him any harm. But none of 'em had any intentions of doing the little colt any harm, and as it was it looked like Smoky had 'em all buffaloed. He'd tear in after some big horse like he was going to eat him up and all that big horse would do was to scatter out like the devil was after him.

Smoky was the boss and pet of the herd for a good two weeks and then one day, here comes another little feller, a little bay colt just two days old and trailing in alongside his mammy. Smoky was left in the background and witnessed the same fuss and commotion that was done over him that morning by the creek. The buckskin horse once again fought his way in that new little feller's heart, and right away he forgot Smoky.

But Smoky never seen anything wrong to that, he went on to playing with every horse that would have him and it wasn't long till he picked up with a young filly and afterwards went to mingling with other young colts.

From then on Smoky had more freedom, he could go out a ways without having some big overgrowed horse tagging along, but he never went far and if he did he always came back a heap faster than when he started out. But them spring days was great for Smoky; he found out a lot of things amongst which was, that grass was good to eat, and water mighty fine to drink when the day was hot. He seen cayotes again and the bigger he got the less he was afraid of 'em till he finally went to chasing every one of 'em he'd see.

Then one day he run acrost another yellow animal. That animal didn't look dangerous, and what's more it was hard for Smoky to make out just what it was, and he was bound to find out. He followed that animal plum to the edge of some willows, and the queer part of it was that animal didn't seem at all in a hurry to get away, it was mumbling along and just taking its time and Smoky was mighty tempted to plant one front foot right in the middle of it and do some pawing, but as luck would have it he didn't have the chance, it'd got in under some willows and all that was sticking out was part of the animal's tail. Smoky took a sniff at it without learning anything outside that it shook a little. There didn't seem to be no danger, so the next sniff he took was a little closer, and that done the trick. Smoky let out a squeal and a snort as he felt his nostrils punctured in half a dozen places with four-inch porcupine quills.

But Smoky was lucky, for if he'd been a couple of inches closer there'd been quills rammed into his nose plum up to his eyes, which would've caused a swelling in such size that he couldn't of been able to eat and most likely starve to death. As it was there was just a few of them quills in his nostrils, and compared to the real dose he might of got, it was just a mild warning to him. Another lesson.

It was a few days later when he met another strange animal, or strange animals, for there was many of 'em. He didn't get much interest out of them somehow, but while they was handy maybe it was just as well for him to have a close look at one. Besides he had nothing else to do, and his mammy wasn't far away.

His instinct had no warning to give as he strutted towards the smallest one of the strangers which he'd picked to investigate. He wasn't afraid of this animal and this animal didn't seem afraid of him so Smoky kept a getting closer till one was within a couple of feet of the other. Both Smoky and this stranger was young, and mighty inquisitive, and neither as yet knowed that they'd sure be seeing plenty of each other's kind as they get older, that they'll be meeting thru the round-ups at the "cutting-grounds," on "day-herd" and on "night-guard," on the long, hot, and dusty trails. A cowboy will be riding Smoky then and keeping a whole herd on the move, a whole herd of the kind that little Smoky was so busy investigating that day. They'll be full grown then, and there'll be other young ones to take the place of them that's trailed in to the shipping point.

But Smoky wasn't as yet worried or even thought on what was to come, neither was the little whitefaced calf he was exchanging squints with; and when the critter called her long-eared, split-hoofed baby to her side, Smoky just kicked up his heels, put his head down, and bucked and crowhopped all the way to where his mammy and the rest of the bunch was grazing.

2

Black Beauty's Early Home

By Anna Sewell

The 1877 novel Black Beauty *that was Anna Sewell's only published work is now considered one of the top ten bestselling novels for children, although it was intended at the time for an adult audience. She died only five months after* Black Beauty's *publication, having lived long enough to see her only novel become a success. Sewell was born in 1820 in Great Yarmouth, Norfolk, into a devout Quaker family. At fourteen, Sewell slipped and severely injured her ankles. For the rest of her life she could not stand without a crutch or walk for any length of time. For greater mobility, she frequently used horse-drawn carriages, which contributed to her love of horses and concern for the humane treatment of animals. Sewell wrote the manuscript of* Black Beauty *in the period between 1871 and 1877. During this time her health was declining; she was often so weak that she was confined to her bed. Writing was a challenge. She dictated the text to her mother and from 1876 began to write on slips of paper that her mother then transcribed. The book is considered to be one of the first English novels to be written from the perspective of a nonhuman animal, in this case a horse. Although it is now considered a children's classic, Sewell originally wrote it for those who worked with horses. She said, "A special aim was to induce kindness, sympathy, and an understanding treatment of horses."*

THE FIRST PLACE THAT I CAN WELL REMEMBER WAS A LARGE PLEASANT meadow with a pond of clear water in it. Some shady trees leaned over it, and rushes and water-lilies grew at the deep end. Over the hedge on one side we looked into a plowed field, and on the other we looked over a gate at our master's house, which stood by the roadside; at the top of the meadow was a grove of fir trees, and at the bottom a running brook overhung by a steep bank.

While I was young I lived upon my mother's milk, as I could not eat grass. In the daytime I ran by her side, and at night I lay down close by her. When it was hot we used to stand by the pond in the shade of the trees, and when it was cold we had a nice warm shed near the grove.

As soon as I was old enough to eat grass my mother used to go out to work in the daytime, and come back in the evening.

There were six young colts in the meadow besides me; they were older than I was; some were nearly as large as grown-up horses. I used to run with them, and had great fun; we used to gallop all together round and round the field as hard as we could go. Sometimes we had rather rough play, for they would frequently bite and kick as well as gallop.

One day, when there was a good deal of kicking, my mother whinnied to me to come to her, and then she said:

"I wish you to pay attention to what I am going to say to you. The colts who live here are very good colts, but they are cart-horse colts, and of course they have not learned manners. You have been well-bred and well-born; your father has a great name in these parts, and your grandfather won the cup two years at the Newmarket races; your grandmother had the sweetest temper of any horse I ever knew, and I think you have never seen me kick or bite. I hope you will grow up gentle and good, and never learn bad ways; do your work with a good will, lift your feet up well when you trot, and never bite or kick even in play."

I have never forgotten my mother's advice; I knew she was a wise old horse, and our master thought a great deal of her. Her name was Duchess, but he often called her Pet.

Our master was a good, kind man. He gave us good food, good lodging, and kind words; he spoke as kindly to us as he did to his little children. We were all fond of him, and my mother loved him very much.

When she saw him at the gate she would neigh with joy, and trot up to him. He would pat and stroke her and say, "Well, old Pet, and how is your little Darkie?" I was a dull black, so he called me Darkie; then he would give me a piece of bread, which was very good, and sometimes he brought a carrot for my mother. All the horses would come to him, but I think we were his favorites. My mother always took him to the town on a market day in a light gig.

There was a plowboy, Dick, who sometimes came into our field to pluck blackberries from the hedge. When he had eaten all he wanted he would have what he called fun with the colts, throwing stones and sticks at them to make them gallop. We did not much mind him, for we could gallop off; but sometimes a stone would hit and hurt us.

One day he was at this game, and did not know that the master was in the next field; but he was there, watching what was going on; over the hedge he jumped in a snap, and catching Dick by the arm, he gave him such a box on the ear as made him roar with the pain and surprise. As soon as we saw the master we trotted up nearer to see what went on.

"Bad boy!" he said, "bad boy! to chase the colts. This is not the first time, nor the second, but it shall be the last. There—take your money and go home; I shall not want you on my farm again." So we never saw Dick any more. Old Daniel, the man who looked after the horses, was just as gentle as our master, so we were well off.

Before I was two years old a circumstance happened which I have never forgotten. It was early in the spring; there had been a little frost in the night, and a light mist still hung over the woods and meadows. I and the other colts were feeding at the lower part of the field when we heard, quite in the distance, what sounded like the cry of dogs. The oldest of the colts raised his head, pricked his ears, and said, "There are the hounds!" and immediately cantered off, followed by the rest of us to the upper part of the field, where we could look over the hedge and see several fields beyond. My mother and an old riding horse of our master's were also standing near, and seemed to know all about it.

"They have found a hare," said my mother, "and if they come this way we shall see the hunt."

And soon the dogs were all tearing down the field of young wheat next to ours. I never heard such a noise as they made. They did not bark, nor howl, nor whine, but kept on a "yo! yo, o, o! yo! yo, o, o!" at the top of their voices. After them came a number of men on horseback, some of them in green coats, all galloping as fast as they could. The old horse snorted and looked eagerly after them, and we young colts wanted to be galloping with them, but they were soon away into the fields lower down; here it seemed as if they had come to a stand; the dogs left off barking, and ran about every way with their noses to the ground.

"They have lost the scent," said the old horse; "perhaps the hare will get off."

"What hare?" I said.

"Oh! I don't know what hare; likely enough it may be one of our own hares out of the woods; any hare they can find will do for the dogs and men to run after"; and before long the dogs began their "yo! yo, o, o!" again, and back they came altogether at full speed, making straight for our meadow at the part where the high bank and hedge overhang the brook.

"Now we shall see the hare," said my mother; and just then a hare wild with fright rushed by and made for the woods. On came the dogs; they burst over the bank, leaped the stream, and came dashing across the field followed by the huntsmen. Six or eight men leaped their horses clean over, close upon the dogs. The hare tried to get through the fence; it was too thick, and she turned sharp round to make for the road, but it was too late; the dogs were upon her with their wild cries; we heard one shriek, and that was the end of her. One of the huntsmen rode up and whipped off the dogs, who would soon have torn her to pieces. He held her up by the leg torn and bleeding, and all the gentlemen seemed well pleased.

As for me, I was so astonished that I did not at first see what was going on by the brook; but when I did look there was a sad sight; two fine horses were down, one was struggling in the stream, and the other was groaning on the grass. One of the riders was getting out of the water covered with mud, the other lay quite still.

"His neck is broke," said my mother.

"And serve him right, too," said one of the colts.

I thought the same, but my mother did not join with us.

"Well, no," she said, "you must not say that; but though I am an old horse, and have seen and heard a great deal, I never yet could make out why men are so fond of this sport; they often hurt themselves, often spoil good horses, and tear up the fields, and all for a hare or a fox, or a stag, that they could get more easily some other way; but we are only horses, and don't know."

While my mother was saying this we stood and looked on. Many of the riders had gone to the young man; but my master, who had been watching what was going on, was the first to raise him. His head fell back and his arms hung down, and every one looked very serious. There was no noise now; even the dogs were quiet, and seemed to know that something was wrong. They carried him to our master's house. I heard afterward that it was young George Gordon, the squire's only son, a fine, tall young man, and the pride of his family.

There was now riding off in all directions to the doctor's, to the farrier's, and no doubt to Squire Gordon's, to let him know about his son. When Mr. Bond, the farrier, came to look at the black horse that lay groaning on the grass, he felt him all over, and shook his head; one of his legs was broken. Then some one ran to our master's house and came back with a gun; presently there was a loud bang and a dreadful shriek, and then all was still; the black horse moved no more.

My mother seemed much troubled; she said she had known that horse for years, and that his name was "Rob Roy"; he was a good horse, and there was no vice in him. She never would go to that part of the field afterward.

Not many days after we heard the church-bell tolling for a long time, and looking over the gate we saw a long, strange black coach that was covered with black cloth and was drawn by black horses; after that came another and another and another, and all were black, while the bell kept tolling, tolling. They were carrying young Gordon to the churchyard to bury him. He would never ride again. What they did with Rob Roy I never knew; but 'twas all for one little hare.

I was now beginning to grow handsome; my coat had grown fine and soft, and was bright black. I had one white foot and a pretty white star on my forehead. I was thought very handsome; my master would not sell me till I was four years old; he said lads ought not to work like men, and colts ought not to work like horses till they were quite grown up.

When I was four years old Squire Gordon came to look at me. He examined my eyes, my mouth, and my legs; he felt them all down; and then I had to walk and trot and gallop before him. He seemed to like me, and said, "When he has been well broken in he will do very well." My master said he would break me in himself, as he should not like me to be frightened or hurt, and he lost no time about it, for the next day he began.

Every one may not know what breaking in is, therefore I will describe it. It means to teach a horse to wear a saddle and bridle, and to carry on his back a man, woman or child; to go just the way they wish, and to go quietly. Besides this he has to learn to wear a collar, a crupper, and a breeching, and to stand still while they are put on; then to have a cart or a chaise fixed behind, so that he cannot walk or trot without dragging it after him; and he must go fast or slow, just as his driver wishes. He must never start at what he sees, nor speak to other horses, nor bite, nor kick, nor have any will of his own; but always do his master's will, even though he may be very tired or hungry; but the worst of all is, when his harness is once on, he may neither jump for joy nor lie down for weariness. So you see this breaking in is a great thing.

I had of course long been used to a halter and a headstall, and to be led about in the fields and lanes quietly, but now I was to have a bit and bridle; my master gave me some oats as usual, and after a good deal of coaxing he got the bit into my mouth, and the bridle fixed, but it was a nasty thing! Those who have never had a bit in their mouths cannot think how bad it feels; a great piece of cold hard steel as thick as a man's finger to be pushed into one's mouth, between one's teeth, and over one's tongue, with the ends coming out at the corner of your mouth, and held fast there by straps over your head, under your throat, round your nose, and under your chin; so that no way in the world can you get rid of the nasty hard thing; it is very bad! yes, very bad! at least I thought so; but I knew my mother always wore one when she went out, and all horses did when they were grown up; and so, what with the nice oats, and what with my master's pats, kind words, and gentle ways, I got to wear my bit and bridle.

Next came the saddle, but that was not half so bad; my master put it on my back very gently, while old Daniel held my head; he then made the girths fast under my body, patting and talking to me all the time; then I had a few oats, then a little leading about; and this he did every day till I began to look for the oats and the saddle. At length, one morning, my master got on my back and rode me round the meadow on the soft grass. It certainly did feel queer; but I must say I felt rather proud to carry my master, and as he continued to ride me a little every day I soon became accustomed to it.

The next unpleasant business was putting on the iron shoes; that too was very hard at first. My master went with me to the smith's forge, to see that I was not hurt or got any fright. The blacksmith took my feet in his hand, one after the other, and cut away some of the hoof. It did not pain me, so I stood still on three legs till he had done them all. Then he took a piece of iron the shape of my foot, and clapped it on, and drove some nails through the shoe quite into my hoof, so that the shoe was firmly on. My feet felt very stiff and heavy, but in time I got used to it.

And now having got so far, my master went on to break me to harness; there were more new things to wear. First, a stiff heavy collar just on my neck, and a bridle with great side-pieces against my eyes called blinkers, and blinkers indeed they were, for I could not see on either side, but only straight in front of me; next, there was a small saddle with a nasty stiff strap that went right under my tail; that was the crupper. I hated the crupper; to have my long tail doubled up and poked through that strap was almost as bad as the bit. I never felt more like kicking, but of course I could not kick such a good master, and so in time I got used to everything, and could do my work as well as my mother.

3

A Horse's Tale

By Mark Twain

The great American humorist and novelist Samuel Clemens, who used the pen name Mark Twain, was a campaigner against cruelty to animals, particularly during the last few years of his life. His greatest weapon was his pen, and his 1904 book A Dog's Tale *told a popular and sentimental story that made the point to a wide audience. In 1907 he followed that book with* A Horse's Tale, *which was supposed to do the same thing for horses.*

It was less successful than the dog book, possibly because of an excess of narrators and possibly because of an equal excess of melodrama. But Mark Twain's brilliant prose and innate humor meant that even a minor book of his was far superior to books written by almost anyone else. The story of Soldier Boy, an army mount, was truly moving, in spite of its sentimentality. Here are the chapters narrated by Soldier Boy and other horses.

—Sharon B. Smith

SOLDIER BOY—PRIVATELY TO HIMSELF

I am Buffalo Bill's horse. I have spent my life under his saddle—with him in it, too, and he is good for two hundred pounds, without his clothes; and there is no telling how much he does weigh when he is out on the warpath and has his batteries belted on. He is over six feet, is young, hasn't

22

an ounce of waste flesh, is straight, graceful, springy in his motions, quick as a cat, and has a handsome face, and black hair dangling down on his shoulders, and is beautiful to look at; and nobody is braver than he is, and nobody is stronger, except myself. Yes, a person that doubts that he is fine to see should see him in his beaded buckskins, on my back and his rifle peeping above his shoulder, chasing a hostile trail, with me going like the wind and his hair streaming out behind from the shelter of his broad slouch. Yes, he is a sight to look at then—and I'm part of it myself.

I am his favorite horse, out of dozens. Big as he is, I have carried him eighty-one miles between nightfall and sunrise on the scout; and I am good for fifty, day in and day out, and all the time. I am not large, but I am built on a business basis. I have carried him thousands and thousands of miles on scout duty for the army, and there's not a gorge, nor a pass, nor a valley, nor a fort, nor a trading post, nor a buffalo range in the whole sweep of the Rocky Mountains and the Great Plains that we don't know as well as we know the bugle calls.

He is Chief of Scouts to the Army of the Frontier, and it makes us very important. In such a position as I hold in the military service one needs to be of good family and possess an education much above the common to be worthy of the place. I am the best-educated horse outside of the hippodrome, everybody says, and the best mannered. It may be so, it is not for me to say; modesty is the best policy, I think. Buffalo Bill taught me the most of what I know, my mother taught me much, and I taught myself the rest. Lay a row of moccasins before me—Pawnee, Sioux, Shoshone, Cheyenne, Blackfoot, and as many other tribes as you please—and I can name the tribe every moccasin belongs to by the make of it. Name it in horse-talk, and could do it in American if I had speech.

I know some of the Indian signs—the signs they make with their hands, and by signal fires at night and columns of smoke by day. Buffalo Bill taught me how to drag wounded soldiers out of the line of fire with my teeth; and I've done it, too; at least I've dragged *him* out of the battle when he was wounded. And not just once, but twice. Yes, I know a lot of things. I remember forms, and gaits, and faces; and you can't disguise a person that's done me a kindness so that I won't know him thereafter wherever I find him. I know the art of searching for a trail, and I know the stale track from the fresh. I can keep a trail all by myself, with Buffalo Bill asleep in the saddle; ask him—he will tell you so. Many a time, when he has ridden all night, he has said to me at dawn, "Take the watch, Boy; if the trail freshens, call me." Then he goes to sleep. He knows he can trust me, because I have a reputation. A scout horse that has a reputation does not play with it.

My mother was all American—no alkali-spider about *her*, I can tell you; she was of the best blood of Kentucky, the bluest Blue-grass aristocracy, very proud and acrimonious—or maybe it is ceremonious. I don't know which it is. But it is no matter; size is the main thing about a word, and that one's up to standard. She spent her military life as colonel of the Tenth Dragoons, and saw a deal of rough service—distinguished service it was, too. I mean, she *carried* the Colonel; but it's all the same. Where would he be without his horse? He wouldn't arrive. It takes two to make a colonel of dragoons. She was a fine dragoon horse, but never got above that. She was strong enough for the scout service, and had the endurance, too, but she couldn't quite come up to the speed required; a scout horse has to have steel in his muscle and lightning in his blood.

My father was a bronco. Nothing as to lineage—that is, nothing as to recent lineage—but plenty good enough when you go a good way back. When Professor Marsh was out here hunting bones for the chapel of Yale University he found skeletons of horses no bigger than a fox, bedded in the rocks, and he said they were ancestors of my father. My mother heard him say it; and he said those skeletons were two million years old, which astonished her and made her Kentucky pretensions look small and pretty antiphonal, not to say oblique. Let me see. . . . I used to know the meaning of those words, but . . . well, it was years ago, and 'tisn't as vivid now as it was when they were fresh. That sort of words doesn't keep, in the kind of climate we have out here. Professor Marsh said those skeletons were fossils. So that makes me part blue grass and part fossil; if there is any older or better stock, you will have to look for it among the Four Hundred, I reckon. I am satisfied with it. And am a happy horse, too, though born out of wedlock.

And now we are back at Fort Paxton once more, after a forty-day scout, away up as far as the Big Horn. Everything quiet. Crows and

Blackfeet squabbling—as usual—but no outbreaks, and settlers feeling fairly easy.

The Seventh Cavalry still in garrison here; also the Ninth Dragoons, two artillery companies, and some infantry. All glad to see me, including General Alison, commandant. The officers' ladies and children well, and called upon me—with sugar. Colonel Drake, Seventh Cavalry, said some pleasant things; Mrs. Drake was very complimentary; also Captain and Mrs. Marsh, Company B, Seventh Cavalry; also the Chaplain, who is always kind and pleasant to me, because I kicked the lungs out of a trader once. It was Tommy Drake and Fanny Marsh that furnished the sugar—nice children, the nicest at the post, I think.

That poor orphan child is on her way from France—everybody is full of the subject. Her father was General Alison's brother; married a beautiful young Spanish lady ten years ago, and has never been in America since. They lived in Spain a year or two, then went to France. Both died some months ago. This little girl that is coming is the only child. General Alison is glad to have her. He has never seen her. He is a very nice old bachelor, but is an old bachelor just the same and isn't more than about a year this side of retirement by age limit; and so what does he know about taking care of a little maid nine years old? If I could have her it would be another matter, for I know all about children, and they adore me. Buffalo Bill will tell you so himself.

I have some of this news from overhearing the garrison gossip, the rest of it I got from Potter, the General's dog. Potter is the Great Dane. He is privileged, all over the post, like Shekels, the Seventh Cavalry's dog, and visits everybody's quarters and picks up everything that is going in the way of news. Potter has no imagination, and no great deal of culture, perhaps, but he has a historical mind and a good memory, and so he is the person I depend upon mainly to post me up when I get back from a scout. That is, if Shekels is out on depredation and I can't get hold of him.

◇◇◇

Little Cathy Alison, the general's niece, soon arrives and becomes a favorite of Buffalo Bill and the rest of the garrison. Soldier Boy becomes both her teacher and her companion. Cathy becomes a skilled rider on his back and is made an honorary officer. Soldier Boy's status increases among the animals of the garrison and his reputation spreads outside its walls, a fact he discovers when a new horse arrives.

SOLDIER BOY AND THE MEXICAN PLUG

"When did you come?"

"Arrived at sundown."

"Where from?"

"Salt Lake."

"Are you in the service?"

"No. Trade."

"Pirate trade, I reckon."

"What do you know about it?"

"I saw you when you came. I recognized your master. He is a bad sort. Trap-robber, horse-thief, squaw-man, renegado—Hank Butters—I know him very well. Stole you, didn't he?"

"Well, it amounted to that."

"I thought so. Where is his pard?"

"He stopped at White Cloud's camp."

"He is another of the same stripe, is Blake Haskins." (*Aside.*) They are laying for Buffalo Bill again, I guess. (*Aloud.*) "What is your name?"

"Which one?"

"Have you got more than one?"

"I get a new one every time I'm stolen. I used to have an honest name, but that was early; I've forgotten it. Since then I've had thirteen *aliases.*"

"Aliases? What is alias?"

"A false name."

"Alias. It's a fine large word, and is in my line; it has quite a learned and cerebrospinal incandescent sound. Are you educated?"

"Well, no, I can't claim it. I can take down bars, I can distinguish oats from shoe-pegs, I can blaspheme a saddle boil with the college-bred, and I know a few other things—not many; I have had no chance, I have always had to work; besides, I am of low birth and no family. You speak my dialect like a native, but you are not a Mexican Plug, you are a gentleman, I can see that; and educated, of course."

"Yes, I am of old family, and not illiterate. I am a fossil."

"A which?"

"Fossil. The first horses were fossils. They date back two million years."

"Great sand and sage-brush! Do you mean it?"

"Yes, it is true. The bones of my ancestors are held in reverence and worship, even by men. They do not leave them exposed to the weather when they find them, but carry them three thousand miles and enshrine them in their temples of learning, and worship them."

"It is wonderful! I knew you must be a person of distinction, by your fine presence and courtly address, and by the fact that you are not subjected to the indignity of hobbles, like myself and the rest. Would you tell me your name?"

"You have probably heard of it—Soldier Boy."

"What!—the renowned, the illustrious?"

"Even so."

"It takes my breath! Little did I dream that ever I should stand face to face with the possessor of that great name. Buffalo Bill's horse! Known from the Canadian border to the deserts of Arizona, and from the eastern marches of the Great Plains to the foothills of the Sierra! Truly this is a memorable day. You still serve the celebrated Chief of Scouts?"

"I am still his property, but he has lent me, for a time, to the most noble, the most gracious, the most excellent, her Excellency Catherine, Corporal-General Seventh Cavalry and Flag-Lieutenant Ninth Dragoons, U.S.A.—on whom be peace!"

"Amen. Did you say *her* Excellency?"

"The same. A Spanish lady, sweet blossom of a ducal house. And truly a wonder; knowing everything, capable of everything; speaking all the languages, master of all sciences, a mind without horizons, a heart of gold, the glory of her race! On whom be peace!"

"Amen. It is marvelous!"

"Verily. I knew many things, she has taught me others. I am educated. I will tell you about her."

"I listen—I am enchanted."

"I will tell a plain tale, calmly, without excitement, without eloquence. When she had been here four or five weeks she was already erudite in military things, and they made her an officer—a double officer. She rode the drill every day, like any soldier; and she could take the bugle and direct the evolutions herself. Then, on a day, there was a grand race, for prizes—none to enter but the children. Seventeen children entered, and she was the youngest. Three girls, fourteen boys—good riders all. It was a steeplechase, with four hurdles, all pretty high. The first prize was a most cunning half-grown silver bugle, and mighty pretty, with red silk cord and tassels. Buffalo Bill was very anxious; for he had taught her to ride, and he did most dearly want her to win that race, for the glory of it. So he wanted her to ride me, but she wouldn't; and she reproached him, and said it was unfair and unright, and taking advantage; for what horse in this post or any other could stand a chance against me? and she was very severe with him, and said, 'You ought to be ashamed—you are proposing to me conduct unbecoming an officer and a gentleman.' So he just tossed her up in the air about thirty feet and caught her as she came down, and said he *was* ashamed; and put up his handkerchief and pretended to cry, which nearly broke her heart, and she petted him, and begged him to forgive her, and said she would do anything in the world he could ask but that; but he said he ought to go hang himself, and he *must*, if he could get a rope; it was nothing but right he should, for he never, never could forgive himself; and then *she* began to cry, and they both sobbed, the way you could hear him a mile, and she clinging around his neck and pleading, till at last he was comforted a little, and gave his solemn promise he wouldn't hang himself till after the race; and wouldn't do it at all if she won it, which made her happy, and she said she would win it or die in the saddle; so then everything was pleasant again and both of them content. He can't help playing jokes on her, he is so fond of her and she is so innocent and unsuspecting; and when she finds it out she cuffs him and is in a fury, but presently forgives him because it's him; and maybe the very next day she's caught with another joke; you see she can't learn any better, because she hasn't any deceit in her, and that kind aren't ever expecting it in another person.

"It was a grand race. The whole post was there, and there was such another whooping and shouting when the seventeen kids came flying down the turf and sailing over the hurdles—oh, beautiful to see! Halfway down, it was kind of neck and neck, and anybody's race and nobody's. Then, what should happen but a cow steps out and puts her head down to munch grass, with her broadside to the battalion, and they a-coming like the wind; they split apart to flank her, but she?—why, she drove the spurs home and soared over that cow like a bird! and on she went, and cleared the last hurdle solitary and alone, the army letting loose the grand yell, and she skipped from the horse the same as if he had been standing still, and made her bow, and everybody crowded around to congratulate, and they gave her the bugle, and she put it to her lips and blew 'boots and saddles' to see how it would go, and BB was as proud as you can't think! And he said, 'Take Soldier Boy, and don't pass him back till I ask for him!' and I can tell you he wouldn't have said that to any other person on this planet. That was two months and more ago, and nobody has been on my back since but the Corporal-General Seventh Cavalry and Flag-Lieutenant of the Ninth Dragoons, U.S.A.—on whom be peace!"

"Amen. I listen—tell me more."

"She set to work and organized the Sixteen, and called it the First Battalion Rocky Mountain Rangers, U.S.A., and she wanted to be bugler, but they elected her Lieutenant-General *and* Bugler. So she ranks her uncle the commandant, who is only a Brigadier. And doesn't she train those little people! Ask the Indians, ask the traders, ask the soldiers; they'll tell you. She has been at it from the first day. Every morning they go clattering down into the plain, and there she sits on my back with her bugle at her mouth and sounds the orders and puts them through the evolutions for an hour or more; and it is too beautiful for anything to see those ponies dissolve from one formation into another, and waltz about, and break, and scatter, and form again, always moving, always graceful, now trotting, now galloping, and so on, sometimes near by, sometimes in the distance, all just like a state ball, you know, and sometimes she can't hold herself any longer, but sounds the 'charge,' and turns me loose! and you can take my word for it, if the battalion hasn't too much of a start we catch up and go over the breastworks with the front line.

"Yes, they are soldiers, those little people; and healthy, too, not ailing any more, the way they used to be sometimes. It's because of her drill.

She's got a fort, now—Fort Fanny Marsh. Major-General Tommy Drake planned it out, and the Seventh and Dragoons built it. Tommy is the Colonel's son, and is fifteen and the oldest in the Battalion; Fanny Marsh is Brigadier-General, and is next oldest—over thirteen. She is daughter of Captain Marsh, Company B, Seventh Cavalry. Lieutenant-General Alison is the youngest by considerable; I think she is about nine and a half or three-quarters. Her military rig, as Lieutenant-General, isn't for business, it's for dress parade, because the ladies made it. They say they got it out of the Middle Ages—out of a book—and it is all red and blue and white silks and satins and velvets; tights, trunks, sword, doublet with slashed sleeves, short cape, cap with just one feather in it; I've heard them name these things; they got them out of the book; she's dressed like a page, of old times, they say. It's the daintiest outfit that ever was—you will say so, when you see it. She's lovely in it—oh, just a dream! In some ways she is just her age, but in others she's as old as her uncle, I think. She is very learned. She teaches her uncle his book. I have seen her sitting by with the book and reciting to him what is in it, so that he can learn to do it himself.

"Every Saturday she hires little Indians to garrison her fort; then she lays siege to it, and makes military approaches by make-believe trenches in make-believe night, and finally at make-believe dawn she draws her sword and sounds the assault and takes it by storm. It is for practice. And she has invented a bugle call all by herself, out of her own head, and it's a stirring one, and the prettiest in the service. It's to call *me*—it's never used for anything else. She taught it to me, and told me what it says: '*It is I, Soldier—come!*' and when those thrilling notes come floating down the distance I hear them without fail, even if I am two miles away; and then—oh, then you should see my heels get down to business!

"And she has taught me how to say good morning and good night to her, which is by lifting my right hoof for her to shake; and also how to say goodbye; I do that with my left foot—but only for practice, because there hasn't been any but make-believe goodbyeing yet, and I hope there won't ever be. It would make me cry if I ever had to put up my left foot in earnest. She has taught me how to salute, and I can do it as well as a soldier. I bow my head low, and lay my right hoof against my cheek. She taught me that because I got into disgrace once, through ignorance. I am privileged, because I am known to be honorable and trustworthy, and because I have a distinguished record in the service; so they don't hobble me nor tie me to stakes or shut me tight in stables, but let me wander around to suit myself. Well, trooping the colors is a very solemn ceremony, and everybody must stand uncovered when the flag goes by, the commandant and all; and once I was there, and ignorantly walked across right in front of the band, which was an awful disgrace: Ah, the Lieutenant-General was so ashamed, and so distressed that I should have done such a thing before all the world, that she couldn't keep the tears back; and then she taught me the salute, so that if I ever did any other unmilitary act through ignorance I could do my salute and she believed everybody would think it was apology enough and would not press the matter. It is very nice and distinguished; no other horse can do it; often the men salute me, and I return it. I am privileged to be present when the Rocky Mountain Rangers troop the colors and I stand solemn, like the children, and I salute when the flag goes by. Of course when she goes to her fort her sentries sing out 'Turn out the guard!' and then ... do you catch that refreshing early morning whiff from the mountain pines and the wild flowers? The night is far spent; we'll hear the bugles before long. Dorcas, the black woman, is very good and nice; she takes care of the Lieutenant-General, and is Brigadier-General Alison's mother, which makes her mother-in-law to the Lieutenant-General. That is what Shekels says. At least it is what I think he says, though I never can understand him quite clearly. He—"

"Who is Shekels?"

"The Seventh Cavalry dog. I mean, if he *is* a dog. His father was a coyote and his mother was a wildcat. It doesn't really make a dog out of him, does it?"

"Not a real dog, I should think. Only a kind of a general dog, at most, I reckon. Though this is a matter of ichthyology, I suppose; and if it is, it is out of my depth, and so my opinion is not valuable, and I don't claim much consideration for it."

"It isn't ichthyology; it is dogmatics, which is still more difficult and tangled up. Dogmatics always are."

"Dogmatics is quite beyond me, quite; so I am not competing. But on general principles it is my opinion that a colt out of a coyote and a wildcat is no square dog, but doubtful. That is my hand, and I stand pat."

"Well, it is as far as I can go myself, and be fair and conscientious. I have always regarded him as a doubtful dog, and so has Potter. Potter is the Great Dane. Potter says he is no dog, and not even poultry—though I do not go quite so far as that."

"And I wouldn't, myself. Poultry is one of those things which no person can get to the bottom of, there is so much of it and such variety. It is just wings, and wings, and wings, till you are weary: turkeys, and geese, and bats, and butterflies, and angels, and grasshoppers, and flying fish, and—well, there is really no end to the tribe; it gives me the heaves just to think of it. But this one hasn't any wings, has he?"

"No."

"Well, then, in my belief he is more likely to be dog than poultry. I have not heard of poultry that hadn't wings. Wings is the *sign* of poultry; it is what you tell poultry by. Look at the mosquito."

"What do you reckon he is, then? He must be something."

"Why, he could be a reptile; anything that hasn't wings is a reptile."

"Who told you that?"

"Nobody told me, but I overheard it."

"Where did you overhear it?"

"Years ago. I was with the Philadelphia Institute expedition in the Badlands under Professor Cope, hunting mastodon bones, and I overheard him say, his own self, that any plantigrade circumflex vertebrate bacterium that hadn't wings and was uncertain was a reptile. Well, then, has this dog any wings? No. Is he a plantigrade circumflex vertebrate bacterium? Maybe so, maybe not; but without ever having seen him, and judging only by his illegal and spectacular parentage, I will bet the odds of a bale of hay to a bran mash that he looks it. Finally, is he uncertain? That is the point—is he uncertain? I will leave it to you if you have ever heard of a more uncertainer dog than what this one is?"

"No, I never have."

"Well, then, he's a reptile. That's settled."

"Why, look here, whatsyourname—"

"Last alias, Mongrel."

"A good one, too. I was going to say, you are better educated than you have been pretending to be. I like cultured society, and I shall cultivate your acquaintance. Now as to Shekels, whenever you want to know about any private thing that is going on at this post or in White Cloud's camp or Thunder-Bird's, he can tell you; and if you make friends with him he'll be glad to, for he is a born gossip, and picks up all the tittle-tattle. Being the whole Seventh Cavalry's reptile, he doesn't belong to anybody in particular, and hasn't any military duties; so he comes and goes as he pleases, and is popular with all the house cats and other authentic sources of private information. He understands all the languages, and talks them all, too. With an accent like gritting your teeth, it is true, and with a grammar that is no improvement on blasphemy—still, with practice you get at the meat of what he says, and it serves. . . . Hark! That's the reveille. . . .

"Faint and far, but isn't it clear, isn't it sweet? There's no music like the bugle to stir the blood, in the still solemnity of the morning twilight, with the dim plain stretching away to nothing and the spectral mountains slumbering against the sky. You'll hear another note in a minute—faint and far and clear, like the other one, and sweeter still, you'll notice. Wait . . . listen. There it goes! It says, '*It is I, Soldier—come!*' . . .

". . . Now then, watch me leave a blue streak behind!"

SOLDIER BOY AND SHEKELS

"Did you do as I told you? Did you look up the Mexican Plug?"

"Yes, I made his acquaintance before night and got his friendship."

"I liked him. Did you?"

"Not at first. He took me for a reptile, and it troubled me, because I didn't know whether it was a compliment or not. I couldn't ask him, because it would look ignorant. So I didn't say anything, and soon liked him very well indeed. Was it a compliment, do you think?"

"Yes, that is what it was. They are very rare, the reptiles; very few left, now-a-days."

"Is that so? What is a reptile?"

"It is a plantigrade circumflex vertebrate bacterium that hasn't any wings and is uncertain."

"Well, it—it sounds fine, it surely does."

"And it is fine. You may be thankful you are one."

"I am. It seems wonderfully grand and elegant for a person that is so humble as I am; but I am thankful, I am indeed, and will try to live up to it. It is hard to remember. Will you say it again, please, and say it slow?"

"Plantigrade circumflex vertebrate bacterium that hasn't any wings and is uncertain."

"It *is* beautiful, anybody must grant it; beautiful, and of a noble sound. I hope it will not make me proud and stuck-up—I should not like to be that. It is much more distinguished and honorable to be a reptile than a dog, don't you think, Soldier?"

"Why, there's no comparison. It is awfully aristocratic. Often a duke is called a reptile; it is set down so, in history."

"Isn't that grand! Potter wouldn't ever associate with me, but I reckon he'll be glad to when he finds out what I am."

"You can depend upon it."

"I will thank Mongrel for this. He is a very good sort, for a Mexican Plug. Don't you think he is?"

"It is my opinion of him; and as for his birth, he cannot help that. We cannot all be reptiles, we cannot all be fossils; we have to take what comes and be thankful it is no worse. It is the true philosophy."

"For those others?"

"Stick to the subject, please. Did it turn out that my suspicions were right?"

"Yes, perfectly right. Mongrel has heard them planning. They are after BB's life, for running them out of Medicine Bow and taking their stolen horses away from them."

"Well, they'll get him yet, for sure."

"Not if he keeps a sharp lookout."

"*He* keep a sharp lookout! He never does; he despises them, and all their kind. His life is always being threatened, and so it has come to be monotonous."

"Does he know they are here?"

"Oh yes, he knows it. He is always the earliest to know who comes and who goes. But he cares nothing for them and their threats; he only laughs when people warn him. They'll shoot him from behind a tree the first he knows. Did Mongrel tell you their plans?"

"Yes. They have found out that he starts for Fort Clayton day after tomorrow, with one of his scouts; so they will leave tomorrow, letting on to go south, but they will fetch around north all in good time."

"Shekels, I don't like the look of it."

Cathy is so proud of her unit that she offers to escort Buffalo Bill to Fort Clayton. Soldier Boy picks up the story in the next chapter.

SOLDIER BOY AND SHEKELS AGAIN

"Well, this is the way it happened. We did the escort duty; then we came back and struck for the plain and put the Rangers through a rousing drill—oh, for hours! Then we sent them home under Brigadier-General Fanny Marsh; then the Lieutenant-General and I went off on a gallop over the plains for about three hours, and were lazying along home in the middle of the afternoon, when we met Jimmy Slade, the drummer-boy, and he saluted and asked the Lieutenant-General if she had heard the news, and she said no, and he said: 'Buffalo Bill has been ambushed and badly shot this side of Clayton, and Thorndike the scout, too; Bill couldn't travel, but Thorndike could, and he brought the news, and Sergeant Wilkes and six men of Company B are gone, two hours ago, hotfoot, to get Bill. And they say—'

"'Go!' she shouts to me—and I went."

"Fast?"

"Don't ask foolish questions. It was an awful pace. For four hours nothing happened, and not a word said, except that now and then she said, 'Keep it up, Boy, keep it up, sweetheart; we'll save him!' I kept it up. Well, when the dark shut down, in the rugged hills, that poor little chap had been tearing around in the saddle all day, and I noticed by the slack knee-pressure that she was tired and tottery, and I got dreadfully afraid; but every time I tried to slow down and let her go to sleep, so I could stop, she hurried me up again; and so, sure enough, at last over she went!

"Ah, that was a fix to be in! for she lay there and didn't stir, and what was I to do? I couldn't leave her to fetch help, on account of the wolves.

There was nothing to do but stand by. It was dreadful. I was afraid she was killed, poor little thing! But she wasn't. She came to, by-and-by, and said, 'Kiss me, Soldier,' and those were blessed words. I kissed her—often; I am used to that, and we like it. But she didn't get up, and I was worried. She fondled my nose with her hand, and talked to me, and called me endearing names—which is her way—but she caressed with the same hand all the time. The other arm was broken, you see, but I didn't know it, and she didn't mention it. She didn't want to distress me, you know.

"Soon the big gray wolves came and hung around, and you could hear them snarl and snap at each other, but you couldn't see anything of them except their eyes, which shone in the dark like sparks and stars. The Lieutenant-General said, 'If I had the Rocky Mountain Rangers here, we would make those creatures climb a tree.' Then she made believe that the Rangers were in hearing, and put up her bugle and blew the 'assembly'; and then, 'boots and saddles'; then the 'trot'; 'gallop'; *charge!* Then she blew the 'retreat,' and said, 'That's for you, you rebels; the Rangers don't ever retreat!'

"The music frightened them away, but they were hungry, and kept coming back. And of course they got bolder and bolder, which is their way. It went on for an hour, then the tired child went to sleep, and it was pitiful to hear her moan and nestle, and I couldn't do anything for her. All the time I was laying for the wolves. They are in my line; I have had experience. At last the boldest one ventured within my lines, and I landed him among his friends with some of his skull still on him, and they did the rest. In the next hour I got a couple more, and they went the way of the first one, down the throats of the detachment. That satisfied the survivors, and they went away and left us in peace.

"We hadn't any more adventures, though I kept awake all night and was ready. From midnight on the child got very restless, and out of her head, and moaned, and said, 'Water, water—thirsty'; and now and then, 'Kiss me, Soldier'; and sometimes she was in her fort and giving orders to her garrison; and once she was in Spain, and thought her mother was with her. People say a horse can't cry; but they don't know, because we cry inside.

"It was an hour after sunup that I heard the boys coming, and recognized the hoof-beats of Pomp and Cæsar and Jerry, old mates of mine; and a welcomer sound there couldn't ever be. Buffalo Bill was in a horse litter, with his leg broken by a bullet, and Mongrel and Blake Haskins's horse were doing the work. Buffalo Bill and Thorndike had killed both of those toughs.

"When they got to us, and Buffalo Bill saw the child lying there so white, he said, 'My God!' and the sound of his voice brought her to herself, and she gave a little cry of pleasure and struggled to get up, but couldn't, and the soldiers gathered her up like the tenderest women, and their eyes were wet and they were not ashamed, when they saw her arm dangling; and so were Buffalo Bill's, and when they laid her in his arms he said, 'My darling, how does this come?' and she said, 'We came to save you, but I was tired, and couldn't keep awake, and fell off and hurt myself, and couldn't get on again.' 'You came to save me, you dear little rat? It was too lovely of you!' 'Yes, and Soldier stood by me, which you know he would, and protected me from the wolves; and if he got a chance he kicked the life out of some of them—for you know he would, BB.' The sergeant said, 'He laid out three of them, sir, and here's the bones to show for it.' 'He's a grand horse,' said BB; 'he's the grandest horse that ever was! and has saved your life, Lieutenant-General Alison, and shall protect it the rest of his life—he's yours for a kiss!' He got it, along with a passion of delight, and he said, 'You are feeling better now, little Spaniard—do you think you could blow the advance?' She put up the bugle to do it, but he said wait a minute first. Then he and the sergeant set her arm and put it in splints, she wincing but not whimpering; then we took up the march for home, and that's the end of the tale; and I'm her horse. Isn't she a brick, Shekels?"

"Brick? She's more than a brick, more than a thousand bricks—she's a reptile!"

"It's a compliment out of your heart, Shekels. God bless you for it!"

After the horses overhear officers talking about the joys of bullfighting, they try to figure out what is so special about the sport. Here the Mexican Plug Mongrel tries to figure it out with the help of another horse.

MONGREL AND THE OTHER HORSE

"Sage-brush, you have been listening?"

"Yes."

"Isn't it strange?"

"Well, no, Mongrel, I don't know that it is."

"Why don't you?"

"I've seen a good many human beings in my time. They are created as they are; they cannot help it. They are only brutal because that is their make; brutes would be brutal if it was *their* make."

"To me, Sage-brush, man is most strange and unaccountable. Why should he treat dumb animals that way when they are not doing any harm?"

"Man is not always like that, Mongrel; he is kind enough when he is not excited by religion."

"Is the bullfight a religious service?"

"I think so. I have heard so. It is held on Sunday."

(*A reflective pause, lasting some moments.*) Then: "When we die, Sage-brush, do we go to heaven and dwell with man?"

"My father thought not. He believed we do not have to go there unless we deserve it."

⋄⋄⋄⋄⋄⋄⋄⋄⋄⋄⋄⋄⋄⋄⋄⋄⋄⋄⋄⋄⋄⋄⋄⋄⋄⋄⋄

General Alison decides to take Cathy to visit her Spanish homeland and gives in to her pleas to bring Soldier Boy along. But Cathy's beloved horse is stolen shortly after their arrival. He picks up his story several months later.

⋄⋄⋄⋄⋄⋄⋄⋄⋄⋄⋄⋄⋄⋄⋄⋄⋄⋄⋄⋄⋄⋄⋄⋄⋄⋄⋄⋄

SOLDIER BOY—TO HIMSELF

It is five months. Or is it six? My troubles have clouded my memory. I have been all over this land, from end to end, and now I am back again since day before yesterday, to that city which we passed through, that last day of our long journey, and which is near her country home. I am a tottering ruin and my eyes are dim, but I recognized it. If she could see me she would know me and sound my call. I wish I could hear it once more;

it would revive me, it would bring back her face and the mountains and the free life, and I would come—if I were dying I would come! She would not know *me*, looking as I do, but she would know me by my star. But she will never see me, for they do not let me out of this shabby stable—a foul and miserable place, with two wrecks like myself for company.

How many times have I changed hands? I think it is twelve times—I cannot remember; and each time it was down a step lower, and each time I got a harder master. They have been cruel, every one; they have worked me night and day in degraded employments, and beaten me; they have fed me ill, and some days not at all. And so I am but bones, now, with a rough and frowsy skin humped and cornered upon my shrunken body—that skin which was once so glossy, that skin which she loved to stroke with her hand. I was the pride of the mountains and the Great Plains; now I am a scarecrow and despised. These piteous wrecks that are my comrades here say we have reached the bottom of the scale, the final humiliation; they say that when a horse is no longer worth the weeds and discarded rubbish they feed to him, they sell him to the bullring for a glass of brandy, to make sport for the people and perish for their pleasure.

To die—that does not disturb me; we of the service never care for death. But if I could see her once more! If I could hear her bugle sing again and say, "It is I, Soldier—come!"

Cathy Alison searches for Soldier Boy, finally tracing him to a bullring. She arrives just in time to realize that Soldier Boy has had his abdomen ripped open by a bull. She rushes into the ring toward him. Soldier Boy staggers toward her and falls at her feet, dying before he realizes that Cathy has also been gored. She lives long enough to be carried away, and before she dies she asks that "Taps" be played for Soldier Boy.

4

White Horse Winter

By Wilbur Daniel Steele

Wilbur Daniel Steele was among the most popular short story writers in the United States at a time when almost every literate person at least occasionally read short stories. Although he was born in North Carolina, Steele lived for many years in Provincetown, Massachusetts, where he discovered some of his favorite themes and settings. He found special inspiration in the lives of the Portuguese fishermen of Cape Cod.

"White Horse Winter," one of Steele's best stories, does center on Portuguese Americans, but at its heart is the magnificent horse of the title. At first, neither the characters nor the readers are quite sure whether the white horse is a dream or a ghost or an illusion. Or could he be real?

—SHARON B. SMITH

THE LITTLE HOUSE WHERE I WAS BORN, AND IN WHICH I PASSED THE earlier years of my life, stands about a hundred yards back from the beach and a little more than a mile down shore from Old Harbor. What we always knew as the "Creek" runs in there, with plenty of water even at low tide to float my father's dory; and the flawless yellow face of a dune used to stand up behind the house, sheltering us from the northerlies that pick the scud from the ocean, a mile back across the Neck, and spatter it in the bay at our front door. My father and mother still live in the house, but the dune has shifted to the westward, and it is colder there on a winter night.

My older sister was born before my father and mother came from the Western Islands, so she had a recollection of green country; but we younger children knew nothing but the water and the sand. Strangely enough, my most vivid remembrance of the water is not from any of its wilder moods: I picture it with the tide out at evening, reflecting the face of the western sky, flat, garish-colored, silent, with a spur of mute fire reaching out at me along the surface of the Creek.

The dunes were the magic land, full of shifting shadows, and deceptive, where a little covey of beach plums made themselves out as a faraway and impenetrable forest, especially when the mist came inland, and a footprint in the sand across a hollow appeared a vast convulsion of nature at the other end of a day's journey. And one felt the dunes always moving, rising up out of the sea, marching silently across the Neck, and advancing upon the little house. I can remember the spring when the sand ate up a pear-tree my father had brought from the Islands.

The dunes entered our lives, and became a part of them. Even now the sight of a strip of sand gets a queer grip on me, and to this day I am apt to catch myself spying out the skyline with an indefinable and portentous dread. I cannot shake off this sensation, although I know perfectly what it is. It is a relic from that time which we have always called, in our family, White Horse Winter.

I remember my father's coming in one October day and standing a long time before the barometer which always hung behind the kitchen door. After a while he said to my mother in his broken English—

"It weel be ver' bad weather tonight—tomorrow."

That night when I was trying to get to sleep, I heard the skirmishers of a great wind feeling at the shingles above my head.

My next recollection is of the tumult of a gale outside, mingled with beating on the door downstairs, and distracted fragments of men's voices calling to one another of a vessel come ashore. I knew it must be at Round Hill or they would not have come past our house.

Then I was out myself, where no boy of ten had any business to be, isolated in the center of a vast disruption, except when an occasional agitated phantom passed in the rocking darkness toward Round Hill Bars. I had an acute consciousness of doing wrong, and with all the fight to keep my feet in the chaos of sand and wind and scud, the thought of what my father would do if he came upon me lay heavy on my mind.

After a time one of the shore dunes came up before me, black, with an aura of distracted sand about its crest and the sky behind it gray with the labor of dawn. The silhouettes of men, and of a few women, were running about over it and pointing to sea with jerking arms. But I was afraid to go up there—still with the fear of my father's anger—so I ran to the northward in the hollow a hundred yards or so before I felt it safe to venture upon the ridge, where I cowered down, a very small and very tired-out boy.

It was a full-rigged ship. Her main and mizzen were already gone, and her foremast writhed in dismal and contorted circles toward the sky, a frail, sensitive needle point marking every onslaught and repulse of the fight below, where the vessel wallowed in the smother between the outer and inner bars. Inshore, on the torn and clamorous beach, the figures of the lifesaving crew moved about their boat with futile gestures, lifting cursed hands to their faces to scream soundless words at one another. The wind was like a blast from the colossal explosion that flared behind the eastern clouds.

But it was the water that fascinated me that morning. The Round Hill Bars make a talking, even in a moderate breeze, which can be heard in our kitchen across the Neck. Now their shouting seemed to me to fill up the whole bowl of the visible world, rumbling around its misty confines in tangled reverberations. I could see the outer bar only as a white, distorted line athwart the gray, but the shoreward shallows were writhing, living things, gnawing at the sky with venomous teeth of spume, and giving birth in agony to the legions which advanced forever and forever upon the land.

My mother used sometimes to sing a little Portuguese song to my brother Antone, the baby. It had a part which ran:

> The herd of the Sea King's White Horses
> Comes up on the shore to graze . . .

It pleased my boy mind, on this morning, to figure them as ravening, stung to frenzy by the lash of the gale, tossing maddened manes, and bellowing, for horses were not common in that fisher country. Try as I might, my eyes would not stay on the wreck, but returned inevitably to those squadrons of white horses advancing out of the mist. They were very fearsome things to me at that time, although I was old enough to know that they were not alive and could not possibly get at me.

Then a tremendous wave broke and flattened out in a smother on the beach, and I was sure for a moment I had seen an actual horse struggling there. The next breaker overwhelmed the place, swirling, thunderous, shot its thin mottled tongue far up the sand and withdrew it seething into the undertow—and now there could be no doubt that a horse was there, screaming, pawing at the treacherous sand, his wide glistening back horribly convulsed, and eyes and nostrils of flame.

Many and many a time since then I have had it all in a dream; and in the dream, even now, I am swept back into something of the elemental terror that held the boy cowering on the ridge of sand while the great white stallion staggered up the face of the dune and stood against the sky, coughing and coughing and coughing.

Of a sudden, I knew that I must run away from that thing, and I scrambled out of my little burrow and ran, not daring to look back, not daring to ease my pace when the sand dragged too cruelly at my shoes— ran and ran—till I found myself in the safe haven of the front room at the little house, and my mother stirring a pan over the kitchen stove.

I staggered out to her, crying that a horse had come out of the water and run after me. She thought that I was feverish, had had a bad dream, and it occurred to me that I need not let her know I had been where I should not have been that morning. She packed me off to bed again, and when I woke in the afternoon I was of even minds myself whether I had dreamed it all or not. Certainly it was cut from the cloth of a dream.

During the weeks that followed I heard a deal about the wreck, from my father and from others who came past on the state road, and stopped to chat. It was a bad affair, that wreck. The shore people could see her men, now and then when the rack drifted aside for a moment, swarming over the deck like ants disturbed by a pail of water. One of these glimpses showed them the crew clustered about the boats on the lee side, and then the lifesavers burned in vain the signal which means, "Do not attempt to leave in your own boats"; the next lifting of the curtain discovered the ship's decks bare of life, and seventeen bodies were dragged from the surf that day.

But a strange thing happened when the lifesavers rowed out to the hulk after the sea had gone down. In the cabin they came upon a young man, dry-clothed, sitting before a fire in the stove, plainly much shaken by the experiences of the night, but still with a grip on himself. He asked if the boats had come ashore all right, and when Captain Hall told him, he seemed taken aback.

"Nothing come ashore?" he asked.

"Nothing alive," said the captain. The other looked into the fire a while, white, and shaking a little. "I was afeared to go with the sailors," he said, after a time.

Of course the story did not come to me in this straight sequence, but merely as haphazard snatches from the gossip of my elders, some of it not clearly till years afterwards—for the details of a great wreck are treasured among people of the sea so long as the generation lasts.

It was almost a week before I went out on the dunes again. Although I was now convinced that I had seen something that was not, still even a bad dream is not a thing for a child to shake off lightly. But my sister Agnes's eighteenth birthday was coming soon now, and it was always a custom in our family to signalize such events with a cake and bayberry candles. So I was off this day to the north of Snail Road, where the bottom of a certain hollow is covered with a mat of bayberry bushes. It takes a good many bayberries to make even a small candle, and the dark was beginning to come down when the basket was filled and I started back across the sand hills toward home.

The dunes were very silent and very misty and very lonely that evening; I trudged along with my small head going about like the mythical owl's, but the dusk remained empty of any horror till I had come across Snail Road and into the region of black sand where one may scoop out a little hole and drink fresh water. I almost always did this, whether I was thirsty or not, but that night I was saved the trouble of scooping the hole—or would have been had I cared to take advantage of the great glistening gash that lay in my path. It was no work of human hands. All about the place the sand was churned and scarred by enormous, deep tracks, and a double thread of them led away over the eastern skyline. Then I was running again, as I had that other morning, running all the way to the little house, careless of the bayberries that strewed my backward trail.

Two nights after, we were all sitting around the fire in our kitchen. There was no wind that evening and the tide was down beyond the flats, so that all was very quiet outside the little house, and a note of distant trumpeting came plain to us through the crisp night. It was surely a queer sound for our country, but its significance passed me till my father spoke to my mother.

"It's the white horse again," he said. My mother nodded, without curiosity or surprise.

"Yes," she answered, "we must keep Zhoe"—that was I, Joe—"off the dunes more."

But they could not keep me off the dunes entirely, now that the white horse had become actual and an object of common gossip. I took an adventurous pleasure in climbing to the top of the hill behind the house and overlooking the country of hummocks. Especially was this fine to do of an early evening, when the light had left the sand and the ridges stood out black against the sky.

I saw him many times from this point of security—always as a dark, far-away silhouette, tremendous, laboring over the back of a dune or standing with his great head flung up and tail streaming on the wind. His presence there gave the whole dune land a new aspect for me—as of a familiar country grown sinister and full of the shadow of disaster. Nights when the wind was northerly, his racketing sometimes came to me in the loft where my cot stood; then I would shiver under the clothes and fall asleep to dream of being lost in a wilderness of shifting dunes, and that great shaggy white beast above me on a ridge, coughing and coughing and coughing. Once he must have come plunging down the face of our own hill, because we were startled by a splashing of sand on the shingles of an outhouse, followed by a great snorting and a ripping of fence timbers. That night even my father and mother were pale.

For I was not the only one who was afraid. Some of the men came out from Old Harbor with lines one day to take the animal, and at first sight of him, suddenly, over the angle of a dune, dropped their entanglements and fled back past our house, running heavily. And that was in the flat sun light of midday. After that men went over to Round Hill Station by other and circuitous routes.

One of these evenings, while I was crouching on the hill with a delightful shiver playing along my spine, a strange man came up and stood a few yards to one side of me, looking out to the eastward. The white horse was there, perhaps a half-mile off, outlined against a bank of silver that came rolling in from the ocean. The newcomer regarded him a long time without moving; then I, being a little afraid of the man, slipped out of the bushes and down the hill to the little house.

The dusk was already thick when he came down the dune and stopped to pass a word with my father, who was working over a net near the gate. I remember my sister Agnes peering curiously at the figure indistinct in the gloom, and my mother whispering to her that it was the man they had taken off the wreck. That made a tremendous impression on me. I was glad when my father asked him to sit a while by the fire.

From my vantage-point behind my mother's chair, I could examine him better than I dared do on the ridge. He was a smallish man, of a wiry build rather uncommon among our own people, whose strength is apt to come upon them with an amount of flesh. His skin was not brown but red, hairy about the wrists—I thought of it as brittle. His hair was almost the color of his skin, his features were heavy. He sat or stood with elbows out and thumbs tucked in his belt, and he had little to say. I can give his age definitely as twenty-eight at that time.

From the moment he entered, the stranger seemed unable to keep his slow-moving gray eyes away from my sister Agnes, who stood lean-ing against the door which led into the front room. Those two were as far apart as the two poles. It is hard for a small boy to know how his brothers and sisters really appear, but looking back out of later years I remember her as rather tall for a girl, full-formed, straight, dark as the rest of us, and with a look of contempt in her black eyes for this alien whom she had no means of comprehending.

For a time my father talked about the wreck, putting questions, hazarding technical opinions in the jargon of the sea. The stranger's replies were monosyllabic and vague. Then in a pause the neighing of the white horse came in to us, and the man started up with an abrupt scraping of his shoes on the boards. I am sure that Agnes believed he was frightened, and that she took no pains to hide it. After that the talk turned naturally on the white horse, going back and forth between my father and mother, for the stranger had even less to say now than before.

Jem Hodges (that was the stranger's name) came the following day and sat on the front porch, watching father who was tarring weir twine in the yard. He had nothing to say—simply sat there with his thumbs tucked in his belt.

Agnes came in and said to my mother, "He's a dummy—I never seen such a dummy, ma."

"I don' know, Aggie," my mother answered her. "He ain't our kind, and you can't tell about things you ain't used to." That was my mother's way.

Agnes flounced out of the kitchen in a manner which had no significance to me then, for my rudimentary wits could perceive no possible connection between her action and the silence of the little man on the porch outside.

I think I can say now what the connection was. Among other things the world has taught me this—that no two men do the same thing in exactly the same way. Jem Hodges was wooing my sister Agnes. Little wonder that her spirit was restive under that wooing, when all the blood of the race in her veins sang of the lover's fervor, the quick eye, the heart speaking in words, the abandon of caresses. And here was a man, fulfilling none of our conventions of beauty, who sat imperturbable, impassive, saying nothing, and making her come to him. I am sure that he did it without planning or analyzing—I think half of it was constraint and all of it instinct. And Agnes might flounce out of the room as she would: sooner or later I saw her again at the front of the house.

This went on for two or three weeks. Jem Hodges came almost every day to sit on the porch a while, after which he sometimes wandered away in the growing evening over our own dune. Again and again I saw him standing there, as on the first evening, for a long time without motion, looking over the hummocks. Sometimes I could hear him whistling under his breath an air that was very strange and outlandish to me, then, who had never heard the like. Many years later I heard one of the great tenors of the world sing the same air, and it thrilled me, but not in the same way.

On the evening of the twenty-eighth of November (I have the date from Agnes) I was ensconced in my bushy retreat, watching the night take hold of the world of sand. Jem Hodges stood on the ridge to the east of me. Every minute that passed robbed his motionless figure of some detail, and lent to it a portion of the flat mystery of the night. I had seen the white horse once that evening, topping a rise far off to the northward, and then no more till I was suddenly aware of a gigantic, indistinct form moving up hill toward me amid a vast *shuf-shuf* of troubled sand.

I was terribly frightened for the instant; then I knew it was a matter only of hopping over the bank behind me and sliding down to the very back door of the little house. I had slipped from the bushes and was almost to the bottom of the smothering slope, when I heard such a plunging in the sand above that my wits came near leaving me again; I made wild and futile plunges, and cried out to my sister, whom I saw in the open doorway. I had no thought in the world but that it was the white horse charging down. I had almost gained the house, a pathetic small figure of panic, when I felt myself brushed aside with a violence which left me sprawling, terrified, on my back in the sand, with a confused impression as of something passing through the doorway where my sister had stood. It was not beyond me at that moment to imagine the white horse, overcarried by the impetus of his charge, blundering right on into the kitchen of the little house.

Jem Hodges had passed completely out of my mind, and it was Jem whom I found in the kitchen, ill at ease, confronted by my sister. Agnes I hardly knew that evening—she was like a new and strange person, aflame with anger and a high, emphatic beauty, speaking tensely, with the nerve twanging upward slur at the end of the phrase which discovered the blood of the Island race through all the veneer of public school. The accumulated unrest of weeks had found a vent at last.

"You—you—oh, you coward!" she reviled him, "you little sneaking coward, you!—an' they call you a man!" Her voice was a whispered shriek, her clenched hands moved before her as though to do him harm.

Jem was white, and still breathing hard.

"A man," Agnes went on. "They call you a man—an' you knock over little children so's you can save your own little hairy hide. You lose your eyesight—and your mind—from seein' a horse walkin' over some sand. . . . Agh!"

Then she turned to me with a fierce gesture of protection.

"Zhoe—poor little Zhoe—he hurt you, didn't he? There, don't cry no more—you're more of a man 'n he is, ain't you Little Zhoe?"

My face was in the folds of her skirt and I still sobbed out the after-swell of the terror, but I could hear Jem's voice speaking. He always seemed to me, when talking, to be expending his words with immense care.

"The horse wouldn't harm Joe," he pronounced.

That was a signal for Agnes to fly at him once more.

"No—won't harm him—you slip that out easy because Zhoe's no folks of yourn—an' never will be either. Agh!—God!—I could kill you if you weren't such a worm!"

"He wouldn't harm Joe, nor nobody."

The man's words were unsteady but assured. Agnes's voice went from her control completely; she came close to him and screamed in his face.

"Harm nobody?—Oh!—Oh!—Little man, go an' bring me that white horse—You been makin' eyes at me—Oh, I seen 'em!—Now if you want me—*me*—go out an' get the white horse that won't harm nobody—with your two bare hands—an' bring him to me."

For that moment, my sister was out of her mind.

Jem came over and laid an absent hand on my shoulder, as if he had thought to comfort me, and then had fallen into abstraction before the act was accomplished. After a moment of vacant quiet he looked up at Agnes.

"An' you tell me that, too," he said.

All that evening I was haunted by a picture of the silent man, with his hard red thumbs tucked in his belt, pursuing a shadow of horror through the black dune country. This distressed me so much that I finally crawled out from beneath the table, where I had been lying, and whispered my fears in my sister's ear. She had been very quiet all evening, but when she understood what I was saying she gave a little bitter laugh and put her arm around me.

"Don't be afeared, Zhoe," she whispered her answer. "The little man is tight behind his own door this night." Then she fell to brooding once more.

When Jem came to the little house the following day he carried a piece of line in one hand. He sat down as usual on the front steps. The picture of him that evening has remained to me the most vivid memory of my young days—why, I cannot say. I peeped out of the front window and saw him there, silhouetted against the blazing waters of the bay—the vast, silent, and expressive shout of the departing day casting out at me the unexpressive man.

Agnes came around a corner and stood, looking down at the line in Jem's hand. He looked down at it, too.

"I been thinkin' it over," he said.

"You're a-scared to do it!" she answered. For a long time they remained there without moving or speaking, both looking down at the line.

"You're a-scared to do it!" Agnes repeated at length, and Jem got up from the steps and went out through the gate toward the dunes. Never have I seen the whole world so saturated with passive flame as it seemed to me, peering from the gloom of the front room that evening.

At supper Agnes talked feverishly of many things, but ate nothing. All of us noticed it, and my mother remarked upon it. The silence outside was so complete that the riffle of the coming tide was audible in the pauses, and once I heard the note of the stallion, far away over the sand. Then my sister broke out into a humming tune—the first and last time I ever knew her to sing at table. I remember wondering why her eyes, which were usually so steady and straight seeing, turned here and there without rest, and why, after the meal, she wandered from window to window, and never stopped to look out at any.

That was to be a gala night for me. My father had been raking up the brush and leaves about the place for a week, heaping them, together with bits of old net and tarry shreds of canvas, in half a dozen piles before the house, and tonight I was allowed to set them off. I had them blazing soon after supper was over, and a fine monstrous spectacle they made for me, who danced up and down the lines full of elemental exultation, and then ran off to call Agnes to see my handiwork.

I could not find her anywhere in the house; I went through all the rooms and out and around the yard. No one knew where she was. My mother thought she had seen her with a shawl over her head, but had taken no particular notice at the time. It didn't matter, at any rate—Agnes often wandered out toward town in the early evening. The rest of us sat on the steps and watched the fires, baby brother and all, but they had lost something of their enchantment for me. I was pursuing an idea, an obscure apprehension.

"I b'lieve Aggie's gone to the dunes," I proclaimed, at length.

"Dunes!" my mother cried out. "No—you're foolish, Zhoe. Why?"

Thus confronted by the direct question, I found my reasonings too diaphanous for a logical answer.

"I dunno," I answered, abashed.

But I had set them worrying. It is a strange fact that fisher-folk are at once the bravest and the most apprehensive people I have any knowledge of. When worried, my mother was generally restless with her hands, while my father betrayed his anxiety by unwonted profanity and by aimless expeditions to inspect the dory mooring in the creek.

These things they did tonight, my mother on the steps, impassive save for her writhing fingers, my father visible in peripatetic red glimpses as he wandered, muttering, about the yard. He called out that he was going to step down and take a look at the boat.

After that, he was gone a long time—half an hour I should say—while the flames died down over the fires, replacing the uncertain flicker in the yard with a smooth pervasive glow. When he at length appeared, I wondered to see sand burrs clinging about the edges of his trousers. The nearest sand burrs I knew of were half a mile off toward Snail Road.

I don't know how long we waited after that. My mother put the baby to bed, and returned to sit with restless hands; my father, muttering curses the while, added bits of driftwood to the fires, with the instinct inbred in sea-people of keeping a beacon alight.

Their coming was as the coming of an apparition seen suddenly in the firelight, tottering forward on limbs too frail for its inexplicable and uncouth frame. Then my mother cried out, and my father's oath was a prayer, and it came to me that the apparition was not one but two figures, one bearing the other.

Jem staggered up between the fires and laid his burden down with her head in my mother's lap. My sister's face was a queer color, her eyes were closed. I was bewildered and afraid.

"Scared," Jem panted. He collapsed rather than sat upon the lowest step. "He never touched her—just scared her—out of her head."

None of us doubted for an instant who "he" was. I ran into the kitchen under my mother's order for water. She worked with a sort of feverish calm over the girl in her lap, while Jem sat, head in hands, and back heaving. After a little he got up and regarded my sister's face.

"She'll come around," he said.

It may have been a question. If it was the answer was at its heels.

Agnes's eyes opened at the sound of the words with a shadow of unutterable horror behind them—her hands went out to him in an agony of rigid appeal. Jem knelt down with an arm about her shoulders.

"You're all right," he comforted her, still expending his words, as it were, with care.

"He came out of the sand—right up out of the sand at me.". . . There was a certain queer quality of raving in Agnes's whisper. She clung to him with the impossible strength of terror. "He came out of the sand—his eyes were red—oh, red—I could see them—and—an' I couldn't run—couldn't step—not step—"

"Yes—yes—Home now, Miss Aggie." Jem's red hand was on her hair, soothing, as one might a child.

"How did I come here?" She put the question abruptly—in her own voice now—took her arms from his neck with a gesture of shame and laid them across my mother's shoulders. It was my mother who answered her query.

"Meester Hodges bring you, Aggie girl." Agnes's eyes went to the little man, but he was lost in abstract contemplation of the nearest fire bed.

My mother went on, "Ain't you goin' to thank Meester Hodges, Aggie?" Jem turned at that, lifting an imperative hand.

"Wait!" said he. "Wait! You told me—to bring the horse."

Agnes cried out, "No!—no!—Oh, please—"

"You told me. Wait—an' don't be afeared." He leaned against a post of the railing, his red skin seeming to take to itself all the dying light of the embers, and began to whistle, low at first, then filling out clear and high and throbbing. He whistled in a peculiar way which I have never observed in any other.

The air was half familiar to me, the one he had played with softly on the dune behind the house. But to me and to my people, bred to the cloying accents of the South, that clear, soaring, sweet thread of Northern melody came as strange and alien and tingling, filling our own familiar night with a quality of expectancy. Jem Hodges was a new man before our eyes; for the first time in our knowledge of him, he was giving utterance to himself. He swept through the melody once, and twice, and paused.

"He's far," he said, and a note of whickering came to us from the east-ward dunes. He caught up the air again, playing with it wonderful things, sweeping the little huddled family of us out of our intimate house and glowing, familiar yard, into a strange, wind-troubled country of his own.

And this time it was the night, not the sea, that gave up the great white stallion, rising to our fence in majestic flight, exploding from the flat darkness.

Jem cried, "No!—no!—don't be afeared!"—for we were making the gestures of panic. The animal came to him, picking a dainty way about the coals for all his tremendous weight, making a wonderfully fine picture with the fiery sheen over his vast deep chest, along the glistening flanks where the sweat stood, turning the four white fetlocks to agitated pinions of flame. Thus, I believe, the horses of the gods came to the ancients.

He stood over us there, heaving, mountainous, filling half the sphere of our sight. But his nose was in the bosom of Jem Hodges's coat, and his ears pricked forward to the breathing of Jem Hodges's song without words. The little man wandered on and on, picking a phrase from here and from there, wooing, recounting, laughing, exulting, weeping, never hating.

When he suddenly began to speak in words, it was as though he had come down a great way, out of his own element.

"It had to be—after all," he said. "After all. . . . Now I suppose I've got to take you on to the rich American leddy? She'll keep you fine—in a fine paddock—you—you of the big wide moorland—free gentleman of half an English county. Ah, it's bad, Baron boy."

Then he was talking to us—to Agnes. "I been lyin' to myself—tryin' to make myself believe Baron was away off and wild—I wanted to have him free like the air—long as he could. The rich leddy will pay five hundred pounds. Why do I need it? We're comfortable on our little place at home. Why?—because father says so an' a man must do what his father says—till he gets a wife an' family of his own. I thought Baron was gone when the ship got wrecked—I was near glad of it—he's no boy to pen up—in a paddock—with a ribbon on, mebbe. An' when I knew he wasn't gone—why—I fair couldn't do it—put it off an' off an' off. Ah, Baron, Baron—they gave me you when I could pick you up in the meadow—but a man's got to do what his father says—"

He fell to musing, then, running his hand over the broad forehead, combing out the silk of the forelock, caressing a fine ear. Then, as to himself—

"Till he gets a wife of his own!"

He spoke to my sister.

"Come here, Miss Aggie."

Agnes went to him and, at his command, laid her fingers on Baron's nose. The animal arched his great neck—oh, an indescribable gesture!— and mouthed the back of her hand. I thought of Agnes at that moment as the bravest girl in all the world. Agnes was a stranger to me that night.

After a little time my mother got up, saying that I ought to have been in my bed long ago. My father came in with us, so that we left only the white horse and my sister and Jem Hodges, standing in a black group against the glow of the fires.

5

How Comanche Came into Camp

By Elbridge Streeter Brooks

◇◇◇

As both an editor and writer, Elbridge Streeter Brooks specializes in books for young readers. His works include biographies of famous Americans, from the Founding Fathers to Civil War generals on both sides of the Mason-Dixon Line. Most of Brooks's work was nonfiction, but his handful of novels often involved a teenage boy in the midst of an extraordinary event in American history. Such was Master of the Strong Hearts: A Story of Custer's Last Rally, *published in 1898, twenty-two years after Custer's death on the Little Bighorn River in Montana Territory.*

It's the story of sixteen-year-old Jack Huntingdon, who in 1875 joins his uncle on a government expedition to the Dakota and Wyoming territories. While exploring on his own, Jack is captured by a band of Sioux. He meets a white man named Red Top, an adoptive member of the band, who introduces him to the renowned Sitting Bull. The legendary Lakota chief sends Jack home to the East to carry the message that the Sioux will never sell their lands.

In Washington Jack meets George Armstrong Custer, who offers him a chance to return to the West. Jack, hoping to meet Red Top again, agrees to go with Custer on a campaign against Sitting Bull. The story reaches its climax in June 1876 when Custer, after dividing his force into three sections, is soundly defeated by Sitting Bull at the Battle of the Little Bighorn. Custer and more than two hundred soldiers and

*civilians, everyone in his personal command, die in and around what
is now called Last Stand Hill.*

*Also dead are all the horses of Custer's unit, or so Jack and the
survivors in the other sections of the regiment believe. Jack and the
soldiers are burying the Seventh Cavalry dead when they discover
that there was indeed one living creature left on the battlefield.*
—SHARON B. SMITH

JACK TURNED SADLY AWAY FROM THE SPOT IN WHICH LAY HIS FRIEND
the renegade. After that day's crowding experience the light-hearted lad
could never more be unfamiliar with death. The Valley of the Little Big
Horn had indeed been to him a veritable valley of death.

He found the troopers still at their sad yet brotherly task; but he
managed to get the trumpeter apart so that he might tell him what he
wished. Briefly he recited Po-to-sha-sha's story and told of the repentant
renegade's last wish.

"Wore the flag next to his heart, did he?" said the trumpeter. "Well,
by George! such a deserter as that is worth forgiving. I reckon he got
more punishment than the service could ever have given him. And
turned Indian, too! Well, Jack, drive ahead. You can count me in on this.
I reckon we can respect his last wishes, even if he did turn redskin."

And so it came to pass that Red Top the renegade had a Christian
burial. For Jack and the trumpeter dug a grave for the squaw man beside
that of his faithful Indian wife; over it they planted the stars and stripes,
and above it, when all was over, the trumpeter played taps, and Po-to-sha-
sha the deserter slept in a soldier's grave.

Jack rode back to the camp in the upper valley that night feeling that,
on that day indeed, he had "supped full of horrors." But "out of sight" is
very soon "out of mind" with a healthy, happy-go-lucky boy, even if he
be strong enough of character and stout enough of heart to never forget,
though he may soon stop thinking, about the sights and scenes of so
memorable a season as that disastrous campaign of the Little Big Horn
in 1876.

Jack found plenty of things to divert his thoughts as he joined the
camp; but that night, after mess, as the men sat around the bivouac fire

smoking and discussing the events that have now become historic in that fatal incident of Custer's last rally, he found himself listening intently as the troopers talked the matter over and freely gave their opinion for or against the general's conduct, and the apparently needless slaughter of more than two hundred gallant men.

Opinions were widely divided. Some declared that the movement was all wrong from the start.

"The general oughtn't to have divided up," said one critic. "If he'd kept the command together and gone in with us all in a bunch he'd 'a' licked 'em, sure as shootin'!"

"That's so," chimed in another; "that's just the way it came out over yonder"—he jerked his head in the direction of that fatal field still known as Custer's Hill. "Didn't you see how they lay around there in three or four little piles? They were too much divided. I tell you, there's nothing an Indian's so afraid of as massing. He likes to get the outfit separated and go for each part."

"I don't see that," said a corporal, long in the Seventh; "that's just the way the general did the thing before, and it never failed till now. If he could have got at 'em early enough, I know it would have been all right, but you see we were a little too late in the day to give them the surprise party we reckoned on."

"Anyway," said one of the self-constituted critics, "the general was too fresh. He was rash, I say—mighty rash. Why didn't he back out when he saw what he'd got to handle, and wait for the rest of us to come up? I don't suppose he thought he was going to fight all the Indians in Christendom. Ten to one is bigger odds than even Custer ought to face. Seems to me he should have known that and pulled back in time."

"They do say," observed another of the critics—one who counted himself well posted on the news of the day—"they do say that the general and old man Grant had a set-to over somethin' or other, down to Washington, and that the President give it to the general hot and heavy. That set him up to make a record for himself out here in the Indian country, and he was just bound to go in and win—the bigger the victory with the smallest outfit, so much the better. And that's how comes it he's layin' out there where he is, and two hundred good fellows alongside of him, instead of legging it after the Indians with us at his heels. Sounds kind of likely now, doesn't it?"

"No, sir, I'll be hanged if it does," exclaimed Jack's friend, the trumpeter. "Say, did you see who was out there on that field? There was the general, and Cap'n Tom, his brother, and Mr. Boston Custer, his other brother, and Cap'n Calhoun, his brother-in-law, and that young Autie Reed, his nephew, to say nothing of those officers who were his closest friends, Keogh and Yates and Cook. Does it stan' to reason that the general would 'a' gone in, selfish-like and just out o' spite, and used up his whole family and his friends, only to make a show? No, sir, it don't. You fellows know such a lot, you make me just sick with your ideas."

But the critics were not silenced by this outburst.

"Well, p'r'aps that ain't so," was the response from one of the most pronounced of them; "but I tell you, the general's tactics were wrong. Why didn't he go slow when he struck that trail that brought us over here? How do we know that he followed orders in hurrying up his fight? General Terry's got a cool head, and just as like as not he told Custer to hold on and wait for him and Gibbon's column as soon as he'd struck the trail."

"Lot you know," said the trumpeter. "Why, I was right by the general's horse ready to sound the advance when General Terry was bidding him good-bye—up there on the Rosebud, you know. And General Terry said to him—I heard him—says he, 'Use your own judgment, Custer; if you do strike a big trail, just you do what you think best.' All he cautioned him was to hold on to his wounded. 'Whatever you do, Custer,' he says, 'hold on to your wounded.' I heard him say that."

"Well, he held on to 'em, sure enough, didn't he?" remarked one of the troopers. "I reckon none of 'em got away. They were all there."

"Right you are, Jimmy," responded a chorus of comrades, and one remarked, "Say, boys, did you see old Butler—sergeant of Cap'n Tom Custer's troop? Did you see where he was? I tell you, he put in his best licks 'fore he threw up the sponge. There he lay, all by his lonesome, down toward the ford, and I'll bet I picked up a pint o' empty ca'tridge shells under him. How he must have laid them Indians out! He was always a rattling good shot, the sergeant was."

"Empty shells!" growled another trooper. "H'm! that don't say much. I tell you, boys, it was the ca'tridges that whipped us. Nine out of ten of them were defective. They were dirty, and they corroded the ejectors so's you couldn't get the empty shells out of the chambers without using your knife to pick 'em out. That's what ailed our guns t' other day. And I tell you it just killed the general's men. How much you going to do when you've got to stop between shots to dig the shells out 'n the ejectors— 'specially when the Indians have got better and newer guns than you have? And where did they get them? At the agencies. Government guns, too. What do you say to that? I call it manslaughter, I do. What redress have poor chaps like us got when the government sends us out here to lick the Indians, and then turns round and sells the Indians guns to kill us with—better guns than ours, too?"

"It's all dirty politics and favoritism and lettin' the Indian agents have a chance to make some money, no matter who's hurt, that does that business," remarked an indignant comrade. "And we get the worst end of the shoddy contracts and the no-account guns—and that does our business."

Whereupon the discussion drifted off into a general arraignment of all in authority over them, as is always the case with all subordinates in warlike or peaceful surroundings, and always has been the case since ever the first man in the world hired another to serve him. Grumbling is the subordinate's privilege, even if it is not his prerogative.

But even criticism and grumbling must end in time, and good humor return, as it did in this case around the glimmering bivouac fires on the bluffs of the Little Big Horn. For, notwithstanding the somber nature of their surroundings, their duties of that ghastly day—the same duties for which they would be detailed on the morrow—the troopers must have their relaxation as certainly as their fault-finding. So before long— before taps were sounded and the weary troopers tumbled into bed—they were all skylarking about their quarters; or, dropping into an absurd step, paraded about the fire, singing that good-humored travesty upon themselves just then a favorite in New York music-halls:

There was Sergeant John McCafferty and Capt'n Donahue,
They made us march and toe the mark in gallant Company Q.

Oh, the drums did roll, upon me soul, and this is the way we go:
Forty miles a day on beans and hay, in the regular army, O!

You can't long keep soldiers or sailors in a somber mood, even though death lies behind them, before them, or all about them! They say there was joking in the ranks even when the six hundred of the Light Brigade—"all that was left of them"—rode out of the death-trap at Balaclava! Dewey's men went skylarking to breakfast in the lull of Manila's fight, and Hobson's comrades put up a bit of "funning" as they rowed into the Spanish clutches at Santiago.

But the trumpeter said to Jack, "It makes me sick, Jack, so it does, to hear those freshies from St. Paul—why, they joined the command after you did, Jack—giving their opinion over the general's tactics, and what he ought to have done! A battle had to come, didn't it? That's what we're here for. If the general hadn't come here, but had struck south to find Crook, or had waited for Terry, why, the Indians wouldn't have hung around till he picked out the time to lick 'em. They'd have just up and got. That's their way. If they'd done so, who'd have got the blame? Custer. He came here; he found 'em; he sailed in to whip 'em. He struck the whole Sioux nation, and got the worst of it. Well, what of it? Isn't it better to stand up and take your medicine like a man, even if it does kill you, than hold back and be afraid to stick your nose out for fear some one'll pull it? General Custer died like a hero; and so did his men; and this country'll never forget 'em, you mark my words."

From all of which Jack Huntingdon was led to infer that the trumpeter thought more of Custer's dash than of Reno's timidity—although no names were mentioned, for the trumpeter was too good a soldier to go against the rules of discipline. And still the never-answered questions stayed with both of them: "Why did not Benteen go with those packs? Why didn't Reno go, too?"

Next day the work of clearing and temporarily marking the battle-field that was a burying ground was concluded, and at once preparations began for a speedy withdrawal. For General Terry, who was, like Reno, no seasoned Indian fighter, felt himself on dangerous and uncertain ground, and decided to fall back at once to the supply camp on the Yellowstone.

He had no inclination to go off "playing tag" with the whole Sioux nation, and wisely deemed discretion the better part of valor. His column, as well as that of General Crook, had been defeated by the well-generalled and warlike Sioux. He wanted reinforcements before he advanced.

So preparations for withdrawal were made. But in the afternoon of the day before departure Jack accompanied a detail sent to make one last survey of the two hundred and sixty graves on and about Custer's Hill. And as they waited there Jack sought once more the twin graves under the cottonwoods, and said a boyish adieu to the good Mi-mi, who had made him the corn-dumplings, and the odd squaw man who had been his friend in time of need. The rent flag still fluttered above the renegade's last resting-place, and Jack with a sigh turned away, going, as he knew, to that civilization which this poor exile longed for, yet would not seek because of his faithfulness to her who had been faithful to him. As he left, Jack somehow found himself saying over and over a scrap that he had heard somewhere, but which he could neither place nor patch out—"in their deaths they were not divided."

"It suits them, anyhow," he declared, "whoever said it."

The dusk was closing in upon the bleak and bluff-like cliffs, the scarred and scarped heights that rampart the fair and now fertile valley of the Little Big Horn, as the detail rode campward across the valley. They were to ascend by the ravine-like coulee up which Reno's men had scrambled in their panic-like flight; but, from their trail, the sharp ridges of the bluffs, touched with the twilight, stood dim and ghostly in the dusk.

As Jack looked his last upon the ridge along which Custer's men had galloped to their death, and where he had taken the long leap that gave him life, he caught every now and then a glimpse of a moving form outlined on the edge of the bluff. At last he pointed it out to his friend the trumpeter.

"It looks like a riderless horse," he said. "But, of course, it can't be."

"The ghost of Custer's troop, I reckon," the trumpeter said, half in fun and half in fear. For superstition touches more people in this world than we are ready to admit. "Looks that way, don't it, Jack? though, of course, that's all foolishness. Hark! hear that! By George! it is a horse—or the ghost of the troop."

They all started as, down from the bluff, came the quavering notes of a neigh.

"The last call of the outpost!" the trumpeter declared, and the whole detail breathed a bit easier as they toiled up the ascent and at last dismounted beside the newly lighted bivouac fire.

But, even as they flung themselves down at mess, once again that quavering neigh of the ghostly troop horse fell upon their ears, and in the distance sounded the approaching tramp of a warhorse. More than one man started to his feet, while the detail that had seen the phantom charger on the bluffs looked at each other in query.

"It's the ghost of the troop horse, Jack," the trumpeter declared. "I wonder is it a warning—or what?"

The trampling sounded nearer; another neigh, quavering, pitiful, almost appealing in its tones, as if begging companionship or welcome, came to their ears, and then, past the challenging outposts and the startled sentries, the ghost of the troop horse came within the lines, and stood trembling before the bivouac fire.

"It's one of ours!" cried Captain McDougall, who stood by. "Stir up that fire, Jack, won't you? Let's see if we know it."

The flare shot up, and in its light the newcomer stood revealed. Bleeding from severe wounds, weak and weary, and with a desire for pity and comfort that was deeply pathetic shining in his eyes, the scarred but beautiful sorrel laid its head against the captain's shoulder as if to claim protection.

Jack sprang forward. "Why! it's Comanche!" he said.

"You're right, Jack. By Jove! it is," cried the captain, flinging his arms about the neck of the sorrel. "Poor Myles Keogh! It's his Comanche. And I believe, boys, he's the only living thing we shall ever see from our side of that battlefield. Let's give him a rousing welcome, boys. Come! three cheers for Comanche!"

And about the bivouac fire the cheers of welcome rang out so lustily that, from all the camp, came officers and men anxious to know the cause and to join again in a salvo of welcome to the noble charger Comanche, sole survivor of the fight, gallant Captain Keogh's splendid Kentucky sorrel.

Next day the shattered command took the backward way, retiring to the supply-camp on the Yellowstone. There Terry was heavily reinforced. Men were hurried also to the strengthening of Crook at the south; and the two commands, uniting in August, 1876, entered upon the protracted search for the Sioux that ended, not in capture, as hoped, but only when Crazy Horse disappeared in the fastnesses of the Dakota Mountains, and Sitting Bull had escaped across the border into British possessions. Once again had the Master of the Strong Hearts proved himself a match for the Long-Swords, against whom he still made bad medicine.

In the end, however, the white man of course triumphed. It was not, in the nature of things, possible for the starving and divided hostiles long to resist the marshaled forces of the United States.

Colonel Miles and Colonel Merritt, both of whom, as general of the army and commander of the Manila expedition, were later to win renown in the war with Spain, pursued the Sioux with energy and determination; the union of the separated Indian bands was prevented and when Lame Deer, the Minniconjou chief, with the last of the resisting hostiles, was surprised and routed on the Rosebud in May, 1877, Crazy Horse, the valiant Ogallala, driven to surrender himself, ran "amuck" on his way to the guard-house at Camp Robinson, and died as a true hostile wished to die—defying the white man.

Three years later, in July, 1881, Sitting Bull himself, pining for his loved home land, crossed the border and, at Standing Rock, surrendered with all his following.

The greatest of all the Sioux wars was over. The prowess of the Long-Swords had overcome the skill, as it had broken the spirit, of the medicine chief, and Custer was avenged.

As for Jack, long before the ending of that summer campaign of 1876, he was speeding to the eastward toward civilization and home. His own "campaign" had not been a success; and yet, in its way, it had been a more surprising success than even his wildest fancy imagined. For he had taken part in the most famous of Indian campaigns, and had a share in the most notable tragedy of all our Indian warfare.

><><><><><><><><><><><><><><><><><><><><><><><><><><><><><><><><><><><><><><><

In reality, Comanche was not the only equine survivor of Last Stand Hill. Several grievously wounded horses were found on the battlefield, still living but too badly injured to save. Other Seventh Cavalry mounts were captured and ended their lives as Indian ponies. But Comanche was the ultimate survivor, living a life of ease and honor at Ft. Riley, Kansas, until his death. He was believed to be twenty-nine years old at the time of his death in 1891.

><><><><><><><><><><><><><><><><><><><><><><><><><><><><><><><><><><><><><><><

6

The Ben Hur Chariot Race

By Lew Wallace

◇◇◇

How can a modern moviegoer like myself ever forget the movie scenes of Charlton Heston commanding a chariot in a desperate race in Rome's coliseum? That race came from a book by a remarkable man, Lew Wallace (1827–1905). He was an American lawyer, Union general in the American Civil War, governor of the New Mexico Territory, politician, diplomat, and author from Indiana. Among his novels and biographies, Wallace is best known for his historical adventure story Ben-Hur: A Tale of the Christ *(1880), a bestselling novel that has been called "the most influential Christian book of the nineteenth century." Here is the great chariot race, without Charlton Heston but exactly as Lew Wallace conceived it.*

◇◇◇

THE CIRCUS AT ANTIOCH STOOD ON THE SOUTH BANK OF THE RIVER, nearly opposite the island, differing in no respect from the plan of such buildings in general.

In the purest sense, the games were a gift to the public; consequently, everybody was free to attend; and, vast as the holding capacity of the structure was, so fearful were the people, on this occasion, lest there should not be room for them, that, early the day before the opening of the exhibition, they took up all the vacant spaces in the vicinity, where their temporary shelter suggested an army in waiting.

At midnight the entrances were thrown wide, and the rabble, surging in, occupied the quarters assigned to them, from which nothing less than an earthquake or an army with spears could have dislodged them. They dozed the night away on the benches, and breakfasted there; and there the close of the exercises found them, patient and sight-hungry as in the beginning.

The better people, their seats secured, began moving towards the Circus about the first hour of the morning, the noble and very rich among them distinguished by litters and retinues of liveried servants.

By the second hour, the efflux from the city was a stream unbroken and innumerable.

Exactly as the gnomon of the official dial up in the citadel pointed the second hour half gone, the legion, in full panoply, and with all its standards on exhibit, descended from Mount Sulpius; and when the rear of the last cohort disappeared in the bridge, Antioch was literally abandoned—not that the Circus could hold the multitude, but that the multitude was gone out to it, nevertheless.

A great concourse on the river shore witnessed the consul come over from the island in a barge of state. As the great man landed, and was received by the legion, the martial show for one brief moment transcended the attraction of the Circus.

At the third hour, the audience, if such it may be termed, was assembled; at last, a flourish of trumpets called for silence, and instantly the gaze of over a hundred thousand persons was directed towards a pile forming the eastern section of the building.

There was a basement first, broken in the middle by a broad arched passage, called the Porta Pompae, over which, on an elevated tribunal magnificently decorated with insignia and legionary standards, the consul sat in the place of honor. On both sides of the passage the basement was divided into stalls termed carceres, each protected in front by massive gates swung to statuesque pilasters. Over the stalls next was a cornice crowned by a low balustrade; back of which the seats arose in theatre arrangement, all occupied by a throng of dignitaries superbly attired. The pile extended the width of the Circus, and was flanked on both sides by towers which, besides helping the architects give grace to their work, served the velaria, or purple awnings, stretched between them so as to throw the whole quarter in a shade that became exceedingly grateful as the day advanced.

This structure, it is now thought, can be made useful in helping the reader to a sufficient understanding of the arrangement of the rest of the interior of the Circus. He has only to fancy himself seated on the tribunal with the consul, facing to the west, where everything is under his eye.

On the right and left, if he will look, he will see the main entrances, very ample, and guarded by gates hinged to the towers.

Directly below him is the arena—a level plane of considerable extent, covered with fine white sand. There all the trials will take place except the running.

Looking across this sanded arena westwardly still, there is a pedestal of marble supporting three low conical pillars of gray stone, much carven. Many an eye will hunt for those pillars before the day is done, for they are the first goal, and mark the beginning and end of the race-course. Behind the pedestal, leaving a passageway and space for an altar, commences a wall ten or twelve feet in breadth and five or six in height, extending thence exactly two hundred yards, or one Olympic stadium. At the farther, or westward, extremity of the wall there is another pedestal, surmounted with pillars which mark the second goal.

The racers will enter the course on the right of the first goal, and keep the wall all the time to their left. The beginning and ending points of the contest lie, consequently, directly in front of the consul across the arena; and for that reason his seat was admittedly the most desirable in the Circus.

Now if the reader, who is still supposed to be seated on the consular tribunal over the Porta Pompae, will look up from the ground arrangement of the interior, the first point to attract his notice will be the marking of the outer boundary-line of the course—that is, a plain-faced, solid wall, fifteen or twenty feet in height, with a balustrade on its cope, like that over the carceres, or stalls, in the east. This balcony, if followed round the course, will be found broken in three places to allow passages of exit and entrance, two in the north and one in the west; the latter very ornate, and called the Gate of Triumph, because, when all is over, the victors will pass out that way, crowned, and with triumphal escort and ceremonies.

At the west end the balcony encloses the course in the form of a half circle, and is made to uphold two great galleries.

Directly behind the balustrade on the coping of the balcony is the first seat, from which ascend the succeeding benches, each higher than the one in front of it; giving to view a spectacle of surpassing interest— the spectacle of a vast space ruddy and glistening with human faces, and rich with varicolored costumes.

The commonalty occupy quarters over in the west, beginning at the point of termination of an awning, stretched, it would seem, for the accommodation of the better classes exclusively.

Having thus the whole interior of the Circus under view at the moment of the sounding of the trumpets, let the reader next imagine the multitude seated and sunk to sudden silence, and motionless in its intensity of interest.

Out of the Porta Pompae over in the east rises a sound mixed of voices and instruments harmonized. Presently, forth issues the chorus of the procession with which the celebration begins; the editor and civic authorities of the city, givers of the games, follow in robes and garlands; then the gods, some on platforms borne by men, others in great four-wheel carriages gorgeously decorated; next them, again, the contestants of the day, each in costume exactly as he will run, wrestle, leap, box, or drive.

Slowly crossing the arena, the procession proceeds to make circuit of the course. The display is beautiful and imposing. Approval runs before it in a shout, as the water rises and swells in front of a boat in motion. If the dumb, figured gods make no sign of appreciation of the welcome, the editor and his associates are not so backward.

The reception of the athletes is even more demonstrative, for there is not a man in the assemblage who has not something in wager upon them, though but a mite or farthing. And it is noticeable, as the classes move by, that the favorites among them are speedily singled out: either their names are loudest in the uproar, or they are more profusely showered with wreaths and garlands tossed to them from the balcony.

If there is a question as to the popularity with the public of the several games, it is now put to rest. To the splendor of the chariots and the

superexcellent beauty of the horses, the charioteers add the personality necessary to perfect the charm of their display. Their tunics, short,
sleeveless, and of the finest woollen texture, are of the assigned colors.
A horseman accompanies each one of them except Ben-Hur, who, for
some reason—possibly distrust—has chosen to go alone; so, too, they are
all helmeted but him. As they approach, the spectators stand upon the
benches, and there is a sensible deepening of the clamor, in which a sharp
listener may detect the shrill piping of women and children; at the same
time, the things roseate flying from the balcony thicken into a storm, and,
striking the men, drop into the chariot-beds, which are threatened with
filling to the tops. Even the horses have a share in the ovation; nor may
it be said they are less conscious than their masters of the honors they
receive.

Very soon, as with the other contestants, it is made apparent that
some of the drivers are more in favor than others; and then the discovery
follows that nearly every individual on the benches, women and children
as well as men, wears a color, most frequently a ribbon upon the breast or
in the hair: now it is green, now yellow, now blue; but, searching the great
body carefully, it is manifest that there is a preponderance of white, and
scarlet and gold.

In a modern assemblage called together as this one is, particularly where
there are sums at hazard upon the race, a preference would be decided by
the qualities or performance of the horses; here, however, nationality was
the rule. If the Byzantine and Sidonian found small support, it was because
their cities were scarcely represented on the benches. On their side, the
Greeks, though very numerous, were divided between the Corinthian and
the Athenian, leaving but a scant showing of green and yellow. Messala's
scarlet and gold would have been but little better had not the citizens of
Antioch, proverbially a race of courtiers, joined the Romans by adopting the color of their favorite. There were left then the country people, or
Syrians, the Jews, and the Arabs; and they, from faith in the blood of the
sheik's four, blent largely with hate of the Romans, whom they desired,
above all things, to see beaten and humbled, mounted the white, making
the most noisy, and probably the most numerous, faction of all.

As the charioteers move on in the circuit, the excitement increases; at the second goal, where, especially in the galleries, the white is the ruling color, the people exhaust their flowers and rive the air with screams.

"Messala! Messala!"

"Ben-Hur! Ben-Hur!"

Such are the cries.

Upon the passage of the procession, the factionists take their seats and resume conversation.

"Ah, by Bacchus! was he not handsome?" exclaims a woman, whose Romanism is betrayed by the colors flying in her hair.

"And how splendid his chariot!" replies a neighbor, of the same proclivities. "It is all ivory and gold. Jupiter grant he wins!"

The notes on the bench behind them were entirely different.

"A hundred shekels on the Jew!"

The voice is high and shrill.

"Nay, be thou not rash," whispers a moderating friend to the speaker.

"The children of Jacob are not much given to Gentile sports, which are too often accursed in the sight of the Lord."

"True, but saw you ever one more cool and assured? And what an arm he has!"

"And what horses!" says a third.

"And for that," a fourth one adds, "they say he has all the tricks of the Romans."

A woman completes the eulogium.

"Yes, and he is even handsomer than the Roman."

Thus encouraged, the enthusiast shrieks again, "A hundred shekels on the Jew!"

"Thou fool!" answers an Antiochian, from a bench well forward on the balcony. "Knowest thou not there are fifty talents laid against him, six to one, on Messala? Put up thy shekels, lest Abraham rise and smite thee."

"Ha, ha! thou ass of Antioch! Cease thy bray. Knowest thou not it was Messala betting on himself?"

Such the reply.

And so ran the controversy, not always good-natured.

When at length the march was ended and the Porta Pompae received back the procession, Ben-Hur knew he had his prayer.

The eyes of the East were upon his contest with Messala.

About three o'clock, speaking in modern style, the program was concluded except the chariot-race. The editor, wisely considerate of the comfort of the people, chose that time for a recess. At once the vomitoria were thrown open, and all who could hastened to the portico outside where the restaurateurs had their quarters. Those who remained yawned, talked, gossiped, consulted their tablets, and, all distinctions else forgotten, merged into but two classes—the winners, who were happy, and the losers, who were grum and captious.

Now, however, a third class of spectators, composed of citizens who desired only to witness the chariot-race, availed themselves of the recess to come in and take their reserved seats; by so doing they thought to attract the least attention and give the least offence. Among these were Simonides and his party, whose places were in the vicinity of the main entrance on the north side, opposite the consul.

As the four stout servants carried the merchant in his chair up the aisle, curiosity was much excited. Presently some one called his name. Those about caught it and passed it on along the benches to the west; and there was hurried climbing on seats to get sight of the man about whom common report had coined and put in circulation a romance so mixed of good fortune and bad that the like had never been known or heard of before.

Ilderim was also recognized and warmly greeted; but nobody knew Balthasar or the two women who followed him closely veiled.

The people made way for the party respectfully, and the ushers seated them in easy speaking distance of each other down by the balustrade overlooking the arena. In providence of comfort, they sat upon cushions and had stools for footrests.

The women were Iras and Esther.

Upon being seated, the latter cast a frightened look over the Circus, and drew the veil closer about her face; while the Egyptian, letting her veil fall upon her shoulders, gave herself to view, and gazed at the scene with the seeming unconsciousness of being stared at, which, in a woman, is usually the result of long social habitude.

The new-comers generally were yet making their first examination of the great spectacle, beginning with the consul and his attendants, when some workmen ran in and commenced to stretch a chalked rope across the arena from balcony to balcony in front of the pillars of the first goal.

About the same time, also, six men came in through the Porta Pompae and took post, one in front of each occupied stall; whereat there was a prolonged hum of voices in every quarter.

"See, see! The green goes to number four on the right; the Athenian is there."

"And Messala—yes, he is in number two."

"The Corinthian—"

"Watch the white! See, he crosses over, he stops; number one it is—number one on the left."

"No, the black stops there, and the white at number two."

"So it is."

These gate-keepers, it should be understood, were dressed in tunics colored like those of the competing charioteers; so, when they took their stations, everybody knew the particular stall in which his favorite was that moment waiting.

"Did you ever see Messala?" the Egyptian asked Esther.

The Jewess shuddered as she answered no. If not her father's enemy, the Roman was Ben-Hur's.

"He is beautiful as Apollo."

As Iras spoke, her large eyes brightened and she shook her jeweled fan. Esther looked at her with the thought, "Is he, then, so much handsomer than Ben-Hur?" Next moment she heard Ilderim say to her father, "Yes, his stall is number two on the left of the Porta Pompae"; and, thinking it was of Ben-Hur he spoke, her eyes turned that way. Taking but the briefest glance at the wattled face of the gate, she drew the veil close and muttered a little prayer.

Presently Sanballat came to the party.

"I am just from the stalls, O sheik," he said, bowing gravely to Ilderim, who began combing his beard, while his eyes glittered with eager inquiry. "The horses are in perfect condition."

Ilderim replied simply, "If they are beaten, I pray it be by some other than Messala."

Turning then to Simonides, Sanballat drew out a tablet, saying, "I bring you also something of interest. I reported, you will remember, the wager concluded with Messala last night, and stated that I left another which, if taken, was to be delivered to me in writing today before the race began. Here it is."

Simonides took the tablet and read the memorandum carefully.

"Yes," he said, "their emissary came to ask me if you had so much money with me. Keep the tablet close. If you lose, you know where to come; if you win"—his face knit hard—"if you win—ah, friend, see to it! See the signers escape not; hold them to the last shekel. That is what they would with us."

"Trust me," replied the purveyor.

"Will you not sit with us?" asked Simonides.

"You are very good," the other returned; "but if I leave the consul, young Rome yonder will boil over. Peace to you; peace to all."

At length the recess came to an end.

The trumpeters blew a call at which the absentees rushed back to their places. At the same time, some attendants appeared in the arena, and, climbing upon the division wall, went to an entablature near the second goal at the west end, and placed upon it seven wooden balls; then returning to the first goal, upon an entablature there they set up seven other pieces of wood hewn to represent dolphins.

"What shall they do with the balls and fishes, O sheik?" asked Balthasar.

"Hast thou never attended a race?"

"Never before; and hardly know I why I am here."

"Well, they are to keep the count. At the end of each round run thou shalt see one ball and one fish taken down."

The preparations were now complete, and presently a trumpeter in gaudy uniform arose by the editor, ready to blow the signal of commencement promptly at his order. Straightway the stir of the people and the hum of their conversation died away. Every face near-by, and every face in the lessening perspective, turned to the east, as all eyes settled upon the gates of the six stalls which shut in the competitors.

The unusual flush upon his face gave proof that even Simonides had caught the universal excitement. Ilderim pulled his beard fast and furious.

"Look now for the Roman," said the fair Egyptian to Esther, who did not hear her, for, with close-drawn veil and beating heart, she sat watching for Ben-Hur.

The structure containing the stalls, it should be observed, was in form of the segment of a circle, retired on the right so that its central point was projected forward, and midway the course, on the starting side of the first goal. Every stall, consequently, was equally distant from the starting-line or chalked rope above mentioned.

The trumpet sounded short and sharp; whereupon the starters, one for each chariot, leaped down from behind the pillars of the goal, ready to give assistance if any of the fours proved unmanageable.

Again the trumpet blew, and simultaneously the gate-keepers threw the stalls open.

First appeared the mounted attendants of the charioteers, five in all, Ben-Hur having rejected the service. The chalked line was lowered to let them pass, then raised again. They were beautifully mounted, yet scarcely observed as they rode forward; for all the time the trampling of eager horses, and the voices of drivers scarcely less eager, were heard behind in the stalls, so that one might not look away an instant from the gaping doors.

The chalked line up again, the gate-keepers called their men; instantly the ushers on the balcony waved their hands, and shouted with all their strength, "Down! down!"

As well have whistled to stay a storm.

Forth from each stall, like missiles in a volley from so many great guns, rushed the six fours; and up the vast assemblage arose, electrified and irrepressible, and, leaping upon the benches, filled the Circus and the air above it with yells and screams. This was the time for which they had so patiently waited!—this the moment of supreme interest treasured up in talk and dreams since the proclamation of the games!

"He is come—there—look!" cried Iras, pointing to Messala.

"I see him," answered Esther, looking at Ben-Hur.

The veil was withdrawn. For an instant the little Jewess was brave. An idea of the joy there is in doing an heroic deed under the eyes of a multitude came to her, and she understood ever after how, at such times, the souls of men, in the frenzy of performance, laugh at death or forget it utterly.

The competitors were now under view from nearly every part of the Circus, yet the race was not begun; they had first to make the chalked line successfully.

The line was stretched for the purpose of equalizing the start. If it were dashed upon, discomfiture of man and horses might be apprehended; on the other hand, to approach it timidly was to incur the hazard of being thrown behind in the beginning of the race; and that was certain forfeit of the great advantage always striven for—the position next the division wall on the inner line of the course.

This trial, its perils and consequences, the spectators knew thoroughly; and if the opinion of old Nestor, uttered that time he handed the reins to his son, were true:

"It is not strength, but art, obtained the prize, And to be swift is less than to be wise."

all on the benches might well look for warning of the winner to be now given, justifying the interest with which they breathlessly watched for the result.

The arena swam in a dazzle of light; yet each driver looked first thing for the rope, then for the coveted inner line. So, all six aiming at the same point and speeding furiously, a collision seemed inevitable; nor that merely. What if the editor, at the last moment, dissatisfied with the start, should withhold the signal to drop the rope? Or if he should not give it in time?

The crossing was about two hundred and fifty feet in width. Quick the eye, steady the hand, unerring the judgment required. If now one look away! or his mind wander! or a rein slip! And what attraction in the ensemble of the thousands over the spreading balcony! Calculating upon the natural impulse to give one glance—just one—in sooth of curiosity or vanity, malice might be there with an artifice; while friendship and love, did they serve the same result, might be as deadly as malice.

The divine last touch in perfecting the beautiful is animation. Can we accept the saying, then these latter days, so tame in pastime and dull in sports, have scarcely anything to compare to the spectacle offered by the six contestants. Let the reader try to fancy it; let him first look down upon the arena, and see it glistening in its frame of dull-gray granite walls; let him then, in this perfect field, see the chariots, light of wheel, very graceful, and ornate as paint and burnishing can make them—Messala's rich with ivory and gold; let him see the drivers, erect and statuesque, undisturbed by the motion of the cars, their limbs naked, and fresh and ruddy with the healthful polish of the baths—in their right hands goads, suggestive of torture dreadful to the thought—in their left hands, held in careful separation, and high, that they may not interfere with view of the steeds, the reins passing taut from the fore ends of the carriage-poles; let him see the fours, chosen for beauty as well as speed; let him see them in magnificent action, their masters not more conscious of the situation and all that is asked and hoped from them—their heads tossing, nostrils in play, now distent, now contracted—limbs too dainty for the sand which they touch but to spurn—limbs slender, yet with impact crushing as hammers—every muscle of the rounded bodies instinct with glorious life, swelling, diminishing, justifying the world in taking from them its ultimate measure of force; finally, along with chariots, drivers, horses, let the reader see the accompanying shadows fly; and, with such distinctness as the picture comes, he may share the satisfaction and deeper pleasure of those to whom it was a thrilling fact, not a feeble fancy. Every age has its plenty of sorrows; Heaven help where there are no pleasures!

The competitors having started each on the shortest line for the position next the wall, yielding would be like giving up the race; and who dared yield? It is not in common nature to change a purpose in mid-career; and the cries of encouragement from the balcony were indistinguishable and indescribable: a roar which had the same effect upon all the drivers.

The fours neared the rope together. Then the trumpeter by the editor's side blew a signal vigorously. Twenty feet away it was not heard. Seeing the action, however, the judges dropped the rope, and not an instant too soon, for the hoof of one of Messala's horses struck it as it fell. Nothing daunted, the Roman shook out his long lash, loosed the reins, leaned forward, and, with a triumphant shout, took the wall.

"Jove with us! Jove with us!" yelled all the Roman faction, in a frenzy of delight.

As Messala turned in, the bronze lion's head at the end of his axle caught the foreleg of the Athenian's right-hand trace-mate, flinging the brute over against its yoke-fellow. Both staggered, struggled, and lost their headway. The ushers had their will at least in part. The thousands held their breath with horror; only up where the consul sat was there shouting.

"Jove with us!" screamed Drusus, frantically.

"He wins! Jove with us!" answered his associates, seeing Messala speed on.

Tablet in hand, Sanballat turned to them; a crash from the course below stopped his speech, and he could not but look that way.

Messala having passed, the Corinthian was the only contestant on the Athenian's right, and to that side the latter tried to turn his broken four; and then; as ill-fortune would have it, the wheel of the Byzantine, who was next on the left, struck the tail-piece of his chariot, knocking his feet from under him. There was a crash, a scream of rage and fear, and the unfortunate Cleanthes fell under the hoofs of his own steeds: a terrible sight, against which Esther covered her eyes.

On swept the Corinthian, on the Byzantine, on the Sidonian.

Sanballat looked for Ben-Hur, and turned again to Drusus and his coterie.

"A hundred sestertii on the Jew!" he cried.

"Taken!" answered Drusus.

"Another hundred on the Jew!" shouted Sanballat.

Nobody appeared to hear him. He called again; the situation below was too absorbing, and they were too busy shouting, "Messala! Messala! Jove with us!"

When the Jewess ventured to look again, a party of workmen were removing the horses and broken car; another party were taking off the man himself; and every bench upon which there was a Greek was vocal with execrations and prayers for vengeance. Suddenly she dropped her hands; Ben-Hur, unhurt, was to the front, coursing freely forward along with the Roman! Behind them, in a group, followed the Sidonian, the Corinthian, and the Byzantine.

The race was on; the souls of the racers were in it; over them bent the myriads.

When the dash for position began, Ben-Hur, as we have seen, was on the extreme left of the six. For a moment, like the others, he was half blinded by the light in the arena; yet he managed to catch sight of his antagonists and divine their purpose. At Messala, who was more than an antagonist to him, he gave one searching look. The air of passionless hauteur characteristic of the fine patrician face was there as of old, and so was the Italian beauty, which the helmet rather increased; but more—it may have been a jealous fancy, or the effect of the brassy shadow in which the features were at the moment cast, still the Israelite thought he saw the soul of the man as through a glass, darkly: cruel, cunning, desperate; not so excited as determined—a soul in a tension of watchfulness and fierce resolve.

In a time not longer than was required to turn to his four again, Ben-Hur felt his own resolution harden to a like temper. At whatever cost, at all hazards, he would humble this enemy! Prize, friends, wagers, honor—everything that can be thought of as a possible interest in the race was lost in the one deliberate purpose. Regard for life even should not hold him back. Yet there was no passion, on his part; no blinding rush of heated blood from heart to brain, and back again; no impulse to fling himself upon Fortune: he did not believe in Fortune; far otherwise. He had his plan, and, confiding in himself, he settled to the task never more observant, never more capable. The air about him seemed aglow with a renewed and perfect transparency.

When not half-way across the arena, he saw that Messala's rush would, if there was no collision, and the rope fell, give him the wall; that the rope would fall, he ceased as soon to doubt; and, further, it came to him, a sudden flash-like insight, that Messala knew it was to be let drop at the last moment (prearrangement with the editor could safely reach that point in the contest); and it suggested, what more Roman-like than for the official to lend himself to a countryman who, besides being so popular, had also so much at stake? There could be no other accounting for the confidence with which Messala pushed his four forward the instant his competitors were prudentially checking their fours in front of the obstruction—no other except madness.

It is one thing to see a necessity and another to act upon it. Ben-Hur yielded the wall for the time.

The rope fell, and all the fours but his sprang into the course under urgency of voice and lash. He drew head to the right, and, with all the speed of his Arabs, darted across the trails of his opponents, the angle of movement being such as to lose the least time and gain the greatest possible advance. So, while the spectators were shivering at the Athenian's mishap, and the Sidonian, Byzantine, and Corinthian were striving, with such skill as they possessed, to avoid involvement in the ruin, Ben-Hur swept around and took the course neck and neck with Messala, though on the outside. The marvellous skill shown in making the change thus from the extreme left across to the right without appreciable loss did not fail the sharp eyes upon the benches; the Circus seemed to rock and rock again with prolonged applause. Then Esther clasped her hands in glad surprise; then Sanballat, smiling, offered his hundred sestertii a second time without a taker; and then the Romans began to doubt, thinking Messala might have found an equal, if not a master, and that in an Israelite!

And now, racing together side by side, a narrow interval between them, the two neared the second goal.

The pedestal of the three pillars there, viewed from the west, was a stone wall in the form of a half-circle, around which the course and opposite balcony were bent in exact parallelism. Making this turn was considered in all respects the most telling test of a charioteer; it was, in fact, the very feat in which Oraetes failed. As an involuntary admission of interest on the part of the spectators, a hush fell over all the Circus, so that for the first time in the race the rattle and clang of the cars plunging after the tugging steeds were distinctly heard. Then, it would seem, Messala observed Ben-Hur, and recognized him; and at once the audacity of the man flamed out in an astonishing manner.

"Down Eros, up Mars!" he shouted, whirling his lash with practiced hand—"Down Eros, up Mars!" he repeated, and caught the well-doing Arabs of Ben-Hur a cut the like of which they had never known.

The blow was seen in every quarter, and the amazement was universal. The silence deepened; up on the benches behind the consul the boldest held his breath, waiting for the outcome. Only a moment thus: then, involuntarily, down from the balcony, as thunder falls, burst the indignant cry of the people.

The four sprang forward affrighted. No hand had ever been laid upon them except in love; they had been nurtured ever so tenderly; and as they grew, their confidence in man became a lesson to men beautiful to see. What should such dainty natures do under such indignity but leap as from death?

Forward they sprang as with one impulse, and forward leaped the car. Past question, every experience is serviceable to us. Where got Ben-Hur the large hand and mighty grip which helped him now so well? Where but from the oar with which so long he fought the sea? And what was this spring of the floor under his feet to the dizzy eccentric lurch with which in the old time the trembling ship yielded to the beat of staggering billows, drunk with their power? So he kept his place, and gave the four free rein, and called to them in soothing voice, trying merely to guide them round the dangerous turn; and before the fever of the people began to abate, he had back the mastery. Nor that only: on approaching the first goal, he was again side by side with Messala, bearing with him the sympathy and admiration of every one not a Roman. So clearly was the feeling shown, so vigorous its manifestation, that Messala, with all his boldness, felt it unsafe to trifle further.

As the cars whirled round the goal, Esther caught sight of Ben-Hur's face—a little pale, a little higher raised, otherwise calm, even placid.

Immediately a man climbed on the entablature at the west end of the division wall, and took down one of the conical wooden balls. A dolphin on the east entablature was taken down at the same time.

In like manner, the second ball and second dolphin disappeared.

And then the third ball and third dolphin.

Three rounds concluded: still Messala held the inside position; still Ben-Hur moved with him side by side; still the other competitors followed as before. The contest began to have the appearance of one of the double races which became so popular in Rome during the later Caesarean period—Messala and Ben-Hur in the first, the Corinthian, Sidonian, and Byzantine in the second. Meantime the ushers succeeded in returning the multitude to their seats, though the clamor continued to run the rounds, keeping, as it were, even pace with the rivals in the course below.

In the fifth round the Sidonian succeeded in getting a place outside Ben-Hur, but lost it directly.

The sixth round was entered upon without change of relative position.

Gradually the speed had been quickened—gradually the blood of the competitors warmed with the work. Men and beasts seemed to know alike that the final crisis was near, bringing the time for the winner to assert himself.

The interest which from the beginning had centred chiefly in the struggle between the Roman and the Jew, with an intense and general sympathy for the latter, was fast changing to anxiety on his account. On all the benches the spectators bent forward motionless, except as their faces turned following the contestants. Ilderim quitted combing his beard, and Esther forgot her fears.

"A hundred sestertii on the Jew!" cried Sanballat to the Romans under the consul's awning.

There was no reply.

"A talent—or five talents, or ten; choose ye!"

He shook his tablets at them defiantly.

"I will take thy sestertii," answered a Roman youth, preparing to write.

"Do not so," interposed a friend.

"Why?"

"Messala hath reached his utmost speed. See him lean over his chariot rim, the reins loose as flying ribbons. Look then at the Jew."

The first one looked.

"By Hercules!" he replied, his countenance falling. "The dog throws all his weight on the bits. I see, I see! If the gods help not our friend, he will be run away with by the Israelite. No, not yet. Look! Jove with us, Jove with us!"

The cry, swelled by every Latin tongue, shook the velaria over the consul's head.

If it were true that Messala had attained his utmost speed, the effort was with effect; slowly but certainly he was beginning to forge ahead. His horses were running with their heads low down; from the balcony their bodies appeared actually to skim the earth; their nostrils showed blood red in expansion; their eyes seemed straining in their sockets. Certainly the good steeds were doing their best! How long could they keep the pace? It was but the commencement of the sixth round. On they dashed. As they neared the second goal, Ben-Hur turned in behind the Roman's car.

The joy of the Messala faction reached its bound: they screamed and howled, and tossed their colors; and Sanballat filled his tablets with wagers of their tendering.

Malluch, in the lower gallery over the Gate of Triumph, found it hard to keep his cheer. He had cherished the vague hint dropped to him by Ben-Hur of something to happen in the turning of the western pillars. It was the fifth round, yet the something had not come; and he had said to himself, the sixth will bring it; but, lo! Ben-Hur was hardly holding a place at the tail of his enemy's car.

Over in the east end, Simonides' party held their peace. The merchant's head was bent low. Ilderim tugged at his beard, and dropped his brows till there was nothing of his eyes but an occasional sparkle of light. Esther scarcely breathed. Iras alone appeared glad.

Along the home-stretch—sixth round—Messala leading, next him Ben-Hur, and so close it was the old story:

> First flew Eumelus on Pheretian steeds;
> With those of Tros bold Diomed succeeds;
> Close on Eumelus' back they puff the wind,
> And seem just mounting on his car behind;
> Full on his neck he feels the sultry breeze,
> And, hovering o'er, their stretching shadow sees.

Thus to the first goal, and round it. Messala, fearful of losing his place, hugged the stony wall with perilous clasp; a foot to the left, and he had been dashed to pieces; yet, when the turn was finished, no man, looking at the wheel-tracks of the two cars, could have said, here went Messala, there the Jew. They left but one trace behind them.

As they whirled by, Esther saw Ben-Hur's face again, and it was whiter than before.

Simonides, shrewder than Esther, said to Ilderim, the moment the rivals turned into the course, "I am no judge, good sheik, if Ben-Hur be not about to execute some design. His face hath that look."

To which Ilderim answered, "Saw you how clean they were and fresh? By the splendor of God, friend, they have not been running! But now watch!"

One ball and one dolphin remained on the entablatures; and all the people drew a long breath, for the beginning of the end was at hand.

First, the Sidonian gave the scourge to his four, and, smarting with fear and pain, they dashed desperately forward, promising for a brief time to go to the front. The effort ended in promise. Next, the Byzantine and the Corinthian each made the trial with like result, after which they were practically out of the race. Thereupon, with a readiness perfectly explicable, all the factions except the Romans joined hope in Ben-Hur, and openly indulged their feeling.

"Ben-Hur! Ben-Hur!" they shouted, and the blent voices of the many rolled overwhelmingly against the consular stand.

From the benches above him as he passed, the favor descended in fierce injunctions.

"Speed thee, Jew!"

"Take the wall now!"

"On! loose the Arabs! Give them rein and scourge!"

"Let him not have the turn on thee again. Now or never!"

Over the balustrade they stooped low, stretching their hands imploringly to him.

Either he did not hear, or could not do better, for halfway round the course and he was still following; at the second goal even still no change!

And now, to make the turn, Messala began to draw in his left-hand steeds, an act which necessarily slackened their speed. His spirit was high; more than one altar was richer of his vows; the Roman genius was still president. On the three pillars only six hundred feet away were fame, increase of fortune, promotions, and a triumph ineffably sweetened by hate, all in store for him! That moment Malluch, in the gallery, saw Ben-Hur lean forward over his Arabs, and give them the reins. Out flew the many-folded lash in his hand; over the backs of the startled steeds it writhed and hissed, and hissed and writhed again and again; and though it fell not, there were both sting and menace in its quick report; and as the man passed thus from quiet to resistless action, his face suffused, his eyes gleaming, along the reins he seemed to flash his will; and instantly not one, but the four as one, answered with a leap that landed them alongside the Roman's car. Messala, on the perilous edge of the goal, heard, but dared not look to see what the awakening portended. From the people he received no sign. Above the noises of the race there was but one voice, and that was Ben-Hur's. In the old Aramaic, as the sheik himself, he called to the Arabs,

"On, Atair! On, Rigel! What, Antares! dost thou linger now? Good horse—oho, Aldebaran! I hear them singing in the tents. I hear the children singing and the women—singing of the stars, of Atair, Antares, Rigel, Aldebaran, victory!—and the song will never end. Well done! Home to-morrow, under the black tent—home! On, Antares! The tribe is waiting for us, and the master is waiting! 'Tis done! 'tis done! Ha, ha! We have overthrown the proud. The hand that smote us is in the dust. Ours the glory! Ha, ha!—steady! The work is done—soho! Rest!"

There had never been anything of the kind more simple; seldom anything so instantaneous.

At the moment chosen for the dash, Messala was moving in a circle round the goal. To pass him, Ben-Hur had to cross the track, and good strategy required the movement to be in a forward direction; that is, on a like circle limited to the least possible increase. The thousands on the benches understood it all: they saw the signal given—the magnificent response; the four close outside Messala's outer wheel; Ben-Hur's inner wheel behind the other's car—all this they saw. Then they heard a crash loud enough to send a thrill through the Circus, and, quicker than thought, out over the course a spray of shining white and yellow flinders flew. Down on its right side toppled the bed of the Roman's chariot. There was a rebound as of the axle hitting the hard earth; another and another; then the car went to pieces; and Messala, entangled in the reins, pitched forward headlong.

To increase the horror of the sight by making death certain, the Sidonian, who had the wall next behind, could not stop or turn out. Into the wreck full speed he drove; then over the Roman, and into the latter's four, all mad with fear. Presently, out of the turmoil, the fighting of horses, the resound of blows, the murky cloud of dust and sand, he crawled, in time to see the Corinthian and Byzantine go on down the course after Ben-Hur, who had not been an instant delayed.

The people arose, and leaped upon the benches, and shouted and screamed. Those who looked that way caught glimpses of Messala, now under the trampling of the fours, now under the abandoned cars. He was still; they thought him dead; but far the greater number followed Ben-Hur in his career. They had not seen the cunning touch of the reins by which, turning a little to the left, he caught Messala's wheel with the iron-shod point of his axle, and crushed it; but they had seen the transformation of the man, and themselves felt the heat and glow of his spirit, the heroic resolution, the maddening energy of action with which, by look, word, and gesture, he so suddenly inspired his Arabs. And such running! It was rather the long leaping of lions in harness; but for the lumbering chariot, it seemed the four were flying. When the Byzantine and Corinthian were halfway down the course, Ben-Hur turned the first goal.

AND THE RACE WAS WON!

The consul arose; the people shouted themselves hoarse; the editor came down from his seat, and crowned the victors.

The fortunate man among the boxers was a low-browed, yellow-haired Saxon, of such brutalized face as to attract a second look from Ben-Hur, who recognized a teacher with whom he himself had been a favorite at Rome. From him the young Jew looked up and beheld Simonides and his party on the balcony. They waved their hands to him. Esther kept her seat; but Iras arose, and gave him a smile and a wave of her fan—favors not the less intoxicating to him because we know, O reader, they would have fallen to Messala had he been the victor.

The procession was then formed, and, midst the shouting of the multitude which had had its will, passed out of the Gate of Triumph.

And the day was over.

7

Wildfire

By Zane Grey

<><><><><><><><><><><><><><><><><><><><><><><><><><><><><><><><><><><><><><><><><><><>

For a man who became the most famous of the western writers, the Ohio-born Zane Grey began life with an improbable name and in unlikely circumstances. His parents named him Pearl Zane Gray. He dropped the "Pearl," changed the spelling of his surname, and shed his career as a dentist as he began to sell stories to outdoor and hunting magazines.

The turning point of Grey's professional life came in 1905 when he traveled to California on his honeymoon. It was the first of many trips out West and provided him with his first look at a life and landscape that he had been only able to imagine. Before he was finished, Zane Grey produced fifty-six Western novels, making him the first millionaire author in American publishing history.

Although his Westerns were filled with menacing villains and worthy heroes, most also included a charming heroine. A romance was often at the heart of a Zane Grey novel. Almost all included horses, usually as secondary characters. Sometimes a horse was at the heart of the story, as in Wildfire.

Lucy Bostil is the eighteen-year-old daughter of John Bostil, a rancher who has made himself rich in the wild borderlands of Utah and Arizona. Bostil loves horses almost as much as he loves Lucy, but the enemies he has made over the years threaten both his horses and his daughter.

The rival Creech family hovers nearby, with young Joel Creech hoping for Lucy's attention and his father refusing to part with the one horse in the region that could challenge Bostil's great racer Sage King. Also nearby is a horse thief named Cordts, who hopes to acquire Sage King, legally or otherwise.

Lucy, one of the most competent riders at Bostil's Ford, is out almost every day aboard the best of her father's horses. One day, aboard Sage King, she comes across a beautiful wild stallion struggling against a rope, with cactus tearing his shiny red coat. She soon finds the man who roped him, the injured wild horse hunter Lin Slone. Lucy helps both man and horse.

Over the next several weeks, Lucy returns again and again to help Slone break and train the horse they now call Wildfire. She decides that Wildfire will challenge Sage King in her father's annual race day.

—Sharon B. Smith

BOSTIL SLEPT THAT NIGHT, BUT HIS SLEEP WAS TROUBLED, AND A strange, dreadful roar seemed to run through it, like a mournful wind over a dark desert. He was awakened early by a voice at his window. He listened. There came a rap on the wood.

"Bostil! . . . Bostil!" It was Holley's voice.

Bostil rolled off the bed. He had slept without removing any apparel except his boots.

"Wal, Hawk, what d'ye mean wakin' a man at this unholy hour?" growled Bostil.

Holley's face appeared above the rude sill. It was pale and grave, with the hawk eyes like glass. "It ain't so awful early," he said. "Listen, boss."

Bostil halted in the act of pulling on a boot. He looked at his man while he listened. The still air outside seemed filled with low boom, like thunder at a distance. Bostil tried to look astounded.

"Hell! . . . It's the Colorado! She's boomin'!"

"Reckon it's hell all right—for Creech," replied Holley. "Boss, why didn't you fetch them horses over?"

Bostil's face darkened. He was a bad man to oppose—to question at times. "Holley, you're sure powerful anxious about Creech. Are you his friend?"

"Haw! I've little use for Creech," replied Holley. But I hold for his hosses as I would for any man's."

"A-huh! An' what's your kick?"

"Nothin'—except you could have fetched them over before the flood come down. That's all."

The old horse trader and his right hand rider looked at each other for a moment in silence. They understood each other. Then Bostil returned to the task of pulling on wet boots and Holley went away.

Bostil opened his door and stepped outside. The eastern ramparts of the desert were bright red with the rising sun. With the night behind him and the morning cool and bright and beautiful, Bostil did not suffer a pang nor feel a regret. He walked around under the cottonwoods where the mockingbirds were singing. The shrill, screeching bray of a burro split the morning stillness, and with that the sounds of the awakening village drowned that sullen, dreadful boom of the river. Bostil went in to breakfast.

He encountered Lucy in the kitchen, and he did not avoid her. He could tell from her smiling greeting that he seemed to her his old self again. Lucy wore an apron and she had her sleeves rolled up, showing round, strong, brown arms. Somehow to Bostil she seemed different. She had been pretty, but now she was more than that. She was radiant. Her blue eyes danced. She looked excited. She had been telling her aunt something, and that worthy woman appeared at once shocked and delighted. But Bostil's entrance had caused a mysterious break in everything that had been going on, except the preparation of the morning meal.

"Now I rode in on some confab or other, that's sure," said Bostil, good-naturedly.

"You sure did, Dad," replied Lucy, with a bright smile.

"Wal, let me sit in the game," he rejoined.

"Dad, you can't even ante," said Lucy.

"Jane, what's this kid up to?" asked Bostil, turning to his sister.

"The good Lord only knows!" replied Aunt Jane, with a sigh.

"Kid? . . . See here, Dad, I'm eighteen long ago. I'm grown up. I can do as I please, go where I like, and anything. . . . Why Dad, I could get—married."

"Haw! Haw!" laughed Bostil. "Jane, hear the girl."

"I hear her, Bostil," sighed Aunt Jane.

"Wal, Lucy, I'd just like to see you fetch some fool lovesick rider around when I'm feelin' good," said Bostil.

Lucy laughed, but there was a roguish, daring flash in her eyes. "Dad, you do seem to have all the young fellows scared. Someday maybe one will ride along—a rider like you used to be—that nobody could bluff . . . and he can have me!"

"A-huh! . . . Lucy, are you in fun?"

Lucy tossed her bright head, but did not answer.

"Jane, what's got into her?" asked Bostil, appealing to his sister.

"Bostil, she's in fun, of course," declared Aunt Jane. "Still, at that, there's some sense in what she says. Come to your breakfast, now."

Bostil took his seat at the table, glad that he could once more be amiable with his womenfolk. "Lucy, tomorrow'll be the biggest day Bostil's Ford has ever seen," he said.

"It sure will be, Dad. The biggest *surprising* day the Ford ever had," replied Lucy.

"Surprisin'?"

"Yes, Dad."

"Who's goin' to get surprised?"

"Everybody."

Bostil said to himself that he had been used to Lucy's banter, but during his moody spell of days past he had forgotten how to take her or else she was different.

"Brackton tells me you've entered a hoss against the field."

"It's an open race, isn't it?"

"Open as the desert, Lucy," he replied. "What's this hoss Wildfire you've entered?"

"Wouldn't you like to know?" taunted Lucy.

"If he's as good as his name you might be in at the finish. . . . But, Lucy, my dear, talkin' good sense now—you ain't a-goin' to go up on some unbroken mustang in this big race?"

"Dad, I'm going to ride a horse."

"But, Lucy, ain't it a risk you'll be takin'—all for fun?"

"Fun! . . . I'm in dead earnest."

Bostil liked the look of her then. She had paled a little; her eyes blazed; she was intense. His question had brought out her earnestness, and straightway Bostil became thoughtful. If Lucy had been a boy she would have been the greatest rider on the uplands; and even girl as she was, superbly mounted, she would have been dangerous in any race.

"Wal, I ain't afraid of your handlin' of a hoss," he said, soberly. "An' as long as you're in earnest I won't stop you. But, Lucy, no bettin'. I won't let you gamble."

"Not even with you?" she asked.

Bostil stared at the girl. What had gotten into her? "What'll you bet?" he queried, with blunt curiosity.

"Dad, I'll go you a hundred dollars in gold that I finish one—two—three."

Bostil threw back his head to laugh heartily. What a chip off the old block she was. "Child, there's some fast hosses that'll be back of the King. You'd be throwin' money away."

Blue fire shone in his daughter's eyes. She meant business, all right, and Bostil thrilled with pride in her.

"Dad, I'll bet you two hundred, even, that I beat the King!" she flashed.

"Wal, of all the nerve!" ejaculated Bostil. "No, I won't take you up. Reckon I never before turned down an even bet. Understand, Lucy, ridin' in the race is enough for you."

"All right, Dad," replied Lucy, obediently.

At that juncture Bostil suddenly shoved back his plate and turned his face to the open door. "Don't I hear a runnin' hoss?"

Aunt Jane stopped the noise she was making, and Lucy darted to the door. Then Bostil heard the sharp, rhythmic hoofbeats he recognized. They shortened to clatter and pound—then ceased somewhere out in front of the house.

"It's the King with Van up," said Lucy, from the door. "Dad, Van's jumped off—he's coming in ... he's running. Something has happened.... There are other horses coming—riders—Indians."

Bostil knew what was coming and prepared himself. Rapid footsteps sounded without.

"Hello, Miss Lucy! Where's Bostil?"

A lean, supple rider appeared before the door. It was Van, greatly excited.

"Come in, boy," said Bostil. "What're you flustered about?"

Van strode in, spurs jangling, cap in hand. "Boss, there's—a sixty-foot raise—in the river!" Van panted.

"Oh!" cried Lucy, wheeling toward her father.

"Wal, Van, I reckon I knowed that," replied Bostil. "Mebbe I'm getting old, but I can still hear.... Listen."

Lucy tiptoed to the door and turned her head sidewise and slowly bowed it till she stiffened. Outside were sounds of birds and horses and men, but when a lull came it quickly filled with a sullen, low boom.

"Highest flood we—ever seen," said Van.

"You've been down?" queried Bostil, sharply.

"Not to the river," replied Van. "I went as far as—where the gulch opens—on the bluff. There was a string of Navajos goin' down. An' some comin' up. I stayed there watchin' the flood, an' pretty soon Somers come up the trail with Blakesley and Brack an' some riders come up the trail an' some riders.... An' Somers hollered out, 'The boat's gone!'"

"Gone!" exclaimed Bostil, his loud cry showing consternation.

"Oh, Dad! Oh, Van!" cried Lucy, with eyes wide and lips parted.

"Sure she's gone. An' the whole place down there—where the willows was an' the sandbar—it was deep under water."

"What will become of Creech's horses?" asked Lucy, breathlessly.

"My God! Ain't it a shame!" went on Bostil, and he could have laughed aloud at his hypocrisy. He felt Lucy's blue eyes riveted upon his face.

"That's what we all was sayin'," went on Van. "While we was watchin' the awful flood an' listenin' to the deep bum—bum—bum of rollin' rocks some one seen Creech an' two Piutes leadin' the hosses up that trail where

92

the slide was. We counted the hosses—nine. An' we saw the roan shine blue in the sunlight."

"Piutes with Creech!" exclaimed Bostil, the deep gloom in his eyes lighting. "By all that's lucky! Mebbe them Indians can climb the horses out of that hole an' find water an' grass enough."

"Mebbe," replied Van, doubtfully. "Sure them Piutes could if there's a chance. But there ain't any grass."

"It won't take much grass travelin' by night."

"So lots of the boys say. But the Navajos they shook their heads. An' Farlane an' Holley, why, they jest held up their hands."

"With them Indians Creech has a chance to get his hosses out," declared Bostil. He was sure of his sincerity, but he was not certain that his sincerity has not the birth of a strange, sudden hope. And then he was able to meet the eyes of his daughter. That was his supreme test.

"Oh, Dad, why, why didn't you hurry Creech's horses over?" said Lucy, with her tears falling.

Something tight within Bostil's breast seemed to ease and lessen. "Why didn't I? . . . Wal, Lucy, I reckon I wasn't in no hurry to oblige Creech. I'm sorry now."

"It won't be so terrible if he doesn't lose the horses," murmured Lucy.

"Where's young Joel Creech?" asked Bostil.

"He stayed on this side last night," replied Van. "Fact is, Joel's the one who first knew the flood was on. Some one said he said he slept in the canyon last night. Anyway, he's ravin' crazy now. An' if he doesn't do harm to some one or hisself I'll miss my guess."

"A-huh!" grunted Bostil. "Right you are."

"Dad, can't anything be done to help Creech now?" appealed Lucy, going close to her father.

Bostil put his arm around her and felt immeasurably relieved to have the golden head press close to his shoulder.

"Child, we can't fly acrost the river. Now don't you cry about Creech's hosses. They ain't starved yet. It's hard luck. But mebbe it'll turn out so Creech'll lose only the race. An', Lucy, it was a dead sure bet he'd have lost that anyway."

Bostil fondled his daughter a moment, the first time in many a day, and then he turned to his rider at the door. "Van, how's the King?"

"Wild to run, Bostil, just plumb wild. There won't be any hoss with the ghost of a show tomorrow."

Lucy raised her drooping head. "Is *that* so, Van Sickle? . . . Listen here. If you and Sage King don't get more wild running tomorrow than you ever had I'll never ride again!" With this retort Lucy left the room.

Van stared at the door and then at Bostil. "What'd I say, Bostil?" he asked, plaintively. "I'm always rilin' her."

"Cheer up, Van. You didn't say much. Lucy is fiery these days. She's got a hoss somewhere an' she's goin' to ride him in the race. She offered to bet on him—against the King! I've a hunch there's a dark hoss goin' to show up here, Van. So don't underrate Lucy an' her mount, whatever he is. She calls him Wildfire. Ever see him?"

"I sure haven't. Fact is, I haven't seen Lucy for days an' days. As for the hunch you gave, I'll say I was figurin' Lucy for some real race. Bostil, she doesn't *make* a hoss run. He'll run just to please her. An' Lucy's lighter 'n a feather. Why Bostil, if she happened to ride out there on Blue Roan or some other hoss as fast I'd—I'd just wilt."

Bostil uttered a laugh full of pride in his daughter. "Wal, she won't show up on Blue Roan," he replied, with grim gruffness. "That's sure as death. . . . Come on out now. I want a look at the King."

Bostil went into the village. All day long he was so busy with a thousand and one things referred to him, put on him, undertaken by him, that he had no time to think. Back in his mind, however, there was a burden of which he was vaguely conscious all the time. He worked late into the night and slept late the next morning.

Never in his life had Bostil been gloomy or retrospective on the day of a race. In the press of matters he had only a word for Lucy, but that earned a saucy, dauntless look. He was glad when he was able to join the procession of villagers, visitors, and Indians moving out toward the sage.

The racecourse lay at the foot of the slope, and now the gray and purple sage was dotted with more horses and Indians, more moving things and colors, than Bostil had ever seen there before. It was a spectacle that stirred him. Many fires sent up blue columns of smoke from before the hastily built brush huts where the Indians cooked and ate. Blankets shone bright in the sun; burros grazed and brayed; horses whistled piercingly across the slope; Indians lolled before the huts or talked in groups, sitting and lounging on their ponies; down in the valley, here and there, were Indians racing, and others were chasing the wiry mustangs. Beyond this gay and colorful spectacle stretched the valley, merging into the desert marked so strikingly and beautifully by the monuments.

Bostil was among the last to ride down to the high bench that overlooked the home end of the racecourse. He calculated that there were a thousand Indians and whites congregated at that point, which was the best vantage-ground to see the finish of a race. And the occasion of his arrival, for all the gaiety, was one of dignity and importance. If Bostil reveled in anything it was in an hour like this. His liberality made this event a great race-day. The thoroughbreds were all there, blanketed, in charge of watchful riders. In the center of the brow of this long bench lay a huge, flat rock, which had been Bostil's seat in the watching of many a race. Here were assembled his neighbors and visitors actively interested in the races, and also the important Indians of both tribes, all waiting for him.

As Bostil dismounted, throwing the bridle to a rider, he saw a face that suddenly froze the thrilling delight of the moment. A tall, gaunt man with cavernous black eyes and huge, drooping black mustache fronted him and seemed waiting. Cordts! Bostil had forgotten. Instinctively Bostil stood on guard. For years he had prepared himself for the moment when he would come face to face with this noted horse-thief.

"Bostil, how are you?" said Cordts. He appeared pleasant, and certainly grateful for being permitted to come there. From his left hand hung a belt containing two heavy guns.

"Hello, Cordts," replied Bostil, slowly unbending. Then he met the other's proffered hand.

"I've bet heavily on the King," said Cordts.

For the moment there could have been no other way to Bostil's good graces, and this remark made the gruff old rider's hard face relax.

"Wal, I was hopin' you'd back some other hoss, so I could take your money," replied Bostil.

Cordts held out the belt and guns to Bostil. "I want to enjoy this race," he said, with a smile that somehow hinted of the years he had packed those guns day and night.

"Cordts, I don't want to take your guns," replied Bostil, bluntly. "I've taken your word an' that's enough."

"Thanks, Bostil. All the same, as I'm your guest, I won't pack them," returned Cordts, and he hung the belt on the horn of Bostil's saddle. "Some of my men are with me. They were all right till they got outside of Brackton's whisky. But now I won't answer for them."

"Wal, you're square to say that," replied Bostil. "An' I'll run this race an' answer for everybody."

Bostil recognized Hutchinson and Dick Sears, but the others of Cordts's gang he did not know. They were a hard-looking lot. Hutchinson was a spare, stoop-shouldered, red-faced squinty-eyed rider, branded all over with the mark of a bad man. And Dick Sears looked his notoriety. He was a little knot of muscle, short and bow-legged, rough in appearance as cactus. He wore a ragged slouch hat pulled low down. His face and stubby beard were dust-colored, and his eyes seemed sullen, watchful. He made Bostil think of a dusty, scaly, hard, desert rattlesnake. Bostil eyed this right-hand man of Cordts's and certainly felt no fear of him, though Sears had the fame of swift and deadly skill with a gun. Bostil felt that he was neither afraid nor loath to face Sears in gun-play, and he gazed at the little horse-thief in a manner that no one could mistake. Sears was not drunk, neither was he wholly free from the unsteadiness caused by the bottle. Assuredly he had no fear of Bostil and eyed him insolently. Bostil turned away to the group of his riders and friends, and he asked for his daughter.

"Lucy's over there," said Farlane, pointing to a merry crowd.

Bostil waved a hand to her, and Lucy, evidently mistaking his action, came forward, leading one of her ponies. She wore a gray blouse with a red scarf, and a skirt over overalls and boots. She looked pale, but she was smiling, and there was a dark gleam of excitement in her blue eyes. She did not have on her sombrero. She wore her hair in a braid, and had a red band tight above her forehead. Bostil took her in all at a glance. She meant business and she looked dangerous. Bostil knew once she slipped out of that skirt she could ride with any rider there. He saw that she had become the center toward which all eyes shifted. It pleased him. She was his, like her mother, and as beautiful and thoroughbred as any rider could wish his daughter.

"Lucy, where's your hoss?" he asked, curiously.

"Never you mind, Dad. I'll be there at the finish," she replied.

"Red's your color for today, then?" he questioned, as he put a big hand on the bright-colored head.

She nodded archly.

"Lucy, I never thought you'd flaunt red in your old Dad's face. Red, when the color of the King is like the sage out yonder. You've gone back on the King."

"No. Dad. I never was for Sage King, else I wouldn't wear red today."

"Child, you sure mean to run in this race—the big one?"

"Sure and certain."

"Wal, the only bitter drop in my cup today will be seein' you get beat. But if you run second I'll give you a present that'll make the purse look sick."

Even the Indian chiefs were smiling. Old Horse, the Navajo, beamed benignly upon this daughter of the friend of the Indians. Silver, his brother chieftain, nodded as if he understood Bostil's pride and regret. Some of the young riders showed their hearts in their eyes. Farlane tried to look mysterious, to pretend he was in Lucy's confidence.

"Lucy, if you are really goin' to race I'll withdraw my hoss so you can win," said Wetherby, gallantly.

Bostil's sonorous laugh rolled down the slope.

"Miss Lucy, I sure hate to run a hoss against yours," said old Cal Blinn. Then Colson, Sticks, Burthwait, the other principals, paid laughing compliments to the bright-haired girl.

Bostil enjoyed this hugely until he caught the strange intensity of regard in the cavernous eye of Cordts. That gave him a shock. Cordts had long wanted this girl as much probably as he wanted Sage King. There were dark and terrible stories that stained the name of Cordts. Bostil regretted his impulse in granting the horse-thief permission to attend the races. Sight of Lucy's fair, sweet face might inflame this Cordts—this

Kentuckian who had boasted of his love of horses and women. Behind Cordts hung the little dust-colored Sears, like a coiled snake, ready to strike. Bostil felt stir in him a long-dormant fire—a stealing along his veins, a passion he hated.

"Lucy, go back to the women till you're ready to come out on your hoss," he said. "An' mind you, be careful today!"

He gave her a meaning glance, which she understood perfectly, he saw, and then he turned to start the day's sport.

The Indian races ran in twos and threes, and on up to a number that crowded the racecourse; the betting and yelling and running; the wild and plunging mustangs; the heat and dust and pounding of hoofs; the excited betting; the surprises and defeats and victories; the trial tests of the principals, jealously keeping off to themselves in the sage; the endless moving, colorful procession, gaudy and swift and thrilling—all these Bostil loved tremendously.

But they were as nothing to what they gradually worked up to—the climax—the great race.

It was afternoon when all was ready for this race, and the sage was bright gray in the westering sun. Everybody was resting, waiting. The tense quiet of the riders seemed to settle upon the whole assemblage. Only the thoroughbreds were restless. They quivered and stamped and tossed their small, fine heads. They knew what was going to happen. They wanted to run. Blacks, bays, and whites were the predominating colors, and the horses and mustangs were alike in those points of race and speed and spirit that proclaimed them thoroughbreds.

Bostil himself took the covering off his favorite. Sage King was on edge. He stood out strikingly in contrast to the other horses. His sage-gray body was as sleek and shiny as satin. He had been trained to the hour. He tossed his head as he champed the bit, and every moment his muscles rippled under his fine skin. Proud, mettlesome, beautiful!

Sage King was the favorite in the betting, the Indians, who were ardent gamblers, plunging heavily on him.

Bostil saddled the horse and was long at the task. Van stood watching. He was pale and nervous. Bostil saw this.

"Van," he said, "it's your race."

The rider reached a quick hand for bridle and horn, and when his foot touched the stirrup Sage King was in the air. He came down, springy—quick, graceful, and then he pranced into line with the other horses.

Bostil waved his hand. Then the troop of riders and racers headed for the starting-point, two miles up the valley. Macomber and Blinn, with a rider and a Navajo, were up there as the official starters of the day.

Bostil's eyes glistened. He put a friendly hand on Cordts's shoulder, an action which showed the stress of the moment. Most of the men crowded around Bostil. Sears and Hutchinson hung close to Cordts. And Holley, keeping near his employer, had keen eyes for other things than horses.

Suddenly he touched Bostil and pointed down the slope. "There's Lucy," he said. "She's ridin' out to join the bunch."

"Lucy! Where? I'd forgotten my girl! . . . Where?"

"There," repeated Holley, and he pointed. Others of the group spoke up, having seen Lucy riding down.

"She's on a red hoss," said one.

"Pears all-fired big to me—her hoss," said another. "Who's got a glass?"

Bostil had the only field glass there and he was using it. Across the round, magnified field of vision moved a giant red horse, his mane waving like a flame. Lucy rode him. They were moving from a jumble of broken rocks a mile down the slope. She had kept her horse hidden there. Bostil felt an added stir in his pulse beat. Certainly he had never seen a horse like this one. But the distance was long, the glass not perfect; he could not trust his sight. Suddenly that sight dimmed.

"Holley, I can't make out nothin'," he complained. "Take the glass. Give me a line on Lucy's mount."

"Boss, I don't need the glass to see that she's up on a hoss," replied Holley, as he took the glass. He leveled it, adjusted it to his eyes, and then looked long. Bostil grew impatient. Lucy was rapidly overhauling the troop of racers on her way to the post. Nothing ever hurried or excited Holley.

"Wal, can't you see any better 'n me?" queried Bostil, eagerly.

"Come on, Holl, give us a tip before she gits to the post," spoke up a rider.

Cordts showed intense eagerness, and all the group were excited. Lucy's advent, on an unknown horse that even her father could not disparage, was the last and unexpected addition to the suspense. They all knew that if this horse was fast, Lucy could be dangerous.

Holley at last spoke; "She's up on a wild stallion. He's red, like fire. He's mighty big—strong. Looks as if he didn't want to go near the bunch. Lord! What action! . . . Bostil, I'd say—a great hoss!"

There was a moment's intense silence in the group round Bostil. Holley was never known to mistake a horse or to be extravagant in judgment or praise.

"A wild stallion!" echoed Bostil. "A-huh! An' she calls him Wildfire. Where'd she get him? . . . Gimme that glass."

But all Bostil could make out was a blur. His eyes were wet. He realized now that his first sight of Lucy on the strange horse had been clear and strong, and it was that which had dimmed his eyes.

"Holley, you use the glass—an' tell us what comes off," said Bostil, as he wiped his eyes with his scarf; he was relieved to find that his sight was clearing. "My God! If I couldn't see this finish!"

Then everybody watched the close, dark mass of horses and riders down the valley. And all waited for Holley to speak. "They're linin' up," began the rider. "Havin' some muss, too, it 'pears. . . . Bostil, that red hoss is raisin' hell! He wants to fight. There! He's up in the air. . . . Boys, he's a devil—a hoss killer like all them wild stallions. He's plungin' at the King—strikin'! There! Lucy's got him down. She's handlin' him. . . . Now they've got the King on the other side. That's better. But Lucy's hoss won't stand. Anyway, it's a runnin' start. . . . Van's got the best position. Foxy Van! . . . He'll be leadin' before the rest know the race's on. . . . Them Indian mustangs are behavin' scandalous. Guess the red stallion scared 'em. Now they're all lined up back of the post. . . . Ah! Gun-smoke! They move. . . . It looks like a go."

Then Holley was silent, strained in watching. So were all the watchers silent. Bostil saw far down the valley, a moving, dark line of horses.

"*They're off! They're off!*" called Holley, thrillingly.

Bostil uttered a deep and booming yell, which rose above the shouts of the men round him and was heard even in the din of Indian cries. Then as quickly as the yells had risen they ceased.

Holley stood up on the rock with leveled glass.

"Mac's dropped the flag. It's a sure go. Now! . . . Van's out there front—inside. The King's got his stride. Boss, the King's stretchin' out! . . . Look! Look! See that red hoss leap! . . . Bostil, he's runnin' down the King! I knowed it. He's like lightnin'. He's pushin' the King over—off the course! See him plunge! Lord! Lucy sticks like a burr. Good, Lucy! Hang on! . . . My Gawd, Bostil, the King's thrown! He's down! . . . He comes up, off the course. The others flash by. . . . Van's out of the race! . . . An', Bostil—an', gentlemen, there ain't anything more to this race than a red hoss!"

Bostil's heart gave a great leap and then seemed to stand still. He was half cold, half hot.

What a horrible, sickening disappointment. Bostil rolled out a cursing query. Holley's answer was short and sharp. The King was out! Bostil raved. He could not see. He could not believe. After all the weeks of preparation, of excitement, of suspense—only this! There was no race. The King was out! The thing did not seem possible. A thousand thoughts flitted through Bostil's mind. Rage, impotent rage, possessed him. He cursed Van, he swore he would kill that red stallion. And someone shook him hard. Someone's incisive words cut into his thick, throbbing ears: "Luck of the game! The King ain't beat! He's only out!"

Then the rider's habit of mind asserted itself and Bostil began to recover. For the King to fall was hard luck. But he had not lost the race! Anguish and pride battled for mastery over him. Even if the King were out it was a Bostil who would win the great race.

"He ain't beat!" muttered Bostil. "It ain't fair! He's run off the track by a wild stallion!"

His dimmed sight grew clear and sharp. And with a gasp he saw the moving, dark line take shape as horses. A bright horse was in the lead. Brighter and larger he grew. Swiftly and more swiftly he came on. The bright color changed to red. Bostil heard Holley calling and Cordts calling—and other voices. But he did not distinguish what was said. The line of horses began to bob, to bunch. The race looked close, despite what Holley had said. The Indians were beginning to lean forward, here and there uttering a short, sharp yell. Everything within Bostil grew together in one great throbbing, tingling mass. His rider's eye, keen once more, caught a gleam of gold above the red, and that gold was Lucy's hair. Bostil forgot the King.

Then Holley bawled into his ear, "They're half-way!"

The race was beautiful. Bostil strained his eyes. He gloried in what he saw—Lucy low over the neck of that red stallion. He could see plainer now. They were coming closer. How swiftly! What a splendid race! But it was too swift—it would not last. The Indians began to yell, drowning the hoarse shouts of the riders. Out of the tail of his eye Bostil saw Cordts and Sears and Hutchinson. They were acting like crazy men. Strange that horse thieves should care! The million thrills within Bostil coalesced into one great shudder of rapture. He grew wet with sweat. His stentorian voice took up the call for Lucy to win.

"Three-quarters!" bawled Holley into Bostil's ear. "An' Lucy's give that wild hoss free rein! Look, Bostil! You never in your life seen a hoss run like that!"

Bostil never had. His heart swelled. Something shook him. Was that his girl—that tight little gray burr half hidden in the huge stallion's flaming mane? The distance had been close between Lucy and the bunched riders.

But it lengthened. How it widened! That flame of a horse was running away from the others. And now they were close—coming into the home stretch. A deafening roar from the onlookers engulfed all other sounds. A straining, stamping, arm-flinging horde surrounded Bostil.

Bostil saw Lucy's golden hair whipping out from the flame-streaked mane. And then he could only see that red brute of a horse. Wildfire before the wind! Bostil thought of leaping prairie flame, storm-driven.

On came the red stallion—on—on! What a tremendous stride! What a marvelous recovery! What ease! What savage action!

He flashed past, low, pointed, long, going faster every magnificent stride—winner by a dozen lengths.

8

The Story of a Jockey

By Richard Harding Davis

Horse racing remained at the forefront of public imagination during the first decades of the twentieth century in spite of roadblocks put up by antigambling crusaders. The drama of the sport attracted the attention of some of the best and best-known writers in the country, including Richard Harding Davis, who rose to fame as an intrepid war correspondent during the Spanish-American War. Davis enjoyed producing stories for young readers in which a moral message was wrapped around an exciting tale, but his reputation as a hard-hitting journalist drew adult readers to these stories as well.

Among the best of his short stories is this one. A young lover of horses rejects the chance of an alluring payoff, preferring to protect his own honor and that of a horse he loves.

—SHARON B. SMITH

YOUNG CHARLEY CHADWICK HAD BEEN BROUGHT UP ON HIS FATHER'S farm in New Jersey. The farm had been his father's before his father died and was still called Chadwick's Meadows in his memory. It was a very small farm and for the most part covered with clover and long, rich grass that were good for pasturing and nothing else. Charley was too young, and Mrs. Chadwick was too much of a housekeeper and not enough of a farmer's wife to make the most out of the farm, and so she let the meadows to the manager of the Cloverdale Stock Farm. This farm is only half a mile back from the Monmouth Park racetrack at Long Branch.

The manager put a number of young colts in it to pasture and took what grass they did not eat to the farm. Charley used to ride these colts back to the big stables at night, and soon grew to ride very well, and to know a great deal about horses and horse breeding and horse racing. Sometimes they gave him a mount at the stables, and he was permitted to ride one of the racehorses around the private track, while the owner took the time from the judges' stand.

There was nothing in his life that he enjoyed like this. He had had very few pleasures, and the excitement and delight of tearing through the air on the back of a great animal, was something he thought must amount to more than anything else in the world. His mother did not approve of his spending his time at the stables, but she found it very hard to refuse him, and he seemed to have a happy faculty of picking up only what was good, and letting what was evil pass by him and leave him unhurt. The good that he picked up was his love for animals, his thoughtfulness for them, and the forbearance and gentleness it taught him to use, with even the higher class of animals who walk on two legs.

He was fond of all the horses, because they were horses; but the one he liked best was Heroine, a big black mare that ran like an express train. He and Heroine were the two greatest friends in the stable. The horse loved him as a horse does love its master sometimes, and though Charley was not her owner, he was in reality her master, for Heroine would have left her stall and carried Charley off to the ends of the continent if he had asked her to run away.

When a man named Oscar Behren bought Heroine, Charley thought he would never be contented again. He cried about it all along the country road from the stables to his home, and cried about it again that night in bed. He knew Heroine would feel just as badly about it as he did, if she could know they were to be separated. Heroine went off to run in the races for which her new master had entered her, and Charley heard of her only through the newspapers.

She won often and became a great favorite, and Charley was afraid she would forget the master of her earlier days before she became so famous. And when he found that Heroine was entered to run at the Monmouth Park racetrack, he became as excited over the prospect of seeing his old friend again as though he were going to meet his promised bride, or a long-lost brother who had accumulated several millions in South America.

He was at the station to meet the Behren horses, and Heroine knew him at once and he knew Heroine, although she was all blanketed up and had grown so much more beautiful to look at that it seemed like a second and improved edition of the horse he had known. Heroine won several races at Long Branch, and though her owner was an unpopular one, and one of whom many queer stories were told, still Heroine was always ridden to win, and win she generally did.

The race for the July Stakes was the big race of the meeting, and Heroine was the favorite. Behren was known to be backing her with thousands of dollars, and it was almost impossible to get anything but even money on her. The day before the race McCallen, the jockey who was to ride her, was taken ill, and Behren was in great anxiety and greatly disturbed as to where he could get a good substitute. Several people told him it made no difference, for the mare was as sure as sure could be, no matter who rode her. Then some one told him of Charley, who had taken out a license when the racing season began, and who had ridden a few unimportant mounts.

Behren looked for Charley and told him he would want him to ride for the July Stakes, and Charley went home to tell his mother about it, in a state of wild delight. To ride the favorite, and that favorite in such a great race, was as much to him as to own and steer the winning yacht in the transatlantic match for the cup.

He told Heroine all about it, and Heroine seemed very well pleased. But while he was standing hidden in Heroine's box stall, he heard something outside that made him wonder.

It was Behren's voice, and he said in a low tone, "Oh, McCallen's well enough, but I didn't want him for this race. He knows too much. The lad I've got now, this country boy, wouldn't know if the mare had the blind staggers."

Charley thought over this a great deal, and all that he had learned on the tracks and around the stables came to assist him in judging what it was that Behren meant, and that afternoon he found out.

The racetrack with the great green enclosures and the grandstand as high as a hill were as empty as a college campus in vacation time, but for a few of the stable boys and some of the owners, and a waiter or two. It was interesting to think what it would be like a few hours later when the trains had arrived from New York with eleven cars each and the passengers hanging from the steps, and the carriages stretched all the way from Long Branch. Then there would not be a vacant seat on the grandstand or a blade of grass untrampled.

Charley was not nervous when he thought of this, but he was very much excited. Howland S. Maitland, who owned a stable of horses and a great many other expensive things, and who was one of those gentlemen who make the racing of horses possible, and Curtis, the secretary of the meeting, came walking towards Charley, looking in at the different horses in the stalls.

"Heroine," said Mr. Maitland, as he read the name over the door. "Can we have a look at her?" he said.

Charley got up and took off his hat. "I am sorry, Mr. Maitland," he said, "but my orders from Mr. Behren are not to allow any one inside. I am sure if Mr. Behren were here he would be very glad to show you the horse; but you see, I'm responsible, sir, and—"

"Oh, that's all right!" said Mr. Maitland pleasantly, as he moved on.

"There's Mr. Behren now," Charley called after him, as Behren turned the corner. "I'll run and ask him."

"No, no, thank you," said Mr. Maitland hurriedly, and Charley heard him add to Mr. Curtis, "I don't want to know the man." It hurt Charley to find that the owner of Heroine and the man for whom he was to ride was held in such bad repute that a gentleman like Mr. Maitland would not know him, and he tried to console himself by thinking that it was better he rode Heroine than some less conscientious jockey whom Behren might order to play tricks with the horse and the public.

Mr. Behren came up with a friend, a red-faced man with a white derby hat. He pointed at Charley with his cane.

"My new jockey," he said. "How's the mare?" he asked.

"Very fit, sir," Charley answered.

"Had her feed yet?"

"No," Charley said.

The feed was in a trough, which the stable boy had lifted outside into the sun. They were mixing it under Charley's supervision, for as a rider he did not stoop to such menial work as carrying the water and feed, but he always overlooked the others when they did it. Behren scooped up a handful and examined it carefully.

"It's not as fresh as it ought to be for the price they ask," he said to the friend with him. Then he threw the handful of feed back into the trough and ran his hand through it again, rubbing it between his thumb and fingers and tasting it critically. Then they passed on up the row.

Charley sat down again on an overturned bucket and looked at the feed trough, then he said to the stable boys, "You fellows can go now and get something to eat if you want to." They did not wait to be urged. Charley carried the trough inside the stable and took up a handful of the feed and looked and sniffed at it. It was fresh from his own barn; he had brought it over himself in a cart that morning.

Then he tasted it with the end of his tongue and his face changed. He glanced around him quickly to see if any one had noticed, and then, with the feed still clenched in his hand, ran out and looked anxiously up and down the length of the stable. Mr. Maitland and Curtis were returning from the other end of the road.

"Can I speak to you a moment, sir?" said Charley anxiously. "Will you come in here just a minute? It's most important, sir. I have something to show you."

The two men looked at the boy curiously and halted in front of the door. Charley added nothing further to what he had said but spread a newspaper over the floor of the stable and turned the feed trough over on it. Then he stood up over the pile and said, "Would you both please taste that?"

There was something in his manner which made questions unnecessary. The two gentlemen did as he asked. Then Mr. Curtis looked into Mr. Maitland's face, which was full of doubt and perplexity, with one of angry suspicion.

"Cooked," he said.

"It does taste strangely," commented the horse owner gravely.

"Look at it; you can see if you look close enough," urged Curtis excitedly. "Do you see that green powder on my finger? Do you know what that is? An ounce of that would turn a horse's stomach as dry as a limekiln. Where did you get this feed?" he demanded of Charley.

"Out of our barn," said the boy. "And no one has touched it except myself, the stable boys, and the owner."

"Who are the stable boys?" demanded Mr. Curtis.

"Who's the owner?" asked Charley.

"Do you know what you are saying?" warned Mr. Maitland sharply. "You had better be careful."

"Careful!" said Charley indignantly. "I will be careful enough." He went over to Heroine, and threw his arm up over her neck. He was terribly excited and trembling all over. The mare turned her head towards him and rubbed her nose against his face.

"That's all right," said Charley. "Don't you be afraid. I'll take care of *you*."

The two men were whispering together. "I don't know anything about you," said Mr. Maitland to Charley. "I don't know what your idea was in dragging me into this. I'm sure I wish I was out of it. But this I do know, if Heroine isn't herself today, and doesn't run as she has run before, and I say it though my own horses are in against her, I'll have you and your owner before the Racing Board, and you'll lose your license and be ruled off every track in the country."

"One of us will," said Charley stubbornly. "All I want you to do, Mr. Maitland, is to put some of that stuff in your pocket. If anything is wrong they will believe what you say, when they wouldn't listen to me. That's why I called you in. I haven't charged any one with anything. I only asked you and Mr. Curtis to taste the feed that this horse was to have eaten. That's all. And I'm not afraid of the Racing Board, either, if the men on it are honest."

Mr. Curtis took some letters out of his pocket and filled the envelopes with the feed, and then put them back in his pocket, and Charley gathered up the feed in a bucket and emptied it out of the window at the back of the stable.

"I think Behren should be told of this," said Mr. Maitland.

Charley laughed; he was still excited and angry. "You had better find out which way Mr. Behren is betting first," he said, "if you can."

"Don't mind the boy. Come away," said Mr. Curtis. "We must look into this."

The Fourth of July holidaymakers had begun to arrive; and there were thousands of them, and they had a great deal of money, and they wanted to bet it all on Heroine. Everybody wanted to bet on Heroine; and the men in the betting ring obliged them.

But there were three men from Boston who were betting on the field against the favorite. They distributed their bets in small sums of money among a great many different bookmakers; even the oldest of the racing men did not know them.

But Mr. Behren seemed to know them. He met one of them openly in front of the grandstand, and the stranger from Boston asked politely if he could trouble him for a light. Mr. Behren handed him his cigar, and while the man puffed at it he said, "We've got $50,000 of it up. It's too much to risk on that powder. Something might go wrong; you mightn't have mixed it properly, or there mayn't be enough. I've known it miss before this. Minerva, she won once with an ounce of it inside her. You'd better fix that jockey."

Mr. Behren's face was troubled, and he puffed quickly at his cigar as the man walked away. Then he turned and moved slowly towards the stables.

A gentleman with a field glass across his shoulder stopped him and asked, "How's Heroine?" and Mr. Behren answered, "Never better; I've $10,000 on her," and passed on with a confident smile.

Charley saw Mr. Behren coming, and bit his lip and tried to make his face look less conscious. He was not used to deception. He felt much more like plunging a pitchfork into Mr. Behren's legs, but he restrained that impulse, and chewed gravely on a straw. Mr. Behren looked carefully around the stable, and wiped the perspiration from his fat red face. The day was warm, and he was excited.

"Well, my boy," he said in a friendly, familiar tone as he seated himself, "it's almost time. I hope you are not rattled."

Charley said "No." He felt confident enough.

"It would be a big surprise if she went back on us, wouldn't it?" suggested the owner gloomily.

"It would, indeed," said Charley.

"Still," said Mr. Behren, "such things have been. Racin' is full of surprises, and horses are full of tricks. I've known a horse, now, get pocketed behind two or three others and never show to the front at all. Though she was the best of the field, too. And I've known horses go wild and jump over the rail and run away with the jock, and sometimes they fall. And sometimes I've had a jockey pull a horse on me and make me drop every cent I had up. You wouldn't do that, would you?" he asked. He looked up at Charley with a smile that might mean anything.

Charley looked at the floor and shrugged his shoulders. "I ride to orders, I do," he said. "I guess the owner knows his own business best. When I ride for a man and take his money I believe he should have his say. Some jockeys ride to win. I ride according to orders."

He did not look up after this, and he felt thankful that Heroine could not understand the language of human beings. Mr. Behren's face rippled with smiles. This was a jockey after his own heart.

"If Heroine should lose," he said, "I say, if she should, for no one knows what might happen, I'd have to abuse you fearful right before all the people. I'd swear at you and say you lost me all my money, and that you should never ride for me again. And they might suspend you for a month or two, which would be very hard on you," he added reflectively.

"But then," he said more cheerfully, "if you had a little money to live on while you were suspended it wouldn't be so hard, would it?" He took a large roll of bank bills from his pocket and counted them, smoothing them out on his fat knee and smiling up at the boy. "It wouldn't be so bad, would it?" he repeated. Then he counted aloud, "Eight hundred, nine hundred, one thousand."

He rose and placed the bills under a loose plank of the floor, and stamped it down on them. "I guess we understand each other, eh?" he said.

"I guess we do," said Charley.

"I'll have to swear at you, you know," said Behren, smiling.

"I can stand that," Charley answered.

As the horses paraded past for the July Stakes, the people rushed forward down the inclined enclosure and crushed against the rail and cheered whichever horse they best fancied.

"Say, you," called one of the crowd to Charley, "you want to win, you do. I've got $5 on that horse you're a-riding."

Charley ran his eyes over the crowd that were applauding and cheering him and Heroine, and calculated coolly that if every one had only $5 on Heroine there would be at least $100,000 on the horse in all.

The man from Boston stepped up beside Mr. Behren as he sat on his dogcart alone.

"The mare looks very fit," he said anxiously. "Her eyes are like diamonds. I don't believe that stuff affected her at all."

"It's all right," whispered Behren calmly. "I've fixed the boy."

The man dropped back off the wheel of the cart with a sigh of relief, and disappeared in the crowd. Mr. Maitland and Mr. Curtis sat together on the top of the former's coach. Mr. Curtis had his hand over the packages of feed in his pockets.

"If the mare don't win," he said, "there will be the worst scandal this track has ever known." The perspiration was rolling down his face. "It will be the death of honest racing."

"I cannot understand it," said Mr. Maitland. "The boy seemed honest, too."

The horses got off together. There were eleven of them. Heroine was amongst the last, but no one minded that because the race was a long one. And within three-quarters of a mile of home Heroine began to shake off the others and came up slowly through the crowd, and her thousands of admirers yelled. And then Maitland's Good Morning and Reilly swerved in front of her, or else Heroine fell behind them, it was hard to tell which, and Lady Betty closed in on her from the right. Her jockey seemed to be trying his best to get her out of the triangular pocket into which she had run. The great crowd simultaneously gave an anxious questioning gasp. Then two more horses pushed to the front, closing the favorite in and shutting her off altogether.

"The horse is pocketed," cried Mr. Curtis, "and not one man out of a thousand would know that it was done on purpose."

"Wait!" said Mr. Maitland.

"Bless that boy!" murmured Behren, trying his best to look anxious. "She can never pull out of that."

They were within half a mile of home. The crowd was panic-stricken and jumping up and down.

"Heroine!" they cried, as wildly as though they were calling for help, or the police. "Heroine!" Charley heard them above the noise of the pounding hoofs, and smiled in spite of the mud and dirt that the great horses in front flung in his face and eyes.

"Heroine," he said, "I think we've scared that crowd about long enough. Now, punish Behren." He sank his spurs into the horse's sides and jerked her head towards a little opening between Lady Betty and Chubb. Heroine sprang at it like a tiger and came neck to neck with the leader. And then, as she saw the wide track empty before her, and no longer felt the hard backward pull on her mouth, she tossed her head with a snort, and flew down the stretch like an express, with her jockey whispering fiercely in her ear.

Heroine won with a grand rush, by three lengths, but Charley's face was filled with anxiety as he tossed up his arm in front of the judges' stand. He was covered with mud and perspiration, and panting with exertion and excitement. He distinguished Mr. Curtis's face in the middle of the wild crowd around him, then patted his legs and hugged and kissed Heroine's head, and danced up and down in the ecstasy of delight.

"Mr. Curtis," he cried, raising his voice above the tumult of the crowd, and forgetting, or not caring, that they could hear, "send some one to the stable, quick. There's a thousand dollars there Behren offered me to pull the horse. It's under a plank near the back door. Get it before he does. That's evidence the Racing Board can't—"

But before he could finish, or before Mr. Curtis could push his way towards him, a dozen stable boys and betting men had sprung away with a yell towards the stable, and the mob dashed after them. It gathered in volume as a landslide does when it goes down hill; and the people in the grandstand and on the coaches stood up and asked what was the matter;

and some cried "Stop thief!" and others cried "Fight!" and others said that a bookmaker had given big odds against Heroine, and was "doing a welsh." The mob swept around the corner of the long line of stables like a charge of cavalry, and dashed at Heroine's lodgings.

The door was open, and on his knees at the other end was Behren, digging at the planks with his fingernails. He had seen that the boy had intentionally deceived him, and his first thought, even before that of his great losses, was to get possession of the thousand dollars that might be used against him. He turned his fat face, now white with terror, over his shoulder, as the crowd rushed into the stable, and tried to rise from his knees; but before he could get up, the first man struck him between the eyes, and others fell on him, pummeling him and kicking him and beating him down.

If they had lost their money, instead of having won, they could not have handled him more brutally. Two policemen and a couple of men with pitchforks drove them back; and one of the officers lifted up the plank, and counted the thousand dollars before the crowd.

Either Mr. Maitland felt badly at having doubted Charley, or else he admired his riding, for he bought Heroine when Behren was ruled off the racetracks and had to sell his horses, and Charley became his head jockey. And just as soon as Heroine began to lose, Mr. Maitland refused to have her suffer such degradation, and said she should stop while she could still win. And then he presented her to Charley, who had won so much and so often with her, and Charley gave up his license and went back to the farm to take care of his mother, and Heroine played all day in the clover fields.

9

"Old Bill"

By Henry C. Wallace

Sentimental horse stories that touch the heart are always welcomed by this reader and editor. This one is excerpted from the book Prairie Gold, *published in 1917.*

WE BURIED OLD BILL TODAY. AS WE CAME BACK TO THE HOUSE IT seemed almost as if we had laid away a member of the family. All afternoon I have been thinking of him, and this evening I want to tell you the story.

Old Bill was a horse, and he was owned by four generations of our family. He was forty-one years old when he died, so you will understand that for many years he was what some might call a "dead-beat boarder." But long ago he had paid in advance for his board as long as he might stay with us. In winter a warm corner of the stable was his as a matter of right, and not a day went by but a lump of sugar, an apple, or some other tidbit found its way to him from the hands of those who loved him. Old Bill was never in the slightest danger of meeting the sad fate of many a faithful old horse in the hands of the huckster or trader.

My grandfather liked a good horse. He loved to draw the lines over a team that trotted up into the bits as if they enjoyed it. He had such a team in a span of eleven-hundred pound mares, full sisters, and well matched both as to appearance and disposition. The old gentleman said they were Morgan bred. Whether they were or not, they had a lot of warm blood in them. He raised several colts from these mares by light horses, but none of them had either the spirit or the quality of their dams. One year a neighbor brought in a Percheron horse, a rangy fellow weighing about seventeen hundred and fifty pounds, clean of limb, and with plenty of life, as were most of the earlier horses of that breed, and grandfather bred these mares to him. The colts foaled the next spring, developed into a fine span, weighing about twelve hundred and fifty each, sound as nuts, willing workers and free movers. Grandfather gave this team to my father the spring he started to farm for himself. They were then three years old, and one of them was Old Bill.

In those days the young farmer's capital was not very large: a team of horses, a cow, two or three pigs, and a few farm implements, the horses being by far the most important part of it. I shall not try to tell of the part these horses played in helping father win out. They were never sick; they were always ready for work. And well do I remember father's grief when Bill's mate slipped on the ice in the barnyard one cold winter day and had to be shot. It was that evening that my father talked of the important part a good horse plays in the life of a farmer, and gave us a little lecture on the treatment of horses and other animals. I was but a lad of ten at that time, but something father said, or the way he said it, made a deep impression on me, and from that time forward I looked upon horses as my friends and treated them as such. What a fine thing it would be if all parents would teach the youngsters at an early age the right way to treat our dumb animals.

Bill was already "Old Bill" when he became mine. He was four years older than I when we started courting together, and my success must have been due in large part to his age and experience. We had but a mile and a half to go, and of a summer evening Bill would trot this off at a pace equal to a much younger horse. When the girl of my affection was snugly seated in the buggy, he would move off briskly for half a mile, after which he dropped to a dignified walk, understanding full well the importance of the business in hand. He knew where it was safe to leave the beaten track and walk quietly along the turf at the side, and he had a positive genius for finding nice shady places where he could browse the overhanging branches, looking back once in a while to see that everything was going along as it should be. I suppose I am old-fashioned, but I don't see how a really first-class job of courting can be done without such a horse as Old Bill. He seemed to take just about as much interest in the matter as I did. One night Jennie brought out a couple of lumps of sugar for him (a hopeful sign to me, by the way), and after that there was no time lost in getting to her house, where Bill very promptly announced our arrival by two or three nickers.

One time I jokingly said to my wife that evidently she married Bill as much as she did me. That remark was a mistake. She admitted it more cheerfully than seemed necessary, and on sundry occasions afterward made free to remind me of it. Sometimes she drew comparisons to my discredit, and if Old Bill could have understood them, he would have enjoyed a real horse laugh. Jennie always said Bill knew more than some real folks.

After the wedding, Old Bill took us on our honeymoon trip—not a very long one, you may be sure—and the three of us settled down to the steady grind of farm life. We asked nothing hard of Old Bill, but he helped chore around, and took Jennie safely where she wanted to go. I felt perfectly at ease when she was driving him. I wish I had a picture of the three of them when she brought out the boy to show to Old Bill. I can close my eyes and see her standing in front of the old horse, with the boy cuddled up in a blanket in her arms. I can see the proud light in her eyes, and I can see Old Bill's sensitive upper lip nuzzling at the blanket. He evidently understood Jennie perfectly, and seemed just as proud as she was.

The youngster learned to ride Old Bill at the age most children are riding broomsticks. Jennie used to put him on Old Bill's back and lead him around, but Old Bill seemed so careful that before a great while she would trust him alone with the boy in the front yard, she sitting on the porch. I remember a scare I had one summer evening. Old Bill did not have much hair left on his withers, but he had a long mane lock just in front of the collar mark, and the youngster held onto this. I was walking up toward the house, where Bill was marching the youngster around in front, Jennie sitting on the porch. Evidently a botfly was bothering Bill's front legs, for he threw his head down quickly, whereupon the youngster, holding tightly to this mane lock, slid down his neck and flopped to the ground. You may be sure I got there in a hurry, almost as quickly as Jennie, who was but a few steps away, calling as I ran: "Did he step on him?" You should have seen the look of scorn Jennie gave me. Such an insult to Old Bill deserved no answer. The old horse seemed as much concerned as we were and Jennie promptly replaced the boy on his back and the ride was resumed, with me relegated to the corner of the porch in disgrace. As if Old Bill would hurt her boy!

Old Bill's later years were full of contentment and happiness, if I know what constitutes horse happiness. In the winter he had the best corner in the stable. In the summer he was the autocrat of the small pasture where we kept the colts. He taught the boy to ride properly and with due respect for his steed. He would give him a gallop now and then, but as a rule he insisted upon a dignified walk, and if the youngster armed himself with a switch and tried to have his way about it, the old fellow would quickly show who was boss by nipping his little legs just hard enough to serve as a warning of what he could do.

Bill had a lot of fun with the mares and colts. We never allowed the colts to follow the mares in the fields, but kept them in the five-acre pasture with Bill for company. At noon, we would lead the mares in after they had cooled off, and let the colts suck, and at night we turned the mares into the pasture with them. Bill had a keen sense of humor. He would fool around until the colts had finished, and then gallop off with all the colts in full tilt after him. Naturally the mares resented this. They followed around in great indignation, but it did them no good. We used to walk over to the pasture fence and watch this little byplay, and I think Bill enjoyed having us there, for he kept up the fun as long as we would watch. He surely was not popular with the mares. They regarded him about as the proud mother regards grandfather when he entices away her darling boy and teaches him tricks of which she does not approve.

Although Bill took delight in teaching the colts mean little tricks during their days of irresponsibility, when they reached the proper age he enjoyed the part he had to play in their training with a grim satisfaction. For more than twenty-five years he was our main reliance in breaking the colts to work. It was amusing to watch a colt the first time he was harnessed and hooked up to the wagon alongside Bill, his halter strap being tied back to the hames on Bill's collar.

Our colts were always handled more or less from infancy, and we had little trouble in harnessing them. When led out to the wagon with Bill, the colt invariably assumed he was out for a good time. But the Bill he found now was not the Bill he had known in the pasture, and he very quickly learned that he was in for real business.

Bill was a very strict disciplinarian; he tolerated no familiarities; with his teeth he promptly suppressed any undue exuberance of spirit; he was kind but firm. As he grew older, he would lose patience now and then with the colts that persisted in their unruly ways. When they lunged forward, he settled back against their plunges with a bored air, as much as to say: "Take it easy, my young friend; you surely don't think you can run away with Old Bill!" When they sulked, he pulled them along for a bit. But if they continued obstreperous he turned upon them with his teeth in an almost savage manner, and the way he would bring them out of the sulky spell was a joy to see.

Finally, when the tired and bewildered colt had settled down to an orderly walk, and had learned to respond to the guiding reins, Bill would reward him with a caress on the neck and other evidences of his esteem.

Old Bill knew the game thoroughly, and was invaluable in this work of training the young ones. But after the first round at the wagon with him, the colts always seemed to feel as if they had lost a boon companion; they kept their friendship for him, but they maintained a very respectful attitude, and never after took liberties unless assured by his manner that they would be tolerated.

I got a collie dog for the youngster when he was about three years old. When he was riding Old Bill, Jack would rush back and forth, in front and behind, barking joyously. Old Bill disliked such frivolity. To him it was a serious occasion. I think he never forgot the time the boy fell off, for nothing could tempt him out of a steady walk until the youngster got to an age when his seat was reasonably secure. When the ride was over, Old Bill would lay back his ears and go after Jack so viciously that the collie would seek refuge under the porch. Except when the boy was about, however, Old Bill and Jack were good friends, and in very cold weather Jack would beg a place in Bill's stall, curling up between his legs, to the apparent satisfaction of both. There was a very real friendship between them, but just as real jealousy for the favors of the little fellow. They were much like human beings in this respect.

Until the last year of his life Bill was a most useful member of the family. Jennie liked a good garden and used to say before we were married that when we had our own home, she would have a garden that was a garden, and that she did not propose to wear herself out with a hoe as her mother had done. She laid out her garden in a long, narrow strip of ground between the pasture and the windbreak, just back of the house, and with Bill's help she had the garden she talked about. Bill plowed the ground and cultivated it, and the care with which he walked the long narrow rows was astonishing. This was another place where he did not want to be bothered with Jack. He was willing Jack should sit at one end and watch the proceedings, but he must keep out of the way.

During the school season Bill's regular job was to take the children to school, a mile away. They rode him, turning him loose to come home alone. He learned to go back for them in the afternoon, and he delivered them at the porch with an air as much as to say: "There are your little folks, safe and sound, thanks to Old Bill." Jennie always met him with an apple or a lump of sugar. She and Old Bill seemed to be in partnership in about everything he could have a part in. They understood each other perfectly, and I don't mind confessing now that once in a great while I felt rather jealous of Old Bill.

Well, as I said in the beginning, we buried Old Bill today. He died peacefully, and, as we say of some esteemed citizen, "full of honors." He was buried on the farm he helped pay for; and, foolish as it may seem to some folks, before long a modest stone will mark his last resting place. And sometimes, of a summer afternoon, if I find Jennie sitting with her needlework in the shade of the big oak tree under which Old Bill rests, I will know that tender memories of a faithful servant are being woven into her neat stitches.

10

World Record Is Set by Man o' War

By the New York Times

WORLD RECORD IS SET BY MAN O' WAR
FROM THE *NEW YORK TIMES*, JUNE 13, 1920
Riddle's Speed Miracle Shatters All Previous Marks for Mile and Three Furlongs
Wins Belmont by a Block
Finishes Half-Furlong before Donnacona
Great Throng Is Amazed

<><><><><><><><><><><><><><><><><><><><><><><><><><><><><><><><><><><><><><><><><><><>

Horse racing found itself in a struggle for its life as the 1920s approached. The sport had survived the antigambling fervor of ten years earlier (reformers had moved on to alcoholic beverages) but the world war had badly damaged the international breeding and racing industries.

By June 13, 1920, when the story of Man o' War's victory in the previous day's Belmont Stakes appeared in the New York Times, *the sport had already begun to climb out of the doldrums, thanks at least partially to the charismatic red colt. Thousands crowded the grandstands when he raced. Millions of dollars were bet on him during his sixteen-month racing career. His Belmont Stakes was fully representative of his career: a great throng was indeed amazed by his accomplishment.*

The Times *article displays the combination of straightforward reporting and adulation that was typical of news coverage of the remarkable horse. It appeared without a byline, customary at the time in racing journalism.*

—Sharon B. Smith

∞∞

Samuel D. Riddle's great race horse, Man o' War, gave at Belmont Park yesterday what was beyond a doubt the greatest exhibition of speed ever witnessed on any racetrack when he shattered the world's record for a mile and three furlongs in winning the $10,000 Belmont Stakes, while a crowd of 25,000 sat stunned by the almost unbelievably brilliant performance. The champion did not just clip the mark, but literally shattered it, for he ran the distance in 2:14 1-5, which is two and three-fifths seconds faster than any horse had ever run it before.

The world's record was previously held by Dean Swift, which ran the mile and three furlongs in 2:16 4-5 at Liverpool, England, in 1908. The next lowest mark was made in the running of the Belmont last year when Sir Barton set a new American record for the distance of 2:17 2-5. The Canadian and Australian records do not even closely approach the English and American marks, which stood until yesterday afternoon.

When the figures were posted there was a hum of amazement in the packed stands. Every one had been expecting Man o' War to lower the record made by Sir Barton last year, but no one was quite ready to believe it would be lowered to the extent of several seconds and take the world's mark with it. Not even his owner had thought he would stage such a performance, for he had not sent his colt out with the expectation of making such wonderful time.

BEST OF ALL TIMES AND CLIMES

The race left no doubt in the minds of all turfmen present that they had seen the greatest horse of this or any other age. Up to this time they had been content to say that he was America's finest product, but after he had crossed the line in the Belmont and his time was flashed there were none among the veterans of the turf who could think of a horse who compared with him. It is safe to say that Man o' War is the superhorse of the ages as far as records go back; a horse the likes of which will probably never be seen by the present generation of horsemen. Man o' War would seem to typify the final goal of breeders, the perfect racehorse, gifted with all the essentials of greatness. The son of Fair Play has set a mark which all horses save himself are likely to shoot at vainly for many years to come.

The Belmont Stakes did not, of course, present a real contest. No one in the great throng had expected that it would. The public as well as horsemen have given up any idea that any three-year-old in the country can make Man o' War get out of a gallop. It was not a race but an exhibition by a great horse and as such it more than satisfied everyone who saw the colt in action. There is pleasure enough for those present in the thought that they have seen the world's greatest racehorse and moreover have been witnesses of his record-making performance. Man o' War finds himself in the position of Alexander of yore, seeking new worlds to conquer, and as there are no horses of his age to race with him he has only the reduction of records for various distances as a stimulus.

DAVID HARUM IS WITHDRAWN

It was the original intention to send two horses against the Fair Play colt in the Belmont Stakes, but W. R. Coe's David Harum was withdrawn and only G. W. Loft's Donnacona was left to act as a running mate. Donnacona is a high class colt, one of the best of his age and it is something of a measure of the greatness of Man o' War that Donnacona finished a sixteenth of a mile back of the winner although doing his best to the end.

There was scarcely any speculation on the race. Man o' War was quoted at the prohibitive odds of 1 to 20 as against 12 to 1 for the Loft colt. Practically the only wagers made were by persons who wanted, for the sake of sentiment, to say that they had made a bet on Man o' War.

The start for the Belmont is made from a chute which leads across the straightaway track into the training track. From this latter the horses turn into the main track at the turn, which leads to the stretch.

As the barrier went up Man o' War popped to the front and jockey Clarence Kummer, wearing his gold stirrups again, let the Fair Play colt run with a fair flight of speed from the beginning. Man o' War never waits for a pacemaker. His habit of running races is to go to the front and bid his rival to come on and catch him.

Through the training track course Man o' War maintained a lead of about two lengths, and was still under restraint, while Donnacona was moving along at a fast clip and apparently had something left. As the horses reached that point where they turned into the main track Donnacona moved up resolutely until he closed the gap of daylight which had appeared between the horses since the start. From the stands it appeared that he was right at the heels of the champion, and the Loft horse was moving with fine speed.

FLASHES AWAY FROM RIVAL

Kummer looked back and, seeing Donnacona, gave Man o' War his head. The son of Fair Play developed a new rate of speed in half a dozen strides. He began to move away from his rival as though the latter was anchored. At the turn into the stretch Man o' War was four lengths in front, and he had not yet been permitted to run as it was quite evident he wished to.

As Man o' War reached the stretch the crowd began to yell to Kummer to let him run, for it was the desire of everyone to see a new record made. Kummer did as they desired. Instead of taking a pull on his mount, as he had done in his previous race, he let Man o' War step along all through the stretch, although at no time urging him. He simply let the colt run freely, and then it became evident how he outclasses the others of his age. He not only left a wide margin between him and Donnacona, but he made a joke of the race as such. He gained a length with every two strides and, although his head was still held high in the air, he increased his lead by a sixteenth of a mile in the distance of the stretch. Man o' War was around the turn and being pulled up as Donnacona crossed the finish line.

There was great cheering for the champion when he came back to the stands and general congratulations for Mr. Riddle for the establishment of the new world's record. Horsemen who watched the race thought the Fair Play colt could have reduced the mark by at least another fraction of a second had he been in the least extended. Though he was fairly flying through the stretch, he was not running at his top speed. Kummer sat perfectly still on him, neither urging nor restraining him, and perhaps one touch of the whip would have taken another two-fifths from the time. This was the first time that Man o' War had ever raced at such a distance, but when he pulled up he was not even breathing hard.

11

How I Bought and Trained Captain

By W. A. Sigsbee, His Owner

When George Wharton James and W. A. Sigsbee met at the Panama-Pacific Exposition in San Francisco in 1915, it was the coming together of two accomplished showmen, an encounter that proved profitable to each of them. James was a respected writer of travelogues and nature books. Sigsbee was an admired trainer of horses. But each made his fortune by presenting himself to the public, James with dramatic readings to audiences and Sigsbee by demonstrating the accomplishments of the horses he had trained.

James was fascinated with what he saw in San Francisco: a horse named Captain who appeared to be able to count, differentiate between colors, make change, and play "Nearer My God to Thee" on the chimes. James believed there was no fraud involved, although he acknowledged that the horse probably didn't understand the words to the hymn. He also thought it was possible that Captain was taking unwitting cues from Sigsbee, even if they weren't visible.

But James was sufficiently impressed to produce a book two years later that told the story of Captain, whom he called "The Horse with the Human Brain." Part of the book was his own analysis, part was a first-person (or first-horse) account of Captain's take on the situation, and part was Sigsbee's story of how he found and trained his famous horse. Here is Sigsbee's contribution.

—Sharon B. Smith

I WAS BROUGHT UP IN THE HORSE BUSINESS. MY FATHER AND UNCLES were horsemen before I was born. They lived in Dane County, Wisconsin, twelve miles from Madison, and there I first saw the light. One of my uncles had trotting horses, and almost as soon as I could do anything I used to go and help him. When I was fourteen years old I was regularly employed by him during my vacations, to help on the farm, in the stables, and to accompany him to the trotting track.

I soon learned to ride as a jockey, and up to the time I was eighteen years old that was my occupation. Then I began to work for myself. I bought, educated or trained, and then sold horses and dogs. I was much interested in them and always seemed to have fair success in their management.

As I grew older I used to go with my own horses to the County and State Fairs, the latter being held at Madison. When I was twenty-four years old I married, settled down on a farm, and as horse-trading seemed to be the business I was especially adapted for, naturally I followed it. Whenever my neighbors wanted a horse that was extra well trained they would come to me, and if I showed them one that could do a few tricks, they liked it nonetheless, and were not unwilling to pay a little extra for the pains I had taken.

The year after I was married I moved to Humboldt, Iowa, where I bought another farm and for four more years continued my work as farmer and horse-trader. Then I bought the Park Hotel, in the town of Humboldt, which I ran for eleven years, never, however, for one moment losing my interest in horses. In fact, it was one of the most profitable parts of my business.

Many farmers, show-men, circus-men, and others came to the town and stopped at my hotel, so I was never away from the atmosphere of the horse ring. Many a time, when they were in a tight place, the show or circus men would come and ask me to help them out, for my reputation as a trainer had spread, and it was pretty generally understood that I was an exceptional hand for teaching horses and dogs rather unusual and interesting tricks.

In time the great circus masters, like Barnum and Bailey, Al Ringling, and others, came to me and asked me to train horses for them, so that my horse business grew, and with it my reputation. Naturally I was always on the lookout for colts that promised well, or horses that seemed extra intelligent, and my eyes were keen for mares that showed a superior order of intelligence that were soon to have colts.

About this time my eyes were attracted to a beautiful mare, evidently with foal. No sooner did I see her than I wanted her. I found on inquiry that she had been bred to a spotted Arabian, as fine and beautiful a creature as she herself was. Satisfied that she was what I wanted, I purchased her. Already I had begun to speculate as to what I should do with her colt. If it was a prettily shaped animal, was as intelligent as the father and mother, I decided it should receive the best education I was capable of giving.

As the days of the mare's time passed I grew more and more anxious. My hopes were raised high, and I was correspondingly expectant and at the same time afraid. What if the colt should prove stupid? I awaited the birth of that colt as eagerly as a royal family awaits the birth of the child of a king, hence you can understand my delight and satisfaction, when the little lady came, that I found her faultless in appearance, neat, trim, dainty, and beautiful, with intelligent eyes and face and every indication of being a most superior animal.

From the hour of her birth I watched her far more closely than many a child is watched. I was in and out of the stable a score of times a day. While she appeared intelligent, I wanted to know with certainty as soon as I could. I was not long in discovering, and this was how it was done. My barn had double doors—one on each side. As it was warm weather I had both doors open to allow a current of air through the building. When the colt was four or five days old, I wished to hitch up the mare and drive her but did not think it wise to let so small and young a colt go along. So I closed the doors and left her inside. She became much excited at being separated from her mother; ran around wildly, whinnied, and generally fretted. But I felt she would have to learn to lose her mother, so I drove away and left her to fight it out as best she could.

The next day I went into the barn and groomed down the mare, the colt apparently paying no attention, but the moment I took the harness from its peg and began to put it upon the mother the little miss ran out of doors. I thought I had scared her in some way and paid no particular attention, but when I was ready to drive away and tried to get her back into the barn she positively refused to go or be driven. She was as resolved to stay out as I was to have her go in, and it was only when I secured additional help that I was able to get her inside.

The same thing occurred on the following day, and then I began to suspect that the colt knew as well as I did what was going on and was resolved not to be left behind. So I called to my wife to come and watch with me, while we experimented. So long as I merely fussed around with the mare, cleaning her, etc., it was all right, but the moment I touched the harness and made it appear I was going to hitch up, out shot the colt from the barn in a moment. We tried this out a dozen times and always with the same result. This occurred when she was nine days old, and with conviction I turned to my wife and exclaimed: "She'll do, the little Trixie; she's got brains, and I'll begin to train her right away." Thus she got her name, and I started upon her education.

In my past experience I had taught many horses to respond to questions with a Yes or No, to paw out numbers, to kiss me, to sit down, lie down, roll over, and other similar simple tricks. I would ask if they would like a drink, a feed of oats, a lump of sugar, etc., and teach them how to answer with a nod of the head, and with a shake when I asked: "Shall I whip you?" or "I guess you don't want any feed today," but with Trixie I determined to go further than this and see if she really could be trained, or, better still, *educated* in any degree.

Thus began Trixie's education, which continued persistently for eighteen months. Every day I kept at it, and it might be interesting here to state that while I was educating Trixie, she was educating me. I learned a great deal about horses and horse nature in those eighteen months. In due time I had trained her so that she could pick out numbers on call, colors, could add, subtract, multiply, and divide; could count with her feet, sit in a chair, on my lap, and answer questions.

I then decided to take her out on the road and give exhibitions with her. But first of all I decided to give a test exhibition at our County Fair, at Humboldt, my own town. Of course I was well known, and my horse training proclivities were the subject of conversation all throughout the country, but few knew how much I had accomplished with Trixie. Hence that first appearance was a great surprise to my neighbors. Needless to say, it was also a wonderful success. Every one was delighted with the exhibition and marveled at the intelligence the beautiful little creature displayed.

I now started to go throughout the country with confidence. I knew what Trixie could do and what the effect of the exhibition would be upon an audience. In those days an educated horse was unknown. There were a few trained circus horses, but a horse like mine excited great wonder and interest. My method was to go to county and other fairs, explain what Trixie could do, and I would undertake to exhibit her before the grand-stand between races. The Fair Associations would engage me, and thus I would earn a good financial return.

Soon after we began to travel I changed the colt's name to *Princess Trixie*, and this was the name by which she was ever afterwards known. About this time I came in contact with William Harrison Barnes, of Sioux City. He had been a newspaper reporter but was naturally a show-man, and shortly before I met him he had drifted into the show busi-ness. He was exhibiting such horses as "The Pacing Wonder," "Johnny, the Guideless Wonder," and when he saw the Princess there was nothing for it but that he should become my partner and go along with us. For four years we traveled together, Barnes making the business arrangements for our appearance at carnivals, state fairs, amusement parks, and under the auspices of various organizations.

Then I sold Princess Trixie to him, continuing to travel with him for four years, after which I returned to Humboldt, bought another farm, and for two or three years did a little desultory training of horses, as before. Let me here, in parenthesis, tell of Princess Trixie's unfortunate end. Barnes showed her all over the country to the great delight of all who ever saw her, until about ten years ago, when she was killed in a railway wreck at Baltimore.

Soon after my return to Humboldt I was urged by Dode Fisk, of Wonewoc, Wisconsin, to plan and organize for him a show of trained horses, dogs, monkeys, etc., with a one-ringed circus. I did so, doing all the training of the animals myself. When we were ready to travel we had a sixteen-wagon show and I was appointed the arena director. For four years I occupied this position, helping build up the show all the time, and at the end of three years we ceased traveling in wagons and became an eleven-car railway show. It was my regular duty to keep the animals in good condition, see that they were healthy and kept up to their work, and to train any new stock we might buy.

Four years of this life tired my wife, and she expressed the desire to get away from a large show. She wanted a rest at home, she said, and then, if I desired to travel she suggested I buy a young horse or a colt, train or educate it, and we would travel with that, without all the hard work, flurry, and daily excitement attendant upon a large show. In the main I agreed with my wife and, anyhow, I felt that she ought to be considered as much as myself, so I began looking out for such a horse as I had in mind. I wanted another Trixie or, better, but scarcely hoped to find one very soon, or very easily.

I was nearer to the end of my search, however, than I supposed, for almost immediately I heard of just such a colt as I was looking for at Oregon, Ill. Right away I went to see him, and there, to my unspeakable delight, I found Captain. His owner was Judge Cartwright, a great lover of and breeder of good horses. Captain was of standard bred trotting stock, and was half brother to the famous Sydney Dillon. His sire was the well-known horse Syed and his dam was the almost equally well-known Robey.

At first sight he pleased me immensely, and I sought to gain all the information possible about him. I learned that as a colt he was very friendly and playful, showing keen intelligence. He also possessed great speed, sometimes pacing in the pasture as fast as his mother could run. This had led his owner, as soon as he was two years old, to train him for ninety days for the development of speed, so that he was able to step his mile in 2:16. He undoubtedly would have made a fast pacing horse with further training. But fate had another destiny in store for him. I resolved to buy him.

Naturally Judge Cartwright hated to part with so promising an animal, but I candidly laid my heart's desire before him. I showed him the influence it would have upon the rising generation if I could demonstrate that animals can reason, that they are capable of thought. Then I expatiated upon the easier life Captain himself would live than if he were to become a regular racehorse, and I appealed to the feeling of pride he—the judge—would possess were I successful—as I knew I should be—at having introduced so world famous a horse as Captain would become, that he had bred and reared. And, finally, to clinch the matter, I produced a certified check for a thousand dollars, which I placed in his hand.

Thus the purchase was made, with the express understanding that Judge Cartwright should always be given the credit for the raising of Captain. Perhaps here I ought to state that the colt's name up to this time had been Sid Bell. As I felt my whole future life's work and fame were going to center on this beautiful, young, and intelligent creature, I renamed him, calling him by the name by which I was known to all my professional associates, Captain Sigsbee.

It was not long before we became intimately acquainted. He was a handsome fellow, a dappled chestnut, fifteen and one half hands high, with broad forehead, large, intelligent eyes, well-shaped ears, deep, sensitive nostrils, mobile mouth, strong nose, a most pleasing face, and perfectly formed in every way.

I was satisfied from the first that in Captain I had a great subject for education. Already I began to plan what I would teach him. I was assured I could go far beyond anything I had hitherto done, even with the clever Trixie. One day in conversation with a group of horsemen, among whom was Al Ringling, the great circus master, I stated some of my expectations. Ringling laughed at me, especially when I declared my intention of so educating a horse that he could do things blindfolded. He freely declared that he had no faith in horse education. He believed that horses could be trained only under the whip and spur.

Said he: "I know you've done some wonderful things with Trixie, but animals are animals, and I don't believe that you can *educate* them. Let me give you some advice. Don't waste your time. Many a man has gone crazy by allowing a fool idea like this of yours to take possession of him."

I defended my ideas, however, and argued that my years of study of the horse had revealed things of horse nature and character few even dreamed of. I was sure they could think and reason. Everybody knew that they had memory, and I was satisfied that I could educate this, or any other intelligent horse, to use his reason, no matter how small it was—in other words to think.

Ringling listened with interest but made no pretense to hide his doubts, and again said I was going crazy when I affirmed my positive conviction that I could, and would, train Captain to take and obey orders *blindfolded*. He was certain it never could be done.

How well I have succeeded the hundreds of thousands who have seen Captain can best tell. It may also be interesting to recount Mr. Ringling's expressions when he saw Captain sometime after I began to give exhibitions with him.

He said: "I confess myself beaten, Sigsbee, I take off my hat to you. What you have accomplished will be a revelation to the world, as it has been to me. In spite of my years of association with horses I never dreamed they had such powers in them. You have opened my eyes, and as others begin to see they will treat their animals with greater consideration, they will think more favorably of them, and no longer treat them as if they were mere brute instruments of their will or pleasure, without feeling or intelligence."

Mr. Ringling well stated what it has been one of my constant endeavors to bring about. I have always loved horses. I wanted to see them better treated, and it is with great satisfaction that I am learning every day that my exhibitions with Princess Trixie and now with Captain are bearing this kind of fruit.

When my purchase of the colt was completed, I took him to my training barn in Chicago and there began his education. The first thing to do was to get well acquainted and gain his affection. This was done by giving him plenty to eat, the best of care, speaking gently and kindly to him, petting him, and giving him dainties now and again, such as carrots, apples, and sugar. My friends and acquaintances often laughed at me, and said I should never accomplish what I was after, but I persevered. They knew I was wasting time, money, and energy for nothing, but "I know" that what "they knew" wasn't so.

It did not take Captain long to learn that I was kind to him; that I was his true and wise friend; and was to be relied upon. These are three things, the importance of which I cannot overestimate. Many people try to be kind to animals, but they are not wise in their treatment, and they are not to be relied upon. I knew that Captain trusted me for the little extra dainties he enjoyed. I never disappointed him. I never lied to him— that is promised him anything I did not intend to perform, and thus he soon learned I was to be trusted.

When left alone he became very uneasy. Like children he wanted companionship of some kind, so I hired a groom, Chili by name, whose duty was to remain with Captain, day and night. He was never to attempt to teach the horse anything, as that would lead to confusion, but was to care for him and be his companion at all times. Chili remained with him for several years and they became very fond of each other. I should never have parted with him, but when we came to San Francisco, he got careless and I had to let him go. Then I was fortunate enough to secure an equally good man in his present groom, Jasper.

Jasper is a natural-born horseman. He has ridden, broken, and owned some very famous horses, and has been on the track for years, hence he thoroughly understands horse-nature, and he and Captain get along famously.

As I have before explained Captain likes company. He strongly resents being left alone. Every night time before he goes to sleep he listens for the footsteps of his groom and if he is not there he signifies his disapproval by pawing, whinnying, etc., and generally keeps it up until Jasper returns and talks to him. Then, content and restful, he goes to sleep.

Once, when he was being brought south by rail, Jasper had to leave him in the Los Angeles freight yards—still in his car—to see that their tickets were properly endorsed, and he was gone for a half an hour or more. When he returned poor Captain was in a complete lather of per-spiration. The unusual noises of the railroad yard in a large city, as he was shut up in a car so that he could not see, had fretted him into a frenzy. As soon as the groom returned he signified his satisfaction with whinnyings and nose-rubbings and in a very short time was cool again.

Every night before he lies down and goes to sleep, he peeks out to see if Jasper is there. If not, he awaits his return, and then stretches out with his head towards the place where Jasper sleeps.

Soon after we arrived in San Diego a lady presented Jasper with a pigeon. The bird was taken to the stable, and Captain became much interested in her. As the pigeon perched on the partition he reached up and nuzzled it in the most affectionate manner. Not only did the pigeon not resent it, but she seemed actually to enjoy it, showing no fear or desire to get away. Now they are almost inseparable friends, and Captain spends hours with his head upon the partition, snuggling close up to the bird. Prior to its coming, Captain often showed considerable nervousness when he heard strange footsteps approaching his stable, or just before a performance, but the presence of the pigeon has changed this. Its mere presence is a soothing influence, and when the show is over he goes back to the stable and greets his bird friend with evident pleasure and affection.

One of my experiences with Captain demonstrated his superior intelligence over most horses. My training barn was two stories high, and a wide pair of stairs led from the ground to the second floor. When my grandson was born Captain took a great liking for him. He loved to "kiss" him and nuzzle him while he was in the cradle, or baby-buggy, or even in his nurse's arms. As the child grew older we used to place him on Captain's back and Captain would march back and forth, as proudly as a king, apparently conscious of the trust we placed in him.

One day while I was working with Captain the child was in the barn, and he kept going up and down the stairs. I noticed that Captain's attention was more often fixed upon the child than upon me and he seemed much interested. Someone called me away for a few moments, and when I returned there was no Captain to be seen. Then I heard a peculiar noise from above, and looking up, what should I see but Captain following the child up the stairs. I am free to confess I got scared, for I couldn't see how I could get him down. But I went up, controlled my fears, and then quietly talked to Captain and told him he'd come up the stairs and now he'd have to go down them. And I backed him down, a step at a time, as easily and as safely as could be. And, strange to say, ever after that, whenever he wanted to go upstairs I let him, and he came down alone. I never had to back him down again. He comes down that way of his own volition.

People often ask me how I train an animal. Personally I would not use the word "train," in speaking of such a horse as Captain, not because it is the wrong word, but because it conveys a wrong idea. I would say "educate," for I firmly believe that horses and dogs and elephants and other animals possess the power of reason, though, of course, in a limited degree. And I believe that by patient and kindly treatment we can "draw out"—educate—the intelligence possessed.

I have no set rules or fixed system by which I work. There are a few principles that control me. First of all I study the animal's nature and disposition. No two animals are alike, any more than any two children are alike. Some animals are very nervous, are easily excited, while others are placid and docile and nothing seems to disturb them. But whatever the natural disposition nothing can be done without gaining the animal's complete confidence.

This I do by uniformly kind treatment. I always speak gently, mildly, never angrily or impatiently. Then I pet the animal at every opportunity, though with some, one must approach them at first, cautiously. As soon as possible get an animal accustomed to the feel of your hands, and to know that they always come gently, and with soothing effect. Find out what they particularly like to eat, and every once in a while, give this to them as a relish, a luxury, a reward for something well done. As I have explained elsewhere horses like carrots, apples, and sugar. Too much of any of these, however, is not good, as their natural food is grass, hay, cereals, and the like. Yet it should never be overlooked that a horse, like a man, can more easily be reached through his stomach than any other way.

Though you must be kind you must also be firm. Many people confound and confuse kindness with mushiness. No animal must be allowed to have his own way, when that way conflicts with his master's will. (Yet a caution, here, is necessary. One who is training either a horse or a child should remember his natural proclivities and tendencies. There should be no attempt to "break the will." It is to be trained, disciplined, brought under control. Hence, never set your will against the will of your animal unless it is in a matter where you know you are right.) For instance, if a horse wants to cut up and frolic when you wish him to attend to business, there are two ways of doing.

One is to leave him alone for a while and then firmly bring him to attention, even though he still desires to continue his fun. Another is to crush the spirit of fun and frolic and not allow him to play at all. This latter method is unnatural, unreasonable, and cruel, and therefore not to be thought of for one moment by any rational or kind man. The former is both kind and *disciplinary*. The horse is allowed to follow his natural instincts, but is also taught to control them at his master's word. This is training and education. A third method is to allow the horse to frolic to his heart's content and then get him to do what you desire. Here there is no discipline whatever. This is the way of "mushiness," and it is often followed by parents and others in handling their children. It is about as bad as the cruel method of suppressing the natural instincts, for an uncontrolled will or appetite soon becomes the child's, animal's, or man's master, and nothing is more disastrous than such a bondage.

Hence be firm in control. It is not necessary to whip to punish. A horse, as well as a child, will learn self-control through appetite, or the giving of something that is a pleasure. Where you have trouble in gaining control, or where the animal is lazy, hold back on the tidbit, or the free run, or something of the kind the horse enjoys. He will soon learn to associate the loss with his disobedience. Equally so be prompt and certain in rewarding his good conduct. It is a good thing in dealing with a stubborn or refractory animal (or child) to let him get "good and hungry." It does not take him long to learn to associate obedience with food, or disobedience with hunger.

Then it is most important that you never lie to an animal. Be strictly truthful. When you promise anything—or by forming a habit imply a promise—do not fail to keep that promise. If your animal expects an apple, a carrot, a piece of sugar, or a frolic at the close of his hour's training, *do not disappoint him*. A horse, a child, instinctively hates a liar. One soon loses confidence, and where there is no confidence there can be no pleasure in working together, and as soon as pleasure goes, the work becomes a burden, a labor, a penalty, and a curse, to be dreaded, shunned, avoided. So win your animal's confidence and then be sure to keep it.

When it comes to actual teaching always be very patient, never excited, always talk gently and keep your voice pitched low, and remember that all animals are curious, possess more or less of the imitative faculty, and have good memories. To remember these things is of great importance. Never lose sight of them. Talk to your animal as you would to a child. Whether you think or believe he understands you, or not, act and talk as if he did. Then *show* him what you want him to do. Do it before him, again and again. Thus you will excite his imitative faculties and at the same time, train his memory.

Occasionally you may be able to give him extra aid. For instance, you want to teach your horse to shake his head to express the idea No! When you say No! tickle the horse's ear, and he will shake his head. Then you also shake your head, and say with emphasis, No! Repeat this several times, and you will find that when you say No! the horse will shake his head without your having to tickle his ear. As soon as he responds to your question with a shake of the head be sure to pet and reward him with a lump of sugar, at the same time talking encouragingly to him.

Then repeat the process, again and again, until it is well fixed in his memory.

Every day go over this same thing; for, if you neglect what he learns today for a week or two, it is very possible he will forget and you will have to begin afresh. Review perpetually, until you know that *he knows*.

In assisting him to nod his head when you want him to signify Yes! when you use the word tap him under the chin. This leads him to throw his head up and down. Soon he will nod at the mere saying of Yes! and later, he will respond with a nod when you ask him a question to which he should reply with the affirmative.

Remember always, in all you do, that you are dealing with an animal whose brainpower is far less than that of an ordinary child, and be *patient, kind, and persevering*. Never allow yourself to believe the animal does not possess intelligence. *Believe* he has it, *hope* he has it, *trust God* that he has it, and work in that belief, hope, trust, and you will accomplish wonders. Faith, hope, and love are the abiding and moving powers of life. With them there is no limit to what can be done, for they belong to the infinite.

12

Sensations of a Cavalry Charge

By Winston Churchill

◇◇◇

After his brave experiences as a young soldier, and before his ultimate triumphs as British prime minister, Winston Churchill worked long and hard on a series of books about history. One of their features was the "you-are-there" feeling he imparts in this account of battles fought on horseback.

◇◇◇

IT IS NOT MY PURPOSE IN THIS RECORD OF PERSONAL IMPRESSIONS TO give a general account of the Battle of Omdurman. The story has been told so often and in such exact military detail that everyone who is interested in the subject is no doubt well acquainted with what took place. I shall only summarize the course of the battle so far as may be necessary to explain my own experiences.

The whole of the Khalifa's army, nearly 60,000 strong, advanced in battle order from their encampment of the night before, topped the swell of ground which hid the two armies from one another, and then rolled down the gently sloping amphitheatre in the arena of which, backed upon the Nile, Kitchener's 20,000 troops were drawn up shoulder to shoulder to receive them. Ancient and modern confronted one another. The weapons, the methods and the fanaticism of the Middle Ages were brought by an extraordinary anachronism into dire collision with the organisation and inventions of the nineteenth century. The result was not surprising. As the successors of the Saracens descended the long smooth slopes which led to the river and their enemy, they encountered the rifle fire of two and a half divisions of trained infantry, drawn up two deep and in close order and supported by at least 70 guns on the riverbank and in the gunboats, all firing with undisturbed efficiency. Under this fire the whole attack withered and came to a standstill, with a loss of perhaps six or seven thousand men, at least 700 yards away from the British-Egyptian line. The Dervish army, however, possessed nearly 20,000 rifles of various kinds, from the most antiquated to the most modern, and when the spearmen could get no farther, these riflemen lay down on the plain and began a ragged, unaimed but considerable fusillade at the dark line of the thorn-fence zariba. Now for the first time they began to inflict losses on their antagonists, and in the short space that this lasted, perhaps two hundred casualties occurred among the British and Egyptian troops.

Seeing that the attack had been repulsed with great slaughter and that he was nearer to the city of Omdurman than the Dervish army, Kitchener immediately wheeled his five brigades into his usual echelon formation, and with his left flank on the river proceeded to march south towards the city, intending thereby to cut off what he considered to be the remnants of the Dervish army from their capital, their base, their food, their water, their home, and to drive them out into the vast deserts which stared on every side. But the Dervishes were by no means defeated. The whole of their left, having overshot the mark, had not even been under fire. The Khalifa's reserve of perhaps 15,000 men was still intact. All these swarms now advanced with undaunted courage to attack the British and Egyptian forces, which were no longer drawn up in a prepared position, but marching freely over the desert. This second shock was far more critical than the first. The charging Dervishes succeeded everywhere in coming to within a hundred or two hundred yards of the troops, and the rear brigade of Soudanese, attacked from two directions, was only saved from destruction by the skill and firmness of its commander, General Hector Macdonald. However, discipline and machinery triumphed over the most desperate valour, and after an enormous carnage, certainly exceeding 20,000 men, who strewed the ground in heaps and swathes "like snowdrifts," the whole mass of the Dervishes dissolved into fragments and into particles and streamed away into the fantastic mirages of the desert.

The Egyptian cavalry and the camel corps had been protecting the right flank of the zariba when it was attacked, and the 21st Lancers were the only horsemen on the left flank nearest to Omdurman. Immediately after the first attack had been repulsed, we were ordered to leave the zariba, ascertain what enemy forces, if any, stood between Kitchener and the city, and if possible drive these forces back and clear the way for the advancing army. Of course as a regimental officer one knows very little of what is taking place over the whole field of battle. We waited by our horses during the first attack close down by the river's edge, sheltered by the steep Nile bank from the bullets which whistled overhead. As soon as the fire began to slacken and it was said on all sides that the attack had been repulsed, a general arrived with his staff at a gallop with instant orders to mount and advance. In two minutes the four squadrons were mounted and trotting out of the zariba in a southerly direction. We ascended again the slopes of Jebel Surgham which had played its part in the first stages of the action, and from its ridges soon saw before us the whole plain of Omdurman with the vast mud city, its minarets and domes, spread before us six or seven miles away.

After various halts and reconnoiterings we found ourselves walking forward in what is called "column of troops." There are four troops in a squadron and four squadrons in a regiment. Each of these troops now followed the other. I commanded the second troop from the rear, comprising between twenty and twenty-five Lancers.

Everyone expected that we were going to make a charge. That was the one idea that had been in all minds since we had started from Cairo. Of course there would be a charge. In those days, before the Boer War, British cavalry had been taught little else. Here was clearly the occasion for a charge. But against what body of enemy, over what ground, in which direction or with what purpose, were matters hidden from the rank and file. We continued to pace forward over the hard sand, peering into the mirage-twisted plain in a high state of suppressed excitement. Presently I noticed, 300 yards away on our flank and parallel to the line on which we were advancing, a long row of blue-black objects, two or three yards apart. I thought there were about a hundred and fifty. Then I became sure that these were men-enemy men-squatting on the ground. Almost at the same moment the trumpet sounded, "Trot"; and the whole column of cavalry began to jingle and clatter across the front of these crouching figures. We were in the lull of the battle and there was perfect silence. Forthwith from every blue-black blob came a white puff of smoke, and a loud volley of musketry broke the odd stillness. Such a target at such a distance could scarcely be missed, and all along the column here and there horses bounded and a few men fell.

The intentions of our colonel had no doubt been to move round the flank of the body of Dervishes he had now located, and who, concealed in a fold of the ground behind their riflemen, were invisible to us, and then to attack them from a more advantageous quarter; but once the fire was opened and losses began to grow, he must have judged it inexpedient to prolong his procession across the open plain. The trumpet sounded "Right wheel into line," and all the sixteen troops swung round towards the blue-black riflemen. Almost immediately the regiment broke into a gallop, and the 21st Lancers were committed to their first charge in war!

I propose to describe exactly what happened to me; what I saw and what I felt. I recalled it to my mind so frequently after the event that the impression is as clear and vivid as it was a quarter of a century ago. The troop I commanded was, when we wheeled into line, the second from the right of the regiment. I was riding a handy, sure-footed, grey Arab polo pony. Before we wheeled and began to gallop, the officers had been marching with drawn swords. On account of my shoulder I had always decided that if I were involved in hand-to-hand fighting, I must use a pistol and not a sword. I had purchased in London a Mauser automatic pistol, then the newest and the latest design. I had practised carefully with this during our march and journey up the river. This then was the weapon with which I determined to fight. I had first of all to return my sword into its scabbard, which is not the easiest thing to do at a gallop. I had then to draw my pistol from its wooden holster and bring it to full cock. This dual operation took an appreciable time, and until it was finished, apart from a few glances to my left to see what effect the fire was producing, I did not look up at the general scene.

Then I saw immediately before me, and now only half the length of a polo ground away, the row of crouching blue figures firing frantically, wreathed in white smoke. On my right and left my neighbouring troop leaders made a good line. Immediately behind was a long dancing row of lances couched for the charge. We were going at a fast but steady gallop.

There was too much trampling and rifle fire to hear any bullets. After this glance to the right and left and at my troop, I looked again towards the enemy. The scene appeared to be suddenly transformed. The blue-black men were still firing, but behind them there now came into view a depression like a shallow sunken road. This was crowded and crammed with men rising up from the ground where they had hidden. Bright flags appeared as if by magic, and I saw arriving from nowhere emirs on horse-back among and around the mass of the enemy. The Dervishes appeared to be ten or twelve deep at the thickest, a great grey mass gleaming with steel, filling the dry watercourse. In the same twinkling of an eye I saw also that our right overlapped their left, that my troop would just strike the edge of their array, and that the troop on my right would charge into air. My subaltern comrade on the right, Wormald of the 7th Hussars, could see the situation too, and we both increased our speed to the very fastest gallop and curved inward like the horns of the moon. One really had not time to be frightened or to think of anything else but these par-ticular necessary actions which I have described. They completely occu-pied mind and senses.

The collision was now very near. I saw immediately before me, not ten yards away, the two blue men who lay in my path. They were perhaps a couple of yards apart. I rode at the interval between them. They both fired. I passed through the smoke conscious that I was unhurt. The trooper immediately behind me was killed at this place and at this moment, whether by these shots or not I do not know. I checked my pony as the ground began to fall away beneath his feet. The clever animal dropped like a cat four or five feet down onto the sandy bed of the watercourse, and in this sandy bed I found myself surrounded by what seemed to be dozens of men. They were not thickly packed enough at this point for me to experience any actual collision with them. Whereas Grenfell's troop, next but one on my left, was brought to a complete standstill and suf-fered very heavy losses, we seemed to push our way through as one has sometimes seen mounted policemen break up a crowd. In less time than it takes to relate, my pony had scrambled up the other side of the ditch. I looked round.

Once again I was on the hard, crisp desert, my horse at a trot. I had the impression of scattered Dervishes running to and fro in all directions. Straight before me a man threw himself on the ground. The reader must remember that I had been trained as a cavalry soldier to believe that if ever cavalry broke into a mass of infantry, the latter would be at their mercy. My first idea therefore was that the man was terrified. But simultaneously I saw the gleam of his curved sword as he drew it back for a ham-stringing cut. I had room and time enough to turn my pony out of his reach, and leaning over on the off side I fired two shots into him at about three yards. As I straightened myself in the saddle, I saw before me another figure with uplifted sword. I raised my pistol and fired. So close were we that the pistol itself actually struck him. Man and sword disappeared below and behind me. On my left, ten yards away, was an Arab horseman in a bright-coloured tunic and steel helmet, with chain mail hangings. I fired at him. He turned aside. I pulled my horse into a walk and looked around again.

In one respect a cavalry charge is very like ordinary life. So long as you are all right, firmly in the saddle, your horse in hand, and well armed, lots of enemies will give you a wide berth. But as soon as you have lost a stirrup, have a rein cut, have dropped your weapon, are wounded, or your horse is wounded, then is the moment when from all quarters enemies rush upon you. Such was the fate of not a few of my comrades in the troops immediately on my left. Brought to an actual standstill in the enemy's mass, clutched at from every side, stabbed at and hacked at by spear and sword, they were dragged from their horses and cut to pieces by the infuriated foe. But this I did not at the time see or understand. My impressions continued to be sanguine. I thought we were masters of the situation, riding the enemy down, scattering them and killing them. I pulled my horse up and looked about me. There was a mass of Dervishes about forty or fifty yards away on my left. They were huddling and clumping themselves together, rallying for mutual protection. They seemed wild with excitement, dancing about on their feet, shaking their spears up and down. The whole scene seemed to flicker. I have an impression, but it is too fleeting to define, of brown-clad Lancers mixed up here and there with this surging mob. The scattered individuals in my immediate neighbourhood made no attempt to molest me. Where was my troop? Where were the other troops of the squadron? Within a hundred yards of me I could not see a single officer or man. I looked back at the Dervish mass. I saw two or three riflemen crouching and aiming their rifles at me from the fringe of it. Then for the first time that morning I experienced a sudden sensation of fear. I felt myself absolutely alone. I thought those riflemen would hit me and the rest devour me like wolves. What a fool I was to loiter like this in the midst of the enemy! I crouched over the saddle, spurred my horse into a gallop and drew clear of the melee. Two or three hundred yards away I found my troop already faced about and partly formed up.

The other three troops of the squadron were reforming close by. Suddenly in the midst of the troop up sprang a Dervish. How he got there I do not know. He must have leaped out of some scrub or hole. All the troopers turned upon him thrusting with their lances; but he darted to and fro causing for the moment a frantic commotion. Wounded several times, he staggered towards me raising his spear. I shot him at less than a yard. He fell on the sand, and lay there dead. How easy to kill a man! But I did not worry about it. I found I had fired the whole magazine of my Mauser pistol, so I put in a new clip of ten cartridges before thinking of anything else.

I was still prepossessed with the idea that we had inflicted great slaughter on the enemy and had scarcely suffered at all ourselves. Three or four men were missing from my troop. Six men and nine or ten horses were bleeding from spear thrusts or sword cuts. We all expected to be ordered immediately to charge back again. The men were ready, though they all looked serious. Several asked to be allowed to throw away their lances and draw their swords. I asked my second sergeant if he had enjoyed himself. His answer was, "Well, I don't exactly say I enjoyed it, sir; but I think I'll get more used to it next time." At this the whole troop laughed.

But now from the direction of the enemy there came a succession of grisly apparitions; horses spouting blood, struggling on three legs, men staggering on foot, men bleeding from terrible wounds, fish-hook spears stuck right through them, arms and faces cut to pieces, bowels protruding, men gasping, crying, collapsing, expiring. Our first task was to succour these; and meanwhile the blood of our leaders cooled. They remembered for the first time that we had carbines. Everything was still in great confusion. But trumpets were sounded and orders shouted, and we all moved off at a trot towards the flank of the enemy. Arrived at a position from which we could enfilade and rake the watercourse, two squadrons were dismounted and in a few minutes with their fire at three hundred yards compelled the Dervishes to retreat. We therefore remained in possession of the field. Within twenty minutes of the time when we had first wheeled into line and began our charge, we were halted and breakfasting in the very watercourse that had so nearly proved our undoing. There one could see the futility of the much vaunted Arme Blanche. The Dervishes had carried off their wounded, and the corpses of thirty or forty enemies were all that could be counted on the ground. Among these lay the bodies of over twenty Lancers, so hacked and mutilated as to be mostly unrecognisable. In all, out of 310 officers and men, the regiment had lost in the space of about two or three minutes five officers and sixty-five men killed and wounded, and 120 horses—nearly a quarter of its strength.

Such were my fortunes in this celebrated episode. It is very rarely that cavalry and infantry, while still both unshaken, are intermingled as the result of an actual collision. Either the infantry keep their heads and shoot the cavalry down, or they break into confusion and are cut down or speared as they run. But the two or three thousand Dervishes who faced the 21st Lancers in the watercourse at Omdurman were not in the least shaken by the stress of battle or afraid of cavalry. Their fire was not good enough to stop the charge, but they had no doubt faced horsemen many a time in the wars with Abyssinia. They were familiar with the ordeal of the charge. It was the kind of fighting they thoroughly understood.

Moreover, the fight was with equal weapons, for the British, too, fought with sword and lance as in the days of old.

13

Philippa's Fox Hunt

By E. OE Somerville and Martin Ross

The British literary tradition before World War II was almost exclusively foxhunting and racing. This excerpt from Some Experiences of an Irish R. M. *might bring back memories for some of that book's appearance on Masterpiece Theater.*

No one can accuse Philippa and me of having married in haste. As a matter of fact, it was but little under five years from that autumn evening on the river when I had said what is called in Ireland "the hard word," to the day in August when I was led to the altar by my best man, and was subsequently led away from it by Mrs. Sinclair Yeates. About two years out of the five had been spent by me at Shreelane in ceaseless warfare with drains, eaveshoots, chimneys, pumps; all those fundamentals, in short, that the ingenuous and improving tenant expects to find established as a basis from which to rise to higher things. As far as rising to higher things went, frequent ascents to the roof to search for leaks summed up my achievements; in fact, I suffered so general a shrinkage of my ideals that the triumph of making the hall-door bell ring blinded me to the fact that the rat-holes in the hall floor were nailed up with pieces of tin biscuit boxes, and that the casual visitor could, instead of leaving a card, have easily written his name in the damp on the walls.

Philippa, however, proved adorably callous to these and similar shortcomings. She regarded Shreelane and its floundering, foundering ménage of incapables in the light of a gigantic picnic in a foreign land; she held long conversations daily with Mrs. Cadogan, in order, as she informed me, to acquire the language; without any ulterior domestic intention she engaged kitchen-maids because of the beauty of their eyes, and house-maids because they had such delightfully picturesque old mothers, and she declined to correct the phraseology of the parlour-maid, whose pain-ful habit it was to whisper "Do ye choose cherry or clarry?" when proffer-ing the wine. Fast-days, perhaps, afforded my wife her first insight into the sterner realities of Irish housekeeping. Philippa had what are known as High Church proclivities, and took the matter seriously.

"I don't know how we are to manage for the servants' dinner to-mor-row, Sinclair," she said, coming in to my office one Thursday morning; "Julia says she 'promised God this long time that she wouldn't eat an egg on a fast-day,' and the kitchen-maid says she won't eat herrings 'without they're fried with onions,' and Mrs. Cadogan says she will 'not go to them extremes for servants.'"

"I should let Mrs. Cadogan settle the menu herself," I suggested.

"I asked her to do that," replied Philippa, "and she only said she 'thanked God she had no appetite!'"

The lady of the house here fell away into unseasonable laughter.

I made the demoralising suggestion that, as we were going away for a couple of nights, we might safely leave them to fight it out, and the problem was abandoned.

Philippa had been much called on by the neighbourhood in all its shades and grades, and daily she and her trousseau frocks presented themselves at hall-doors of varying dimensions in due acknowledgment of civilities. In Ireland, it may be noted, the process known in England as "summering and wintering" a newcomer does not obtain; sociability and curiosity alike forbid delay. The visit to which we owed our escape from the intricacies of the fast-day was to the Knoxes of Castle Knox, relations in some remote and tribal way of my landlord, Mr. Flurry of that ilk. It involved a short journey by train, and my wife's longest basket-trunk; it also, which was more serious, involved my being lent a horse to go out cubbing the following morning.

At Castle Knox we sank into an almost forgotten environment of draught-proof windows and doors, of deep carpets, of silent servants instead of clattering belligerents. Philippa told me afterwards that it had only been by an effort that she had restrained herself from snatching up the train of her wedding-gown as she paced across the wide hall on little Sir Valentine's arm. After three weeks at Shreelane she found it difficult to remember that the floor was neither damp nor dusty.

I had the good fortune to be of the limited number of those who got on with Lady Knox, chiefly, I imagine, because I was as a worm before her, and thankfully permitted her to do all the talking.

"Your wife is extremely pretty," she pronounced autocratically, surveying Philippa between the candle-shades; "does she ride?"

Lady Knox was a short square lady, with a weather-beaten face, and an eye decisive from long habit of taking her own line across country and elsewhere. She would have made a very imposing little coachman, and would have caused her stable helpers to rue the day they had the presumption to be born; it struck me that Sir Valentine sometimes did so.

"I'm glad you like her looks," I replied, "as I fear you will find her thoroughly despicable otherwise; for one thing, she not only can't ride, but she believes that I can!"

"Oh come, you're not as bad as all that!" my hostess was good enough to say; "I'm going to put you up on Sorcerer to-morrow, and we'll see you at the top of the hunt—if there is one. That young Knox hasn't a notion how to draw these woods."

"Well, the best run we had last year out of this place was with Flurry's hounds," struck in Miss Sally, sole daughter of Sir Valentine's house and home, from her place half-way down the table. It was not difficult to see that she and her mother held different views on the subject of Mr. Flurry Knox.

"I call it a criminal thing in any one's great-great-grandfather to rear up a preposterous troop of sons and plant them all out in his own country," Lady Knox said to me with apparent irrelevance. "I detest collaterals. Blood may be thicker than water, but it is also a great deal nastier. In this country I find that fifteenth cousins consider themselves near relations if they live within twenty miles of one!"

Having before now taken in the position with regard to Flurry Knox, I took care to accept these remarks as generalities, and turned the conversation to other themes.

"I see Mrs. Yeates is doing wonders with Mr. Hamilton," said Lady Knox presently, following the direction of my eyes, which had strayed away to where Philippa was beaming upon her left-hand neighbour, a mildewed-looking old clergyman, who was delivering a long dissertation, the purport of which we were happily unable to catch.

"She has always had a gift for the Church," I said.

"Not curates?" said Lady Knox, in her deep voice.

I made haste to reply that it was the elders of the Church who were venerated by my wife.

"Well, she has her fancy in old Eustace Hamilton; he's elderly enough!" said Lady Knox. "I wonder if she'd venerate him as much if she knew that he had fought with his sister-in-law, and they haven't spoken for thirty years! though for the matter of that," she added, "I think it shows his good sense!"

"Mrs. Knox is rather a friend of mine," I ventured.

"Is she? H'm! Well, she's not one of mine!" replied my hostess, with her usual definiteness. "I'll say one thing for her, I believe she's always been a sportswoman. She's very rich, you know, and they say she only married old Badger Knox to save his hounds from being sold to pay his debts, and then she took the horn from him and hunted them herself. Has she been rude to your wife yet? No? Oh, well, she will. It's a mere question of time. She hates all English people. You know the story they tell of her? She was coming home from London, and when she was getting her ticket the man asked if she had said a ticket for York. 'No, thank God, Cork!' says Mrs. Knox."

"Well, I rather agree with her!" said I; "but why did she fight with Mr. Hamilton?"

"Oh, nobody knows. I don't believe they know themselves! Whatever it was, the old lady drives five miles to Fortwilliam every Sunday, rather than go to his church, just outside her own back gates," Lady Knox said with a laugh like a terrier's bark. "I wish I'd fought with him myself," she said; "he gives us forty minutes every Sunday."

As I struggled into my boots the following morning, I felt that Sir Valentine's acid confidences on cub-hunting, bestowed on me at midnight, did credit to his judgment. "A very moderate amusement, my dear

Major," he had said, in his dry little voice; "you should stick to shooting. No one expects you to shoot before daybreak."

It was six o'clock as I crept downstairs, and found Lady Knox and Miss Sally at breakfast, with two lamps on the table, and a foggy daylight oozing in from under the half-raised blinds. Philippa was already in the hall, pumping up her bicycle, in a state of excitement at the prospect of her first experience of hunting that would have been more comprehensible to me had she been going to ride a strange horse, as I was. As I bolted my food I saw the horses being led past the windows, and a faint twang of a horn told that Flurry Knox and his hounds were not far off.

Miss Sally jumped up.

"If I'm not on the Cockatoo before the hounds come up, I shall never get there!" she said, hobbling out of the room in the toils of her safety habit. Her small, alert face looked very childish under her riding-hat; the lamp-light struck sparks out of her thick coil of golden-red hair: I wondered how I had ever thought her like her prim little father.

She was already on her white cob when I got to the hall-door, and Flurry Knox was riding over the glistening wet grass with his hounds, while his whip, Dr. Jerome Hickey, was having a stirring time with the young entry and the rabbit-holes. They moved on without stopping, up a back avenue, under tall and dripping trees, to a thick laurel covert, at some little distance from the house. Into this the hounds were thrown, and the usual period of fidgety inaction set in for the riders, of whom, all told, there were about half-a-dozen. Lady Knox, square and solid, on her big, confidential iron-grey, was near me, and her eyes were on me and my mount; with her rubicund face and white collar she was more than ever like a coachman.

"Sorcerer looks as if he suited you well," she said, after a few minutes of silence, during which the hounds rustled and crackled steadily through the laurels; "he's a little high on the leg, and so are you, you know, so you show each other off."

Sorcerer was standing like a rock, with his good-looking head in the air and his eyes fastened on the covert. His manners, so far, had been those of a perfect gentleman, and were in marked contrast to those of Miss Sally's cob, who was sidling, hopping, and snatching unappeasably at his bit. Philippa had disappeared from view down the avenue ahead. The fog was melting, and the sun threw long blades of light through the trees; everything was quiet, and in the distance the curtained windows of the house marked the warm repose of Sir Valentine, and those of the party who shared his opinion of cubbing.

"Hark! hark to cry there!"

It was Flurry's voice, away at the other side of the covert. The rustling and brushing through the laurels became more vehement, then passed out of hearing.

"He never will leave his hounds alone," said Lady Knox disapprovingly.

Miss Sally and the Cockatoo moved away in a series of heraldic capers towards the end of the laurel plantation, and at the same moment I saw Philippa on her bicycle shoot into view on the drive ahead of us.

"I've seen a fox!" she screamed, white with what I believe to have been personal terror, though she says it was excitement; "it passed quite close to me!"

"What way did he go?" bellowed a voice which I recognised as Dr. Hickey's, somewhere in the deep of the laurels.

"Down the drive!" returned Philippa, with a pea-hen quality in her tones with which I was quite unacquainted.

An electrifying screech of "Gone away!" was projected from the laurels by Dr. Hickey.

"Gone away!" chanted Flurry's horn at the top of the covert.

"This is what he calls cubbing!" said Lady Knox, "a mere farce!" but none the less she loosed her sedate monster into a canter.

Sorcerer got his hind-legs under him, and hardened his crest against the bit, as we all hustled along the drive after the flying figure of my wife. I knew very little about horses, but I realised that even with the hounds tumbling hysterically out of the covert, and the Cockatoo kicking the gravel into his face, Sorcerer comported himself with the manners of the best society. Up a side road I saw Flurry Knox opening half of a gate and cramming through it; in a moment we also had crammed through, and the turf of a pasture field was under our feet. Dr. Hickey leaned forward and took hold of his horse; I did likewise, with the trifling difference that my horse took hold of me, and I steered for Flurry Knox with single-hearted purpose, the hounds, already a field ahead, being merely an exciting and noisy accompaniment of this endeavour. A heavy stone wall was the first occurrence of note. Flurry chose a place where the top was loose, and his clumsy-looking brown mare changed feet on the rattling stones like a fairy. Sorcerer came at it, tense and collected as a bow at full stretch, and sailed steeply into the air; I saw the wall far beneath me, with an unsuspected ditch on the far side, and I felt my hat following me at the full stretch of its guard as we swept over it, then, with a long slant, we descended to earth some sixteen feet from where we had left it, and I was possessor of the gratifying fact that I had achieved a good-sized "fly," and had not perceptibly moved in my saddle. Subsequent disillusioning experience has taught me that but few horses jump like Sorcerer, so gallantly, so sympathetically, and with such supreme mastery of the subject; but none the less the enthusiasm that he imparted to me has never been extinguished, and that October morning ride revealed to me the unsuspected intoxication of fox-hunting.

Behind me I heard the scrabbling of the Cockatoo's little hoofs among the loose stones, and Lady Knox, galloping on my left, jerked a maternal chin over her shoulder to mark her daughter's progress. For my part, had there been an entire circus behind me, I was far too much occupied with ramming on my hat and trying to hold Sorcerer, to have looked round, and all my spare faculties were devoted to steering for Flurry, who had taken a right-handed turn, and was at that moment surmounting a bank of uncertain and briary aspect. I surmounted it also, with the swiftness and simplicity for which the Quaker's methods of bank jumping had not prepared me, and two or three fields, traversed at the same steeplechase pace, brought us to a road and to an abrupt check. There, suddenly, were the hounds, scrambling in baffled silence down into the road from the opposite bank, to look for the line they had overrun, and there, amazingly, was Philippa, engaged in excited converse with several men with spades over their shoulders.

"Did ye see the fox, boys?" shouted Flurry, addressing the group.

"We did! we did!" cried my wife and her friends in chorus; "he ran up the road!"

"We'd be badly off without Mrs. Yeates!" said Flurry, as he whirled his mare round and clattered up the road with a hustle of hounds after him.

It occurred to me as forcibly as any mere earthly thing can occur to those who are wrapped in the sublimities of a run, that, for a young woman who had never before seen a fox out of a cage at the Zoo, Philippa was taking to hunting very kindly. Her cheeks were a most brilliant pink, her blue eyes shone.

"Oh, Sinclair!" she exclaimed, "they say he's going for Aussolas, and there's a road I can ride all the way!"

"Ye can, Miss! Sure we'll show you!" chorussed her cortège.

Her foot was on the pedal ready to mount. Decidedly my wife was in no need of assistance from me.

Up the road a hound gave a yelp of discovery, and flung himself over a stile into the fields; the rest of the pack went squealing and jostling after him, and I followed Flurry over one of those infinitely varied erections, pleasantly termed "gaps" in Ireland. On this occasion the gap was made of three razor-edged slabs of slate leaning against an iron bar, and Sorcerer conveyed to me his thorough knowledge of the matter by a lift of his hind-quarters that made me feel as if I were being skilfully kicked downstairs. To what extent I looked it, I cannot say, nor providentially can Philippa, as she had already started. I only know that undeserved good luck restored to me my stirrup before Sorcerer got away with me in the next field.

What followed was, I am told, a very fast fifteen minutes; for me time was not; the empty fields rushed past uncounted, fences came and went in a flash, while the wind sang in my ears, and the dazzle of the early sun was in my eyes. I saw the hounds occasionally, sometimes pouring over a green bank, as the charging breaker lifts and flings itself, sometimes driving across a field, as the white tongues of foam slide racing over the sand; and always ahead of me was Flurry Knox, going as a man goes who knows his country, who knows his horse, and whose heart is wholly and absolutely in the right place.

Do what I would, Sorcerer's implacable stride carried me closer and closer to the brown mare, till, as I thundered down the slope of a long field, I was not twenty yards behind Flurry. Sorcerer had stiffened his neck to iron, and to slow him down was beyond me; but I fought his head away to the right, and found myself coming hard and steady at a stonefaced bank with broken ground in front of it. Flurry bore away to the left, shouting something that I did not understand. That Sorcerer shortened his stride at the right moment was entirely due to his own judgment; standing well away from the jump, he rose like a stag out of the tussocky ground, and as he swung my twelve stone six into the air the obstacle revealed itself to him and me as consisting not of one bank but of two, and between the two lay a deep grassy lane, half choked with furze. I have often been asked to state the width of the bohereen, and can only reply that in my opinion it was at least eighteen feet; Flurry Knox and Dr. Hickey, who did not jump it, say that it is not more than five. What Sorcerer did with it I cannot say; the sensation was of a towering flight with a kick back in it, a biggish drop, and a landing on cee-springs, still on the downhill grade. That was how one of the best horses in Ireland took one of Ireland's most ignorant riders over a very nasty place.

A sombre line of fir-wood lay ahead, rimmed with a grey wall, and in another couple of minutes we had pulled up on the Aussolas road, and were watching the hounds struggling over the wall into Aussolas demesne.

"No hurry now," said Flurry, turning in his saddle to watch the Cockatoo jump into the road, "he's to ground in the big earth inside. Well, Major, it's well for you that's a big-jumped horse. I thought you were a dead man a while ago when you faced him at the bohereen!"

I was disclaiming intention in the matter when Lady Knox and the others joined us.

"I thought you told me your wife was no sportswoman," she said to me, critically scanning Sorcerer's legs for cuts the while, "but when I saw her a minute ago she had abandoned her bicycle and was running across country like——"

"Look at her now!" interrupted Miss Sally. "Oh!—oh!" In the interval between these exclamations my incredulous eyes beheld my wife in mid-air, hand in hand with a couple of stalwart country boys, with whom she was leaping in unison from the top of a bank on to the road.

Every one, even the saturnine Dr. Hickey, began to laugh; I rode back to Philippa, who was exchanging compliments and congratulations with her escort.

"Oh, Sinclair!" she cried, "wasn't it splendid? I saw you jumping, and everything! Where are they going now?"

"My dear girl," I said, with marital disapproval, "you're killing yourself. Where's your bicycle?"

"Oh, it's punctured in a sort of lane, back there. It's all right; and then they"—she breathlessly waved her hand at her attendants—"they showed me the way."

"Begor! you proved very good, Miss!" said a grinning cavalier.

"Faith she did!" said another, polishing his shining brow with his white flannel coat-sleeve, "she lepped like a haarse!"

"And may I ask how you propose to go home?" said I.

"I don't know and I don't care! I'm not going home!" She cast an entirely disobedient eye at me. "And your eye-glass is hanging down your back and your tie is bulging out over your waistcoat!"

The little group of riders had begun to move away.

"We're going on into Aussolas," called out Flurry; "come on, and make my grandmother give you some breakfast, Mrs. Yeates; she always has it at eight o'clock."

The front gates were close at hand, and we turned in under the tall beech-trees, with the unswept leaves rustling round the horses' feet, and the lovely blue of the October morning sky filling the spaces between smooth grey branches and golden leaves. The woods rang with the voices of the hounds, enjoying an untrammelled rabbit hunt, while the Master and the Whip, both on foot, strolled along unconcernedly with their bridles over their arms, making themselves agreeable to my wife, an occasional touch of Flurry's horn, or a crack of Dr. Hickey's whip, just indicating to the pack that the authorities still took a friendly interest in their doings.

Down a grassy glade in the wood a party of old Mrs. Knox's young horses suddenly swept into view, headed by an old mare, who, with her tail over her back, stampeded ponderously past our cavalcade, shaking and swinging her handsome old head, while her youthful friends bucked and kicked and snapped at each other round her with the ferocious humour of their kind.

"Here, Jerome, take the horn," said Flurry to Dr. Hickey; "I'm going to see Mrs. Yeates up to the house, the way these tomfools won't gallop on top of her."

From this point it seems to me that Philippa's adventures are more worthy of record than mine, and as she has favoured me with a full account of them, I venture to think my version may be relied on.

Mrs. Knox was already at breakfast when Philippa was led, quaking, into her formidable presence. My wife's acquaintance with Mrs. Knox was, so far, limited to a state visit on either side, and she found but little comfort in Flurry's assurances that his grandmother wouldn't mind if he brought all the hounds in to breakfast, coupled with the statement that she would put her eyes on sticks for the Major.

Whatever the truth of this may have been, Mrs. Knox received her guest with an equanimity quite unshaken by the fact that her boots were in the fender instead of on her feet, and that a couple of shawls of varying dimensions and degrees of age did not conceal the inner presence of a magenta flannel dressing-jacket. She installed Philippa at the table and plied her with food, oblivious as to whether the needful implements with which to eat it were forthcoming or no. She told Flurry where a vixen had reared her family, and she watched him ride away, with some biting comments on his mare's hocks screamed after him from the window.

The dining-room at Aussolas Castle is one of the many rooms in Ireland in which Cromwell is said to have stabled his horse (and probably no one would have objected less than Mrs. Knox had she been consulted in the matter). Philippa questions if the room had ever been tidied up since, and she endorses Flurry's observation that "there wasn't a day in the year you wouldn't get feeding for a hen and chickens on the floor." Opposite to Philippa, on a Louis Quinze chair, sat Mrs. Knox's woolly dog, its suspicious little eyes peering at her out of their setting of pink lids and dirty white wool. A couple of young horses outside the windows tore at the matted creepers on the walls, or thrust faces that were half-shy, half-impudent, into the room. Portly pigeons waddled to and fro on the broad window-sill, sometimes flying in to perch on the picture-frames, while they kept up incessantly a hoarse and pompous cooing.

Animals and children are, as a rule, alike destructive to conversation; but Mrs. Knox, when she chose, bien entendu, could have made herself agreeable in a Noah's ark, and Philippa has a gift of sympathetic attention that personal experience has taught me to regard with distrust as well as respect, while it has often made me realise the worldly wisdom of Kingsley's injunction:

"Be good, sweet maid, and let who will be clever."

Family prayers, declaimed by Mrs. Knox with alarming austerity, followed close on breakfast, Philippa and a vinegar-faced henchwoman forming the family. The prayers were long, and through the open window as they progressed came distantly a whoop or two; the declamatory tones staggered a little, and then continued at a distinctly higher rate of speed.

"Ma'am! Ma'am!" whispered a small voice at the window.

Mrs. Knox made a repressive gesture and held on her way. A sudden outcry of hounds followed, and the owner of the whisper, a small boy with a face freckled like a turkey's egg, darted from the window and dragged a donkey and bath-chair into view. Philippa admits to having lost the thread of the discourse, but she thinks that the "Amen" that immediately ensued can hardly have come in its usual place. Mrs. Knox shut the book abruptly, scrambled up from her knees, and said, "They've found!"

In a surprisingly short space of time she had added to her attire her boots, a fur cape, and a garden hat, and was in the bath-chair, the small boy stimulating the donkey with the success peculiar to his class, while Philippa hung on behind.

The woods of Aussolas are hilly and extensive, and on that particular morning it seemed that they held as many foxes as hounds. In vain was the horn blown, and the whips cracked, small rejoicing parties of hounds, each with a fox of its own, scoured to and fro: every labourer in the vicinity had left his work, and was sedulously heading every fox with yells that would have befitted a tiger hunt, and sticks and stones when occasion served.

"Will I pull out as far as the big rosy-dandhrum, ma'am?" inquired the small boy; "I seen three of the dogs go in it, and they yowling."

"You will," said Mrs. Knox, thumping the donkey on the back with her umbrella; "here! Jeremiah Regan! Come down out of that with that pitchfork! Do you want to kill the fox, you fool?"

"I do not, your honour, ma'am," responded Jeremiah Regan, a tall young countryman, emerging from a bramble brake.

"Did you see him?" said Mrs. Knox eagerly.

"I seen himself and his ten pups drinking below at the lake ere yestherday, your honour, ma'am, and he as big as a chestnut horse!" said Jeremiah.

"Faugh! Yesterday!" snorted Mrs. Knox; "go on to the rhododendrons, Johnny!"

The party, reinforced by Jeremiah and the pitchfork, progressed at a high rate of speed along the shrubbery path, encountering en route Lady Knox, stooping on to her horse's neck under the sweeping branches of the laurels.

"Your horse is too high for my coverts, Lady Knox," said the Lady of the Manor, with a malicious eye at Lady Knox's flushed face and dinged hat; "I'm afraid you will be left behind like Absalom when the hounds go away!"

"As they never do anything here but hunt rabbits," retorted her ladyship, "I don't think that's likely."

Mrs. Knox gave her donkey another whack, and passed on.

"Rabbits, my dear!" she said scornfully to Philippa. "That's all she knows about it. I declare it disgusts me to see a woman of that age making such a Judy of herself! Rabbits indeed!"

Down in the thicket of rhododendron everything was very quiet for a time. Philippa strained her eyes in vain to see any of the riders; the horn blowing and the whip cracking passed on almost out of hearing. Once or twice a hound worked through the rhododendrons, glanced at the party, and hurried on, immersed in business. All at once Johnny, the donkey-boy, whispered excitedly: "Look at he! Look at he!" and pointed to a boulder of grey rock that stood out among the dark evergreens. A big yellow cub was crouching on it; he instantly slid into the shelter of the bushes, and the irrepressible Jeremiah, uttering a rending shriek, plunged into the thicket after him. Two or three hounds came rushing at the sound, and after this Philippa says she finds some difficulty in recalling the proper order of events; chiefly, she confesses, because of the wholly ridiculous tears of excitement that blurred her eyes.

"We ran," she said, "we simply tore, and the donkey galloped, and as for that old Mrs. Knox, she was giving cracked screams to the hounds all the time, and they were screaming too; and then somehow we were all out on the road!"

What seems to have occurred was that three couple of hounds, Jeremiah Regan, and Mrs. Knox's equipage, amongst them somehow hustled the cub out of Aussolas demesne and up on to a hill on the farther side of the road. Jeremiah was sent back by his mistress to fetch Flurry, and the rest of the party pursued a thrilling course along the road, parallel with that of the hounds, who were hunting slowly through the gorse on the hillside.

"Upon my honour and word, Mrs. Yeates, my dear, we have the hunt to ourselves!" said Mrs. Knox to the panting Philippa, as they pounded along the road. "Johnny, d'ye see the fox?"

"I do, ma'am!" shrieked Johnny, who possessed the usual field-glass vision bestowed upon his kind. "Look at him over-right us on the hill above! Hi! The spotty dog have him! No, he's gone from him! *Gwan out o' that!*" This to the donkey, with blows that sounded like the beating of carpets, and produced rather more dust.

They had left Aussolas some half a mile behind, when, from a strip of wood on their right, the fox suddenly slipped over the bank on to the road just ahead of them, ran up it for a few yards and whisked in at a small entrance gate, with the three couple of hounds yelling on a red-hot scent, not thirty yards behind. The bath-chair party whirled in at their heels, Philippa and the donkey considerably blown, Johnny scarlet through his freckles, but as fresh as paint, the old lady blind and deaf to all things save the chase. The hounds went raging through the shrubs beside the drive, and away down a grassy slope towards a shallow glen, in the bottom of which ran a little stream, and after them over the grass bumped the bath-chair. At the stream they turned sharply and ran up the glen towards the avenue, which crossed it by means of a rough stone viaduct.

"'Pon me conscience, he's into the old culvert!" exclaimed Mrs. Knox; "there was one of my hounds choked there once, long ago! Beat on the donkey, Johnny!"

At this juncture Philippa's narrative again becomes incoherent, not to say breathless. She is, however, positive that it was somewhere about here that the upset of the bath-chair occurred, but she cannot be clear as to whether she picked up the donkey or Mrs. Knox, or whether she herself was picked up by Johnny while Mrs. Knox picked up the donkey. From my knowledge of Mrs. Knox I should say she picked up herself and no one else. At all events, the next salient point is the palpitating moment when Mrs. Knox, Johnny, and Philippa successively applying an eye to the opening of the culvert by which the stream trickled under the viaduct, while five dripping hounds bayed and leaped around them, discovered by more senses than that of sight that the fox was in it, and furthermore that one of the hounds was in it too.

"There's a sthrong grating before him at the far end," said Johnny, his head in at the mouth of the hole, his voice sounding as if he were talking into a jug, "the two of them's fighting in it; they'll be choked surely!"

"Then don't stand gabbling there, you little fool, but get in and pull the hound out!" exclaimed Mrs. Knox, who was balancing herself on a stone in the stream.

"I'd be in dread, ma'am," whined Johnny.

"Balderdash!" said the implacable Mrs. Knox. "In with you!"

I understand that Philippa assisted Johnny into the culvert, and presume that it was in so doing that she acquired the two Robinson Crusoe bare footprints which decorated her jacket when I next met her.

"Have you got hold of him yet, Johnny?" cried Mrs. Knox up the culvert.

"I have, ma'am, by the tail," responded Johnny's voice, sepulchral in the depths.

"Can you stir him, Johnny?"

"I cannot, ma'am, and the wather is rising in it."

"Well, please God, they'll not open the mill dam!" remarked Mrs. Knox philosophically to Philippa, as she caught hold of Johnny's dirty ankles. "Hold on to the tail, Johnny!"

She hauled, with, as might be expected, no appreciable result. "Run, my dear, and look for somebody, and we'll have that fox yet!"

Philippa ran, whither she knew not, pursued by fearful visions of bursting mill-dams, and maddened foxes at bay. As she sped up the avenue she heard voices, robust male voices, in a shrubbery, and made for them. Advancing along an embowered walk towards her was what she took for one wild instant to be a funeral; a second glance showed her that it was a party of clergymen of all ages, walking by twos and threes in the dappled shade of the over-arching trees. Obviously she had intruded her sacrilegious presence into a Clerical Meeting. She acknowledges that at this awe-inspiring spectacle she faltered, but the thought of Johnny, the hound, and the fox, suffocating, possibly drowning together in the culvert, nerved her. She does not remember what she said or how she said it, but I fancy she must have conveyed to them the impression that old Mrs. Knox was being drowned, as she immediately found herself heading a charge of the Irish Church towards the scene of disaster.

Fate has not always used me well, but on this occasion it was mercifully decreed that I and the other members of the hunt should be privileged to arrive in time to see my wife and her rescue party precipitating themselves down the glen.

"Holy Biddy!" ejaculated Flurry, "is she running a paper-chase with all the parsons? But look! For pity's sake will you look at my grandmother and my Uncle Eustace?"

Mrs. Knox and her sworn enemy the old clergyman, whom I had met at dinner the night before, were standing, apparently in the stream, tugging at two bare legs that projected from a hole in the viaduct, and arguing at the top of their voices. The bath-chair lay on its side with the donkey grazing beside it, on the bank a stout Archdeacon was tendering advice, and the hounds danced and howled round the entire group.

"I tell you, Eliza, you had better let the Archdeacon try," thundered Mr. Hamilton.

"Then I tell you I will not!" vociferated Mrs. Knox, with a tug at the end of the sentence that elicited a subterranean lament from Johnny. "Now who was right about the second grating? I told you so twenty years ago!"

Exactly as Philippa and her rescue party arrived, the efforts of Mrs. Knox and her brother-in-law triumphed. The struggling, sopping form of Johnny was slowly drawn from the hole, drenched, speechless, but clinging to the stern of a hound, who, in its turn, had its jaws fast in the hindquarters of a limp, yellow cub.

"Oh, it's dead!" wailed Philippa, "I did think I should have been in time to save it!"

"Well, if that doesn't beat all!" said Dr. Hickey.

14

The Chimaera

By Nathaniel Hawthorne

The Chimaera, *an alternate name for Pegasus, was published in Hawthorne's* A Wonder Book for Girls and Boys *(1851). The 1883 edition features illustrations by Walter Crane. In Greek mythology, a chimaera is a fire-breathing female creature with the body of a lion.*

ONCE, IN THE OLD, OLD TIMES (FOR ALL THE STRANGE THINGS WHICH I tell you about happened long before anybody can remember), a fountain gushed out of a hillside, in the marvelous land of Greece. And, for aught I know, after so many thousand years, it is still gushing out of the very selfsame spot. At any rate, there was the pleasant fountain, welling freshly forth and sparkling adown the hillside, in the golden sunset, when a handsome young man named Bellerophon drew near its margin. In his hand he held a bridle studded with brilliant gems, and adorned with a golden bit. Seeing an old man, and another of middle age, and a little boy, near the fountain, and likewise a maiden, who was dipping up some of the water in a pitcher, he paused, and begged that he might refresh himself with a draught.

"This is very delicious water," he said to the maiden as he rinsed and filled her pitcher, after drinking out of it. "Will you be kind enough to tell me whether the fountain has a name?"

"Yes, it is called the Fountain of Pirene," answered the maiden; and then she added, "My grandmother has told me that this clear fountain was once a beautiful woman, and when her son was killed by the arrow of the huntress Diana, she melted all away into tears. And so the water, which you find so cool and sweet, is the sorrow of that poor mother's heart!"

"I should not have dreamed," observed the young stranger, "that so clear a wellspring, with its gush and gurgle, and its cheery dance out of the shade into the sunlight, had so much as one teardrop in its bosom! And this, then, is Pirene! I thank you, pretty maiden, for telling me its name. I have come from a faraway country to find this very spot."

A middle-aged country fellow (he had driven his cow to drink out of the spring) stared hard at young Bellerophon, and at the handsome bridle which he carried in his hand.

"The watercourses must be getting low, friend, in your part of the world," remarked he, "if you come so far only to find the Fountain of Pirene. But, pray, have you lost a horse? I see you carry the bridle in your hand; and a pretty one it is, with that double row of bright stones upon it. If the horse was as fine as the bridle, you are much to be pitied for losing him."

"I have lost no horse," said Bellerophon, with a smile. "But I happen to be seeking a very famous one, which, as wise people have informed me, must be found hereabouts, if any where. Do you know whether the winged horse Pegasus still haunts the Fountain of Pirene, as he used to do in your forefathers' day?"

But then the country fellow laughed.

Some of you, my little friends, have probably heard that this Pegasus was a snow-white steed, with beautiful silvery wings, who spent most of his time on the summit of Mount Helicon. He was as wild, and as swift, and as buoyant, in his flight through the air, as any eagle that ever soared into the clouds. There was nothing else like him in the world. He had no mate; he had never been backed or bridled by a master; and for many a long year, he led a solitary and happy life.

Oh, how fine a thing it is to be a winged horse! Sleeping at night, as he did, on a lofty mountaintop, and passing the greater part of the day in the air, Pegasus seemed hardly to be a creature of the earth. Whenever he was seen, up very high above people's heads, with the sunshine on his silvery wings, you would have thought that he belonged to the sky, and that, skimming a little too low, he had got astray among our mists and vapors, and was seeking his way back again. It was very pretty to behold him to plunge into the fleecy bosom of a bright cloud, and be lost in it for a moment or two, and then break forth from the other side. Or, in a sullen rainstorm, when there was a grey pavement of clouds over the whole sky, it would sometimes happen that the winged horse descended right through it, and the glad light of the upper region would gleam after him. In another instant, it is true, both Pegasus and the pleasant light would be gone away together. But anyone who was fortunate enough to see this wondrous spectacle felt cheerful the whole day afterwards, and as much longer as the storm lasted.

In the summertime, and in the beautifullest of weather, Pegasus often alighted on the solid earth, and, closing his silvery wings, would gallop over hill and dale for pastime, as fleetly as the wind. Oftener than in any other place, he had been seen near the Fountain of Pirene, drinking the delicious water, or rolling himself upon the soft grass of the margin. Sometimes, too (but Pegasus was very dainty in his food), he would crop a few of the clover blossoms that happened to be the sweetest.

To the Fountain of Pirene, therefore, people's great-grandfathers had been in the habit of going (as long as they were youthful, and retained their faith in winged horses), in hopes of getting a glimpse at the beautiful Pegasus. But, of late years, he had been very seldom seen. Indeed, there were many of the country folks, dwelling within half an hour's walk of the fountain, who had never beheld Pegasus, and did not believe that there was any such creature in existence. The country fellow to whom Bellerophon was speaking chanced to be one of those incredulous persons.

And that was the reason he laughed.

"Pegasus indeed!" cried he, turning up his nose as high as such a flat nose could be turned up, "Pegasus, indeed! A winged horse, truly! Why, friend, are you in your senses? Of what use would wings be to a horse? Could he drag the plough so well, think you? To be sure, there might be a little saving in the expense of shoes, but then, how would a man like to see his horse flying out of the stable window? Yes, or whisking him above the clouds, when he only wanted to ride to mill? No, no! I don't believe in Pegasus. There never was such a ridiculous kind of horse-fowl made!"

"I have some reason to think otherwise," said Bellerophon, quietly.

And then he turned to the old, grey man, who was leaning on a staff, and listening very attentively, with his head stretched forward, and one hand at his ear, because, for the last twenty years, he had been getting rather deaf.

"And what do you say, venerable sir?" inquired he. "In your younger days, I should imagine, you must frequently have seen the winged steed!"

"Ah, young stranger, my memory is very poor!" said the aged man. "When I was a lad, if I remember rightly, I used to believe there was such a horse, and so did everybody else. But, nowadays, I hardly know what to think, and very seldom think about the winged horse at all. If I ever saw the creature, it was a long, long while ago; and to tell you the truth, I doubt whether I ever did see him. One day, to be sure, when I was quite a youth, I remember seeing some hoof-tramps round about the brink of the fountain. Pegasus might have made those hoofmarks, and so might some other horse."

"And have you never seen him, my fair maiden?" asked Bellerophon of the girl, who stood with the pitcher on her head, while this talk went on. "You certainly could see Pegasus, if anybody can, for your eyes are very bright."

"Once I thought I saw him," replied the maiden, with a smile and a blush. "It was either Pegasus, or a large white bird, a very great way up in the air. And one other time, as I was coming to the fountain with my pitcher, I heard a neigh. Oh, such a brisk and melodious neigh as that was! My very heart leaped with delight at the sound. But, it startled me, nevertheless, so that I ran home without filling my pitcher."

"That was truly a pity," said Bellerophon.

And he turned to the child, whom I mentioned at the beginning of the story, and who was gazing at him, as children are apt to gaze at strangers, with his rosy mouth wide open.

"Well, my little fellow," cried Bellerophon, playfully pulling one of his curls, "I suppose you have often seen the winged horse."

"That I have," answered the child very readily. "I saw him yesterday, and many times before."

"You are a fine little man!" said Bellerophon, drawing the child closer to him. "Come, tell me all about it."

"Why," replied the child, "I often come here to sail little boats in the fountain, and to gather pretty pebbles out of its basin. And sometimes, when I look down into the water, I see the image of the winged horse, in the picture of the sky that is there. I wish he would come down and take me on his back, and let me ride him up to the moon! But, if I so much as stir to look at him, he flies far away out of sight."

And Bellerophon put his faith in the child, who had seen the image of Pegasus in the water, and in the maiden who had heard him neigh so melodiously, rather than in the middle-aged clown, who believed only in cart horses, or in the old man who had forgotten the beautiful things of his youth.

Therefore, he haunted about the Fountain of Pirene for a great many days afterwards. He kept continually on the watch, looking upward at the sky, or else down into the water, hoping forever that he should see either the reflected image of the winged horse, or the marvelous reality. He held the bridle, with its bright gems and golden bit, always ready in his hand. The rustic people, who dwelt in the neighborhood, and drove their cattle to the fountain to drink, would often laugh at poor Bellerophon, and sometimes take him pretty severely to task. They told him that an able-bodied young man, like himself, ought to have better business than to be wasting his time in such idle pursuit. They offered to sell him a horse, if he wanted one, and when Bellerophon declined the purchase, they tried to drive a bargain with him for his fine bridle.

Even the country boys thought him so very foolish that they used to have a great deal of sport about him, and were rude enough not to care a fig, although Bellerophon saw and heard it. One little urchin, for example, would play Pegasus, and cut the oddest imaginable capers, by way of flying; while one of his schoolfellows would scamper after him holding forth a twist of bulrushes, which was intended to represent Bellerophon's ornamental bridle. But the gentle child, who had seen the picture of Pegasus in the water, comforted the young stranger more than all the naughty boys could torment him. The dear little fellow, in his play hours, often sat down beside him, and without speaking a word, would look down into the fountain and up towards the sky, with so innocent a faith, that Bellerophon could not help feeling encouraged.

Well was it for Bellerophon that the child had grown so fond of him, and was never weary of keeping him company. Every morning the child gave him a new hope to put in his bosom, instead of yesterday's withered one.

"Dear Bellerophon," he would cry, looking up hopefully into his face, "I think we shall see Pegasus today!"

One morning the child spoke to Bellerophon even more hopefully than usual.

"Dear, dear Bellerophon," cried he, "I know not why it is, but I feel as if we shall certainly see Pegasus today!"

And all that day he would not stir a step from Bellerophon's side; so they ate a crust of bread together, and drank some of the water from the fountain. In the afternoon, there they sat, and Bellerophon had thrown his arm around the child, who likewise had put one of his little hands into Bellerophon's. The latter was lost in his own thoughts, and was fixing his eyes vacantly on the trunks of the trees that overshadowed the fountain, and on the grapevines that clambered up among the branches. But the gentle child was gazing down into the water. He was grieved, for Bellerophon's sake, that the hope of another day should be deceived, like so many before it; and two or three quiet teardrops fell from his eyes, and mingled with what were said to be the many tears of Pirene, when she wept for her slain children.

But, when he least thought of it, Bellerophon felt the pressure of the child's little hand, and heard a soft, almost breathless whisper.

"See there, dear Bellerophon, there is an image in the water."

The young man looked down into the dimpling mirror of the fountain, and saw what he took to be the reflection of a bird which seemed to be flying at a great height in the air, with a gleam of sunshine on its snowy or silvery wings.

"What a splendid bird it must be!" said he. "And how very large it looks, though it must really be flying higher than the clouds!"

"It makes me tremble!" whispered the child. "I am afraid to look up into the air! It is very beautiful, and yet I dare only look at its image in the water. Dear Bellerophon, do you not see that it is not bird? It is the winged horse Pegasus!"

Bellerophon's heart began to throb! He gazed keenly upward, but could not see the winged creature, whether bird or horse; because, just then, it had plunged into the fleecy depths of a summer cloud. It was but a moment, however, before the object reappeared, sinking lightly down out of the cloud, although still a vast distance from the earth. Bellerophon caught the child in his arms, and shrank back with him, so that they were both hidden among the thick shrubbery which grew all around the fountain. Not that he was afraid of any harm, but he dreaded lest, if Pegasus caught a glimpse of them, he would fly far away, and alight in some inaccessible mountaintop. For it really was the winged horse. After they had expected him so long, he was coming to quench his thirst with the water of Pirene.

Nearer and nearer came the aerial wonder, flying in great circles, as you may have seen a dove when about to alight. Downward came Pegasus, in those wide, sweeping circles, which grew narrower, and narrower still, as he gradually approached the earth. The nigher the view of him, the more beautiful he was, and the more marvelous the sweep of his silvery wings. At last, with so slight a pressure as hardly to bend the grass about the fountain, or imprint a hoof-tramp in the sand of its margin, he alighted, and, stooping his wild head, began to drink. He drew in the water, with long and pleasant sighs, and tranquil pauses of enjoyment; and then another draught, and another, and another. For, nowhere in the world, or up among the clouds, did Pegasus love any water as he loved this of Pirene. And when his thirst was slaked, he cropped a few of the honey blossoms of the clover, delicately tasting them, but not caring to make a hearty meal, because the herbage, just beneath the clouds, on the lofty sides of Mount Helicon, suited his palate better than this ordinary grass.

After thus drinking to his heart's content, and in his dainty fashion, condescending to take a little food, the winged horse began to caper to and fro, and dance, as it were, out of mere idleness and sport. There was never a more playful creature made than this very Pegasus. So there he frisked, in a way that delights me to think about, fluttering his great wings as lightly as ever did a linnet, and running little races, half on earth and half in air, and which I know not whether to call a flight or a gallop. When a creature is perfectly able to fly, he sometimes chooses to run, just for the pastime of the thing; and so did Pegasus, although it cost him some little trouble to keep his hoofs so near the ground. Bellerophon, meanwhile, holding the child's hand, peeped forth from the shrubbery, and thought that never was any sight so beautiful as this, nor ever a horse's eyes so wild and spirited as those of Pegasus. It seemed a sin to think of bridling him and riding on his back.

Once or twice, Pegasus stopped, and snuffed the air, pricking up his ears, tossing his head, and turning it on all sides, as if he partly suspected some mischief or other. Seeing nothing, however, and hearing no sound, he soon began his antics again.

At length—not that he was weary, but only idle and luxurious—Pegasus folded his wings, and lay down on the soft green turf. But, being too foll of aerial life to remain quiet for many moments together, he soon rolled over on his back, with his four slender legs in the air. It was beautiful to see him, this one solitary creature, whose mate had never been created, but who needed no companion, and, living a great many hundred years, was as happy as the centuries were long. The more he did such things as mortal horses are accustomed to do, the less earthly and the more wonderful he seemed. Bellerophon and the child almost held their breath, partly from a delightful awe, but still more because they dreaded lest the slightest stir or murmur should send him up, with the speed of an arrow-flight into the farthest blue of the sky.

Finally, when he had had enough of rolling over and over, Pegasus turned himself about, and, indolently, like an other horse, put out his forelegs, in order to rise from the ground; and Bellerophon, who had guessed that he would do so, darted suddenly from the thicket, and leaped astride of his back.

Yes, there he sat, on the back of the winged horse!

But what a bound did Pegasus make, when, for the first time, he felt the weight of a mortal man upon his loins! A bound, indeed! Before he had time to draw a breath, Bellerophon found himself five hundred feet aloft, and still shooting upward, while the winged horse snorted and trembled with terror and anger. Upward he went, up, up, up, until he plunged into the cold misty bosom of a cloud, at which, only a little while before, Bellerophon had been gazing, and fancying it a very pleasant spot. Then again, out of the heart of the cloud, Pegasus shot down like a thunderbolt, as if he meant to dash both himself and his rider headlong against a rock. Then he went through about a thousand of the wildest caprioles that had ever been performed either by a bird or a horse.

I cannot tell you half that he did. He skimmed straightforward, and sideways, and backward. He reared himself erect, with his forelegs on a wreath of mist and his hind legs on nothing at all. He flung his heels behind, and put his head between his legs, with his wings pointing right upward. At about two miles' height above the earth, he turned a somerset, so that Bellerophon's heels were where his head should have been, and he seemed to look down into the sky, instead of up. He twisted his head about, and looking Bellerophon in the face, with fire flashing from his eyes, made a terrible attempt to bite him. He fluttered his pinions so wildly that one of the silver feathers was shaken out, and, floating earthward, was picked up by the child, who kept it as long as he lived, in memory of Pegasus and Bellerophon.

But the latter (who, as you may judge, was as good a horseman as ever galloped) had been watching his opportunity, and at last clapped the golden bit of the enchanted bridle between the winged steed's jaws. No sooner was this done, than Pegasus became as manageable as if he had taken food all his life out of Bellerophon's hand. To speak what I really feel, it was almost a sadness to see so wild a creature grow suddenly so tame. And Pegasus seemed to feel it so, likewise. He looked round to Bellerophon with tears in his beautiful eyes instead of the fire that so recently flashed from them. But when Bellerophon patted his head, and spoke a few authoritative, yet kind and soothing words; another look came into the eyes of Pegasus; for he was glad at heart, after so many lonely centuries, to have found a companion and a master.

Thus it always is with winged horses, and with all such wild and solitary creatures. If you can catch and overcome them, it is the surest way to win their love.

15

Strider—The Story of a Horse

By Leo Tolstoy

In some of his research for horse chapters in another book, editor Steven D. Price tells us that Tolstoy himself once estimated he had spent seven years of his life in the saddle. A fellow writer, Ivan Turgenev, once encountered Tolstoy whispering to a mangy old nag the two had encountered on a walk in the country. "I could have listened forever," Turgenev later wrote. "He had got inside the very soul of the poor beast and taken me with him."

I

HIGHER AND HIGHER RECEDED THE SKY, WIDER AND WIDER SPREAD THE streak of dawn, whiter grew the pallid silver of the dew, more lifeless the sickle of the moon, and more vocal the forest. People began to get up, and in the owner's stable-yard the sounds of snorting, the rustling of litter, and even the shrill angry neighing of horses crowded together and at variance about something, grew more and more frequent.

"Hold on! Plenty of time! Hungry?" said the old huntsman, quickly opening the creaking gate. "Where are you going?" he shouted, threateningly raising his arm at a mare that was pushing through the gate.

The keeper, Nester, wore a short Cossack coat with an ornamental leather girdle, had a whip slung over his shoulder, and a hunk of bread wrapped in a cloth stuck in his girdle. He carried a saddle and bridle in his arms.

The horses were not at all frightened or offended at the horseman's sarcastic tone: they pretended that it was all the same to them and moved leisurely away from the gate; only one old brown mare, with a thick mane, laid back an ear and quickly turned her back on him. A small filly standing behind her and not at all concerned in the matter took this opportunity to whinny and kick out at a horse that happened to be near.

"Now then!" shouted the keeper still louder and more sternly, and he went to the opposite corner of the yard. Of all the horses in the enclosure (there were about a hundred of them), a piebald gelding, standing by himself in a corner under the penthouse and licking an oak post with half-closed eyes, displayed least impatience.

It is impossible to say what flavor the piebald gelding found in the post, but his expression was serious, and thoughtful while he licked.

"Stop that!" shouted the groom, drawing nearer to him and putting the saddle and a glossy saddlecloth on the manure heap beside him.

The piebald gelding stopped licking and without moving gave Nester a long look. The gelding did not laugh, nor grow angry, nor frown, but his whole belly heaved with a profound sigh and he turned away. The horseman put his arm round the gelding's neck and placed the bridle on him.

"What are you sighing for?" said Nester.

The gelding switched his tail as if to say, "Nothing in particular, Nester!" Nester put the saddlecloth and saddle on him, and this caused the gelding to lay back his ears, probably to express dissatisfaction, but he was only called a "good-for-nothing" for it and his saddle-girths were tightened.

At this the gelding blew himself out, but a finger was thrust into his mouth and a knee hit him in the stomach, so that he had to let out his breath. In spite of this, when the saddlecloth was being buckled on he again laid back his ears and even looked round. Though he knew it would do no good he considered it necessary to show that it was disagreeable to him and that he would always express his dissatisfaction with it. When he was saddled he thrust forward his swollen-off foot and began champing his bit, this too for some reason of his own, for he ought to have known by that time that a bit cannot have any flavor at all.

Nester mounted the gelding by the short stirrup, unwound his long whip, straightened his coat out from under his knee, seated himself in the manner peculiar to coachmen, huntsman, and horsemen, and jerked the reins. The gelding lifted his head to show his readiness to go where ordered, but did not move. He knew that before starting there would be much shouting and that Nester, from the seat on his back, would give many orders to Vaska, the other groom, and to the horses. And Nester did shout: "Vaska! Hullo, Vaska. Have you let out the brood mares? Where are you going, you devil? Now then! Are you asleep? . . . Open the gate! Let the brood mares get out first!" and so on.

The gate creaked. Vaska, cross and sleepy, stood at the gate post holding his horse by the bridle and letting the other horses pass out. The horses followed one another and stepped carefully over the straw, smelling at it: fillies, yearling colts with their manes and tails cut, suckling foals, and mares in foal carrying their burden heedfully passed one by one through the gateway. The fillies sometimes crowded together in twos and threes, throwing their heads across one another's backs and hitting their hoofs against the gate, for which they received a rebuke from the grooms every time. The foals sometimes darted under the legs of the wrong mares and neighed loudly in response to the short whinny of their own mothers.

A playful filly directly had got out at the gate, bent her head sideways, kicked up her hind legs, and squealed, but all the same she did not dare to run ahead of old dappled Zhuldyba who at a slow and heavy pace, swinging her belly from side to side, marched as usual ahead of all the other horses.

In a few minutes the enclosure that had been so animated became deserted, the posts stood gloomily under the empty penthouse, and only trampled straw mixed with manure was to be seen. Used as he was to that desolate sight it probably depressed the piebald gelding. As if making a bow he slowly lowered his head and raised it again, sighed as deeply as the tightly drawn girth would allow, and hobbling along on his stiff and crooked legs, shambled after the herd, bearing old Nester on his bony back.

"I know that as soon as we get out on the road he will begin to strike a light and smoke his wooden pipe with its brass mountings and little chain," thought the gelding. "I am glad of it because early in the morning when it is dewy I like that smell, it reminds me of much that was pleasant. But it's annoying that when his pipe is between his teeth the old man always begins to swagger and thinks himself somebody and sits sideways, always sideways—and that side hurts. However, it can't be helped! Suffering for the pleasure of others is nothing new to me. I have even begun to find a certain equine pleasure in it. Let him swagger, poor fellow! Of course he can only do that when he is alone and no one see him—let him sit sideways!" thought the gelding, and stepping carefully on his crooked legs he went along the middle of the road.

II

Having driven the horses to the riverside where they were to graze, Nester dismounted and unsaddled. Meanwhile the herd had begun gradually to spread over the untrampled meadow, covered with dew and by the mist that rose from it and the encircling river.

When he had taken the bridle off the piebald gelding, Nester scratched him under the neck, in response to which the gelding expressed his gratitude and satisfaction by closing his eyes. "He likes it, the old dog!" muttered Nester. The gelding, however, did not really care for the scratching at all and pretended that it was agreeable merely out of courtesy. He nodded his head in assent to Nester's words, but suddenly Nester, quite unexpectedly and without any reason, perhaps imagining that too much familiarity might give the gelding a wrong idea of his importance, pushed the gelding's head away from himself without any warning and, swinging the bridle, struck him painfully with the buckle on his lean leg, and then without saying a word went up to the hillock to a tree stump beside which he generally seated himself.

Though this action grieved the piebald gelding he gave no indication of it, but, leisurely switching his scanty tail, sniffed at something and, biting off some wisps of grass merely to divert his mind, walked to the river. He took no notice whatever of the antics of the young mares, colts, and foals around him, who were filled with the joy of the morning, and knowing that, especially at his age, it is healthier to have a good drink on an empty stomach and to eat afterwards, he chose a spot where the bank was widest and least steep, and wetting his hoofs and fetlocks, dipped his muzzle in the water and began to suck it up through his torn lips, to expand his filling sides, and from pleasure to switch his scanty tail with its half bald stump.

An aggressive chestnut filly, who always teased the old fellow and did all kinds of unpleasant things to him, now came up to him in the water as if attending to some business of her own but in reality merely to foul the water before his nose. But the piebald gelding, who had already had his fill, as though not noticing the filly's intention quietly drew one foot after the other out of the mud in which they had sunk, jerked his head, and stepping aside from the youthful crowd, started grazing. Sprawling his feet apart in different ways and not trampling the grass needlessly, he went on eating without unbending himself for exactly three hours. Having eaten till his belly hung down from his steep skinny ribs like a sack, he balanced himself equally on his four sore legs so as to have a little pain as possible, especially in his off foreleg which was the weakest, and fell asleep.

Old age is sometimes majestic, sometimes ugly, and sometimes pathetic. But old age can be both ugly and majestic, and the gelding's old age was just of that kind.

He was tall, rather over fifteen hands high. His spots were black, or rather they had been black, but had now turned a dirty brown. He had three spots, one on his head, starting from a crooked bald patch on the side of his nose and reaching halfway down his neck. His long mane, filled with burrs, was white in some places and brownish in others. Another spot extended down his off side to the middle of his belly; the third, on his croup, touched part of his tail and went halfway down his quarters. The rest of the tail was whitish and speckled. The big bony head, with deep hollows over the eyes and a black hanging lip that had been torn at some time, hung low and heavily on his neck, which was so lean that it looked as though it were carved of wood. The pendant lip revealed a blackish bitten tongue and the yellow stumps of the worn lower teeth. The ears, one of which was slit, hung low on either side, and only occasionally moved lazily to drive away the pestering flies. Of the forelock, one tuft which was still long hung back behind an ear; the uncovered forehead was dented and rough, and the skin hung down like bags on his broad jawbones. The veins of his neck had grown knotty and twitched and shuddered at every touch of a fly. The expression of his face was one of stern patience, thoughtfulness, and suffering.

His forelegs were crooked to a bow at the knees, there were swellings over both hoofs, and on one leg, on which the piebald spot reached halfway down, there was a swelling at the knee as big as a fist. The hind legs were in better condition, but apparently long ago his haunches had been so rubbed that in places the hair would not grow again. The leanness of his body made all four legs look disproportionately long. The ribs, though straight, were so exposed and the skin so tightly drawn over them, that it seemed to have dried fast to the spaces between. His back and withers were covered with marks of old lashings, and there was a fresh sore behind, still swollen and festering; the black dock of his tail, which showed the vertebrae, hung down long and almost bare. On his dark-brown croup, near the tail, was a scar, as though of a bite, the size of a man's hand and covered with white hair. Another scarred sore was visible on one of his shoulders. His tail and hocks were dirty because of chronic bowel troubles. The hair on the whole body, though short, stood out straight. Yet in spite of the hideous old age of this horse one involuntary paused to reflect when one saw him, and an expert would have said at once that he had been a remarkably fine horse in his day. The expert would even have said that there was only one breed in Russia that could furnish such breadth of bone, such immense knees, such hoofs, such slender cannons, such a well-shaped neck, and above all such a skull, such eyes—large, black, and clear—and such a thoroughbred network of veins on head and neck, and such delicate skin and hair.

There was really something majestic in that horse's figure and in the terrible union in him of repulsive indications of decrepitude, emphasized by the motley color of his hair, and his manner which expressed the self-confidence and calm assurance that go with beauty and strength. Like a living ruin he stood alone in the midst of the dewy meadow, while not far from him could be heard the tramping, snorting, and youthful neighing and whinnying of the scattered herd.

III

The sun had risen above the forest and now shone brightly on the grass and the winding river. The dew was drying up and condensing into drops, the last of the morning mist was dispersing like tiny smoke clouds. The cloudlets were becoming curly but there was as yet no wind. Beyond the river the verdant rye stood bristling, its ears curling into little horns, and there was an odor of fresh verdure and blossom. A cuckoo called rather hoarsely from the forest, and Nester, lying on his back in the grass, was counting the calls to ascertain how many years he still had to live. The larks were rising over the rye and the meadow. A belated hare, finding himself among the horses, leaped into the open, sat down by a bush, and pricked his ears to listen. Vaska fell asleep with his head in the grass; the fillies, making a still wider circle around him, scattered over the field below. The old mares went about snorting and made a shiny track across the dewy grass, always choosing a place where no one would disturb them. They no longer grazed but only nibbled at choice tufts of grass. The whole herd was moving imperceptibly in one direction.

And again it was old Zhuldyba who, stepping sedately in front of the others, showed the possibility of going farther. Black Mushka, a young mare who had foaled for the first time, with uplifted tail kept whinnying and snorting at her bluish foal; the young filly Satin, sleek and brilliant, bending her head till her black silky forelock hid her forehead and eyes, played with the grass, nipping off a little and tossing it and stamping her leg with its shaggy fetlock all wet with dew. One of the older foals, probably imagining he was playing some kind of game, with his curly tail raised like a plume, ran for the twenty-sixth time round his mother, who quietly went on grazing, having grown accustomed to her son's ways, and only occasionally glanced askance at him with one of her large black eyes.

One of the very youngest foals, black, with a big head, a tuft sticking up in astonishment between his ears, and a little tail still twisted to one side as it had been in his mother's womb, stood motionless, his ears pricked and his dull eyes fixed, gazing at the frisking and prancing foal—whether admiring or condemning him it is hard to say. Some of the foals were sucking and butting with their noses, some—heaven knows why—despite their mother's call were running at an awkward little trot in quite the opposite direction as if searching for something and then, for no apparent reason, stopping and neighing with desperate shrillness. Some lay on their sides in a row, some were learning to eat grass, some again were scratching themselves behind their ears with their hind legs. Two mares still in foal were walking apart from the rest and while slowly moving their legs continued to graze. The others evidently respected their condition, and none of the young ones ventured to come near to disturb them. If any saucy youngsters thought of approaching them, the mere movement of an ear or tail sufficed to show them all how improper such behavior was.

The colts and yearling fillies, pretending to be grownup and sedate, rarely jumped or joined the merry company. They grazed in a dignified manner, curving their close-cropped swan-like necks, and flourished their little broom-like tails as if they also had long ones. Just like the grownups they lay down, rolled over, or rubbed one another. The merriest group was composed of the two- and three-year-old fillies and mares not yet in foal. They almost always walked about together like a separate merry virgin crowd. Among them you could hear sounds of tramping, whinnying, neighing, and snorting. They drew close together, put their heads over one another's necks, sniffed at one another, jumped, and sometimes at a semi-trot, semi-amble, with tails lifted like an oriflamme, raced proudly and coquettishly past their companions. The most beautiful and spirited of them was the mischievous chestnut filly. What she devised the others did; wherever she went the whole crowd of beauties followed. That morning the naughty one was in a specially playful mood. She was seized with a joyous fit, just as human beings sometimes are. Already at the riverside she had played a trick on the old gelding, and after that she ran along through the water pretending to be frightened by something, gave a hoarse squeal, and raced full speed into the field so that Vaska had to gallop after her and the others who followed her. Then after grazing a little she began rolling, then teasing the old mares by dashing in front of them, then she drove away a small foal from the dam and chased it as if meaning to bite it. Its mother was frightened and stopped grazing, while the little foal cried in a piteous tone, but the mischievous one did not touch him at all, she only wanted to frighten him and give a performance for the benefit of her companions, who watched her escapade approvingly. Then she set out to turn the head of a little roan horse with which a peasant was ploughing in a rye field far beyond the river. She stopped, proudly lifted her head somewhat to one side, shook herself, and neighed in a sweet, tender, long-drawn voice. Mischief, feeling, and a certain sadness were expressed in that call. There was in it the desire for and the promise of love, and a pining for it.

"There in the thick reeds is a corn-crake running backwards and forwards and calling passionately to his mate; there is the cuckoo, and the quails are singing of love, and the flowers are sending their fragrant dust to each other by the wind. And I too am young and beautiful and strong." The mischievous one's voice said, "but it has not yet been allowed me to know the sweetness of that feeling, and not only to experience it, but no lover—not a single one—has ever seen me!"

And this neighing, sad and youthful and fraught with feeling, was borne over the lowland and the field to the roan horse far away. He pricked up his ears and stopped. The peasant kicked him with his bast shoe, but the little horse was so enchanted by the silvery sound of the distant neighing that he neighed too. The peasant grew angry, pulled at the reins, and kicked the little roan so painfully in the stomach with his bast shoes that he could not finish his neigh and walked on. But the little roan felt a sense of sweetness and sadness, and for a long time the sounds of unfinished and passionate neighing, and of the peasant's angry voice, were carried from the distant rye field over to the herd.

If the sound of her voice alone so overpowered the little roan that he forgot his duty, what would have happened had he seen the naughty beauty as she stood pricking her ears, breathing in the air with dilated nostrils, ready to run, trembling with her whole beautiful body, and calling to him?

But the mischievous one did not brood long over her impressions. When the neighing of the roan died away she gave another scornful neigh, lowered her head, and began pawing the ground, and then she went to wake and tease the piebald gelding. The piebald gelding was the constant martyr and butt of those happy youngsters. He suffered more from them than at the hands of men. He did no harm to either.

People needed him, but why should these young horses torment him?

IV

He was old, they were young; he was lean, they were sleek; he was miserable, they were gay; and so he was quite alien to them, an outsider, an utterly different creature whom it was impossible for them to pity. Horses only have pity on themselves and very occasionally on those in whose skins they can easily imagine themselves to be. But was it the old gelding's fault that he was old, poor, and ugly?

One might think not, but in equine ethics it was, and only those were right who were strong, young, and happy—those who had life still before them, whose every muscle quivered with superfluous energy, and whose tails stood erect. Maybe the piebald gelding himself understood this and in his quiet moments was ready to agree that it was his fault that he had already lived his life, and that he had to pay for that life, but after all he was a horse and often could not suppress a sense of resentment, sadness, and indignation when he looked at those youngsters who tormented him for what would befall them all at the end of their lives. Another cause of the horse's lack of pity was their aristocratic pride. Every one of them traced back its pedigree, through father or mother, to the famous Creamy, while the piebald was of unknown parentage. He was a chance comer, purchased three years before at a fair for eighty assignat rubles.

The chestnut filly, as if taking a stroll, passed close by the piebald gelding's nose and pushed him. He knew at once what it was, and without opening his eyes laid back his ears and showed his teeth. The filly wheeled round as if to kick him. The gelding opened his eyes and stepped aside. He did not want to sleep anymore and began to graze. The mischief-maker, followed by her companions, again approached the gelding. A very stupid two-year-old white-spotted filly who always imitated the chestnut in everything went up with her and, as irritators always do, went to greater lengths than the instigator. The chestnut always went up as if intent on business of her own and passed by the gelding's nose without looking at him, so that he really did not know whether to be angry or not, and that was really funny.

She did the same now, but the white-spotted one, who followed her and had grown particularly lively, bumped right against the gelding with her chest. He again showed his teeth, whinnied, and with an agility one could not have expected of him, rushed after her and bit her flank. The white-spotted one kicked out with all her strength and dealt the old horse a heavy blow on his thin bare ribs. He snorted heavily and was going to rush at her again but bethought himself, and drawing a deep sigh, stepped aside. The whole crowd of young ones must have taken as a personal affront the impertinence the piebald gelding had permitted himself to offer to the white-spotted one and for the rest of the day did not let him graze in peace for a moment, so that the keeper had to quiet them several times and could not understand what had come over them.

The gelding felt so offended that he went up himself to Nester when the old man was getting ready to drive the horses home and felt happier and quieter when he was saddled and the old man had mounted him.

God knows what the gelding was thinking as he carried old Nester on his back; whether he thought bitterly of the pertinacious and merciless youngsters or forgave his tormentors with the contemptuous and silent pride suited old age. At all events he did not betray his thoughts till he reached home.

That evening as Nester drove the horses past the huts of the domestic serfs, he noticed a peasant horse and cart tethered to his porch; some friends had come to see him. When driving the horses in he was in such a hurry that he let the gelding in without unsaddling him and, shouting to Vaska to do it, shut the gate and went to his friends. Whether because of the affront to the white-spotted filly—Creamy's great-granddaughter—by that "mangy trash" bought at the horse fair, who did not know his father or mother, and the consequent outrage to the aristocratic sentiment of the whole herd, or because the gelding with his high saddle and without a rider presented a strangely fantastic spectacle to the horses, at any rate something quite unusual occurred that night in the paddock. All the horses, young and old, ran after the gelding, showing their teeth and driving him all round the yard; one heard the sound of hoofs striking against his bare ribs, and his deep moaning. He could no longer endure this, nor could he avoid the blows. He stopped in the middle of the paddock, his face expressing first the repulsive weak malevolence of helpless old age, and then despair: he dropped his ears, and then something happened that caused all the horses to quiet down. The oldest of the mares,

Vyazapurikha, went up to the gelding, sniffed at him, and sighed. The gelding sighed too.

V

In the middle of the moonlit paddock stood the tall gaunt figure of the gelding, still wearing the high saddle with its prominent peak at the bow. The horses stood motionless and in deep silence around him as if they were learning something new and unexpected.

This is what they learned from him . . . .

First Night

Yes, I am the son of Affable I and of Baba. My pedigree name is Muzhik, and I was nicknamed Strider by the crowd because of my long and sweeping strides, the like of which was nowhere to be found in all Russia. There is no more thoroughbred horse in the world. I should never have told you this. What good would it have done? You would never have recognized me: even Vyazapnrikha, who was with me in Khrenovoa, did not recognize me till now. You would not have believed me if Vyazapurikha were not here to be my witness, and I should never have told you this. I don't need equine sympathy. But you wished it Yes, I am that Strider whom connoisseurs are looking for and cannot find—that Strider whom the count himself knew and got rid of from his stud because I outran Swan, his favorite.

When I was born, I did not know what "piebald" meant—I thought I was just a horse. I remember that the first remark we heard about my color struck my mother and me deeply.

I suppose I was born in the night; by the morning, having been licked over by my mother, I already stood on my feet. I remember I kept wanting something and that everything seemed very surprising and yet very simple. Our stalls opened into a long war passage and had latticed doors through which everything could be seen.

My mother offered me her teats but I was still so innocent that I poked my nose now between her forelegs and now under her udder. Suddenly she glanced at the latticed door and, lifting her leg over me, stepped aside. The groom on duty was looking into our stall through the lattice.

"Why, Baba has foaled!" he said, and began to draw the bolt. He came in over the fresh bedding and put his arms around me. "Just look, Taras!" he shouted, "what a piebald he is—a regular magpie!"

I darted away from him and fell on my knees.

"Look at him—the little devil!"

My mother became disquieted but did not take my part; she only stepped a little to one side with a very deep sigh. Other grooms came to look at me, and one of them ran to tell the stud groom.

Everybody laughed when they looked at my spots, and they gave me all kinds of strange names, but neither I nor my mother understood these words. Till then there had been no piebalds among all my relatives. We did not think there was anything bad in it. Everybody even praised my strength and my form.

"See what a frisky fellow!" said the groom. "There's no holding him."

Before long the stud groom came and began to express astonishment at my color; he even seemed aggrieved.

"And who does the little monster take after?" he said. "The general won't keep him in the stud. Oh, Baba, you have played me a trick!" he addressed my mother. "You might at least have dropped one with just a star—but this one is all piebald!"

My mother did not reply but as usual on such occasions drew a sigh. "And what devil does he take after—he's just like a peasant horse!" he continued. "He can't be left in the stud—he'd shame us. But he's well built—very well!" said he, and so did everyone who saw me.

A few days later the general himself came and looked at me, and again everyone seemed horrified at something, and abused me and my mother for the color of my hair. "But he's a fine colt—very fine!" said all who saw me.

Until spring we all lived separately in the brood mares' stable, each with our mother, and only occasionally when the snow on the stable roofs began to melt in the sun were we let out with our mothers into the large paddock strewn with fresh straw. There I first came to know all my near and my distant relations. Here I saw all the famous mares of the day coming out from different doors with their little foals. There was the old mare Dutch, Fly (Creamy's daughter), Ruddy the riding horse,

Wellwisher—all celebrities at that time. They all gathered together with their foals, walking about in the sunshine, rolling on the fresh straw and sniffing at one another like ordinary horses. I have never forgotten the sight of that paddock full of the beauties of that day. It seems strange to you to think and hard to believe, that I was ever young and frisky, but it was so. This same Vyazapurikha was then a yearling filly whose mane had just been cut; a dear, merry, lively little thing, but—and I do not say it to offend her—although among you she is now considered a remarkable thoroughbred she was then among the poorest horses in the stud. She will herself confirm this.

My mottled appearance, which men so disliked, was very attractive to all the horses; they all came round me, admired me, and frisked about with me. I began to forget what men said about my mottled appearance and felt happy. But I soon experienced the first sorrow of my life and the cause of it was my mother. When the thaw had set in, the sparrows twittered under the eaves, spring was felt more strongly in the air, and my mother's treatment of me changed.

Her whole disposition changed: she would frisk about without any reason and run round the yard, which did not at all accord with her dignified age, then she would consider and begin to neigh, and would bite and kick her sister mares, and then begin to sniff at me and snort discontentedly; then on going out into the sun she would lay her head across the shoulder of her cousin, Lady Merchant, dreamily rub her back, and push me away from her teats.

One day the stud groom came and had a halter put on her and she was led out of the stall. She neighed and I answered and rushed after her, but she did not even look back at me. The strapper, Taras, seized me in his arms while they were closing the door after my mother had been led out.

I bolted and upset the strapper on the straw, but the door was shut and I could only hear the receding sound of my mother's neighing; and that neigh did not sound like a call to me but had another expression. Her voice was answered from afar by a powerful voice—that of Dobry I, as I learned later, who was being led by two grooms—one on each side, to meet my mother.

I don't remember how Taras got out of my stall: I felt too sad, for I knew that I had lost my mother's love forever. "And it's all because I am piebald!" I thought, remembering what people said about my color, and such passionate anger overcame me that I began to beat my head and knees against the walls of the stall and continued till I was sweating all over and quite exhausted.

After a while my mother came back to me. I heard her run up the passage at a trot and with an unusual gait. They opened the door for her and I hardly knew her—she had grown so much younger and more beautiful. She sniffed at me, snorted, and began to whinny. Her whole demeanor showed that she no longer loved me.

She told me of Dobry's beauty and her love of him. Those meetings continued and the relations between my mother and me grew colder and colder.

Soon after that we were let out to pasture. I now discovered new joys which made up to me for the loss of my mother's love. I had friends and companions. Together we learned to eat grass, to neigh like the grown-ups, and to gallop round our mothers with lifted tails. That was a happy time. Everything was forgiven me, everybody loved me, admired me, and looked indulgently at anything I did. But that did not last long.

Soon afterwards something dreadful happened to me.

The gelding heaved a deep sigh and walked away from the other horses.

The dawn had broken long before. The gates creaked. Nester came in, and the horses separated. The keeper straightened the saddle on the gelding's back and drove the horses out.

VI

Second Night

As soon as the horses had been driven in they again gathered round the piebald, who continued:

In August they separated me from my mother and I did not feel particularly grieved. I saw that she was again heavy (with my brother, the famous Usan) and that I could no longer be to her what I had been. I was not jealous but felt that I had become indifferent to her. Besides, I knew that having left my mother I should be put in the general division of foals, where we were kept two or three together and were every day let out in a crowd into the open. I was in the same stall with Darling. Darling was a saddle horse, who was subsequently ridden by the emperor and portrayed in pictures and sculpture. At that time he was a mere foal, with a soft glossy coat, a swanlike neck, and straight slender legs taut as the strings of an instrument. He was always lively, good-tempered, and amiable, always ready to gambol, exchange licks, and lay tricks on horse or man. Living together as we did we involuntarily made friends, and our friendship lasted the whole of our youth. He was merry and giddy. Even then he began to make love, courted the fillies, and laughed at my guilelessness. To my misfortune, vanity led me to imitate him, and I was soon carried away and fell in love. And this early tendency of mine was the cause of the greatest change in my fate. It happened that I was carried away.... Vyazapurilcha was a year older than I, and we were special friends, but towards the autumn I noticed that she began to be shy with me....

But I will not speak of that unfortunate period of my first love; she herself remembers my mad passion, which ended for me in the most important change of my life.

The strappers rushed to drive her away and to beat me. That evening I was shut up in a special stall where I neighed all night as if foreseeing what was to happen next.

In the morning the general, the stud groom, the stablemen and the strappers came into the passage where my stall was, and there was a terrible hubbub. The general said that he would have everybody flogged, and that it would not do to keep young stallions. The stud groom promised that he would have everything attended to. They grew quiet and went away. I did not understand anything, but could see that they were planning something concerning me.

The day after that I ceased neighing forever. I became what I am now.

The whole world changed in my eyes. Nothing mattered anymore; I became self-absorbed and began to brood. At first everything seemed repulsive to me. I even ceased to eat, drink, or walk, and there was no idea of playing. Now and then it occurred to me to give a kick, to gallop, or to start neighing, but immediately came the question: Why? What for? And all my energy died away.

One evening I was being exercised just when the horses were driven back from pasture. I saw in the distance a cloud of dust enveloping the indistinct but familiar outlines of all our brood mares. I heard their cheerful snorting and the trampling of their feet. I stopped, though the cord of the halter by which the groom was leading me cut the nape of my neck, and I gazed at the approaching drove as one gazes at happiness that is lost forever and cannot return. They approached, and I could distinguish one after another all the familiar, beautiful, stately, healthy, sleek figures. Some of them also turned to look at me. I was unconscious of the pain the groom's jerking at my halter inflicted. I forgot myself and from old habit involuntarily neighed and began to trot, but my neighing sounded sad, ridiculous, and meaningless. No one in the drove made sport of me, but I noticed that out of decorum many of them turned away from me. They evidently felt it repugnant, pitiable, indelicate, and above all ridiculous, to look at my thin, expressionless neck, my large head (I had grown lean in the meantime), my long, awkward legs, and the silly awkward gait with which by force of habit I trotted round the groom. No one answered my neighing—they all looked away. Suddenly I understood it all, understood how far I was forever removed from them, and I do not remember how I got home with the groom.

Already before that I had shown a tendency towards gravity and thoughtfulness, but now a decided change came over me. My being piebald, which aroused such curious contempt in men, my terrible and unexpected misfortune, and also my peculiar position in the stud farm which I felt but was unable to explain made me retire into myself. I pondered over the injustice of men, who blamed me for being piebald; I pondered on the inconstancy of mother-love and feminine love in general and on its dependence on physical conditions; and above all I pondered on the characteristics of that strange race of animals with whom we are so closely connected, and whom we call men—those characteristics which were the source of my own peculiar position in the stud farm, which I felt but could not understand.

The meaning of this peculiarity in people and the characteristic on which it is based was shown to me by the following occurrence:

It was in winter at holiday time. I had not been fed or watered all day. As I learned later this happened because the lad who fed us was drunk. That day the stud groom came in, saw that I had no food, began to use bad language about the missing lad, and then went away.

Next day the lad came into our stable with another groom to give us hay. I noticed that he was particularly pale and sad and that in the expression of his long back especially there was something significant which evoked compassion.

He threw the hay angrily over the grating. I made a move to put my head over his shoulder but he struck me such a painful blow on the nose with his fist that I started back. Then he kicked me in the belly with his boot.

"If it hadn't been for this scurvy beast," he said, "nothing would have happened!"

"How's that?" inquired the other groom.

"You see, he doesn't go to look after the count's horses but visits his own twice a day."

"What, have they given him the piebald?" asked the other.

"Given it, or sold it—the devil only knows! The count's horses might all starve—he wouldn't care—but just dare to leave 'his' colt without food! 'Lie down!' he says, and they begin walloping me! No Christianity in it. He has more pity on a beast than on a man. He must be an infidel—he counted the strokes himself, the barbarian! The general never flogged like that! My whole back is covered with welts. There's no Christian soul in him!"

What they said about flogging and Christianity I understood well enough, but I was quite in the dark as to what they meant by the words "his colt," from which I perceived that people considered that there was some connection between me and the head groom. What the connection was I could not at all understand then. Only much later when they separated me from the other horses did I learn what it meant. At that time I could not at all understand what they meant by speaking of "me" as being a man's property. The words "my" horse applied to me, a live horse, seemed to me as strange as to say "my land"; "my air," or "my water."

But those words had an enormous effect on me. I thought of them constantly and only after long and varied relations with men did I at last understand the meaning they attach to these strange words, which indicate that men are guided in life not by deeds but by words. They like not so much to do or abstain from doing anything, as to be able to apply conventional words to different objects. Such words, considered very important among them, are "my" and "mine," which they apply to various things, creatures, or objects; even to land, people, and horses. They have agreed that of any given thing only one person may use the word "mine" and he who in this game of theirs may use that conventional word about the greatest number of things is considered the happiest. Why this is so I do not know, but it is so. For a long time I tried to explain it by some direct advantage they derive from it, but this proved wrong.

For instance, many of those who called me "their" horse did not ride me, quite other people rode me, nor did they feed me—quite other people did that. Again it was not those who called me "their" horse who treated me kindly, but coachmen, veterinaries, and in general, quite other people. Later on, having widened my field of observation, I became convinced that not only as applied to us horses, but in regard to other things, the idea of "mine" has no other basis than a low, mercenary instinct in men, which they call the feeling or right of property. A man who never lives in it says "my house" but only concerns himself with its building and maintenance, and a tradesman talks of "my cloth business" but has none of his clothes made of the best cloth that is in his shop.

There are people who call land theirs, though they have never seen that land and never walked on it. There are people who call other people theirs but have never seen those others, and the whole relationship of the owners to the owned is that they do them harm.

There are men who call women their women or their wives; yet these women live with other men. And men strive in life not to do what they think right but to call as many things as possible "their own."

I am now convinced that in this lies the essential difference between men and us. Therefore, not to speak of other things in which we are superior to men, on this ground alone we may boldly say that in the scale of living creatures we stand higher than man. The activity of men, at any rate of those I have had to do with, is guided by words, while ours is guided by deeds.

It was this right to speak of me as "my horse" that the stud groom had obtained, and that was why he had the stable lad flogged. This discovery much astonished me and, together with the thoughts and opinions aroused in men by my piebald color, and the thoughtfulness produced in me by my mother's betrayal, caused me to become the serious and thoughtful gelding that I am.

I was thrice unfortunate: I was piebald, I was a gelding, and people considered that I did not belong to God and to myself, as is natural to all living creatures, but that I belonged to the stud groom.

Their thinking this about me had many consequences. The first was that I was kept apart from the other horses, was better fed, more often taken out on the line, and was broken in at an earlier age. I was first harnessed in my third year. I remember how the stud groom, who imagined I was his, himself began to harness me with a crowd of other grooms, expecting me to prove unruly or to resist. They put ropes round me to lead me into the shafts, put a cross of broad straps on my back and fastened it to the shafts so that I could not kick, while I was only awaiting an opportunity to show my readiness and love of work.

They were surprised that I started like an old horse. They began to break me and I began to practice trotting. Every day I made greater and greater progress, so that after three months the general himself and many others approved of my pace. But strange to say, just because they considered me not as their own, but as belonging to the head groom, they regarded my paces quite differently.

The stallions who were my brothers were raced, their records were kept, people went to look at them, drove them in gilt sulkies, and expensive horse cloths were thrown over them. I was driven in a common sulky to Chesmenka and other farms on the head groom's business. All this was the result of my being piebald, and especially of my being in their opinion, not the count's, but the head groom's property.

Tomorrow, if we are alive, I will tell you the chief consequence for me of this right of property the head groom considered himself to have."

All that day the horses treated Strider respectfully, but Nester's treatment of him was as rough as ever. The peasant's little roan horse neighed again on coming up to the herd, and the chestnut filly again coquettishly replied to him.

VII
Third Night

The new moon had risen and its narrow crescent lit up Strider's figure as he once again stood in the middle of the stable-yard. The other horses crowded round him.

The gelding continued:

For me the most surprising consequence of my not being the count's, nor God's, but the head groom's, was that the very thing that constitutes our chief merit—a fast pace—was the cause of my banishment. They were driving Swan round the track, and the head groom, returning from Chesmenka, drove me up and stopped there. Swan went past. He went well, but all the same he was showing off and had not the exactitude I had developed in myself—so that directly one foot touched the ground another instantaneously lifted and not the lightest effort was lost but every atom of exertion carried me forward. Swan went by us. I pulled towards the ring and the head groom did not check me. "Here, shall I try my piebald?" he shouted, and when next Swan came abreast of us he let me go. Swan was already going fast, and so I was left behind during the first round, but in the second I began to gain on him, drew near to his sulky, drew level—and passed him. They tried us again—it was the same thing. I was the faster. And this dismayed everybody. The general asked that I should be sold at once to some distant place, so that nothing more should be heard of me: "Or else the count will get to know of it and there will be trouble!" So they sold me to a horse dealer as a shaft horse. I did not remain with him long. A hussar who came to buy remounts bought me. All this was so unfair, so cruel, that I was glad when they took me away from Khrenova and parted me forever from all that had been familiar and dear to me. It was too painful for me among them. They had love, honor, freedom, before them! I had labor, humiliation, humiliation, labor, to the end of my life. And why? Because I was piebald, and because of that had to become somebody's horse. . . .

Strider could not continue that evening. An event occurred in the enclosure that upset all the horses. Kupchikha, a mare big with foal, who had stood listening to the story, suddenly turned away and walked slowly into the shed, and there began to groan so that it drew the attention of all the horses. Then she lay down, then got up again, and again lay down. The old mares understood what was happening to her, but the young ones became excited and, leaving the gelding, surrounded the invalid. Towards morning there was a new foal standing unsteadily on its little legs. Nester shouted to the groom, and the mare and foal were taken into a stall and the other horses driven to the pasture without them.

VIII

Fourth Night

In the evening when the gate was closed and all had quieted down, the piebald continued:

I have had the opportunity to make many observations both of men and horses during the time I passed from hand to hand.

I stayed longest of all with two masters: a prince (an officer of hussars), and later with an old lady who lived near the church of St. Nicholas the Wonder Worker.

The happiest years of my life I spent with the officer of hussars. Though he was the cause of my ruin, and though he never loved anything or anyone, I loved and still love him for that very reason.

What I liked about him was that he was handsome, happy, rich, and therefore never loved anybody.

You understand that lofty equine feeling of ours. His coldness and my dependence on him gave special strength to my love for him. "Kill me, drive me till my wind is broken!" I used to think in our good days, "and I shall be all the happier."

He bought me from an agent to whom the head groom had sold me for eight hundred rubles, and he did so just because no one else had piebald horses. That was my best time. He had a mistress. I knew this because I took him to her every day and sometimes took them both out.

His mistress was a handsome woman, and he was handsome, and his coachman was handsome, and I loved them all because they were. Life was worth living then. This was how our time was spent: in the morning the groom came to rub me down—not the coachman himself but the groom. The groom was a lad from among the peasants. He would open the door, let out the steam from the horses, throw out the droppings, take off our rugs, and begin to fidget over our bodies with a brush, and lay whitish streaks of dandruff from a currycomb on the boards of the floor that was dented by our rough horseshoes. I would playfully nip his sleeve and paw the ground. Then we were led out one after another to the trough filled with cold water, and the lad would admire the smoothness of my spotted coat which he had polished, my foot with its broad hoof my legs straight as an arrow, my glossy quarters, and my back wide enough to sleep on. Hay was piled into the high racks, and the oak cribs were filled with oats. Then Feofan, the head coachman, would come in.

Master and coachman resembled each other. Neither of them was afraid of anything or cared for anyone but himself, and for that reason everybody liked them. Feofan wore a red shirt, black velveteen knicker-bockers, and a sleeveless coat. I liked it on a holiday when he would come into the stable, his hair pomaded, and wearing his sleeveless coat, and would shout, "Now then, beastie, have you forgotten?" and push me with the handle of the stable fork, never so as to hurt me but just as a joke. I immediately knew that it was a joke and laid back an ear, making my teeth click.

We had a black stallion, who drove in a pair. At night they used to put me in harness with him. That Polkan, as he was called, did not understand a joke but was simply vicious as the devil. I was in the stall next to his and sometimes we bit each other seriously. Feofan was not afraid of him. He would come up and give a shout: it looked as if Polkan would kill him, but no, he'd miss, and Feofan would put the harness on him.

Once, he and I bolted down Smiths Bridge Street. Neither my master nor the coachman was frightened: they laughed, shouted at the people, checked us, and turned so that no one was run over.

In their service I lost my best qualities and half my life. They ruined me by watering me wrongly, and they foundered me. . . . Still, for all that, it was the best time of my life. At twelve o'clock they would come to harness me, black my hoofs, moisten my forelock and mane, and put me in the shafts.

The sledge was of plaited cane upholstered with velvet. The reins were of silk, the harness had silver buckles, sometimes there was a cover of silken flynet, and altogether it was such that when all the traces and straps were fastened it was difficult to say where the harness ended and the horse began. We were harnessed at ease in the stable. Feofan would come, broader at the hips than at the shoulders, his red belt up under his arms. He would examine the harness, take his seat, wrap his coat round him, put his foot into the sledge stirrup, let off some joke, and for appearance's sake always hang a whip over his arm though he hardly ever hit me, and would say "Let go!" and, playfully stepping from foot to foot I would move out of the gate, and the cook who had come out to empty the slops would stop on the threshold, and the peasant who had brought wood into the yard would open his eyes wide. We would come out, go a little way, and stop. Footmen would come out and other coachmen, and a chatter would begin. Everybody would wait: sometimes we had to stand for three hours at the entrance, moving a little way, turning back, and standing again.

At last there would be a stir in the hall: Old Tikhon with his paunch would rush out in his dress coat and cry, "Drive up!" (In those days there was not that stupid way of saying, "Forward!" as if one did not know that we moved forward and not back.) Feofan would cluck, drive up, and the prince would hurry out carelessly, as though there were nothing remarkable about the sledge, or the horse, or Feofan—who bent his back and stretched out his arms so that it seemed it would be impossible for him to keep them long in that position. The prince would have a shako on his head and wear a fur coat with a grey beaver collar hiding his rosy, black-browed, handsome face, that should never have been concealed. He would come out clattering his saber, his spurs, and the brass backs of the heels of his overshoes, stepping over the carpet as if in a hurry and taking no notice of me or Feofan whom everybody but he looked at and admired. Feofan would cluck, I would tug at the reins, and respectably, at a foot pace, we would draw up to the entrance and stop. I would turn my eyes on the prince and jerk my thoroughbred head with its delicate forelock. The prince would be in good spirits and sometimes jest with Feofan. Feofan would reply, half turning his handsome head, and without lowering his arms would make a scarcely perceptible movement with the reins which I understand. And then one, two, three. . . . with ever wider and wider strides, every muscle quivering, and sending the muddy snow against the front of the sledge, I would go. In those days, too, there was none of the present-day stupid habit of crying "Oh!" as if the coachman were in pain, instead of the sensible "Be off! Take care!" Feofan would shout, "Be off! Look out there!" and the people would step aside and stand craning their necks to see the handsome gelding, the handsome coachman, and the handsome gentleman. . . .

I was particularly fond of passing a trotter. When Feofan and I saw at a distance a turn-out worthy of the effort, we would fly like a whirlwind and gradually gain on it. Now, throwing the dirt right to the back of the sledge, I would draw level with the occupant of the vehicle and snort above his head:

Then I would reach the horse's harness and the arch of his troika, and then would no longer see it but only hear its sounds in the distance behind. And the prince, Feofan, and I, would all be silent, and pretend to be merely going on our own business and not even notice those with slow horses whom we happened to meet on our way. I liked to pass another horse but also liked to meet a good trotter. An instant, a sound, a glance, and we had passed each other and were flying in opposite directions. . . .

The gate creaked and voices of Nester and Vaska were heard.

Fifth Night

The weather began to break up. It had been dull since morning and there was no dew; but it was warm and the mosquitoes were troublesome. As soon as the horses were driven in they collected round the piebald, and he finished his story as follows:

The happy period of my life was soon over. I lived in that way only two years. Towards the end of the second winter the happiest event of my life occurred, and following it came my greatest misfortune. It was during carnival week. I took the prince to the races. Glossy and Bull were running. I don't know what people were doing in the pavilion, but I know the prince came out and ordered Feofan to drive onto the track. I remember how they took me in and placed me beside Glossy. He was harnessed to a racing sulky and I, just as I was, to a town sledge. I outstripped him at the turn. Roars of laughter and howls of delight greeted me.

When I was led in, a crowd followed me and five or six people offered the prince thousands for me.

He only laughed, showing his white teeth. "No," he said, "this isn't a horse, but a friend. I wouldn't sell him for mountains of gold. Au revoir, gentleman!" He unfastened the sledge apron and got in.

"To Ostozenka Street!" That was where his mistress lived, and off we flew. . . .

That was our last happy day. We reached her home.

He spoke of her as "his," but she loved someone else and had run away with him. The prince learned this at her lodgings. It was five o'clock, and without unharnessing me he started in pursuit of her. They did what had never been done to me before—struck me with the whip and made me gallop. For the first time I fell out of step and felt ashamed and wished to correct it, but suddenly I heard the prince shout in an unnatural voice: "Get on!" The whip whistled through the air and cut me, and I galloped, striking my foot against the iron front of the sledge. We overtook her after going sixteen miles. I got him there but trembled all night long and could not eat anything. In the morning they gave me water. I drank it and after that was never again the horse that I had been. I was ill, and they tormented me and maimed me—doctoring me, as people call it. My hoofs came off, I had swellings and my legs grew bent; my chest sank in and I became altogether limp and weak. I was sold to a horse dealer who fed me carrots and something else and made something of me quite unlike myself, though good enough to deceive one who did not know. My strength and my pace were gone.

When purchasers came the dealer also tormented me by coming into my stall and beating me with a heavy whip to frighten me and madden me. Then he would rub down the stripes on my coat and lead me out.

An old woman bought me of him. She always drove to the Church of St. Nicholas the Wonder Worker, and she used to have her coachman flogged. He used to weep in my stall and I learned that tears have a pleasant, salty taste. Then the old woman died. Her steward took me to the country and sold me to a hawker. Then I over-ate myself with wheat and grew still worse. They sold me to a peasant. There I ploughed, and had hardly anything to eat, my foot got cut by a ploughshare, and I again became ill. Then a gypsy took me in exchange for something. He tormented me terribly and finally sold me to the steward here. And here I am.

All were silent. A sprinkling of rain began to fall.

IX

The Evening After

As the herd returned home the following evening they encountered their master with a visitor. Zhuldyba when nearing the house looked askance at the two male figures: one was the young master in his straw hat, the other a tall, stout, bloated military man. The old mare gave the man a side glance and, swerving, went near him; the others, the young ones, were flustered and hesitated, especially when the master and his visitor purposely stepped among them, pointing something out to each other and talking.

"That one, the dapple grey, I bought of Voekov," said the master. "And where did you get that young black mare with the white legs?"

"She's a fine one!" said the visitor. They looked over many of the horses going forward and stopping them. They noticed the chestnut filly too.

"That is one I kept of Khrenova's saddle-horse breed"; said the master.

They could not see all the horses as they walked past, and the master called to Nester, and the old man, tapping the sides of the piebald with his heels, trotted forward. The piebald limped on one leg but moved in a way that showed that as long as his strength lasted he would not murmur on any account, even if they wanted him to run in that way to the end of the world. He was even ready to gallop and tried to do so with his right leg.

"There, I can say for certain there is no better horse in Russia than this one," said the master, pointing to one of the mares. The visitor admired it. The master walked about excitedly, ran forward, and showed his visitor all the horses, mentioning the origin and pedigree of each. The visitor evidently found the master's talk dull but devised some questions to show interest.

"Yes, yes," he said absent-mindedly.

"Just look," said the master, not answering a question. "Look at her legs. . . . She cost me a lot but has a third foal already in harness."

"And trots well?" asked the guest.

So they went past all the horses till there were no more to show. Then they were silent. "Well, shall we go now?"

"Yes, let's go."

They went through the gate. The visitor was glad the exhibition was over and that he could now go to the house where they could eat and drink and smoke, and he grew perceptibly brighter. As he went past Nester, who sat on the piebald waiting for orders, the visitor slapped the piebald's crupper with his big fat hand.

"What an ornamented one!" he said. "I once had a piebald like him; do you remember my telling you of him?"

The master, finding that it was not his horse that was being spoken about, paid no attention but kept looking round at his own herd.

Suddenly above his ear he heard a dull, weak, senile neigh. It was the piebald that had begun to neigh and had broken off as if ashamed.

Neither the visitor nor the master paid any attention to this neighing, but went into the house.

In the flabby old man Strider had recognized his beloved master, the once brilliant, handsome, and wealthy Serpukhovskoy.

X

It kept on drizzling. In the stable-yard it was gloomy, but in the master's house it was very different. The table was laid in a luxurious drawing room for a luxurious evening tea, and at it sat the host, the hostess, and their guest.

The hostess, her pregnancy made very noticeable by her figure, her strained convex pose, her plumpness, and especially by her large eyes with their mild inward look, sat by the samovar.

The host held in his hand a box of special, ten-year-old cigars, such as he said no one else had, and he was preparing to boast about them to his guest. The host was a handsome man of about twenty-five, fresh-looking, well cared for, and well groomed. In the house he was wearing a new loose thick suit made in London. Large expensive pendants hung from his watch-chain. His gold-mounted turquoise shirt studs were also large and massive. He had a beard à la Napoleon III, and the tips of his moustache stuck out in a way that could only have been learned in Paris.

The hostess wore a dress of silk gauze with a large floral pattern of many colors, and large gold hairpins of a peculiar pattern held up her thick, light-brown hair—beautiful though not all her own. On her arms and hands she wore many bracelets and rings, all of them expensive.

The tea service was of delicate china and the samovar of silver. A footman, resplendent in dress coat, white waistcoat and necktie, stood like a statue by the door awaiting orders. The furniture was elegantly carved and upholstered in bright colors, the wallpaper dark with a large flowered pattern. Beside the table, tinkling the silver bells on its collar, was a particularly fine whippet, whose difficult English name its owners, neither of whom knew English, pronounced.

In the corner, surrounded by plants, stood an inlaid piano. Everything gave the impression of newness, luxury, and rarity. Everything was good, but it all bore an imprint of superfluity, wealth, and the absence of intellectual interests.

The host, a lover of trotting races, was sturdy and full-blooded—one of that never-dying race which drives about in sable coats, throws expensive bouquets to actresses, drinks the most expensive wines with the most fashionable labels at the most expensive restaurants, offers prizes engraved with the donor's name, and keeps the most expensive mistresses.

Nikita Serpukhovskoy, their guest, was a man of over forty, tall, stout, bald-headed, with heavy moustache and whiskers. He must once have been very handsome but had now evidently sunk physically, morally, and financially.

He had such debts that he had been obliged to enter the government service to avoid imprisonment for debt and was now on his way to a provincial town to become the head of a stud farm, a post some important relatives had obtained for him.

He wore a military coat and blue trousers of a kind only a rich man would have had made for himself. His shirt was of similar quality and so was his English watch. His boots had wonderful soles as thick as a man's finger.

Nikita Serpukhovskoy had during his life run through a fortune of two million rubles, and was now a hundred and twenty thousand in debt. In cases of that kind there always remains a certain momentum of life enabling a man to obtain credit and continue living almost luxuriously for another ten years.

These ten years were however coming to an end, the momentum was exhausted, and life was growing hard for Nikita. He was already beginning to drink—that is, to get fuddled with wine, a thing that used not to happen, though strictly speaking he had never begun or left off drinking. His decline was most noticeable in the restlessness of his glance (his eyes had grown shifty) and in the uncertainty of his voice and movements. This restlessness struck one the more as it had evidently got hold of him only recently, for one could see that he had all his life been accustomed not to be afraid of anything or anybody and had only recently, through heavy suffering, reached this state of fear so unnatural to him.

His host and hostess noticed this and exchanged glances which showed that they understood one another and were only postponing till bedtime a detailed discussion of the subject, putting up meanwhile with poor Nikita and even showing him attentions.

The sight of his young host's good fortune humiliated Serpukhovskoy, awakening a painful envy in him as he recalled his own irrecoverable past.

"Do you mind my smoking a cigar, Marie?" he asked, addressing the lady in the peculiar tone acquired only by experience—the tone, polite and friendly but not quite respectful, in which men who know the world speak to kept women in contradistinction to wives. Not that he wished to offend her: on the contrary he now wished rather to curry favor with her and with her keeper, though he would on no account have acknowledged the fact to himself. But he was accustomed to speak in that way to such women. He knew she would herself be surprised and even offended were he to treat her as a lady. Besides he had to retain a certain shade of a respectful tone for his friend's real wife. He always treated his friend's mistresses with respect, not because he shared the so-called convictions promulgated in periodicals (he never read trash or that kind) about the respect due to the personality of every man, about the meaninglessness of marriage, and so forth, but because all decent men do so and he was a decent, though fallen, man.

He took a cigar. But his host awkwardly picked up a whole handful and offered them to him.

"Just see how good these are. Take them!"

Serpukhovskoy pushed aside the hand with the cigars, and a gleam of offense and shame showed itself in his eyes.

"Thank you!" He took out his cigar case. "Try mine!"

The hostess was sensitive. She noticed his embarrassment and hastened to talk to him. "I am very fond of cigars. I should smoke myself if everyone about me did not smoke." And she smiled her pretty, kindly smile.

He smiled in return, but irresolutely. Two of his teeth were missing.

"No, take this!" the tactless host continued. "The others are weaker. Fritz, bring another box. There are two there."

The German footman brought another box.

"Do you prefer big ones? Strong ones? These are very good. Take them all!" he continued, forcing them on his guest.

He was evidently glad to have someone to boast to of the rare things he possessed, and he noticed nothing amiss. Serpukhovskoy lit his cigar and hastened to resume the conversation they had begun.

"So, how much did you pay for Atlasny?" he asked.

"He cost me a great deal, not less than five thousand, but at any rate I am already safe on him. What colts he gets, I tell you!"

"Do they trot?" asked Serpukhovskoy.

"They trot well! His colt took three prizes this year: in Tula, in Moscow, and in Petersburg; he raced Voekov's Raven. That rascal, the driver, let him make four false steps or he'd have left the other behind the flag."

"He's a bit green. Too much Dutch blood in him, that's what I say," remarked Serpukhovskoy.

"Well, but what about the mares? I'll show Goody to you tomorrow. I gave three thousand for her. For Amiable I gave two thousand."

And the host again began to enumerate his possessions. The hostess saw that this hurt Serpukhovskoy and that he was only pretending to listen. "Will you have some more tea?" she asked.

"I won't," replied the host and went on talking. She rose, the host stopped her, embraced her, and kissed her.

As he looked at them Serpukhovskoy for their sakes tried to force a smile, but after the host had got up, embraced her, and let her to the portiere, Serpukhovskoy's face suddenly changed. He sighed heavily, and a look of despair showed itself on his flabby face. Even malevolence appeared on it.

The host returned and smilingly sat down opposite him. They were silent awhile.

XI

"Yes, you were saying you bought him of Voekov," remarked Serpukhovskoy with assumed carelessness.

"Oh, yes, that was of Atlasny, you know. I always meant to buy some mares of Dubovitzki, but he had nothing but rubbish left."

"He has failed. . . ." said Serpukhovskoy, and suddenly stopped and glanced round. He remembered that he owed that bankrupt twenty thousand rubles, and if it came to talking of being bankrupt it was certainly said that he was one. He laughed.

Both again sat silent for a long time. The host considered what he could brag about to his guest. Serpukhovskoy was thinking what he could say to show that he did not consider himself bankrupt. But the minds of both worked with difficulty, in spite of efforts to brace themselves up with cigars.

"When are we going to have a drink?" thought Serpukhovskoy.

"I must certainly have a drink or I shall die of ennui with this fellow," thought the host.

"Will you be remaining here long?" Serpukhovskoy asked.

"Another month. Well, shall we have supper, eh? Fritz, is it ready?"

They went into the dining room. There under a hanging lamp stood a table on which were candles and all sorts of extraordinary things: syphons, and little dolls fastened to corks, rare wine in decanters, unusual hors-d'oeuvres, and vodka. They had a drink, ate a little, drank again, ate again, and their conversation got into swing. Serpukhovskoy was flushed and began to speak without timidity.

They spoke of women and of who kept this one or that, a gypsy, a ballet girl, or a Frenchwoman.

"And have you given up Mathieu?" asked the host. That was the woman who had ruined Serpukhovskoy.

"No, she left me. Ah, my dear fellow, when I recall what I have got through in my life. Now I am really glad when I have a thousand rubles, and am glad to get away from everybody. I can't stand it in Moscow. But what's the good of talking!"

The host found it tiresome to listen to Serpukhovskoy. He wanted to speak about himself—to brag. But Serpukhovskoy also wished to talk about himself, about his brilliant past. His host filled his glass for him and waited for him to stop, so that he might tell him about himself and how his stud was now arranged as no one had ever had a stud arranged before. And that Marie loved him with her heart and not merely for his wealth.

"I wanted to tell you that in my stud. . . ." he began, but Serpukhovskoy interrupted him.

"I may say that there was a time," Serpukhovskoy began, "when I liked to live well and knew how to do it. Now you talk about trotting—tell me which is your fastest horse."

The host, glad of an opportunity to tell more about his stud, was beginning, when Serpukhovskoy again interrupted him.

"Yes, yes," he said, "but you breeders do it just out of vanity and not for pleasure, not for the joy of life. It was different with me. You know I told you I had a driving horse, a piebald with just the same kind of spots as the one your keeper was riding. Oh, what a horse that was! You can't possibly know: it was in 1842, when I had just come to Moscow; I went to a horse dealer and there I saw a well-bred piebald gelding. I liked him. The price?

One thousand rubles. I liked him, so I took him and began to drive with him. I never had, and you have not and never will have, such a horse. I never knew one like him for speed and for strength. You were a boy then and couldn't have known, but you may have heard of him. All Moscow was talking about him."

"Yes, I heard of him"; the host unwillingly replied. "But what I wished to say about mine. . . ."

"Ah, then you did hear! I bought him just as he was, without pedigree and without a certificate; it was only afterwards that I got to know Voekov and found out. He was a colt by Affable I. Strider—because of his long strides. On account of his piebald spots he was removed from the Khrenova stud and given to the head keeper, who had him castrated and sold him to the horse dealer. There are no such horses now, my dear chap. Ah, those were the days! Ah, vanished youth!" And he sang the words of the gypsy song. He was getting tipsy. "Ah, those were the good times. I was twenty-five and had eighty thousand rubles a year, not a single grey hair, and all my teeth like pearls. . . . Whatever I touched succeeded, and now it is all ended . . . ."

"But there was not the same mettlesomeness then," said the host, availing himself of the pause.

"Let me tell you that my first horses began to trot without . . ."

"Your horses! But they used to be more mettlesome . . ."

"How—more mettlesome?"

"Yes, more mettlesome! I remember as if it were today how I drove him once to the trotting races in Moscow. No horse of mine was running. I did not care for trotters, mine were thoroughbreds: General Chaulet, Mahomet. I drove up with my piebald. My driver was a fine fellow, I was fond of him, but he also took to drink. . . . Well, so I got there."

"'Serpukhovskoy,' I was asked, 'When are you going to keep trotters?' 'The devil take your lubbers!' I replied. 'I have a piebald hack that can outpace all your trotters!' 'Oh no, he won't!' 'I'll bet a thousand rubles!' Agreed, and they started. He came in five seconds ahead and I won the thousand rubles. But what of it? I did a little over sixty-six miles in three hours with a troyka of thoroughbreds. All Moscow knows it."

And Serpukhovskoy began to brag so glibly and continuously that his host could not get a single word in and sat opposite him with a dejected countenance, filling up his own and his guest's glass every now and then by way of distraction.

The dawn was breaking and still they sat there. It became intolerably dull for the host. He got up.

"If we are to go to bed, let's go," said Serpukhovskoy rising, and reeling and puffing, he went to the room prepared for him.

The host was lying beside his mistress. "No, he is unendurable"; he said. "He gets drunk and swaggers incessantly."

"And he makes up to me."

"I'm afraid he'll be asking for money."

Serpukhovskoy was lying on the bed in his clothes, breathing heavily.

"I must have been lying a lot," he thought. "Well, no matter! The wine was good, but he is an awful swine. There's something cheap about him. And I'm an awful swine," he said to himself and laughed aloud. "First I used to keep women and now I'm kept. Yes, the Winkler girl will support me. I take money of her. Serves him right. Still, I must undress. Can't get my boots off. Hullo! Hullo!" he called out, but the man who had been told off to wait on him had long since gone to bed.

He sat down, took off his coat and waistcoat and somehow managed to kick off his trousers, but for a long time could not get his boots off—his soft stomach being in the way. He got one off at last, and struggled for a long time with the other, panting and becoming exhausted. And so with his foot in the boot-top he rolled over and began to snore, filling the room with a smell of tobacco, wine, and disagreeable old age.

XII

If Strider recalled anything that night, he was distracted by Vaska, who threw a rug over him, galloped off on him, and kept him standing till morning at the door of a tavern, near a peasant horse. They licked one another. In the morning when Strider returned to the herd he kept rubbing himself.

Five days passed. They called in a veterinary, who said cheerfully: "It's the itch; let me sell him to the gypsies."

"What's the use? Cut his throat, and get it done today."

The morning was calm and clear. The herd went to pasture, but Strider was left behind. A strange man came—thin, dark, and dirty, in a coat splashed with something black. It was the knacker. Without looking at Strider he took him by the halter they had put on him and led him away. Strider went quietly without looking round, dragging along as usual and catching his hind feet in the straw.

When they were out of the gate he strained towards the well, but the knacker jerked his halter, saying: "Not worth while."

The knacker and Vaska, who followed behind, went to a hollow behind the brick barn and stopped as if there were something peculiar about this very ordinary place. The knacker, handing the halter to Vaska, took off his coat, rolled up his sleeves, and produced a knife and a whetstone from his boot leg. The gelding stretched towards the halter meaning to chew it a little from dullness, but he could not reach it. He sighed and closed his eyes. His nether lip hung down, disclosing his worn yellow teeth, and he began to drowse to the sound of the sharpening of the knife. Only his swollen, aching, outstretched leg kept jerking. Suddenly he felt himself being taken by the lower jaw and his head lifted. He opened his eyes. There were two dogs in front of him; one was sniffing at the knacker, the other was sitting and watching the gelding as if expecting something from him. The gelding looked at them and began to rub his jaw against the arm that was holding him.

"Want to doctor me probably—well, let them!" he thought.

And in fact he felt that something had been done to his throat. It hurt, and he shuddered and gave a kick with one foot, but restrained himself and waited for what would follow. . . . Then he felt something liquid streaming down his neck and chest. He heaved a profound sigh and felt much better.

The whole burden of his life was eased.

He closed his eyes and began to droop his head.

No one was holding it. Then his legs quivered and his whole body swayed. He was not so much frightened as surprised.

Everything was so new to him. He was surprised and started forward and upward, but instead of this, in moving from the spot his legs got entangled, he began to fall sideways, and trying to take a step fell forward and down on his left side.

The knacker waited till the convulsions had ceased, drove away the dogs that had crept nearer, took the gelding by the legs, turned him on his back, told Vaska to hold a leg, and began to skin the horse.

"It was a horse, too," remarked Vaska.

"If he had been better fed, the skin would have been fine," said the knacker.

The herd returned downhill in the evening, and those on the left saw down below something red, round which dogs were busy and above which hawks and crows were flying. One of the dogs, pressing its paws against the carcass and swinging his head, with a crackling sound tore off what it had seized hold of. The chestnut filly stopped, stretched out her head and neck, and sniffed the air for a long time. They could hardly drive her away.

At dawn, in a ravine of the old forest, down in an overgrown glade, big-headed wolf cubs were howling joyfully. There were five of them: four almost alike and one with a head bigger than his body. A lean old wolf who was shedding her coat, dragging her full belly with its hanging dugs along the ground, came out of the bushes and sat down in front of the cubs. The cubs came and stood round her in a semicircle. She went to the smallest, and bending her knee and holding her muzzle down, made some convulsive movements, and opening her large sharp-toothed jaws disgorged a large piece of horseflesh. The bigger cubs rushed towards her, but she moved threateningly at them and let the little one have it all. The little one, growling as if in anger, pulled the horseflesh under him and began to gorge. In the same way the mother wolf coughed up a piece for the second, the third, and all five of them, and then lay down in front of them to rest.

A week later only a large skull and two shoulder blades lay behind the barn; the rest had all been taken away. In summer a peasant, collecting bones, carried away these shoulder blades and skull and put them to use.

The dead body of Serpukhovskoy, which had walked about the earth eating and drinking, was put under ground much later. Neither his skin, nor his flesh, nor his bones were of any use.

Just as for the last twenty years his body that had walked the earth had been a great burden to everybody, so the putting away of that body was again an additional trouble to people. He had not been wanted by anybody for a long time and had only been a burden, yet the dead who bury their dead found it necessary to clothe that swollen body, which at once began to decompose, in a good uniform and good boots and put it into a new and expensive coffin with tassels at its four corners, and then to place that coffin in another coffin of lead, to take it to Moscow and there dig up some long buried human bones, and to hide in that particular spot this decomposing maggoty body in its new uniform and polished boots, and cover it all up with earth.

16

Blue Murder

By Wilbur Daniel Steele

◇◇

We featured Wilbur Daniel Steele back in chapter 4. Now, in yet another of his great short stories, he show us how a horse story can also be a mystery story.

◇◇

AT MILL CROSSING IT WAS ALREADY PAST SUNSET. THE RAYS, REDDER for what autumn leaves were left, still laid fire along the woods crowning the stony slopes of Jim Bluedge's pastures; but then the line of the dusk began and from that level it filled the valley, washing with transparent blue the buildings scattered about the bridge, Jim's house and horse sheds and hay barns, Frank's store, and Camden's blacksmith shop.

The mill had been gone fifty years, but the falls which had turned its wheel still poured in the bottom of the valley, and when the wind came from the Footstool way their mist wet the smithy, built of the old stone on the old foundations, and their pouring drowned the clink of Camden's hammer.

Just now they couldn't drown Camden's hammer, for he wasn't in the smithy; he was at his brother's farm. Standing inside the smaller of the horse paddocks behind the sheds, he drove in stakes, one after another, cut green from saplings, and so disposed as to cover the more glaring of the weaknesses in the five foot fence. From time to time, when one was done and another to do, he rested the head of his sledge in the pocket of his leather apron (he was never without it; it was as though it had grown on him, lumpy with odds and ends of his trade-bolts and nails and rusty pliers and old horseshoes) and, standing so, he mopped the sweat from his face and looked up at the mountain.

Of the three brothers he was the dumb one. He seldom had anything to say. It was providential (folks said) that of the three enterprises at the Crossing one was a smithy; fix while he was a strong, big, hungry-muscled fellow, he never would have had the shrewdness to run the store or the farm. He was better at pounding-pounding while the fire reddened and the sparks flew, and thinking, and letting other people wonder what he was thinking of.

Blossom Bluedge, his brother's wife, sat perched on the top bar of the paddock gate, holding her skirts around her ankles with a trifle too much care to be quite unconscious, and watched him work. When he looked at the mountain he was looking at the mares, half a mile up the slope, grazing in a line as straight as soldiers, their heads all one way. But Blossom thought it was the receding light he was thinking of, and her own sense of misgiving returned and deepened.

"You'd have thought Jim would be home before this, wouldn't you, Cam?"

Her brother-in-law said nothing.

"Cam, look at me!"

It was nervousness, but it wasn't all nervousness—she was the prettiest girl in the valley; a small part of it was mingled coquetry and pique.

The smith began to drive another stake, swinging the hammer from high overhead, his muscles playing in fine big rhythmical convulsions under the skin of his arms and chest, covered with short blond down. Studying him cornerwise, Blossom muttered, "Well, don't look at me, then!"

He was too dumb for any use. He was as dumb as this: when all three of the Bluedge boys were after her a year ago, Frank, the storekeeper, had brought her candy; chocolates wrapped in silver foil in a two-pound Boston box. Jim had laid before her the Bluedge farm and with it the dominance of the valley. And Camden, to the daughter of Ed Beck, the apple grower, Camden brought a box of apples!—and been bewildered too, when, for all she could help it, she had had to clap a hand over her mouth and run into the house to have her giggle.

A little more than just bewildered, perhaps. Had she, or any of them, ever speculated about that? He had been dumb enough before; but that was when he started being as dumb as he was now.

Well, if he wanted to be dumb, let him be dumb. Pouting her pretty lips and arching her fine brows, she forgot the unimaginative fellow and turned to the ridge again. And now, seeing the sun was quite gone, all the day's vague worries and dreads—held off by this and that—could not be held off much longer. For weeks there had been so much talk, so much gossip and speculation and doubt.

"Camden," she reverted suddenly. "Tell me one thing. Did you hear—"

She stopped there. Some people were coming into the kitchen yard, dark forms in the growing darkness. Most of them lingered at the porch, sitting on the steps and lighting their pipes. The one that came out was Frank, the second of her brothers-in-law. She was glad. Frank wasn't like Camden; he would talk. Turning and taking care of her skirts, she gave him a bright and sisterly smile.

"Well, Frankie, what's the crowd?"

Far from avoiding the smile, as Camden's habit was, the storekeeper returned it with a brotherly wink for good measure. "Oh, they're tired of waiting down the road, so they come up here to see the grand arrival." He was something of a man of the world; in his calling he acquired a fine turn for skepticism. "Don't want to miss being on hand to see what flaws they can pick in Jim's five hundred dollars' worth of experiment."

"Frank, ain't you the least bit worried over Jim? So late?"

"Don't see why."

"All the same, I wish either you or Cam could've gone with him."

"Don't see why. Had all the men from Perry's stable there in Twinshead to help him get the animal off the freight, and he took an extra rope and the log-chain and the heavy wagon, so I guess no matter how wild and woolly the devil is he'll scarcely be climbing over the tailboard. Besides, them Western horses ain't such a big breed; even a stallion."

"All the same—(look the other way, Frankie)." Flipping her ankles over the rail, Blossom jumped down beside him.

"Listen, Frank, tell me something. Did you hear—did you hear the reason Jim's getting him cheap was because he killed a man out West there, what's-its-name, Wyoming?"

Frank was taking off his sleeve protectors, the pins in his mouth. It was Camden, at the bars, speaking in his sudden deep rough way: "Who the hell told you that?"

Frank got the pins out of his mouth. "I guess what it is, Blossie, what's mixed you up is his having that name 'Blue Murder.'"

"No sir! I got some sense and some ears. You don't go fooling me."

Frank laughed indulgently and struck her shoulder with a light hand. "Don't worry. Between two horsemen like Jim and Cam—"

"Don't Cam me! He's none of my horse. I told Jim once—" Breaking off, Camden hoisted his weight over the fence and stood outside, his feet spread and his hammer in both hands, an attitude that would have looked a little ludicrous had anyone been watching him.

Jim had arrived. With a clatter of hoofs and a rattle of wheels he was in the yard and come to a standstill, calling aloud as he threw the lines over the team, "Well, friends, here we are."

The curious began to edge around, closing a cautious circle. The dusk had deepened so that it was hard to make anything at any distance of Jim's "experiment" but a blurry silhouette anchored at the wagon's tail. The farmer put an end to it, crying from his eminence, "Now, now, clear out and don't worry him; give him some peace tonight, for Lord's sake! Git!" He jumped to the ground and began to whack his arms, chilled with driving, only to have them pinioned by Blossom's without warning.

"Oh, Jim, I'm so glad you come. I been so worried; gi' me a kiss!"

The farmer reddened, eyeing the cloud of witnesses. He felt awkward and wished she could have waited. "Get along, didn't I tell you fellows?" he cried with a trace of the Bluedge temper. "Go and wait in the kitchen then; I'll tell you all about everything soon's I come in. . . . Well now—wife—"

"What's the matter?" she laughed, an eye over her shoulder. "Nobody's looking that matters. I'm sure Frank don't mind. And as for Camden—"

Camden wasn't looking at them. Still standing with his hammer two-fisted and his legs spread, his chin down and his thoughts to himself (the dumb head) he was looking at Blue Murder, staring at that other dumb head, which, raised high on the motionless column of the stallion's neck, seemed hearkening with an exile's doubt to the new sounds of this new universe, testing with wide nostrils the taint in the wind of equine strangers, and studying with eyes accustomed to far horizons these dark pastures that went up in the air.

Whatever the smith's cogitations, presently he let the hammer down and said aloud, "So you're him, eh?"

Jim put Blossom aside, saying "Got supper ready? I'm hungry!" Excited by the act of kissing and the sense of witnesses to it, she fussed with her hair and started kitchenwards as he turned to his brothers.

"Well, what do you make of him?"

"Five hundred dollars," said Frank. "However, it's your money."

Camden was shorter. "Better put him in."

"All right; let them bars down while I and Frank lead him around."

"No thanks!" The storekeeper kept his hands in his pockets. "I just cleaned up, thanks. Cam's the boy for horses."

"He's none o' my horse!" Camden wet his lips, shook his shoulders, and scowled. "Be damned, no!" He never had the right words, and it made him mad. Hadn't he told Jim from the beginning that he washed his hands of this fool Agricultural College squandering, "and a man-killer to the bargain?"

"Unless"; Frank put in slyly, "unless Cam's scared."

"Oh, is Cam scared?"

"Scared?" And still to the brothers' enduring wonder, the big dense fellow would rise to that boyhood bait. "Scared? The hell I'm scared of any horse ever wore a shoe! Come on, I'll show you! I'll show you!"

"Well, be gentle with him, boys, he may be brittle." As Frank sauntered off around the shed he whistled the latest tune.

In the warmth and light of the kitchen he began to fool with his pretty sister-in-law, feigning princely impatience and growling with a wink at the assembled neighbors, "When do we eat?"

But she protested, "Land, I had everything ready since five, ain't I? And now if it ain't you it's them to wait for. I declare for men!"

At last one of the gossips got in a word.

"What you make of Jim's purchase, Frank?"

"Well, it's Jim's money, Darred. If I had the running of this farm—" Frank began drawing up chairs noisily, leaving it at that.

Darred persisted. "Don't look to me much like an animal for women and children to handle, not yet awhile."

"Cowboys han'les 'em, pa." That was Darred's ten-year-old, big-eyed.

Blossom put the kettle back, protesting, "Leave off, or you'll get me worried to death; all your talk. . . . I declare, where are those bad boys?"

Opening the door, she called into the dark, "Jim! Cam! Land's sake!"

Subdued by distance and the intervening sheds, she could hear them at their business—sounds, muffled and fragmentary, soft thunder of hoofs, snorts, puffings, and the short words of men in action: "Aw, leave him be in the paddock tonight." . . .

"With them mares there, you damn fool?" . . .

"Damn fool, eh? Try getting him in at that door and see who's the damn fool!" . . . "Come on, don't be so scared." . . . "Scared, eh? Scared?"

Why was it she always felt that curious tightening of all her powers of attention when Camden Bluedge spoke? Probably because he spoke so rarely, and then so roughly, as if his own thickness made him mad. Never mind.

"Last call for supper in the dining car, boys!" she called and closed the door. Turning back to the stove, she was about to replace the tea water for the third time when, straightening up, she said, "What's that?"

No one else had heard anything. They looked at one another.

"Frank, go—go see what—go tell the boys to come in."

Frank hesitated, feeling foolish, then went to the door.

Then everyone in the room was out of his chair.

There were three sounds. The first was human and incoherent. The second was incoherent, too, but it wasn't human. The third was a crash, a ripping and splintering of wood.

When they got to the paddock they found Camden crawling from beneath the wreckage of the fence where a gap was opened on the pasture side.

He must have received a blow on the head, for he seemed dazed. He didn't seem to know they were there. At a precarious balance—one hand at the back of his neck—he stood facing up the hill, gaping after the diminuendo of floundering hoofs, invisible above.

So seconds passed. Again the beast gave tongue, a high wild horning note, and on the black of the stony hill to the right of it a faint shower of sparks blew like fireflies where the herding mares wheeled. It seemed to awaken the dazed smith. He opened his mouth. "Almighty God!" Swinging, he flung his arms towards the shed. "There! There!"

At least someone brought a lantern. They found Jim Bluedge lying on his back in the corner of the paddock near the door to the shed. In the lantern light, and still better in the kitchen when they had carried him in, they read the record of the thing which Camden, dumb in good earnest now, seemed unable to tell them with anything but his strange unfocused stare.

The bloody offense to the skull would have been enough to kill the man, but it was the second, full on the chest above the heart, that told the tale. On the caved grating of the ribs, already turning blue under the yellowish down, the iron shoe had left its mark; and when, laying back the rag of shirt, they saw that the toe of the shoe was upward and the cutting calkends down, they knew all they wanted to know of that swift, black, crushing episode.

No outlash of heels in fright. Here was a forefoot. An attack aimed and frontal; an onslaught reared, erect; beast turned biped; red eyes mad to white eyes aghast.... And only afterward, when it was done, the blood-fright that serves the horse for conscience; the blind rush down the enclosure; the fence gone down....

No one had much to say. No one seemed to know what to do.

As for Camden, he was no help. He simply stood propped on top of his logs of legs where someone had left him. From the instant when with his "Almighty God!" he had been brought back to memory, instead of easing its hold as the minutes passed, the event to which he remained the only living human witness seemed minute by minute to tighten its grip. It set its sweat-beaded stamp on his face, distorted his eyes, and tied his tongue. He was no good to anyone.

As for Blossom, even now—perhaps more than ever now—her dependence on physical touch was the thing that ruled her. Down on her knees beside the lamp they had set on the floor, she plucked at one of the dead man's shoes monotonously, and as it were, idly, swaying the toe like an inverted pendulum from side to side. That was all. Not a word. And when Frank, the only one of the three with any sense, got her up finally and led her away to her room, she clung to him.

It was lucky that Frank was a man of affairs. His brother was dead, and frightfully dead, but there was tomorrow for grief. Just now there were many things to do. There were people to be gotten rid of. With short words and angry gestures he cleared them out, all but Darred and a man named White, and to these he said, "Now first thing, Jim can't stay here." He ran and got a blanket from a closet. "Give me a hand and we'll lay him in the ice house overnight. Don't sound so good, but it's best, poor fellow. Cam, come along!"

He waited a moment, and as he studied the wooden fool the blood poured back into his face. "Wake up, Cam! You great big scared stiff, you!"

Camden brought his eyes out of nothingness and looked at his brother. A twinge passed over his face, convulsing the mouth muscles. "Scared?"

"Yes, you're scared!" Frank's lip lifted, showing the tips of his teeth. "And I'll warrant you something; if you wasn't the scared stiff you was, this hellish damn thing wouldn't have happened, maybe. Scared! You a blacksmith! Scared of a horse!"

"Horse!" Again that convulsion of the mouth muscles, something between irony and an idiot craft. "Why don't you go catch 'im?"

"Hush it! Don't waste time by going loony now, for God's sake. Come!"

"My advice to anybody—" Camden looked crazier than ever, knotting his brows—"My advice to anybody is to let somebody else go catch that—that—" Opening the door, he faced out into the night, his head sunk between his shoulders and the fingers working at the ends of his hanging arms; and before they knew it he began to swear. They could hardly hear because his teeth were locked and his breath soft. There were all the vile words he had ever heard in his life, curses and threats and abominations, vindictive, violent, obscene. He stopped only when at a sharp word from Frank he was made aware that Blossom had come back into the room.

Even then he didn't seem to comprehend her return but stood blinking at her, and at the rifle she carried, with his distraught bloodshot eyes.

Frank comprehended. Hysteria had followed the girl's blankness. Stepping between her and the body on the floor, he spoke in a persuasive, unhurried way. "What are you doing with that gun, Blossie? Now, now, you don't want that gun, you know you don't."

It worked. Her rigidity lessened appreciably. Confusion gained.

"Well, but—oh, Frank—well but, when we going to shoot him?"

"Yes, yes, Blossie—now, yes—only you best give me that gun, that's the girlie."

When he had got the weapon he put an arm around her shoulders. "Yes, yes 'course we're going to shoot him; what you think? Don't want an animal like that running round. Now first thing in the morning—"

Hysteria returned. With its strength she resisted his leading.

"No, now! Now!"

"He's gone and killed Jim! Killed my husband! I won't have him left alive another minute! I won't! Now! No sir, I'm going myself, I am! Frank, I am! Cam!"

At his name, appealed to in that queer screeching way, the man in the doorway shivered all over, wet his lips, and walked out into the dark.

"There, you see?" Frank was quick to capitalize on anything. "Cam's gone to do it. Cam's gone, Blossie! . . . Here, one of you—Darred, take this gun and run, give it to Camden, that's the boy."

"You sure he'll kill him, Frank? You sure?"

"Sure as daylight. Now you come along back to your room like a good girl and get some rest. Come, I'll go with you."

When Frank returned to the kitchen ten minutes later, Darred was back.

"Well, now, let's get at it and carry out poor Jim; he can't lay here. . . . Where's Cam gone now, damn him!"

"Cam? Why, he's gone and went."

"Went where?"

"Up the pasture, like you said."

"Like I—" Frank went an odd color. He walked to the door. Between the light on the sill and the beginnings of the stars where the woods crowned the mountain was all one blackness. One stillness too. He turned on Darred. "But look, you never gave him that gun, even."

"He didn't want it."

"Lord's sake. What did he say?"

"Said nothing. He'd got the log-chain out of the wagon and when I caught him he was up hunting his hammer in under that wreck at the fence. Once he found it he started off up. 'Cam,' says I, 'here's a gun, want it?' He seem not to. Just when on walking up."

"How'd he look?"

"Look same's you seen him looking. Sick."

"The damned fool!" . . .

Poor dead Jim! Poor fool Camden! As the storekeeper went about his business, and afterwards when, the ice-house door closed on its tragic tenant and White and Darred gone off home, he roamed the yard, driven here and there, soft-footed, waiting, hearkening—his mind was for a time not on his own property but the plaything of thoughts diverse and wayward. Jim. His brother, so suddenly and so violently gone. The stallion. That beast that had kicked him to death. With anger and hate and pitiless impatience of time he thought of the morrow, when they would catch him and take their revenge with guns and clubs. Behind these speculations, covering the background of his consciousness and stringing his nerves to endless vigil, spread the wall of the mountain; silent from instant to instant but devising under its black silence (who could know what instant to come) a neigh, a yell, a spark-line of iron hoofs on rolling flints, a groan. And still behind that and deeper into the borders of the unconscious, the storekeeper thought of the farm that had lost its master, the rich bottoms, the broad, well-stocked pastures, the fat barns, and the comfortable house whose chimneys and gable ends fell into changing shapes of perspective against the stars as he wandered here and there. . . .

Jim gone . . . and Camden, at any moment. . . .

His face grew hot. An impulse carried him a dozen steps. "I ought to go up. Ought to take the gun and go up." But there shrewd sanity put on the brakes. "Where's the use? Couldn't find him in the dark. Besides I oughtn't to leave Blossom here alone."

With that he went around towards the kitchen, thinking to go in. But the sight of the lantern, left burning out near the sheds, sent his ideas off on another course. At any rate it would give his muscles and nerves something to work on. Taking the lantern and entering the paddock, he fell to patching the gap into the pasture, using broken boards from the wreck. As he worked his eyes chanced to fall on footprints in the dung-mixed earth—Camden's footprints, leading away beyond the little ring of light. And beside them, taking off from the landing place of that prodigious leap, he discerned the trail of the stallion. After a moment he got down on his knees where the earth was softest, holding the lantern so that its light fell full.

He gave over his fence building. Returning to the house his gait was no longer that of the roamer; his face, caught by the periodic flare of the swinging lantern, was the face of another man. In its expression there was a kind of fright and a kind of calculating eagerness. He looked at the dock on the kitchen shelf, shook it, and read it again. He went to the telephone and tumbled at the receiver. He waited till his hand quit shaking, then removed it from the hook.

"Listen, Darred," he said when he had got the farmer at last, "get White and whatever others you can and come over first thing it's light. Come a-riding and bring your guns. No, Cam ain't back."

He heard Blossom calling. Outside her door he passed one hand down over his face, as he might have passed a wash rag to wipe off what was there. Then he went in.

"What's the matter, Blossie? Can't sleep?"

"No, I can't sleep. Can't think. Can't sleep. Oh, Frankie!"

He sat down beside the bed.

"Oh, Frankie, Frankie, hold my hand!"

She looked almost homely, her face bleached out and her hair a mess on the pillow. But she would get over that. And the short sleeve of the nightgown on the arm he held was edged with pretty lace.

"Got your watch here?" he asked. She gave it to him from under the pillow. This too he shook as if he couldn't believe it was going.

Pretty Blossom Beck. Here for a wonder he sat in her bedroom and held her hand. One brother was dead and the other was on the mountain.

But little by little, as he sat and dreamed so, nightmare crept over his brain. He had to arouse and shake himself. He had to set his thoughts resolutely in other roads. . . . Perhaps there would be even the smithy. The smithy, the store, the farm. Complete. The farm, the farmhouse, the room in the farmhouse, the bed in the room, the wife in the bed. Complete beyond belief. If. . . . Worth dodging horror for. If . . .

"Frank, has Cam come back?"

"Cam? Don't worry about Cam. Where's that watch again?"

Far from rounding up their quarry in the early hours after dawn, it took the riders, five of them, till almost noon simply to make certain that he wasn't to be found—not in any of the pastures. Then when they discovered the hole in the fence far up in the woods beyond the crest where Blue Murder had led the mares in a break for the open country of hills and ravines to the south, they were only beginning.

The farmers had left their work undone at home and, as the afternoon lengthened and with it the shadows in the hollow places, they began to eye one another behind their leader's back. Yet they couldn't say it; there was something in the storekeeper's air today, something zealous and pitiless and fanatical, that shut them up and pulled them plodding on.

Frank did the trailing. Hopeless of getting anywhere before sundown in that unkempt wilderness of a hundred square miles of scrub, his companions slouched in their saddles and rode more and more mechanically, knee to knee, and it was he who made the casts to recover the lost trail and, dismounting to read the dust, cried back, "He's still with 'em," and with gestures of imperious excitement beckoned them on.

"Which you mean?" Darred asked him once. "Cam or the horse?"

Frank wheeled his beast and spurred back at the speaker. It was extraordinary. "You don't know what you're talking about!" he cried, with a causelessness and a disordered vehemence that set them first staring, then speculating. "Come on, you dumb heads; don't talk—ride!"

By the following day, when it was being told in all the farmhouses, the story might vary in details and more and more as the tellings multiplied, but in its fundamentals it remained the same. In one thing they certainly all agreed: they used the same expression—"It was like Frank was drove. Drove in a race against something, and not sparing the whip."

They were a good six miles to the south of the fence. Already the road back home would have to be followed three parts in the dark.

Darred was the spokesman. "Frank, I'm going to call it a day."

The others reined up with him but the man ahead rode on. He didn't seem to hear. Darred lifted his voice. "Come on, call it a day, Frank. Tomorrow, maybe. But you see we've run it out and they're not here."

"Wait," said Frank. over his shoulder, still riding on into the pocket.

White's mount, a mare, laid back her ears, shied, and stood trembling. After a moment she whinnied.

It was as if she had whinnied for a dozen. A crashing in the woods above them to the left and the avalanche came—down streaming, erupting, wheeling, wheeling away with volleying snorts, a dark rout.

Darred, reining his horse, began to shout, "Here they go this way, Frank!" But Frank was yelling, "Up here, boys! This way, quick!"

It was the same note, excited, feverish, disordered, breaking like a child's. When they neared him they saw he was off his horse, rifle in hand, and down on his knees to study the ground where the woods began. By the time they reached his animal the impetuous fellow had started up into the cover, his voice trailing, "Come on, spread out and come on!"

One of the farmers got down. When he saw the other three keeping their saddles he swung up again.

White spoke this time. "Be darned if I do!" He lifted a protesting hail. "Come back here Frank! You're crazy! It's getting dark!"

It was Frank's own fault. They told him plainly to come back and he wouldn't listen.

For a while they could hear his crackle in the mounting underbrush. Then that stopped, whether he had gone too far for their ears or whether he had come to a halt to give his own ears a chance. . . . Once, off to the right, a little higher up under the low ceiling of the trees that darkened moment by moment with the rush of night, they heard another movement, another restlessness of leaves and stones. Then that was still, and everything was still.

Darred ran a sleeve over his face and swung down. "God alive, boys!"

It was the silence. All agreed there—the silence and the deepening dusk.

The first they heard was the shot. No voice. Just the one report. Then after five breaths of another silence a crashing of growth, a charge in the darkness under the withered scrub, continuous and diminishing.

They shouted "Frank!" No answer. They called, "Frank Bluedge!"

Now, since they had to, they did. Keeping contact by word, and guided partly by directional memory (and mostly in the end by luck), after a time they found the storekeeper in a brake of ferns, lying across his gun.

They got him down to the open, watching behind them all the while. Only then, by the flares of successive matches, under the noses of the snorting horses, did they look for the damage done.

They remembered the stillness and the gloom; it must have been quite black in there. The attack had come from behind—equine and pantherine at once, and planned and cunning. A deliberate lunge with a forefoot again; the shoe which had crushed the backbone between the shoulder blades was a fore shoe; that much they saw by the match flares in the red wreck.

They took no longer getting home than they had to, but it was longer than they wished. With Frank across his own saddle, walking their horses and with one or another ahead to pick the road (it was going to rain, and even the stars were lost), they made no more than a creeping speed.

None of them had much to say on the journey. Finding the break in the boundary fence and feeling through the last of the woods, the lights of their farms began to show in the pool of blackness below, and Darred uttered a part of what had lain in their minds during the return.

"Well, that leaves Cam."

None followed it up. None cared to go any closer than he was to the real question. Something new, alien, menacing and pitiless had come into the valley of their lives with that beast they had never really seen; they felt its oppression, every one, and kept the real question back in their minds: "Does it leave Cam?"

It answered itself. Camden was at home when they got there.

He had come in a little before them, empty-handed.

Empty-headed, too. When Blossom, who had waited all day, part of the time with neighbor women who had come in and part of the time alone to the point of going mad—when she saw him coming down the pasture, his feet stumbling and his shoulders dejected, her first feeling was relief. Her first words, however, were "Did you get him, Cam?" And all he would answer was, "Gi' me something to eat, can't you? Gi' me a few hours' sleep, can't you? Then wait!"

He looked as if he would need more than a few hours' sleep. Propped on his elbows over his plate, it seemed as though his eyes would close before his mouth would open.

His skin was scored by thorns and his shirt was in ribbons under the straps of his iron-sagged apron, but it was not by these marks that his twenty-odd hours showed; it was by his face. While yet his eyes were open and his wits still half awake, his face surrendered. The flesh relaxed into lines of stupor, a putty-formed, putty-colored mask of sleep.

Once he let himself be aroused. This was when, to an abstracted query as to Frank's whereabouts, Blossom told him Frank had been out with four others since dawn. He heaved clear of the table and opened his eyes at her, showing the red around the rims.

He spoke with the thick tongue of the drunkard. "If anybody but me lays hand on that stallion, I'll kill him. I'll wring his neck."

Then he relapsed into his stupidity, and not even the arrival of the party bringing his brother's body home seemed able to shake him so far clear of it again.

At first, when they had laid Frank on the floor where on the night before they had laid Jim, he seemed hardly to comprehend.

"What's wrong with Frank?"

"Some more of Jim's 'experiment.'"

"Frank see him? He's scared, Frank is. Look at his face there."

"He's dead, Cam."

"Dead, you say? Frank dead? Dead of fright; is that it?"

Even when, rolling the body over they showed him what was what, he appeared incapable of comprehension, of amazement, of passion, or of any added grief. He looked at them all with a kind of befuddled protest.

Returning to his chair and his plate, he grumbled, "Le' me eat first, can't you? Can't you gi' me a little time to sleep?"

"Well, you wouldn't do much tonight anyway, I guess."

At White's words Blossom opened her mouth for the first time.

"No, nothing tonight, Cam. Cam! Camden! Say! Promise!"

"And then tomorrow, Cam, what we'll do is get every last man in the valley, and we'll go at this right. We'll lay hand on that devil—"

Camden swallowed his mouthful of cold steak with difficulty. His obsession touched, he showed them the rims of his eyes again.

"You do and I'll wring your necks. The man that touches that animal before I do gets his neck wrang. That's all you need to remember."

"Yes, yes—no—that is—" Poor Blossom. "Yes, Mr. White, thanks; no, Cam's not going out tonight. . . . No, Cam, nobody's going to interfere—nor nothing. Don't you worry there. . . ."

Again poor Blossom! Disaster piled too swiftly on disaster; no discipline but instinct left. Caught in fire and flood and earthquake and not knowing what to come, and no creed but "save him who can!"—by hook or crook of wile or smile. With the valley of her life emptied out, and its emptiness repeopled monstrously and pressing down black on the roof under which (now that Frank was gone to the ice house too and the farmers back home) one brother was left of three—she would tread softly, she would talk or she would be dumb, as her sidelong glimpses of the awake-asleep man's face above the table told her was the instant's need; or if he would eat, she would magic out of nothing something, anything, or if he would sleep, he could sleep, so long as he slept in that house where she could know he was sleeping.

Only one thing. If she could touch him. If she could touch and cling.

Lightning filled the windows. After a moment the thunder came avalanching down the pasture and brought up against the clapboards of the house. At this she was behind his chair. She put out a hand. She touched his shoulder. The shoulder was bare, the shirt ripped away; it was caked with sweat and with the blackening smears of scratches, but for all its exhaustion it was flesh alive—a living man to touch.

Camden blundered up. "What the hell!" He started off two steps and wheeled on her. "Why don't you get off to bed for Goll sake!"

"Yes, Cam, yes—right off, yes."

"Well, I'm going, I can tell you. For Goll sake, I need some sleep!"

"Yes, that's right, yes, Cam, good night, Cam—only—only you promise—promise you won't go out—nowheres."

"Go out? Not likely I won't! Not likely! Get along."

It took her no time to get going then—quick and quiet as a mouse.

Camden lingered to stand at one of the windows where the lightning came again, throwing the black barns and paddocks at him from the white sweep of the pastures crowned by woods.

As it had taken her no time to go, it took Blossom no time to undress and get in bed. When Camden was on his way to his room he heard her calling, "Cam! Just a second, Cam!"

In the dark outside her door he drew one hand down over his face, wiping off whatever might be there. Then he entered.

"Yes? What?"

"Cam, set by me a minute, won't you? And Cam, oh Cam, hold my hand."

As he slouched down, his fist enclosing her fingers, thoughts awakened and ran and fastened on things. They fastened, tentatively at first, upon the farm. Jim gone. Frank gone. The smithy, the store, and the farm. The whole of Mill Crossing. The trinity. The three in one. . . .

"Tight, Cam, for pity's sake! Hold it tight!"

His eyes, falling to his fist, strayed up along the arm it held. The sleeve, rumpled near the shoulder, was trimmed with pretty lace. . . .

"Tighter, Cam!"

A box of apples. That memory hidden away in the cellar of his mind. Hidden away, clamped down in the dark, till the noxious vapors, the murderous vapors of its rotting had filled the shut-up house he was. . . . A box of red apples for the apple grower's girl. . . . the girl who sniggered and ran away from him to laugh at him. . . .

And here, by the unfolding of a devious destiny, he sat in that girl's bedroom, holding that girl's hand. Jim who had got her, Frank who had wanted her, lay side by side out there in the ice house under the lightning. While he, the "dumb one"—the last to be thought of with anything but amusement and the last to be feared—his big hot fist enclosing her

imprecating hand now, and his eyes on the pretty lace at her shoulder—
He jumped up with a gulp and a clatter of iron.

"What the—" He flung her hand away. "What the—hell!" He swallowed. "Damn you, Blossie Beck!" He stared at her with repugnance and mortal fright. "Why, you—you-you—"

He moderated his voice with an effort, wiping his brow. "Good night. You must excuse me, Blossie. I wasn't meaning—I mean—I hope you sleep good. I shall. Good night!"

In his own brain was the one word "Hurry!"

She lay and listened to his boots going along the hall and heard the closing of his door. She ought to have put out the lamp. But even with the shades drawn, the lightning around the edges of the window unnerved her; in the dark alone it would have been more than she could bear.

She lay so still she felt herself nearing exhaustion from the sustained rigidity of her limbs. Rain came and with the rain, wind. Around the eaves it neighed like wild stallions; down the chimneys it moaned like men.

Slipping out of bed and pulling on a bathrobe she ran from her room, barefooted, and along the hall to Camden's door.

"Cam!" she called. "Oh, Cam!" she begged. "Please, please!"

And now he wouldn't answer her.

New lightning, diffused through all the sky by the blown rain, ran at her along the corridor. She pushed the door open. The lamp was burning on the bureau but the room was empty and the bed untouched.

Taking the lamp she skittered down to the kitchen. No one was there. . . .

"Hurry!"

Camden had reached the woods when the rain came. Lighting the lantern he had brought, he made his way on to the boundary fence. There, about a mile to the east of the path the others had taken that day, he pulled the rails down and tumbled the stones together in a pile. Then he proceeded another hundred yards, holding the lantern high and peering through the streaming crystals of the rain.

Blue Murder was there. Neither the chain nor the sapling had given way. The lantern and, better than the lantern, a globe of lightning, showed the tethered stallion glistening and quivering, his eyes all whites at the man's approach.

"Gentle, boy; steady, boy!" Talking all the while in the way he had with horses, Camden put a hand on the taut chain and bore with a gradually progressive weight, bringing the dark head nearer. "Steady, boy, gentle there, damn you; gentle!"

Was he afraid of horses? Who said he was afraid of horses?

The beast's head was against the man's chest, held there by an arm thrown over the bowed neck. As he smoothed the forehead and fingered the nose with false caresses, Camden's "horse talk" ran on—the cadence one thing, the words another.

"Steady, Goll damn you; you're going to get yours. Cheer up, cheer up, the worst is yet to come. Come now! Come easy! Come along!"

When he had unloosed the chain, he felt for and found with his free hand his hammer hidden behind the tree. Throwing the lantern into the brush where it flared for an instant before dying, he led the stallion back as far as the break he had made in the fence. Taking a turn with the chain around the animal's nose, like an improvised hackamore, he swung from the stone pile to the slippery back. A moment's shying, a sliding caracole of amazement and distrust, a crushing of knees, a lash of the chain end, and that was all there was to that. Blue Murder had been ridden before. . . .

In the smithy, chambered in the roaring of the falls and the swish and shock of the storm, Camden sang as he pumped his bellows, filling the cave beneath the rafters with red. The air was nothing, the words were mumbo-jumbo, but they swelled his chest. His eyes, cast from time to time at his wheeling prisoner had lost their look of helplessness and surly distraction.

Scared? He? No, no, no! Now that he wasn't any longer afraid of time, he wasn't afraid of anything on earth.

"Shy, you devil!" He wagged his exalted head.

"Whicker, you hellion! Whicker all you want to, stud horse! Tomorrow they're going to get you, the numb fools! Tomorrow they can have you. I got you tonight!"

He was more than other men; he was enormous.

Fishing an iron shoe from that inseparable apron pocket of his, he thrust it into the coals and blew and blew. He tried it and it was burning red. He tried it again and it was searing white. Taking it out on the anvil he began to beat it, swinging his hammer one-handed, gigantic. So in the crimson light, irradiating iron sparks, he was at his greatest. Pounding, pounding. A man in the dark of night with a hammer about him can do wonders; with a horseshoe about him he can cover up a sin. And if the dark of night in a paddock won't hold it, then the dark of undergrowth on a mountainside will. . . .

Pounding, pounding; thinking, thinking in a great halo of hot stars. Feeding his hungry, his insatiable muscles.

"Steady, now, you blue bastard! Steady, boy!"

What he did not realize in his feverish exhaustion was that his muscles were not insatiable. In the thirty-odd hours past they had had a feast spread before them and they had had their fill. . . . More than their fill.

As with the scorching iron in his tongs he approached the stallion, he had to step over the nail box he had stepped over five thousand times in the routine of every day.

A box of apples, eh? Apples to snigger at, eh? But whose girl are you now? . . . Scared, eh?

His foot was heavier of a sudden than it should have been. This five thousand and first time, by the drag of the tenth of an inch, the heel caught the lip of the nail box.

He tried to save himself from stumbling. At the same time, instinctively, he held the iron flame in his tongs away.

There was a scream out of a horse's throat; a whiff of hair and burnt flesh.

There was a lash of something in the red shadows. There was another sound and another wisp of stench. . . .

When, guided by the stallion's whinnying, they found the smith next day, they saw by the cant of his head that his neck was broken, and they perceived that he too had on him the mark of a shoe. It lay up on one side of his throat and the broad of a cheek.

It wasn't blue, this time, however—it was red. It took them some instants in the sunshine pouring through the wide door to comprehend this phenomenon.

It wasn't sunk in by a blow this time; it was burned in, a brand.

Darred called them to look at the stallion, chained behind the forge.

"Almighty God!" The words sounded funny in his mouth. They sounded the funnier in that they were the same ones the blundering smithy had uttered when, staring uphill from his clever wreckage of the paddock fence, he had seen the mares striking sparks from the stones where the stallion struck none. And he, of all men, a smith!

"Almighty God!" called Darred. "What do you make of these here feet?"

One fore hoof was freshly pared for shoeing; the other three hoofs were as virgin as any yearling's on the plains. Blue Murder had never yet been shod. . . .

17

The Horse of Hurricane Reef

By Charles Tenney Jackson

◇◇◇

The title of this tale promises an adventure narrative, and Charles Tenney Jackson delivers exactly that.

◇◇◇

"THE MARES ARE FOR WHOEVER IS MAN ENOUGH TO TAKE THEM," retorted Jean Abadie from the bow of the barge which the towing launch was shoving into the mud shoal on the bay side of Ile Dautrive. "Rojas has given them up. The white stallion killed his son, Emile, four years ago. No man of the camps around here will land on this reef; he has a name, that wild white devil!"

"You see, M'sieu Lalande, it is not stealing"; added Pierre as he stopped the motor and looked at the stranger in the stern seat.

"It is stealing," grunted Joe Lalande, "else why do we come under cover of storm to rope the colts and mares? Well, no matter. Once we get them aboard and up to the Mississippi plantations, I will show you something, you shrimp-seine Cajuns. Throwing a rope, eh? Over westward they never yet showed me a horse I could not break."

The two seine-haulers from Sanchez's platform looked at him doubtfully. "Over westward," to the men of Barataria Bay, began at the dim marsh shore and stretched to infinity. A native never ventured so far; out there anything might be possible. But no man had faced the exiled king of Dautrive reef. Pierre muttered again how they would get the young mares—they would first shoot the white stallion. It was the hurricane month; they knew well enough that an obliterating sea would come this

230

week over the dunes and marshes. Old Rojas, living with his grandchildren, orphaned by the white brute's savagery, on the far west point of the island, would never know what happened to the five mares and colts. More than once the gale off the Gulf had left the shell-beached *chenaies* far up the bay strewn with the dead cattle of the people of the reefs.

The big Lalande laughed as he followed through the salt grass to the first low dunes. "Shoot him! You'll shoot no horse with me! You say he's so bad; show him to me! I'll rope and load him, too, my friends, or he will finish me. If we lift Rojas's animals we take 'em all."

The Cajuns laughed in nervous disbelief. Lalande, a native also, who had returned this season to haul seine in Sanchez's company, might have been a great man with the pitching broncos he told of, but Rojas's great white stallion—well, this boaster would see! The brute would allow no seine crew to land on the Ile Dautrive; they told of his charging upon the fishing skiffs clear out to the surf line. Sanchez, the boss, had shot him once as he fled to his lugger, leaving the bleeding stallion to rend and trample an abandoned seine.

Grand-père Rojas, in his camp across the shoal depression that cut through the reef, had never tried to reclaim the wild mares and the colts of the white stud's breed. The generations of them lived on the coarse reef grass and the rain pools; an oysterman had no use for horses, anyhow. His son, Emile, had tried this foolish experiment of raising horses on the reef, and given his life under the stallion's hoofs. *Grand-père* had shrugged and let the breed go wild; yet, as Lalande muttered when Jean and Pierre proposed to use his skill in lifting the younger animals, the horses were his to the scrawniest colt. But Lalande had come. He would show the shrimpers; and even if they only roped and dragged the least unruly one to the barge, Lalande could break them and Pierre sell them on the plantations. Yet it was horse stealing. Lalande would not gloss that over, but something else had drawn him here—the stories the islanders told of the white stallion's savagery.

"Old Rojas's son, I will be the avenger," he grunted, sullenly, and came on the day Pierre had chosen for the secret raid.

Abadie had stopped on the sandy trail broken through the mangroves to the top of the sand ridge. "Bon Dieu!" he whispered, pointing. "His track, Lalande! Big as a bucket! Eh bien! I'd rather face a hurricane than this white tiger!"

Lalande had stepped out in the open sand patch. From here the dunes fell sway to the Gulf beach. Already the sea was rising. Between Dautrive and the outer bar curious, oily currents were twisting in unwonted directions, and beyond them the surf broke in white, serried teeth gleaming against the black southeast. The sky was ribboned in black lines streaming northerly; the wind came in fitful smashes against the mangrove thickets and then seemed sucked up to howl in the writhing clouds.

"There'll have to be quick work," muttered Pierre. "I tell you this is bad, this sea. We waited too long, M'sieu Lalande. We better be back across the bay, and try for the colts another time."

Lalande's gray eyes narrowed surlily. He straightened his powerful figure above the wind-slanting bushes. The two other raiders had crept back through the brush. It was disconcerting to find the animals crossing their trail behind. "If he smells a man he will never let up on us, Lalande," muttered Jean. "Kill him, then!"

The white leader had crossed the trail of the raiders. He turned, broke through the brush, and gained the ridge forty yards from them. Lalande could see him now against the black skyline very plainly. A tremendous brute towering above the others, his shaggy mane flowing backward in the wind, his muzzle outstretched, his neck tensed until the powerful muscles bulged the satin skin. He was suspicious; he stood there, a challenging figure to the storm, but his eyes were roving watchfully into the thickets as a tiger scenting prey.

Lalande glanced back. His comrades had slunk below the mangroves. They were brave, hardy men of the hurricane coast, but the evil name of the sea horse of Ile Dautrive seemed to hold them nerveless. The horse was coming on along the top of the ridge, slowly crashing through the brush with alert glances right and left. His pink nostrils quivered, his iron-gray tail raised and swept in the wind puffs.

"They will shoot," muttered Lalande. "If he trails them the cowards will shoot." And he stepped more in the open, and then shouted, "Come, thieves, let the colts go! I will need you on the throw-line to check and choke this brute!" Breast-high in the windswept thickets, he was laughing and coiling his rope. This was a foe for a strong man who boasted!

The great horse suddenly upreared with a neigh that was like the roar of a lion. No man had so much as ever put a finger on him; he had beaten the brains from one, broken the leg of another, and smashed two seine skiffs in the shallows for invaders. He had been the lord of the reef. Now he reared again and again as he plunged through the mangroves watching for the fugitives as a cat would a mouse under a flimsy cover of straw.

His satiny flanks were toward Lalande; apparently he had not yet discovered the man behind him in this hunt for the others. And then, out of pure panic as the white stallion broke near him, Jean Abadie fired. Lalande cursed and sprang down the slope of dunes after him. He knew he would need their help when he roped this horse; it was no starveling cayuse of the Texas range. But he saw now that the two islanders were skulking for the boat in the last fringe of the mangroves. They would never make it; out in the open the white stallion would crush them both ere they covered half the marsh grass, unless, indeed, they killed him.

The brute saw them now; he swerved in a tremendous rush below the man on the higher sand. Lalande was whirling his rope, and when he heard the hiss of it through the air he laughed, for he knew the throw was true.

"*Eh, bien*, devil! You and me!" He went down sprawling, seeking a root of the tough mangroves to snub the line. He caught one, then it was jerked out; and he went trundling and rolling over and over through the sands hanging to the lariat. He might as well have roped a torpedo. The horse was in the open now rearing and bucking, but with his savage eyes still on the fugitives. They were floundering through the water. Jean was jerking the mooring lines from the barge, and Pierre poling the launch back from the swamp grass. The stallion was surging on with the line cutting deep in his neck, but they could not see this in the welter of spray he threw in his charge.

Joe Lalande was on his back in the high grass, bruised and dizzy from his ride on the throw-rope. It was lying out taut through the grass; and for a time the man did not stir. The stallion was plunging somewhere out there, still implacable with fury to get at the shrimpers. Then, Lalande heard the first throb of the motor. They were getting away, leaving him, then? They must think him killed—a good end for a braggart who would rather fight the stud than steal the mares!

He lay in the grass listening, without even resentment. The wide reach of the bay northward was flecked with white surges rising between those curious, oily bulges of water, the first stir of the creeping tides which come upon the Gulf shores before the hurricane winds. Lalande remembered enough of his boyhood among the island folk to know that. Pierre was right; they had waited too long for this week of storm to raid Rojas's wild horses.

He crept around on the jerking line. Above the grass billows he saw the brute. He was whirling madly in the shallows fighting this strange, choking clutch on his neck. Then he charged back up the dunes, and Lalande barely had time to lie out on the end ere he was dragged again. But when the stallion plunged into the thickets, no human strength could hold. He felt his fingers breaking in the tangle of rope and roots, his face ground into the sand and pounded by showers of sand from the brute's hoofs.

Lalande staggered to his feet presently, cleared his eyes, and followed a crashing trail over the sand ridge. Northward he saw the launch rocking its way across the pass with whiplike streamers of wind hitting the water beyond. Everywhere the coast folk would be debating whether to quit their platform camps and take to the luggers or trust to the oaks of the *chenaies* and their moorings. The hurricane month, and a sea coming up past Cuba! Île Derniere had vanished under the waves; La Caminada gone with six hundred souls; these were traditions of the coast, but the natives knew what a hurricane tide meant on the low, loose sand islands that fringed the Louisiana swamps.

Lalande paused on the highest ridge. There was that sullen glisten of the sea, cut through with patches of white, and the green-back horizon gaping to east and west and blotting out with gray squalls. The great wind had not come yet beyond these first squadrons. The big man shrugged as he regarded it. The hurricane tide was shoving frothy fingers out over the shoals. Across the sandy stretch westward he could just see the shack camp of *Grand-père* Rojas on the highest ridge of Dautrive. A few ragged oaks showed white against the sky. The old man ought to be leaving with his orphaned grandchildren, taking his stout oyster lugger and making for the solid land fourteen miles north across the bay.

"It is no place for little ones," muttered Lalande in the Cajun patois. "These people never will leave quick enough before the storms. I can see the old man's lugger still riding behind the point. He is a fool, Old Rojas, afraid to put foot on this end of the reef because of the white stud, but stubborn against the sea which comes like a million white horses."

He went warily on the crushed trail. That throwrope would foul somewhere in the mangroves; that stallion would choke himself to a stupor, for not all the strength in the world can avail against lungs bursting for air. Then he saw the mares. They were huddled in a hollow of the dunes, the colts about them as if confused, uncertain, their shaggy coats ruffled in the wind. That wind was moaning now, high and far; not so bad here on the reef, but striking in slants on the sea as if the sky had opened to let an arrow loose. A hundred miles away as yet, that Gulf hurricane wind, but mounting; sixty, eighty, a hundred miles an hour—a hundred and twenty-five in the bursts that presently drove the sand dunes into smoke.

The rim of wet sand beyond the dry, hummocky space was covered with sheets of black water racing from the surf line, breaking on the shoals.

And here Lalande saw what he had sought. There was the white mound in the ripples. With a cry he dashed for it. The horse was down. He had not thought it would come so soon. But the end of the trailing rope had fouled a great drift heap, and the brute had kept on charging and fighting until he choked and fell in the first wash of the sea. The slipnoose was bound to cut him down if he kept on hurling his weight against it, Lalande knew.

He wished he had seen the last magnificent fight against it on the sands; but now he walked quickly around the fallen brute, and knelt to touch his distended, quivering nostrils. The eyes were shut but bulging under a film. The great sides were heaving, a rumbling groan found escape somehow; it was as if the mighty heart was breaking with a last throb against this mysterious power choking its strength away.

"Eh, soldier!" whispered Lalande, and felt high on the horse's neck.

A sudden apprehension took him. Perhaps the thong had killed the renegade? He did not mean that; he was filled with a great exultant joy in this savage. He had stalked and subdued him alone! He stood above this outstretched, trembling body in the first sea ripples, laughing.

"Come, boy! The fight's not done yet! Not the end yet." He twisted his fingers into the taut rope, forced on the dragging driftwood, and eased the tension bit by bit. The rope was buried in the white skin; he worked hurriedly, fearing it was too late.

"Come, come; this will not do—" he was whispering into the stallion's tense ear, fighting at the rope. Then came a fierce, convulsive blow, an explosive sigh, a struggle, and the stallion lay quiet again. He was breathing in great, resurging sighs. His filmed eyes opened slowly. Lalande kept patting his muzzle while he hitched the noose into a knot that would not choke again. He did not know why he did this, only it seemed fair. He was looking close into the brute's eyes which were beginning to glow with sense again; and to withdraw the choking hitch seemed only justice.

Lalande stood up and looked down at the white stallion. The water was roaring out there now. The skyline was blown white as feathers. The mangroves were slanting; and he suddenly realized that the wind was hard as a plank against his cheek. Not bursting, but steadily lying against the land. There was no rain, yet the air was full of water streaming in white lines through a growing darkness.

"Get up!" he shouted. "The sea is coming. This is no place to be! Comrade, on your feet!"

And the great horse did so. First plunging up, but with his haunches squatted in the water as he looked slowly about. Then to all fours and standing with his tail whipped about on his heaving flanks. He seemed watching that wall of blow water from the Gulf. Watching steadily, undaunted. The sands under the racing froth seemed trembling; one could hardly see the mangrove dunes not a hundred yards away.

Lalande swiftly turned his eyes from the ridge at a sound. It had seemed a shriek above the tumult. Then he leaped, and the wind appeared to lift him above the shaking earth.

For the great stud was on him. Upreared above him, a shaggy hoof coming not an inch's breadth from his skull.

Just a glimpse of those red, savage eyes; and the impact of those huge feet almost upon his own. Then Lalande ran. The hurricane wind flung him onward, but he could hear the rush of the white stallion. The entangled rope checked the charge only enough to allow the man to hurl himself into the first mangroves, crawl under them in a whirlwind of rising sands, and keep on crawling. When he stopped, he knew the horse was crashing in the thickets hunting him. He saw him as a wraith against the sky, plunging his head low enough to ferret out his enemy, blowing explosively and hurling the tough mangrove clumps aside.

Lalande kept on his stealthy crawl. He lay, finally, in a water-riven dusk under the lee of the dunes, listening. "Dieu!" he panted. "I said, a soldier! The hurricane could not stop that hate of men!"

For half an hour he did not move. The brute had lost his trail. And when Lalande crawled to the top of the dunes he could not stand. All over the weather side the sea had risen. It was white. White, that was all he could say. And the wind? It did not seem a wind, merely a crushing of one's skull and lungs. When he tried to turn away it threw him headlong, but he got to his feet on the northerly, lee side of the sand ridge and fought on.

The sand was dissolving under his feet, and now he saw the water of the bay streaming by him. The inner marshes were gone; the hurricane tide was on, and sixty miles inland it would rush to batter on the cypress forests and the back levees of the plantation lands. Lalande had no illusions about Ile Dautrive—he had been a lad on this coast—but he kept on, for the highest ridge was at the western point. Across the sand shoal, beyond this point, was still higher land, a clay fragment in which grew a few stout oaks. By these Old Rojas's camp had stood. It did not stand there now, thought Lalande. Nothing built by man on the reef would stand. *Grand-père* and the children of the man whom the white stallion had killed must certainly have taken to the lugger—escaped before the hurricane tide rushed upon the flimsy shack. Surely, yes. Rojas was no fool!

Lalande kept on, clinging to the thickets when the worst clutch of the wind was on him. The roaring of it all was so steady that actually he seemed in a great silence, as if a new element had enveloped him—a normal thing, this shock and unceasing tenseness of feeling and of sound. Through it he strode steadily himself, a strong man with neither fear nor curiosity—a mere dull plunge on to the last foothold of that reef which was churning to gruel behind his steps. He could not miss the point; there was no other spot to reach, and the hurricane was guide as well as captor.

And his mind was upon the lord of Dautrive Island. "He will go. Perhaps he is gone now. And the mares and colts, all off the reef by now." And a grim satisfaction came that the white stud had turned on him at the last. It was fine to think of. The savage had not cringed. "I do not want anything that can be stolen," he murmured, and spat the sea spray from his sore lips. "His mares and colts, he fights for them—that devil!"

And he began shouting profane, fond challenges and adulations to his conqueror somewhere in this white chaos of a night. A whipping wisp of scud was that charging shape above the torn thickets; any single shriek of the storm, his trumpeted challenge in return. Lalande boasted to his soul that he was seeking his foe; if it was the last stroke of his hand he wished it raised to taunt the white, oncoming devil.

Even the storm glimmer had faded when he felt the water shoaling from his armpits to his waist. This was the west point, the highest, and here, with hands locked to the stoutest of the mangroves, he would have to let the sea boil over him as long as a strong man could—then go.

On the western high point at last, and nothing to see, nothing to feel but the submerged bushes and the earth dissolving so that he had to keep his feet moving to avoid each becoming the center of a whirlpool.

"It is a storm," Lalande grunted. "Two white devils on this reef." He remembered seeing space, of mirrored calm, peaceful coves over which they told him orange trees had bloomed in cottage yards of the reef dwellers. The sea had devoured the islands in a night, dug the hole, and lain down in it like a fed tiger. Lalande, crowded closer to the stouter thickets, put out his hand in the dark. He touched a wet, warm surface, heaving slightly.

The skin of a brute. He smoothed the hair in the rushing water, felt along. A wall of steely flesh broadside to the tidal wave. Lalande softly slipped his hand over the huge round flank. The water was swirling about them both to the man's armpits now: Lalande knew. They were on the highest point, but ahead lay the shoal pass. The sea was eating away this point; what was left was sinking, flicked off into the meeting currents around Dautrive and swept inland. The island would be silt on some cane planter's back fields forty miles up the Mississippi delta within the week.

But for the last of his domain the lord of Dautrive was fighting with his last foothold. The white devil of the sea was doing what man could not do. Lalande laughed in the blackness. The stallion could not feel his soft touch in all that beating welter of sand and debris churning around him. He rested his arm across the unseen back—the brute would think it was a driftwood branch. The man stepped forward. There was no other foothold now, it seemed. He reached his hand to the shoulder, up to feel the stiff, wet mane. He laughed and patted the bulged muscles.

"We go, you and I," he grumbled. The mangroves were slatted out on the tide rush, tearing loose, reeling past them. "Eh, friend? The last—"

And then he knew that the horse had whirled, upreared in the blackness with a scream of fury. Lalande sprang to the left, into deep, moiling water.

He felt the plunge of his foe just missing him once more. But another body struck him and then was whirled off in the meeting tides. He collided with a colt in the dark; and now he guessed that the white stallion's breed had been gathered on the refuge shielded to the last by his huge bulk against the inexorable seas.

They were gone now. There was no more foothold on Dautrive either for the exiles or the man who had come to subdue them. Lalande knew he must not go with the tidal wave. It was death anywhere out there. The water would rush fifty miles inland over the battered reefs. So he fought powerfully back to get a handhold on the mangrove thickets through a whirlpool of dissolving sand.

But the man could not breast those surges through the dark; he felt himself driven farther back in a tangle of foam and debris, and suddenly came a whip-like tightening about his legs. He was dragged under and out across the current until he fought down to grasp this thing that had him.

It was his throw-rope, the new and heavy line he had brought to conquer the white stud that the island men feared. Lalande plunged up and along it. The rope was tight and surging athwart the drift. When he got his head above water he knew he was clear of the disintegrating sand point, overwhelmed by the rollers in the pass and stung by the spray, but moving.

An unseen guide, a mighty power was drawing aslant the inshore tide. Lalande hauled along until he felt the rhythmic beat of the stallion's stroke; along until he touched his flank. When he could put his hand to his long mane, Lalande laughed. He hung there, and felt the brute plunge higher at this contact. Once, twice, and then the stud settled to his fight.

The lord of Dautrive could not shake him off or rend him with teeth or hoof. He was being ridden through the blackness and the sea.

Lalande began shouting. He could not resist the impulse of defiance: the great horse had been merciless to him on the island, so now he howled at him whenever he could keep the salt water from his teeth.

"Eh, bien! Big fellow, you see I am here! If you go, I go! Lalande is with you—devil! Fight! Fight on; a man is on your back at last. A last ride, too, white devil!"

For he had no hope of anything except to be battered to a pulp by the drift logs and wreckage in the pass or drowned over the flooded marshes. But the stallion would not give to the northward tide; always he kept fighting to windward and westerly. When he plunged on these tacks Lalande swung out straight over his back, but clinging lightly and calling his taunting courage to the brute.

"The west ridge," muttered the rider. "He knows that, the oaks and the clay soil. If anything hangs together in this sea it will be that." So he clung in the dark. Nothing but the incessant battles of the horse's broadside in the hurricane tide kept that feeling in Lalande's heart that the swimmer was trying to cross the pass to Rojas's oak grove. The white devil was blind in the white sea, but he remembered that Lalande could feel the leg strokes steady and true even when the waves lifted or buried them, or when they were half drowned in the whipped foam among patches of reef wreckage. The man was fighting at this debris to keep it from the stallion's neck when he felt something else streaming along his flanks. It appeared to be submerged bushes or thick, long grass twisting about beneath them. And there was a changed note to the hurricane's tumult.

Lalande swung up on the stallion's back, listening. The swells of the pass were slower here, huge and strangling, but not with the fierce rush they had battled. The horse was swimming more to seaward, almost head on now, and once he arose as if his forefeet had struck the earth.

"He has found the marsh," muttered Lalande. "Night of wonders; nothing else!"

Still that powerful, steady stroke under the man's clinging limbs. The brute was seeking whatever land might be above the water. Then Lalande began to think, as again he felt the forefeet touch bottom.

"Then we fight again, eh, tiger? Shake me off and come at me! Make the oaks and we'll see!"

The horse plunged past a torn oak stump which smashed him in the side. He was in water to his withers, but Lalande knew he was climbing. He got a foothold, leaned against the tide rushing through the oak grove, and kept on. Against the man and the horse there crushed another trunk, denuded of leaves, swinging by its roots, staggering them with its blows. The sea was over this also, Lalande knew. If it came higher there was no hope here.

Then the stallion stopped. He stood belly deep in the lee of another oak trunk which Lalande could feel in the utter dark. And the man sat silent astride the white king of Dautrive who had lost his domain and his subjects. He moved his legs across the heaving flanks—a sort of stealthy challenge. He wanted the white stud to know that he, Joe Lalande, was there astride him. He laughed and leaned to pat the unseen arch of the neck.

And then again came that furious, uprearing plunge of the great brute. His head came about in a side blow, his teeth tearing at Lalande's face as the rider swerved out under this twisting, maddened attack. He heard that trumpet cry again of the wild horse seeking him as he dragged himself about the oak tree in the water. He stood clutching the rope, trying to make out the brute's form.

Then he knew that the swells riding through the twisted oaks were slowed; the yelling of the winds more fitful, higher; and a sort of check came to the clutch on his body against the tree. Lalande seemed to stand in a frothy eddy as if the sea had stopped running and was foaming to an apex about him. And he knew what it meant, the moment that always comes in the Gulf hurricanes. The wind was dying off and changing. The sea could do no more. It had piled its flood as far inland and as high as even its strength could hold. Its whirling center was now over the coast, the wind whipping fitfully, now southwest, westerly, northward, and beginning to rise again. But there came one moment when it was almost a calm, silence except for that roaring in the sky.

"*La revanche*," muttered the man. "Now comes the worst—the rush of the tide back to sea. The good God help them all, these Cajuns who have not found refuge up the bay. *La revanche*—that is when they die!"

He felt about his oak trunk, wondering if it were still rooted firmly. The white stallion must be just about the torn branches, for Lalande still had the trailing line. And then came something that numbed him with uncanny fear. A voice out in the dark, a child's cry among the oaks.

"*La revanche*! *Grand-père*, it is coming! Get the lines the other way, *Grand-père*—"

Lalande went plunging toward the spot. "*Nom de Dieu*! It is not possible? Rojas!" He shouted, and stumbled among wreckage of trees and timbers around his waist. "Rojas, you are in the grove?"

A dim light glowed behind a blanket. He saw a boy had snatched this moment of the falling wind to try the lantern. When Lalande waded to the spot an old man straightened up on the other side of a sunken raft. Upon it, under the blankets, were lashed the forms of Rojas's children, the orphans of Emile, who had once sought to tame the white horse of Île Dautrive. Old Rojas held the lantern close to his white beard. He seemed as frightened as was the small boy by the stranger's coming.

Old Rojas had been trying to spike a cross-piece to his shattered raft. His lugger had been smashed in the first reach of the hurricane, and he had torn up the planks of his camp floor to build this refuge anchored to the biggest oaks of the grove. They knew what to do, these Cajuns of the reefs, when they were caught by the hurricane tide. Cut the mast from the lugger and drift inland, seize an anchorage before the dreaded *revanche* took them seaward; or if not that, hang to one's oak stumps!

Lalande did not waste the precious moments with a single question.

"A brave fight, old man. I see you made a brave fight! Give me your raft-lines. The other way around now, and to the stoutest trees. This sea, it is like a mad tiger when it has to go back defeated! Come." He took the mooring-line and plunged off in the waist-deep froth.

"Day of wonders!" mumbled Old Rojas. "A man on the reef—living. A big man, strong after the hurricane! It is impossible!" He went hammering his raft as it surged and plunged by his shoulders, ordering the youngster to make himself fast once more in the life ropes which held them all to the shaking planks. There was no whimper from the four children. They raised big dark eyes, staring from *Grand-père* to the strange man who was battling back in the first seaward rush of the waters to make them fast against *la revanche*. The wind was smiting again. It appeared to fall out of the blackness to the north, blast after blast, rising swifter, smiting the piled-up waters, hurling them over the reef islands with thrice the speed they had come in.

The dim lantern went out. The fugitives tied themselves on again. If the worn lines held and the raft kept together they might live. "Name of Names!" grumbled Old Rojas. "A man coming to us out of the sea? He said he would make fast for us. If not, my children—well, we must trust him."

Lalande had struggled off into the new rush of the wind with the raft-lines. They were frayed and ragged. He made them fast to his own throw-rope. He would get this rope off the stallion somehow, and make it fast to the big oak. If not—he shrugged, well, then, nothing! Every wreck of a lugger, plank of a camp, drift log, tree, that was loose would be miles in the open Gulf tomorrow to eddy endlessly in *la revanche*.

The old man's mooring-lines would not reach the big oak. Lalande had thought that, combined, they might last the night out, but the sea and wind were whipping fast on him in the dark. He had to plunge out shoulder deep to the tree, feeling of his line.

"The white devil is there and quiet," he grumbled. "If he would let me slip the rope from his shoulders and tie it to the tree!" He breasted the brimming tides over the submerged isle past the oak, his hand cautiously out to the dark. "Devil!" he called softly. "This is for Emile Rojas's young ones. The rope, devil! We've fought, you and I, but now let me have it."

The line was tight past the oak stump. The weight of the raft was already coming strongly on it as the tide began to seethe through the shattered grove. Lalande could hardly keep his feet, or his eyes open in the bitter spray. Then he was off his feet; he was hanging to the line, fighting out on it, calling to his foe, reaching for him. The brute must be swimming now, for the footing had gone from under them both.

Lalande felt a plunging on the line. It was too late now to hope to get the rope to the oak. The fighting horse was on it, and it began to give slowly past the man's hands. *La revanche* was bearing them on, the raft, the man, and the white devil who was its sole anchor, now. Lalande clung with one arm to the oak and drew in on the line. The dead weight of the raft had its way. The bucking, plunging brute, now touching the ground, now surging in the tide, was being drawn to him. Lalande began to call again. He had a great sense of pity for the stud. There were things that could not be withstood even by his lion heart; yet even the sea might not conquer except for this choking drag of the raft that held Rojas's grandchildren.

Lalande touched the stallion's muzzle now, coming on fighting with the obstinate ferocity of a white shark. He crouched in the crotch of the oak and held out his arms to the stallion's neck. When finally the brute crashed upon the sunken oak, Lalande reached his fingers to the cleft where the throw-rope cut into his neck. He dragged on the line, vainly trying to ease that tension. Once he thought of his knife; he might cut that choking grip from the white stud's throat. Then Lalande lay back in the crotch above the plunging hoofs and eased the great head above his own shoulder. Dragging on the line with all his power, he kept up his whispering as the hurricane tide rushed under them, swinging the oak on its roots, twisting it seaward, and sucking the earth away in whirls where Rojas's house had stood.

"I tell you we are still here, you and I," called Lalande after a while. "You and I, devil! You and I—smashed up together, my face against your own! *Eh, bien!* Be quiet, Emile Rojas may be watching his children, and you in this storm? Remember that, white devil, you have returned for them!" He laughed and shouted in the dark, his arm around the neck of the horse working his fingers under the rope, trying to take some of the strain upon his own flesh and bone. And presently he grumbled, "And remember, also, I am not a thief. Not a thief, eh?"

They clung that way five hours, until the crest of *la revanche* was passed. The sun even got through the huge rifts of black clouds streaming south by the time Old Rojas stirred about from his creaking raft in the scrub oaks. Everywhere a brown, dirty, sullen sea setting out, flecked with drift and wreckage, and of all Île Dautrive nothing showed but those few battered, branchless trees.

The stout old man waded waist-deep from his raft where now Emile's young ones sat up stiff and drowsy from the sea's nightlong flailing. He followed his mooring-line out to where it sogged under water by the big oak. The eldest boy had stood up looking after him.

"*Grand-père!*" screamed the lad suddenly. "Look! The white horse has come! By the tree, with the man!"

Old Rojas waded and struggled there, too astounded to speak. The sight was a queer one, indeed. The white horse was drawn against the oak crotch, pinned in there, in fact; and the rope from his neck also crushed the strange man against his shoulder. Joe Lalande appeared to be crucified against the satin coat of the stallion. But he lifted his free arm faintly when the old man floundered near them.

"M'sieu?" gasped Rojas. "You here?" He had to touch Lalande's drenched body ere he could believe that the man lived. Then he fell to loosening the slacked rope so that Lalande lurched down from the horse's neck into the water where he could hardly stand but clung to the tree trunk watching the animal. The rope had cut through Lalande's arm and shoulder until it made a long red-scarred mark from neck to elbow. He could not speak for a time with his salt-swollen lips.

"Yes, I am here," he whispered at last, and staggered weakly.

"Name of God, the white horse!" cried the old man. He put his hand out to touch the smooth side, but as if fearing him even now. Lalande was trying to discover whether or not the heart of the white stallion still beat; and then he turned away, his eyes closing wearily. He seemed to be shaken by a sob, a grief that the islander could not comprehend.

"What's the matter, M'sieu? We are safe; the boats will find us. Le bon Dieu! That was a storm! I have never seen a greater on this reef!"

Then he looked curiously at the still form of his old enemy. "Eh, bien! It took a white sea to kill this white devil, my friend!"

"It was not the sea," grumbled Lalande. "The touch of a rope on his neck, M'sieu. I saw his heart break last night, but it was for the children of Emile. A rope and the touch of my hand upon his neck, they were not to be endured, M'sieu." Then Lalande turned away, as if speaking to the lord of Dautrive against the tree: "At least you must know this, white devil, the hand on you was not the hand of a thief."

18

The Round-Up

By Theodore Roosevelt

◇◇◇

Our twenty-sixth president wrote an amazing forty-two books and countless articles on personal experiences and adventures around the world. This portrait of ranch life, which he lived vigorously, is from Ranch Life and the Hunting Trail, *1888.*

◇◇◇

DURING THE WINTERTIME THERE IS ORDINARILY BUT LITTLE WORK done among the cattle. There is some line riding, and a continual lookout is kept for the very weak animals; but most of the stock are left to shift for themselves, undisturbed. Almost every stock-grower's association forbids branding any calves before the spring round-up. If great bands of cattle wander off the range, parties may be fitted out to go after them and bring them back; but this is only done when absolutely necessary, as when the drift of the cattle has been towards an Indian reservation or a settled granger country, for the weather is very severe, and the horses are so poor that their food must be carried along.

The bulk of the work is done during the summer, including the late spring and early fall, and consists mainly in a succession of round-ups, beginning, with us, in May and ending towards the last of October. But a good deal may be done by riding over one's range. Frequently, too, herding will be practiced on a large scale.

Still more important is the "trail" work; cattle, while driven from one range to another, or to a shipping point for beef, being said to be "on the trail." For years, the over-supply from the vast breeding ranches to the south, especially in Texas, has been driven northward in large herds, either to the shipping towns along the great railroads, or else to the fattening ranges of the Northwest; it having been found, so far, that while the calf crop is larger in the South, beeves become much heavier in the North. Such cattle, for the most part, went along tolerably well-marked routes or trails, which became for the time being of great importance, flourishing—and extremely lawless—towns growing up along them; but with the growth of the railroad system, and above all with the filling up of the northern ranges, these trails have steadily become of less and less consequence, though many herds still travel on them on their way to the already crowded ranges of western Dakota and Montana, or to the Canadian regions beyond. The trail work is something by itself. The herds may be on the trail several months, averaging fifteen miles or fewer a day. The cowboys accompanying each have to undergo much hard toil, of a peculiarly same and wearisome kind, on account of the extreme slowness with which everything must be done, as trail cattle should never be hurried. The foreman of a trail outfit must be not only a veteran cowhand, but also a miracle of patience and resolution.

Round-up work is far less irksome, there being an immense amount of dash and excitement connected with it; and when once the cattle are on the range, the important work is done during the round-up. On cow ranches, or wherever there is breeding stock, the spring round-up is the great event of the season, as it is then that the bulk of the calves are branded. It usually lasts six weeks, or thereabouts; but its end by no means implies rest for the stockman. On the contrary, as soon as it is over, wagons are sent to work out-of-the-way parts of the country that have been passed over, but where cattle are supposed to have drifted; and by the time these have come back the first beef round-up has begun, and thereafter beeves are steadily gathered and shipped, at least from among the larger herds, until cold weather sets in; and in the fall there is another round-up, to brand the late calves and see that the stock is got back on the range. As all of these round-ups are of one character, a description of the most important, taking place in the spring, will be enough.

In April we begin to get up the horses. Throughout the winter very few have been kept for use, as they are then poor and weak, and must be given grain and hay if they are to be worked. The men in the line camps need two or three apiece, and each man at the home ranch has a couple more; but the rest are left out to shift for themselves, which the tough, hardy little fellows are well able to do. Ponies can pick up a living where cattle die; though the scanty feed, which they may have to uncover by pawing off the snow, and the bitter weather often make them look very gaunt by springtime. But the first warm rains bring up the green grass, and then all the livestock gain flesh with wonderful rapidity. When the spring round-up begins the horses should be as fat and sleek as possible. After running all winter free, even the most sober pony is apt to betray an inclination to buck; and, if possible, we like to ride every animal once or twice before we begin to do real work with him. Animals that have escaped for any length of time are almost as bad to handle as if they had never been broken. One of the two horses mentioned in a preceding article as having been gone eighteen months has, since his return, been suggestively dubbed "Dynamite Jimmy," on account of the incessant and eruptive energy with which he bucks. Many of our horses, by the way, are thus named from some feat or peculiarity. Wire Fence, when being broken, ran into one of the abominations after which he is now called; Hackamore once got away and remained out for three weeks with a hackamore, or breaking-halter, on him; Macaulay contracted the habit of regularly getting rid of the huge Scotchman to whom he was entrusted; Bulberry Johnny spent the hour or two after he was first mounted in a large patch of thorny bulberry bushes, his distracted rider unable to get him to do anything but move round sidewise in a circle; Fall Back would never get to the front; Water Skip always jumps mud puddles; and there are a dozen others with names as purely descriptive.

The stock-growers of Montana, of the western part of Dakota, and even of portions of extreme northern Wyoming—that is, of all the grazing lands lying in the basin of the Upper Missouri—have united and formed themselves into the great Montana Stock-Growers' Association. Among the countless benefits they have derived from this course, not the least has been the way in which the various round-ups work in with and supplement one another. At the spring meeting of the association, the entire territory mentioned above, including perhaps a hundred thousand square miles, is mapped out into round-up districts, which generally are changed but slightly from year to year, and the times and places for the round-ups to begin refixed so that those of adjacent districts may be run with a view to the best interests of all. Thus the stockmen along the Yellowstone have one round-up; we along the Little Missouri have another; and the country lying between, through which the Big Beaver flows, is almost equally important to both. Accordingly, one spring, the Little Missouri round-up, beginning May 25 and working downstream, was timed so as to reach the mouth of the Big Beaver about June 1, the Yellowstone round-up beginning at that date and place. Both then worked up the Beaver together to its head, when the Yellowstone men turned to the west and we went back to our own river; thus the bulk of the strayed cattle of each were brought back to their respective ranges. Our own round-up district covers the Big and Little Beaver creeks, which rise near each other, but empty into the Little Missouri nearly a hundred and fifty miles apart, and so much of the latter river as lies between their mouths.

The captain or foreman of the round-up, upon whom very much of its efficiency and success depends, is chosen beforehand. He is, of course, an expert cowman, thoroughly acquainted with the country; and he must also be able to command and to keep control of the wild rough-riders he has under him—a feat needing both tact and firmness.

At the appointed day all meet at the place from which the round-up is to start. Each ranch, of course, has most work to be done in its own roundup district, but it is also necessary to have representatives in all those surrounding it. A large outfit may employ a dozen cowboys, or over, in the home district, and yet have nearly as many more representing its interest in the various ones adjoining. Smaller outfits generally club together to run a wagon and send outside representatives, or else go along with their stronger neighbors, their paying part of the expenses. A large outfit, with a herd of twenty thousand cattle or more, can, if necessary, run a round-up entirely by itself, and is able to act independently of outside help; it is therefore at a great advantage compared with those that can take no step effectively without their neighbor's consent and assistance.

If the starting point is some distance off, it may be necessary to leave home three or four days in advance. Before this we have got everything in readiness; have overhauled the wagons, shod any horse whose forefeet are tender—as a rule, all our ponies go barefooted—and left things in order at the ranch. Our outfit may be taken as a sample of everyone else's. We have a stout four-horse wagon to carry the bedding and the food; in its rear a mess-chest is rigged to hold the knives, forks, cans, etc. All our four team-horses are strong, willing animals, though of no great size, being originally just "broncos" or unbroken native horses, like the others. The teamster is also cook: a man who is a really first-rate hand at both driving and cooking—and our present teamster is both—can always command his price. Besides our own men, some cowboys from neighboring ranches and two or three representatives from other round-up districts are always along, and we generally have at least a dozen "riders," as they are termed—that is, cowboys, or "cow-punchers," who do the actual cattle work—with the wagon. Each of these has a string of eight or ten ponies; and to take charge of the saddle-band, thus consisting of a hundred-odd head, there are two herders, always known as "horse wranglers"—one for the day and one for the night. Occasionally there will be two wagons, one to carry the bedding and one the food, known, respectively, as the bed and the mess wagon; but this is not usual.

While traveling to the meeting point the pace is always slow, as it is an object to bring the horses on the ground as fresh as possible. Accordingly, we keep at a walk almost all day, and the riders, having nothing else to do, assist the wranglers in driving the saddle-band, three or four going in front, and others on the side, so that the horses shall keep on a walk. There is always some trouble with the animals at the starting out, as they are very fresh and are restive under the saddle. The herd is likely to stampede, and any beast that is frisky or vicious is sure to show its worst side. To do really effective cow-work a pony should be well broken; but many even of the old ones have vicious traits, and almost every man will have in his string one or two young horses, or broncos, hardly broken at all. In consequence, very many of my horses have to this day traits not calculated to set a timid or a clumsy rider at his ease. One or two run away and cannot be held by even the strongest bit; others can hardly be bridled or saddled until they have been thrown; two or three have a tendency to fall over backward; and half of them buck more or less, some so hard that only an expert can sit on them.

In riding these wild, vicious horses, and in careering over such very bad ground, especially at night, accidents are always occurring. A man who is merely an ordinary rider is certain to have a pretty hard time. On my first round-up I had a string of nine horses, four of them broncos, only broken to the extent of having each been saddled once or twice. One of them it was an impossibility to bridle or to saddle single-handed; it was very difficult to get on or off him, and he was exceedingly nervous if a man moved his hands or feet; but he had no bad tricks. The second soon became perfectly quiet. The third turned out to be one of the worst buckers on the ranch; once, when he bucked me off, I managed to fall on a stone and broke a rib. The fourth had a still worse habit, for he would balk and then throw himself over backward; once, when I was not quick enough, he caught me and broke something in the point of my shoulder, so that it was some weeks before I could raise the arm freely. My hurts were far from serious, and did not interfere with my riding and working as usual through the round-up; but I was heartily glad when it ended, and ever since have religiously done my best to get none but gentle horses in my own string. However, everyone gets falls from or with his horse now and then in cow country; and even my men, good riders though they are, are sometimes injured. One of them once broke his ankle; another a rib; another was on one occasion stunned, remaining unconscious for some hours; and yet another had certain of his horses buck under him so hard and long as finally to hurt his lungs and make him cough blood. Fatal accidents occur annually in almost every district, especially if there is much work to be done among stampeded cattle at night; but on my own ranch none of my men has ever been seriously hurt, though on one occasion a cowboy from another ranch, who was with my wagon, was killed, his horse falling and pitching him heavily on his head.

For bedding, each man has two or three pairs of blankets, and a tarpaulin or small wagon-sheet. Usually, two or three sleep together. Even in June the nights are generally cool and pleasant, and it is chilly in the early mornings; although this is not always so, and when the weather stays hot and mosquitoes are plenty; the hours of darkness, even in midsummer, seem painfully long. In the Bad Lands proper we are not often bothered very seriously by these winged pests; but in the low bottoms of the Big Missouri, and beside many of the reedy ponds and great sloughs out on the prairie, they are a perfect scourge. During the very hot nights, when they are especially active, the bedclothes make a man feel absolutely smothered, and yet his only chance for sleep is to wrap himself tightly up, head and all, and even then some of the pests will usually force their way in. At sunset I have seen the mosquitoes rise up from the land like a dense cloud, to make the hot, stifling night one long torture; the horses would neither lie down nor graze, traveling restlessly to and fro till daybreak, their bodies streaked and bloody, and the insects settling on them so as to make them all one color, a uniform gray; while the men, after a few hours' tossing about in the vain attempt to sleep, rose, built a little fire of damp sagebrush, and thus endured the misery as best they could until it was light enough to work.

But if the weather is fine, a man will never sleep better nor more pleasantly than in the open air after a hard day's work on the round-up; nor will an ordinary shower or gust of wind disturb him in the least, for he simply draws the tarpaulin over his head and goes on sleeping. But now and then we have a windstorm that might better be called a whirlwind and has to be met very differently; and two or three days or nights of rain ensure the wetting of the blankets, and therefore shivering discomfort on the part of the would-be sleeper. For two or three hours all goes well; and it is rather soothing to listen to the steady patter of the great raindrops on the canvas. But then it will be found that a corner has been left open through which the water can get in, or else the tarpaulin will begin to leak somewhere; or perhaps the water will have collected in a hollow underneath and have begun to soak through. Soon a little stream trickles in, and every effort to remedy matters merely results in a change for the worse. To move out of the way ensures getting wet in a fresh spot; and the best course is to lie still and accept the evils that have come with what fortitude one can. Even thus, the first night a man can sleep pretty well; but if the rain continues, the second night, when the blankets are already damp, and when the water comes through more easily, is apt to be the most unpleasant.

Of course, a man can take little spare clothing on a round-up; at the very outside two or three clean handkerchiefs, a pair of socks, a change of under-clothes, and the most primitive kind of washing apparatus, all wrapped up in a stout jacket which is to be worn when night-herding. The inevitable "slicker," or oilskin coat, which gives complete protection from the wet, is always carried behind the saddle.

At the meeting place there is usually a delay of a day or two to let everyone come in; and the plain on which the encampment is made becomes a scene of great bustle and turmoil. The heavy four-horse wagons jolt in from different quarters, the horse wranglers rushing madly to and fro in the endeavor to keep the different saddle-bands from mingling, while the "riders," or cowboys, with each wagon jog along in a body. The representative, from outside districts ride in singly or by twos and threes, every man driving before him his own horses, one of them loaded with his bedding. Each wagon wheels out of the way into some camping place not too near the others, the bedding is tossed out on the ground, and then everyone is left to do what he wishes, while the different wagon bosses, or foremen, seek out the captain of the round-up to learn what his plans are.

There is a good deal of rough but effective discipline and method in the way in which a round-up is carried on. The captain of the whole has as lieutenants the various wagon foremen, and in making demands for men to do some special service he will usually merely designate some foreman to take charge of the work and let him parcel it out among his men to suit himself. The captain of the roundup or the foreman of a wagon may himself be a ranchman; if such is not the case, and the ranchman nevertheless comes along, he works and fares precisely as do the other cowboys.

While the head men are gathered in a little knot, planning out the work, the others are dispersed over the plain in every direction, racing, breaking rough horses, or simply larking with one another. If a man has an especially bad horse, he usually takes such an opportunity, when he has plenty of time, to ride him; and while saddled he is surrounded by a crowd of most unsympathetic associates who greet with uproarious mirth any misadventure. A man on a bucking horse is always considered fair game, every squeal and jump of the bronco being hailed with cheers of delighted irony for the rider and shouts to "stay with him." The antics of a vicious bronco show infinite variety of detail, but are all modeled on one general plan. When the rope settles round his neck the fight begins, and it is only after much plunging and snorting that a twist is taken over his nose, or else a hackamore—a species of severe halter, usually made of plaited hair—slipped on his head. While being bridled he strikes viciously with his forefeet, and perhaps has to be blindfolded or thrown down; and to get the saddle on him is quite as difficult. When saddled, he may get rid of his exuberant spirits by bucking under the saddle, or may reserve all his energies for the rider. In the latter case, the man, keeping tight hold with his left hand of the cheek-strap, so as to prevent the horse from getting his head down until he is fairly seated, swings himself quickly into the saddle. Up rises the bronco's back into an arch; his head, the ears laid straight back, goes down between his forefeet, and, squealing savagely, he makes a succession of rapid, stiff-legged, jarring bounds. Sometimes he is a "plunging" bucker, who runs forward all the time while bucking; or he may buck steadily in one place, or "sunfish"—that is, bring first one shoulder down almost to the ground and then the other—or else he may change ends while in the air. A first-class rider will sit throughout it all without moving from the saddle, quirting (Spanish term for a short flexible riding whip used throughout cowboy land) his horse all the time, though his hat may be jarred off his head and his revolver out of its sheath. After a few jumps, however, the average man grasps hold of the horn of the saddle—the delighted onlookers meanwhile earnestly advising him not to "go to leather"—and is contented to get through the affair in any shape, provided he can escape without being thrown off. An accident is of necessity borne with a broad grin, as any attempt to resent the raillery of the bystanders—which is perfectly good-humored—would be apt to result disastrously. Cowboys are certainly extremely good riders. As a class they have no superiors. Of course, they would at first be at a disadvantage in steeple-chasing or fox-hunting, but their average of horsemanship is without doubt higher than that of the men who take part in these latter amusements. A cowboy would learn to ride across the country in a quarter of the time it would take a cross-country rider to learn to handle a vicious bronco or to do good cow-work round and in a herd.

On such a day, when there is no regular work, there will often be horse races, as each outfit is pretty sure to have some running pony which it believes can outpace any other. These contests are always short-distance dashes, for but a few hundred yards. Horse racing is a mania with most plainsmen, white or red. A man with a good racing pony will travel all about with it, often winning large sums, visiting alike cow ranches, frontier towns, and Indian encampments. Sometimes the race is "pony against pony," the victor taking both steeds. In racing, the men ride bareback, as there are hardly any light saddles in the cow country. There will be intense excitement and very heavy betting over a race between two well-known horses, together with a good chance of blood being shed in the attendant quarrels. Indians and whites often race against each other as well as among themselves. I have seen several such contests, and in every case but one the white man happened to win. A race is usually run between two thick rows of spectators, on foot and on horseback, and as the racers pass, these rows close in behind them, every man yelling and shouting with all the strength of his lungs, and all waving their hats and cloaks to encourage the contestants, or firing off their revolvers and saddle guns. The little horses are fairly maddened, as is natural enough, and run as if they were crazy: were the distances any longer, some would be sure to drop in their tracks.

Besides the horse races, which are, of course, the main attraction, the men at a round-up will often get up wrestling matches or foot races. In fact, everyone feels that he is off for a holiday; for after the monotony of a long winter, the cowboys look forward eagerly to the round-up, where the work is hard, it is true, but exciting and varied, and treated a good deal as a frolic. There is no eight-hour law in cowboy land; during round-up time we often count ourselves lucky if we get off with much fewer than sixteen hours; but the work is done in the saddle, and the men are spurred on all the time by the desire to outdo one another in feats of daring and skillful horsemanship. There is very little quarreling or fighting, and though the fun often takes the form of rather rough horseplay, yet the practice of carrying dangerous weapons makes cowboys show far more rough courtesy to each other and far less rudeness to strangers than is the case among, for instance, Eastern miners, or even lumbermen—when a quarrel may very probably result fatally, a man thinks twice before going into it; warlike people or classes always treat one another with a certain amount of consideration and politeness. The moral tone of a cow camp, indeed, is rather high than otherwise. Meanness, cowardice, and dishonesty are not tolerated. There is a high regard for truthfulness and keeping one's word, intense contempt for any kind of hypocrisy, and a hearty dislike for a man who shirks his work. Many of the men gamble and drink, but many do neither; and the conversation is not worse than in most bodies composed wholly of male human beings. A cowboy will not submit tamely to an insult, and is very ready to avenge his own wrongs; nor has he an over-wrought fear of shedding blood. He possesses, in fact, few of the emascu-lated, milk-and-water moralities admired by the pseudo-philanthropists; but he does possess, to a very high degree, the stern, manly qualities that are so valuable to a nation.

The method of work is simple. The mess-wagons and loose horses, after breaking camp in the morning, move on in a straight line for some few miles, going into camp again before midday; and the day herd, consist-ing of all the cattle that have been found far off their range, and which are to be brought back there, and of any others that it is necessary to gather, follows on afterwards. Meanwhile, the cowboys scatter out and drive in all the cattle from the country round about, going perhaps ten or fifteen miles back from the line of march, and meeting at the place where camp has already been pitched. The wagons always keep some little distance from one another, and the saddle-bands do the same, so that the horses may not get mixed. It is rather picturesque to see the four-horse teams filing down at a trot through a pass among the buttes—the saddle-bands being driven along at a smart place to one side or behind, the teamsters cracking their whips, and the horse wranglers calling and shouting as they ride rapidly from side to side behind the horses, urging on the stragglers by dexterous touches with the knotted ends of their long lariats that are left trailing from the saddle. The country driven over is very rough, and it is often necessary to double up teams and put on eight horses to each wagon in going up an unusually steep pitch, or hauling through a deep mud-hole, or over a river crossing where there is quicksand.

The speed and thoroughness with which a country can be worked depends, of course, very largely upon the number of riders. Ours is prob-ably about an average round-up as regards size. The last spring I was out, there were half a dozen wagons along; the saddle-bands numbered about a hundred each; and the morning we started, sixty men in the saddle splashed along the shallow ford of the river that divided the plain where we had camped from the valley of the long winding creek up which we were first to work.

In the morning, the cook is preparing breakfast long before the first glimmer of dawn. As soon as it is ready, probably about 3 o'clock, he utters a long-drawn shout, and all the sleepers feel it is time to be up on the instant, for they know there can be no such thing as delay on the round-up, under penalty of being set afoot. Accordingly, they bundle out, rubbing their eyes and yawning, draw on their boots and trousers—if they have taken the latter off—roll up and cord their bedding, and usually without any attempt at washing crowd over to the little smoldering fire, which is placed in a hole dug in the ground, so that there may be no risk of its spreading. The men are rarely very hungry at breakfast, and it is a meal that has to be eaten in shortest order, so it is perhaps the least important. Each man, as he comes up, grasps a tin cup and plate from the messbox, pours out his tea or coffee, with sugar, but of course no milk, helps himself to one or two of the biscuits that have been baked in a Dutch oven, and perhaps also to a slice of the fat pork swimming in the grease of the frying pan, ladles himself out some beans, if there are any; and squats down on the ground to eat his breakfast. The meal is not an elaborate one; nevertheless a man will have to hurry if he wishes to eat it before hearing the foreman sing out, "Come, boys, catch your horses"; when he must drop everything and run out to the wagon with his lariat. The night wrangler is now bringing in the saddle-band, which he has been up all night guarding. A rope corral is rigged up by stretching a rope from each wheel of one side of the wagon, making a V-shaped space, into which the saddle horses are driven. Certain men stand around to keep them inside, while the others catch the horses; many outfits have one man do all the roping. As soon as each has caught his horse—usually a strong, tough animal, the small, quick ponies being reserved for the work round the herd in the afternoon—the band, now in charge of the day wrangler, is turned loose, and everyone saddles up as fast as possible. It still lacks some time of being sunrise, and the air has in it the peculiar chill of the early morning. When all are saddled, many of the horses bucking and dancing about, the riders from the different wagons all assemble at the one where the captain is sitting, already mounted. He waits a very short time—for laggards receive but scant mercy—before announcing the proposed camping place and parceling out the work among those present. If, as is usually the case, the line of march is along a river or creek, he appoints some man to take a dozen others and drive down (or up) it ahead of the day herd, so that the latter will not have to travel through other cattle; the day herd itself being driven and guarded by a dozen men detached for that purpose. The rest of the riders are divided into two bands, placed under men who know the country, and start out, one on each side, to bring in every head for fifteen miles back. The captain then himself rides down to the new camping place, so as to be there as soon as any cattle are brought in.

Meanwhile, the two bands, a score of riders in each, separate and make their way in opposite directions. The leader of each tries to get such a "scatter" on his men that they will cover completely all the land gone over. This morning work is called circle riding, and is peculiarly hard in the Bad Lands on account of the remarkably broken, rugged nature of the country. The men come in on lines that tend to a common center—as if the sticks of a fan were curved. As the band goes out, the leader from time to time detaches one or two men to ride down through certain sections of the country, making the shorter, or what are called inside, circles, while he keeps on; and finally, retaining as companions the two or three whose horses are toughest, makes the longest or outside circle himself, going clear back to the divide, or whatever the point may be that marks the limit of the round-up work, and then turning and working straight to the meeting place. Each man, of course, brings in every head of cattle he can see.

These long, swift rides in the glorious spring mornings are not soon to be forgotten. The sweet, fresh air with a touch of sharpness thus early in the day, and the rapid motion of the fiery little horse combine to make a man's blood thrill and leap with sheer buoyant light-heartedness and eager, exultant pleasure in the boldness and freedom of the life he is leading. As we climb the steep sides of the first range of buttes, wisps of wavering mist still cling in the hollows of the valley; when we come out on the top of the first great plateau, the sun flames up over its edge, and in the level, red beams the galloping horsemen throw long, fantastic shadows. Black care rarely sits behind a rider whose pace is fast enough; at any rate, not when he first feels the horse move under him.

Sometimes we trot or pace, and again we lope or gallop; the few who are to take the outside circle must needs ride both hard and fast. Although only grass-fed, the horses are tough and wiry; and moreover, are each used but once in four days or thereabouts, so they stand the work well. The course out lies across great grassy plateaus, among knife-like ridge crests, among winding valleys and ravines, and over acres of barren, sun-scorched buttes that look grimly grotesque and forbidding, while in the Bad Lands the riders unhesitatingly go down and over places where it seems impossible that a horse should even stand. The line of horsemen will quarter down the site of a butte, where every pony has to drop from ledge to ledge like a goat, and will go over the shoulder of the soapstone cliff, when wet and slippery, with a series of plunges and scrambles which, if unsuccessful, would land horses and riders in the bottom of the canyon-like washout below. In descending a clay butte after a rain, the pony will put all four feet together and slide down to the bottom almost or quite on his haunches. In very wet weather the Bad Lands are absolutely impassable; but if the ground is not slippery, it is a remarkable place that can shake the matter-of-course confidence felt by the rider in the capacity of his steed to go anywhere.

19

Esmé

By Saki (H. H. Munro)

◇◇

The British literary equestrian heritage is the force behind this splendid story by a leading short story writer and playwright of his time, H. H. Munro (1870–1916), who used the pen name Saki. This tale is from his book The Chronicles of Clovis, *1911.*

◇◇

"ALL HUNTING STORIES ARE THE SAME," SAID CLOVIS; "JUST AS ALL TURF stories are the same, and all—"

"My hunting story isn't a bit like any you've ever heard," said the Baroness. "It happened quite a while ago, when I was about twenty-three. I wasn't living apart from my husband then; you see, neither of us could afford to make the other a separate allowance. In spite of everything that proverbs may say, poverty keeps together more homes than it breaks up. But we always hunted with different packs. All this has nothing to do with the story."

"We haven't arrived at the meet yet. I suppose there was a meet," said Clovis.

"Of course there was a meet," said the Baroness; "all the usual crowd were there, especially Constance Broddle. Constance is one of those strapping florid girls that goes so well with autumn scenery or Christmas decorations in church. 'I feel a presentiment that something dreadful is going to happen,' she said to me. 'Am I looking pale?'

"She was looking about as pale as a beet root that has suddenly heard bad news.

"'You're looking nicer than usual,' I said, 'but that's so easy for you.' Before she had got the right bearings of this remark we had settled down to business; hounds had found a fox lying out in some gorse bushes."

"I knew it," said Clovis. "In every foxhunting story that I've ever heard there's been a fox and some gorse bushes."

"Constance and I were well mounted," continued the Baroness serenely, "and we had no difficulty in keeping ourselves in the first flight, though it was a fairly stiff run. Towards the finish, however, we must have held rather too independent a line, for we lost the hounds, and found ourselves plodding aimlessly along miles away from anywhere. It was fairly exasperating, and my temper was beginning to let itself go by inches, when on pushing our way through an accommodating hedge, we were gladdened by the sight of hounds in full cry in a hollow just beneath us.

"'There they go,' cried Constance, and then added in a gasp, 'In Heaven's name, what are they hunting?'

"It was certainly no mortal fox. It stood more than twice as high, had a short, ugly head, and an enormous thick neck.

"'It's a hyaena,' I cried; 'it must have escaped from Lord Pabham's Park.'

"At that moment the hunted beast turned and faced its pursuers, and the hounds (there were only about six couple then) stood round in a half-circle and looked foolish. Evidently they had broken away from the rest of the pack on the trail of this alien scent, and were not quite sure how to treat the quarry now they had got him.

"The hyaena hailed our approach with unmistakable relief and demonstrations of friendliness. It had probably been accustomed to uniform kindness from humans, while its first experience of a pack of hounds had left a bad impression. The hounds looked more than ever embarrassed as their quarry paraded its sudden intimacy with us, and the faint toot of a horn in the distance was seized on as a welcome signal for unobtrusive departure. Constance and I and the hyaena were left alone in the gathering twilight.

"'What are we to do?' asked Constance.

"'What a person you are for questions,' I said.

"'Well, we can't stay here all night with a hyaena,' she retorted.

"'I don't know what your ideas of comfort are,' I said; 'but I shouldn't think of staying here all night even without a hyaena. My home may be an unhappy one, but at least it has hot and cold water laid on, and domestic service, and other conveniences which we shouldn't find here. We had better make for that ridge of trees to the right; I imagine the Crowley road is just beyond.'

"We trotted off slowly along a faintly marked cart track, with the beast following cheerfully at our heels.

"'What on earth are we to do with the hyaena?' came the inevitable question.

"'What does one generally do with hyaenas?' I asked crossly.

"'I've never had anything to do with one before,' said Constance.

"'Well, neither have I. If we even knew its sex we might give it a name. Perhaps we might call it Esmé. That would do in either case.'

"There was still sufficient daylight for us to distinguish wayside objects, and our listless spirits gave an upward perk as we came upon a small half-naked gypsy brat picking blackberries from a low-growing bush. The sudden apparition of two horsewomen and a hyaena set it off crying, and in any case we should have scarcely gleaned any useful geographical information from that source; but there was a probability that we might strike a gypsy encampment somewhere along our route. We rode on hopefully but uneventfully for another mile or so.

"'I wonder what that child was doing there,' said Constance presently.

"'Picking blackberries, obviously.'

"'I don't like the way it cried,' pursued Constance; 'somehow its wail keeps ringing in my ears.'

"I did not chide Constance for her morbid fancies; as a matter of fact the same sensation, of being pursued by a persistent fretful wail, had been forcing itself on my rather overtired nerves. For company's sake I hulloed to Esme, who had lagged somewhat behind. With a few springy bounds he drew up level, and then shot past us.

"The wailing accompaniment was explained. The gypsy child was firmly, and I expect painfully, held in his jaws.

"'Merciful Heaven!' screamed Constance, 'what on earth shall we do? What are we to do?'

"I am perfectly certain that at the Last Judgment Constance will ask more questions than any of the examining Seraphs.

"'Can't we do something?' she persisted tearfully, as Esme cantered along easily in front of our tired horses.

"Personally I was doing everything that occurred to me at the moment. I stormed and scolded and coaxed in English and French and gamekeeper language; I made absurd, ineffectual cuts in the air with my hunting crop; I hurled my sandwich case at the brute; in fact, I really don't know what more I could have done. And still we lumbered on through the deepening dusk, with the dark uncouth shape lumbering ahead of us, and a drone of lugubrious music floating in our ears. Suddenly Esme bounded aside into some thick bushes, where we could not follow; the wail rose to a shriek and then stopped altogether. This part of the story I always hurry over, because it is really rather horrible. When the beast joined us again, after an absence of a few minutes, there was an air of patient understanding about him, as though he knew that he had done something of which we disapproved, but which he felt to be thoroughly justifiable.

"'How can you let that ravening beast trot by your side?' asked Constance. She was looking more than ever like an albino beet root.

"'In the first place, I can't prevent it,' I said, 'and in the second place, whatever else he may be, I doubt if he's ravening at the present moment.'

"Constance shuddered. 'Do you think the poor little thing suffered much,' came another of her futile questions.

"'The indications were all that way,' I said. 'On the other hand, of course, it may have been crying from sheer temper. Children sometimes do.'

"It was nearly pitch-dark when we emerged suddenly into the high road. A flash of lights and the whir of a motor went past us at the same moment at uncomfortably close quarters. A thud and a sharp screeching yowl followed a second later. The car drew up, and when I had ridden back to the spot I found a young man bending over a dark motionless mass lying by the roadside.

"'You have killed my Esme,' I exclaimed bitterly.

"'I'm so awfully sorry,' said the young man; 'I keep dogs myself, so I know what you must feel about it. I'll do anything I can in reparation.'

"'Please bury him at once,' I said; 'that much I think I may ask of you.'

"'Bring the spade, William,' he called to the chauffeur. Evidently hasty roadside interments were contingencies that had been provided against.

"The digging of a sufficiently large grave took some time. 'I say, what a magnificent fellow,' said the motorist as the corpse was rolled over into the trench. I'm afraid he must have been rather a valuable animal.'

"'He took second in the puppy class at Binningham last year,' I said resolutely.

"Constance snorted loudly.

"'Don't cry, dear,' I said brokenly; 'it was all over in a moment. He couldn't have suffered much.'

"'Look here,' said the young fellow desperately, 'you simply must let me do something by way of reparation.'

"I refused sweetly, but as he persisted I let him have my address.

"Of course, we kept our own counsel as to the earlier episodes of the evening. Lord Pabham never advertised the loss of his hyaena; when a strictly fruit-eating animal strayed from his park a year or two previously he was called upon to give compensation in eleven cases of sheep-worrying and practically to restock his neighbor's poultry yards, and an escaped hyaena would have mounted up to the something on the scale of a government grant. The gypsies were equally unobtrusive over their missing offspring; I don't suppose in large encampments they really know to a child or two how many they've got."

The Baroness paused reflectively, and then continued: "There was a sequel to the adventure, though. I got through the post a charming little diamond brooch, with the name Esme set in a sprig of rosemary. Incidentally, too, I lost the friendship of Constance Broddle. You see, when I sold the brooch I quite properly refused to give her any share of the proceeds. I pointed out that the Esme part of the affair was my own invention, and the hyaena part of it belonged to Lord Pabham, if it really was his hyaena, of which, of course, I've no proof."

20

The Story of the Pony Express

By Glenn D. Bradley

◇◇

It's hard to imagine that fewer than two centuries ago it took weeks for a letter to travel from the East to West Coast. But when the first "express" package was delivered, it was thanks to the horse. The Pony Express was a harrowing journey for the rough men and tough horses that carried the mail over challenging terrain and through hostile territory. Glenn D. Bradley's The Story of the Pony Express, *excerpted here, provides a fascinating account of its first riders and the challenges they faced.*

—Jessie Shiers

◇◇

(Editor's Note: This chapter includes footnotes linking important historical data and the story of Mark Twain's experience with the Pony Express.)

The First Trip and Triumph
On March 26, 1860, there appeared simultaneously in the *St. Louis Republic* and the *New York Herald* the following notice:

To San Francisco in 8 days by the Central Overland California and Pike's Peak Express Company. The first courier of the Pony Express will leave the Missouri River on Tuesday April 3rd at 5 o'clock p.m. and will run regularly weekly hereafter, carrying a letter mail only. The point of departure on the Missouri River will be in telegraphic connection with the East and will be announced in due time.

Telegraphic messages from all parts of the United States and Canada in connection with the point of departure will be received up to 5 o'clock p.m. of the day of leaving and transmitted over the Placerville and St. Joseph telegraph wire to San Francisco and intermediate points by the connecting express, in 8 days.

The letter mail will be delivered in San Francisco in ten days from the departure of the Express. The Express passes through Forts Kearney, Laramie, Bridger, Great Salt Lake City, Camp Floyd, Carson City, The Washoe Silver Mines, Placerville, and Sacramento.

Letters for Oregon, Washington Territory, British Columbia, the Pacific Mexican ports, Russian Possessions, Sandwich Islands, China, Japan and India will be mailed in San Francisco.

Special messengers, bearers of letters to connect with the express the 3rd of April, will receive communications for the courier of that day at No. 481 Tenth St., Washington City, up to 2:45 p.m. on Friday, March 30, and in New York at the office of J. B. Simpson, Room No. 8, Continental Bank Building, Nassau Street, up to 6:30 a.m. of March 31.

Full particulars can be obtained on application at the above places and from the agents of the Company.

This sudden announcement of the long desired fast mail route aroused great enthusiasm in the West and especially in St. Joseph, Missouri, Salt Lake City, and the cities of California, where preparations to celebrate the opening of the line were at once begun. Slowly the time passed, until the afternoon of the eventful day, April 3rd, that was to mark the first step in annihilating distance between the East and West. A great crowd had assembled on the streets of St. Joseph, Missouri. Flags were flying and a brass band added to the jubilation. The Hannibal and St. Joseph Railroad had arranged to run a special train into the city, bringing the through mail from connecting points in the East. Everybody was anxious and excited. At last the shrill whistle of a locomotive was heard, and the train rumbled in—on time. The pouches were rushed to the post office where the express mail was made ready.

The people now surge about the old "Pike's Peak Livery Stables," just South of Pattee Park. All are hushed with subdued expectancy. As the moment of departure approaches, the doors swing open and a spirited horse is led out. Nearby, closely inspecting the animal's equipment is a wiry little man scarcely twenty years old.

Time to go! Everybody back! A pause of seconds, and a cannon booms in the distance—the starting signal. The rider leaps to his saddle and starts. In less than a minute he is at the post office where the letter pouch, square in shape with four padlocked pockets, is awaiting him. Dismounting only long enough for this pouch to be thrown over his saddle, he again springs to his place and is gone. A short sprint and he has reached the Missouri River wharf. A ferry boat under a full head of steam is waiting. With scarcely checked speed, the horse thunders onto the deck of the craft. A rumbling of machinery, the jangle of a bell, the sharp toot of a whistle and the boat has swung clear and is headed straight for the opposite shore. The crowd behind breaks into tumultuous applause. Some scream themselves hoarse; others are strangely silent; and some—strong men—are moved to tears.

The noise of the cheering multitude grows faint as the Kansas shore draws near. The engines are reversed; a swish of water, and the craft grates against the dock. Scarcely has the gang plank been lowered than horse and rider dash over it and are off at a furious gallop. Away on the jet black steed goes Johnnie Frey, the first rider, with the mail that must be hurled by flesh and blood over 1,966 miles of desolate space—across the plains, through North-eastern Kansas and into Nebraska, up the valley of the Platte, across the Great Plateau, into the foothills and over the summit of the Rockies, into the arid Great Basin, over the Wahsatch range, into the valley of Great Salt Lake, through the terrible alkali deserts of Nevada, through the parched Sink of the Carson River, over the snowy Sierras, and into the Sacramento Valley—the mail must go without delay. Neither storms, fatigue, darkness, rugged mountains, burning deserts, nor savage Indians were to hinder this pouch of letters. The mail must *go*; and its schedule, incredible as it seemed, *must* be made. It was a sublime undertaking, than which few have ever put the fibre of Americans to a severer test.

The managers of the Central Overland California and Pike's Peak Express Company had laid their plans well. Horses and riders for fresh relays, together with station agents and helpers, were ready and waiting at the appointed places, ten or fifteen miles apart over the entire course. There was no guess-work or delay.

After crossing the Missouri River, out of St. Joseph, the official route[1] of the westbound Pony Express ran at first west and south through Kansas to Kennekuk; then northwest, across the Kickapoo Indian reservation, to Granada, Log Chain, Seneca, Ash Point, Guittards, Marysville, and Hollenberg. Here the valley of the Little Blue River was followed, still in a northwest direction. The trail crossed into Nebraska near Rock Creek and pushed on through Big Sandy and Liberty Farm, to Thirty-two-mile Creek. From thence it passed over the prairie divide to the Platte River, the valley of which was followed to Fort Kearney. This route had already been made famous by the Mormons when they journeyed to Utah in 1847. It had also been followed by many of the California gold-seekers in 1848–49 and by Gen. Albert Sidney Johnston and his army when they marched west from Fort Leavenworth to suppress the "Mormon War" of 1857–58.

For about three hundred miles out of Fort Kearney, the trail followed the prairies; for two-thirds of this distance, it clung to the south bank of the Platte, passing through Plum Creek and Midway.[2] At Cottonwood Springs the junction of the North and South branches of the Platte was reached. From here the course moved steadily westward, through Fremont's Springs, O'Fallon's Bluffs, Alkali, Beauvais Ranch, and Diamond Springs to Julesburg, on the South fork of the Platte. Here the stream was forded and the rider then followed the course of Lodge Pole Creek in a northwesterly direction to Thirty Mile Ridge. Thence he journeyed to Mud Springs, Court-House Rock, Chimney Rock, and Scott's Bluffs to Fort Laramie. From this point he passed through the foot-hills to the base of the Rockies, then over the mountains through South Pass and to Fort Bridger. Then to Salt Lake City, Camp Floyd, Ruby Valley, Mountain Wells, across the Humboldt River in Nevada to Bisbys', Carson City, and to Placerville,

---

1. Root and Connelley's Overland Stage to California.

2. So called because it was about half way between the Missouri River and Denver.

California; thence to Folsom and Sacramento. Here the mail was taken by a fast steamer down the Sacramento River to San Francisco.

A large part of this route traversed the wildest regions of the Continent. Along the entire course there were but four military posts and they were strung along at intervals of from two hundred and fifty to three hundred and fifty miles from each other. Over most of the journey there were only small way stations to break the awful monotony. Topographically, the trail covered nearly six hundred miles of rolling prairie, intersected here and there by streams fringed with timber. The nature of the mountainous regions, the deserts, and alkali plains as avenues of horseback travel is well understood. Throughout these areas the men and horses had to endure such risks as rocky chasms, snow slides, and treacherous streams, as well as storms of sand and snow. The worst part of the journey lay between Salt Lake City and Sacramento, where for several hundred miles the route ran through a desert, much of it a bed of alkali dust where no living creature could long survive. It was not merely these dangers of dire exposure and privation that threatened, for wherever the country permitted of human life, Indians abounded. From the Platte River valley westward, the old route sped over by the Pony Express is today substantially that of the Union Pacific and Southern Pacific Railroads.

In California, the region most benefited by the express, the opening of the line was likewise awaited with the keenest anticipation. Of course there had been at the outset a few dissenting opinions, the gist of the opposing sentiment being that the Indians would make the operation of the route impossible. One newspaper went so far as to say that it was "Simply inviting slaughter upon all the foolhardy young men who had been engaged as riders." But the California spirit would not down. A vast majority of the people favored the enterprise and clamored for it; and before the express had been long in operation, all classes were united in the conviction that they could not do without it.

At San Francisco and Sacramento, then the two most important towns in the far West, great preparations were made to celebrate the first outgoing and incoming mails. On April 3rd, at the same hour the express started from St. Joseph,[3] the eastbound mail was placed on board a steamer

---

3. Reports as to the precise hour of starting do not all agree. It was probably late in the afternoon or early in the evening, no later than 6:30.

at San Francisco and sent up the river, accompanied by an enthusiastic delegation of business men. On the arrival of the pouch and its escort at Sacramento, the capital city, they were greeted with the blare of bands, the firing of guns, and the clanging of gongs. Flags were unfurled and floral decorations lined the streets. That night the first rider for the East, Harry Roff, left the city on a white broncho. He rode the first twenty miles in fifty-nine minutes, changing mounts once. He next took a fresh horse at Folsom and pushed on fifty-five miles farther to Placerville. Here he was relieved by "Boston," who carried the mail to Friday Station, crossing the Sierras en route. Next came Sam Hamilton who rode through Geneva, Carson City, Dayton, and Reed's Station to Fort Churchill, seventy-five miles in all. This point, one hundred and eighty-five miles out of Sacramento had been reached in fifteen hours and twenty minutes, in spite of the Sierra Divide where the snow drifts were thirty feet deep and where the Company had to keep a drove of pack mules moving in order to keep the passageway clear. From Fort Churchill into Ruby Valley went H. J. Faust; from Ruby Valley to Shell Creek the courier was "Josh" Perkins; then came Jim Gentry who carried the mail to Deep Creek, and he was followed by "Let" Huntington who pushed on to Simpson's Springs. From Simpson's to Camp Floyd rode John Fisher, and from the latter place Major Egan carried the mail into Salt Lake City, arriving April 7, at 11:45 p.m.[4] The obstacles to fast travel had been numerous because of snow in the mountains, and stormy spring weather with its attendant discomfort and bad going. Yet the schedule had been maintained, and the last seventy-five miles into Salt Lake City had been ridden in five hours and fifteen minutes.

At that time Placerville and Carson City were the terminals of a local telegraph line. News had been flashed back from Carson on April 4 that the rider had passed that point safely. After that came an anxious wait until April 12 when the arrival of the westbound express announced that all was well.

The first trip of the Pony Express westbound from St. Joseph to Sacramento was made in nine days and twenty-three hours. Eastbound, the run was covered in eleven days and twelve hours. The average time of

4. Authorities differ somewhat as to the personnel of the first trip; also as to the number of letters carried.

these two performances was barely half that required by the Butterfield stage over the Southern route. The pony had clipped ten full days from the schedule of its predecessor, and shown that it could keep its schedule—which was as follows:

From St. Joseph to Salt Lake City—124 hours.
From Salt Lake City to Carson City—218 hours, from starting point.
From Carson City to Sacramento—232 hours, from starting point.
From Sacramento to San Francisco—240 hours, from starting point.

From the very first trip, expressions of genuine appreciation of the new service were shown all along the line. The first express which reached Salt Lake City eastbound on the night of April 7, led the *Deseret News*, the leading paper of that town to say that: "Although a telegraph is very desirable, we feel well-satisfied with this achievement for, the present." Two days later, the first westbound express bound from St. Joseph reached the Mormon capital. Oddly enough this rider carried news of an act to amend a bill just proposed in the United States Senate, providing that Utah be organized into Nevada Territory under the name and leadership of the latter.[5] Many of the Mormons, like numerous persons in California, had at first believed the Pony Express an impossibility, but now that it had been demonstrated wholly feasible, they were delighted with its success, whether it brought them good news or bad; for it had brought Utah within six days of the Missouri River and within seven days of Washington City. Prior to this, under the old stage coach régime, the people of that territory had been accustomed to receive their news of the world from six weeks to three months old.

Probably no greater demonstrations were ever held in California cities than when the first incoming express arrived. Its schedule having been announced in the daily papers a week ahead, the people were ready with their welcome. At Sacramento, as when the pony mail had first come up from San Francisco, practically the whole town turned out.

5. On account of the Mormon outbreak and the troubles of 1857–1858, there was at this time much ill-feeling in Congress against Utah. Matters were finally smoothed out and the bill in question was of course dropped. Utah was loyal to the Union throughout the Civil War.

Stores were closed and business everywhere suspended. State officials and other citizens of prominence addressed great crowds in commemoration of the wonderful achievement. Patriotic airs were played and sung and no attempt was made to check the merry-making of the populace. After a hurried stop to deliver local mail, the pouch was rushed aboard the fast sailing steamer *Antelope*, and the trip down the stream begun. Although San Francisco was not reached until the dead of night, the arrival of the express mail was the signal for a hilarious reception. Whistles were blown, bells jangled, and the California Band turned out. The city fire department, suddenly aroused by the uproar, rushed into the street, expecting to find a conflagration, but on recalling the true state of affairs, the firemen joined in with spirit. The express courier was then formally escorted by a huge procession from the steamship dock to the office of the Alta Telegraph, the official Western terminal, and the momentous trip had ended.

The first Pony Express from St. Joseph brought a message of congratulation from President Buchanan to Governor Downey of California, which was first telegraphed to the Missouri River town. It also brought one or two official government communications, some New York, Chicago, and St. Louis newspapers, a few bank drafts, and some business letters addressed to banks and commercial houses in San Francisco—about eighty-five pieces of mail in all.[6] And it had brought news from the East only nine days on the road.

At the outset, the Express reduced the time for letters from New York to the Coast from twenty-three days to about ten days. Before the line had been placed in operation, a telegraph wire, allusion to which has been made, had been strung two hundred and fifty miles Eastward from San Francisco through Sacramento to Carson City, Nevada. Important official business from Washington was therefore wired to St. Joseph, then forwarded by pony rider to Carson City where it was again telegraphed to Sacramento or San Francisco as the case required, thus saving twelve or fifteen hours in transmission on the last lap of the journey. The usual schedule for getting dispatches from the Missouri River to the Coast was eight days, and for letters, ten days.

---

6. Eastbound the first rider carried about seventy letters.

After the triumphant first trip, when it was fully evident that the Pony Express[7] was a really established enterprise, the *St. Joseph Free Democrat* broke into the following panegyric:

> *Take down your map and trace the footprints of our quadrupedantic animal: From St. Joseph on the Missouri to San Francisco, on the Golden Horn—two thousand miles—more than half the distance across our boundless continent; through Kansas, through Nebraska, by Fort Kearney, along the Platte, by Fort Laramie, past the Buttes, over the Rocky Mountains, through the narrow passes and along the steep defiles, Utah, Fort Bridger, Salt Lake City, he witches Brigham with his swift ponyship—through the valleys, along the grassy slopes, into the snow, into sand, faster than Thor's Thialfi, away they go, rider and horse—did you see them? They are in California, leaping over its golden sands, treading its busy streets. The courser has unrolled to us the great American panorama, allowed us to glance at the homes of one million people, and has put a girdle around the earth in forty minutes. Verily the riding is like the riding of Jehu, the son of Nimshi for he rideth furiously. Take out your watch. We are eight days from New York, eighteen from London. The race is to the swift.*

The Pony Express had been tried at the tribunal of popular opinion and given a hearty endorsement. It had yet to win the approval of shrewd statesmanship.

About a hundred years back, such a system was in vogue in various countries of Europe.

Early in the nineteenth century before the telegraph was invented, a New York newspaper man named David Hale used a Pony Express system to collect state news. A little later, in 1830, a rival publisher, Richard Haughton, political editor of the *New York Journal of Commerce* borrowed the same idea. He afterward founded the *Boston Atlas*, and by making

---

7. The idea of a Pony Express was not a new one in 1859. Marco Polo relates that Genghis Khan, ruler of Chinese Tartary, had such a courier service about one thousand years ago. This ambitious monarch, it is said, had relay stations twenty-five miles apart, and his riders sometimes covered three hundred miles in twenty-four hours.

relays of fast horses and taking advantage of the services offered by a few short lines of railroad then operating in Massachusetts, he was enabled to print election returns by nine o'clock on the morning after election.

This idea was improved by James W. Webb, Editor of the *New York Courier* and *Enquirer*, a big daily of that time. In 1832, Webb organized an express rider line between New York and Washington. This undertaking gave his paper much valuable prestige.

In 1833, Hale and Hallock of the *Journal of Commerce* started a rival line that enabled them to publish Washington news within forty-eight hours, thus giving their paper a big "scoop" over all competitors. Papers in Norfolk, Va., two hundred and twenty-nine miles south-east of Washington actually got the news from the capitol out of the *New York Journal of Commerce* received by the ocean route, sooner than news printed in Washington could be sent to Norfolk by boat directly down the Potomac River.

The California Pony Express of historic fame was imitated on a small scale in 1861 by the *Rocky Mountain News* of Denver, then, as now, one of the great newspapers of the West. At that time, this enterprising daily owned and published a paper called the *Miner's Record* at Tarryall, a mining community some distance out of Denver. The *News* also had a branch office at Central City, forty-five miles up in the mountains. As soon as information from the War arrived over the California Pony Express and by stage out of old Julesburg from the Missouri River—Denver was not on the Pony Express route—it was hurried to these outlying points by fast horsemen. Thanks to this enterprise, the miners in the heart of the Rockies could get their War news only four days late.

RIDERS AND FAMOUS RIDES

Bart Riles, the pony rider, died this morning from wounds received at Cold Springs, May 16.

The men at Dry Creek Station have all been killed and it is thought those at Robert's Creek have met with the same fate.

Six Pike's Peakers found the body of the station keeper horribly mutilated, the station burned, and all the stock missing from Simpson's.

Eight horses were stolen from Smith's Creek on last Monday, supposedly by road agents.

The above are random extracts from frontier newspapers, printed while the Pony Express was running. The Express could never have existed on its high plane of efficiency, without an abundance of cool-headed, hardened men; men who knew not fear and who were expert—though sometimes in vain—in all the wonderful arts of self-preservation practiced on the old frontier. That these employees could have performed even the simplest of their duties, without stirring and almost incredible adventures, it is needless to assert.

The faithful relation of even a considerable number of the thrilling experiences to which the "Pony" men were subjected would discount fiction. Yet few of these adventures have been recorded. Today, after a lapse of over fifty years, nearly all of the heroes who achieved them have gone out on that last long journey from which no man returns. While history can pay the tribute of preserving some anecdotes of them and their collective achievements, it must be forever silent as to many of their personal acts of heroism.

While lasting praise is due the faithful station men who, in their isolation, so often bore the murderous attacks of Indians and bandits, it is, perhaps, to the riders that the seeker of romance is most likely to turn. It was the riders' skill and fortitude that made the operation of the line possible. Both riders and hostlers shared the same privations, often being reduced to the necessity of eating wolf meat and drinking foul or brackish water.

While each rider was supposed to average seventy-five miles a trip, riding from three to seven horses, accidents were likely to occur, and it was not uncommon for a man to lose his way. Such delays meant serious trouble in keeping the schedule, keyed up, as it was, to the highest possible speed. It was confronting such emergencies, and in performing the duties of comrades who had been killed or disabled while awaiting their turns to ride, that the most exciting episodes took place.

Among the more famous riders[8] was Jim Moore who later became a ranchman in the South Platte Valley, Nebraska. Moore made his greatest ride on June 8, 1860. He happened to be at Midway Station, half way

---

8. Root and Connelley.

between the Missouri River and Denver, when the westbound messenger arrived with important Government dispatches to California. Moore "took up the run," riding continuously one hundred and forty miles to old Julesburg, the end of his division. Here he met the eastbound messenger, also with important missives, from the Coast to Washington. By all the rules of the game Moore should have rested a few hours at this point, but his successor, who would have picked up the pouch and started eastward, had been killed the day before. The mail must go, and the schedule must be sustained. Without asking any favors of the man who had just arrived from the West, Moore resumed the saddle, after a delay of only ten minutes, without even stopping to eat, and was soon pounding eastward on his return trip. He made it, too, in spite of lurking Indians, hunger and fatigue, covering the round trip of two hundred and eighty miles in fourteen hours and forty-six minutes an average speed of over eighteen miles an hour. Furthermore, his westbound mail had gone through from St. Joseph to Sacramento on a record-making run of eight days and nine hours.

William James, always called "Bill" James, was a native of Virginia. He had crossed the plains with his parents in a wagon train when only five years old. At eighteen, he was one of the best Pony Express riders in the service. James's route lay between Simpson's Park and Cole Springs, Nevada, in the Smoky Valley range of mountains. He rode only sixty miles each way but covered his round trip of one hundred and twenty miles in twelve hours, including all stops. He always rode California mustangs, using five of these animals each way. His route crossed the summits of two mountain ridges, lay through the Shoshone Indian country, and was one of the loneliest and most dangerous divisions on the line. Yet "Bill" never took time to think about danger, nor did he ever have any serious trouble.

Theodore Rand rode the Pony Express during the entire period of its organization. His run was from Box Elder to Julesburg, one hundred and ten miles and he made the entire distance both ways by night. His schedule, night run though it was, required a gait of ten miles an hour, but Rand often made it at an average of twelve, thus saving time on the through schedule for some unfortunate rider who might have trouble and delay. Originally, Rand used only four or five horses each way, but this number, in keeping with the revised policy of the Company, was afterward doubled, an extra mount being furnished him every twelve or fifteen miles.

Johnnie Frey who has already been mentioned as the first rider out of St. Joseph, was little more than a boy when he entered the pony service. He was a native Missourian, weighing less than one hundred and twenty-five pounds. Though small in stature, he was every inch a man. Frey's division ran from St. Joseph to Seneca, Kansas, eighty miles, which he covered at an average of twelve and one half miles an hour, including all stops. When the war started, Frey enlisted in the Union army under General Blunt. His short but worthy career was cut short in 1863 when he fell in a hand-to-hand fight with rebel bushwhackers in Arkansas. In this, his last fight, Frey is said to have killed five of his assailants before being struck down.

Jim Beatley, whose real name was Foote, was another Virginian, about twenty-five years of age. He rode on an eastern division, usually west out of Seneca. On one occasion, he traveled from Seneca to Big Sandy, fifty miles and back, doubling his route twice in one week. Beatley was killed by a stage hand in a personal quarrel, the affair taking place on a ranch in Southern Nebraska in 1862.

William Boulton was one of the older riders in the service; his age at that time is given at about thirty-five. Boulton rode for about three months with Beatley.[9] On one occasion, while running between Seneca and Guittards', Boulton's horse gave out when five miles from the latter station. Without a moment's delay, he removed his letter pouch and hurried the mail in on foot, where a fresh horse was at once provided and the schedule resumed.

Melville Baughn, usually known as "Mel," had a pony run between Fort Kearney and Thirty-two-mile Creek. Once while "laying off" between trips, a thief made off with his favorite horse. Scarcely had the miscreant gotten away when Baughn discovered the loss. Hastily saddling another steed, "Mel" gave pursuit, and though handicapped, because the outlaw had the pick of the stable, Baughn's superior horsemanship, even on an inferior mount, soon told. After a chase of several miles, he

---

9. Pony riders often alternated "runs" with each other over their respective divisions in the same manner as do railroad train crews at the present time.

forced the fellow so hard that he abandoned the stolen animal at a place called Loup Fork, and sneaked away. Recovering the horse, Baughn then returned to his station, found a mail awaiting him, and was off on his run without further delay. With him and his fellow employees, running down a horse thief was but a trifling incident and an annoyance merely because of the bother and delay which it necessitated. Baughn was afterward hanged for murder at Seneca, but his services to the Pony Express were above reproach.

Another Eastern Division man was Jack Keetly, who also rode from St. Joseph to Seneca, alternating at times with Frey and Baughn. Keetley's greatest performance, and one of the most remarkable ever achieved in the service, was riding from Rock Creek to St. Joseph; then back to his starting point and on to Seneca, and from Seneca once more to Rock Creek—three hundred and forty miles without rest. He traveled continuously for thirty-one hours, his entire run being at the rate of eleven miles an hour. During the last five miles of his journey, he fell asleep in the saddle and in this manner concluded his long trip.

Don C. Rising, who afterwards settled in Northern Kansas, was born in Painted Post, Steuben County, New York, in 1844, and came West when thirteen years of age. He rode in the pony service nearly a year, from November, 1860, until the line was abandoned the following October, most of his service being rendered before he was seventeen. Much of his time was spent running eastward out of Fort Kearney until the telegraph had reached that point and made the operation of the Express between the fort and St. Joseph no longer necessary. On two occasions, Rising is said to have maintained a continuous speed of twenty miles an hour while carrying important dispatches between Big Sandy and Rock Creek.

One rider who was well known as "Little Yank" was a boy scarcely out of his teens and weighing barely one hundred pounds. He rode along the Platte River between Cottonwood Springs and old Julesburg and frequently made one hundred miles on a single trip.

Another man named Hogan, of whom little is known, rode northwesterly out of Julesburg across the Platte and to Mud Springs, eighty miles.

Jimmy Clark rode between various stations east of Fort Kearney, usually between Big Sandy and Hollenburg. Sometimes his run took him as far West as Liberty Farm on the Little Blue River.

James W. Brink, or "Dock" Brink as he was known to his associates, was one of the early riders, entering the employ of the Pony Express Company in April, 1860. While "Dock" made a good record as a courier, his chief fame was gained in a fight at Rock Creek station, in which Brink and Wild Bill[10] "cleaned out" the McCandless gang of outlaws, killing five of their number.

Charles Cliff had an eighty-mile pony run when only seventeen years of age, but, like Brink, young Cliff gained his greatest reputation as a fighter—in his case fighting Indians. It seems that while Cliff was once freighting with a small train of nine wagons, it was attacked by a party of one hundred Sioux Indians and besieged for three days until a larger train approached and drove the redskins away. During the conflict, Cliff received three bullets in his body and twenty-seven in his clothing, but he soon recovered from his injuries, and was afterward none the less valuable to the Pony Express service.

J. G. Kelley, later a citizen of Denver, was a veteran pony man. He entered the employ of the company at the outset, and helped Superintendent Roberts to lay out the route across Nevada. Along the Carson River, tiresome stretches of corduroy road had to be built. Kelley relates that in constructing this highway willow trees were cut near the stream and the trunks cut into the desired lengths before being laid in place. The men often had to carry these timbers in their arms for three hundred yards, while the mosquitoes swarmed so thickly upon their faces and hands as to make their real color and identity hard to determine.

At the Sink of the Carson,[11] a great depression of the river on its course through the desert, Kelley assisted in building a fort for protecting the line against Indians. Here there were no rocks nor timber, and so

---

10. "Wild Bill" Hickock was one of the most noted gun fighters that the West ever produced. As marshal of Abilene, Kansas, and other wild frontier towns he became a terror to bad men and compelled them to respect law and order when under his jurisdiction. Probably no man has ever equaled him in the use of the six shooter. Numerous magazine articles describing his career can be found.

11. Inman and Cody, Salt Lake Trail.

the structure had to be built of adobe mud. To get this mud to a proper consistency, the men tramped it all day with their bare feet. The soil was soaked with alkali, and as a result, according to Kelley's story, their feet were swollen so as to resemble "hams."

They next erected a fort at Sand Springs, twenty miles from Carson Lake, and another at Cold Springs, thirty-two miles east of Sand Springs. At Cold Springs, Kelley was appointed assistant station-keeper under Jim McNaughton. An outbreak of the Pah-Ute Indians was now in progress, and as the little station was in the midst of the disturbed area, there was plenty of excitement.

One night while Kelley was on guard his attention was attracted by the uneasiness of the horses. Gazing carefully through the dim light, he saw an Indian peering over the outer wall or stockade. The orders of the post were to shoot every Indian that came within range, so Kelley blazed away, but missed his man. In the morning, many tracks were found about the place. This wild shot had probably frightened the prowlers away, saving the station from attack, and certain destruction.

During this same morning, a Mexican pony rider came in, mortally wounded, having been shot by the savages from ambush while passing through a dense thicket in the vicinity known as Quaking Asp Bottom. Although given tender care, the poor fellow died within a few hours after his arrival. The mail was waiting and it must go. Kelley, who was the lightest man in the place—he weighed but one hundred pounds—was now ordered by the boss to take the dead man's place, and go on with the dispatches. This he did, finishing the run without further incident. On his return trip he had to pass once more through the aspen thicket where his predecessor had received his death wound. This was one of the most dangerous points on the entire trail, for the road zigzagged through a jungle, following a passageway that was only large enough to admit a horse and rider; for two miles a man could not see more than thirty or forty feet ahead. Kelley was expecting trouble, and went through like a whirlwind, at the same time holding a repeating rifle in readiness should trouble occur. On having cleared the thicket, he drew rein on the top of a hill, and, looking back over his course, saw the bushes moving in a suspicious manner. Knowing there was no live stock in that locality and that wild game rarely abounded there, he sent several shots in the direction of the moving underbrush. The motion soon ceased, and he galloped onward, unharmed.

A few days later, two United States soldiers, while traveling to join their command, were ambushed and murdered in the same thicket.

This was about the time when Major Ormsby's command was massacred by the Utes in the disaster at Pyramid Lake,[12] and the Indians everywhere in Nevada were unusually aggressive and dangerous. There were seldom more than three or four men in the little station and it is remarkable that Kelley and his companions were not all killed.

One of Kelley's worst rides, in addition to the episode just related, was the stretch between Cold Springs and Sand Springs for thirty-seven miles without a drop of water along the way.

Once, while dashing past a wagon train of immigrants, a whole fusillade of bullets was fired at Kelley who narrowly escaped with his life. Of course he could not stop the mail to see why he had been shot at, but on his return trip he met the same crowd, and in unprintable language told them what he thought of their lawless and irresponsible conduct. The only satisfaction he could get from them in reply was the repeated assertion, "We thought you was an Indian!"[13] Nor was Kelley the only pony rider who took narrow chances from the guns of excited immigrants. Traveling rapidly and unencumbered, the rider, sunburned and blackened by exposure, must have borne on first glance no little resemblance to an Indian; and especially would the mistake be natural to excited wagon-men who were always in fear of dashing attacks from mounted Indians—attacks in which a single rider would often be deployed to ride past the white men at utmost speed in order to draw their fire. Then when their guns were empty a hidden band of savages would make a furious onslaught. It was the established rule of the West in those days, in case of suspected danger,

---

12. Bancroft.

13. Indians would sometimes gaze in open-mouthed wonder at the on-rushing ponies. To some of them, the "pony outfit" was "bad medicine" and not to be molested. There was a certain air of mystery about the wonderful system and untiring energy with which the riders followed their course. Unfortunately, a majority of the red men were not always content to watch the Express in simple wonder. They were too frequently bent upon committing deviltry to refrain from doing harm whenever they had a chance.

to shoot first, and make explanations afterward; to do to the other fellow as he would do to you, and do it first!

Added to the perils of the wilderness deserts, blizzards, and wild Indians—the pony riders, then, had at times to beware of their white friends under such circumstances as have been narrated. And that added to the tragical romance of their daily lives. Yet they courted danger and were seldom disappointed, for danger was always near them.

21

Mark Twain's Pony Express Adventure

By Mark Twain

From his book Roughing It, *one of America's greatest writers shares his early experiences with the Pony Express.*

IN A LITTLE WHILE ALL INTEREST WAS TAKEN UP IN STRETCHING OUR necks and watching for the "pony-rider"—the fleet messenger who sped across the continent from St. Joe to Sacramento, carrying letters nineteen hundred miles in eight days! Think of that for perishable horse and human flesh and blood to do! The pony-rider was usually a little bit of a man, brimful of spirit and endurance. No matter what time of the day or night his watch came on, and no matter whether it was winter or summer, raining, snowing, hailing, or sleeting, or whether his "beat" was a level straight road or a crazy trail over mountain crags and precipices, or whether it lead through peaceful regions or regions that swarmed with hostile Indians, he must be always ready to leap into the saddle and be off like the wind!

There was no idling-time for a pony-rider on duty. He rode fifty miles without stopping, by daylight, moonlight, starlight, or through the blackness of darkness—just as it happened. He rode a splendid horse that was born for a racer and fed and lodged like a gentleman; kept him at his utmost speed for ten miles, and then, as he came crashing up to the station where stood two men holding fast a fresh, impatient steed, the transfer of rider and mailbag was made in the twinkling of an eye, and away flew the eager pair and were out of sight before the spectator could get hardly the ghost of a look.

Both rider and horse went "flying light." The rider's dress was thin, and fitted close; he wore a "round-about," and a skull-cap, and tucked his pantaloons into his boot-tops like a race-rider. He carried no arms—he carried nothing that was not absolutely necessary, for even the postage on his literary freight was worth five dollars a letter.

"HERE HE COMES"

He got but little frivolous correspondence to carry—his bag had business letters in it, mostly. His horse was stripped of all unnecessary weight, too. He wore a little wafer of a racing-saddle, and no visible blanket. He wore light shoes, or none at all. The little flat mail-pockets strapped under the rider's thighs would each hold about the bulk of a child's primer. They held many and many an important business chapter and newspaper letter, but these were written on paper as airy and thin as gold leaf, nearly, and thus bulk and weight were economized. The stagecoach traveled about a hundred to a hundred and twenty-five miles a day (twenty-four hours), the pony-rider about two hundred and fifty. There were about eighty pony-riders in the saddle all the time, night and day, stretching in a long, scattering procession from Missouri to California, forty flying eastward, and forty towards the west, and among them making four hundred gallant horses earn a stirring livelihood and see a deal of scenery every single day in the year.

We had had a consuming desire, from the beginning, to see a pony-rider, but somehow or other all that passed us and all that met us managed to streak by in the night, and so we heard only a whiz and a hail, and the swift phantom of the desert was gone before we could get our heads out of the windows. But now we were expecting one along every moment, and would see him in broad daylight. Presently the driver exclaims: "HERE HE COMES!"

Every neck is stretched further, and every eye strained wider. Away across the endless dead level of the prairie a black speck appears against the sky, and it is plain that it moves. Well, I should think so!

CHANGING HORSES

In a second or two it becomes a horse and rider, rising and falling, rising and falling—sweeping towards us nearer and nearer—growing more and more distinct, more and more sharply defined—nearer and still nearer, and the flutter of the hoofs comes faintly to the ear—another instant a whoop and a hurrah from our upper deck, a wave of the rider's hand, but no reply; and man and horse burst past our excited faces, and go winging away like a belated fragment of a storm!

So sudden is it all, and so like a flash of unreal fancy, that but for the flake of white foam left quivering and perishing on a mail-sack after the vision had flashed by and disappeared, we might have doubted whether we had seen any actual horse and man at all, maybe.

22

The Pacing Mustang

By Ernest Thompson Seton

*One of America's most renowned writers of nature stories has some-
thing different for us here. "The Pacing Mustang" is the tale of a horse
that will not be ridden by anyone. For Wild West enthusiasts, it is
an exciting adventure story. For horse lovers, it is an account with a
tragic, yet powerful, ending that exemplifies both the importance of a
good horse to the men who won the West as well as the fighting spirit of
a truly untamable horse. Why most horses have allowed themselves to
be domesticated by human beings, given their sheer size and strength,
is a mystery. While many horses will tolerate unbelievable amounts of
hard work and abuse, there are those horses that are legendary for their
independent spirit. "The Pacing Mustang" is one of them.*

—Jessie Shiers

I

Jo CALONE THREW DOWN HIS SADDLE ON THE DUSTY GROUND, TURNED
his horses loose, and went clanking into the ranchhouse.

"Nigh about chuck time?" he asked.

"Seventeen minutes," said the cook glancing at the Waterbury, with
the air of a train starter, though this show of precision had never yet been
justified by events.

"How's things on the Perico?" said Jo's pard.

"Hotter'n hinges," said Jo. "Cattle seem O.K.; lots of calves."

"I seen that bunch o' mustangs that waters at Antelope Springs; couple o' colts along; one little dark one, a fair dandy; a born pacer. I run them a mile or two, and he led the bunch, an' never broke his pace. Cut loose, an' pushed them jest for fun, an' darned if I could make him break."

"You didn't have no reefreshments along?" said Scarth, incredulously.

"That's all right, Scarth. You had to crawl on our last bet, an' you'll get another chance soon as you're man enough."

"Chuck," shouted the cook, and the subject was dropped. Next day the scene of the roundup was changed, and the mustangs were forgotten.

A year later the same corner of New Mexico was worked over by the roundup, and again the mustang bunch was seen. The dark colt was now a black yearling, with thin, clean legs and glossy flanks; and more than one of the boys saw with his own eyes this oddity—the mustang was a born pacer. Jo was along, and the idea now struck him that that colt was worth having. To an Easterner this thought may not seem startling or original, but in the West, where an unbroken horse is worth $5, and where an ordinary saddlehorse is worth $15 or $20, the idea of a wild mustang being desirable property does not occur to the average cowboy, for mustangs are hard to catch, and when caught are merely wild animal prisoners, perfectly useless and untamable to the last. Not a few of the cattle-owners make a point of shooting all mustangs at sight, they are not only useless cumberers of the feeding-grounds, but commonly lead away domestic horses, which soon take to wild life and are thenceforth lost.

Wild Jo Calone knew a "bronk right down to subsoil." "I never seen a white that wasn't soft, nor a chestnut that wasn't nervous, nor a bay that wasn't good if broke right, nor a black that wasn't hard as nails, an' full of the old Harry. All a black bronk wants is claws to be wus'n Daniel's hull outfit of lions."

Since, then, a mustang is worthless vermin, and a black mustang ten times worse than worthless, Jo's pard "didn't see no sense in Jo's wantin' to corral the yearling," as he now seemed intent on doing. But Jo got no chance to try that year.

He was only a cow-puncher on $25 a month, and tied to hours. Like most of the boys, he always looked forward to having a ranch and an outfit of his own. His brand, the hogpen, of sinister suggestion, was already registered at Santa Fe, but of horned stock it was borne by a single old cow, so as to give him a legal right to put his brand on any maverick (or unbranded animal) he might chance to find.

Yet each fall, when paid off, Jo could not resist the temptation to go to town with the boys and have a good time "while the stuff held out." So that his property consisted of little more than his saddle, his bed, and his old cow. He kept on hoping to make a strike that would leave him well fixed with a fair start, and when the thought came that the Black Mustang was his mascot, he only needed a chance to "make the try."

The roundup circled down to the Canadian River, and back in the fall by the Don Carlos Hills, and Jo saw no more of the Pacer, though he heard of him from many quarters, for the colt, now a vigorous, young horse, rising three, was beginning to be talked of.

Antelope Springs is in the middle of a great level plain. When the water is high it spreads into a small lake with a belt of sedge around it; when it is low there is a wide flat of black mud, glistening white with alkali in places, and the spring a water-hole in the middle. It has no flow or outlet and is fairly good water, the only drinking-place for many miles.

This flat, or prairie as it would be called farther north, was the favorite feeding-ground of the Black Stallion, but it was also the pasture of many herds of range horses and cattle. Chiefly interested was the "L cross F" outfit. Foster, the manager and part owner, was a man of enterprise. He believed it would pay to handle a better class of cattle and horses on the range, and one of his ventures was ten half-blooded mares, tall, clean-limbed, deer-eyed creatures that made the scrub cow-ponies look like pitiful starvelings of some degenerate and quite different species.

One of these was kept stabled for use, but the nine, after the weaning of their colts, managed to get away and wandered off on the range.

A horse has a fine instinct for the road to the best feed, and the nine mares drifted, of course, to the prairie of Antelope Springs, twenty miles to the southward. And when, later that summer Foster went to round them up, he found the nine indeed, but with them and guarding them with an air of more than mere comradeship was a coal-black stallion, prancing around and rounding up the bunch like an expert, his jet-black coat a vivid contrast to the golden hides of his harem.

The mares were gentle, and would have been easily driven homeward but for a new and unexpected thing. The Black Stallion became greatly aroused. He seemed to inspire them too with his wildness, and flying this way and that way drove the whole band at full gallop where he would. Away they went, and the little cow-ponies that carried the men were easily left behind.

This was maddening, and both men at last drew their guns and sought a chance to drop that "blasted stallion." But no chance came that was not 9 to 1 of dropping one of the mares. A long day of manoeuvring made no change. The Pacer, for it was he, kept his family together and disappeared among the southern sand-hills. The cattlemen on their jaded ponies set out for home with the poor satisfaction of vowing vengeance for their failure on the superb cause of it.

One of the most aggravating parts of it was that one or two experiences like this would surely make the mares as wild as the Mustang, and there seemed to be no way of saving them from it.

Scientists differ on the power of beauty and prowess to attract female admiration among the lower animals, but whether it is admiration or the prowess itself, it is certain that a wild animal of uncommon gifts soon wins a large following from the harems of his rivals. And the great Black Horse, with his inky mane and tail and his green-lighted eyes, ranged through all that region and added to his following from many bands till not less than a score of mares were in his "bunch." Most were merely humble cow-ponies turned out to range, but the nine great mares were there, a striking group by themselves. According to all reports, this bunch was always kept rounded up and guarded with such energy and jealously that a mare, once in it, was a lost animal so far as man was concerned, and the ranchmen realized soon that they had gotten on the range a mustang that was doing them more harm than all other sources of loss put together.

II

It was December, 1893. I was new in the country, and was setting out from the ranch-house on the Pinavetitos, to go with a wagon to the Canadian

River. As I was leaving, Foster finished his remark by: "And if you get a chance to draw a bead on that accursed mustang, don't fail to drop him in his tracks."

This was the first I had heard of him, and as I rode along I gathered from Burns, my guide, the history that has been given. I was full of curiosity to see the famous three-year-old, and was not a little disappointed on the second day when we came to the prairie on Antelope Springs and saw no sign of the Pacer or his band.

But on the next day, as we crossed the Alamosa Arroyo, and were rising to the rolling prairie again, Jack Burns, who was riding on ahead, suddenly dropped flat on the neck of his horse, and swung back to me in the wagon, saying: "Get out your rifle, here's that—stallion."

I seized my rifle, and hurried forward to a view over the prairie ridge. In the hollow below was a band of horses, and there at one end was the Great Black Mustang. He had heard some sound of our approach, and was not unsuspicious of danger. There he stood with head and tail erect, and nostrils wide, an image of horse perfection and beauty, as noble an animal as ever ranged the plains, and the mere notion of turning that magnificent creature into a mass of carrion was horrible. In spite of Jack's exhortation to "shoot quick," I delayed, and threw open the breach, whereupon he, always hot and hasty, swore at my slowness, growled, "Gi' me that gun," and as he seized it I turned the muzzle up, and accidentally the gun went off.

Instantly the herd below was all alarm, the great black leader snorted and neighed and dashed about. And the mares bunched, and away all went in a rumble of hoofs, and a cloud of dust.

The Stallion careered now on this side, now on that, and kept his eye on all and led and drove them far away. As long as I could see I watched, and never once did he break his pace.

Jack made Western remarks about me and my gun, as well as that mustang, but I rejoiced in the Pacer's strength and beauty, and not for all the mares in the bunch would I have harmed his glossy hide.

III

There are several ways of capturing wild horses. One is by creasing—that is, grazing the animal's nape with a rifle-ball so that he is stunned long enough for hobbling.

"Yes! I seen about a hundred necks broke trying it, but I never seen a mustang creased yet," was Wild Jo's critical remark.

Sometimes, if the shape of the country abets it, the herd can be driven into a corral; sometimes with extra fine mounts they can be run down, but by far the commonest way, paradoxical as it may seem, is to walk them down.

The fame of the Stallion that never was known to gallop was spreading. Extraordinary stories were told of his gait, his speed, and his wind, and when old Montgomery of the "triangle-bar" outfit came out plump at Well's Hotel in Clayton, and in presence of witnesses said he'd give one thousand dollars cash for him safe in a boxcar, providing the stories were true, a dozen young cow-punchers were eager to cut loose and win the purse, as soon as present engagements were up. But Wild Jo had had his eye on this very deal for quite a while; there was no time to lose, so ignoring present contracts he rustled all night to raise the necessary equipment for the game.

By straining his already overstrained credit, and taxing the already overtaxed generosity of his friends, he got together an expedition consisting of twenty good saddle-horses, a mess-wagon, and a fortnight's stuff for three men—himself, his "pard," Charley, and the cook.

Then they set out from Clayton, with the avowed intention of walking down the wonderfully swift wild horse. The third day they arrived at Antelope Springs, and as it was about noon they were not surprised to see the black Pacer marching down to drink with all his band behind him. Jo kept out of sight until the wild horses each and all had drunk their fill, for a thirsty animal always travels better than one laden with water.

Jo then rode quietly forward. The Pacer took alarm at half a mile, and led his band away out of sight on the soapweed mesa to the southeast. Jo followed at a gallop till he once more sighted them, then came back and instructed the cook, who was also teamster, to make for Alamosa Arroyo in the south. Then away to the southeast he went after the mustangs.

After a mile or two he once more sighted them, and walked his horse quietly till so near that they again took alarm and circled away to the south. An hour's trot, not on the trail, but cutting across to where they ought to go, brought Jo again in close sight. Again he walked quietly toward the herd, and again there was the alarm and fright. And so they passed the afternoon, but circled ever more and more to the south, so that when the sun was low they were, as Jo had expected, not far from Alamosa Arroyo. The band was again close at hand, and Jo, after starting them off, rode to the wagon, while his pard, who had been taking it easy, took up the slow chase on a fresh horse.

After supper the wagon moved on to the upper ford of the Alamosa, as arranged, and there camped for the night.

Meanwhile, Charley followed the herd. They had not run so far as at first, for their pursuer made no sign of attack, and they were getting used to his company. They were more easily found, as the shadows fell, on account of a snow-white mare that was in the bunch. A young moon in the sky now gave some help, and relying on his horse to choose the path, Charley kept him quietly walking after the herd, represented by that ghost-white mare, till they were lost in the night. He then got off, unsaddled and picketed his horse, and in his blanket quickly went to sleep.

At the first streak of dawn he was up, and within a short half-mile, thanks to the snowy mare, he found the band. At his approach, the shrill neigh of the Pacer bugled his troop into a flying squad. But on the first mesa they stopped, and faced about to see what this persistent follower was, and what he wanted. For a moment or so they stood against the sky to gaze, and then deciding that he knew him as well as he wished to, that black meteor flung his mane on the wind, and led off at his tireless, even swing, while the mares came streaming after.

Away they went, circling now to the west, and after several repetitions of this same play, flying, following, and overtaking, and flying again, they passed, near noon, the old Apache look-out, Buffalo Bluff. And here, on watch, was Jo. A long thin column of smoke told Charley to come to camp, and with a flashing pocket-mirror he made response. Jo, freshly mounted, rode across, and again took up the chase, and back came Charley to camp to eat and rest, and then move on up stream.

All that day Jo followed, and managed, when it was needed, that the herd should keep the great circle, of which the wagon cut a small chord. At sundown he came to Verde Crossing, and there was Charley with a fresh horse and food, and Jo went on in the same calm, dogged way. All the evening he followed, and far into the night, for the wild herd was now getting somewhat used to the presence of the harmless strangers, and were more easily followed; moreover, they were tiring out with perpetual traveling. They were no longer in the good grass country, they were not grain-fed like the horses on their track, and above all, the slight but continuous nervous tension was surely telling. It spoiled their appetites, but made them very thirsty. They were allowed, and as far as possible encouraged, to drink deeply at every chance. The effect of large quantities of water on a running animal is well known; it tends to stiffen the limbs and spoil the wind. Jo carefully guarded his own horse against such excess, and both he and his horse were fresh when they camped that night on the trail of the jaded mustangs.

At dawn he found them easily close at hand, and though they ran at first they did not go far before they dropped into a walk. The battle seemed nearly won now, for the chief difficulty in the "walk-down" is to keep track of the herd the first two or three days when they are fresh.

All that morning Jo kept in sight, generally in close sight, of the band. About ten o'clock, Charley relieved him near Jos. Peak and that day the mustangs walked only a quarter of a mile ahead with much less spirit than the day before and circled now more north again. At night Charley was supplied with a fresh horse and followed as before.

Next day the mustangs walked with heads held low, and in spite of the efforts of the Black Pacer at times they were less than a hundred yards ahead of their pursuer.

The fourth and fifth days passed the same way, and now the herd was nearly back to Antelope Springs. So far all had come out as expected. The chase had been in a great circle with the wagon following a lesser circle. The wild herd was back to its starting-point, worn out; and the hunters were back, fresh and on fresh horses. The herd was kept from drinking till late in the afternoon and then driven to the Springs to swell themselves with a perfect water gorge. Now was the chance for the skilful ropers on the grain-fed horses to close in, for the sudden heavy drink was ruin-ation, almost paralysis, of wind and limb, and it would be easy to rope and hobble them one by one.

There was only one weak spot in the programme, the Black Stallion, the cause of the hunt, seemed made of iron, that ceaseless swinging pace seemed as swift and vigorous now as on the morning when the chase began. Up and down he went rounding up the herd and urging them on by voice and example to escape. But they were played out. The old white mare that had been such help in sighting them at night, had dropped out hours ago, dead beat. The half-bloods seemed to be losing all fear of the horsemen, the band was clearly in Jo's power. But the one who was the prize of all the hunt seemed just as far as ever out of reach.

Here was a puzzle. Jo's comrades knew him well and would not have been surprised to see him in a sudden rage attempt to shoot the Stallion down. But Jo had no such mind. During that long week of following he had watched the horse all day at speed and never once had he seen him gallop.

The horseman's adoration of a noble horse had grown and grown, till now he would as soon have thought of shooting his best mount as firing on that splendid beast.

Jo even asked himself whether he would take the handsome sum that was offered for the prize. Such an animal would be a fortune in himself to sire a race of pacers for the track.

But the prize was still at large—the time had come to finish up the hunt. Jo's finest mount was caught. She was a mare of Eastern blood, but raised on the plains. She never would have come into Jo's possession but for a curious weakness. The loco is a poisonous weed that grows in these regions. Most stock will not touch it; but sometimes an animal tries it and becomes addicted to it.

It acts somewhat like morphine, but the animal, though sane for long intervals, has always a passion for the herb and finally dies mad. A beast with the craze is said to be locoed. And Jo's best mount had a wild gleam in her eye that to an expert told the tale.

But she was swift and strong and Jo chose her for the grand finish of the chase. It would have been an easy matter now to rope the mares, but was no longer necessary. They could be separated from their black leader and driven home to the corral. But that leader still had the look of untamed strength. Jo, rejoicing in a worthy foe, went bounding forth to try the odds. The lasso was flung on the ground and trailed to take out every kink, and gathered as he rode into neatest coils across his left palm. Then putting on the spur the first time in that chase he rode straight for the Stallion a quarter of a mile beyond. Away he went, and away went Jo, each at his best, while the fagged-out mares scattered right and left and let them pass. Straight across the open plain the fresh horse went at its hardest gallop, and the Stallion, leading off, still kept his start and kept his famous swing.

It was incredible, and Jo put on more spur and shouted to his horse, which fairly flew, but shortened up the space between by not a single inch. For the Black One whirled across the flat and up and passed a soap-weed mesa and down across a sandy treacherous plain, then over a grassy stretch where prairie dogs barked, then hid below, and on came Jo, but there to see, could he believe his eyes, the Stallion's start grown longer still, and Jo began to curse his luck, and urge and spur his horse until the poor uncertain brute got into such a state of nervous fright, her eyes began to roll, she wildly shook her head from side to side, no longer picked her ground—a badger-hole received her foot and down she went, and Jo went flying to the earth. Though badly bruised, he gained his feet and tried to mount his crazy beast. But she, poor brute, was done for—her off foreleg hung loose.

There was but one thing to do. Jo loosed the cinch, put Lightfoot out of pain, and carried back the saddle to the camp. While the Pacer steamed away till lost to view.

This was not quite defeat, for all the mares were manageable now, and Jo and Charley drove them carefully to the "L cross F" corral and claimed a good reward. But Jo was more than ever bound to own the Stallion. He had seen what stuff he was made of, he prized him more and more, and only sought to strike some better plan to catch him.

IV

The cook on that trip was Bates—Mr. Thomas Bates, he called himself at the post office where he regularly went for the letters and remittance which never came. Old Tom Turkeytrack, the boys called him, from his cattle-brand, which he said was on record at Denver, and which, according to his story, was also borne by countless beef and saddle stock on the plains of the unknown North.

When asked to join the trip as a partner, Bates made some sarcastic remarks about horses not fetching $12 a dozen, which had been literally true within the year, and he preferred to go on a very meagre salary. But no one who once saw the Pacer going had failed to catch the craze. Turkeytrack experienced the usual change of heart. He now wanted to own that mustang. How this was to be brought about he did not clearly see till one day there called at the ranch that had "secured his services," as he put it, one, Bill Smith, more usually known as Horseshoe Billy, from his cattle-brand. While the excellent fresh beef and bread and the vile coffee, dried peaches and molasses were being consumed, he of the horseshoe remarked, in tones which percolated through a huge stop-gap of bread: "Wall, I seen that thar Pacer today, nigh enough to put a plait in his tail."

"What, you didn't shoot?"

"No, but I come mighty near it."

"Don't you be led into no sich foolishness," said a "double-bar H" cow-puncher at the other end of the table. "I calc'late that maverick 'ill carry my brand before the moon changes."

"You'll have to be pretty spry or you'll find a 'triangle dot' on his weather side when you get there."

"Where did you run across him?"

"Wail, it was like this; I was riding the flat by Antelope Springs and I sees a lump on the dry mud inside the rush belt. I knowed I never seen that before, so I rides up, thinking it might be some of our stock, an' seen it was a horse lying plumb flat. The wind was blowing like—from him to me, so I rides up close and seen it was the Pacer, dead as a mackerel. Still, he didn't look swelled or cut, and there wa'n't no smell, an' I didn't know what to think till I seen his ear twitch off a fly and then I knowed he was sleeping. I gits down me rope and coils it, and seen it was old and pretty shaky in spots, and me saddle a single cinch, an' me pony about 700 again a 1,200 lbs. stallion, an' I sez to meself, sez I: 'Tain't no use, I'll only break me cinch and git throwed an' lose me saddle.' So I hits the saddle-horn a crack with the hondu, and I wish't you'd a seen that mustang. He lept six foot in the air an' snorted like he was shunting cars. His eyes fairly bugged out an' he lighted out lickety split for California, and he orter be there about now if he kep' on like he started—and I swear he never made a break the hull trip."

The story was not quite so consecutive as given here. It was much punctuated by present engrossments, and from first to last was more or less infiltrated through the necessaries of life, for Bill was a healthy young man without a trace of false shame. But the account was complete and everyone believed it, for Billy was known to be reliable. Of all those who heard, old Turkeytrack talked the least and probably thought the most, for it gave him a new idea.

During his after-dinner pipe he studied it out and deciding that he could not go it alone, he took Horseshoe Billy into his council and the result was a partnership in a new venture to capture the Pacer; that is, the $5,000 that was now said to be the offer for him safe in a boxcar.

Antelope Springs was still the usual watering-place of the Pacer. The water being low left a broad belt of dry black mud between the sedge and the spring. At two places this belt was broken by a well-marked trail made by the animals coming to drink. Horses and wild animals usually kept to these trails, though the horned cattle had no hesitation in taking a short cut through the sedge.

In the most used of these trails the two men set to work with shovels and dug a pit 15 feet long, 6 feet wide and 7 feet deep. It was a hard twenty hours work for them as it had to be completed between the Mustang's drinks, and it began to be very damp work before it was finished. With poles, brush, and earth it was then cleverly covered over and concealed. And the men went to a distance and hid in pits made for the purpose.

About noon the Pacer came, alone now since the capture of his band. The trail on the opposite side of the mud belt was little used, and old Tom, by throwing some fresh rushes across it, expected to make sure that the Stallion would enter by the other, if indeed he should by any caprice try to come by the unusual path.

What sleepless angel is it watches over and cares for the wild animals? In spite of all reasons to take the usual path, the Pacer came along the other. The suspicious-looking rushes did not stop him; he walked calmly to the water and drank. There was only one way now to prevent utter failure; when he lowered his head for the second draft which horses always take, Bates and Smith quit their holes and ran swiftly toward the trail behind him, and when he raised his proud head Smith sent a revolver shot into the ground behind him.

Away went the Pacer at his famous gait straight to the trap. Another second and he would be into it. Already he is on the trail, and already they feel they have him, but the Angel of the wild things is with him, that incomprehensible warning comes, and with one mighty bound he clears the fifteen feet of treacherous ground and spurns the earth as he fades away unharmed, never again to visit Antelope Springs by either of the beaten paths.

V

Wild Jo never lacked energy. He meant to catch that Mustang, and when he learned that others were bestirring themselves for the same purpose he at once set about trying the best untried plan he knew—the plan by which the coyote catches the fleeter jackrabbit, and the mounted Indian the far swifter antelope—the old plan of the relay chase.

The Canadian River on the south, its affluent, the Pinavetitos Arroyo, on the northeast, and the Don Carlos Hills with the Ute Creek Canyon on the west, formed a sixty-mile triangle that was the range of the Pacer. It was believed that he never went outside this, and at all times Antelope Springs was his headquarters.

Jo knew this country well, all the water-holes and canon crossings as well as the ways of the Pacer.

If he could have gotten fifty good horses he could have posted them to advantage so as to cover all points, but twenty mounts and five good riders were all that proved available.

The horses, grain-fed for two weeks before, were sent on ahead; each man was instructed how to play his part and sent to his post the day before the race. On the day of the start Jo with his wagon drove to the plain of Antelope Springs and, camping far off in a little draw, waited.

At last he came, that coal-black Horse, out from the sand-hills at the south, alone as always now, and walked calmly down to the Springs and circled quite around it to sniff for any hidden foe. Then he approached where there was no trail at all and drank.

Jo watched and wished that he would drink a hogs-head. But the moment that he turned and sought the grass Jo spurred his steed. The Pacer heard the hoofs, then saw the running horse, and did not want a nearer view but led away. Across the flat he went down to the south, and kept the famous swinging gait that made his start grow longer. Now through the sandy dunes he went, and steadying to an even pace he gained considerably and Jo's too-laden horse plunged through the sand and sinking fetlock deep, he lost at every bound. Then came a level stretch where the runner seemed to gain, and then a long decline where Jo's horse dared not run his best, so lost again at every step.

But on they went, and Jo spared neither spur nor quirt. A mile—a mile—and another mile, and the far-off rock at Arriba loomed up ahead.

And there Jo knew fresh mounts were held, and on they dashed. But the night-black mane out level on the breeze ahead was gaining more and more.

Arriba Canon reached at last, the watcher stood aside, for it was not wished to turn the race, and the Stallion passed—dashed down, across and up the slope, with that unbroken pace, the only one he knew.

And Jo came bounding on his foaming steed, and on the waiting mount, then urged him down the slope and up upon the track, and on the upland once more drove in the spurs, and raced and raced, and raced, but not a single inch he gained.

Ga-lump, ga-lump, ga-lump, with measured beat he went—an hour—an hour, and another hour—Arroyo Alamosa just ahead with fresh relays, and Jo yelled at his horse and pushed him on and on. Straight for the place the Black One made, but on the last two miles some strange foreboding turned him to the left, and Jo foresaw escape in this, and pushed his jaded mount at any cost to head him off, and hard as they had raced this was the hardest race of all, with gasps for breath and leather squeaks at every straining bound. Then cutting right across, Jo seemed to gain, and drawing his gun he fired shot after shot to toss the dust, and so turned the Stallion's head and forced him back to take the crossing to the right.

Down they went. The Stallion crossed and Jo sprang to the ground. His horse was done, for thirty miles had passed in the last stretch, and Jo himself was worn out. His eyes were burnt with flying alkali dust. He was half blind so he motioned to his "pard" to "go ahead and keep him straight for Alamosa ford."

Out shot the rider on a strong, fresh steed, and away they went—up and down on the rolling plain—the Black Horse flecked with snowy foam. His heaving ribs and noisy breath showed what he felt—but on and on he Went.

And Tom on Ginger seemed to gain, then lose and lose, when in an hour the long decline of Alamosa came.

And there a freshly mounted lad took up the chase and turned it west, and on they went past towns of prairie dogs, through soapweed tracts and cactus brakes by scores, and pricked and wrenched rode on. With dust and sweat the Black was now a dappled brown, but still he stepped the same. Young Carrington, who followed, bad hurt his steed by pushing at the very start, and spurred and urged him now to cut across a gulch at which the Pacer shied. Just one misstep and down they went.

The boy escaped, but the pony lies there yet, and the wild Black Horse kept on.

This was close to old Gallego's ranch where Jo himself had cut across refreshed to push the chase. Within thirty minutes he was again scorching the Pacer's trail.

Far in the west the Carlos Hills were seen, and there Jo knew fresh men and mounts were waiting, and that way the indomitable rider tried to turn, the race, but by a sudden whim, of the inner warning born perhaps—the Pacer turned. Sharp to the north he went, and Jo, the skilful wrangler, rode and rode and yelled and tossed the dust with shots, but down on a gulch the wild black meteor streamed and Jo could only follow. Then came the hardest race of all; Jo, cruel to the Mustang, was crueller to his mount and to himself. The sun was hot, the scorching plain was dim in shimmering heat, his eyes and lips were burnt with sand and salt, and yet the chase sped on. The only chance to win would be if he could drive the Mustang back to the Big Arroyo Crossing. Now almost for the first time he saw signs of weakening in the Black. His mane and tail were not just quite so high, and his short half mile of start was down by more than half, but still he stayed ahead and paced and paced and paced.

An hour and another hour, and still they went the same. But they turned again, and night was near when Big Arroyo ford was reached—fully twenty miles. But Jo was game, he seized the waiting horse. The one he left went gasping to the stream and gorged himself with water till he died.

Then Jo held back in hopes the foaming Black would drink. But he was wise; he gulped a single gulp, splashed through the stream and then passed on with Jo at speed behind him. And when they last were seen the Black was on ahead just out of reach and Jo's horse bounding on.

It was morning when Jo came to camp on foot. His tale was briefly told: eight horses dead—five men worn out—the matchless Pacer safe and free.

"Tain't possible; it can't be done. Sorry I didn't bore his hellish carcass through when I had the chance," said Jo, and gave it up.

VI

Old Turkeytrack was cook on this trip. He had watched the chase with as much interest as anyone, and when it failed he grinned into the pot and said: "That mustang's mine unless I'm a darned fool." Then falling back on Scripture for a precedent, as was his habit, he still addressed the pot: "Reckon the Philistines tried to run Samson down and they got done up, an' would a stayed don only for a nat'ral weakness on his part. An' Adam would a loafed in Eden yit it ony for a leetle failing, which we all onder stand. An' it aint $5,000 I'll take for him nuther."

Much persecution had made the Pacer wilder than ever. But it did not drive him away from Antelope Springs. That was the only drinking-place with absolutely no shelter for a mile on every side to hide an enemy. Here he came almost every day about noon, and after thoroughly spying the land approached to drink.

His had been a lonely life all winter since the capture of his harem, and of this old Turkeytrack was fully aware. The old cook's chum had a nice little brown mare which he judged would serve his ends, and taking a pair of the strongest hobbles, a spade, a spare lasso, and a stout post he mounted the mare and rode away to the famous Springs.

A few antelope skimmed over the plain before him in the early freshness of the day. Cattle were lying about in groups, and the loud, sweet song of the prairie lark was heard on every side. For the bright snowless winter of the mesas was gone and the springtime was at hand. The grass was greening and all nature seemed turning to thoughts of love.

It was in the air, and when the little brown mare was picketed out to graze she raised her nose from time to time to pour forth a long shrill whinny that surely was her song, if song she had, of love.

Old Turkeytrack studied the wind and the lay of the land. There was the pit he had labored at, now opened and filled with water that was rank with drowned prairie dogs and mice. Here was the new trail the animals were forced to make by the pit. He selected a sedgy clump near some smooth, grassy ground, and first firmly sunk the post, then dug a hole large enough to hide in, and spread his blanket in it. He shortened up the little mare's tether, till she could scarcely move; then on the ground between he spread his open lasso, tying the long end to the post, then covered the rope with dust and grass, and went into his hiding-place.

About noon, after long waiting, the amorous whinny of the mare was answered from the high ground, away to the west, and there, black against the sky, was the famous Mustang.

Down he came at that long swinging gait, but grown crafty with much pursuit, he often stopped to gaze and whinny, and got answer that surely touched his heart.

Nearer he came again to call, then took alarm, and paced all around in a great circle to try the wind for his foes, and seemed in doubt. The Angel whispered "Don't go." But the brown mare called again. He circled nearer still, and neighed once more, and got reply that seemed to quell all fears, and set his heart aglow.

Nearer still he pranced, till he touched Solly's nose with his own, and finding her as responsive as he well could wish, thrust aside all thoughts of danger, and abandoned himself to the delight of conquest, until, as he pranced around, his hind legs for a moment stood within the evil circle of the rope. One deft sharp twitch, the noose flew tight, and he was caught.

A snort of terror and a bound in the air gave Tom the chance to add the double hitch. The loop flashed up the line, and snake-like bound those mighty hoofs.

Terror lent speed and double strength for a moment, but the end of the rope was reached, and down he went a captive, a hopeless prisoner at last. Old Tom's ugly, little crooked form sprang from the pit to complete the mastering of the great glorious creature whose mighty strength had proved as nothing when matched with the wits of a little old man. With snorts and desperate bounds of awful force the great beast dashed and struggled to be free; but all in vain. The rope was strong.

The second lasso was deftly swung, and the forefeet caught, and then with a skilful move the feet were drawn together, and down went the raging Pacer to lie a moment later "hog-tied" and helpless on the ground. There he struggled till worn out, sobbing great convulsive sobs while tears ran down his cheeks.

Tom stood by and watched, but a strange revulsion of feeling came over the old cow-puncher. He trembled nervously from head to foot, as he had not done since he roped his first steer, and for a while could do nothing but gaze on his tremendous prisoner. But the feeling soon passed away. He saddled Delilah, and taking the second lasso, roped the great horse about the neck, and left the mare to hold the Stallion's head, while he put on the hobbles. This was soon done, and sure of him now old Bates was about to loose the ropes, but on a sudden thought he stopped. He had quite forgotten, and had come unprepared for something of importance. In Western law the Mustang was the property of the first man to mark him with his brand; how was this to be done with the nearest branding-iron twenty miles away?

Old Tom went to his mare, took up her hoofs one at a time, and examined each shoe. Yes! one was a little loose; he pushed and pried it with the spade, and got it off. Buffalo chips and kindred fuel were plentiful about the plain, so a fire was quickly made, and he soon had one arm of the horseshoe red hot, then holding the other wrapped in his sock he rudely sketched on the left shoulder of the helpless mustang a turkeytrack, his brand, the first time really that it had ever been used. The Pacer shuddered as the hot iron seared his flesh, but it was quickly done, and the famous Mustang Stallion was a maverick no more.

Now all there was to do was to take him home. The ropes were loosed, the Mustang felt himself freed, thought he was free, and sprang to his feet only to fall as soon as he tried to take a stride. His forefeet were strongly tied together, his only possible gait a shuffling walk, or else a desperate labored bounding with feet so unnaturally held that within a few yards he was inevitably thrown each time he tried to break away. Tom on the light pony headed him off again and again, and by dint of driving, threatening, and maneuvering, contrived to force his foaming, crazy captive northward toward the Pinavetitos Canyon. But the wild horse would not drive, would not give in. With snorts of terror or of rage and maddest bounds, he tried and tried to get away. It was one long cruel fight; his glossy sides were thick with dark foam, and the foam was stained with blood. Countless hard falls and exhaustion that a long day's chase was powerless to produce were telling on him; his straining bounds first this way and then that, were not now quite so strong, and the spray he snorted as he gasped was half a spray of blood. But his captor, relentless, masterful and cool, still forced him on. Down the slope toward the canyon they had come, every yard a fight, and now they were at the head of the draw that took the trail down to the only crossing of the canon, the northmost limit of the Pacer's ancient range.

From this the first corral and ranch-house were in sight. The man rejoiced, but the Mustang gathered his remaining strength for one more desperate dash. Up, up the grassy slope from the trail he went, defied the swinging, slashing rope and the gunshot fired in air, in vain attempt to turn his frenzied course. Up, up and on, above the sheerest cliff he dashed then sprang away into the vacant air, down—down—two hundred downward feet to fall, and land upon the rocks below, a lifeless wreck—but free.

23

The Maltese Cat

By Rudyard Kipling

The Maltese Cat is perhaps the greatest polo story ever written. Like Black Beauty, it is written from the perspective of the horses. We learn that the horses understand and love the game as much , if not more, as the human players. For the ponies—unlike their riders who have jobs and families—polo is all they know and care about. Many riders today can sense this about their own mounts—a jumper lives for the show ring, where he is allowed the privilege of jumping big fences at a gallop. An eventer seems to spend his every waking moment waiting for his next chance to tackle the cross-country course. This competitive spirit in the horse is what makes him so important to his human companions.

—JESSIE SHIERS

THEY HAD GOOD REASON TO BE PROUD, AND BETTER REASON TO BE afraid, all twelve of them; for though they had fought their way, game by game, up the teams entered for the polo tournament, they were meeting the Archangels that afternoon in the final match; and the Archangels men were playing with half a dozen ponies apiece. As the game was divided into six quarters of eight minutes each, that meant a fresh pony after every halt. The Skidars' team, even supposing there were no accidents, could only supply one pony for every other change; and two to one is heavy odds. Again, as Shiraz, the grey Syrian, pointed out, they were meeting the pink and pick of the polo-ponies of Upper India, ponies that had cost from a thousand rupees each, while they themselves were a cheap lot gathered, often from country-carts, by their masters, who belonged to a poor but honest native infantry regiment.

"Money means pace and weight," said Shiraz, rubbing his black-silk nose dolefully along his neat-fitting boot, "and by the maxims of the game as I know it—"

"Ah, but we aren't playing the maxims," said The Maltese Cat. "We're playing the game; and we've the great advantage of knowing the game. Just think a stride, Shiraz! We've pulled up from bottom to second place in two weeks against all those fellows on the ground here. That's because we play with our heads as well as our feet."

"It makes me feel undersized and unhappy all the same," said Kittiwynk, a mouse-coloured mare with a red brow-band and the cleanest pair of legs that ever an aged pony owned. "They've twice our style, these others."

Kittiwynk looked at the gathering and sighed. The hard, dusty polo-ground was lined with thousands of soldiers, black and white, not counting hundreds and hundreds of carriages and drags and dogcarts, and ladies with brilliant-coloured parasols, and officers in uniform and out of it, and crowds of natives behind them; and orderlies on camels, who had halted to watch the game, instead of carrying letters up and down the station; and native horse-dealers running about on thin-eared Biluchi mares, looking for a chance to sell a few first-class polo-ponies. Then there were the ponies of thirty teams that had entered for the Upper India Free-for-All Cup—nearly every pony of worth and dignity, from Mhow to Peshawar, from Allahabad to Multan; prize ponies, Arabs, Syrian, Barb, country-bred, Deccanee, Waziri, and Kabul ponies of every colour and shape and temper that you could imagine. Some of them were in mat-roofed stables, close to the polo-ground, but most were under saddle, while their masters, who had been defeated in the earlier games, trotted in and out and told the world exactly how the game should be played.

It was a glorious sight, and the come and go of the little, quick hooves, and the incessant salutations of ponies that had met before on other polo-grounds or race-courses were enough to drive a four-footed thing wild.

But the Skidars' team were careful not to know their neighbours, though half the ponies on the ground were anxious to scrape acquaintance with the little fellows that had come from the North, and, so far, had swept the board.

"Let's see," said a soft gold-coloured Arab, who had been playing very badly the day before, to The Maltese Cat; "didn't we meet in Abdul Rahman's stable in Bombay, four seasons ago? I won the Paikpattan Cup next season, you may remember?"

"Not me," said The Maltese Cat, politely. "I was at Malta then, pulling a vegetable-cart. I don't race. I play the game."

"Oh!" said the Arab, cocking his tail and swaggering off.

"Keep yourselves to yourselves," said The Maltese Cat to his companions. "We don't want to rub noses with all those goose-rumped half-breeds of Upper India. When we've won this Cup they'll give their shoes to know us."

"We sha'n't win the Cup," said Shiraz. "How do you feel?"

"Stale as last night's feed when a muskrat has run over it," said Polaris, a rather heavy-shouldered grey; and the rest of the team agreed with him.

"The sooner you forget that the better," said The Maltese Cat, cheerfully. "They've finished tiffin in the big tent. We shall be wanted now. If your saddles are not comfy, kick. If your bits aren't easy, rear, and let the saises know whether your boots are tight."

Each pony had his sais, his groom, who lived and ate and slept with the animal, and had betted a good deal more than he could afford on the result of the game. There was no chance of anything going wrong, but to make sure, each sais was shampooing the legs of his pony to the last minute. Behind the saises sat as many of the Skidars' regiment as had leave to attend the match—about half the native officers, and a hundred or two dark, black-bearded men with the regimental pipers nervously fingering the big, beribboned bagpipes. The Skidars were what they call a Pioneer regiment, and the bagpipes made the national music of half their men. The native officers held bundles of polo-sticks, long cane-handled mallets, and as the grand stand filled after lunch they arranged themselves by ones and twos at different points round the ground, so that if a stick were broken the player would not have far to ride for a new one. An impatient British Cavalry Band struck up "If you want to know the time, ask a p'leeceman!" and the two umpires in light dust-coats danced out on two little excited ponies. The four players of the Archangels' team followed, and the sight of their beautiful mounts made Shiraz groan again.

"Wait till we know," said The Maltese Cat. "Two of 'em are playing in blinkers, and that means they can't see to get out of the way of their own side, or they may shy at the umpires' ponies. They've all got white web-reins that are sure to stretch or slip!"

"And," said Kittiwynk, dancing to take the stiffness out of her, "they carry their whips in their hands instead of on their wrists. Hah!"

"True enough. No man can manage his stick and his reins and his whip that way," said The Maltese Cat. "I've fallen over every square yard of the Malta ground, and I ought to know."

He quivered his little, flea-bitten withers just to show how satisfied he felt; but his heart was not so light. Ever since he had drifted into India on a troop-ship, taken, with an old rifle, as part payment for a racing debt, The Maltese Cat had played and preached polo to the Skidars' team on the Skidars' stony pologround. Now a polo-pony is like a poet. If he is born with a love for the game, he can be made. The Maltese Cat knew that bamboos grew solely in order that poloballs might be turned from their roots, that grain was given to ponies to keep them in hard condition, and that ponies were shod to prevent them slipping on a turn. But, besides all these things, he knew every trick and device of the finest game in the world, and for two seasons had been teaching the others all he knew or guessed.

"Remember," he said for the hundredth time, as the riders came up, "you must play together, and you must play with your heads. Whatever happens, follow the ball. Who goes out first?"

Kittiwynk, Shiraz, Polaris, and a short high little bay fellow with tremendous hocks and no withers worth speaking of (he was called Corks) were being girthed up, and the soldiers in the background stared with all their eyes.

"I want you men to keep quiet," said Lutyens, the captain of the team, "and especially not to blow your pipes."

"Not if we win, Captain Sahib?" asked the piper.

"If we win you can do what you please," said Lutyens, with a smile, as he slipped the loop of his stick over his wrist, and wheeled to canter to his place. The Archangels' ponies were a little bit above themselves on account of the many-coloured crowd so close to the ground. Their riders were excellent players, but they were a team of crack players instead of a crack team; and that made all the difference in the world. They honestly meant to play together, but it is very hard for four men, each the best of the team he is picked from, to remember that in polo no brilliancy in hitting or riding makes up for playing alone. Their captain shouted his orders to them by name, and it is a curious thing that if you call his name aloud in public after an Englishman you make him hot and fretty. Lutyens said nothing to his men, because it had all been said before. He pulled up Shiraz, for he was playing "back," to guard the goal. Powell on Polaris was half-back, and Macnamara and Hughes on Corks and Kittiwynk were forwards. The tough, bamboo ball was set in the middle of the ground, one hundred and fifty yards from the ends, and Hughes crossed sticks, heads up, with the Captain of the Archangels, who saw fit to play forward; that is a place from which you cannot easily control your team. The little click as the cane-shafts met was heard all over the ground, and then Hughes made some sort of quick wrist-stroke that just dribbled the ball a few yards. Kittiwynk knew that stroke of old, and followed as a cat follows a mouse. While the Captain of the Archangels was wrenching his pony round, Hughes struck with all his strength, and next instant Kittiwynk was away, Corks following close behind her, their little feet pattering like raindrops on glass.

"Pull out to the left," said Kittiwynk between her teeth; "it's coming your way, Corks!"

The back and half-back of the Archangels were tearing down on her just as she was within reach of the ball. Hughes leaned forward with a loose rein, and cut it away to the left almost under Kittiwynk's foot, and it hopped and skipped off to Corks, who saw that, if he was not quick it would run beyond the boundaries. That long bouncing drive gave the Archangels time to wheel and send three men across the ground to head off Corks. Kittiwynk stayed where she was; for she knew the game. Corks was on the ball half a fraction of a second before the others came up, and Macnamara, with a backhanded stroke, sent it back across the ground to Hughes, who saw the way clear to the Archangels' goal, and smacked the ball in before any one quite knew what had happened.

"That's luck," said Corks, as they changed ends. "A goal in three minutes for three hits, and no riding to speak of."

"Don't know," said Polaris. "We've made 'em angry too soon. Shouldn't wonder if they tried to rush us off our feet next time."

"Keep the ball hanging, then," said Shiraz. "That wears out every pony that is not used to it."

Next time there was no easy galloping across the ground. All the Archangels closed up as one man, but there they stayed, for Corks, Kittiwynk, and Polaris were somewhere on the top of the ball, marking time among the rattling sticks, while Shiraz circled about outside, waiting for a chance.

"We can do this all day," said Polaris, ramming his quarters into the side of another pony. "Where do you think you're shoving to?"

"I'll—I'll be driven in an ekka if I know," was the gasping reply, "and I'd give a week's feed to get my blinkers off. I can't see anything."

"The dust is rather bad. Whew! That was one for my off-hock. Where's the ball, Corks?"

"Under my tail. At least, the man's looking for it there! This is beautiful. They can't use their sticks, and it's driving 'em wild. Give old Blinkers a push and then he'll go over."

"Here, don't touch me! I can't see. I'll—I'll back out, I think," said the pony in blinkers, who knew that if you can't see all round your head, you cannot prop yourself against the shock.

Corks was watching the ball where it lay in the dust, close to his near foreleg, with Macnamara's shortened stick tap-tapping it from time to time. Kittiwynk was edging her way out of the scrimmage, whisking her stump of a tail with nervous excitement.

"Ho! They've got it," she snorted. "Let me out!" and she galloped like a rifle-bullet just behind a tall lanky pony of the Archangels, whose rider was swinging up his stick for a stroke.

"Not today, thank you," said Hughes, as the blow slid off his raised stick, and Kittiwynk laid her shoulder to the tall pony's quarters, and shoved him aside just as Lutyens on Shiraz sent the ball where it had come from, and the tall pony went skating and slipping away to the left. Kittiwynk, seeing that Polaris had joined Corks in the chase for the ball up the ground, dropped into Polaris' place, and then "time" was called.

The Skidars' ponies wasted no time in kicking or fuming. They knew that each minute's rest meant so much gain, and trotted off to the rails, and their saises began to scrape and blanket and rub them at once.

"Whew!" said Corks, stiffening up to get all the tickle of the big vulcanite scraper. "If we were playing pony for pony, we would bend those Archangels double in half an hour. But they'll bring up fresh ones and fresh ones and fresh ones after that—you see."

"Who cares?" said Polaris. "We've drawn first blood. Is my hock swelling?"

"Looks puffy," said Corks. "You must have had rather a wipe. Don't let it stiffen. You'll be wanted again in half an hour."

"What's the game like?" said The Maltese Cat.

"Ground's like your shoe, except where they put too much water on it," said Kittiwynk. "Then it's slippery. Don't play in the centre. There's a bog there. I don't know how their next four are going to behave, but we kept the ball hanging, and made 'em lather for nothing. Who goes out? Two Arabs and a couple of country-breds! That's bad. What a comfort it is to wash your mouth out!"

Kitty was talking with a neck of a lather-covered soda-water bottle between her teeth, and trying to look over her withers at the same time. This gave her a very coquettish air.

"What's bad?" said Grey Dawn, giving to the girth and admiring his well-set shoulders.

"You Arabs can't gallop fast enough to keep yourselves warm—that's what Kitty means," said Polaris, limping to show that his hock needed attention. "Are you playing back, Grey Dawn?"

"Looks like it," said Grey Dawn, as Lutyens swung himself up. Powell mounted The Rabbit, a plain bay country-bred much like Corks, but with mulish ears. Macnamara took Faiz-Ullah, a handy, short-backed little red Arab with a long tail, and Hughes mounted Benami, an old and sullen brown beast, who stood over in front more than a polo-pony should.

"Benami looks like business," said Shiraz. "How's your temper, Ben?" The old campaigner hobbled off without answering, and The Maltese Cat looked at the new Archangel ponies prancing about on the ground. They were four beautiful blacks, and they saddled big enough and strong enough to eat the Skidars' team and gallop away with the meal inside them.

"Blinkers again," said The Maltese Cat. "Good enough!"

"They're chargers—cavalry chargers!" said Kittiwynk, indignantly. "They'll never see thirteen-three again."

"They've all been fairly measured, and they've all got their certificates," said The Maltese Cat, "or they wouldn't be here. We must take things as they come along, and keep your eyes on the ball."

The game began, but this time the Skidars were penned to their own end of the ground, and the watching ponies did not approve of that.

"Faiz-Ullah is shirking—as usual," said Polaris, with a scornful grunt.

"Faiz-Ullah is eating whip," said Corks. They could hear the leather-thonged polo-quirt lacing the little fellow's well-rounded barrel. Then The Rabbit's shrill neigh came across the ground.

"I can't do all the work," he cried, desperately.

"Play the game—don't talk," The Maltese Cat whickered; and all the ponies wriggled with excitement, and the soldiers and the grooms gripped the railings and shouted. A black pony with blinkers had singled out old Benami, and was interfering with him in every possible way. They could see Benami shaking his head up and down, and flapping his under lip.

"There'll be a fall in a minute," said Polaris. "Benami is getting stuffy."

The game flickered up and down between goalpost and goalpost, and the black ponies were getting more confident as they felt they had the legs of the others. The ball was hit out of a little scrimmage, and Benami and The Rabbit followed it, Faiz-Ullah only too glad to be quiet for an instant.

The blinkered black pony came up like a hawk, with two of his own side behind him, and Benami's eye glittered as he raced. The question was which pony should make way for the other, for each rider was perfectly willing to risk a fall in a good cause. The black, who had been driven nearly crazy by his blinkers, trusted to his weight and his temper; but Benami knew how to apply his weight and how to keep his temper. They met, and there was a cloud of dust. The black was lying on his side, all the breath knocked out of his body. The Rabbit was a hundred yards up the ground with the ball, and Benami was sitting down. He had slid nearly ten yards on his tail, but he had had his revenge, and sat cracking his nostrils till the black pony rose.

"That's what you get for interfering. Do you want any more?" said Benami, and he plunged into the game. Nothing was done that quarter, because Faiz-Ullah would not gallop, though Macnamara beat him whenever he could spare a second. The fall of the black pony had impressed his companions tremendously, and so the Archangels could not profit by Faiz-Ullah's bad behaviour.

But as The Maltese Cat said when "time" was called, and the four came back blowing and dripping, Faiz-Ullah ought to have been kicked all round Umballa. If he did not behave better next time The Maltese Cat promised to pull out his Arab tail by the roots and—eat it.

There was no time to talk, for the third four were ordered out.

The third quarter of a game is generally the hottest, for each side thinks that the others must be pumped; and most of the winning play in a game is made about that time.

Lutyens took over The Maltese Cat with a pat and a hug, for Lutyens valued him more than anything else in the world; Powell had Shikast, a little grey rat with no pedigree and no manners outside polo; Macnamara mounted Bamboo, the largest of the team; and Hughes Who's Who, alias The Animal. He was supposed to have Australian blood in his veins, but he looked like a clothes-horse, and you could whack his legs with an iron crowbar without hurting him.

They went out to meet the very flower of the Archangels' team; and when Who's Who saw their elegantly booted legs and their beautiful satin skins, he grinned a grin through his light, well-worn bridle.

"My word!" said Who's Who. "We must give 'em a little football. These gentlemen need a rubbing down."

"No biting," said The Maltese Cat, warningly; for once or twice in his career Who's Who had been known to forget himself in that way.

"Who said anything about biting? I'm not playing tiddly-winks. I'm playing the game."

The Archangels came down like a wolf on the fold, for they were tired of football, and they wanted polo. They got it more and more. Just after the game began, Lutyens hit a ball that was coming towards him rapidly, and it rolled in the air, as a ball sometimes will, with the whirl of a frightened partridge. Shikast heard, but could not see it for the minute, though he looked everywhere and up into the air as The Maltese Cat had taught him. When he saw it ahead and overhead he went forward with Powell as fast as he could put foot to ground. It was then that Powell, a quiet and level-headed man, as a rule, became inspired, and played a stroke that sometimes comes off successfully after long practice. He took his stick in both hands, and, standing up in his stirrups, swiped at the ball in the air, Munipore fashion. There was one second of paralysed astonishment, and then all four sides of the ground went up in a yell of applause and delight as the ball flew true (you could see the amazed Archangels ducking in their saddles to dodge the line of flight, and looking at it with open mouths), and the regimental pipes of the Skidars squealed from the railings as long as the pipers had breath.

Shikast heard the stroke; but he heard the head of the stick fly off at the same time. Nine hundred and ninety-nine ponies out of a thousand would have gone tearing on after the ball with a useless player pulling at their heads; but Powell knew him, and he knew Powell; and the instant he felt Powell's right leg shift a trifle on the saddle-flap, he headed to the boundary, where a native officer was frantically waving a new stick. Before the shouts had ended, Powell was armed again.

Once before in his life The Maltese Cat had heard that very same stroke played off his own back, and had profited by the confusion it wrought. This time he acted on experience, and leaving Bamboo to guard the goal in case of accidents, came through the others like a flash, head and tail low—Lutyens standing up to ease him—swept on and on before the other side knew what was the matter, and nearly pitched on his head between the Archangels' goalpost as Lutyens kicked the ball in after a straight scurry of a hundred and fifty yards. If there was one thing more than another upon which The Maltese Cat prided himself, it was on this quick, streaking kind of run half across the ground. He did not believe in taking balls round the field unless you were clearly overmatched. After this they gave the Archangels five-minuted football; and an expensive fast pony hates football because it rumples his temper.

Who's Who showed himself even better than Polaris in this game. He did not permit any wriggling away, but bored joyfully into the scrimmage as if he had his nose in a feed-box and was looking for something nice. Little Shikast jumped on the ball the minute it got clear, and every time an Archangel pony followed it, he found Shikast standing over it, asking what was the matter.

"If we can live through this quarter," said The Maltese Cat, "I sha'n't care. Don't take it out of yourselves. Let them do the lathering."

So the ponies, as their riders explained afterwards, "shut-up." The Archangels kept them tied fast in front of their goal, but it cost the Archangels' ponies all that was left of their tempers; and ponies began to kick, and men began to repeat compliments, and they chopped at the legs of Who's Who, and he set his teeth and stayed where he was, and the dust stood up like a tree over the scrimmage until that hot quarter ended.

They found the ponies very excited and confident when they went to their saises; and The Maltese Cat had to warn them that the worst of the game was coming.

"Now we are all going in for the second time," said he, "and they are trotting out fresh ponies. You think you can gallop, but you'll find you can't; and then you'll be sorry."

"But two goals to nothing is a halter-long lead," said Kittiwynk, prancing.

"How long does it take to get a goal?" The Maltese Cat answered. "For pity's sake, don't run away with a notion that the game is half-won just because we happen to be in luck now! They'll ride you into the grand stand, if they can; you must not give 'em a chance. Follow the ball."

"Football, as usual?" said Polaris. "My hock's half as big as a nose-bag."

"Don't let them have a look at the ball, if you can help it. Now leave me alone. I must get all the rest I can before the last quarter."

He hung down his head and let all his muscles go slack, Shikast, Bamboo, and Who's Who copying his example.

"Better not watch the game," he said. "We aren't playing, and we shall only take it out of ourselves if we grow anxious. Look at the ground and pretend it's fly-time."

They did their best, but it was hard advice to follow. The hooves were drumming and the sticks were rattling all up and down the ground, and yells of applause from the English troops told that the Archangels were pressing the Skidars hard. The native soldiers behind the ponies groaned and grunted, and said things in undertones, and presently they heard a long-drawn shout and a clatter of hurrahs!

"One to the Archangels," said Shikast, without raising his head. "Time's nearly up. Oh, my sire and dam!"

"Faiz-Ullah," said The Maltese Cat, "if you don't play to the last nail in your shoes this time, I'll kick you on the ground before all the other ponies."

"I'll do my best when my time comes," said the little Arab, sturdily.

The saises looked at each other gravely as they rubbed their ponies' legs. This was the time when long purses began to tell, and everybody knew it. Kittiwynk and the others came back, the sweat dripping over their hooves and their tails telling sad stories.

"They're better than we are," said Shiraz. "I knew how it would be."

"Shut your big head," said The Maltese Cat; "we've one goal to the good yet."

"Yes; but it's two Arabs and two country-breds to play now," said Corks. "Faiz-Ullah, remember!" He spoke in a biting voice.

As Lutyens mounted Grey Dawn he looked at his men, and they did not look pretty. They were covered with dust and sweat in streaks. Their yellow boots were almost black, their wrists were red and lumpy, and their eyes seemed two inches deep in their heads; but the expression in the eyes was satisfactory.

"Did you take anything at tiffin?" said Lutyens; and the team shook their heads. They were too dry to talk.

"All right. The Archangels did. They are worse pumped than we are."

"They've got the better ponies," said Powell. "I sha'n't be sorry when this business is over."

That fifth quarter was a painful one in every way. Faiz-Ullah played like a little red demon, and The Rabbit seemed to be everywhere at once, and Benami rode straight at anything and everything that came in his way; while the umpires on their ponies wheeled like gulls outside the shifting game. But the Archangels had the better mounts—they had kept their racers till late in the game—and never allowed the Skidars to play football. They hit the ball up and down the width of the ground till Benami and the rest were outpaced. Then they went forward, and time and again Lutyens and Grey Dawn were just, and only just, able to send the ball away with a long, spitting backhander. Grey Dawn forgot that he was an Arab; and turned from grey to blue as he galloped. Indeed, he forgot too well, for he did not keep his eyes on the ground as an Arab should, but stuck out his nose and scuttled for the dear honour of the game. They had watered the ground once or twice between the quarters, and a careless waterman had emptied the last of his skinful all in one place near the Skidars' goal. It was close to the end of the play, and for the tenth time Grey Dawn was bolting after the ball, when his near hind-foot slipped on the greasy mud, and he rolled over and over, pitching Lutyens just clear of the goalpost; and the triumphant Archangels made their goal. Then "time" was called—two goals all; but Lutyens had to be helped up, and Grey Dawn rose with his near hind-leg strained somewhere.

"What's the damage?" said Powell, his arm around Lutyens.

"Collar-bone, of course," said Lutyens, between his teeth. It was the third time he had broken it in two years, and it hurt him.

Powell and the others whistled.

"Game's up," said Hughes.

"Hold on. We've five good minutes yet, and it isn't my right hand. We'll stick it out."

"I say," said the Captain of the Archangels, trotting up, "are you hurt, Lutyens? We'll wait if you care to put in a substitute. I wish—I mean—the fact is, you fellows deserve this game if any team does. Wish we could give you a man, or some of our ponies—or something."

"You're awfully good, but we'll play it to a finish, I think."

The Captain of the Archangels stared for a little. "That's not half bad," he said, and went back to his own side, while Lutyens borrowed a scarf from one of his native officers and made a sling of it. Then an Archangel galloped up with a big bath-sponge, and advised Lutyens to put it under his armpit to ease his shoulder, and between them they tied up his left arm scientifically; and one of the native officers leaped forward with four long glasses that fizzed and bubbled.

The team looked at Lutyens piteously, and he nodded. It was the last quarter, and nothing would matter after that. They drank out the dark golden drink, and wiped their moustaches, and things looked more hopeful.

The Maltese Cat had put his nose into the front of Lutyens' shirt and was trying to say how sorry he was.

"He knows," said Lutyens, proudly. "The beggar knows. I've played him without a bridle before now—for fun."

"It's no fun now," said Powell. "But we haven't a decent substitute."

"No," said Lutyens. "It's the last quarter, and we've got to make our goal and win. I'll trust The Cat."

"If you fall this time, you'll suffer a little," said Macnamara.

"I'll trust The Cat," said Lutyens.

"You hear that?" said The Maltese Cat, proudly, to the others. "It's worth while playing polo for ten years to have that said of you. Now then, my sons, come along. We'll kick up a little bit, just to show the Archangels this team haven't suffered."

And, sure enough, as they went on to the ground, The Maltese Cat, after satisfying himself that Lutyens was home in the saddle, kicked out three or four times, and Lutyens laughed. The reins were caught up any-how in the tips of his strapped left hand, and he never pretended to rely on them. He knew The Cat would answer to the least pressure of the leg, and by way of showing off—for his shoulder hurt him very much—he bent the little fellow in a close figure-of-eight in and out between the goalposts. There was a roar from the native officers and men, who dearly loved a piece of dugabashi (horse-trick work), as they called it, and the pipes very quietly and scornfully droned out the first bars of a common bazaar tune called "Freshly Fresh and Newly New," just as a warning to the other regiments that the Skidars were fit. All the natives laughed.

"And now," said The Maltese Cat, as they took their place, "remember that this is the last quarter, and follow the ball!"

"Don't need to be told," said Who's Who.

"Let me go on. All those people on all four sides will begin to crowd in—just as they did at Malta. You'll hear people calling out, and moving forward and being pushed back; and that is going to make the Archangel ponies very unhappy. But if a ball is struck to the boundary, you go after it, and let the people get out of your way. I went over the pole of a four-in-hand once, and picked a game out of the dust by it. Back me up when I run, and follow the ball."

There was a sort of an all-round sound of sympathy and wonder as the last quarter opened, and then there began exactly what The Maltese Cat had foreseen. People crowded in close to the boundaries, and the Archangels' ponies kept looking sideways at the narrowing space. If you know how a man feels to be cramped at tennis—not because he wants to run out of the court, but because he likes to know that he can at a pinch—you will guess how ponies must feel when they are playing in a box of human beings.

"I'll bend some of those men if I can get away," said Who's Who, as he rocketed behind the ball; and Bamboo nodded without speaking. They were playing the last ounce in them, and The Maltese Cat had left the goal undefended to join them. Lutyens gave him every order that he could to bring him back, but this was the first time in his career that the little wise grey had ever played polo on his own responsibility, and he was going to make the most of it.

"What are you doing here?" said Hughes, as The Cat crossed in front of him and rode off an Archangel.

"The Cat's in charge—mind the goal!" shouted Lutyens, and bowing forward hit the ball full, and followed on, forcing the Archangels towards their own goal.

"No football," said The Maltese Cat. "Keep the ball by the boundaries and cramp 'em. Play open order, and drive 'em to the boundaries."

Across and across the ground in big diagonals flew the ball, and whenever it came to a flying rush and a stroke close to the boundaries the Archangel ponies moved stiffly. They did not care to go headlong at a wall of men and carriages, though if the ground had been open they could have turned on a sixpence.

"Wriggle her up the sides," said The Cat. "Keep her close to the crowd. They hate the carriages. Shikast, keep her up this side."

Shikast and Powell lay left and right behind the uneasy scuffle of an open scrimmage, and every time the ball was hit away Shikast galloped on it at such an angle that Powell was forced to hit it towards the boundary; and when the crowd had been driven away from that side, Lutyens would send the ball over to the other, and Shikast would slide desperately after it till his friends came down to help. It was billiards, and no football, this time—billiards in a corner pocket; and the cues were not well chalked.

"If they get us out in the middle of the ground they'll walk away from us. Dribble her along the sides," cried The Maltese Cat.

So they dribbled all along the boundary, where a pony could not come on their right-hand side; and the Archangels were furious, and the umpires had to neglect the game to shout at the people to get back, and several blundering mounted policemen tried to restore order, all close to the scrimmage, and the nerves of the Archangels' ponies stretched and broke like cobwebs.

Five or six times an Archangel hit the ball up into the middle of the ground, and each time the watchful Shikast gave Powell his chance to send it back, and after each return, when the dust had settled, men could see that the Skidars had gained a few yards.

Every now and again there were shouts of "Side! Off side!" from the spectators; but the teams were too busy to care, and the umpires had all they could do to keep their maddened ponies clear of the scuffle.

At last Lutyens missed a short easy stroke, and the Skidars had to fly back helter-skelter to protect their own goal, Shikast leading. Powell stopped the ball with a backhander when it was not fifty yards from the goalposts, and Shikast spun round with a wrench that nearly hoisted Powell out of his saddle.

"Now's our last chance," said The Cat, wheeling like a cockchafer on a pin. "We've got to ride it out. Come along."

Lutyens felt the little chap take a deep breath, and, as it were, crouch under his rider. The ball was hopping towards the right-hand boundary, an Archangel riding for it with both spurs and a whip; but neither spur nor whip would make his pony stretch himself as he neared the crowd. The Maltese Cat glided under his very nose, picking up his hind legs sharp, for there was not a foot to spare between his quarters and the other pony's bit. It was as neat an exhibition as fancy figure-skating. Lutyens hit with all the strength he had left, but the stick slipped a little in his hand, and the ball flew off to the left instead of keeping close to the boundary. Who's Who was far across the ground, thinking hard as he galloped. He repeated stride for stride The Cat's manoeuvres with another Archangel pony, nipping the ball away from under his bridle, and clearing his opponent by half a fraction of an inch, for Who's Who was clumsy behind. Then he drove away towards the right as The Maltese Cat came up from the left; and Bamboo held a middle course exactly between them. The three were making a sort of Government-broad-arrow-shaped attack; and there was only the Archangels' back to guard the goal; but immediately behind them were three Archangels racing all they knew, and mixed up with them was Powell sending Shikast along on what he felt was their last hope. It takes a very good man to stand up to the rush of seven crazy ponies in the last quarters of a Cup game, when men are riding with their necks for sale, and the ponies are delirious. The Archangels' back missed his stroke and pulled aside just in time to let the rush go by. Bamboo and Who's Who shortened stride to give The Cat room, and Lutyens got the goal with a clean, smooth, smacking stroke that was heard all over the field. But there was no stopping the ponies. They poured through the goalposts in one mixed mob, winners and losers together, for the pace had been terrific. The Maltese Cat knew by experience what would happen, and, to save Lutyens, turned to the right with one last effort, that strained a back-sinew beyond hope of repair. As he did so he heard the right-hand goalpost crack as a pony cannoned into it—crack, splinter and fall like a mast. It had been sawed three parts through in case of accidents, but it upset the pony nevertheless, and he blundered into another, who blundered into the left-hand post, and then there was confusion and dust and wood. Bamboo was lying on the ground, seeing stars; an Archangel pony rolled beside him, breathless and angry; Shikast had sat down dog-fashion to avoid falling over the others, and was sliding along on his little bobtail in a cloud of dust; and Powell was sitting on the ground, hammering with his stick and trying to cheer. All the others were shouting at the top of what was left of their voices, and the men who had been spilt were shouting too. As soon as the people saw no one was hurt, ten thousand native and English shouted and clapped and yelled, and before any one could stop them the pipers of the Skidars broke on to the ground, with all the native officers and men behind them, and marched up and down, playing a wild Northern tune called "Zakhme Began," and through the insolent blaring of the pipes and the high-pitched native yells you could hear the Archangels' band hammering, "For they are all jolly good fellows," and then reproachfully to the losing team, "Ooh, Kafoozalum! Kafoozalum! Kafoozalum!"

Besides all these things and many more, there was a Commander-in-chief, and an Inspector-General of Cavalry, and the principal veterinary officer of all India standing on the top of a regimental coach, yelling like schoolboys; and brigadiers and colonels and commissioners, and hundreds of pretty ladies joined the chorus. But The Maltese Cat stood with his head down, wondering how many legs were left to him; and Lutyens watched the men and ponies pick themselves out of the wreck of the two goalposts, and he patted The Maltese Cat very tenderly.

"I say," said the Captain of the Archangels, spitting a pebble out of his mouth, "will you take three thousand for that pony—as he stands?"

"No thank you. I've an idea he's saved my life," said Lutyens, getting off and lying down at full length. Both teams were on the ground too, waving their boots in the air, and coughing and drawing deep breaths, as the saises ran up to take away the ponies, and an officious water-carrier sprinkled the players with dirty water till they sat up.

"My aunt!" said Powell, rubbing his back, and looking at the stumps of the goalposts, "That was a game!"

They played it over again, every stroke of it, that night at the big dinner, when the Free-for-All Cup was filled and passed down the table, and emptied and filled again, and everybody made most eloquent speeches. About two in the morning, when there might have been some singing, a wise little, plain little, grey little head looked in through the open door.

"Hurrah! Bring him in," said the Archangels; and his sais, who was very happy indeed, patted The Maltese Cat on the flank, and he limped in to the blaze of light and the glittering uniforms, looking for Lutyens. He was used to messes, and men's bedrooms, and places where ponies are not usually encouraged, and in his youth had jumped on and off a mess-table for a bet. So he behaved himself very politely, and ate bread dipped in salt, and was petted all round the table, moving gingerly; and they drank his health, because he had done more to win the Cup than any man or horse on the ground.

That was glory and honour enough for the rest of his days, and The Maltese Cat did not complain much when the veterinary surgeon said that he would be no good for polo any more. When Lutyens married, his wife did not allow him to play, so he was forced to be an umpire; and his pony on these occasions was a flea-bitten grey with a neat polo-tail, lame all round, but desperately quick on his feet, and, as everybody knew, Past Pluperfect Prestissimo Player of the Game.

24

Jerry Strann and the Gift Horse

By Max Brand

*Horses helped pioneers navigate the wilderness and made western
expansion possible. In "Jerry Strann and the Gift Horse" we witness
that special ability that horses have to know exactly who is riding
them. Satan, the magnificent black stallion in this story, loves his
owner and is as gentle as a lamb with him. But when stranger Jerry
Strann steps into the saddle, the horse cringes "with the horror of a
man who shivers at the touch of an unclean animal" and becomes like
a demon. This tale illustrates two fundamental characters of the Old
West: the man who will take no price for his favorite horse, and the
horse who cannot be ridden by anyone but his owner. Excerpted from*
The Night Horseman.

THE WRATH OF THE LORD SEEMS LESS TERRIBLE WHEN IT IS LOCALISED, and the world at large gave thanks daily that the range of Jerry Strann was limited to the Three B's. As everyone in the mountain-desert knows, the Three B's are Bender, Buckskin, and Brownsville; they make the points of a loose triangle that is cut with canyons and tumbled with mountains, and that triangle was the chosen stamping ground of Jerry Strann. Jerry was not born in the region of the Three B's and why it should have been chosen specially by him was matter which the inhabitants could not puzzle out; but they felt that for their sins the Lord had probably put his wrath among them in the form of Jerry Strann.

He was only twenty-four, this Jerry, but he was already grown into a proverb. Men of the Three B's reckoned their conversational dates by the visits of the youth; if a storm hung over the mountains someone might remark: "It looks like Jerry Strann is coming," and such a remark was always received in gloomy silence; mothers had been known to hush their children by chanting: "Jerry Strann will get you if you don't watch out." Yet he was not an ogre with a red knife between his teeth. He stood at exactly the perfect romantic height; he was just six feet tall; he was as graceful as a young cotton-wood in a windstorm and he was as strong and tough as the roots of the mesquite. He was one of those rare men who are beautiful without being unmanly. His face was modelled with the care a Praxiteles would lavish on a Phoebus. His brown hair was thick and dark and every touch of wind stirred it, and his hazel eyes were brilliant with an enduring light—the inextinguishable joy of life.

Consider that there was no malice in Jerry Strann. But he loved strife as the young Apollo loved strife—or a pure-blooded bull terrier. He fought with distinction and grace and abandon and was perfectly willing to use fists or knives or guns at the pleasure of the other contracting party. In another age, with armour and a golden chain and spurs, Jerry Strann would have been—but why think of that? Swords are not forty-fives, and the Twentieth Century is not the Thirteenth. He was, in fact, born just six hundred years too late. From his childhood he had thirsted for battle as other children thirst for milk: and now he rode anything on hoofs and threw a knife like a Mexican—with either hand—and at short range he did snap shooting with two revolvers that made rifle experts sick at heart.

However, the men of the Three B's, as everyone understands, are not gentle or long-enduring, and you will wonder why this young destroyer was allowed to range at large so long. There was a vital reason. Up in the mountains lived Mac Strann, the hermit-trapper, who hated everything in the wide world except his young brother, the beautiful, wild, and sunny Jerry Strann. And Mac Strann loved his brother as much as he hated everything else; it is impossible to state it more strongly. It was not long before the men of the Three B's discovered how Mac Strann felt about his brother. After Jerry's famous Hallowe'en party in Buckskin, for instance, Williamson, McKenna, and Rath started out to rid the country of the disturber. They went out to hunt him as men go out to hunt a wild mustang. And they caught him and bent him down—those three stark men—and he lay in bed for a month; but before the month was over Mac Strann came down from his mountain and went to Buckskin and gathered Williamson and McKenna and Rath in one public place. And when the morning came Williamson and McKenna and Rath had left this vale of tears and Mac Strann was back on his mountain. He was not even arrested. For there was a devilish cunning about the fellow and he made his victims, without exception, attack him first; then he destroyed them, suddenly and surely, and retreated to his lair. Things like this happened once or twice and then the men of the Three B's understood that it was not wise to lay plots for Jerry Strann. They accepted him, as I have said before, as men accept the wrath of God.

Let it not be thought that Jerry Strann was a solitary like his brother. When he went out for a frolic the young men of the community gathered around him, for Jerry paid all scores and the red-eye flowed in his path like wine before the coming of Bacchus; where Jerry went there was never a dull moment, and young men love action. So it happened that when he rode into Brownsville this day he was the leader of a cavalcade. Rumour rode before them, and doors were locked and windows were darkened, and men sat in the darkness within with their guns across their knees. For Brownsville lay at the extreme northern tip of the triangle and it was rarely visited by Jerry; and it is well established that men fear the unfamiliar more than the known.

As has been said, Jerry headed the train of revellers, partially because it was most unwise to cut in ahead of Jerry and partially because there was not a piece of horseflesh in the Three B's which could outfoot his chestnut. It was a gelding out of the loins of the north wind and sired by the devil himself, and its spirit was one with the spirit of Jerry Strann; perhaps because they both served one master. The cavalcade came with a crash of racing hoofs in a cloud of dust. But in the middle of the street Jerry raised his right arm stiffly overhead with a whoop and brought his chestnut to a sliding stop; the cloud of dust rolled lazily on ahead. The young men gathered quickly around the leader, and there was silence as they waited for him to speak—a silence broken only by the wheezing of the horses, and the stench of sweating horseflesh was in every man's nostrils.

"Who owns that hoss?" asked Jerry Strann, and pointed.

He had stopped just opposite O'Brien's hotel, store, blacksmith shop, and saloon, and by the hitching rack was a black stallion. Now, there are some men who carry tidings of their inward strength stamped on their foreheads and written in their eyes. In times of crises crowds will turn to such men and follow them as soldiers follow a captain; for it is patent at a glance that this is a man of men. It is likewise true that there are horses which stand out among their fellows, and this was such a horse. He was such a creature that, if he had been led to a barrier, the entire crowd at the race track would rise as one man and say: "What is that horse?" There were points in which some critics would find fault; most of the men of the mountain-desert, for instance, would have said that the animal was too lightly and delicately limbed for long endurance; but as the man of men bears the stamp of his greatness in his forehead and his eyes, so it was with the black stallion. When the thunder of the cavalcade had rushed upon him down the street he had turned with catlike grace and raised his head to see; and his forehead and his eyes arrested Jerry Strann like a lev-elled rifle. Looking at that proud head one forgot the body of the horse, the symmetry of curves exquisite beyond the sculptor's dream, the arching neck and the steel muscles; one was only conscious of the great spirit. In Human beings we refer to it as "personality."

After a little pause, seeing that no one offered a suggestion as to the identity of the owner, Strann said, softly: "That hoss is mine."

It caused a stir in the crowd of his followers. In the mountain-desert one may deal lightly with a man's wife and lift a random cow or two and settle the score, at need, with a snug "forty-five" chunk of lead. But with horses it is different. A horse in the mountain-desert lies outside of all laws—and above all laws. It is greater than honour and dearer than love, and when a man's horse is taken from him the men of the desert gather together and hunt the thief whether it be a day or whether it be a month, and when they have reached him they shoot him like a dog and leave his flesh to the buzzards and his bones to the merciless stars. For all of this there is a reason. But Jerry Strann swung from his mount, tossed the reins over the head of the chestnut, and walked towards the black with hungry eyes. He was careless, also, and venturing too close—the black whirled with his sudden, catlike agility, and two black hoofs lashed within a hair's breadth of the man's shoulder. There was a shout from the crowd, but Jerry Strann stepped back and smiled so that his teeth showed.

"Boys," he said, but he was really speaking to himself, "there's nothing in the world I want as bad as I want that hoss. Nothing! I'm going to buy him; where's the owner?"

"Don't look like a hoss a man would want to sell, Jerry," came a suggestion from the cavalcade, who had dismounted and now pressed behind their leader.

Jerry favoured the speaker with another of his enigmatic smiles: "Oh," he chuckled, "he'll sell, all right! Maybe he's inside. You gents stick out here and watch for him; I'll step inside."

And he strode through the swinging doors of the saloon.

It was a dull time of day for O'Brien, so he sat with his feet on the edge of the bar and sipped a tall glass of beer; he looked up at the welcome click of the doors, however, and then was instantly on his feet. The good red went out of his face and the freckles over his nose stood out like ink marks.

"There's a black hoss outside," said Jerry, "that I'm going to buy. Where's the owner?"

"Have a drink," said the bartender, and he forced an amiable smile.

"I got business on my hands, not drinking," said Jerry Strann.

"Lost your chestnut?" queried O'Brien in concern.

"The chestnut was all right until I seen the black. And now he ain't a hoss at all. Where's the gent I want?"

The bartender had fenced for time, as long as possible.

"Over there," he said, and pointed.

It was a slender fellow sitting at a table in a corner of the long room, his sombrero pushed back on his head. He was playing solitaire and his back was towards Jerry Strann, who now made a brief survey, hitched his cartridge belt, and approached the stranger with a grin. The man did not turn; he continued to lay down his cards with monotonous regularity, and while he was doing it he said in the gentlest voice that had ever reached the ear of Jerry Strann: "Better stay where you are, stranger. My dog don't like you."

And Jerry Strann perceived, under the shadow of the table, a blacker shadow, huge and formless in the gloom, and two spots of incandescent green twinkling towards him. He stopped; he even made a step back; and then he heard a stifled chuckle from the bartender.

If it had not been for that untimely mirth of O'Brien's probably nothing of what followed would have passed into the history of the Three B's.

THE GIFT-HORSE

"Your dog is your own dog," remarked Jerry Strann, still to the back of the card-playing stranger, "but this ain't your back-yard. Keep your eye on him, or I'll fix him so he won't need watching!"

So saying he made another step forward, and it brought a snarl from the dog; not one of those high-whining noises, but a deep guttural that sounded like indrawn breath. The gun of Jerry Strann leaped into his hand.

"Bart," said the gentle-voiced stranger, "lie down and don't talk." And he turned in his chair, pulled his hat straight, and looked mildly upon the gunman. An artist would have made much of that picture, for there was in this man, as in Strann, a singular portion of beauty. It was not, however, free from objection, for he had not the open manliness of the larger of the two. Indeed, a feminine grace and softness marked him; his wrists were as round as a girl's, and his hands as slender and as delicately finished. Whether it be the white-hot sun of summer or the hurricane snows of winter, the climate of the mountain-desert roughens the skin, and it cuts away spare flesh, hewing out the face in angles; but with this man there were no rough edges, but all was smoothed over and rounded with painful care; as if nature had concentrated in that birth to show what she could do. Such fine workmanship, perhaps, would be appreciated more by women than by men; for men like a certain weight and bulk of bone and muscle—whereas this fellow seemed as light of body as he was of hand. He sat now watching Strann with the utmost gravity. He had very large brown eyes of a puzzling quality; perhaps that was because there seemed to be no thought behind them and one caught the mystery and the wistfulness of some animals from a glance at him.

The effect of that glance on Strann was to make him grin again, and he at once banished the frown from his forehead and put away his gun; the big dog had slunk deeper into the shadow and closer to his master.

"I'm Strann. Maybe you've heard of me."

"My name is Barry," said the other. "I'm sorry that I haven't heard of you before."

And the sound of his voice made Jerry Strann grin again; it was such a low, soft voice with the velvet of a young girl's tone in it; moreover, the brown eyes seemed to apologise for the ignorance concerning Strann's name.

"You got a hoss out in front."

A nod of agreement.

"What's your price?"

"None."

"No price? Look here," argued Strann, "everything's got a price, and I got to have that hoss, understand? Got to! I ain't bargaining. I won't try to beat you down. You just set a figger and I'll cover it. I guess that's square!"

"He ain't a gentle hoss," said Barry. "Maybe you wouldn't like him."

"Oh, that's all right about being gentle," chuckled Strann. Then he checked his mirth and stared piercingly at the other to make out if there were a secret mockery. It could not, however, be possible. The eyes were as gravely apologetic as ever. He continued: "I seen the hell-fire in him. That's what stopped me like a bullet. I like 'em that way. Much rather have 'em with a fight. Well, let's have your price. Hey, O'Brien, trot out your red-eye; I'm going to do some business here!"

O'Brien came hastily, with drinks, and while they waited Strann queried politely: "Belong around these parts?"

"No," answered the other softly.

"No? Where you come from?"

"Over there," said Barry, and waved a graceful hand towards half the points of the compass.

"H-m-m!" muttered Strann, and once more he bent a keen gaze upon his companion. The drinks were now placed before them. "Here," he concluded, "is to the black devil outside!" And he swallowed the liquor at a gulp, but as he replaced the empty glass on the table he observed, with breathless amazement, that the whiskey glass of the stranger was still full; he had drunk his chaser!

"Now, by God!" said Strann in a ringing voice, and struck a heavy hand upon the top of the table. He regained his control, however, instantly. "Now about that price!"

"I don't know what horses are worth," replied Barry.

"To start, then—five hundred bucks in cold cash—gold!—for your—what's his name?"

"Satan."

"Eh?"

"Satan."

"H-m-m!" murmured Strann again. "Five hundred for Satan, then. How about it?"

"If you can ride him," began the stranger.

"Oh, hell," smiled Strann with a large and careless gesture, "I'll ride him, all right."

"Then I would let you take him for nothing," concluded Barry.

"You'd—what?" said Strann. Then he rose slowly from his chair and shouted; instantly the swinging doors broke open and a throng of faces appeared at the gap. "Boys, this gent here is going to give me the black—ha, ha, ha!—if I can ride him!" He turned back on Barry. "They've heard it," he concluded, "and this bargain is going to stick just this way. If your hoss can throw me the deal's off. Eh?"

"Oh, yes," nodded the brown-eyed man.

"What's the idea?" asked one of Jerry's followers as the latter stepped through the doors of the saloon onto the street.

"I dunno," said Jerry. "That gent looks kind of simple; but it ain't my fault if he made a rotten bargain. Here, you!"

And he seized the bridle-reins of the black stallion. Speed, lightning speed, was what saved him, for the instant his fingers touched the leather Satan twisted his head and snapped like an angry dog. The teeth clicked beside Strann's shoulder as he leaped back. He laughed savagely.

"That'll be took out of him," he announced, "and damned quick!"

Here the voice of Barry was heard, saying: "I'll help you mount, Mr. Strann." And he edged his way through the little crowd until he stood at the head of the stallion.

"Look out!" warned Strann in real alarm, "or he'll take your head off!"

But Barry was already beside his horse, and, with his back towards those vicious teeth, he drew the reins over its head. As for the stallion, it pricked one ear forward and then the other, and muzzled the man's shoulder confidingly. There was a liberal chorus of astonished oaths from the gathering.

"I'll hold his head while you get on," suggested Barry, turning his mild eyes upon Strann again.

"Well," muttered the big man, "may I be eternally damned!" He added: "All right. Hold his head, and I'll ride him without pulling leather. Is that square?"

Barry nodded absently. His slender fingers were patting the velvet nose of the stallion and he was talking to it in an affectionate under-tone—meaningless words, perhaps, such as a mother uses to soothe a child. When Strann set his foot in the stirrup and gathered up the reins the black horse cringed and shuddered; it was not a pleasant thing to see; it was like a dog crouching under the suspended whip. It was worse than that; it was almost the horror of a man who shivers at the touch of an unclean animal. There was not a sound from the crowd; and every grin was wiped out. Jerry Strann swung into the saddle lightly.

There he sat, testing the stirrups. They were too short by inches but he refused to have them lengthened. He poised his quirt and tugged his hat lower over his eyes.

"Turn him loose!" he shouted. "Hei!"

And his shrill yell went down the street and the echoes sent it barking back from wall to wall; Barry stepped back from the head of the black. But for an instant the horse did not stir. He was trembling violently, but his blazing eyes were fixed upon the face of his owner. Barry raised his hand.

And then it happened. It was like the release of a coiled watch-spring; the black whirled as a top spins and Strann sagged far to the left; before he could recover the stallion was away in a flash, like a racer leaving the barrier and reaching full speed in almost a stride. Not far—hardly the breadth of the street—before he pitched up in a long leap as if to clear a barrier, landed stiff-legged with a sickening jar, whirled again like a spinning top, and darted straight back. And Jerry Strann pulled leather—with might and main—but the short stirrups were against him, and above all the suddenness of the start had taken him off guard for all his readiness. When the stallion dropped stiff-legged Jerry was thrown forward and an unlucky left foot jarred loose from the stirrup; and when the horse whirled Strann was flung from the saddle. It was a clean fall. He twisted over in the air as he fell and landed in deep dust. The black stallion had reached his master and now he turned, in that same catlike manner, and watched with pricking ears as Strann dragged himself up from the dust.

There was no shout of laughter—no cheer for that fall, and without a smile they watched Strann returning. Big O'Brien had seen from his open door and now he laid a hand on the shoulder of one of the men and whispered at his ear: "There's going to be trouble; bad trouble, Billy. Go for Fatty Matthews—he's a deputy marshal now—and get him here as quick as you can. Run!"

The other spared time for a last glance at Strann and then hurried down the street.

Now, a man who can lose and smile is generally considered the most graceful of failures, but the smile of Jerry Strann as he walked slowly back worried his followers.

"We all hit dust sometime," he philosophized. "But one try don't prove nothin'. I ain't near through with that hoss!"

Barry turned to Strann. If there had been mockery in his eyes or a smile on his lips as he faced Jerry there would have been a gun play on the spot; but, instead, the brown eyes were as dumbly apologetic as ever.

"We didn't talk about two tries," he observed.

"We talk about it now," said Strann.

There was one man in the crowd a little too old to be dangerous and therefore there was one man who was in a position to speak openly to Strann. It was big O'Brien.

"Jerry, you named your game and made your play and lost. I guess you ain't going to turn up a hard loser. Nobody plays twice for the same pot."

The hazel eye of Strann was grey with anguish of the spirit as he looked from O'Brien to the crowd and from the crowd to Satan, and from Satan to his meek-eyed owner. Nowhere was there a defiant eye or a glint of scorn on which he could wreak his wrath. He stood poised in his anger for the space of a breath; then, in the sharp struggle, his better nature conquered.

"Come on in, all of you," he called. "We'll liquor, and forget this."

25

How Blister Got His Name

By John Taintor Foote

◇◇

John Taintor Foote (1881–1950) not only wrote books and stories about the sporting life he lived in hunting and fishing adventures, he was equally adept at turning them into fiction, as he shows here in one of his favorite subjects, horse racing. Foote also succeeded in writing screenplays for Hollywood.

◇◇

HOW MY OLD-YOUNG FRIEND "BLISTER" JONES ACQUIRED HIS REMARKable nickname, I learned one cloudless morning late in June.

Our chairs were tipped against number 84 in the curving line of boxstalls at Latonia. Down the sweep of whitewashed stalls the upper doors were yawning wide, and from many of these openings, velvet black in the sunlight, sleek snaky heads protruded.

My head rested in the center of the lower door of 84. From time to time a warm moist breath, accompanied by a gigantic sigh, would play against the back of my neck; or my hat would be pushed a bit farther over my eyes by a wrinkling muzzle—for Tambourine, gazing out into the green of the center-field, felt a vague longing and wished to tell me about it.

The track, a broad tawny ribbon with a lace-work edging of white fence, was before us; the "upper-turn" with its striped five-eighths pole, not fifty feet away. Some men came and set up the starting device at this red and white pole, and I asked Blister to explain to me just what it meant.

"Goin' to school two-year-olds at the barrier," he explained. And presently—mincing, sidling, making futile leaps to get away, the boys on their

336

backs standing clear above them in the short stirrups—a band of deer-like young thoroughbreds assembled, thirty feet or so from the barrier.

Then there was trouble. Those sweet young things performed, with the rapidity of thought, every lawless act known to the equine brain. They reared. They plunged. They bucked. They spun. They surged together. They scattered like startled quail. I heard squeals, and saw vicious shiny hoofs lash out in every direction; and the dust spun a yellow haze over it all.

"Those jockeys will be killed!" I gasped.

"Jockeys!" exclaimed Blister contemptuously. "Them ain't jockeys—they're exercise-boys. Do you think a jock would school a two-year-old?"

A man, who Blister said was a trainer, stood on the fence and acted as starter. Language came from this person in volcanic blasts, and the seething mass, where infant education was brewing, boiled and boiled again.

"That bay filly's a nice-lookin' trick, Four Eyes!" said Blister, pointing out a two-year-old standing somewhat apart from the rest. "She's by Hamilton 'n' her dam's Alberta, by Seminole."

The bay filly, I soon observed, had more than beauty—she was so obviously the outcome of a splendid and selected ancestry. Even her manners were aristocratic. She faced the barrier with quiet dignity and took no part in the whirling riot except to move disdainfully aside when it threatened to engulf her. I turned to Blister and found him gazing at the filly with a far-away look in his eyes.

"Ole Alberta was a grand mare," he said presently. "I see her get away last in the Crescent City Derby 'n' be ten len'ths back at the quarter. But she come from nowhere, collared ole Stonebrook in the stretch, looked him in the eye the last eighth 'n' outgamed him at the wire. She has a hundred 'n' thirty pounds up at that.

"Ole Alberta dies when she has this filly," he went on after a pause. "Judge Dillon, over near Lexington, owned her, 'n' Mrs. Dillon brings the filly up on the bottle. See how nice that filly stands? Handled every day since she was foaled, 'n' never had a cross word. Sugar every mawnin' from Mrs. Dillon. That's way to learn a colt somethin'."

At last the colts were formed into a disorderly line.

"Now, boys, you've got a chance—come on with 'em!" bellowed the starter. "Not too fast . . ." he cautioned. "Awl-r-r-right . . . let 'em go-o-!"

They were off like rockets as the barrier shot up, and the bay filly flashed into the lead. Her slender legs seemed to bear her as though on the breast of the wind. She did not run—she floated—yet the gap between herself and her struggling schoolmates grew ever wider.

"Oh, you Alberta!" breathed Blister. Then his tone changed. "Most of these wise Ikes talk about the sire of a colt, but I'll take a good dam all the time for mine!"

Standing on my chair, I watched the colts finish their run, the filly well in front.

"She's a wonder!" I exclaimed, resuming my seat.

"She acts like she'll deliver the goods," Blister conceded. "She's got a lot of step, but it takes more'n that to make a race hoss. We'll know about her when she goes the route, carryin' weight against class."

The colts were now being led to their quarters by stable-boys. When the boy leading the winner passed, he threw us a triumphant smile.

"I guess she's bad!" he opined.

"Some baby," Blister admitted. Then with disgust: "They've hung a fierce name on her though."

"Ain't it the truth!" agreed the boy.

"What is her name?" I asked, when the pair had gone by.

"They call her Trez Jolly," said Blister. "Now, ain't that a hell of a name? I like a name you can kind-a warble." He had pronounced the French phrase exactly as it is written, with an effort at the "J" following the sibilant.

"Très Jolie—it's French," I explained, and gave him the meaning and proper pronunciation.

"Traysyolee!" he repeated after me. "Say, I'm a rube right. Tra-aysyole-e in the stretch byano-o-se!" he intoned with gusto. "You can warble that!" he exclaimed.

"I don't think much of Blister—for beauty," I said. "Of course, that isn't your real name."

"No; I had another once," he replied evasively. "But I never hears it much. The old woman calls me 'thatdambrat,' 'n' the old man the same, only more so. I gets Blister handed to me by the bunch one winter at the New Awlin' meetin'."

"How?" I inquired.

"Wait till I get the makin's 'n' I'll tell you," he said, as he got up and entered a stall.

"One winter I'm swipin' fur Jameson," he began, when he returned with tobacco and papers. "We ships to New Awlins early that fall. We have twelve dogs—half of 'em hop-heads 'n' the other half dinks.

"In them days I ain't much bigger 'n a peanut, but I sure thinks I'm a clever guy. I figger they ain't a gazabo on the track can hand it to me.

"One mawnin' there's a bunch of us ginnies settin' on the fence at the wire, watchin' the workouts. Some trainers 'n' owners is standin' on the track rag-chewin'.

"A bird owned by Cal Davis is finishin' a mile-'n'-a-quarter, under wraps, in scan'lous fast time. Cal is standin' at the finish with his clock in his hand lookin' real contented. All of a sudden the bird makes a stagger, goes to his knees 'n' chucks the boy over his head. His swipe runs out 'n' grabs the bird 'n' leads him in a-limpin'.

"Say! That bird's right-front tendon is bowed like a barrel stave!

"This Cal Davis is a big owner. He's got all kinds of kale—'n' he don't fool with dinks. He gives one look at the bowed tendon.

"'Anybody that'll lead this hoss off the track, gets him 'n' a month's feed,' he says.

"Before you could spit I has that bird by the head. His swipe ain't goin' to let go of him, but Cal says: 'Turn him loose, boy!' 'N' I'm on my way with the bird.

"That's the first one I ever owns. Jameson loans me a stall fur him. That night a ginnie comes over from Cal's barn with two bags of oats in a wheelbarrow.

"A newspaper guy finds out about the deal, 'n' writes it up so everybody is hep to me playin' owner. One day I see the starter point me out to Colonel King, who's the main squeeze in the judge's stand, 'n' they both laugh.

"I've got all winter before we has to ship, 'n' believe me I sweat some over this bird. I done everythin' to that tendon, except make a new one. In a month I has it in such shape he don't limp, 'n' I begins to stick mile gallops 'n' short breezers into him. He has to wear a stiff bandage on the dinky leg, 'n' I puts one on the left-fore, too—it looks better.

"It ain't so long till I has this bird cherry ripe. He'll take a-holt awful strong right at the end of a stiff mile. One day I turns him loose, fur three-eighths, 'n' he runs it so fast he makes me dizzy.

"I know he's good, but I wants to know how good, before I pays entrance on him. I don't want the clockers to get wise to him, neither!

"Joe Nickel's the star jock that year. I've seen many a good boy on a hoss, but I think Joe's the best judge of pace I ever see. One day he's comin' from the weighin'-room, still in his silks. His valet's with him carryin' the saddle. I steps up 'n' says: 'Kin I see you private a minute, Joe?'

"'Sure thing, kid,' he says. 'N' the valet skidoos.

"'Joe,' I says, 'I've got a bird that's right. I don't know just how good he is, but he's awful good. I want to get wise to him before I crowds my dough on to the 'Sociation. Will you give him a work?'

"It takes an awful nerve to ask a jock like Nickel to work a hoss out, but he's the only one can judge pace good enough to put me wise, 'n' I'm desperate.

"'It's that Davis cripple, ain't it?' he asks.

"'That's him,' I says.

"He studies a minute, lookin' steady at me.

"'I'm your huckleberry,' he says at last. 'When do you want me?'

"'Just as she gets light to-morrow mawnin',' I says quick, fur I hasn't believed he'd come through, 'n' I wants to stick the gaff into him 'fore he changes his mind.

"He give a sigh. I knowed he was no early riser.

"'All right,' he says. 'Where'll you be?'

"'At the half-mile post,' I says. 'I'll have him warmed up fur you.'

"'All right,' he says again—'n' that night I don't sleep none.

"When it begins to get a little gray next mawnin' I takes the bird out 'n' gallops him a slow mile with a stiff breezer at the end. But durin' the night I gives up thinkin' Joe'll be there, 'n' I nearly falls off when I comes past the half-mile post, 'n' he's standin' by the fence in a classy overcoat 'n' kid gloves.

"He takes off his overcoat, 'n' comes up when I gets down, 'n' gives a look at the saddle.

"'I can't ride nothin' on that thing,' he says. 'Slip over to the jocks' room 'n' get mine. It's on number three peg—here's the key.'

"It's gettin' light fast 'n' I'm afraid of the clockers.

"'The sharp-shooters'll be out in a minute,' I says.

"'I can't help it,' says Joe. 'I wouldn't ride a bull on that saddle!'

"I see there's no use to argue, so I beats it across the center-field, cops the saddle 'n' comes back. I run all the way, but it's gettin' awful light.

"'Send him a mile in forty-five 'n' see what he's got left,' I says, as I throws Joe up.

"'Right in the notch—if he's got the step,' he says.

"I click Jameson's clock on them, as they went away—Joe whisperin' in the bird's ear. The back-stretch was the stretch, startin' from the half. I seen the bird's mouth wide open as they come home, 'n' Joe has double wraps on him. 'He won't beat fifty under that pull!' I says to myself. But when I stops the clock at the finish it was at forty-four-'n'-three-quarters. Joe ain't got a clock to go by neither—that's judgin' pace!—take it from me!

"'He's diseased with speed,' says Joe, when he gets down. 'He can do thirty-eight sure—just look at my hands!'

"I does a dance a-bowin' to the bird, 'n' Joe stands there laughin' at me, squeezin' the blood back into his mitts.

"We leads the hoss to the gate, 'n' there's a booky's clocker named Izzy Goldberg.

"'You an exercise-boy now?' he asks Joe.

"'Not yet,' says Joe. 'Mu cousin here owns this trick, 'n' I'm givin' him a work.'

"'Up kind-a early, ain't you? Say! He's good, ain't he, Joe?' says Izzy; 'n' looks at the bird close.

"'Naw, he's a mutt,' says Joe.

"'What's he doin' with his mouth open at the end of that mile?' Izzy says, 'n' laughs.

"'He only runs it in fifty,' says Joe, careless. 'I takes hold of him 'cause he's bad in front, 'n' he's likely to do a flop when he gets tired. So long, Bud!' Joe says to me, 'n' I takes the bird to the barn.

"I'm not thinkin' Izzy ain't wise. It's a cinch Joe don't stall him. Every booky would hear about that workout by noon. Sure enough the Item's pink sheet has this among the tips the next day: 'Count Noble'—that was the bird's name—'a mile in forty-four. Pulled to a walk at the end. Bet the works on him; his first time out, boys!'

"That was on a Saturday. On Monday I enters the bird among a bunch of dogs to start in a five furlong sprint Thursday. I'm savin' every soomarkee I gets my hands on 'n' I pays the entrance to the secretary like it's a mere bag of shells. Joe Nickel can't ride fur me—he's under contract. I meets him the day before my race.

"'You're levelin' with your hoss, ain't you?' he says. 'I'll send my valet in with you, 'n' after you get yours on, he'll bet two hundred fur me.'

"'Nothin' doin', Joe!' I says. 'Stay away from it. I'll tell you when I gets ready to level. You can't bet them bookies nothin'—they're wise to him.'

"'Look-a-here, Bud!' says Joe. 'That bird'll cake-walk among them crabs. No jock can make him lose, 'n' not get ruled off.'

"'Leave that to me,' I says.

"Just as I figgers—my hoss opens up eight-to-five in the books.

"I gives him all the water he'll drink afore he goes to the post, 'n' I has bandages on every leg. The paddock judge looks at them bandages, but he knows the bird's a cripple, 'n' he don't feel 'em.

"'Them's to hold his legs on, ain't they?' he says, 'n' grins.

"'Surest thing you know,' I says. But I feels some easier when he's on his way—there's seven pounds of lead in each of them bandages.

"I don't want the bird whipped when he ain't got a chance.

"'This hoss backs up if you use the bat on him,' I says to the jock, as he's tyin' his reins.

"'He backs up anyway, I guess,' he says, as the parade starts.

"The bird gets away good, but I'd overdone the lead in his socks. He finished a nasty last—thirty len'ths back.

"'Roll over, kid!' says the jock, when I go up to slip him his fee. 'Not fur ridin' that hippo. It 'ud be buglary—he couldn't beat a piano!'

"I meets Colonel King comin' out of the judge's stand that evenin'.

"An owner's life has its trials and tribulations—eh, my boy?' he says.

"'Yes, sir!' I says. That's the first time Colonel King ever speaks to me, 'n' I swells up like a toad. 'I'm gettin' to be all the gravy 'round here,' I says to myself.

"Two days after this they puts an overnight mile run fur maidens on the card, 'n' I slips the bird into it. I knowed it was takin' a chance so soon after his bad race, but it looks so soft I can't stay 'way from it. I goes to Cal Davis, 'n' tells him to put a bet down.

"'Oh, ho!' he says. 'Lendin' me a helpin' hand, are you?' Then I tells him about Nickel.

"'Did Joe Nickel work him out for you?' he says. 'The best is good enough fur you, ain't it? I'll see Joe, 'n' if it looks good to him I'll take a shot at it. Much obliged to you.'

"'Don't never mention it,' I says.

"'How do you mean that?' he says, grinnin'.

"'Both ways,' says I.

"'The mawnin' of the race, I'm givin' the bird's bad leg a steamin', when a black swipe named Duckfoot Johnson tells me I'm wanted on the phone over to the secretary's office, 'n' I gets Duckfoot to go on steamin' the leg while I'm gone.

"'It's a feed man on the phone, wantin' to know when he gets sixteen bucks I owe him.

"'The bird'll bring home your coin at four o'clock this afternoon,' I tells him.

"'Well, that's lucky,' he says. 'I thought it was throwed to the birds, 'n' I didn't figure they'd bring it home again.'

"When I gets back there's a crap game goin' on in front of the stall, 'n' Duckfoot's shootin'. There's a hot towel on the bird's leg, 'n' it's been there too long. I takes it off 'n' feel where small blisters has begun to raise under the hair—a little more 'n' it 'ud been clear to the bone. I cusses Duckfoot good, 'n' rubs vaseline into the leg."

I interrupted Blister long enough to inquire: "Don't they blister horses sometimes to cure them of lameness?"

"Sure," he replied. "But a hoss don't work none fur quite a spell afterwards. A blister, to do any good, fixes him so he can't hardly raise his leg fur two weeks.

"Well," he went on, "the race fur maidens was the last thing on the card. I'm in the betting-ring when they chalks up the first odds, 'n' my hoss opens at twenty-five-to-one. The two entrance moneys have about cleaned me. I'm only twenty green men strong. I peels off ten of 'em 'n' shoved up to a booky.

"'On the nose fur that one,' I says, pointin' to the bird's name.

"'Quit your kiddin',' he says. 'What 'ud you do with all that money? This fur yours.''N' he rubs to twelve-to-one.

"'Ain't you the liberal gink?' I says, as he hands me the ticket.

"'I starts fur the next book, but say!—the odds is just meltin' away. Joe's 'n' Cal's dough is comin' down the line, 'n' the gazabos, thinkin' it's wise money, trails. By post-time the bird's a one-to-three shot.

"I've give the mount to Sweeney, 'n' like a nut I puts him hep to the bird, 'n' he tells his valet to bet a hundred fur him. The bird has on socks again, but this time they're empty, 'n' the race was a joke. He breaks fifth at the get-away, but he just mows them dogs down. Sweeney keeps thinkin' about that hundred, I guess, 'cause he rode the bird all the way, 'n' finished a million len'ths in front.

"I cashes my ticket, 'n' starts fur the barn to sleep with that bird, when here comes Joe Nickel.

"'He run a nice race,' he says, grinnin', 'n' hands me six hundred bucks.

"'What's this fur?' I says. 'You better be careful . . . I got a weak heart.'

"'I win twelve hundred to the race,' he says. 'N' we splits it two ways.'

"'Nothin' doin',' I says, 'n' tries to hand him back the wad.

"'Go awn!' he says, 'I'll give you a soak in the ear. I bet that money fur you, kiddo.'

"I looks at the roll 'n' gets wobbly in the knees. I never see so much kale before—not at one time. Just then we hears the announcer sing out through a megaphone:

"'The o-o-owner of Count Nobul-l-l-l is wanted in the judge's stand!'

"'Oy, oy!' says Joe. 'You'll need that kale—you're goin' to lose your happy home. It's Katy bar the door fur yours, Bud!'

"'Don't worry—watch me tell it to 'em,' I says to Joe, as I stuffs the roll 'n' starts fur the stand. I was feelin' purty good.

"'Wait a minute,' says Joe, runnin' after me. 'You can't tell them people nothin'. You ain't wise to that bunch yet. Bud—why, they'll kid you silly before they hand it to you, 'n' then change the subject to somethin' inter-estin', like where to get pompono cooked to suit 'em. I've been up against it,' he says, "n' I'm tellin' you right. Just keep stallin' around when you get in the stand, 'n' act like you don't know the war's over.'

"'Furget it,' I says. 'I'll show those big stiffs where to head in. I'll hypnotize the old owls. I'll give 'em a song 'n' dance that's right!'

"As I goes up the steps I see the judges settin' in their chairs, 'n' I takes off my hat. Colonel King ain't settin', he's standin' up with his hands in his pockets. Somehow, when I sees him I begins to wilt—he looks so clean. He's got a white mustache, 'n' his face is kind-a brown 'n' pink. He looks at me a minute out of them blue eyes of his.

"'Are you the owner of Count Noble, Mr.—er—?'

"'Jones, sir,' I says.

"'Jones?' says the colonel.

"'Yes, sir,' I says.

"'Mr. Jones,' says the colonel, 'how do you account for the fact that on Thursday Count Noble performs disgracefully, and on Saturday runs like a stake horse? Have the days of the week anything to do with it?'

"I never says nothin'. I just stands there lookin' at him, foolin' with my hat.

"'This is hell,' I thinks.

"'The judges are interested in this phenomenon, Mr. Jones, and we have sent for you, thinking perhaps you can throw a little light on the matter,' says the colonel, 'n' waits fur me again.

"'Come on . . . get busy!' I says to myself. 'You can kid along with a bunch of bums, 'n' it sounds good—don't get cold feet the first time some class opens his bazoo at you!' But I can't make a noise like a word, on a bet.

"'The judges, upon looking over the betting sheets of the two races in which your horse appeared, find them quite interesting,' says the colonel. 'The odds were short in the race he did not win; they remained unchanged—in fact, rose—since only a small amount was wagered on his chances. On the other hand, these facts are reversed in today's race, which he won. It seems possible that you and your friends who were pessimists on Thursday became optimists today, and benefited by the change. Have you done so?'

"I see I has to get some sort-a language out of me.

"'He was a better hoss today—that's all I knows about it,' I says.

"'The first part of your statement seems well within the facts,' says the colonel. 'He was, apparently, a much better horse today. But these gentlemen and myself, having the welfare of the American thoroughbred at heart, would be glad to learn by what method he was so greatly improved.'

"I don't know why I ever does it, but it comes to me how Duckfoot leaves the towel on the bird's leg, 'n' I don't stop to think.

"'I blistered him,' I says.

"'You—what?' says the colonel. I'd have give up the roll quick, sooner'n spit it out again, but I'm up against it.

"'I blisters him,' I says.

"The colonel's face gets red. His eyes bung out 'n' he turns 'round 'n' starts to cough 'n' make noises. The rest of them judges does the same. They holds on to each other 'n' does it. I know they're givin' me the laugh fur that fierce break I makes.

"'You're outclassed, kid!' I says to myself. 'They'll tie a can to you, sure. The gate fur yours!'

"Just then Colonel King turns round, 'n' I see I can't look at him no more. I looks at my hat, waitin' fur him to say I'm ruled off. I've got a lump in my throat, 'n' I think it's a bunch of bright conversation stuck there. But just then a chunk of water rolls out of my eye, 'n' hits my hat—pow! It looks bigger'n Lake Erie, 'n' 'fore I kin jerk the hat away—pow!—comes another one. I knows the colonel sees 'em, 'n' I hopes I croak.

"'Ahem—,' he says.

"'Now I get mine!' I says to myself.

"'Mr. Jones,' says the colonel, 'n' his voice is kind-a cheerful. 'The judges will accept your explanation. You may go if you wish.'"

Just as I'm goin' down the steps the colonel stops me.

"'I have a piece of advice for you, Mr. Jones,' he says. His voice ain't cheerful neither. It goes right into my gizzard. I turns and looks at him. 'Keep that horse blistered from now on!' says the colonel.

"Some ginnies is in the weighin'-room under the stand, 'n' hears it all. That's how I gets my name."

26

The White Dandy Story

By Velma Caldwell Melville

◇◇

Another advocate of animal rights was a Wisconsin woman named Velma Caldwell Melville, who was widely published in women's magazines of the late nineteenth century. Melville was an active supporter of Henry Bergh, a wealthy New Yorker who founded the Society for the Prevention of Cruelty to Animals in 1866. Twelve years later Melville was struck by the worldwide success of Black Beauty. *Anna Sewell, the book's English author, intended it as a morality tale for people who worked with horses, but its message of the horrors of mistreatment for working horses struck a chord with a much wider audience.*

Melville decided that North America needed its own version of Black Beauty. *Her book featured a horse named White Dandy and was written entirely in his voice. As in the original, other horse characters tell their stories of abuse.*

From his earliest days, White Dandy knows nothing but kindness. His job as a riding and driving horse for Dr. Richard Wallace suits him perfectly and he's an enthusiastic worker as the doctor goes about his rounds. While Dr. Wallace demands much, he is equally demanding that the hostlers who care for his beloved horse do their jobs kindly.

Dr. Wallace's brother Fred, also a doctor, is less careful, and White Dandy notices how the horses used by the doctor and his sons can be treated with thoughtlessness and occasional cruelty. The memories of these incidents frighten White Dandy when his master makes a momentous decision.

—SHARON B. SMITH

$\Diamond$

ONE AUTUMN MASTER DETERMINED TO "GO WEST." WHY HE WENT I DO not know, but he was to stay "some months," they said. How I did hope he would take me along, but he did not.

"Be kind to Dandy," was his parting injunction, as usual, to Herman, the man who had succeeded Park Winters as hostler. Of course, I did not know what going West means, and could not think that "some months" were longer than the time he had spent in Chicago. The morning he started he came into my stall and talked to me a long while. Among other things he said: "Be a good boy, Dandy, and when I come home we'll go and live at the farm—you and I."

I did miss him so! The days were all dreary, and I dreaded to go to sleep at night, because I would be obliged to awake to a fresh sense of my loss. I cannot begin to give all my experience during his absence, but will note a few instances. Of a truth, I realized as never before what it is to be a horse.

Dr. and Mrs. Wallace were not a happy couple. The latter was less outspoken than in the early days of her married life, but she was equally as self-willed, only more cunning and underhanded about it. Fred drank all the time, but people could not ordinarily tell when he was intoxicated. The barn boys said he could "carry a good deal." The two boys, Chet and Carm, were wild and lawless. The former was smart and a great student, though. Poor Carm, better but weaker, was always in disgrace. His teacher and father called him a "numbskull," and gradually the latter came to indulge Chet in everything and deny Carm just as prodigally.

There were two other children in the house now—Tommy and Elizabeth, or "Bobby," as the little girl called herself, and others fell into the habit. I liked Bobby from the time Master first held the little yellow-haired creature on my back for a ride; and she always clapped her little hands on seeing me, and cried, "Dandy! Dandy!" I liked her for herself, and also because Dr. Dick loved her. It did me good to know that he had this little child to pet and think about.

Things went well enough for a week or so after Master left, then Chet began to drive me. Sometimes when the doctor would use me for a long drive in the day, soon after dark, while I was yet eating my supper, the boy, with some companion, would come into the barn and put my harness on. Herman would object, and there would be a fuss between them, always ending in my being hitched in a buggy or road cart and driven out. It was the second time that this occurred that I discovered that Chet was under the influence of liquor, as was also his companion, and they carried bottles with them. Chet used the whip freely and I went as fast as I could, but the oftener they touched those bottles the harder they drove.

After what seemed to me hours of agony, they pulled up before a brilliantly lighted old building out in the country, hitched me, and staggered in. The wind was raw and cold, and the sweat pouring off me. I surely thought Chet would remember my blanket, but he didn't, and there I had to stand one, two, three, four, or more dreadful hours. Long before they came out I was alternately chilling and burning. I ached and trembled.

They drove home as fast as they came, whipping nearly all the way, though I was doing my best. Herman swore profusely (people did not do that around the barn when Master was home) as he rubbed me down rapidly with a coarse cloth before blanketing me closely. How I felt!

And thirsty—it did seem I must have water or choke, but he gave me none for some reason. By morning I was so stiff I could scarcely move, my breath was short and came hard, and my skin was hot. Dr. Fred ordered me early.

"I don't think Dandy is able to go out, sir, today," Herman replied. "The young gentlemen had him out all night almost, and he is all stiffened up."

Dr. Fred muttered something and ordered out the bays, calling out to Herman, as he drove off, to get Dr. Dick's box of horse medicine and give me aconite—two-drop doses of the tincture every two hours—until the fever was gone; then to alternate bryonia, and thus according to directions given in the book with the box.

I noticed that I began to feel better pretty soon, and by afternoon Mrs. Wallace said she wanted me hitched up. Herman demurred, but had to finally give in. I was as stiff as ever when I got home again.

That very night Chet harnessed me again, despite Herman's angry protest, and drove me ten miles. If only he had taken the trouble to look in my eyes, I am sure he must have seen how wretched I felt. This time he carelessly threw a blanket over me, but did not buckle it over my chest, and in a little while the wind had blown it half off me. It would have been entirely off—and it might as well have been—but for a corner catching on the top of the collar.

That time gray was showing in the east before he started for home. With vile, profane words he bade me "Get up," emphasizing by stinging blows of the whip, saying to his companion that he must make the ten miles before his father was up. I suppose no man was ever compelled to stand tied to a post all night; if there had, he would surely be going up and down the earth preaching mercy and justice to those who have the power over horses. Another thing made that night especially wearing was the fact that I was tied short, and my front feet were much lower than my back ones. Such a strain as I was on!

It does seem that horses deserve the little consideration necessary to tie them in a decent spot. I have heard many of my kind speak of this matter. In some villages the hitching places along the sidewalks are most uncomfortable, the animals being obliged to stand on a twist, ofttimes with the front feet lower and in a mud puddle. Is it any wonder we sometimes protest by vigorously pawing the sidewalks, if we can reach them? Give us fair play.

Well, I was too lame to get out at all, after that night, for a week. I had rheumatism. Had Master been there to treat me, I might have recovered, but Herman knew nothing about horse doctoring, and so it ran on. If I did get a little better, it was only to be overdriven and exposed. Another time there was to be a horse race five miles off, and Chet drove Prince and I in the buggy.

Then I found out how it hurts a heavy-bodied, short-legged horse to be driven with a light-bodied, long-limbed one. He drove, as usual, just as fast as he could make us go, uphill and down the same. More than once I thought I should fall, and by the time he stopped I was whiter than even nature intended me to be, being covered with foam. Prince was not nearly so tired, but he said it irritated and fretted him to be driven with a horse of my build.

It was only a little country horse race, and the animals were chiefly working ones with neither inclination, strength, nor training for the race-track. The men were wild with excitement, and betting was going on all around. After a while three men got on their horses' backs and started. The crowd yelled and clapped their hands; the riders buried the cruel spurs in the horses' sides, and leaned as far forward as possible.

Of course, some one had to beat, and it was a long-legged, bony creature that won the first heat. Three times the same ones run, and twice the long-legged one won, but the others had done their best; yes, more than that, I may say.

Poor things! There they stood, sweat and blood covering their sides, every nerve and muscle overstrained, and their masters cursing them for their defeat. The entire afternoon was consumed in this manner. Among others Prince was taken on the track. I knew by his eye, and the poise of his head he did not like it, but he behaved nicely until a cruel-looking fellow got on his back and dug the rowels in; with one bound he was off, and the rider had hard work to keep his seat. He won the heat, and I was scarcely enjoying his victory when, quick as a flash, he reached out and catching the fellow by the shoulder flung him headlong some feet away.

Someone caught the bridle strap, and, as soon as the fellow could pick himself up, he flew at the offender, dealing him a blow between the eyes with a club chancing to be handy. "Hold on!" Chet cried, but another, and another blow followed. My noble gray friend staggered, gathered up, staggered again, then fell. A half-dozen convulsive shivers passed over his frame and he was dead.

In a fury of anger and terror the young master sprang upon Prince's slayer. They grappled, but strong hands separated them, and Chet had only to put my harness in the buggy, get on my back, and ride sorrowfully homeward. Dr. Fred was in a temper, to be sure, and immediately had an officer after the man who had killed his horse.

All night and, for many nights, I could not close my eyes without seeming to see poor Prince in the death throes, and all because he dared to resent unfair treatment. I heard Herman say that the fellow had paid for the horse, that Chet and his father had had a quarrel, and that Mrs. Wallace insisted on the former leaving home.

"Yes, she's mighty keen fer the first woman's boys to leave home," remarked an old man who worked around the barn. "She's wantin''em out of the way so her young uns 'll git the property."

"Guess there won't be enough to fight over if Dr. Dick stays away long," Herman replied.

Speaking of horse races reminds me to say that if all racehorses, or those that are made to run, could tell their stories they would fill volumes with tales of injustice and suffering. All animals will, if humanely treated, do their best for their masters; but a kind word and reassuring pat will go much further toward winning a race than all the spurs and curses in the world. Many a race has been lost through the very efforts made to win it.

Coolness and self-possession are indispensable in both horse and rider. I remember being at a state fair with my master some years later, and witnessing a race. Among the competitors was a handsome little black horse, all grit and goodness, but, owing to its owner being partly intoxicated, it lost the stake, in consequence incurring his wrath. And how he did pound the noble little beast! A number of disapprovals arose from the multitude, but no one ventured to interfere. The animal was his, you know.

I had no idea before that year's experience that little things—at least what men call little things—could so affect the health and spirits of a horse. I had even felt a little scornful sometimes when I saw strong-looking animals go along with drooping heads, and noticed how dull and stupid they looked. But when I came to endure hardships and have no petting (though Herman was better to me than most men are to their own horses) I felt differently about it. We need encouragement.

Chet did not take me out after Prince's tragic death for some time, but Dr. Fred drove me a great deal, as there was only the bays and myself then. Topsy had had no regular breaking yet, but Chet declared his intention of attending to the matter at once. When he did undertake it he frightened the poor thing almost to death, and what the outcome would have been I can only surmise, had not a humane man noticed him one day and chided him for his method, or rather lack of method.

"Let me show you my way," he said.

I suppose Chet was getting tired of the job, so surrendered. From being always handled, Topsy was all right, so long as no harness was introduced, or any unusual noise made near her; but at the first unfamiliar sight or sound she was a bunch of terrified, prancing nerves, expecting the worst, and usually getting it, in the form of a whipping.

"She's got to learn that I'm boss," was a favorite expression of Chet's.

"Well, my boy," said the gentleman, "I suppose it is necessary for a horse to know it has a master, but it is equally necessary for us to recognize that they have rights, and also that bullying an animal is not being, in a manly sense, its master. Now I have broken scores of horses, and never yet whipped but one, and I have always hated myself for doing that."

Then he began to gently rub Topsy's head and neck with his hands, and later with a brush. She seemed to enjoy this, and when he let the latter gradually pass over her shoulders and back, she offered no resistance. He worked with her fifteen minutes or longer, then turned her into the little enclosure she occupied during the day.

I think I neglected to say I was resting out at the farm for a day or two when this occurred. In two or three hours the man came again, and repeated the handling and brushing, only this time he touched the whole body, talking kindly and reassuring all the while.

"She is going to be an uncommonly easy subject, I predict," he announced.

"But who'd have patience for such slow getting on?" Chet scornfully asked.

"I should imagine a little time apparently wasted in the beginning less loss than a fine horse ruined in the end," the old man quietly answered.

When he let the young mare go that time she seemed slow to leave him, though he had brushed her even to her heels. The next time he handled her with greater freedom, brushing and talking and finally showing her a little sack of straw. She eyed it a while, smelled it, and then seemed not to care for it.

The man now began to rub her with this, gradually increasing the noise it made. Of course, she was a little shy of this, and inclined to go away. A few gentle touches of the brush reassured her. Then he put a halter on her. She had often worn one before. After this he applied the straw again, stopping every little while to brush and smooth her. In a little time she paid no attention either to the noise or the touch of the sack.

The next day he gave her four lessons of similar character. Later he rattled tin cans and the like about her from head to heels, and had small boys blow tin horns in all directions. Topsy told me afterwards that so long as she could hear that man's voice or feel his touch, she was not afraid of anything.

Afterward he gradually introduced the bridle and harness. Like all horses, she objected to the bit, and I fancy people would make more fuss than we do, if they had to wear it. It was the first night that Topsy was at the livery barn after her "breaking," and she was saying she minded the bit worst of all. An old horse replied that well she might hate it.

"For years," she said, "my tongue has been in a measure paralyzed. It always hangs out of my mouth when the bit is in, and I can't help it. Sometimes it is more helpless than others and I almost starve. I get better at times where some one owns me who puts a bit in my mouth that don't hurt; but I am getting used up anyway, and change hands often, and the majority of bits makes the trouble worse."

"I was once troubled that way," spoke up another horse, "and my master kept changing bits until he got one that was all right and then I got over it."

"I, too, had a paralyzed tongue," said another, "but it was not the bit, it was genuine paralysis—might have been caused by that in the first place, though I never thought of it. Anyway they applied electricity to the nerves and gave me some medicine three times a day—'strychnia,' they called it, one-hundredth of a grain at a dose. I soon got well."

"My tongue was all torn to pieces once with a frosty bit," put in another. "And how I did suffer! No one noticed it until it was all ulcerated, and I could not eat and scarcely drink. My master was one of those careless fellows who never examines his horse, and seems to forget that, however much they suffer, they can't speak for themselves. He did not know what to do for me and so sent for a neighbor, who told him to use alum wash until the ulcers were all gone, and leave the bit out until my mouth got well, meanwhile feeding me soft food."

And still another spoke of her teeth becoming long and rough, and lacerating her tongue badly. She said they filed the teeth and wet her tongue and mouth with a lotion made of calendula and water.

Topsy was a beauty in harness, and Chet was proud of her in his way, but from the first I feared hers would be a hard life, but my darkest forebodings came short of the dread reality. Among other experiences that winter was one in horseshoeing. Master had been exceedingly particular always about my feet, but Herman was like a majority of other men; knew nothing of the business himself and trusted entirely to the smith, who chanced to be a new one.

I had often heard Master and the good blacksmith in the old home denounce the fashion of trimming the frog and thinning the sole until it yielded to the pressure of the thumb, and that was just what this smith did. And then he put on great, heavy shoes, driving in spikes rather than nails. I admit that I kicked and plunged, but it was all wrong, and I knew it; then the last spike went through into the foot. This made me rear and plunge worse than ever, and the blacksmith struck me with the hammer.

"See here, Dr. Dick Wallace won't stand that," cried Herman. "He allows no man to strike Dandy."

"Don't reckon he's better than other horses," he answered.

"Folks might differ on that," said Herman.

Well, I got out of there at last, but my foot hurt intolerably, and I limped. Herman spoke of it to Dr. Fred, but the latter was in one of his gruff moods, and only answered: "It most always lames 'em at first."

That night a man came for a doctor in great haste; some one had taken poison by mistake. Dandy was ordered. If I could have spoken, how soon I would have convinced Herman that, with that terrible torture in my foot, I could not go, but I could only mutely look at him, and he, half asleep, paid no attention. It was a good many miles we went, and the doctor drove like mad. It seemed to me that running through fire would have been easy compared with the pain in my foot, aggravated by the ceaseless concussion of the hard roads.

With a blanket thrown over me, I was left tied in a shed. How I longed to lie down on something! All I could do was to hold up that leg. The pains extended clear into my shoulders, and the cords of my neck were growing stiff.

After a long time, a man came out and unhitched me from the road cart. The moment I was free I lay down. Directly the man ran and brought Dr. Fred. They bade me get up, and, rather than to disobey, I tried it, but the moment I threw any weight on that foot had to immediately lay down again. Presently the man noticed me holding that foot, and asked if I was not newly shod. Then Dr. Fred remembered.

"Well, Dandy," he said, "we must get home. Try it once more." I got on my feet, but had to hold that one up for awhile. Gradually I compelled myself to put it down, for I knew we must go, as he had said. That was long years ago, but even now I can feel some of the agony of that slow journey.

He went with Herman and me to the shop, and fiercely ordered that shoe removed. The smith was not nearly so independent then. When the doctor saw the heavy thing he raved more than ever.

"Do you put such shoes as those on a horse like this?" he cried. The result was that all the shoes came off, and I was put in my stall till my feet got well.

"An ounce at the toe means a pound at the withers," quoted the old stable man. "And there's truth in it; glad the doctor had sense enough to refuse them."

It was four weeks before I could be shod again, and in the meantime I had a very sore foot. They gave me aconite to keep down my fever, and used arnica on my foot after paring away the horn and poulticing until suppuration ceased. My one thought was: "Will Master never come home?"

And so the winter and spring passed. "Several months," I thought as much! My experience was pretty much the same right through, but I felt years older when once again I rested my head on my beloved Master's shoulder.

There was a new stable boy when he came back; Paddy, they called him. Dr. Fred and Herman had quarreled some time before. There was a new span of horses, too; John and Jean. The old stable man privately told Master of some of my hardships, and with tears in his eyes, the latter whispered: "Forgive me, Dandy."

27

The Great Match Race: Eclipse and Sir Henry

By an Old Turfman

Working horses made up the great majority of the three million or so horses who lived in the United States during the first half of the nineteenth century. But the relatively small number of sporting horses drew a disproportionate amount of attention and money. Horse racing, for both sporting and gambling purposes, was almost universally popular. The sport found itself standing in for the regional conflict between North and South several times during the decades leading up to the Civil War, never more so than in the Great Match Race of 1823.

This is how the match was proposed by newspaper advertisements to horsemen North and South during the early months of 1823:

Great match race . . . over the Union Course, Long Island, May 27th, 1823. Heats four miles, for $20,000. The Southern gentlemen to be allowed to name their horse at the starting post.

A writer who described himself as "An Old Turfman," actually Cadwallader R. Colden, manager of the Union Course itself, told the story of the race a few years later.

—SHARON B. SMITH

DOUBTS WERE ENTERTAINED BY SOME OF THE NEW YORK SPORTSMEN to the last moment whether this great match would be contested by the Virginia gentlemen. They, it was perfectly understood, had left Virginia, with five horses, selected from the best racers which North Carolina and Virginia could boast of, and proceeded to the estate of Mr. Bela Badger, adjacent to Bristol, in Pennsylvania, distant from the Union Course, about ninety miles, where, having a fine course upon which to exercise and try their horses, they had made a halt.

The horses selected for this great occasion, as also to contend for the three purse races to be run for, on the three days subsequent to the match, heats of four, three, and two miles, were Betsey Richards, five years old; her full brother, John Richards, four years; Sir Henry, four years; Flying Childers, five years; all by Sir Archy; and Washington, four years old, by Timoleon, a son of Sir Archy. With one of the three first named, it was the intention of Mr. William R. Johnston to run the match. Of these, at the time he left home, John Richards was his favorite; his next choice was Sir Henry, and thirdly, the mare; although some of the Southern gentlemen (and amongst others Gen. Wynn) gave their opinion in favor of running the mare, fearing lest Henry might get frightened by so large a crowd of people and swerve from the track.

Unfortunately for the Virginians, their favorite, John Richards, in a trial race, while at Mr. Badger's, met with an accident, by receiving a cut in the heel or frog of one of his forefeet, which rendered it necessary to throw him out of train; Washington also fell amiss, and he and Richards were left behind at Mr. Badger's. With the other three the Southern sportsmen proceeded to the Union Course, where they arrived five or six days previous to that fixed upon for the match.

The ill-fortune which befell the Virginians by laming their best horse in the onset seemed to pursue them, for scarcely had they arrived at Long Island and become fixed in their new quarters, when Mr. Johnston, the principal on their part, upon whose management and attention their success in a great measure depended, was seized with indisposition, so sudden and violent, as to confine him not only to his room, but to his bed, which he was unable to leave on the day of the race. Thus the Southrons, deprived of their leader, whose skill and judgment, whether in the way of stable preparation, or generalship in the field, could be supplied by none other, had to face their opponents under circumstances thus far disadvantageous and discouraging. Notwithstanding these unexpected and untoward events, they met the coming contest manfully, having full and unimpaired confidence in their two remaining horses, Sir Henry and Betsey Richards, and backed their opinion to the moment of starting.

At length the rising sun gave promise that the eventful day would prove fine and unclouded. I was in the field at the peep of dawn and observed that the Southern horse and mare, led by Harry Curtis in their walk, were both plated, treated alike, and both in readiness for the approaching contest. It was yet unknown to the Northern sportsmen which was to be their competitor.

The road from New York to the course, a distance of eight miles, was covered by horsemen and a triple line of carriages in an unbroken chain, from the dawn of day until one o'clock, the appointed hour of starting. The stands on the ground for the reception of spectators were crowded to excess at an early hour, and the club house, and balcony extending along its whole front, was filled by ladies; the whole track, or nearly so, for a mile distance in circuit, was lined on the inside by carriages and horsemen, and the throng of pedestrians surpassed all belief—*not less than sixty thousand spectators were computed to be in the field.*

About half past twelve o'clock Sir Henry made his appearance on the course as the champion of the South and was soon confronted by his antagonist. I shall now endeavor to give a brief description of these noted racers. Sir Henry is a dark sorrel or chestnut color, with one hind foot white, and a small star in the forehead; his mane and tail about two shades lighter than that of his body; he has been represented as being fifteen hands and one inch high, but having taken his measure, his exact height is only fourteen hands three and a half inches. His form is compact, bordering upon what is termed pony-built, with a good shoulder, fine clean head, and all those points which constitute a fine forehand; his barrel is strong, and well ribbed up towards the hip; waist rather short; chinbone strong, rising or arched a little over the loin, indicative of ability to carry weight; sway short; the loin full and strong; haunches strong and well let down; hindquarters somewhat high and sloping off from the coupling to the croup; thighs full and muscular, without being fleshy; hocks, or houghs, strong, wide, and pretty well let down; legs remarkably fine, with a full proportion of bone; back sinew, or Achilles tendon, large, and well detached from the canon bone; stands firm, clear, and even, moves remarkably well, with his feet in line; possesses great action and muscular power, and although rather under size, the exquisite symmetry of his form indicates uncommon strength and hardihood. He was bred by Mr. Lemuel Long, near Halifax, in the state of North Carolina, and foaled on the 17th day of June, 1819. He was sired by Sir Archy (son of imported chestnut Diomed), his dam by Diomed, . . .

Eclipse is a dark sorrel horse with a star, the near hind foot white, said to be fifteen hands three inches in height, but in fact measures, by the standard, only fifteen hands and two inches. He possesses great power and substance, being well spread and full made throughout his whole frame, his general mould being much heavier than what is commonly met with in the thoroughbred blood-horse; he is, however, right in the cardinal points, very deep in the girth, with a good length of waist; loin wide and strong; shoulder by no means fine, being somewhat thick and heavy, yet strong and deep; breast wide, and apparently too full, and too much spread for a horse of great speed; arms long, strong, and muscular; head by no means fine; neck somewhat defective, the junction with the head having an awkward appearance, and too fleshy, and bagging too much upon the underside, near the throttle; his forelegs, from the knee downwards, are short and strong, with a large share of bone and sinew; upon the whole his forehand is too heavy.

To counterbalance this, his hindquarters are as near perfection as it is possible to imagine. From the hooks, or hip bone, to the extremity of the hindquarter, including the whole sweep from the hip to the hough, he has not an equal; with long and full muscular thighs, let down almost to the houghs, which are also particularly long, and well let down upon the cannon bone; legs short, with large bone and strong tendon, well detached, upon which he stands clear and even. Although his form throughout denotes uncommon strength, yet to the extraordinary fine construction of his hindquarters, I conceive him indebted for his great racing powers, continuance, and ability, equal to any weight. I have closely observed him in his gallops; if he has a fault, it is that of falling a little too heavy on his forefeet, and dwelling a little too long on the ground; but then the style and regularity with which he brings up his haunches, and throws his gaskins forward, overbalance other defects.

He was sired by Duroc, a Virginia horse, bred by Wade Moseby, Esq., and got by imported chestnut Diomed, out of Amanda, by Grey Diomed, a son of old Medley. His (Eclipse's) dam was the noted gray mare Miller's Damsel, got by imported Messenger. He was bred by Gen. Nathaniel Coles, of Queens County, Long Island, and foaled on the 25th of May, 1814.

All horses date their age from the 1st of May. Thus a horse foaled any time in the year 1819, would be considered four years old on the 1st day of May, 1828. Consequently, Sir Henry, although not four years old complete until the 17th day of June, had, on the 27th of May, to carry the regulated weight (agreeably to the then rules of the course) for a four year old, viz. 108 pounds. Eclipse, being nine years old, carried weight for an aged horse, 126 pounds.

At length the appointed hour arrived, the word was given to saddle, and immediately afterwards to mount. Eclipse was rode by William Crafts, dressed in a crimson jacket and cap, and Sir Henry by a Virginia boy, of the name of John Walden, dressed in a sky blue jacket, with cap of the same color. The custom on the Union Course is to run to the left about, or with the left hand next to the poles; Eclipse, by lot, had the left, or inside station at the start. Sir Henry took his ground about twenty-five feet wide of him, to the right, with the evident intention of making a run in a straight line for the lead. The preconcerted signal was a single tap of the drum. All was now breathless anxiety; the horses came up evenly; the eventful signal was heard, they went off handsomely together; Henry, apparently quickest, made play from the score, obtained the lead, and then took a hard pull. By the time they had gone the first quarter of a mile, which brought them round the first turn, to the commencement of what is termed the back side of the course, which is a straight run, comprising the second quarter of a mile, he was full three lengths ahead; this distance he with little variation maintained, running steadily with a hard pull during the first, second, third, and for about three-fourths of the fourth round or mile, the pace, all this time, a killing one.

It may be proper to note that the course is nearly an oval of one mile, with this small variation, that the back and front are straight lines of about a quarter of a mile each, connected at each extremity by semicircles of also a quarter of a mile each. When the horses were going the last round, being myself well mounted, I took my station at the commencement of the stretch or last quarter, where I expected a violent exertion would be made at this last straight run in, when they left the straight part on the back of the course and entered upon the last turn.

Henry was, as heretofore, not less than three lengths in the clear ahead. They had not proceeded more than twenty rods upon the first part of the sweep when Eclipse made play, and the spur and whip were both applied freely; when they were at the extreme point or center of the sweep, I observed the right hand of Crafts disengaged from his bridle, making free use of his whip; when they had swept about three-fourths of the way round the turn and had advanced within twenty-five rods of my station, I clearly saw that Crafts was making every exertion with both spur and whip to get Eclipse forward, and scored him sorely, both before and behind the girths; at this moment Eclipse threw his tail into the air, and flirted it up and down, after the manner of a tired horse or one in distress and great pain; and John Buckley, the jockey (and present trainer), who I kept stationed by my side, observed, "Eclipse is done."

When they passed me about the commencement of the stretch, seventy to eighty rods from home, the space between them was about sixteen feet, or a full length and a half in the clear. Here the rider of Henry turned his head round and took a view for an instant of his adversary; Walden used neither whip nor spur, but maintained a hard and steady pull, under which his horse appeared accustomed to run. Craft continued to make free use of the whip; his right hand in so doing was necessarily disengaged from the bridle, his arm often raised high in air, his body thrown abroad, and his seat loose and unsteady; not having strength to hold and gather his horse with one hand, and at the same time keep his proper position; in order to acquire a greater purchase, he had thrown his body quite back to the cantle of the saddle, stuck his feet forward by way of bracing himself with the aid of the stirrups, and in this style, he was belaboring his horse, going in the last quarter.

Buckley exclaimed, (and well he might) "Good G——d, look at Billy." From this place to the winning post, Eclipse gained but a few feet, Henry coming ahead about a length in the clear. The shortest time of this heat, as returned by the judges on the stand, was 7 minutes 37½ seconds. Many watches, and mine (which was held by a gentleman on the stand) among others, made it 7 minutes 40 seconds; and this time the Southern gentlemen reported.

I pushed immediately up to the winning post, in order to view the situation of the respective horses after this very trying and severe heat; for it was in fact running the whole four miles. Sir Henry was less distressed than I expected to find him; Eclipse also bore it well, but of the two, he appeared the most jaded; the injudicious manner in which he had been rode, had certainly annoyed, and unnecessarily distressed him; the cause of his throwing out his tail, and flirting it up and down, as already observed, was now apparent; Craft, in using his whip wildly, had struck him too far back, and had cut him not only upon his sheath, but had made a deep incision upon his testicles, and it was no doubt the violent pain occasioned thereby, that caused the noble animal to complain, and motion with his tail, indicative of the torture he suffered. The blood flowed profusely from one or both of these foul cuts, and trickling down the inside of his hind legs, appeared conspicuously upon the white hind foot, and gave a more doleful appearance to the discouraging scene of a lost heat.

The incapacity of Crafts to manage Eclipse (who required much urging, and at the same time to be pulled hard) was apparent to all; he being a slender made lad, in body weight about 100 lbs. only. A person interested in the event, seeing Buckley, who had rode the horse on a former occasion, with me, requested that I would keep him within call, and ready to ride in case of an emergency. It was, however, soon settled and announced that Mr. Purdy would ride him the second heat, upon which, long faces grew shorter, and Northern hope revived—six to four was, nevertheless, offered on the Southern horse, but no takers.

The horses, after a lapse of 30 minutes, were called up for a second heat. I attentively viewed Eclipse while saddling, and was surprised to find that to appearance he had not only entirely recovered, but seemed full of mettle, lashing and reaching out with his hind feet, anxious and impatient to renew the contest. Mr. Purdy having mounted his favorite was perfectly at home and self-confident. The signal being again given, he went off rapidly from the start; Sir Henry being now entitled to the inside, took the track, and kept the lead, followed closely by Eclipse, whom Mr. Purdy at once brought to his work, knowing that game and stoutness was his play, and his only chance of success, that of driving his speedy adversary, up to the top of his rate, without giving him the least respite.

Henry went steadily on, nearly at the top of his speed, keeping a gap open between himself and Eclipse of about twenty feet without much variation for about two miles and seven-eighths, or until towards the conclusion of the third mile they had arrived nearly opposite the four-mile distance post. Here Purdy made his run, and when they had advanced forty rods further, which brought them to the end of the third mile, was close up, say nose and tail. They now entered upon the fourth and last mile, which commences with a turn or sweep the moment you leave the starting post. Here the crowd was immense; I was at this moment on horseback, stationed down the stretch or straight run, a short distance below the winning post, in company with a friend, and Buckley the jockey, who kept close to me during the whole race. We pushed out into the center, or open space of the ground, in order to obtain a more distinct view of the struggle, which we saw making for the lead; every thing depended upon this effort of Purdy; well he knew it; his case was a desperate one, and required a desperate attempt; it was to risk all, for all; he did not hesitate.

When the horses had got about one third of the way round the sweep, they had so far cleared the crowd as to afford us a distinct view of them a little before they reached the center of the turn; Eclipse had lapped Henry about head and girth and appeared evidently in the act of passing. Here Buckley vociferated, "see Eclipse! Look at Purdy!" By heaven on the inside! I was all attention.

Purdy was on the left hand or inside of Henry. I felt alarmed for the consequence, satisfied that he had thus hazarded all; I feared that Walden would take advantage of his position, and by reining in, force him against or inside one of the poles; when they had proceeded a little more than half way round the sweep, the horses were a dead lap; when about three-fourths round, Eclipse's quarter covered Henry's head and neck, and just as they had finished the bend, and were entering upon the straight run, which extends along the back part of the course, Eclipse for the first time was fairly clear, and ahead.

He now with the help of the persuaders, which were freely bestowed, kept up his run, and continued gradually, though slowly, to gain during the remaining three quarters of a mile and came in about two lengths ahead. As they passed up the stretch or last quarter of a mile, the shouting, clapping of hands, waving of handkerchiefs, long and loud applause sent forth by the Eclipse party, exceeded all description; it seemed to roll along the track as the horses advanced, resembling the loud and reiterated shout of contending armies.

I have been thus particular in stating that Mr. Purdy made his pass on the inside, understanding that many gentlemen and particularly Mr. Stevens, the principal in the match on the part of Eclipse (and for aught I know Mr. Purdy himself), insist that the *go by* was given on the outside. After the heat was over, I found that my friend Mr. M. Buckley and myself were far from the only persons that had observed the mode in which Mr. Purdy ran up and took the inside track from his adversary.

The circumstance was in the mouths of hundreds. In corroboration of which, I will quote a passage from the *New York Evening Post*, of May 28th, 1823, giving a description of this second heat:

> Henry took the lead as in the first heat until about two-thirds around on the third mile, when Purdy seized with a quickness and dexterity peculiar to himself, the favorable moment that presented, when appearing to aim at the outside, he might gain the inside, made a dash at him accordingly, and *passed him on the left*.

Here, then, the observations of many independent of my friend Mr. M. Buckley, or myself, added to the instantaneous and striking remark of B., which did not fail to rivet my peculiar attention, form a wonderful coincidence. Thus circumstanced, and long conversant with turf matters, rules, and practices, and familiar with sights of this kind, it was impossible I could be mistaken. I was not mistaken, the honest belief of some gentlemen to the contrary notwithstanding. Time, this second heat, 7 minutes, 49 seconds.

It was now given out, that in place of the boy Walden, who had rode Sir Henry the two preceding heats, that Arthur Taylor, a trainer of great experience, and long a rider, equaled by few, and surpassed by none, would ride him this last and decisive heat. At the expiration of 30 minutes the horses were once more summoned to the starting post, and Purdy and Taylor mounted; the word being given, they went off at a quick rate; Purdy now taking the lead, and pushing Eclipse from the score; and indeed, the whole four miles, applying the whip and spur incessantly; evidently resolved to give Sir Henry no respite but to cause him, if determined to trail, to employ all his speed and strength without keeping any thing in reserve for the run in.

Sir Henry continued to trail, apparently under a pull, never attempting to come up, until they had both fairly entered the straight run towards the termination of the last mile and had advanced within about sixty rods from home. Here Sir Henry being about five yards behind, made a dash, and ran up to Eclipse so far as to cover his quarter or haunch with his head, and for a moment had the appearance of going past; he made a severe struggle for about two hundred yards, when he again fell in the rear, and gave up the contest.

Thus terminated the most interesting race ever run in the United States. Besides the original stake of $20,000 each, it was judged that upwards of $900,000 changed hands. In this last heat Sir Henry carried 110 lbs. being two pounds over his proper weight; it not being possible to bring Arthur Taylor to ride less, and although a small horse and wanting twenty days of being four years old, he made the greatest run ever witnessed in America. Time, this heat, 8 minutes, 24 seconds.

Thus the three heats, or twelve miles, were run in 528 minutes, 50 seconds, or an average of 7 minutes, 57 seconds each heat; or 1 minute, 59 seconds per mile.

28

Horses

By Stephen Crane

◇◇◇

Stephen Crane (1871–1900) is always remembered as the author of
The Red Badge of Courage, *his Civil War novel. He was a writer
with immense talent, that showed in his many short stories and as a
war correspondent. He wrote* The Red Badge of Courage *without
experiencing any action as a soldier in the Civil War. This short story
joins another Crane masterpiece,* The Open Boat, *in the collection*
The Open Boat and Other Stories. *The setting in this story, Mexico, was familiar ground to Crane. His amazing life was cut short in
1900 when tuberculosis took him at age twenty-eight.*

◇◇◇

RICHARDSON PULLED UP HIS HORSE, AND LOOKED BACK OVER THE TRAIL
where the crimson serape of his servant flamed amid the dusk of the
mesquit. The hills in the west were carved into peaks, and were painted
the most profound blue. Above them the sky was of that marvellous tone
of green—like still, sun-shot water—which people denounce in pictures.

José was muffled deep in his blanket, and his great toppling sombrero
was drawn low over his brow. He shadowed his master along the dim-
ming trail in the fashion of an assassin. A cold wind of the impending
night swept over the wilderness of mesquit.

"Man," said Richardson in lame Mexican as the servant drew near, "I
want eat! I want sleep! Understand—no? Quickly! Understand?"

"Si, señor," said José, nodding. He stretched one arm out of his blanket and pointed a yellow finger into the gloom. "Over there, small village. Si, señor."

They rode forward again. Once the American's horse shied and breathed quiveringly at something which he saw or imagined in the darkness, and the rider drew a steady, patient rein, and leaned over to speak tenderly as if he were addressing a frightened woman. The sky had faded to white over the mountains, and the plain was a vast, pointless ocean of black.

Suddenly some low houses appeared squatting amid the bushes. The horsemen rode into a hollow until the houses rose against the sombre sundown sky, and then up a small hillock, causing these habitations to sink like boats in the sea of shadow.

A beam of red firelight fell across the trail. Richardson sat sleepily on his horse while his servant quarrelled with somebody—a mere voice in the gloom—over the price of bed and board. The houses about him were for the most part like tombs in their whiteness and silence, but there were scudding black figures that seemed interested in his arrival.

José came at last to the horses' heads, and the American slid stiffly from his seat. He muttered a greeting, as with his spurred feet he clicked into the adobe house that confronted him. The brown stolid face of a woman shone in the light of the fire. He seated himself on the earthen floor and blinked drowsily at the blaze. He was aware that the woman was clinking earthenware, and hieing here and everywhere in the manoeuvres of the housewife. From a dark corner there came the sound of two or three snores twining together.

The woman handed him a bowl of tortillas. She was a submissive creature, timid and large-eyed. She gazed at his enormous silver spurs, his large and impressive revolver, with the interest and admiration of the highly-privileged cat of the adage. When he ate, she seemed transfixed off there in the gloom, her white teeth shining.

José entered, staggering under two Mexican saddles, large enough for building-sites. Richardson decided to smoke a cigarette, and then changed his mind. It would be much finer to go to sleep. His blanket hung over his left shoulder, furled into a long pipe of cloth, according to the Mexican fashion. By doffing his sombrero, unfastening his spurs and his revolver belt, he made himself ready for the slow, blissful twist into the blanket. Like a cautious man he lay close to the wall, and all his property was very near his hand.

The mesquit brush burned long. José threw two gigantic wings of shadow as he flapped his blanket about him—first across his chest under his arms, and then around his neck and across his chest again—this time over his arms, with the end tossed on his right shoulder. A Mexican thus snugly enveloped can nevertheless free his fighting arm in a beautifully brisk way, merely shrugging his shoulder as he grabs for the weapon at his belt. (They always wear their serapes in this manner.)

The firelight smothered the rays which, streaming from a moon as large as a drum-head, were struggling at the open door. Richardson heard from the plain the fine, rhythmical trample of the hoofs of hurried horses. He went to sleep wondering who rode so fast and so late. And in the deep silence the pale rays of the moon must have prevailed against the red spears of the fire until the room was slowly flooded to its middle with a rectangle of silver light.

Richardson was awakened by the sound of a guitar. It was badly played—in this land of Mexico, from which the romance of the instrument ascends to us like a perfume. The guitar was groaning and whining like a badgered soul. A noise of scuffling feet accompanied the music. Sometimes laughter arose, and often the voices of men saying bitter things to each other, but always the guitar cried on, the treble sounding as if some one were beating iron, and the bass humming like bees. "Damn it—they're having a dance," he muttered, fretfully. He heard two men quarrelling in short, sharp words, like pistol shots; they were calling each other worse names than common people know in other countries. He wondered why the noise was so loud. Raising his head from his saddle pillow, he saw, with the help of the valiant moonbeams, a blanket hanging flat against the wall at the further end of the room. Being of opinion that it concealed a door, and remembering that Mexican drink made men very drunk, he pulled his revolver closer to him and prepared for sudden disaster.

Richardson was dreaming of his far and beloved north.

"Well, I would kill him, then!"

"No, you must not!"

"Yes, I will kill him! Listen! I will ask this American beast for his beautiful pistol and spurs and money and saddle, and if he will not give them—you will see!"

"But these Americans—they are a strange people. Look out, señor."

Then twenty voices took part in the discussion. They rose in quavering shrillness, as from men badly drunk. Richardson felt the skin draw tight around his mouth, and his knee-joints turned to bread. He slowly came to a sitting posture, glaring at the motionless blanket at the far end of the room. This stiff and mechanical movement, accomplished entirely by the muscles of the waist, must have looked like the rising of a corpse in the wan moonlight, which gave everything a hue of the grave.

My friend, take my advice and never be executed by a hangman who doesn't talk the English language. It, or anything that resembles it, is the most difficult of deaths. The tumultuous emotions of Richardson's terror destroyed that slow and careful process of thought by means of which he understood Mexican. Then he used his instinctive comprehension of the first and universal language, which is tone. Still, it is disheartening not to be able to understand the detail of threats against the blood of your body.

Suddenly, the clamour of voices ceased. There was a silence—a silence of decision. The blanket was flung aside, and the red light of a torch flared into the room. It was held high by a fat, round-faced Mexican, whose little snake-like moustache was as black as his eyes, and whose eyes were black as jet. He was insane with the wild rage of a man whose liquor is dully burning at his brain. Five or six of his fellows crowded after him. The guitar, which had been thrummed doggedly during the time of the high words, now suddenly stopped. They contemplated each other. Richardson sat very straight and still, his right hand lost in his blanket. The Mexicans jostled in the light of the torch, their eyes blinking and glittering.

The fat one posed in the manner of a grandee. Presently his hand dropped to his belt, and from his lips there spun an epithet—a hideous word which often foreshadows knife-blows, a word peculiarly of Mexico, where people have to dig deep to find an insult that has not lost its savour.

The American did not move. He was staring at the fat Mexican with a strange fixedness of gaze, not fearful, not dauntless, not anything that could be interpreted. He simply stared.

The fat Mexican must have been disconcerted, for he continued to pose as a grandee, with more and more sublimity, until it would have been easy for him to have fallen over backward. His companions were swaying very drunkenly. They still blinked their little beady eyes at Richardson. Ah, well, sirs, here was a mystery! At the approach of their menacing company, why did not this American cry out and turn pale, or run, or pray them mercy? The animal merely sat still, and stared, and waited for them to begin. Well, evidently he was a great fighter! Or perhaps he was an idiot? Indeed, this was an embarrassing situation, for who was going forward to discover whether he was a great fighter or an idiot?

To Richardson, whose nerves were tingling and twitching like live wires, and whose heart jolted inside him, this pause was a long horror; and for these men, who could so frighten him, there began to swell in him a fierce hatred—a hatred that made him long to be capable of fighting all of them, a hatred that made him capable of fighting all of them. A 44-calibre revolver can make a hole large enough for little boys to shoot marbles through; and there was a certain fat Mexican with a moustache like a snake who came extremely near to have eaten his last tomale merely because he frightened a man too much.

José had slept the first part of the night in his fashion, his body hunched into a heap, his legs crooked, his head touching his knees. Shadows had obscured him from the sight of the invaders. At this point he arose, and began to prowl quakingly over toward Richardson, as if he meant to hide behind him.

Of a sudden the fat Mexican gave a howl of glee. José had come within the torch's circle of light. With roars of ferocity the whole group of Mexicans pounced on the American's servant. He shrank shuddering away from them, beseeching by every device of word and gesture. They pushed him this way and that. They beat him with their fists. They stung him with their curses. As he grovelled on his knees, the fat Mexican took him by the throat and said—"I am going to kill you!" And continually they turned their eyes to see if they were to succeed in causing the initial demonstration by the American. But he looked on impassively. Under the blanket his fingers were clenched, as iron, upon the handle of his revolver.

Here suddenly two brilliant clashing chords from the guitar were heard, and a woman's voice, full of laughter and confidence, cried from without—"Hello! hello! Where are you?" The lurching company of Mexicans instantly paused and looked at the ground. One said, as he stood with his legs wide apart in order to balance himself—"It is the girls. They have come!" He screamed in answer to the question of the woman—"Here!" And without waiting he started on a pilgrimage toward the blanket-covered door. One could now hear a number of female voices giggling and chattering.

Two other Mexicans said—"Yes, it is the girls! Yes!" They also started quietly away. Even the fat Mexican's ferocity seemed to be affected. He looked uncertainly at the still immovable American. Two of his friends grasped him gaily—"Come, the girls are here! Come!" He cast another glower at Richardson. "But this——," he began. Laughing, his comrades hustled him toward the door. On its threshold, and holding back the blanket, with one hand, he turned his yellow face with a last challenging glare toward the American. José, bewailing his state in little sobs of utter despair and woe, crept to Richardson and huddled near his knee. Then the cries of the Mexicans meeting the girls were heard, and the guitar burst out in joyous humming.

The moon clouded, and but a faint square of light fell through the open main door of the house. The coals of the fire were silent, save for occasional sputters. Richardson did not change his position. He remained staring at the blanket which hid the strategic door in the far end. At his knees José was arguing, in a low, aggrieved tone, with the saints. Without, the Mexicans laughed and danced, and—it would appear from the sound—drank more.

In the stillness and the night Richardson sat wondering if some serpent-like Mexican were sliding towards him in the darkness, and if the first thing he knew of it would be the deadly sting of a knife. "Sssh," he whispered, to José. He drew his revolver from under the blanket, and held it on his leg. The blanket over the door fascinated him. It was a vague form, black and unmoving. Through the opening it shielded were to come, probably, threats, death. Sometimes he thought he saw it move. As grim white sheets, the black and silver of coffins, all the panoply of death, affect us, because of that which they hide, so this blanket, dangling before a hole in an adobe wall, was to Richardson a horrible emblem, and a horrible thing in itself. In his present mood he could not have been brought to touch it with his finger.

The celebrating Mexicans occasionally howled in song. The guitarist played with speed and enthusiasm. Richardson longed to run. But in this vibrating and threatening gloom his terror convinced him that a move on his part would be a signal for the pounce of death. José, crouching abjectly, mumbled now and again. Slowly, and ponderous as stars, the minutes went.

Suddenly Richardson thrilled and started. His breath for a moment left him. In sleep his nerveless fingers had allowed his revolver to fall and clang upon the hard floor. He grabbed it up hastily, and his glance swept apprehensively over the room. A chill blue light of dawn was in the place. Every outline was slowly growing; detail was following detail. The dread blanket did not move. The riotous company had gone or fallen silent. He felt the effect of this cold dawn in his blood. The candour of breaking day brought his nerve. He touched José. "Come," he said. His servant lifted his lined yellow face, and comprehended. Richardson buckled on his spurs and strode up; José obediently lifted the two great saddles. Richardson held two bridles and a blanket on his left arm; in his right hand he had his revolver. They sneaked toward the door.

The man who said that spurs jingled was insane. Spurs have a mellow clash—clash—clash. Walking in spurs—notably Mexican spurs—you remind yourself vaguely of a telegraphic linesman. Richardson was inexpressibly shocked when he came to walk. He sounded to himself like a pair of cymbals. He would have known of this if he had reflected; but then, he was escaping, not reflecting. He made a gesture of despair, and from under the two saddles José tried to make one of hopeless horror. Richardson stooped, and with shaking fingers unfastened the spurs. Taking them in his left hand, he picked up his revolver, and they slunk on toward the door. On the threshold he looked back. In a corner he saw, watching him with large eyes, the Indian man and woman who had been his hosts. Throughout the night they had made no sign, and now they neither spoke nor moved. Yet Richardson thought he detected meek satisfaction at his departure.

The street was still and deserted. In the eastern sky there was a lemon-coloured patch. José had picketed the horses at the side of the house. As the two men came round the corner Richardson's beast set up a whinny of welcome. The little horse had heard them coming. He stood facing them, his ears cocked forward, his eyes bright with welcome.

Richardson made a frantic gesture, but the horse, in his happiness at the appearance of his friends, whinnied with enthusiasm. The American felt that he could have strangled his well-beloved steed. Upon the threshold of safety, he was being betrayed by his horse, his friend! He felt the same hate that he would have felt for a dragon. And yet, as he glanced wildly about him, he could see nothing stirring in the street, nothing at the doors of the tomb-like houses.

José had his own saddle-girth and both bridles buckled in a moment. He curled the picket-ropes with a few sweeps of his arm. The American's fingers, however, were shaking so that he could hardly buckle the girth. His hands were in invisible mittens. He was wondering, calculating, hoping about his horse. He knew the little animal's willingness and courage under all circumstances up to this time; but then—here it was different. Who could tell if some wretched instance of equine perversity was not about to develop? Maybe the little fellow would not feel like smoking over the plain at express speed this morning, and so he would rebel, and kick, and be wicked. Maybe he would be without feeling of interest, and run listlessly. All riders who have had to hurry in the saddle know what it is to be on a horse who does not understand the dramatic situation. Riding a lame sheep is bliss to it. Richardson, fumbling furiously at the girth, thought of these things.

Presently he had it fastened. He swung into the saddle, and as he did so his horse made a mad jump forward. The spurs of José scratched and tore the flanks of his great black beast, and side by side the two horses raced down the village street. The American heard his horse breathe a quivering sigh of excitement. Those four feet skimmed. They were as light as fairy puff balls. The houses glided past in a moment, and the great, clear, silent plain appeared like a pale blue sea of mist and wet bushes. Above the mountains the colours of the sunlight were like the first tones, the opening chords of the mighty hymn of the morning.

The American looked down at his horse. He felt in his heart the first thrill of confidence. The little animal, unurged and quite tranquil, moving his ears this way and that way with an air of interest in the scenery, was nevertheless bounding into the eye of the breaking day with the speed of a frightened antelope. Richardson, looking down, saw the long, fine reach of forelimb as steady as steel machinery. As the ground reeled past, the long, dried grasses hissed, and cactus plants were dull blurs. A wind whirled the horse's mane over his rider's bridle hand.

José's profile was lined against the pale sky. It was as that of a man who swims alone in an ocean. His eyes glinted like metal, fastened on some unknown point ahead of him, some fabulous place of safety. Occasionally his mouth puckered in a little unheard cry; and his legs, bended back, worked spasmodically as his spurred heels sliced his charger's sides.

Richardson consulted the gloom in the west for signs of a hard-riding, yelling cavalcade. He knew that, whereas his friends the enemy had not attacked him when he had sat still and with apparent calmness confronted them, they would take furiously after him now that he had run from them—now that he had confessed himself the weaker. Their valour would grow like weeds in the spring, and upon discovering his escape they would ride forth dauntless warriors. Sometimes he was sure he saw them. Sometimes he was sure he heard them. Continually looking backward over his shoulder, he studied the purple expanses where the night was marching away. José rolled and shuddered in his saddle, persistently disturbing the stride of the black horse, fretting and worrying him until the white foam flew, and the great shoulders shone like satin from the sweat.

At last, Richardson drew his horse carefully down to a walk. José wished to rush insanely on, but the American spoke to him sternly. As the two paced forward side by side, Richardson's little horse thrust over his soft nose and inquired into the black's condition.

Riding with José was like riding with a corpse. His face resembled a cast in lead. Sometimes he swung forward and almost pitched from his seat. Richardson was too frightened himself to do anything but hate this man for his fear. Finally, he issued a mandate which nearly caused José's eyes to slide out of his head and fall to the ground, like two coins: "Ride behind me—about fifty paces."

"Señor——" stuttered the servant. "Go," cried the American furiously. He glared at the other and laid his hand on his revolver. José looked at his master wildly. He made a piteous gesture. Then slowly he fell back, watching the hard face of the American for a sign of mercy. But Richardson had resolved in his rage that at any rate he was going to use the eyes and ears of extreme fear to detect the approach of danger; so he established his panic-stricken servant as a sort of outpost.

As they proceeded, he was obliged to watch sharply to see that the servant did not slink forward and join him. When José made beseeching circles in the air with his arm, he replied by menacingly gripping his revolver. José had a revolver too; nevertheless it was very clear in his mind that the revolver was distinctly an American weapon. He had been educated in the Rio Grande country.

Richardson lost the trail once. He was recalled to it by the loud sobs of his servant.

Then at last José came clattering forward, gesticulating and wailing. The little horse sprang to the shoulder of the black. They were off.

Richardson, again looking backward, could see a slanting flare of dust on the whitening plain. He thought that he could detect small moving figures in it.

José's moans and cries amounted to a university course in theology. They broke continually from his quivering lips. His spurs were as motors. They forced the black horse over the plain in great headlong leaps. But under Richardson there was a little insignificant rat-coloured beast who was running apparently with almost as much effort as it takes a bronze statue to stand still. The ground seemed merely something to be touched from time to time with hoofs that were as light as blown leaves. Occasionally Richardson lay back and pulled stoutly at the bridle to keep from abandoning his servant. José harried at his horse's mouth, flopped about in the saddle, and made his two heels beat like flails. The black ran like a horse in despair.

Crimson serapes in the distance resemble drops of blood on the great cloth of plain. Richardson began to dream of all possible chances. Although quite a humane man, he did not once think of his servant. José being a Mexican, it was natural that he should be killed in Mexico; but for himself, a New Yorker——! He remembered all the tales of such races for life, and he thought them badly written.

The great black horse was growing indifferent. The jabs of José's spurs no longer caused him to bound forward in wild leaps of pain. José had at last succeeded in teaching him that spurring was to be expected, speed or no speed, and now he took the pain of it dully and stolidly, as an animal who finds that doing his best gains him no respite. José was turned into a raving maniac. He bellowed and screamed, working his arms and his heels like one in a fit. He resembled a man on a sinking ship, who appeals to the ship. Richardson, too, cried madly to the black horse. The spirit of the horse responded to these calls, and quivering and breathing heavily he made a great effort, a sort of a final rush, not for himself apparently, but because he understood that his life's sacrifice, perhaps, had been invoked by these two men who cried to him in the universal tongue. Richardson had no sense of appreciation at this time—he was too frightened; but often now he remembers a certain black horse.

From the rear could be heard a yelling, and once a shot was fired—in the air, evidently. Richardson moaned as he looked back. He kept his hand on his revolver. He tried to imagine the brief tumult of his capture—the flurry of dust from the hoofs of horses pulled suddenly to their haunches, the shrill, biting curses of the men, the ring of the shots, his own last contortion. He wondered, too, if he could not somehow manage to pelt that fat Mexican, just to cure his abominable egotism.

It was José, the terror-stricken, who at last discovered safety. Suddenly he gave a howl of delight and astonished his horse into a new burst of speed. They were on a little ridge at the time, and the American at the top of it saw his servant gallop down the slope and into the arms, so to speak, of a small column of horsemen in grey and silver clothes. In the dim light of the early morning they were as vague as shadows, but Richardson knew them at once for a detachment of Rurales, that crack cavalry corps of the Mexican army which polices the plain so zealously, being of themselves the law and the arm of it—a fierce and swift-moving body that knows little of prevention but much of vengeance. They drew up suddenly, and the rows of great silver-trimmed sombreros bobbed in surprise.

Richardson saw José throw himself from his horse and begin to jabber at the leader. When he arrived he found that his servant had already outlined the entire situation, and was then engaged in describing him, Richardson, as an American señor of vast wealth, who was the friend of almost every governmental potentate within two hundred miles. This seemed profoundly to impress the officer. He bowed gravely to Richardson and smiled significantly at his men, who unslung their carbines.

The little ridge hid the pursuers from view, but the rapid thud of their horses' feet could be heard. Occasionally they yelled and called to each other. Then at last they swept over the brow of the hill, a wild mob of almost fifty drunken horsemen. When they discerned the pale-uniformed Rurales, they were sailing down the slope at top speed.

If toboggans half-way down a hill should suddenly make up their minds to turn round and go back, there would be an effect something like that produced by the drunken horsemen. Richardson saw the Rurales serenely swing their carbines forward, and, peculiar-minded person that he was, felt his heart leap into his throat at the prospective volley. But the officer rode forward alone.

It appeared that the man who owned the best horse in this astonished company was the fat Mexican with the snaky moustache, and, in consequence, this gentleman was quite a distance in the van. He tried to pull up, wheel his horse, and scuttle back over the hill as some of his companions had done, but the officer called to him in a voice harsh with rage. "——!" howled the officer. "This señor is my friend, the friend of my friends. Do you dare pursue him,——?——!——!——!——!" These dashes represent terrible names, all different, used by the officer.

The fat Mexican simply grovelled on his horse's neck. His face was green: it could be seen that he expected death. The officer stormed with magnificent intensity: "——!——!——!" Finally he sprang from his saddle, and, running to the fat Mexican's side, yelled—"Go!" and kicked the horse in the belly with all his might. The animal gave a mighty leap into the air, and the fat Mexican, with one wretched glance at the contemplative Rurales, aimed his steed for the top of the ridge. Richardson gulped again in expectation of a volley, for—it is said—this is a favourite method for disposing of objectionable people. The fat, green Mexican also thought that he was to be killed on the run, from the miserable look he cast at the troops. Nevertheless, he was allowed to vanish in a cloud of yellow dust at the ridge-top.

José was exultant, defiant, and, oh! bristling with courage. The black horse was drooping sadly, his nose to the ground. Richardson's little animal, with his ears bent forward, was staring at the horses of the Rurales as if in an intense study. Richardson longed for speech, but he could only bend forward and pat the shining, silken shoulders. The little horse turned his head and looked back gravely.

29

Memoirs of a Conquistador

By Bernal Di'Az Del Castillo
Translated by John Ingram Lockhart (1844)

Although North America was home to its ancestors, the horse had evolved, migrated, and become extinct in its homeland by the time the Spanish conquistadores arrived in the late fifteenth century. Columbus was the first to return the horse to the Americas when he landed at the Caribbean island of Marie-Galante in 1493 on his second voyage to the New World. The first identifiable Spanish horses to set foot on the North American continent were the fifteen mounts of the soldiers of Hernan Cortes, who arrived to conquer Mexico in February 1519. Historian and soldier Bernal Díaz del Castillo, who came along for the conquest, leaves us descriptions of the individual horses in his history of the expedition.

—SHARON B. SMITH

FOR MEMORY'S SAKE I WILL HERE LIKEWISE DESCRIBE THE HORSES AND mares which we took with us on our expedition. Cortes had a dark chestnut stallion, which died afterwards at St. Juan de Ulua. Pedro de Alvarado and Hernando Lopez d'Avila had jointly an excellent brown mare, which had been broken in for the field of battle as well as for tournaments.

After our arrival in New Spain, Alvarado bought Lopez's share, or perhaps took forcible possession of it. Alonso Hernandez Puertocarrero had a gray-colored mare, which Cortes had purchased for him with the golden borders of his state robe; it was capitally trained for the field of battle. Juan Velasquez de Leon's mare was of the same color, a noble and powerful animal, full of fire and eager for battle: we commonly termed it the "short tail."

Christobal de Oli had a dark brown fine-spirited horse. Francisco de Montejo and Alonso de Avila had between them a sorrel-colored horse, but of little use in battle. Francisco de Morla had likewise a dark chestnut stallion, one full of fire and wonderfully swift. The light-colored horse of Juan de Escalante was not worth much. The gray-colored mare of Diego de Ordas, which would never foal, was neither very swift. Gonzalo Dominiguez had a small dark-brown nag, a very swift and noble animal.

Also the brown-colored horse of Pedro Gonzalez de Truxillo was a swift animal. Moron, who was a native of Vaimo, had a small horse, which was pretty well trained. Vaena, of Trinidad, had a darkish-colored horse, though a bad leaper. The light-colored chestnut galloway of De Lares was, on the other hand, a splendid animal and a capital runner.

Ortiz, the musician, and a certain Bartolome Garcia, who had applied himself to the art of mining, had between them a very good dark-colored horse, which they named the Arriero (mule driver), and was one of the best animals of the whole corps. Juan Sedeño, of the Havana, had a fine chestnut mare, which foaled on board. This Sedeño was considered to be the most wealthy man amongst us; for he had a ship of his own, a horse, a few Negroes to attend upon him, and his own lading of cassava and cured bacon. Just about this time horses and Negroes were only to be purchased for very high prices, which accounts for the small number of the former we had with us on this expedition.

◇◇

Later Diaz explains how the conquistadores used their horses. On March 12, 1519, Cortes and his retinue anchored off the Yucatán Peninsula. The following day warriors from the village of Potonchán attacked the handful of dismounted soldiers who had disembarked. The Spaniards managed to fight off the attackers and capture the town. Diaz picks up the story.

◇◇

Cortes being now certain that the Indians would renew the attack, immediately ordered all our horses to be brought on shore, and every one, our wounded not excepted, to hold himself in readiness. When our horses, which had been such a length of time at sea, now stepped on firm ground again, they appeared very awkward and full of fear; however, the day following, they had regained their usual liveliness and agility. There were also six or seven of our men, all young and otherwise strong fellows, who were attacked with such severe pains in the groins that they could not walk without support. No one could guess the cause of this; it was only said they had lived too freely at Cuba, and that the pain was occasioned by the heat, and the weight of their arms; Cortes, therefore, ordered them again on board. The cavaliers, who were to fight on horseback, were commanded to hang bells around their horses' necks, and Cortes impressed on their minds not to rush at the Indians with their lances before they had been dispersed, and then even to aim at their faces only. The following men were selected to fight on horseback:

Christobal de Oli, Pedro de Alvarado, Alonso Hernandez Puertocarrero, and Juan de Escalante. Francisco de Montejo and Alonso de Avila were to use the horses of Ortiz the musician, and of a certain Bartolome Garcia, though neither was worth much. Further, there were Velasquez de Leon, Francisco de Morla, and one of the Lares (for there was another excellent horseman among us of that name), and Gonzalo Dominiguez, both superior horsemen; lastly, there were Moron de Bayamo and Pedro de Truxillo. Then comes Cortes, who placed himself at their head. Mesa had charge of the artillery, while the rest of our men were commanded by Diego de Ordas, who, though he knew nothing of the cavalry service, excelled as a crossbow man and musketeer.

The morning following, which was the day of annunciation to the holy Virgin, we attended mass very early, and arranged ourselves under our ensign Antonio de Villareal. We now put ourselves in motion, and marched towards some extensive bean fields, where Francisco de Lugo and Pedro de Alvarado had fought the previous battle.

There was a village in this neighborhood called Cintla, belonging to the Tabascans, which lay about four miles from our headquarters. Cortes, on account of the bogs, which our horses could not pass, was obliged to take a circuitous route. Our other troops, however, under Diego de Ordas, came up with the Indians near Cintla, where they had arranged themselves on the plain: if they felt equal ardor for the combat as we did, they could now satisfy themselves, for this was a battle in every sense of the word which we here fought, fearful in the extreme, as will be seen.

What followed was the Battle of Cintla. In the midst of close combat between dismounted Spaniards and a full force of Mayans, the natives appeared repeatedly to be gaining the upper hand.

In one of these moments Cortes came galloping up with the horse. Our enemies being still busily engaged with us did not immediately observe this, so that our cavalry easily dashed in among them from behind. The nature of the ground was quite favorable for its maneuvers and as it consisted of strong active fellows, most of the horses being, moreover, powerful and fiery animals, our small body of cavalry in every way made the best use of their weapons. When we, who were already hotly engaged with the enemy, espied our cavalry, we fought with renewed energy, while the latter, by attacking them in the rear at the same time, now obliged them to face about. The Indians, who had never seen any horses before, could not think otherwise than that horse and rider were one body. Quite astounded at this to them so novel a sight, they quitted the plain and retreated to a rising ground.

The Spanish victory at Cintla was an important step to the conquest of the Aztec Empire. That happened eleven months later.

30

The Dun Horse

By George Bird Grinnell

As the founder of the National Audubon Society, naturalist George Bird Grinnell may be best known for his love of American birds. But his admiration for Native American culture was equally important to him. He devoted much of his life to gathering the histories and legends of several tribes of the Great Plains, including the Pawnee, who honored him with the name "White Wolf." Grinnell's 1899 compilation of the Pawnee legends included the story of a dun pony who saved his master from ridicule and starvation and then assured him a future of prosperity and respect.

—SHARON B. SMITH

MANY YEARS AGO THERE LIVED IN THE PAWNEE TRIBE AN OLD WOMAN and her grandson, a boy about sixteen years old. These people had no relations and were very poor. They were so poor that they were despised by the rest of the tribe. They had nothing of their own; and always, after the village started to move the camp from one place to another, these two would stay behind the rest, to look over the old camp and pick up anything that the other Indians had thrown away as worn out or useless. In this way they would sometimes get pieces of robes, worn out moccasins with holes in them, and bits of meat.

Now, it happened one day, after the tribe had moved away from the camp, that this old woman and her boy were following along the trail behind the rest, when they came to a miserable old worn-out dun horse, which they supposed had been abandoned by some Indians. He was thin and exhausted, was blind of one eye, had a bad sore back, and one of his forelegs was very much swollen. In fact, he was so worthless that none of the Pawnees had been willing to take the trouble to try to drive him along with them. But when the old woman and her boy came along, the boy said, "Come now, we will take this old horse, for we can make him carry our pack." So the old woman put her pack on the horse, and drove him along, but he limped and could only go very slowly.

The tribe moved up on the North Platte until they came to Court House Rock. The two poor Indians followed them and camped with the others. One day while they were here, the young men who had been sent out to look for buffalo came hurrying into camp and told the chiefs that a large herd of buffalo were near and that among them was a spotted calf.

The Head Chief of the Pawnees had a very beautiful daughter, and when he heard about the spotted calf, he ordered his old crier to go about through the village and call out that the man who killed the spotted calf should have his daughter for his wife. For a spotted robe is ti-war'-uks-ti—big medicine.

The buffalo were feeding about four miles from the village, and the chiefs decided that the charge should be made from there. In this way, the man who had the fastest horse would be the most likely to kill the calf. Then all the warriors and the young men picked out their best and fastest horses, and made ready to start. Among those who prepared for the charge was the poor boy on the old dun horse. But when they saw him, all the rich young braves on their fast horses pointed at him and said, "Oh, see; there is the horse that is going to catch the spotted calf"; and they laughed at him, so that the poor boy was ashamed, and rode off to one side of the crowd, where he could not hear their jokes and laughter.

When he had ridden off some little way the horse stopped and turned his head round, and spoke to the boy. He said, "Take me down the creek, and plaster me all over with mud. Cover my head and neck and body and legs." When the boy heard the horse speak, he was afraid; but he did as he was told. Then the horse said, "Now mount, but do not ride back to the warriors, who laugh at you because you have such a poor horse. Stay right here until the word is given to charge." So the boy stayed there.

And presently all the fine horses were drawn up in line and pranced about, and were so eager to go that their riders could hardly hold them in; and at last the old crier gave the word, "Loo-ah!—Go!" Then the Pawnees all leaned forward on their horses and yelled, and away they went.

Suddenly, away off to the right, was seen the old dun horse. He did not seem to run. He seemed to sail along like a bird. He passed all the fastest horses, and in a moment he was among the buffalo. First he picked out the spotted calf, and charging up alongside of it, U-ra-rish! Straight flew the arrow. The calf fell. The boy drew another arrow, and killed a fat cow that was running by. Then he dismounted and began to skin the calf, before any of the other warriors had come up. But when the rider got off the old dun horse, how changed he was! He pranced about and would hardly stand still near the dead buffalo. His back was all right again; his legs were well and fine; and both his eyes were clear and bright.

The boy skinned the calf and the cow that he had killed, and then he packed all the meat on the horse, and put the spotted robe on top of the load, and started back to the camp on foot, leading the dun horse. But even with this heavy load the horse pranced all the time, and was scared at everything he saw. On the way to camp, one of the rich young chiefs of the tribe rode up by the boy and offered him twelve good horses for the spotted robe, so that he could marry the Head Chief's beautiful daughter; but the boy laughed at him and would not sell the robe.

Now, while the boy walked to the camp leading the dun horse, most of the warriors rode back, and one of those that came first to the village went to the old woman and said to her, "Your grandson has killed the spotted calf." And the old woman said, "Why do you come to tell me this? You ought to be ashamed to make fun of my boy, because he is poor." The warrior said, "What I have told you is true," and then he rode away. After a little while another brave rode up to the old woman, and said to her, "Your grandson has killed the spotted calf." Then the old woman began to cry, she felt so badly because every one made fun of her boy, because he was poor.

Pretty soon the boy came along, leading the horse up to the lodge where he and his grandmother lived. It was a little lodge, just big enough for two, and was made of old pieces of skin that the old woman had picked up, and was tied together with strings of rawhide and sinew. It was the meanest and worst lodge in the village. When the old woman saw her boy leading the dun horse with the load of meat and the robes on it, she was very surprised. The boy said to her, "Here, I have brought you plenty of meat to eat, and here is a robe, that you may have for yourself. Take the meat off the horse." Then the old woman laughed, for her heart was glad. But when she went to take the meat from the horse's back, he snorted and jumped about, and acted like a wild horse. The old woman looked at him in wonder, and could hardly believe that it was the same horse. So the boy had to take off the meat, for the horse would not let the old woman come near him.

That night the horse spoke again to the boy and said, "Wa-ti-hes Chah'-ra-rat wa-ta. Tomorrow the Sioux are coming—a large war party. They will attack the village, and you will have a great battle. Now, when the Sioux are all drawn up in line of battle, and are all ready to fight, you jump on to me, and ride as hard as you can, right into the middle of the Sioux, and up to their Head Chief, their greatest warrior, and count coup on him, and kill him, and then ride back. Do this four times, and count coup on four of the bravest Sioux, and kill them, but don't go again. If you go the fifth time, maybe you will be killed, or else you will lose me. La-ku'-ta-chix—remember." So the boy promised.

The next day it happened as the horse had said, and the Sioux came down and formed in line of battle. Then the boy took his bow and arrows, and jumped on the dun horse, and charged into the midst of them. And when the Sioux saw that he was going to strike their Head Chief, they all shot their arrows at him, and the arrows flew so thickly across each other that they darkened the sky, but none of them hit the boy. And he counted coup on the Chief, and killed him, and then rode back. After that he charged again among the Sioux, where they were gathered thickest, and counted coup on their bravest warrior, and killed him. And then twice more, until he had gone four times as the horse had told him.

But the Sioux and the Pawnees kept on fighting, and the boy stood around and watched the battle. And at last he said to himself, "I have been four times and have killed four Sioux, and I am all right, I am not hurt anywhere; why may I not go again?" So he jumped on the dun horse, and charged again. But when he got among the Sioux, one Sioux warrior drew an arrow and shot. The arrow struck the dun horse behind the fore-legs and pierced him through. And the horse fell down dead. But the boy jumped off, and fought his way through the Sioux, and ran away as fast as he could to the Pawnees.

Now, as soon as the horse was killed, the Sioux said to each other: "This horse was like a man. He was brave. He was not like a horse." And they took their knives and hatchets, and hacked the dun horse and gashed his flesh, and cut him into small pieces.

The Pawnees and Sioux fought all day long, but toward night the Sioux broke and fled.

The boy felt very badly that he had lost his horse, and, after the fight was over, he went out from the village to where it had taken place, to mourn for his horse. He went to the spot where the horse lay, and gath-ered up all the pieces of flesh, which the Sioux had cut off, and the legs and the hoofs, and put them all together in a pile. Then he went off to the top of a hill near by, and sat down and drew his robe over his head, and began to mourn for his horse.

As he sat there, he heard a great windstorm coming up, and it passed over him with a loud rushing sound, and after the wind came a rain. The boy looked down from where he sat to the pile of flesh and bones, which was all that was left of his horse, and he could just see it through the rain. And the rain passed by, and his heart was very heavy, and he kept on mourning.

And pretty soon came another rushing wind, and after it a rain; and as he looked through the driving rain toward the spot where the pieces lay, he thought that they seemed to come together and take shape, and that the pile looked like a horse lying down, but he could not see well for the thick rain.

After this came a third storm like the others; and now when he looked toward the horse he thought he saw its tail move from side to side two or three times, and that it lifted its head from the ground. The boy was afraid, and wanted to run away, but he stayed. And as he waited, there came another storm. And while the rain fell, looking through the rain, the boy saw the horse raise himself up on his forelegs and look about. Then the dun horse stood up.

The boy left the place where he had been sitting on the hilltop, and went down to him. When the boy had come near to him, the horse spoke and said: "You have seen how it has been this day; and from this you may know how it will be after this. But Ti-ra'-wa has been good, and has let me come back to you. After this, do what I tell you; not any more, not any less." Then the horse said: "Now lead me off, far away from the camp, behind that big hill, and leave me there tonight, and in the morning come for me," and the boy did as he was told.

And when he went for the horse in the morning, he found with him a beautiful white gelding, much more handsome than any horse in the tribe. That night the dun horse told the boy to take him again to the place behind the big hill, and to come for him the next morning; and when the boy went for him again, he found with him a beautiful black gelding. And so for ten nights, he left the horse among the hills, and each morning he found a different colored horse, a bay, a roan, a gray, a blue, a spotted horse, and all of them finer than any horses that the Pawnees had ever had in their tribe before.

Now the boy was rich, and he married the beautiful daughter of the Head Chief, and when he became older he was made Head Chief himself. He had many children by his beautiful wife, and one day when his oldest boy died, he wrapped him in the spotted calf robe and buried him in it. He always took good care of his old grandmother, and kept her in his own lodge until she died. The dun horse was never ridden except at feasts, and when they were going to have a doctors' dance, but he was always led about with the Chief wherever he went. The horse lived in the village for many years, until he became very old. And at last he died.

31

His Love for His Old Gray Horse

By Laura Spencer Portor and Charles Marshall Graves

∞∞∞

Laura Spencer Portor was a prolific contributor to women's magazines, a professional journalist who wrote on subjects ranging from Shakespeare to mice-infested old houses. She wrote ghost stories and science fiction novels and stories for children. Charles Marshall Graves, also a journalist, was an expert on Edgar Allan Poe.

They were an unlikely combination to put together a short biography of the great Confederate warhorse Traveller, the mount of General Robert E. Lee. But Graves was, early in his career, an editor of the Richmond Times-Dispatch *and had corresponded with many former Confederates. By time this story was published, he was an editor and executive at the* New York Times *and would have been considered more than qualified to write about Lee and his famous horse. This 1908 article remains one of the most important sources of information about Traveller.*

—Sharon B. Smith

∞∞∞

In that part of Virginia now known as West Virginia, and in the meadows of one of the most lovely parts of Greenbrier County, near the White Sulphur Springs, there was grazing, in the summer days of 1859, a two-year-old colt named "Jeff Davis." He was a handsome gray, with dark points; was well proportioned and muscular, with deep chest and short back, strong haunches, flat legs, small head, broad forehead, delicate ears, quick eye, small feet, and full mane and tail.

There were other horses, too, raised with him, who had many of his good points, and who, when he or they were ridden or driven that summer to the fair at Lewisburg, stood almost as good a chance as he of winning honors for their owner. Yet, after the judges had stood about fanning themselves in the hot sun, comparing and discussing and examining all the colts entered in "Jeff Davis's" class, it was to "Jeff Davis" that the little group returned oftenest; and that evening as the horses came home over the mountain roads it was "Jeff Davis" who picked his way, perhaps, with the proudest and most springing gait; for it fluttered at one side of his high head the honor that it would seem a horse would be likely most to covet—two short streamers of blue ribbon. This was the colt's first taste of distinction.

The following summer, when the stream of dusty country vehicles again went creaking by on the road to the Lewisburg Fair, the gray colt and a few of his comrades were again called out from the others one morning and their heads again turned toward Lewisburg.

Once more there was the lazy hubbub of the fair, the judges fanning themselves in the hot sun, and everything as it had been the year before. Once more, returning home, it was the gray colt from whose bridle fluttered the honorable blue ribbon.

But by the time another year had come around County Fairs had begun to seem little things indeed compared with the big national events and interests and the rumors of war that were stirring the country. Stable boys and farm hands, masters and chance guests, talked of little else. If the gray colt were to see more of the world it was likely indeed now to be more than the Lewisburg Fair. Instead of dusty vehicles creaking on their slow way, he might have cantered any day to the meadow bars to look at troops of soldiers riding past, or at an occasional messenger in military garb galloping on in haste.

One day one of these messengers stopped. He was a quartermaster of the Third Regiment of Infantry of the Wise legion, then camped at and near Big Sewell Mountain; and he came in search of a horse of the Greenbrier stock for the use, during the war, of his brother, a major in the same regiment.

The best horses in the stables and meadow were shown him. He considered them all carefully; then he considered the gray colt a little more carefully, put a few questions, stroked him and considered again. Finally, the others were led back by the stable boys. Some gold was counted out by the soldier, and saddle and bridle were put on "Jeff Davis."

As the gray colt and the soldier rode away, as the road turned and the mountains folded in, shutting the home lands from view, they were shutting in at the same time all the treasures of peace, of home meadow and the quiet, dewy mornings and the cool, untroubled evenings. But the gray colt did not look back. His gait was rapid, his head high; he sniffed from side to side in eager contentment. "Jeff Davis" himself was off to the war. If he had been heretofore a companion to peaceful days and stable boys, here was indeed a new outlook.

When the quartermaster drew rein and dismounted, "Jeff Davis" found himself in the midst of a camp. Those about him were soldiers, all of them. Groups of Confederates admired his fine points, his easy gait, and asked where he came from. In time he became known among them by the name of his home county, "Greenbrier." Scarcely a day went by when someone did not have a word of praise or admiration for him.

One autumn day General Lee arrived in camp. The gray colt had never seen the commander, although there had been plenty of talk about him among men and officers. When he did see him he saw a man of gentle but soldierly bearing, who looked at him not critically, as had the quartermaster and the judges at the county fair; not so critically as kindly, and with a sort of gentle comradeship; and who stroked him and said to "Greenbrier's" master: "Major, I shall need that horse before the war is over."

After that they met often. The General always had a kind word to say to "my colt," as he called the proud stepping gray. But this was not to last long as General Lee soon left camp to take up his command in South Carolina. Several months later, however, the Third Regiment was also ordered to that state.

It was the quartermaster who rode the gray colt now, for the major, ill of a fever, had remained in Virginia. One day, near Pocotaligo, General

Lee chanced to see the major's horse again. There was the usual greeting and praise. The general's liking for "Greenbrier" was by this time so well known that the quartermaster ventured to offer the colt as a gift. This the commander declined; but if the major would be willing to sell the horse—in that case General Lee would like to use him for a week to become acquainted with his qualities. The following day "Greenbrier" was led to the stables of General Lee.

At the end of the week he was returned to the quartermaster with the message that he suited entirely, but that General Lee could not use so valuable a horse in such times of peril unless he were his own.

Upon this the major, who was still in Virginia, was consulted. He wrote at once for the quartermaster to say that if General Lee would not accept the horse as a gift, the quartermaster might let him have "Greenbrier" for the amount originally paid. So the matter was closed. The gray colt was led once more to the commander's stable, and was renamed by his new master "Traveller."

No one has ever set down authentically what the ambitions of a high-spirited horse might be, but it seems reasonable to suppose that of all the praise and distinction that had come to the gray colt this was by all odds the best: to carry up and down the ranks, himself a "Confederate Gray," the most noted and honored man of the Confederate Army—the best-loved man in the South.

When the army returned to Virginia, "Traveller" accompanied as one of General Lee's warhorses. At first he merely relieved the other horses ridden by General Lee; but as his endurance was more and more proven, and his fidelity more and more tried, he came oftener into requisition. In time the several other horses failed or sank under the duties of war, at once so cruel and so exacting. But the spirited gray seemed never to waver from fear, nor stumble from fatigue; so at last it was he, and he alone, who carried his beloved master. Where his master went, he too went; they were indeed from this time on never separated.

What lay ahead of him only they knew who followed in those days the actual fortunes of war. We can at best just guess at such things. Again and again he saw the blue lines meet the gray, and one or the other break pitifully. Again and again he saw bloody banners rally and lead on the broken forces, reformed into superhuman bravery and courage. Battle followed battle. Event crowded on event. There were days and nights when the saddle was scarcely off his back.

He was learning life in no mean school. Manassas, Sharpsburg, Fredericksburg, Chancellorsville, Gettysburg, Rappahannock—these were teaching him, as they taught thousands at home and on the battlefields, the big and awful truths of war.

Yet the strain and misery could not have been altogether unsoftened to one so beloved. There was time for many a sympathetic word from the general he carried. He did not now bear him so often in front of even and untouched ranks, lined up in proud review; it was oftener in front of broken ones, war-stained, smoke-grimed; or it was often the wounded and dying now who remembered, and lifted their heads, or attempted a cheer as he went past, bearing his loved master and theirs.

Men and officers who have together faced death, who have shared victory or bitter defeat, are bound by no slight bonds. Wherever the gray horse went bearing General Lee a shout went up. Or when those of another section heard wild cheering, but could not see either horse or rider, there, too, affection kindled, and a smile went over the war-grimed faces: "There goes Marse Robert on 'Old Traveller'!" they said, with renewed courage.

The days were long and full, and unlike enough to the old, quiet Greenbrier days. But there was even more to be borne; days of still greater stress ahead, and need of still greater bravery.

The campaign of '64, which commenced at Orange, led the brave horse through the fearful fire of the Wilderness, Spotsylvania, Cold Harbor, Petersburg. The fortunes of war were utterly changing now. The master whom he had carried through many victories he bore now through much defeat. The gay and gallant and sanguine soldiers that he had known in '61 were worn and hunger-stricken. The proud ranks were for the most part torn and decimated. The men who cheered now as he passed had faces furrowed with hunger and suffering; many of them staggered from weakness; their clothes were tattered and the feet of many were bare and bleeding. Their cause was already a lost cause. Yet for another winter still the brilliant fight continued. Along the lines of defenses from the Chickahominy, north of Richmond, to Hatcher's Run, south of the Appomattox,

"Traveller" was to be seen daily. Heavy odds were closing in. The war was nearing its end. The stricken South could hold her own but little longer. One day the last stand was taken; the last struggle made; the last smoke of battle cleared away. Defense was no longer possible. The cause which had led so many must be abandoned.

The story of Lee's surrender at Appomattox need not be retold. If "Traveller" himself could have told it we should have heard most, no doubt, of the few brief words of farewell which his master spoke to his tattered soldiers; and of how the ragged men crowded, sobbing, to touch their General's hand, or his uniform, or just to lay hands on good old "Traveller."

From that day on there was no more war, but only the memory of war, for the "Confederate Gray." From Appomattox "Traveller" carried his beloved master, now a prisoner of war on parole, to Richmond. As the well-known horse and rider came unexpected through the streets, Southern citizens and Northern soldiers, recognizing them, raised their hats in silent respect or emotion as the two passed by. At East Franklin Street, where General Lee dismounted and made his way to his waiting family, sympathetic crowds gathered around the gray horse who had carried him so well and so long, and some put their arms about "Traveller's" neck and sobbed there and kissed him.

After the war, when General Lee took up his duties at Lexington, "Traveller" was still his master's beloved friend and companion. When work for the day was finished "Traveller" would be brought from the stable and his master would ride in paths now of memory and quietness. Or in the summer "Traveller" would sometimes carry General Lee to the mountains of the White Sulphur in Greenbrier. There the gray horse saw once more his old haunts of quiet and peace; once more he took his way along the very mountain roads where, as a proud young colt, he had in former years returned from the Lewisburg Fair with the blue ribbon, his first honor, fluttering from his bridle knot.

There were honors in plenty for him now. His master often rode him on visits to friends and relatives on the plantations throughout Virginia. Everywhere he was welcomed royally. As war had taught him courage, so peace taught him now the gentler virtues and softer honors of life. He learned to know the loving touch of women's hands, the glad welcome and caresses of little children, and all the quiet, daily lovelinesses that still bloomed in a land so lately visited by war.

So quiet pleasure followed on quiet pleasure until 1870. In the autumn of that year his master lay stricken and on his deathbed. The physicians, making an effort to rouse him, reminded him that he must make haste to get well, for old "Traveller" had been standing in the stable and needed exercise. But General Lee, knowing that his end was near, shook his head. "Traveller" still waited. And the kind hand and gentle voice did not come to him again. From then on he was to miss the familiar touch on his bridle.

After that he was petted even more than before. He might browse as he chose about his master's house, or stand at the veranda whinnying softly for the caresses and attentions he had grown to love.

But "Traveller" did not long survive his master.

One June day following General Lee's death he was browsing about the yard, and, seeing someone on the piazza, advanced whinnying for the petting and the lump of sugar he always expected. It was noticed that he was slightly lame. General Lee's son examined the lame hoof and found a very small nail in it. The nail was extracted. The wound it left was very slight, and did not even bleed, and nothing more was thought of the matter.

In the course of a few days the hostler reported that "Traveller" was not well. There was no veterinary surgeon in Lexington, but a physician was summoned who found that the horse was suffering from lockjaw. The two physicians who had attended General Lee in his last illness now devoted themselves to his famous warhorse. His sufferings were great. All that skill and devotion could do to relieve them was done. When he was no longer able to stand, a mattress was laid on the stable floor for him.

The little town of Lexington was deeply sympathetic. Not only the people of the town, but the farmers of the neighborhood as well, came to offer suggestions and condolences. But nothing was of any avail. The good warhorse died very shortly, beloved and mourned by all who had known him.

As long as General Lee's name is remembered that of his gray warhorse "Traveller" will be lovingly associated with it. Nor will it be only an association of names. The qualities which have endeared General Lee to so many—courage, bravery, gentleness, fidelity, and fortitude—these qualities were shared by "Traveller," the friend and companion and faithful servant of his master, and for these things he too shall be remembered.

32

A Ride with a Mad Horse in a Freight-Car

By W. H. H. Murray

◇◇

Beyond his religion, clergyman William Henry Harrison Murray loved two things above all: the Adirondack Mountains of New York and horses. Publication of his 1869 book Adventures in the Wilderness, *a collection of essays and stories about events and life in the mountains of Northeastern New York, marked the beginning of outdoor writing in North America. The book's success earned him the nickname of "Adirondack" Murray. His book* The Perfect Horse *followed in 1873. This massive volume on horse selection and training is still used today.*

The two loves of W. H. H. Murray came together in the short story that anchored Adventures in the Wilderness. *"A Ride with a Mad Horse in a Freight-Car" is considered Murray's masterpiece, even though it takes place in circumstances he never experienced himself and features a relationship between a horse and a man that is somewhat improbable. But it is still a remarkably moving story, one that perfectly expresses the potential for love between a human being and a horse.*

—SHARON B. SMITH

◇◇

SHOULD THE READER EVER VISIT THE SOUTH INLET OF RACQUETTE Lake—one of the loveliest bits of water in the Adirondack wilderness—at the lower end of the pool below the falls, on the left-hand side going up, he will see the charred remnants of a campfire. It was there that the following story was first told—told, too, so graphically, with such vividness, that I found little difficulty, when writing it out from memory two months later, in recalling the exact words of the narrator in almost every instance.

It was in the month of July, 1868, that John and I, having located our permanent camp on Constable's Point, were lying off and on, as sailors say, about the lake, pushing our explorations on all sides out of sheer love of novelty and abhorrence of idleness. We were returning, late one afternoon of a hot, sultry day, from a trip to Shedd Lake, a lonely, out-of-the-way spot which few sportsmen have ever visited, and had reached the falls on South Inlet just after sunset. As we were getting short of venison, we decided to lie by awhile and float down the river on our way to camp, in hope of meeting a deer. To this end we had gone ashore at this point, and, kindling a small fire, were waiting for denser darkness. We had barely started the blaze, when the tap of a carelessly handled paddle against the side of a boat warned us that we should soon have company, and in a moment two boats glided around the curve below and were headed directly toward our bivouac. The boats contained two gentlemen and their guides. We gave them a cordial, hunter-like greeting, and, lighting our pipes, were soon engaged in cheerful conversation, spiced with story-telling. It might have been some twenty minutes or more when another boat, smaller than you ordinarily see even on those waters, containing only the paddler, came noiselessly around the bend below, and stood revealed in the reflection of the firelight. I chanced to be sitting in such a position as to command a full view of the curve in the river, or I should not have known of any approach, for the boat was so sharp and light, and he who urged it along so skilled at the paddle, that not a ripple, no, nor the sound of a drop of water falling from blade or shaft, betrayed the paddler's presence.

If there is anything over which I become enthusiastic, it is such a boat and such paddling. To see a boat of bark or cedar move through the water noiselessly as a shadow drifts across a meadow, no jar or creak above, no gurgling of displaced water below, no whirling and rippling wake astern, is something bordering so nearly on the weird and ghostly, that custom can never make it seem other than marvelous to me.

Thus, as I sat half reclining, and saw that little shell come floating airily out of the darkness into the projection of the firelight, as a feather might come blown by the night-wind, I thought I had never seen a prettier or more fairylike sight. None of the party save myself were so seated as to look down stream, and I wondered which of the three guides would first discover the presence of the approaching boat.

Straight on it came. Light as a piece of finest cork it sat upon and glided over the surface of the river; no dip and roll, no drip of falling water as the paddle shaft gently rose and sank. The paddler, whoever he might be, knew his art thoroughly. He sat erect and motionless. The turn of the wrists, and the easy elevation of his arms as he feathered his paddle, were the only movements visible. But for these the gazer might deem him a statue carved from the material of the boat, a mere inanimate part of it. I have boated much in bark canoe and cedar shell alike, and John and I have stolen on many a camp that never knew our coming or our going, with paddles which touched the water as snowflakes touch the earth; and well I knew, as I sat gazing at this man, that not one boatman, red man or white, in a hundred could handle a paddle like that.

The quick ear of John, when the stranger was within thirty feet of the landing, detected the lightest possible touch of a lily pad against the side of the boat as it just grazed it glancing by, and his "hist" and sudden motion toward the river drew the attention of the whole surprised group thither. The boat glided to the sand so gently as barely to disturb a grain, and the paddler, noiseless in all his movements, stepped ashore and entered our circle.

"Well, stranger," said John, "I don't know how long your fingers have polished a paddle shaft, but it isn't every man who can push a boat up ten rods of open water within twenty feet of my back without my knowing it."

The stranger laughed pleasantly, and, without making any direct reply, lighted his pipe and joined in the conversation. He was tall in stature, wiry, and bronzed. An ugly cicatrice stretched on the left side of his face from temple almost down to chin. His eyes were dark gray, frank, and genial. I concluded at once that he was a gentleman, and had seen service. Before he joined us, we had been whiling away the time by story-telling, and John was at the very crisis of an adventure with a panther, when his quick ear detected the stranger's approach. Explaining this to him, I told

John to resume his story, which he did. Thus half an hour passed quickly, all of us relating some experience.

At last I proposed that Mr. Roberts—for so we will call him—should entertain us; "and," continued I, "if I am right in my surmise that you have seen service and been under fire, give us some adventure or incident which may have befallen you during the war."

He complied, and then and there, gentle reader, I heard from his lips the story, which, for the entertainment of friends, I afterward wrote out. It left a deep impression upon all who heard it around our campfire under the pines that night; and from the mind of one I know has never been erased the impression made by the story which I have named "A Ride with a Mad Horse in a Freight-Car."

"Well," said the stranger, as he loosened his belt and stretched himself in an easy, recumbent position, "it is not more than fair that I should throw something into the stock of common entertainment; but the story I am to tell you is a sad one, and I fear will not add to the pleasure of the evening. As you desire it, however, and it comes in the line of the request that I would narrate some personal episode of the war, I will tell it, and trust the impression will not be altogether unpleasant.

"It was at the battle of Malvern Hill—a battle where the carnage was more frightful, as it seems to me, than in any this side of the Alleghenies during the whole war—that my story must begin. I was then serving as major in the ——th Massachusetts Regiment—the old ——th, as we used to call it, and a bloody time the boys had of it too. About 2:00 p.m. we had been sent out to skirmish along the edge of the wood in which, as our generals suspected, the Rebs lay massing for a charge across the slope, upon the crest of which our army was posted. We had barely entered the underbrush when we met the heavy formations of Magruder in the very act of charging. Of course, our thin line of skirmishers was no impediment to those onrushing masses. They were on us and over us before we could get out of the way. I do not think that half of those running, screaming masses of men ever knew that they had passed over the remnants of as plucky a regiment as ever came out of the old Bay State.

"But many of the boys had good reason to remember that afternoon at the base of Malvern Hill, and I among the number; for when the last line of Rebs had passed over me, I was left among the bushes with the breath nearly trampled and an ugly bayonet gash through my thigh; and mighty little consolation was it for me at that moment to see the fellow who run me through lying stark dead at my side, with a bullet hole in his head, his shock of coarse black hair matted with blood, and his stony eyes looking into mine.

"Well, I bandaged up my limb the best I might, and started to crawl away, for our batteries had opened, and the grape and canister that came hurtling down the slope passed but a few feet over my head. It was slow and painful work, as you can imagine, but at last, by dint of perseverance, I had dragged myself away to the left of the direct range of the batteries, and, creeping to the verge of the wood, looked off over the green slope. I understood by the crash and roar of the guns, the yells and cheers of the men, and that hoarse murmur which those who have been in battle know, but which I cannot describe in words, that there was hot work going on out there; but never have I seen, no, not in that three days' desperate *mêlée* at the Wilderness, nor at that terrific repulse we had at Cold Harbor, such absolute slaughter as I saw that afternoon on the green slope of Malvern Hill.

"The guns of the entire army were massed on the crest, and thirty thousand of our infantry lay, musket in hand, in front. For eight hundred yards the hill sank in easy declension to the wood, and across this smooth expanse the Rebs must charge to reach our lines. It was nothing short of downright insanity to order men to charge that hill; and so his generals told Lee, but he would not listen to reason that day, and so he sent regiment after regiment, and brigade after brigade, and division after division, to certain death. Talk about Grant's disregard of human life, his effort at Cold Harbor—and I ought to know, for I got a minie in my shoulder that day—was hopeful and easy work to what Lee laid on Hill's and Magruder's divisions at Malvern.

"It was at the close of the second charge, when the yelling mass reeled back from before the blaze of those sixty guns and thirty thousand rifles, even as they began to break and fly backward toward the woods, that I saw from the spot where I lay a riderless horse break out of the confused and flying mass, and, with mane and tail erect and spreading nostril, come dashing obliquely down the slope. Over fallen steeds and heaps of the dead she leaped with a motion as airy as that of the flying fox when, fresh and unjaded, he leads away from the hounds, whose sudden cry has broken him off from hunting mice amid the bogs of the meadow. So this riderless horse came vaulting along.

"Now from my earliest boyhood I have had what horsemen call a 'weakness' for horses. Only give me a colt of wild, irregular temper and fierce blood to tame, and I am perfectly happy. Never did lash of mine, singing with cruel sound through the air, fall on such a colt's soft hide. Never did yell or kick send his hot blood from heart to head deluging his sensitive brain with fiery currents, driving him to frenzy or blinding him with fear; but touches, soft and gentle as a woman's, caressing words, and oats given from the open palm, and unfailing kindness, were the means I used to 'subjugate' him. Sweet subjugation, both to him who subdues and to him who yields! The wild, unmannerly, and unmanageable colt, the fear of horsemen the country round, finding in you, not an enemy but a friend, receiving his daily food from you, and all those little 'nothings' which go as far with a horse as a woman, to win and retain affection, grows to look upon you as his protector and friend, and testifies in countless ways his fondness for you.

"So when I saw this horse, with action so free and motion so graceful, amid that storm of bullets, my heart involuntarily went out to her, and my feelings rose higher and higher at every leap she took from amid the whirlwind of fire and lead. And as she plunged at last over a little hillock out of range and came careering toward me as only a riderless horse might come, her head flung wildly from side to side, her nostrils widely spread, her flank and shoulders flecked with foam, her eye dilating, I forgot my wound and all the wild roar of battle, and, lifting myself involuntarily to a sitting posture as she swept grandly by, gave her a ringing cheer.

"Perhaps in the sound of a human voice of happy mood amid the awful din she recognized a resemblance to the voice of him whose blood moistened her shoulders and was even yet dripping from saddle and housings, be that as it may, no sooner had my voice sounded than she flung her head with a proud upward movement into the air, swerved sharply to the left, neighed as she might to a master at morning from her stall, and came trotting directly up to where I lay, and, pausing, looked down upon me as it were in compassion. I spoke again, and stretched out my hand caressingly. She pricked her ears, took a step forward and lowered her nose until it came in contact with my palm. Never did I fondle anything more tenderly, never did I see an animal which seemed to court and appreciate human tenderness as that beautiful mare. I say 'beautiful.' No other word might describe her. Never will her image fade from my memory while memory lasts.

"In weight she might have turned, when well conditioned, nine hundred and fifty pounds. In color she was a dark chestnut, with a velvety depth and soft look about the hair indescribably rich and elegant. Many a time have I heard ladies dispute the shade and hue of her plush-like coat as they ran their white, jeweled fingers through her silken hair. Her body was round in the barrel, and perfectly symmetrical. She was wide in the haunches, without projection of the hipbones, upon which the shorter ribs seemed to lap. High in the withers as she was, the line of her back and neck perfectly curved, while her deep, oblique shoulders and long thick forearm, ridgy with swelling sinews, suggesting the perfection of stride and power. Her knees across the pan were wide, the cannon-bone below them short and thin; the pasterns long and sloping; her hoofs round, dark, shiny, and well set on. Her mane was a shade darker than her coat, fine and thin, as a thoroughbred's always is whose blood is without taint or cross. Her ear was thin, sharply pointed, delicately curved, nearly black around the borders, and as tremulous as the leaves of an aspen. Her neck rose from the withers to the head in perfect curvature, hard, devoid of fat, and well cut up under the chops. Her nostrils were full, very full, and thin almost as parchment. The eyes, from which tears might fall or fire flash, were well brought out, soft as a gazelle's, almost human in their intelligence, while over the small bony head, over neck and shoulders, yea, over the whole body and clean down to the hoofs, the veins stood out as if the skin were but tissue-paper against which the warm blood pressed, and which it might at any moment burst asunder.

"'A perfect animal,' I said to myself, as I lay looking her over—an animal which might have been born from the wind and the sunshine, so cheerful and so swift she seems; an animal which a man would present as his choicest gift to the woman he loved, and yet one which that woman, wife or lady love, would give him to ride when honor and life depended on bottom and speed.

"All that afternoon the beautiful mare stood over me, while away to the right of us the hoarse tide of battle flowed and ebbed. What charm, what delusion of memory, held her there? Was my face to her as the face of her dead master, sleeping a sleep from which not even the wildest roar of battle, no, nor her cheerful neigh at morning, would ever wake him? Or is there in animals some instinct, answering to our intuition, only more potent, which tells them whom to trust and whom to avoid? I know not, and yet some such sense they may have, they must have, or why else should this mare so fearlessly attach herself to me?

"By what process of reason or instinct I know not, but there she chose me for her master; for when some of my men at dusk came searching, and found me, and, laying me on a stretcher, started toward our lines, the mare, uncompelled, of her own free will, followed at my side; and all through that stormy night of wind and rain, as my men struggled along through the mud and mire toward Harrison's Landing, the mare followed, and ever after, until she died, was with me, and was mine, and I, so far as man might be, was hers. I named her Gulnare.

"As quickly as my wound permitted, I was transported to Washington, whither I took the mare with me. Her fondness for me grew daily, and soon became so marked as to cause universal comment. I had her boarded while in Washington at the corner. The groom had instructions to lead her around to the window against which was my bed, at the hospital, twice every day, so that by opening the sash I might reach out my hand and pet her. But the second day, no sooner had she reached the street, than she broke suddenly from the groom and dashed away at full speed. I was lying, bolstered up in bed, reading, when I heard the rush of flying feet, and in an instant, with a loud, joyful neigh, she checked herself in front of my window. And when the nurse lifted the sash, the beautiful creature thrust her head through the aperture, and rubbed her nose against my shoulder like a dog. I am not ashamed to say that I put both my arms around her neck, and, burying my face in her silken mane, kissed her again and again. Wounded, weak, and away from home, with only strangers to wait upon me, and scant service at that, the affection of this lovely creature for me, so tender and touching, seemed almost human, and my heart went out to her beyond any power of expression, as to the only being, of all the thousands around me, who thought of me and loved me.

"Shortly after her appearance at my window, the groom, who had divined where he should find her, came into the yard. But she would not allow him to come near her, much less touch her. If he tried to approach she would lash out at him with her heels most spitefully, and then, laying back her ears and opening her mouth savagely, would make a short dash at him, and, as the terrified African disappeared around the corner of the hospital, she would wheel, and, with a face bright as a happy child's, come trotting to the window for me to pet her. I shouted to the groom to go back to the stable, for I had no doubt but that she would return to her stall when I closed the window. Rejoiced at the permission, he departed. After some thirty minutes, the last ten of which she was standing with her slim, delicate head in my lap, while I braided her foretop and combed out her silken mane, I lifted her head, and, patting her softly on either cheek, told her that she must go. I gently pushed her head out of the window and closed it, and then, holding up my hand, with the palm turned toward her, charged her, making the appropriate motion, to 'go away right straight back to her stable.' For a moment she stood looking steadily at me, with an indescribable expression of hesitation and surprise in her clear, liquid eyes, and then, turning lingeringly, walked slowly out of the yard.

"Twice a day for nearly a month, while I lay in the hospital, did Gulnare visit me. At the appointed hour the groom would slip her headstall, and, without a word of command, she would dart out of the stable, and, with her long, leopard-like lope, go sweeping down the street and come dashing into the hospital yard, checking herself with the same glad neigh at my window; nor did she ever once fail, at the closing of the sash, to return directly to her stall. The groom informed me that every morning and evening, when the hour of her visit drew near, she would begin to chafe and worry, and, by pawing and pulling at the halter, advertise him that it was time for her to be released.

"But of all exhibitions of happiness, either by beast or man, hers was the most positive on that afternoon when, racing into the yard, she found me leaning on a crutch outside the hospital building. The whole corps of nurses came to the doors, and all the poor fellows that could move themselves—for Gulnare had become a universal favorite, and the boys looked for her daily visits nearly, if not quite, as ardently as I did—crawled to the windows to see her.

"What gladness was expressed in every movement! She would come prancing toward me, head and tail erect, and, pausing, rub her head against my shoulder, while I patted her glossy neck; then suddenly, with a sidewise spring, she would break away, and with her long tail elevated until her magnificent brush, fine and silken as the golden hair of a blonde, fell in a great spray on either flank, and, her head curved to its proudest arch, pace around me with that high action and springing step peculiar to the thoroughbred. Then like a flash, dropping her brush and laying back her ears and stretching her nose straight out, she would speed away with that quick, nervous, low-lying action which marks the rush of racers, when side by side and nose to nose lapping each other, with the roar of cheers on either hand and along the seats above them, they come straining up the home stretch. Returning from one of these arrowy flights, she would come curveting back, now pacing sidewise as on parade, now dashing her hind feet high into the air, and anon vaulting up and springing through the air, with legs well under her, as if in the act of taking a five-barred gate, and finally would approach and stand happy in her reward—my caress.

"The war, at last, was over. Gulnare and I were in at the death with Sheridan at the Five Forks. Together we had shared the pageant at Richmond and Washington, and never had I seen her in better spirits than on that day at the capital. It was a sight indeed to see her as she came down Pennsylvania Avenue. If the triumphant procession had been all in her honor and mine, she could not have moved with greater grace and pride. With dilating eye and tremulous ear, ceaselessly champing her bit, her heated blood bringing out the magnificent lacework of veins over her entire body, now and then pausing, and with a snort gathering herself back upon her haunches as for a mighty leap, while she shook the froth from her bits, she moved with a high, prancing step down the magnificent street, the admired of all beholders.

"Cheer after cheer was given, huzza after huzza rang out over her head from roofs and balcony, bouquet after bouquet was launched by fair and enthusiastic admirers before her; and yet, amid the crash and swell of music, the cheering and tumult, so gentle and manageable was she, that, though I could feel her frame creep and tremble under me as she moved through that whirlwind of excitement, no check or curb was needed, and the bridle-lines—the same she wore when she came to me at Malvern Hill—lay unlifted on the pommel of the saddle.

"Never before had I seen her so grandly herself. Never before had the fire and energy, the grace and gentleness, of her blood so revealed themselves. This was the day and the event she needed. And all the royalty of her ancestral breed—a race of equine kings—flowing as without taint or cross from him that was the pride and wealth of the whole tribe of desert rangers, expressed itself in her.

"I need not say that I shared her mood. I sympathized in her every step. I entered into all her royal humors. I patted her neck and spoke loving and cheerful words to her. I called her my beauty, my pride, my pet. And did she not understand me? Every word! Else why that listening ear turned back to catch my softest whisper; why the responsive quiver through the frame, and the low, happy neigh?

"'Well,' I exclaimed, as I leaped from her back at the close of the review—alas! that words spoken in lightest mood should portend so much!—'well, Gulnare, if you should die, your life has had its triumph. The nation itself, through its admiring capital, has paid tribute to your beauty, and death can never rob you of your fame.' And I patted her moist neck and foam-flecked shoulders, while the grooms were busy with head and loins.

"That night our brigade made its bivouac just over Long Bridge, almost on the identical spot where four years before I had camped my company of three months' volunteers. With what experiences of march and battle were those four years filled! For three of these years Gulnare had been my constant companion. With me she had shared my tent, and not rarely my rations, for in appetite she was truly human, and my steward always counted her as one of our 'mess.' Twice had she been wounded— once at Fredericksburg, through the thigh; and once at Cold Harbor, where a piece of shell tore away a part of her scalp. So completely did it stun her, that for some moments I thought her dead, but to my great joy she shortly recovered her senses. I had the wound carefully dressed by our brigade surgeon, from whose care she came in a month with the edges of the wound so nicely united that the eye could with difficulty detect the scar.

"This night, as usual, she lay at my side, her head almost touching mine. Never before, unless when on a raid and in face of the enemy, had I seen her so uneasy. Her movements during the night compelled wakefulness on my part. The sky was cloudless, and in the dim light I lay and watched her. Now she would stretch herself at full length, and rub her head on the ground. Then she would start up, and, sitting on her haunches, like a dog, lift one foreleg and paw her neck and ears. Anon she would rise to her feet and shake herself, walk off a few rods, return and lie down again by my side.

"I did not know what to make of it, unless the excitement of the day had been too much for her sensitive nerves. I spoke to her kindly and petted her. In response she would rub her nose against me, and lick my hand with her tongue—a peculiar habit of hers—like a dog. As I was passing my hand over her head, I discovered that it was hot, and the thought of the old wound flashed into my mind, with a momentary fear that something might be wrong about her brain, but after thinking it over I dismissed it as incredible. Still I was alarmed. I knew that something was amiss, and I rejoiced at the thought that I should soon be at home where she could have quiet, and, if need be, the best of nursing.

"At length the morning dawned, and the mare and I took our last meal together on Southern soil—the last we ever took together. The brigade was formed in line for the last time, and as I rode down the front to review the boys she moved with all her old battle grace and power. Only now and then, by a shake of the head, was I reminded of her actions during the night. I said a few words of farewell to the men whom I had led so often to battle, with whom I had shared perils not a few, and by whom, as I had reason to think, I was loved, and then gave, with a voice slightly unsteady, the last order they would ever receive from me: 'Brigade, Attention, Ready to break ranks, *Break Ranks.*'

"The order was obeyed. But ere they scattered, moved by a common impulse, they gave first three cheers for me, and then, with the same heartiness and even more power, three cheers for Gulnare. And she, standing there, looking with her bright, cheerful countenance full at the men, pawing with her forefeet, alternately, the ground, seemed to understand the compliment; for no sooner had the cheering died away than she arched her neck to its proudest curve, lifted her thin, delicate head into the air, and gave a short, joyful neigh.

"My arrangements for transporting her had been made by a friend the day before. A large, roomy car had been secured, its floor strewn with bright, clean straw, a bucket and a bag of oats provided, and everything done for her comfort. The car was to be attached to the through express, in consideration of fifty dollars extra, which I gladly paid, because of the greater rapidity with which it enabled me to make my journey.

"As the brigade broke up into groups, I glanced at my watch and saw that I had barely time to reach the cars before they started. I shook the reins upon her neck, and with a plunge, startled at the energy of my signal, away she flew. What a stride she had! What an elastic spring! She touched and left the earth as if her limbs were of spiral wire. When I reached the car my friend was standing in front of it, the gangplank was ready, I leaped from the saddle and, running up the plank into the car, whistled to her; and she, timid and hesitating, yet unwilling to be separated from me, crept slowly and cautiously up the steep incline and stood beside me.

"Inside I found a complete suit of flannel clothes with a blanket and, better than all, a lunch basket. My friend explained that he had bought the clothes as he came down to the depot, thinking, as he said, 'that they would be much better than your regimentals,' and suggested that I doff the one and don the other. To this I assented the more readily as I reflected that I would have to pass one night at least in the car, with no better bed than the straw under my feet.

"I had barely time to undress before the cars were coupled and started. I tossed the clothes to my friend with the injunction to pack them in my trunk and express them on to me, and waved him my adieu. I arrayed myself in the nice, cool flannel and looked around. The thoughtfulness of my friend had anticipated every want. An old cane-seated chair stood in one corner. The lunch basket was large and well supplied. Amid the oats I found a dozen oranges, some bananas, and a package of real Havana cigars. How I called down blessings on his thoughtful head as I took the chair and, lighting one of the fine-flavored *figaros*, gazed out on the fields past which we were gliding, yet wet with morning dew. As I sat dreamily admiring the beauty before me, Gulnare came and, resting her head upon my shoulder, seemed to share my mood.

"As I stroked her fine-haired, satin-like nose, recollection quickened and memories of our companionship in perils thronged into my mind. I rode again that midnight ride to Knoxville, when Burnside lay entrenched, desperately holding his own, waiting for news from Chattanooga of which I was the bearer, chosen by Grant himself because of the reputation of my mare. What riding that was! We started, ten riders of us in all, each with the same message. I parted company the first hour out with all save one, an iron-gray stallion of Messenger blood. Jack Murdock rode him, who learned his horsemanship from buffalo and Indian hunting on the plains—not a bad school to graduate from.

"Ten miles out of Knoxville the gray, his flanks dripping with blood, plunged up abreast of the mare's shoulders and fell dead; and Gulnare and I passed through the lines alone. I had ridden the terrible race without whip or spur. With what scenes of blood and flight she would ever be associated!

"And then I thought of home, unvisited for four long years—that home I left a stripling, but to which I was returning a bronzed and brawny man. I thought of Mother and Bob—how they would admire her!—of old Ben, the family groom, and of that one who shall be nameless, whose picture I had so often shown to Gulnare as the likeness of her future mistress; had they not all heard of her, my beautiful mare, she who came to me from the smoke and whirlwind, my battle gift? How they would pat her soft, smooth sides, and tie her mane with ribbons, and feed her with all sweet things from open and caressing palm! And then I thought of one who might come after her to bear her name and repeat at least some portion of her beauty—a horse honored and renowned the country through, because of the transmission of the mother's fame.

"About three o'clock in the afternoon a change came over Gulnare. I had fallen asleep upon the straw, and she had come and awakened me with a touch of her nose. The moment I started up I saw that something was the matter. Her eyes were dull and heavy. Never before had I seen the light go out of them. The rocking of the car as it went jumping and vibrating along seemed to irritate her. She began to rub her head against the side of the car. Touching it, I found that the skin over the brain was hot as fire. Her breathing grew rapidly louder and louder. Each breath was drawn with a kind of gasping effort. The lids with their silken fringe drooped wearily over the lusterless eyes. The head sank lower and lower, until the nose almost touched the floor. The ears, naturally so lively and erect, hung limp and widely apart. The body was cold and senseless. A pinch elicited no motion. Even my voice was at last unheeded. To word and touch there came, for the first time in all our intercourse, no response.

"I knew as the symptoms spread what was the matter. The signs bore all one way. She was in the first stages of phrenitis, or inflammation of the brain. In other words, *my beautiful mare was going mad.*

"I was well versed in the anatomy of the horse. Loving horses from my very childhood, there was little in veterinary practice with which I was not familiar. Instinctively, as soon as the symptoms had developed themselves, and I saw under what frightful disorder Gulnare was laboring, I put my hand into my pocket for my knife, in order to open a vein. There was no knife there. Friends, I have met with many surprises. More than once in battle and scout have I been nigh death; but never did my blood desert my veins and settle so around the heart, never did such a sickening sensation possess me, as when, standing in that car with my beautiful mare before me marked with those horrible symptoms, I made that discovery.

"My knife, my sword, my pistols even, were with my suit in the care of my friend, two hundred miles away. Hastily, and with trembling fingers, I searched my clothes, the lunch basket, my linen; not even a pin could I find. I shoved open the sliding door, and swung my hat and shouted, hoping to attract some brakeman's attention. The train was thundering along at full speed, and none saw or heard me. I knew her stupor would not last long. A slight quivering of the lip, an occasional spasm running through the frame, told me too plainly that the stage of frenzy would soon begin.

"'My God,' I exclaimed in despair, as I shut the door and turned toward her, 'must I see you die, Gulnare, when the opening of a vein would save you? Have you borne me, my pet, through all these years of peril, the icy chill of winter, the heat and torment of summer, and all the thronging dangers of a hundred bloody battles, only to die torn by fierce agonies, when so near a peaceful home?'

"But little time was given me to mourn. My life was soon to be in peril, and I must summon up the utmost power of eye and limb to escape the violence of my frenzied mare. Did you ever see a mad horse when his madness is on him? Take your stand with me in that car, and you shall see what suffering a dumb creature can endure before it dies. In no malady does a horse suffer more than in phrenitis, or inflammation of the brain. Possibly in severe cases of colic, probably in rabies in its fiercest form, the pain is equally intense. These three are the most agonizing of all the diseases to which the noblest of animals is exposed.

"Had my pistols been with me, I should then and there, with whatever strength Heaven granted, have taken my companion's life, that she might be spared the suffering which was so soon to rack and wring her sensitive frame. A horse laboring under an attack of phrenitis is as violent as a horse can be. He is not ferocious as is one in a fit of rabies. He may kill his master, but he does it without design. There is in him no desire of mischief for its own sake, no cruel cunning, no stratagem and malice. A rabid horse is conscious in every act and motion. He recognizes the man he destroys. There is in him an insane *desire to kill*. Not so with the phrenetic horse. He is unconscious in his violence. He sees and recognizes no one. There is no method or purpose in his madness. He kills without knowing it.

"I knew what was coming. I could not jump out, that would be certain death. I must abide in the car, and take my chance of life. The car was fortunately high, long, and roomy. I took my position in front of my horse, watchful, and ready to spring. Suddenly her lids, which had been closed, came open with a snap, as if an electric shock had passed through her, and the eyes, wild in their brightness, stared directly at me. And what eyes they were! The membrane grew red and redder until it was of the color of blood, standing out in frightful contrast with the transparency of the cornea. The pupil gradually dilated until it seemed about to burst out of the socket. The nostrils, which had been sunken and motionless, quivered, swelled, and glowed. The respiration became short, quick and gasping. The limp and dripping ears stiffened and stood erect, pricked sharply forward, as if to catch the slightest sound. Spasms, as the car swerved and vibrated, ran along her frame. More horrid than all, the lips slowly contracted, and the white, sharp-edged teeth stood uncovered, giving an indescribable look of ferocity to the partially opened mouth.

"The car suddenly reeled as it dashed around a curve, swaying her almost off her feet, and, as a contortion shook her, she recovered herself, and rearing upward as high as the car permitted, plunged directly at me. I was expecting the movement, and dodged. Then followed exhibitions of pain, which I pray God I may never see again. Time and again did she dash herself upon the floor, and roll over and over, lashing out with her feet in all directions. Pausing a moment, she would stretch her body to its extreme length, and, lying upon her side, pound the floor with her head as if it were a maul. Then like a flash she would leap to her feet, and whirl round and round until from very giddiness she would stagger and fall. She would lay hold of the straw with her teeth, and shake it as a dog shakes a struggling woodchuck; then dashing it from her mouth, she would seize hold of her own sides, and rend herself. Springing up, she would rush against the end of the car, falling all in a heap from the violence of the concussion.

"For some fifteen minutes without intermission the frenzy lasted. I was nearly exhausted. My efforts to avoid her mad rushes, the terrible tension of my nervous system produced by the spectacle of such exquisite and prolonged suffering, were weakening me beyond what I should have thought it possible an hour before for anything to weaken me. In fact, I felt my strength leaving me. A terror such as I had never yet felt was taking possession of my mind. I sickened at the sight before me, and at the thought of agonies yet to come.

"'My God,' I exclaimed, 'must I be killed by my own horse in this miserable car!' Even as I spoke the end came. The mare raised herself until her shoulders touched the roof, then dashed her body upon the floor with a violence which threatened the stout frame beneath her. I leaned, panting and exhausted, against the side of the car. Gulnare did not stir. She lay motionless, her breath coming and going in lessening respirations. I tottered toward her, and, as I stood above her, my ear detected a low gurgling sound. I cannot describe the feeling that followed. Joy and grief contended within me. I knew the meaning of that sound.

"Gulnare, in her frenzied violence, had broken a blood vessel, and was bleeding internally. Pain and life were passing away together. I knelt down by her side. I laid my head upon her shoulders, and sobbed aloud. Her body moved a little beneath me, as if she would be nearer me, looked once more with her clear eyes into my face, breathed a long breath, straightened her shapely limbs, and died. And there, holding the head of my dead mare in my lap, while the great warm tears fell one after another down my cheeks, I sat until the sun went down, the shadows darkened in the car, and night drew her mantle, colored like my grief, over the world."

33

The Camp of the Wild Horse

By Washington Irving

White Americans also hunted wild horses. Their techniques were different, as were the uses they had for the animals they captured. The famous New York writer Washington Irving, who had lived abroad for seventeen years, returned to the United States in 1832 with an urge to see his country and prove he hadn't lost his feeling for his native land. Irving, already renowned for his stories "Rip van Winkle" and the "Legend of Sleepy Hollow," immediately embarked on a tour of what is now Oklahoma. He turned the journals he kept on the trip into A Tour on the Prairies, *a masterpiece of early Western travel literature. In this chapter, he describes the exhilaration of the wild horse hunt.*

—SHARON B. SMITH

WE HAD ENCAMPED IN A GOOD NEIGHBORHOOD FOR GAME, AS THE reports of rifles in various directions speedily gave notice. One of our hunters soon returned with the meat of a doe tied up in the skin and slung across his shoulders. Another brought a fat buck across his horse. Two other deer were brought in, and a number of turkeys. All the game was thrown down in front of the captain's fire, to be portioned out among the various messes. The spits and camp kettles were soon in full employ, and throughout the evening there was a scene of hunters' feasting and profusion.

We had been disappointed this day in our hopes of meeting with buffalo, but the sight of the wild horse had been a great novelty and gave a turn to the conversation of the camp for the evening. There were several anecdotes told of a famous gray horse that has ranged the prairies of this neighborhood for six or seven years, setting at naught any attempt of the hunters to capture him. They say he can pace and rack (or amble) faster than the fleetest horses can run. Equally marvelous accounts were given of a black horse on the Brazos, who grazed the prairies on that river's banks in Texas. For years he outstripped all pursuit. His fame spread far and wide; offers were made for him to the amount of a thousand dollars; the boldest and most hard-riding hunters tried incessantly to make prize of him, but in vain. At length he fell a victim to his gallantry; being decoyed under a tree by a tame mare, and a noose dropped over his head by a boy perched among the branches.

The capture of the wild horse is one of the most favorite achievements of the prairie tribes; and, indeed, it is from this source that the Indian hunters chiefly supply themselves. The wild horses that range those vast grassy plains, extending from the Arkansas to the Spanish settlements, are of various forms and colors, betraying their various descents. Some resemble the common English stock, and are probably descended from horses that have escaped from our border settlements. Others are of a low but strong make, and are supposed to be of the Andalusian breed, brought out by the Spanish discoverers.

Some fanciful speculatists have seen in them descendants of the Arab stock brought into Spain from Africa, and thence transferred to this country; and have pleased themselves with the idea that their sires may have been of the pure coursers of the desert, that once bore Mahomet and his warlike disciples across the sandy plains of Arabia!

The habits of the Arab seem to have come with the steed. The introduction of the horse on the boundless plains of the far West changed the whole mode of living of their inhabitants. It gave them that facility of rapid motion, and of sudden and distant change of place, so dear to the roving propensities of man. Instead of lurking in the depths of gloomy forests, and patiently threading the mazes of a tangled wilderness on foot, like his brethren of the north, the Indian of the West is a rover of the plain; he leads a brighter and more sunshiny life, almost always on horse-back, on vast flowery prairies and under cloudless skies.

I was lying by the captain's fire late in the evening, listening to stories about these coursers of the prairies and weaving speculations of my own, when there was a clamor of voices and a loud cheering at the other end of the camp, and word was passed that Beatte, the half-breed, had brought in a wild horse.

In an instant every fire was deserted; the whole camp crowded to see the Indian and his prize. It was a colt about two years old, well grown, finely limbed, with bright prominent eyes, and a spirited yet gentle demeanor. He gazed about him with an air of mingled stupefaction and surprise at the men, the horses, and the campfires; while the Indian stood before him with folded arms, having hold of the other end of the cord which noosed his captive, and gazing on him with a most imperturbable aspect. Beatte, as I have before observed, has a greenish olive complexion; with a strongly-marked countenance not unlike the bronze casts of Napoleon; and as he stood before his captive horse, with folded arms and fixed aspect, he looked more like a statue than a man.

If the horse, however, manifested the least restiveness, Beatte would immediately worry him with the lariat, jerking him first on one side then on the other, so as almost to throw him on the ground; when he had thus rendered him passive, he would resume his statue-like attitude and gaze at him in silence.

The whole scene was singularly wild: the tall grove partially illumined by the flashing fires of the camp; the horses tethered here and there among the trees; the carcasses of deer hanging around; and in the midst of all the wild huntsman and his wild horse, with an admiring throng of rangers, almost as wild.

In the eagerness of their excitement, several of the young rangers sought to get the horse by purchase or barter, and even offered extravagant terms; but Beatte declined all their offers. "You give great price now," said he; "tomorrow you take back, and say, 'D——d Indian!'"

The young men importuned him with questions about the mode in which he took the horse, but his answers were dry and laconic; he evidently retained some pique at having been undervalued and sneered at by the young rangers, and at the same time looked down upon them with contempt as greenhorns, little versed in the noble science of woodcraft.

Afterwards, however, when he was seated by our fire, I readily drew from him an account of his exploit; for, though taciturn among strangers, and little prone to boast of his actions, yet his taciturnity, like that of all Indians, had its times of relaxation.

He informed me that, on leaving the camp, he had returned to the place where we had lost sight of the wild horse. Soon getting upon its track, he followed it to the banks of the river. Here, the prints being more distinct in the sand, he perceived that one of the hoofs was broken and defective, so he gave up the pursuit.

As he was returning to the camp, he came upon a gang of six horses, which immediately made for the river. He pursued them across the stream, left his rifle on the river bank, and, putting his horse to full speed, soon came up with the fugitives. He attempted to noose one of them; but the lariat hitched on one of his ears, and he shook it off. The horses dashed up a hill; he followed hard at their heels; when, of a sudden, he saw their tails whisking in the air, indicating that they were plunging down a precipice. It was too late to stop. He shut his eyes, held in his breath, and went over with them—neck or nothing. The descent was between twenty and thirty feet, but they all came down safe upon a sandy bottom.

He now succeeded in throwing his noose round a fine young horse. As he galloped alongside of him, the two horses passed each side of a sapling, and the end of the lariat was jerked out of his hand. He regained it, but an intervening tree obliged him again to let it go. Having once more caught it, and coming to a more open country, he was enabled to play the young horse with the line until he gradually checked and subdued him, so as to lead him to the place where he had left his rifle.

He had another formidable difficulty in getting him across the river, where both horses stuck for a time in the mire, and Beatte was nearly unseated from his saddle by the force of the current and the struggles of his captive. After much toil and trouble, however, he got across the stream, and brought his prize safe into the camp.

For the remainder of the evening the camp remained in a high state of excitement: nothing was talked of but the capture of wild horses;

every youngster of the troop was for this harum-scarum kind of chase; every one promised himself to return from the campaign in triumph, bestriding one of these wild coursers of the prairies. Beatte had suddenly risen to great importance; he was the prime hunter, the hero of the day; offers were made him by the best mounted rangers to let him ride their horses in the chase, provided he would give them a share of the spoil. Beatte bore his honors in silence, and closed with none of the offers. Our stammering, chattering, gasconading little Frenchman, however, made up for his taciturnity by vaunting as much upon the subject as if it were he that had caught the horse. Indeed, he held forth so learnedly in the matter, and boasted so much of the many horses he had taken, that he began to be considered an oracle, and some of the youngsters were inclined to doubt whether he were not superior even to the taciturn Beatte.

The excitement kept the camp awake later than usual. The hum of voices, interrupted by occasional peals of laughter, was heard from the groups around the various fires, and the night was considerably advanced before all had sunk to sleep.

With the morning dawn the excitement revived, and Beatte and his wild horse were again the gaze and talk of the camp. The captive had been tied all night to a tree, among the other horses. He was again led forth by Beatte, by a long halter, or lariat, and, on his manifesting the least restiveness, was, as before, jerked and worried into passive submission. He appeared to be gentle and docile by nature, and had a beautifully mild expression of the eye. In his strange and forlorn situation, the poor animal seemed to seek protection and companionship in the very horse that had aided to capture him.

Seeing him thus gentle and tractable, Beatte, just as we were about to march, strapped a light pack upon his back, by way of giving him the first lesson in servitude. The native pride and independence of the animal took fire at this indignity. He reared, and plunged, and kicked, and tried in every way to get rid of the degrading burden. The Indian was too potent for him. At every paroxysm he renewed the discipline of the halter, until the poor animal, driven to despair, threw himself prostrate on the ground, and lay motionless, as if acknowledging himself vanquished. A stage hero representing the despair of a captive prince could not have played his part more dramatically. There was absolutely a moral grandeur in it.

The imperturbable Beatte folded his arms, and stood for a time looking down in silence upon his captive, until, seeing him perfectly subdued, he nodded his head slowly, screwed his mouth into a sardonic smile of triumph, and, with a jerk of the halter, ordered him to rise. He obeyed, and from that time forward offered no resistance. During that day he bore his pack patiently and was led by the halter; but in two days he followed voluntarily at large among the supernumerary horses of the troop.

I could not but look with compassion upon this fine young animal, whose whole course of existence had been so suddenly reversed. From being a denizen of these vast pastures, ranging at will from plain to plain and mead to mead, cropping of every herb and flower, and drinking of every stream, he was suddenly reduced to perpetual and painful servitude, to pass his life under the harness and the curb, amid, perhaps, the din and dust and drudgery of cities. The transition in his lot was such as sometimes takes place in human affairs, and in the fortunes of towering individuals: one day, a prince of the prairies; the next day, a packhorse!

34

The American Cavalry Horse

By Captain Wilmot E. Ellis

In retrospect 1905 seems late to be writing about the importance of the cavalry horse, but mounted soldiers still had value to an army for a few more years. Captain Wilmot E. Ellis was able to describe the kind of horses needed by the cavalry during the last decades of the nineteenth century, when they offered the only means of battlefield transportation. Ellis was a perfect candidate to provide a look backward. Later in his career junior officers complained to the army's Office of the Inspector General that the then-colonel Ellis was "an old army fossil." He retired soon after, tired of what the army had become—an organization where horses had only ceremonial duties. These are his ideas about the making of a good cavalry horse.

—SHARON B. SMITH

A NATION'S STRENGTH IN WAR DEPENDS NOT ONLY UPON ITS MEN, BUT also upon its horses. Every army needs cavalry and the efficiency of cavalry hinges, to a great extent, upon the quality and quantity of the supply of horses.

The United States has more horses than any other country except Russia, owning about sixteen millions to Russia's twenty-five millions. The animal was first carried to America by the Spaniards early in the sixteenth century. The wild herds which abounded in the Southwest until quite recently were probably the direct descendants of horses abandoned in that region by De Soto and other explorers.

Later colonists brought animals from several European countries. Wherever the settler went, the horse went with him and helped him to subdue the soil, to fight his enemies, and to face the hardships of life in a new world. Naturally, the pioneers' stock was usually poor; but before the Revolution, as the wealth of the colonists increased, the importation of English thoroughbreds had effected a marked improvement in the prevailing types.

Since those days, horse-breeding as an industry has grown with the growth of the country, though like any other industry it has had its ups and downs. At the present time it is prosperous, after surviving some particularly hard knocks.

More than once the prophets have shaken their heads and declared that the days of the horse were numbered. The electric car has driven him from the street railway service—surely a welcome release from an intolerable slavery. The bicycle and the automobile have disputed his possession of the roads, and the traction engine is doing some of his work on the farm. And a few years ago certain military experts, real or pretended, were loudly asserting that even his usefulness in warfare was practically over, for the development of the long-range rifle and the machine gun had rendered cavalry obsolete.

This last prediction was completely falsified during the recent war in South Africa, when the British government found itself compelled to spend several million dollars in buying horses abroad. Its agents found their best and most satisfactory market in the United States. They organized a great depot at Lathrop, Missouri, and their large purchases did much to stimulate the breeding of saddle horses in that and neighboring states.

The demand was increased by the expansion of our own cavalry establishment from ten to fifteen regiments in 1901. Many of the Western breeders are now making a specialty of supplying the cavalry with mounts, and it is gratifying to note that a distinct type of animal, specially adapted to the use of mounted soldiers, is beginning to appear.

Hitherto the United States army has usually purchased its horses by contract made through the quartermaster's department, but the results have not proved entirely satisfactory. The system has proved extravagant, as several middlemen are involved, and the government frequently pays as much as a hundred and twenty-five dollars for a sixty-dollar horse. The last army appropriation bill provides for purchase in open market, and cavalry officers feel that this policy will result in economy to Uncle Sam and an improvement in the quality of mounts. Some foreign war offices, notably that of Austria, conduct their own stock farms. This scheme has been advocated for the United States by prominent cavalry officers, but the experiment has never been tried, principally because it contravenes the time-honored policy that the government should not come into competition with private enterprise.

The horses presented for sale are passed upon by a board, ordinarily composed of an officer of the quartermaster's department, a cavalry officer, and an army veterinarian. The officers pass upon the horses with particular reference to "form," and the animals that they accept are minutely inspected by the veterinarian for soundness. Each horse—technically referred to as a "remount"—successfully passing the scrutiny of the inspectors is branded "U. S." on the left fore shoulder. Later it is branded on the hoof of the near fore foot with the designation of the company to which it is assigned.

The regulation cavalry horse must be a gelding of hardy color, sound and well-bred, gentle under the saddle, free from vicious habits, with free and prompt action at the walk, trot, and gallop, without blemish or defect, of a kind disposition, and with easy mouth and gait. Its height must be between fifteen hands and a quarter and sixteen hands; his weight between nine hundred and fifty and eleven hundred and fifty pounds.

The prescribed age is from four to eight years, but animals under five years are seldom accepted, and the best authorities recommend a minimum age of six years when hard field service is anticipated. There are other more or less technical requirements as to the points of a well-built, hardy, and active saddle horse. These specifications have been summed up in the following maxim: "Many good, few indifferent, no bad points."

It is manifestly out of the question to furnish thoroughbreds for cavalry service, for the supply of suitable ones is limited, the expense would be much greater, and these high-strung, mettlesome animals demand an amount of care quite inconsistent with the exigencies of active field work. Officers—who in our service are required to purchase their own mounts—usually provide themselves with thoroughbred chargers, or at least with very well-bred ones. Just now, however, most cavalry officers of moderate means do not feel disposed to purchase expensive animals, on account of the risk incurred in the Philippine service.

Our government does not reimburse its officers for losses of mounts in time of war, and only under very limited conditions does it repay them in time of peace. The equine mortality in the Philippines has been large. The enervating climate affects horses as well as men, and a disease called *surra* has caused serious loss.

Our two great official centers of instruction in military horseman-ship—besides the cavalry regiments, each of which, of course, is in itself a school of training—are West Point, for cadets, and the Fort Riley Cavalry School, for the younger officers. At both places the instructors are senior officers. In the United States service, civilians have never been employed as riding masters.

There is nothing unduly conservative about the American cavalry instruction, and our officers are keen to avail themselves of all useful nov-elties. For instance, the West Point cadets have taken up the use of the double-reined bridle and the typical hunting and polo saddle. Not long ago, in quest of new ideas, an officer was detailed for a two years' course at the great French cavalry school at Saumur.

There is an analogy, not altogether fanciful, between the experiences of the equine recruit and the soldier recruit, or the "plebe" at West Point. The horse, fresh from the freedom of the ranch, finds himself among strange surroundings. The troop herd to which he is admitted receives him with calm indifference, but to himself it is a matter of such serious import that he is apt to grow feverish and excited in his new environment.

All the horses of a particular troop, as far as practicable, are of the same color, and the newcomer is assigned according to the shade of his coat. He is allowed to run freely with the troop herd in the corral and on the range. During this period he is "sized up" by the old troop horses, and often receives an admonitory kick or bite if inclined to be too frisky.

In order to steady him, he is picketed and stalled with old and gen-tle troop horses as neighbors. He is gradually introduced to the stir and activity of military life, being led by a soldier mounted on a quiet animal through those parts of the post where drills and ceremonies are being held.

The training in the riding school is begun by teaching the horse to take the snaffle bit properly, and to respond to the pressure of the rein on his neck, and to that of his rider's legs. He is next fixed in the regulation gaits of the walk, trot, and gallop, and taught to jump ditches and hurdles. Simultaneously with these exercises he is gradually accustomed to the saber and to the discharge of firearms.

Freedom from fear is not as difficult to acquire as it might seem, for the ordinary horse, if he has not been abused, readily learns to fear nothing except what his memory associates with physical pain. As soon as the horse responds satisfactorily to the snaffle, he is fitted with a curb bit. The curb is the regulation bit of the service, principally because by its use the trooper can manage the horse at all times, employing the left hand alone, with the pressure of the legs as an aid. Bitting is a science in itself, to which the efficient cavalry officer attaches the utmost importance.

The Rarey system plays an important part in the training of the American cavalry horse. It is an elaborate and detailed system formulated before the Civil War by John S. Rarey, a famous American horse-breaker of his day. With slight modifications, it has been embodied in the United States Cavalry Drill Regulations, and is employed to subdue stubborn animals. It is also brought into general use in the latter stages of training, to complete a cavalry charger's education, and to impress upon him once for all that man is master.

One of the most useful of these advanced exercises is the throwing of the horse. The animal is first equipped with the surcingle and watering-bridle. The trooper attaches one end of a long strap to the pastern of the off foreleg, and passes the other end through a ring on the top of the surcingle. The horse's near foreleg is then tied up by means of a short strap. Taking the free end of the long strap in his hand, the soldier places himself opposite the animal's croup on the near side, and urges his mount to step forward. As it does so, the trooper pulls on the long strap, which brings it to its knees. When it ceases to plunge, the trooper leans back on the strap, and the horse will gradually lie down on the near side.

The horse is prevented from rising by passing the reins under the surcingle and pulling his head to the right if he makes any attempt to change his position. Before allowing him to rise, the straps should be removed from his legs. After several repetitions of this exercise, the horse will usually lie down without making it necessary to use the straps.

As a rule, each trooper has his own horse to care for and to ride—an arrangement which leads the soldier to take pride in his charge and to establish that understanding between horse and man which is so essential to cavalry efficiency. It is this mutual confidence which enables our gritty, active cavalrymen to furnish such fine exhibitions of horsemanship and daredevil riding.

These showy exercises, however, are but a small part of cavalry routine. The trooper has to think of discipline and drill, of carbine and revolver practice, of saber exercises; of such practical details as bitting, saddling, packing, feeding, shoeing, and stable management, of the duties of mounted reconnaissance, and of the maintenance of men and horses in the hardy form that has made our records for forced marches unsurpassed in the history of the world. So manifold is his service, and so indispensable is he to an army in the field, that it is easy to understand why all the leading nations of Europe are increasing their mounted forces, and why the American military student views with alarm any proposed reduction of our own modest-sized cavalry establishment.

35

Anecdotes of American Horses

Author Unknown

This affectionate tale of two working horses in western New York dur-
ing the time of the Erie Canal appeared in one of the publications
known as "the knowledge magazines." These were extremely low-
priced compilations of fact-based articles aimed at middle-class read-
ers, products of the expanding public education system. The variety of
topics in the knowledge magazines was breathtaking. The volume that
includes the story of ferry horse Grizzle and farm horse Charlie also
includes a biography of the British spy John Andre, a treatise on the
botany of bogs, an explanation of how to milk a cow, and a reflection
on babyhood. This horse story is typical of the magazines: easy to read,
brief, and intriguing.

—SHARON B. SMITH

A SHORT DISTANCE BELOW FORT ERIE, AND ABOUT A MILE FROM WHERE
the river Niagara escapes over a barrier of rock from the depths of Lake
Erie, a ferry has long been established across that broad and there exceedingly rapid river, the distance from shore to shore being a little over one-
third of a mile. On the Canada side of the river is the small village of
Waterloo, and opposite thereto on the United States side is the large village of Blackrock—distant from the young and flourishing city of Buffalo
two miles.

In completing the Erie Canal, a pier or dam was erected up and down
the river and opposite to Blackrock at no great distance from the shore,

for the purpose of raising the waters of the Niagara to such a height that they might be made to supply an adjoining section of the Erie Canal. This pier was (and is) a great obstruction to the ferryboats; for previous to its erection passengers embarked from *terra-firma* on one side of the river and were landed without any difficulty on the other; but after this dam was constructed it became necessary to employ two sets of boats—one to navigate the river, and the other the basin—so that all passengers, as well as goods or luggage, had to be landed upon this narrow wall or pier, and re-shipped.

Shortly after the erection of the pier-dam, a boat propelled by horses was established between this pier and the Canada shore. The horses moved upon a circular platform which consequently was put in motion, to which other machinery was connected, that acted upon the paddle wheels attached to the sides of the boat. The boat belonged to persons connected with the ferry on the American side of the river; but, owing to the barrier formed by the pier, the horses employed on the boat were stabled at night in the village of Waterloo. I well recollect the first day this boat began to ply, for the introduction of a boat of that description, in those days, and in such a situation, was considered an event of some magnitude.

The two horses (for that boat had but two) worked admirably, considering the very few lessons they had had (upon the treadmill, as it was called) previous to their introduction upon the main river. One of the horses employed on the new ferryboat had once been a dapple gray, but at the period I am speaking of he had become white. He was still hale and hearty, for he had a kind and indulgent master. The first evening after the horses had been a short time in the stable, to which they were strangers, they were brought out for the purpose of being watered at the river, the common custom at this place. The attendant was mounted upon the bay horse—the white one was known to be so gentle and docile that he was allowed to drink where he pleased.

I happened to be standing close by in company with my friend W———n, the ferry contractor on the Canada side, and thus had an opportunity of witnessing the whole proceedings of old Grizzle, the name that the white horse still went by. The moment he got round the corner of the building, so as to have a view of his home on the opposite side, he stopped and gazed intently.

He then advanced to the brink of the river, then he again stopped and looked earnestly across for a short time, then waded into the water until it had reached his chest, drank a little, lifted his head and, with his lips closed, and his eyes fixed upon some object on the farther shore, remained for a short time perfectly motionless.

Apparently having made up his mind to the task, he then waded farther into the river until the water reached his ribs, when off he shot into deep water without a moment's more hesitation. The current being so strong and rapid, the river boiling and turmoiling over a rocky bed at the rate of six miles the hour, it was impossible for the courageous and attached animal to keep a direct course across, although he breasted the waves heroically, and swam with remarkable vigor.

Had he been able to steer his way directly across, the pier wall would have proved an insurmountable barrier. As it was, the strength of the current forced him down to below where the lower extremity of this long pier abuts upon an island, the shore of which being low and shelving, he was enabled to effect a landing with comparative ease. Having regained *terra-firma*, he shook the water from his dripping flanks, but he did not halt over a few minutes, when he plunged into the basin and soon regained his native shore.

The distance from where Grizzle took the water to where he effected a landing on the island was about seven hundred yards; but the efforts made to swim directly across, against the powerful current, must have rendered the undertaking a much more laborious one. At the commencement of his voyage, his arched neck and withers were above the surface, but before he reached the island nothing but his head was visible to us.

He reached his own stable door, that home for which he had risked so much, to the no small astonishment of his owner. This unexpected visit evidently made a favorable impression upon his master, for he was heard to vow that if old Grizzle performed the same feat a second time, for the future he should remain on his own side of the river and never be sent to the mill again. Grizzle was sent back to work the boat on the following day, but he embraced the very first opportunity that occurred of escaping, swam back in the way he had done before, and his owner, not being a person to break the promise he had once made, never afterwards dispossessed him of the stall he had long been accustomed to, but treated him with marked kindness and attention.

During my residence on the headwaters of the Susquehanna, I owned a small American horse of the name of Charlie that was very remarkable for his attachment to my own person, as well as for his general good qualities. He was a great favorite with all the family; and being a favorite, he was frequently indulged with less work and more to eat than any of the other horses on the farm.

At a short distance from the dwelling-house was a small but luxuriant pasture, where, during the summer, Charlie was often permitted to graze. When this pasture had been originally reclaimed from its wild forest state, about ten years previous to the period of which I am speaking, four or five large trees of the sugar maple species had been left standing when the rest were cut down, and means had afterwards been found to prevent their being scorched by the fire at the time the rest of the timber had been consumed. Though remarkably fine trees of their kind, they were, however, no great ornament, their stems being long and bare, their heads small and by no means full of leaves, the case generally with trees that have grown up in close contact with each other in the American forests. But if they were no ornament, they might serve as shade-trees.

Beneath one of these trees Charlie used to seek shelter, as well from the heat of the meridian sun, as from the severe thunder gusts that occasionally ravage that part of the country. On an occasion of this sort Charlie had taken his stand close to his favorite tree, his tail actually pressing against it, his head and body in an exact line with the course of the wind; apparently understanding the most advantageous position to escape the violence of the storm, and quite at home, as it were, for he had stood in the same place some scores of times.

The storm came on and raged with such violence that the tree under which the horse had taken shelter was literally torn up by the roots. I happened to be standing at a window from whence I witnessed the whole scene. The moment Charlie heard the roots giving way behind him, that is, on the contrary side of the tree from where he stood, and probably feeling the uprooted tree pressing against his tail, he sprang forward and barely cleared the ground upon which, at the next moment, the top of the huge forest tree fell with such a force that the crash was tremendous, for every limb and branch were actually riven asunder.

I have many a time seen horses alarmed, nay, exceedingly frightened; but never in my life did I witness any thing of the sort that bore the slightest comparison to Charlie's extreme terror; and yet Charlie, on ordinary occasions, was by no means a coward. He galloped, he reared his mane and tossed his head, he stopped short and snorted wildly, and then he darted off at the top of his speed in a contrary direction, and then as suddenly stopped and set off in another, until long after the storm had considerably abated, and it was not until after the lapse of some hours that he ventured to reconnoiter—but that at a considerable distance—the scene of his narrow escape.

For that day at least his appetite had been completely spoiled, for he never offered to stoop his head to the ground while daylight continued. The next day his apprehension seemed somewhat abated, but his curiosity had been excited to such a pitch that he kept pacing from place to place, never sailing to halt as he passed within a moderate distance of the prostrate tree, gazing thereat in utter bewilderment, as if wholly unable to comprehend the scene he had witnessed the preceding day.

After this occurrence took place I kept this favorite horse several years, and during the summer months he usually enjoyed the benefit of his old pasture. But it was quite clear that he never forgot, on any occasion, the narrow escape he had had; for neither the burning rays of the noontide summer sun, nor the furious raging of the thunderstorm, could compel Charlie to seek shelter under one of the trees that still remained standing in his small pasture.

36

The Cumbersome Horse

By H. C. Bunner

Henry Cuyler Bunner was probably best known as an editor of Puck
Magazine, *a publication that managed to find humor in politics. But
he was also a poet, a novelist, and an author of short stories.*

*Bunner specialized in ironic takes on life in Manhattan, a world
in which horses rarely figured. But one of his best-known works was
the story of an old farm horse who insisted that a promise be kept, no
matter how inconvenient.*

—SHARON B. SMITH

IT IS NOT TO BE DENIED THAT A SENSE OF DISAPPOINTMENT PERVADED
Mr. Brimmington's being in the hour of his first acquaintance with the
isolated farmhouse which he had just purchased, sight unseen, after long
epistolary negotiations with Mr. Hiram Skinner, postmaster, carpenter,
teamster, and real estate agent of Bethel Corners, who was now driving
him to his new domain.

Perhaps the feeling was of a mixed origin. Indian Summer was much
colder up in the Pennsylvania hills than he had expected to find it; and
the hills themselves were much larger and bleaker and barer, and far more
indifferent in their demeanor toward him, than he had expected to find
them. Then Mr. Skinner had been something of a disappointment, himself. He was too familiar with his big, knobby, red hands; too furtive with
his small, close-set eyes; too profuse of tobacco-juice, and too raspingly
loquacious. And certainly the house itself did not meet his expectations

when he first saw it, standing lonely and desolate in its ragged meadows of stubble and wild grass on the unpleasantly steep mountainside.

And yet Mr. Skinner had accomplished for him the desire of his heart. He had always said that when he should come into his money—forty thousand dollars from a maiden aunt—he would quit forever his toilsome job of preparing Young Gentlemen for admission to the Larger Colleges and Universities, and would devote the next few years to writing his long-projected "History of Prehistoric Man." And to go about this task he had always said that he would go and live in perfect solitude—that is, all by himself and a chore-woman—in a secluded farmhouse, situated upon the southerly slope of some high hill; an old farmhouse—a Revolutionary farmhouse, if possible—a delightful, long, low, rambling farmhouse; a farmhouse with floors of various levels—a farmhouse with crooked stairs, and with nooks and corners and quaint cupboards—this—this had been the desire of Mr. Brimmington's heart.

Mr. Brimmington, when he came into his money at the age of forty-five, fixed on Pike County, Pennsylvania, as a mountainous country of good report. A postal guide informed him that Mr. Skinner was the postmaster of Bethel Corners; so Mr. Brimmington wrote to Mr. Skinner.

The correspondence between Mr. Brimmington and Mr. Skinner was long enough and full enough to have settled a treaty between two nations. It ended by a discovery of a house lonely enough and aged enough to fill the bill. Several hundred dollars' worth of repairs were needed to make it habitable, and Mr. Skinner was employed to make them. Toward the close of a cold November day, Mr. Brimmington saw his purchase for the first time.

In spite of his disappointment, he had to admit, as he walked around the place in the early twilight, that it was just what he had bargained for. The situation, the dimensions, the exposure, were all exactly what had been stipulated. About its age there could be no question. Internally, its irregularity—indeed, its utter failure to conform to any known rules of domestic architecture—surpassed Mr. Brimmington's wildest expectations. It had stairs eighteen inches wide; it had rooms of strange shapes and sizes; it had strange, shallow cupboards in strange places; it had no hallways; its windows were of odd design, and whoso wanted variety in floors could find it there. And along the main wall of Mr. Brimmington's study there ran a structure some three feet and a half high and nearly as deep, which Mr. Skinner confidently assured him was used in old times as a wall bench or a dresser, indifferently.

"You might think," said Mr. Skinner, "that all that space inside there was jest wasted; but it ain't so. Them seats is jest filled up inside with braces so's that you can set on them good and solid." And then Mr. Skinner proudly called attention to the two coats of gray paint spread over the entire side of the house, walls, ceilings and woodwork, blending the original portions and the Skinner restorations in one harmonious, homogeneous whole.

Mr. Skinner might have told him that this variety of gray paint is highly popular in some rural districts, and is made by mixing lamp-black and ball-blue with a low grade of white lead. But he did not say it; and he drove away as soon as he conveniently could, after formally introducing him to Mrs. Sparhawk, a gaunt, stern-faced, silent, elderly woman. Mrs. Sparhawk was to take charge of his bachelor establishment during the daytime. Mrs. Sparhawk cooked him a meal for which she very properly apologized. Then she returned to her kitchen to "clean up." Mr. Brimmington went to the front door, partly to look out upon his property, and partly to turn his back on the gray paint. There were no steps before the front door, but a newly graded mound or earthwork about the size of a half-hogshead. He looked out upon his apple-orchard, which was further away than he had expected to find it. It had been out of bearing for ten years, but this Mr. Brimmington did not know. He did know, however, that the whole outlook was distinctly dreary.

As he stood there and gazed out into the twilight, two forms suddenly approached him. Around one corner of the house came Mrs. Sparhawk on her way home. Around the other came an immensely tall, whitish shape, lumbering forward with a heavy tread. Before he knew it, it had scrambled up the side of his mound with a clumsy, ponderous rush, and was thrusting itself directly upon him when he uttered so lusty a cry of dismay that it fell back startled; and, wheeling about a great long body that swayed on four misshapen legs, it pounded off in the direction it had come from, and disappeared around the corner. Mr. Brimmington turned to Mrs. Sparhawk in disquiet and indignation.

"Mrs. Sparhawk," he demanded; "what is that?"

"It's a horse," said Mrs. Sparhawk, not at all surprised, for she knew that Mr. Brimmington was from the city. "They hitch 'em to wagons here."

"I know it is a horse, Mrs. Sparhawk," Mr. Brimmington rejoined with some asperity, "but whose horse is it, and what is it doing on my premises?"

"I don't rightly know whose horse it *is*," replied Mrs. Sparhawk; "the man that used to own it, he's dead now."

"But what," inquired Mr. Brimmington sternly, "is the animal doing here?"

"I guess he b'longs here," Mrs. Sparhawk said. She had a cold, even, impersonal way of speaking, as though she felt that her safest course in life was to confine herself strictly to such statements of fact as might be absolutely required of her.

"But, my good woman," replied Mr. Brimmington, in bewilderment, "how can that be? The animal can't certainly belong on my property unless he belongs to me, and that animal certainly is not mine."

Seeing him so much at a loss and so greatly disturbed in mind, Mrs. Sparhawk relented a little from her strict rule of life, and made an attempt at explanation. "He b'longed to the man who owned this place first off; and I don' know for sure, but I've heard tell that he fixed it some way so's that the horse would sort of go with the place."

Mr. Brimmington felt irritation rising within him. "But," he said, "it's preposterous! There was no such consideration in the deed. No such thing can be done, Mrs. Sparhawk, without my acquiescence!"

"I don't know nothin' about that," said Mrs. Sparhawk; "what I do know is, the place has changed hands often enough since, and the horse has always went with the place."

There was an unsettled suggestion in the first part of this statement of Mrs. Sparhawk that gave a shock to Mr. Brimmington's nerves. He laughed uneasily.

"Oh, er, yes! I see. Very probably there's been some understanding. I suppose I am to regard the horse as a sort of lien upon the place—a—what do they call it?—an encumbrance. Yes," he repeated, more to himself than to Mrs. Sparhawk, "an encumbrance. I've got a gentleman's country place with a horse encumbrant."

Mrs. Sparhawk heard him, however. "It *is* a sorter cumbersome horse," she said. And without another word she gathered her shawl about her shoulders, and strode off into the darkness.

Mr. Brimmington turned back into the house, and busied himself with a vain attempt to make his long-cherished furniture look at home in his new leaden-hued rooms. The ungrateful task gave him the blues and, after an hour of it, he went to bed.

He was dreaming leaden-hued dreams, oppressed, uncomfortable dreams, when a peculiarly weird and uncanny series of thumps on the front of the house awoke him with a start. The thumps might have been made by a giant with a weaver's beam, but he must have been a very drunken giant to group his thumps in such a disorderly parody of time and sequence.

Mr. Brimmington had too guileless and clean a heart to be the prey of undefined terrors. He rose, ran to the window and opened it. The moonlight lit up the raw, frosty landscape with a cold, pale, diffused radiance, and Mr. Brimmington could plainly see right below him the cumbersome horse, cumbersomely trying to maintain a footing on the top of the little mound before the front door. When, for a fleeting instant, he seemed to think that he had succeeded in this feat, he tried to bolt through the door. As soon, however, as one of his huge knees smote the panel, his hind feet lost their grip on the soft earth, and he wobbled back down the incline, where he stood shaking and quivering, until he could muster wind enough for another attempt to make a catapult of himself. The veil-like illumination of the night, which turned all things else to a dim, silvery gray, could not hide the scars and bruises and worn places that spotted the animal's great, gaunt, distorted frame. His knees were as big as a man's head. His feet were enormous. His joints stood out from his shriveled carcass like so many pine knots. Mr. Brimmington gazed at him, fascinated, horrified, until a rush more desperate and uncertain than the rest threatened to break his front door in.

"Hi!" shrieked Mr. Brimmington; "go away!"

It was the horse's turn to get frightened. He lifted his long, coffin-shaped head toward Mr. Brimmington's window, cast a sort of blind, cross-eyed, ineffectual glance at him, and with a long-drawn, wheezing, cough-choked whinny he backed down the mound, got himself about, end for end, with such extreme awkwardness that he hurt one poor knee on a hitching post that looked to be ten feet out of his way, and limped off to the rear of the house.

The sound of that awful, rusty, wind-broken whinny haunted Mr. Brimmington all the rest of that night. It was like the sound of an orchestra run down, or of a man who is utterly tired of the whooping cough and doesn't care who knows it.

The next morning was bright and sunshiny, and Mr. Brimmington awoke in a more cheerful frame of mind than he would naturally have expected to find himself in after his perturbed night. He found himself inclined to make the best of his purchase and to view it in as favorable a light as possible. He went outside and looked at it from various points of view, trying to find and if possible to dispose of the reason for the vague sense of disappointment which he felt, having come into possession of the rambling old farmhouse, which he had so much desired.

He decided, after a long and careful inspection, that it was the *proportions* of the house that were wrong. They were certainly peculiar. It was singularly high between joints in the first story, and singularly low in the second. In spite of its irregularity within, it was uncompromisingly square on the outside. There was something queer about the pitch of its roof, and it seemed strange that so modest a structure with no hallway whatever should have vestibule windows on each side of its doors, both front and rear.

But here an idea flashed into Mr. Brimmington's mind that in an instant changed him from a carping critic to a delighted discoverer. He was living in a Block House! Yes; that explained—that accounted for all the strangeness of its architecture. In an instant he found his purchase invested with a beautiful glamour of adventurous association. Here was the stout and well-planned refuge to which the grave settlers of an earlier day had fled to guard themselves against the attack of the vindictive redskins. He saw it all. A moat, crossed no doubt by drawbridges, had surrounded the building. In the main room below, the women and children had huddled while their courageous defenders had poured a leaden hail upon the foe through loopholes in the upper story. He walked around the house for some time, looking for loopholes.

So pleased was Mr. Brimmington at his theory that the morning passed rapidly away, and when he looked at his watch he was surprised to find that it was nearly noon. Then he remembered that Mr. Skinner had promised to call on him at eleven, to make anything right that was not right. Glancing over the landscape he saw Mr. Skinner approaching by a circuitous track. He was apparently following the course of a snake fence, which he could readily have climbed. This seemed strange, as his way across the pastureland was seemingly unimpeded. Thinking of the pastureland made Mr. Brimmington think of the white horse, and casting his eyes a little further down the hill he saw that animal slowly and painfully steering a parallel course to Mr. Skinner, on the other side of the fence. Mr. Skinner went out of sight behind a clump of trees, and when he arrived it was not upon the side of the house where Mr. Brimmington had expected to see him appear.

As they were about to enter the house Mr. Brimmington noticed the marks of last night's attack upon his front door, and he spoke to Mr. Skinner about the horse.

"Oh, yes," said Mr. Skinner, with much ingenuousness; "that horse. I was meaning to speak to you about that horse. Fact is, I've kinder got that horse on my hands, and if it's no inconvenience to you, I'd like to leave him where he is for a little while."

"But it would be very inconvenient, indeed, Mr. Skinner," said the new owner of the house. "The animal is a very unpleasant object; and, moreover, it attempted to break into my front door last night."

Mr. Skinner's face darkened. "Sho!" he said; "you don't mean to tell me that?"

But Mr. Brimmington did mean to tell him that, and Mr. Skinner listened with a scowl of unconcealed perplexity and annoyance. He bit his lip reflectively for a minute or two before he spoke.

"Too bad you was disturbed," he said at length. "You'll have to keep the bars up to that meadow and then it won't happen again."

"But, indeed, it must not happen again," said Mr. Brimmington. "The horse must be taken away."

"Well, you see it's this way, friend," returned Mr. Skinner, with a rather ugly air of decision. "I really ain't got no choice in the matter. I'd like to oblige you, and if I'd known as far back that you would have objected to the animal I'd have had him took somewheres. But, as it is, there ain't no such a thing as getting that there horse off this here place till the frost's out of the ground. You can see for yourself that that horse, the condition he's in now, couldn't no more go up nor down this hill than he could fly. Why, I came over here a-foot this morning on purpose not to take them horses of mine over this road again. It can't be done, sir."

"Very well," suggested Mr. Brimmington. "Kill the horse."

"I ain't killin' no horses," said Mr. Skinner. "You may if you like; but I'd advise you not to. There's them as mightn't like it."

"Well, let them come and take their horse away, then," said Mr. Brimmington.

"Just so," assented Mr. Skinner. "It's they who are concerned in the horse, and they have a right to take him away. I would if I was any ways concerned, but I ain't." Here he turned suddenly upon Mr. Brimmington.

"Why, look here," he said, "you ain't got the heart to turn that there horse out of that there pasture where he's been for fifteen years! It won't do you no sorter hurt to have him stay there till spring. Put the bars up, and he won't trouble you no more."

"But," objected Mr. Brimmington, weakly, "even if the poor creature were not so unsightly, he could not be left alone all winter in that pasture without shelter."

"That's just where you're mistaken," Mr. Skinner replied, tapping his interlocutor heavily upon the shoulder. "He don't mind it not one mite. See that shed there?" And he pointed to a few wind-racked boards in the corner of the lot. "There's hoss-shelter; and as for feed, why there's feed enough in that meadow for two such as him."

In the end, Mr. Brimmington, being utterly ignorant of the nature and needs of horseflesh, was over-persuaded, and he consented to let the unfortunate white horse remain in his pasture lot to be the sport of the winter's chill and bitter cruelty. Then he and Mr. Skinner talked about some new paint.

It was the dead vast and middle of Mr. Brimmington's third night in his new house, when he was absolutely knocked out of a calm and peaceful slumber by a crash so appalling that he at first thought that the side of the mountain had slid down upon his dwelling. This was followed by other crashes, thumps, the tearing of woodwork and various strange and gruesome noises. Whatever it might be, Mr. Brimmington felt certain that it was no secret midnight marauder, and he hastened to the eighteen-inch stairway without even waiting to put on a dressing gown. A rush of cold air came up from below, and he had no choice but to scuttle back for a bathrobe and a candle while the noises continued, and the cold air floated all over the house.

There was no difficulty in locating the sounds. Mr. Brimmington presented himself at the door of the little kitchen, pulled it open, and, raising the light above his head, looked in. The rush of wind blew out his light, but not before he had had time to see that it was the white horse that was in the kitchen, and that he had gone through the floor.

Subsequent investigation proved that the horse had come in through the back door, carrying that and its two vestibule windows with him, and that he had first trampled and then churned the thin floor into matchwood. He was now reposing on his stomach, with his legs hanging down between the joists into the hollow under the house—for there was no cellar. He looked over his shoulder at his host and emitted his bloodcurdling wail.

"My gracious!" said Mr. Brimmington.

That night Mr. Brimmington sat up with the horse, both of them wrapped, as well as Mr. Brimmington could do it, in bedclothes. There is not much you can do with a horse when you have to sit up with him under such circumstances. The thought crossed Mr. Brimmington's mind of reading to him, but he dismissed it.

In the interview the next day, between Mr. Brimmington and Mr. Skinner, the aggressiveness was all on Mr. Brimmington's side, and Mr. Skinner was meek and wore an anxious expression. Mr. Brimmington had, however, changed his point of view. He now realized that sleeping out of winter nights might be unpleasant, even painful to an aged and rheumatic horse. And, although he had cause of legitimate complaint against the creature, he could no longer bear to think of killing the animal with whom he had shared that cold and silent vigil.

He commissioned Mr. Skinner to build for the brute a small but commodious lodging, and to provide a proper stock of provender—commissions which Mr. Skinner gladly and humbly accepted. As to the undertaking to get the horse out of his immediate predicament, however, Mr. Skinner absolutely refused to touch the job.

"That horse don't like me," said Mr. Skinner; "I know he don't; I seen it in his eyes long ago. If you like, I'll send you two or three men and a block-and-tackle, and they can get him out; but not me; no, sir!"

Mr. Skinner devoted that day to repairing damages, and promised on the morrow to begin the building of the little barn. Mr. Brimmington was glad there was going to be no greater delay, when, early in the evening, the sociable white horse tried to put his front feet through the study window.

But of all the noises that startled Mr. Brimmington, in the first week of his sojourn in the farmhouse, the most alarming awakened him about eight o'clock of the following morning. Hurrying to his study, he gazed in wonder upon a scene unparalleled even in the History of Prehistoric Man. The boards had been ripped off the curious structure which was supposed to have served the hardy settlers for a wall bench and a dresser, indifferently.

This revealed another structure in the form of a long crib or bin, within which, apparently trying to back out through the wall, stood Mr. Skinner, holding his toolbox in front of him as if to shield himself, and fairly yelping with terror. The front door was off its hinges, and there stood Mrs. Sparhawk wielding a broom to keep out the white horse, who was viciously trying to force an entrance. Mr. Brimmington asked what it all meant; and Mrs. Sparhawk, turning a desperate face upon him, spoke with the vigor of a woman who has kept silence too long.

"It means," she said, "that this here house of yours is this here horse's stable; *and the horse knows it*; and that there was the horse's manger. This here horse was old Colonel Josh Pincus's regimental horse, and so provided for in his will; and this here man Skinner was to have the caring of him until he should die a natural death, and then he was to have this stable; and till then the stable was left to the horse. And now he's taken the stable away from the horse, and patched it up into a dwelling-house for a fool from New York City; and the horse don't like it; and the horse don't like Skinner. And when he come back to git that manger for your barn, the horse sot onto him. And that's what's the matter, Mr. Skimmerton."

"Mrs. Sparhawk," began Mr. Brimmington—

"I *ain't* no Sparhawk!" fairly shouted the enraged woman, as with a furious shove she sent the Cumbersome Horse staggering down the doorway mound; "this here's Hiram Skinner, the meanest man in Pike County, and I'm his wife, let out to do day's work. You've had one week of him—how would you have liked twenty years?"

37

Chu Chu

By Bret Harte

‹‹

Bret Harte, born Francis Brett Harte in Albany, New York, in 1836, was one of the most famous writers in North America during the last quarter of the nineteenth century. Magazines paid the unheard of sum of $1,000 each for some of his colorful short stories of life in the rowdy mining camps and isolated ranches of California. Harte came by the color honestly, having worked in the gold camps, as a guard on a stage-coach line, and as a reporter and editor for several Western newspapers.

Bret Harte had great affection for both horses and Californios, the descendants of the aristocratic Spanish settlers of the early part of the nineteenth century. Both are featured in "Chu Chu," the story of a beautiful wild mare who was never quite tamed.

—SHARON B. SMITH

‹‹

I DO NOT BELIEVE THAT THE MOST ENTHUSIASTIC LOVER OF THAT "USE-ful and noble animal," the horse, will claim for him the charm of geniality, humor, or expansive confidence. Any creature who will not look you squarely in the eye, whose only oblique glances are inspired by fear, distrust, or a view to attack; who has no way of returning caresses, and whose favorite expression is one of head-lifting disdain, may be "noble" or "useful," but can be hardly said to add to the gaiety of nations. Indeed, it may be broadly stated that, with the single exception of goldfish, of all animals kept for the recreation of mankind the horse is alone capable of exciting a passion that shall be absolutely hopeless. I deem these general remarks

444

necessary to prove that my unreciprocated affection for Chu Chu was not purely individual or singular. And I may add that to these general characteristics she brought the waywardness of her capricious sex.

She came to me out of the rolling dust of an emigrant wagon, behind whose tailboard she was gravely trotting. She was a half-broken filly in which character she had at different times unseated everybody in the train and, although covered with dust, she had a beautiful coat and the most lambent gazelle-like eyes I had ever seen. I think she kept these latter organs purely for ornament, apparently looking at things with her nose, her sensitive ears, and, sometimes, even a slight lifting of her slim near foreleg. On our first interview I thought she favored me with a coy glance, but as it was accompanied by an irrelevant "Look out!" from her owner, the teamster, I was not certain.

I only know that after some conversation, a good deal of mental reservation, and the disbursement of considerable coin, I found myself standing in the dust of the departing emigrant wagon with one end of a forty-foot riata in my hand, and Chu Chu at the other. I pulled invitingly at my own end, and even advanced a step or two towards her. She then broke into a long disdainful pace, and began to circle round me at the extreme limit of her tether. I stood admiring her free action for some moments, not always turning with her, which was tiring until I found that she was gradually winding herself up on me.

Her frantic astonishment when she suddenly found herself thus brought up against me was one of the most remarkable things I ever saw and nearly took me off my legs. Then, when she had pulled against the riata until her narrow head and prettily arched neck were on a perfectly straight line with it, she as suddenly slackened the tension and condescended to follow me, at an angle of her own choosing. Sometimes it was on one side of me, sometimes on the other.

Even then the sense of my dreadful contiguity apparently would come upon her like a fresh discovery, and she would become hysterical. But I do not think that she really saw me. She looked at the riata and sniffed it disparagingly; she pawed some pebbles that were near me tentatively with her small hoof; she started back with a Robinson Crusoe–like horror of my footprints in the wet gully, but my actual personal presence she ignored. She would sometimes pause, with her head thoughtfully between her forelegs, and apparently say: "There is some extraordinary presence here: animal, vegetable, or mineral I can't make out which but it's not good to eat, and I loathe and detest it."

When I reached my house in the suburbs, before entering the "fifty vara" lot enclosure, I deemed it prudent to leave her outside while I informed the household of my purchase, and with this object I tethered her by the long riata to a solitary sycamore which stood in the center of the road, the crossing of two frequented thoroughfares. It was not long, however, before I was interrupted by shouts and screams from that vicinity, and on returning thither I found that Chu Chu, with the assistance of her riata, had securely wound up two of my neighbors to the tree, where they presented the appearance of early Christian martyrs. When I released them it appeared that they had been attracted by Chu Chu's graces, and had offered her overtures of affection, to which she had characteristically rotated, with this miserable result.

I led her, with some difficulty, warily keeping clear of the riata, to the enclosure from whose fence I had previously removed several bars. Although the space was wide enough to have admitted a troop of cavalry she affected not to notice it, and managed to kick away part of another section on entering. She resisted the stable for some time, but after carefully examining it with her hoofs and an affectedly meek outstretching of her nose, she consented to recognize some oats in the feed-box without looking at them and was formally installed. All this while she had resolutely ignored my presence. As I stood watching her she suddenly stopped eating; the same reflective look came over her.

"Surely I am not mistaken, but that same obnoxious creature is somewhere about here," she seemed to say, and shivered at the possibility.

It was probably this which made me confide my unreciprocated affection to one of my neighbors, a man supposed to be an authority on horses, and particularly of that wild species to which Chu Chu belonged. It was he who, leaning over the edge of the stall where she was complacently and, as usual, obliviously munching, absolutely dared to toy with a pet lock of hair which she wore over the pretty star on her forehead.

"Ye see, Captain," he said, with jaunty easiness, "Hosses is like women; ye don't want ter use any standoffishness or shyness with them; a steady but careless sort o' familiarity, a kind o' free but firm handlin', just like this, to let her see who's master."

We never clearly knew how it happened, but when I picked up my neighbor from the doorway, amid the broken splinters of the stall rail, and a quantity of oats that mysteriously filled his hair and pockets, Chu Chu was found to have faced around the other way, and was contemplating her forelegs, with her hind ones in the other stall.

My neighbor spoke of damages while he was in the stall, and of physical coercion when he was out of it again. But here Chu Chu, in some marvelous way, righted herself, and my neighbor departed hurriedly with a brimless hat and an unfinished sentence.

My next intermediary was Enriquez Saltello, a youth of my own age, and the brother of Consuelo Saltello, whom I adored. As a Spanish Californian he was presumed, on account of Chu Chu's half-Spanish origin, to have superior knowledge of her character, and I even vaguely believed that his language and accent would fall familiarly on her ear. There was the drawback, however, that he always preferred to talk in a marvelous English, combining Castilian precision with what he fondly believed to be California slang.

"To confer then as to this horse, which is not observe me a Mexican plug! Ah, no! you can your boots bet on that. She is of Castilian stock, believe me, and strike me dead! I will myself at different times overlook and affront her in the stable, examine her as to the assault, and why she should do this thing. When she is of the exercise I will also accost and restrain her. Remain tranquil, my friend! When a few days shall pass much shall be changed, and she will be as another. Trust your uncle to do this thing! Comprehend me? Everything shall be lovely, and the goose hang high!"

Conformably with this he "overlooked" her the next day, with a cigarette between his yellow-stained finger tips, which made her sneeze in a silent pantomimic way, and certain Spanish blandishments of speech, which she received with more complacency. But I don't think she ever even looked at him. In vain he protested that she was the "dearest" and "littlest" of his "little loves"; in vain he asserted that she was his patron saint and that it was his soul's delight to pray to her; she accepted the compliment with her eyes fixed upon the manger. When he had exhausted his whole stock of endearing diminutives, adding a few playful and more audacious sallies, she remained with her head down, as if inclined to meditate upon them. This he declared was at least an improvement on her former performances. It may have been my own jealousy, but I fancied she was only saying to herself, "Gracious! can there be two of them?"

"Courage and patience, my friend," he said, as we were slowly quitting the stable. "This horse is young and has not yet the habitude of the person. Tomorrow, at another season, I shall give to her a foundling ('fondling,' I have reason to believe, was the word intended by Enriquez) and we shall see. It shall be as easy as to fall away from a log. A little more of this chin music which your friend Enriquez possesses, and some tapping of the head and neck, and you are there. You are ever the right side up. Houpla! But let us not precipitate this thing. The more haste, we do not so much accelerate ourselves." He appeared to be suiting the action to the word as he lingered in the doorway of the stable.

"Come on," I said.

"Pardon," he returned, with a bow that was both elaborate and evasive, "but you shall yourself precede me. The stable is yours."

"Oh, come along!" I continued, impatiently. To my surprise he seemed to dodge back into the stable again. After an instant he reappeared.

"Pardon! But I am restrain! Of a truth, in this instant I am grasp by the mouth of this horse in the coattail of my dress! She will that I should remain. It would seem"—he disappeared again—"that"—he was out once more—"the experiment is a success! She reciprocate. She is, of a truth, gone on me. It is love!"

A stronger pull from Chu Chu here sent him in again but he was out now triumphantly with half his garment torn away. "I shall coquet."

Nothing daunted, however, the gallant fellow was back next day with a Mexican saddle and attired in the complete outfit of a *vaquero*. Overcome though he was by heavy deerskin trousers, open at the side from the knees down, and fringed with bullion buttons, an enormous flat sombrero and a stiff, short, embroidered velvet jacket, I was more concerned at the ponderous saddle and equipments intended for the slim Chu Chu. That these would hide and conceal her beautiful curves and contour, as well as overweight her, seemed certain; that she would resist them all to the last seemed equally clear.

Nevertheless, to my surprise, when she was led out, and the saddle thrown deftly across her back, she was passive. Was it possible that some drop of her old Spanish blood responded to its clinging embrace? She did not either look at it or smell it. But when Enriquez began to tighten the "cinch" or girth a more singular thing occurred. Chu Chu visibly distended her slender barrel to twice its dimensions; the more he pulled the more she swelled, until I was actually ashamed of her. Not so Enriquez. He smiled at us, and complacently stroked his thin moustache.

"It is ever so! She is the child of her grandmother! Even when you shall make saddle this old Castilian stock, it will make large. It will become a balloon! It is a trick. It is a little game believe me. For why?"

I had not listened, as I was at that moment astonished to see the saddle slowly slide under Chu Chu's belly, and her figure resume, as if by magic, its former slim proportions. Enriquez followed my eyes, lifted his shoulders, shrugged them, and said smilingly, "Ah, you see!"

When the girths were drawn in again with an extra pull or two from the indefatigable Enriquez, I fancied that Chu Chu nevertheless secretly enjoyed it, as her sex is said to appreciate tight lacing. She drew a deep sigh, possibly of satisfaction, turned her neck, and apparently tried to glance at her own figure—Enriquez promptly withdrawing to enable her to do so easily. Then the dread moment arrived. Enriquez, with his hand on her mane, suddenly paused, and with exaggerated courtesy lifted his hat and made an inviting gesture.

"You will honor me to precede."

I shook my head laughingly.

"I see," responded Enriquez, gravely. "You have to attend the obsequies of your aunt, who is dead, at two of the clock. You have to meet your broker, who has bought you fifty share of the Comstock Lode at this moment or you are loss! You are excuse! Attend! Gentlemen, make your bets! The band has arrived to play! Here we are!"

With a quick movement the alert young fellow had vaulted into the saddle. But, to the astonishment of both of us, the mare remained perfectly still. There was Enriquez, bolt upright in the stirrups, completely overshadowing, by his saddle-flaps, leggings, and gigantic spurs, the fine proportions of Chu Chu, until she might have been a placid Rosinante, bestridden by some youthful Quixote. She closed her eyes; she was going to sleep! We were dreadfully disappointed. This clearly would not do. Enriquez lifted the reins cautiously! Chu Chu moved forward slowly— then stopped, apparently lost in reflection.

"Affront her on this side."

I approached her gently. She shot suddenly into the air, coming down again on perfectly stiff legs with a springless jolt. This she instantly followed by a succession of other rocket-like propulsions, utterly unlike a leap, all over the enclosure. The movements of the unfortunate Enriquez were equally unlike any equitation I ever saw. He appeared occasionally over Chu Chu's head, astride of her neck and tail, or in the free air, but never in the saddle. His rigid legs, however, never lost the stirrups but came down regularly, accentuating her springless hops. More than that, the disproportionate excess of rider, saddle, and accoutrements was so great that he had at times the appearance of lifting Chu Chu forcibly from the ground by superior strength, and of actually contributing to her exercise.

As they came towards me, a wild, tossing, and flying mass of hoofs and spurs, it was not only difficult to distinguish them apart, but to ascertain how much of the jumping was done by Enriquez separately. At last Chu Chu brought matters to a close by making for the low-stretching branches of an oak tree which stood at the corner of the lot. In a few moments she emerged from it—but without Enriquez!

I found the gallant fellow disengaging himself from the fork of a branch in which he had been firmly wedged, but still smiling and confident, and his cigarette between his teeth. Then for the first time he removed it, and seating himself easily on the branch with his legs dangling down, he blandly waved aside my anxious queries with a gentle reassuring gesture.

"Remain tranquil, my friend. This does not count! I have conquer—you observe—for why? I have never for once arrive at the ground! Consequent she is disappoint! She will ever that I should! But I have got her when the hair is not long! Your uncle Henry"—with an angelic wink—"is fly! He is ever a bully boy, with the eye of glass! Believe me. Behold! I am here! Big Injun! Whoop!"

He leaped lightly to the ground. Chu Chu, standing watchfully at a little distance, was evidently astonished at his appearance. She threw out her hind hoofs violently, shot up into the air until the stirrups crossed each other high above the saddle, and made for the stable in a succession of rabbit-like bounds, taking the precaution to remove the saddle on entering by striking it against the lintel of the door.

"You observe," said Enriquez, blandly, "she would make that thing of *me*. Not having the good occasion, she is dissatisfied. Where are you now?"

Two or three days afterwards he rode her again with the same result—accepted by him with the same heroic complacency. As we did not, for certain reasons, care to use the open road for this exercise, and as it was impossible to remove the tree, we were obliged to submit to the inevitable. On the following day I mounted her—undergoing the same experience as Enriquez, with the individual sensation of falling from a third-story window on top of a counting-house stool, and the variation of being projected over the fence. When I found that Chu Chu had not accompanied me, I saw Enriquez at my side.

"More than ever it is become necessary that we should do this thing again," he said, gravely, as he assisted me to my feet. "Courage, my noble General! God and Liberty! Once more on to the breach! Charge, Chestare, charge! Come on, Don Stanley! 'Ere we are!"

He helped me none too quickly to catch my seat again, for it apparently had the effect of the turned peg on the enchanted horse in the "Arabian Nights," and Chu Chu instantly rose into the air. But she came down this time before the open window of the kitchen, and I alighted easily on the dresser. The indefatigable Enriquez followed me.

"Won't this do?" I asked, meekly.

"It is better for you arrive not on the ground," he said, cheerfully, "but you should not once but a thousand times make trial! Ha! Go and win! Never die and say so! There you are!"

Luckily, this time I managed to lock the rowels of my long spurs under her girth, and she could not unseat me. She seemed to recognize the fact after one or two plunges, when, to my great surprise, she suddenly sank to the ground and quietly rolled over me. The action disengaged my spurs, but, righting herself without getting up, she turned her beautiful head and absolutely looked at me, still in the saddle. I felt myself blushing. But the voice of Enriquez was at my side.

"Arise, my friend; you have conquer! It is she who has arrive at the ground. You are all right. It is done; believe me, it is finish. No more shall she make this thing. From this instant you shall ride her as the cow as the rail of this fence and remain tranquil. For she is broke! Ta-ta! Regain your hats, gentlemen! Pass in your checks! It is over! How are you now?" He lit a fresh cigarette, put his hands in his pockets, and smiled at me blandly.

For all that, I ventured to point out that the habit of alighting in the fork of a tree, or the disengaging of oneself from the saddle on the ground, was attended with inconvenience, and even ostentatious display. But Enriquez swept the objections away with a single gesture.

"It is the principal—the bottom fact—at which you arrive. The next come of himself! Many horse have achieve to mount the rider by the knees, and relinquish after this same fashion. My grandfather had a barb of this kind—but she has gone dead, and so have my grandfather. Which is sad and strange! Otherwise I shall make of them both an instant example!"

I ought to have said that although these performances were never actually witnessed by Enriquez's sister—for reasons which he and I thought sufficient—the dear girl displayed the greatest interest in them, and, perhaps aided by our mutually complimentary accounts of the other, looked upon us both as invincible heroes. It is possible also that she overestimated our success, for she suddenly demanded that I should ride Chu Chu to her house, that she might see her.

It was not far; by going through a back lane I could avoid the trees which exercised such a fatal fascination for Chu Chu. There was a pleading, child-like entreaty in Consuelo's voice that I could not resist, with a slight flash from her lustrous dark eyes that I did not care to encourage. So I resolved to try it at all hazards. My equipment for the performance was modeled after Enriquez's previous costume, with the addition of a few fripperies of silver and stamped leather, out of compliment to Consuelo, and even with a faint hope that it might appease Chu Chu. She certainly looked beautiful in her glittering accoutrements, set off by her jet-black shining coat. With an air of demure abstraction she permitted me to mount her, and even for a hundred yards or so indulged in a mincing maidenly amble that was not without a touch of coquetry. Encouraged by this, I addressed a few terms of endearment to her, and in the exuberance of my youthful enthusiasm I even confided to her my love for Consuelo, and begged her to be "good" and not disgrace herself and me before my Dulcinea. In my foolish trustfulness I was rash enough to add a caress, and to pat her soft neck. She stopped instantly with a hysteric shudder. I knew what was passing through her mind; she had suddenly become aware of my baleful existence.

The saddle and bridle Chu Chu was becoming accustomed to, but who was this living, breathing object that had actually touched her? Presently her oblique vision was attracted by the fluttering movement of a fallen oak leaf in the road before her. She had probably seen many oak leaves many times before; her ancestors had no doubt been familiar with them on the trackless hills and in field and paddock; but this did not alter her profound conviction that I and the leaf were identical, that our baleful touch was something indissolubly connected. She reared before that innocent leaf, she revolved round it, and then fled from it at the top of her speed.

The lane passed before the rear wall of Saltello's garden. Unfortunately, at the angle of the fence stood a beautiful Madroño tree, brilliant with its scarlet berries and endeared to me as Consuelo's favorite haunt, under whose protecting shade I had more than once avowed my youthful passion. By the irony of fate Chu Chu caught sight of it, and with a succession of spirited bounds instantly made for it. In another moment I was beneath it, and Chu Chu shot like a rocket into the air. I had barely time to withdraw my feet from the stirrups, to throw up one arm to protect my glazed sombrero and grasp an overhanging branch with the other, before Chu Chu darted off. But to my consternation, as I gained a secure perch on the tree, and looked about me, I saw her—instead of running away— quietly trot through the gate into Saltello's garden.

Need I say that it was to the beneficent Enriquez that I again owed my salvation? Scarcely a moment elapsed before his bland voice rose in a concentrated whisper from the corner of the garden below me. He had divined the dreadful truth!

"For the love of God, collect to yourself many kinds of this berry! All you can! Your full arms round! Rest tranquil. Leave to your old uncle to make for you a delicate exposure. At the instant!"

He was gone again. I gathered, wonderingly, a few of the larger clusters of parti-colored fruit and patiently waited. Presently he reappeared, and with him the lovely Consuelo, her dear eyes filled with an adorable anxiety.

"Yes," continued Enriquez to his sister, with a confidential lowering of tone but great distinctness of utterance, "it is ever so with the American! He will ever make *first* the salutation of the flower or the fruit, picked to himself by his own hand, to the lady where he call. It is the custom of the American hidalgo! My God! . . . It is so! Without doubt he is in this instant doing this thing. That is why he have let go his horse to precede him here; it is always the etiquette to offer this things on the feet. Ah, I behold! It is he!—Don Francisco! Even now he will descend from this tree! Ah! You make the blush, little sister! (archly). I will retire. I am discreet; two is not company for the one. I make tracks. I am gone."

How far Consuelo entirely believed and trusted her ingenious brother I do not know, nor even then cared to inquire. For there was a pretty mantling of her olive cheek as I came forward with my offering, and a certain significant shyness in her manner that were enough to throw me into a state of hopeless imbecility. And I was always miserably conscious that Consuelo possessed an exalted sentimentality and a predilection for the highest medieval romance, in which I knew I was lamentably deficient. Even in our most confidential moments I was always aware that I weakly lagged behind this daughter of a gloomily distinguished ancestry in her frequent incursions into a vague but poetic past. There was something of the dignity of the Spanish *châtelaine* in the sweetly grave little figure that advanced to accept my specious offering. I think I should have fallen on my knees to present it, but for the presence of the all-seeing Enriquez. But why did I even at that moment remember that he had early bestowed upon her the nickname of "Pomposa"? This, as Enriquez himself might have observed, was "sad and strange."

I managed to stammer out something about the Madroño berries being at her "disposicion" (the tree was in her own garden), and she took the branches in her little brown hand with a soft response to my unutterable glances. But here Chu Chu, momentarily forgotten, executed a happy diversion. To our astonishment she gravely walked up to Consuelo, and, stretching out her long slim neck, not only sniffed curiously at the berries, but even protruded a black underlip towards the young girl herself. In another instant Consuelo's dignity melted. Throwing her arms around Chu Chu's neck she embraced and kissed her. Young as I was, I understood the divine significance of a girl's vicarious effusiveness at such a moment and felt delighted. But I was the more astonished that the usually sensitive horse not only submitted to these caresses, but actually responded to the extent of affecting to nip my mistress's little right ear.

This was enough for the impulsive Consuelo. She ran hastily into the house, and in a few moments reappeared in a bewitching riding skirt gathered round her waist. In vain Enriquez and myself joined in earnest entreaty; the horse was hardly broken for even a man's riding yet; the saints alone could tell what the nervous creature might do with a woman's skirt flapping at her side! We begged for delay, for reflection, for at least time to change the saddle but with no avail. Consuelo was determined, indignant, distressingly reproachful! Ah, well! If Don Pancho (an ingenious diminutive of my Christian name) valued his horse so highly—if he were jealous of the evident devotion of the animal to herself, he would—But here I succumbed! And then I had the felicity of holding that little foot for one brief moment in the hollow of my hand, of readjusting the skirt as she threw her knee over the saddle horn, of clasping her tightly only half in fear as I surrendered the reins to her grasp. And to tell the truth, as Enriquez and I fell back, although I had insisted upon still keeping hold of the end of the riata, it was a picture to admire. The petite figure of the young girl, and the graceful folds of her skirt, admirably harmonized with Chu Chu's lithe contour, and as the mare arched her slim neck and raised her slender head under the pressure of the reins, it was so like the lifted velvet-capped toreador crest of Consuelo herself that they seemed of one race.

"I would not that you should hold the riata," said Consuelo, petulantly.

I hesitated. Chu Chu looked, certainly, very amiable. I let go. She began to amble towards the gate, not mincingly as before, but with a freer and fuller stride. In spite of the incongruous saddle, the young girl's seat was admirable. As they neared the gate she cast a single mischievous glance at me, jerked at the rein, and Chu Chu sprang into the road at a rapid canter. I watched them fearfully and breathlessly, until at the end of the lane I saw Consuelo rein in slightly, wheel easily, and come flying back. There was no doubt about it; the horse was under perfect control. Her second subjugation was complete and final.

Overjoyed and bewildered, I overwhelmed them with congratulations; Enriquez alone retaining the usual brotherly attitude of criticism and a superior toleration of a lover's enthusiasm. I ventured to hint to Consuelo (in what I believed was a safe whisper) that Chu Chu only showed my own feelings towards her.

"Without doubt," responded Enriquez, gravely. "She have of herself assist you to climb to the tree to pull to yourself the berry for my sister." But I felt Consuelo's little hand return my pressure, and I forgave and even pitied him.

From that day forward Chu Chu and Consuelo were not only firm friends but daily companions. In my devotion I would have presented the horse to the young girl, but with flattering delicacy she preferred to call it mine.

"I shall ride it for you, Pancho," she said. "I shall feel," she continued, with exalted although somewhat vague poetry, "that it is of *you*. You love the beast—it is therefore of a necessity *you*, my Pancho! It is *your* soul I shall ride like the wings of the wind—your love in this beast shall be my only cavalier forever."

I would have preferred something whose vicarious qualities were less uncertain than I still felt Chu Chu's to be, but I kissed the girl's hand submissively. It was only when I attempted to accompany her in the flesh, on another horse, that I felt the full truth of my instinctive fears. Chu Chu would not permit anyone to approach her mistress's side. My mounted presence revived in her all her old blind astonishment and disbelief in my existence; she would start suddenly, face about, and back away from me in utter amazement, as if I had been only recently created, or with an affected modesty as if I had been just guilty of some grave indecorum towards her sex which she really could not stand. The frequency of these exhibitions in the public highway were not only distressing to me as a simple escort, but as it had the effect on the casual spectators of making Consuelo seem to participate in Chu Chu's objections, I felt that, as a lover, it could not be borne. Any attempt to coerce Chu Chu ended in her running away. And my frantic pursuit of her was open to equal misconstruction.

"Go it, miss, the little dude is gainin' on you!" shouted by a drunken teamster to the frightened Consuelo, once checked me in mid-career. Even the dear girl herself saw the uselessness of my real presence, and after a while was content to ride with "my soul."

Notwithstanding this, I am not ashamed to say that it was my custom, whenever she rode out, to keep a slinking and distant surveillance of Chu Chu on another horse, until she had fairly settled down to her pace. A little nod of Consuelo's round black-and-red toreador hat, or a kiss tossed from her riding whip was reward enough!

I remember a pleasant afternoon when I was thus awaiting her in the outskirts of the village. The eternal smile of the Californian summer had begun to waver and grow less fixed; dust lay thick on leaf and blade; the dry hills were clothed in russet leather; the trade winds were shifting to the south with an ominous warm humidity. A few days longer and the rains would be here.

It so chanced that this afternoon my seclusion on the roadside was accidentally invaded by a village belle—a Western young lady somewhat older than myself and of a flirtatious reputation. As she persistently, and—as I now have reason to believe—mischievously lingered, I had only a passing glimpse of Consuelo riding past at an unaccustomed speed which surprised me at the moment. But as I reasoned later that she was only trying to avoid a merely formal meeting, I thought no more about it.

It was not until I called at the house to fetch Chu Chu at the usual hour and found that Consuelo had not yet returned that a recollection of Chu Chu's furious pace again troubled me. An hour passed—it was getting towards sunset but there were no signs of Chu Chu nor her mistress. I became seriously alarmed. I did not care to reveal my fears to the family, for I felt myself responsible for Chu Chu. At last I desperately saddled my horse and galloped off in the direction she had taken. It was the road to Rosario, and the *hacienda* of one of her relations, where she sometimes halted.

The road was a very unfrequented one, twisting like a mountain river; indeed, it was the bed of an old watercourse, between brown hills of wild oats, and debouching at last into a broad blue lake-like expanse of alfalfa meadows. In vain I strained my eyes over the monotonous level; nothing appeared to rise above or move across it. In the faint hope that she might have lingered at the *hacienda*, I was spurring on again, when I heard a slight splashing on my left. I looked around. A broad patch of fresher-colored herbage and a cluster of dwarfed alders indicated a hidden spring. I cautiously approached its quaggy edges, when I was shocked by what appeared to be a sudden vision! Mid-leg deep in the center of a greenish pool stood Chu Chu! But without a strap or buckle of harness upon her—as naked as when she was foaled.

For a moment I could only stare at her in bewildered terror. Far from recognizing me, she seemed to be absorbed in a nymph-like contemplation of her own graces in the pool. Then I called "Consuelo!" and galloped frantically around the spring. But there was no response, nor was there anything to be seen but the all-unconscious Chu Chu. The pool, thank Heaven, was not deep enough to have drowned anyone; there were no signs of a struggle on its quaggy edges. The horse might have come from a distance! I galloped on, still calling. A few hundred yards farther I detected the vivid glow of Chu Chu's scarlet saddle blanket in the brush near the trail. My heart leaped—I was on the track. I called again; this time a faint; reply, in accents I knew too well, came from the field beside me.

Consuelo was there, reclining beside a manzanita bush which screened her from the road, in what struck me, even at that supreme moment, as a judicious and picturesquely selected couch of scented Indian grass and dry tussocks. The velvet hat with its balls of scarlet plush was laid carefully aside; her lovely blue-black hair retained its tight coils undishevelled; her eyes were luminous and tender. Shocked as I was at her apparent helplessness, I remember being impressed with the fact that it gave so little indication of violent usage or disaster.

I threw myself frantically on the ground beside her. "You are hurt, Consita! For Heaven's sake! What has happened?"

She pushed my hat back with her little hand and tumbled my hair gently. "Nothing. *You* are here, Pancho—it is enough! What shall come after this—when I am perhaps gone among the grave—make nothing! *You* are here I am happy. For a little, perhaps—not much."

"But," I went on, desperately, "was it an accident? Were you thrown? Was it Chu Chu?"—for somehow, in spite of her languid posture and voice, I could not, even in my fears, believe her seriously hurt.

"Beat not the poor beast, Pancho. It is not from *her* comes this thing. She have make nothing—believe me! I have come upon your assignation with Miss Smith! I make but to pass you—to fly—to never come back! I have say to Chu Chu, 'Fly!' We fly many miles. Sometimes together, sometimes not so much! Sometimes in the saddle, sometimes on the neck. Many things remain in the road; at the end, I myself remain! I have say, 'Courage, Pancho will come!' Then I say, 'No, he is talk with Miss Smith!' I remember not more. I have creep here on the hands. It is finish!"

I looked at her distractedly. She smiled tenderly and slightly smoothed down and rearranged a fold of her dress to cover her delicate little boot.

"But," I protested, "you are not much hurt, dearest. You have broken no bones. Perhaps," I added, looking at the boot, "only a slight sprain. Let me carry you to my horse; I will walk beside you home. Do, dearest Consita!"

She turned her lovely eyes towards me sadly. "You comprehend not, my poor Pancho! It is not of the foot, the ankle, the arm, or the head that I can say, 'she is broke!' I would it were even so. But"—she lifted her sweet lashes slowly—"I have derange my inside. It is an affair of my family. My grandfather have once tumble over the bull at a rodeo. He speak no more; he is dead. For why? He has derange his inside. Believe me, it is of the family. You comprehend? The Saltellos are not as the other peoples for this. When I am gone, you will bring to me the berry to grow upon my tomb, Pancho, the berry you have picked for me. The little flower will come too, the little star will arrive, but Consuelo, who loves you, she will come not more! When you are happy and talk in the road to the Smith, you will not think of me. You will not see my eyes, Pancho; this little grass"—she ran her plump little fingers through a tussock—"will hide them; and the small animals in the black coats that live here will have much sorrow but you will not. It is better so! My father will not that I, a Catholique, should marry into a camp-meeting, and live in a tent, and make howl like the coyote." (It was one of Consuelo's bewildering beliefs that there was only one form of dissent—Methodism!) "He will not that I should marry a man who possesses not the many horses, ox, and cow, like him. But I care not. *You* are my only religion, Pancho! I have enough of the horse, and ox, and cow when *you* are with me! Kiss me, Pancho. Perhaps it is for the last time—the finish! Who knows?"

There were tears in her lovely eyes; I felt that my own were growing dim; the sun was sinking over the dreary plain to the slow rising of the wind; an infinite loneliness had fallen upon us, and yet I was miserably conscious of some dreadful unreality in it all. A desire to laugh, which I felt must be hysterical, was creeping over me; I dared not speak. But her dear head was on my shoulder, and the situation was not unpleasant.

Nevertheless, something must be done! This was the more difficult as it was by no means clear what had already been done. Even while I supported her drooping figure I was straining my eyes across her shoulder for succor of some kind. Suddenly the figure of a rapid rider appeared upon the road. It seemed familiar. I looked again it was the blessed Enriquez! A sense of deep relief came over me. I loved Consuelo; but never before had lover ever hailed the irruption of one of his beloved's family with such complacency.

"You are safe, dearest; it is Enriquez."

I thought she received the information coldly. Suddenly she turned upon me her eyes, now bright and glittering. "Swear to me at the instant, Pancho, that you will not again look upon Miss Smith, even for once."

I was simple and literal. Miss Smith was my nearest neighbor, and, unless I was stricken with blindness, compliance was impossible. I hesitated but swore.

"Enough—you have hesitate—I will no more." She rose to her feet with grave deliberation.

For an instant, with the recollection of the delicate internal organization of the Saltellos on my mind, I was in agony lest she should totter and fall, even then, yielding up her gentle spirit on the spot. But when I looked again she had a hairpin between her white teeth, and was carefully adjusting her toreador hat. And beside us was Enriquez cheerful, alert, voluble, and undaunted.

"Eureka! I have found! We are all here! It is a little public—eh! A little too much of a front seat for a *tête-à-tête*, my young friends," he said, glancing at the remains of Consuelo's bower, "but for the accounting of taste there is none. What will you? The meat of the one man shall envenom the meat of the other. But," (in a whisper to me) "as to this horse—this Chu Chu, which I have just pass—why is she undress? Surely you would not make an exposition of her to the traveler to suspect! And if not, why so?"

I tried to explain, looking at Consuelo, that Chu Chu had run away, that Consuelo had met with a terrible accident, had been thrown, and I feared had suffered serious internal injury. But to my embarrassment, Consuelo maintained a half scornful silence, and an inconsistent freshness of healthful indifference, as Enriquez approached her with an engaging smile.

"Ah, yes, she have the headache and the molligrubs. She will sit on the damp stone when the gentle dew is falling. I comprehend. Meet me in the lane when the clock strike nine! But," in a lower voice, "of this undress horse I comprehend nothing! Look you—it is sad and strange."

He went off to fetch Chu Chu, leaving me and Consuelo alone. I do not think I ever felt so utterly abject and bewildered before in my life. Without knowing why, I was miserably conscious of having in some way offended the girl for whom I believed I would have given my life, and I had made her and myself ridiculous in the eyes of her brother. I had again failed in my slower Western nature to understand her high romantic Spanish soul. Meantime she was smoothing out her riding habit, and looking as fresh and pretty as when she first left her house.

"Consita," I said, hesitatingly, "you are not angry with me?"

"Angry?" she repeated haughtily, without looking at me. "Oh, no! Of a possibility it is Miss Smith who is angry that I have interrupt her *tête-à-tête* with you, and have send here my brother to make the same with me."

"But," I said, eagerly, "Miss Smith does not even know Enriquez!"

Consuelo turned on me a glance of unutterable significance. "Ah!" she said, darkly, "you *think!*"

Indeed I *knew*. But here I believe I understood Consuelo and was relieved. I even ventured to say gently, "And are you better?"

She drew herself up to her full height, which was not much. "Of my health, what is it? A nothing. Yes! Of my soul, let us not speak."

Nevertheless, when Enriquez appeared with Chu Chu she ran towards her with outstretched arms. Chu Chu protruded about six inches of upper lip in response—apparently under the impression, which I could quite understand, that her mistress was edible. And, I may have been mistaken, but their beautiful eyes met in an absolute and distinct glance of intelligence!

During the home journey Consuelo recovered her spirits, and parted from me with a magnanimous and forgiving pressure of the hand. I do not know what explanation of Chu Chu's original escapade was given to Enriquez and the rest of the family; the inscrutable forgiveness extended to me by Consuelo precluded any further inquiry on my part. I was willing to leave it a secret between her and Chu Chu. But, strange to say, it seemed to complete our own understanding and precipitated, not only our lovemaking, but the final catastrophe which culminated that romance. For we had resolved to elope. I do not know that this heroic remedy was absolutely necessary from the attitude of either Consuelo's family or my own; I am inclined to think we preferred it, because it involved no previous explanation or advice. Need I say that our confidant and firm ally was Consuelo's brother—the alert, the linguistic, the ever-happy, ever-ready Enriquez! It was understood that his presence would not only give a certain mature respectability to our performance but I do not think we would have contemplated this step without it. During one of our riding excursions we were to secure the services of a Methodist minister in the adjoining county, and later, that of the Mission Padre—when the secret was out.

"I will give her away," said Enriquez confidently. "It will on the instant propitiate the old shadbelly who shall perform the affair, and withhold his jaw. A little chin-music from your uncle Harry shall finish it! Remain tranquil, and forget not a ring! One does not always, in the agony and dissatisfaction of the moment, a ring remember. I shall bring two in the pocket of my dress."

If I did not entirely participate in this roseate view, it may have been because Enriquez, although a few years my senior, was much younger-looking, and with his demure devilry of eye, and his upper lip close shaven for this occasion, he suggested a depraved acolyte rather than a responsible member of a family. Consuelo had also confided to me that her father—possibly owing to some rumors of our previous escapade—had forbidden any further excursions with me alone. The innocent man did not know that Chu Chu had forbidden it also, and that even on this momentous occasion both Enriquez and myself were obliged to ride in opposite fields like out-flankers. But we nevertheless felt the full guilt of disobedience added to our desperate enterprise.

Meanwhile, although pressed for time, and subject to discovery at any moment, I managed at certain points of the road to dismount and walk beside Chu Chu (who did not seem to recognize me on foot), holding Consuelo's hand in my own, with the discreet Enriquez leading my horse in the distant field. I retain a very vivid picture of that walk—the ascent of a gentle slope towards a prospect as yet unknown, but full of glorious possibilities; the tender dropping light of an autumn sky, slightly filmed with the promise of the future rains, like foreshadowed tears; and the half-frightened, half-serious talk into which Consuelo and I had insensibly fallen.

And then, I don't know how it happened, but as we reached the summit Chu Chu suddenly reared, wheeled, and the next moment was flying back along the road we had just traveled, at the top of her speed! It might have been that, after her abstracted fashion, she only at that moment detected my presence, but so sudden and complete was her evolution that before I could regain my horse from the astonished Enriquez she was already a quarter of a mile on the homeward stretch, with the frantic Consuelo pulling hopelessly at the bridle.

We started in pursuit. But a horrible despair seized us. To attempt to overtake her, to even follow at the same rate of speed, would not only excite Chu Chu, but endanger Consuelo's life. There was absolutely no help for it—nothing could be done. The mare had taken her determined, long, continuous stride, the road was a straight, steady descent all the way back to the village, Chu Chu had the bit between her teeth, and there was no prospect of swerving her. We could only follow hopelessly, idiotically, furiously, until Chu Chu dashed triumphantly into the Saltellos' courtyard, carrying the half-fainting Consuelo back to the arms of her assembled and astonished family.

It was our last ride together. It was the last I ever saw of Consuelo before her transfer to the safe seclusion of a convent in Southern California. It was the last I ever saw of Chu Chu, who in the confusion of that rencontre was overlooked in her half-loosed harness, and allowed to escape through the back gate to the fields. Months afterwards it was said that she had been identified among a band of wild horses in the Coast Range, as a strange and beautiful creature who had escaped the brand of the rodeo and had become a myth.

There was another legend that she had been seen, sleek, fat, and gorgeously caparisoned, issuing from the gateway of the Rosario, before a lumbering Spanish cabriole in which a short, stout matron was seated but I will have none of it. For there are days when she still lives, and I can see her plainly still climbing the gentle slope towards the summit, with Consuelo on her back, and myself at her side, pressing eagerly forward towards the illimitable prospect that opens in the distance.

38

In Which True Becomes Justin Morgan

By Eleanor Waring Burnham

<><><><><><><><><><><><><><><><><><><><><><><><><><><><><><><><><><><><><><><><>

The Morgan horse emerged in New England during the first quarter of the nineteenth century in a time and place where good agricultural records were kept, particularly of horses that proved to be useful and valuable. We know something of the second generation and a great deal about later generations of Morgans but comparatively little about the father of the breed, even though he became well known during his own lifetime.

The mysterious origins of the first Morgan horse led to fiction and nonfiction accounts of his early life. In Eleanor Waring Burnham's book Justin Morgan, Founder of His Race, *readers got some of both approaches. Burnham produced a fictionalized narrative of one of the several versions of the horse's early years. It was a technique that Burnham had successfully used in her previous novels.*

In her story, Burnham begins with a mare she names Gipsey, who has produced a handsome bay colt, the son of a stallion named True Briton. Their owner, a farmer in West Springfield, Massachusetts, names the colt True Briton the Second, soon shortened to True. Gipsey has a prophetic message for True. "When other horses now famous are forgotten," she says, "your memory will live on."

True becomes a favorite pet of his owner, especially when he saves his master's life by running for help when the elderly farmer is injured. But the farmer reluctantly sells True to a singing teacher from Vermont, a kindly young man named Justin Morgan.

After a sojourn among well-bred horses and distinguished people in Hartford, Connecticut, True travels to Vermont with his new master, who is proud to show off the sturdy little horse to his hardworking neighbors. Illness and financial problems force the singing teacher to rent True to Robert Evans for fifteen dollars so the farmer can clear a new field.

It was hard work but True revels in it, enjoying the admiration from Evans and his neighbors for the amount of work he could do. Evans enjoyed the admiration just as much. In this chapter, True receives a new name.

—Sharon B. Smith

⬦⬦⬦

Once or twice a week it was the custom among the farmers waiting at Chase's Mill to pass the time testing their strength or that of their horses. It was healthful sport and kept them and their beasts in trim. Many were the jugs of Medford rum consumed on these occasions, and anyone having a horse to try, or a new test of strength for the men, was welcomed.

Running their horses short distances for small stakes came to be very popular. A course of eighty rods was measured, starting at the mill and extending along the highway; a line was drawn across the road, called a "scratch," the horses were ranged in a row, and at the drop of a hat away they went, cheered by the crowd.

It so happened that Evans and True, who never finished their work until dusk, were rarely at these tests. Evans, himself, was too tired to join in the sports, but True often thought he would like to try his strength against the larger, heavier horses.

One day, coming along the River Road to the mill, his heavy farm harness and tug chains still dangling on True, they passed Master Justin Morgan—he stood under a maple tree and was lilting an old French song learned from the Canadian lumbermen, called "A la Claire Fontaine." True and Evans paused to listen. Everyone liked Master Morgan for his sweet voice and gentle manners.

When the song was finished Evans gave the singer a neighborly greeting and strode on to the mill, True following him, more like a dog than a horse. The sun was gone and the evening shadows were beginning to fall, but there were still lingering along the horizon long streaks of crimson and gold that tinged the river with color.

In evident discussion, near a log at the mill, stood a group of farmers. Evans and True approached. Nathan Nye, friendly and jovial, whittling a birch stick, looked up as Evans said: "How be ye all?"

"Why not give Bob's horse a show?" he asked, a twinkle in his keen blue eyes, a smile brightening his genial face.

Horses and oxen were hitched to the limbs of trees or grazed near at hand, quite without interest in whatever was taking place. Sledges and wagons rested their shafts on the ground, seeming to wait patiently.

"Is it a pulling bee?" asked Evans, leaning against True's side.

"Yaas, but I guess it's about over, now," drawled a lank youth, coming out of the mill with a sack of meal on his shoulder.

"Anybody but you in a hurry to be going homealong?" questioned Nye, crushingly.

The youth did not answer, but went on to his sledge.

"There's a jug of Medford rum in the store for the owner of the horse that can get that there log on my runway this evening," explained Miller Chase to Evans.

"Now I want to know!" exclaimed Evans, carelessly, "Why didn't you say so before? You seem to be making quite a chore of a very simple thing; I'll just have my little horse do it for you in a jiffy!"

A shout of derisive laughter greeted his remark.

"Now do tell!" cried Hiram Sage, sarcastically.

"That pony pull a log my Jim refused?" scoffed another.

"My 'pony,' as you call him," laughed Evans, good-naturedly, "has never refused me yet." He placed his arm over True's neck; the horse rattled his chains musically, and reached for a low-handing bough.

"Work is play for this animal," Evans went on. "We've been in the logging field all day, but that don't make a mite o' difference to the Morgan horse. Come, show us your log!" True shook himself again and went on chewing leaves.

"Why, that beast's naught but a colt!" said Jim's owner, scornfully.

"Colt or no, he's the finest bit o' horseflesh this side of The Plains of Abraham!" Evans contended, hotly. "Give him his head and he goes like a shot and doesn't pull an ounce, and as for drawing a load—when this horse starts, *something's* got to come! That is," he added with a laugh, "as long as the tugs last!"

"Well, stop your bragging," said the sarcastic Hiram; "actions speak louder than words. Hitch him up that there 'something' and let us see it 'come.'" Miller Chase stepped forward, hospitably.

"First come in, men, and fix up your bets over a mug," he said.

They went inside the shop, all talking at once, and left True nibbling among the grasses and weeds. When they had disappeared he glanced at the log which the other horses had refused—horses much larger and heavier than he. The opportunity he had hoped for had come!

"But can I do it?" he asked himself.

The answer was, he *could*, and *would*. He was spurred to the greatest effort of his life by the taunt that he was a "pony." At any rate he was over fourteen hands and weighed nine hundred and fifty pounds!

"As I understand it," Evans was saying, as the men came out of the shop, "the agreement is that my horse has got to pull that big log ten rods onto the logway, *in three pulls*, or I lose?"

"That's the idea, exactly," assented Miller Chase.

Evans took hold of True's bridle confidently, and led him to the enormous log, where he fastened the tugs properly. Then he stepped one side and looked the young horse straight in the eye.

True returned his look—they might almost have been said to have exchanged a wink.

At this thought, Evans shouted with laughter.

"Gentlemen," he said, when he could speak seriously, "I am ashamed to ask my horse to pull a little weight like that *on a test*—couldn't two or three of you get on and ride?"

Then Evans was *sure* he saw a twinkle in True's eye.

A loud laugh greeted the proposal. "But, man, that there's a dead lift!" expostulated the miller.

"Well, mine's a live horse," Evans cried, with a grin. "Get on there! Justin Morgan's waitin' for to take you to drive!"

From this day the young horse was called *Justin Morgan's*. It was an easy transition to drop the possessive "s," after a while, and call him "Justin Morgan." With much hilarity three men climbed up on the log.

By this time darkness had fallen and Master Chase ran to get his lanthorn, swinging it back and forth, as he returned.

"Mind you don't fall off," Evans warned the men. "'Something' is about to 'come.'"

And "something" did!

Justin Morgan's horse gathered himself together, almost crouching, and waited for the word to start. When it was given, his chest muscles strained, his wide nostrils were scarlet and dilated, and this scion of Arabia's proud breed moved off as if inspired by Allah himself for an almost miraculous feat.

The bystanders, craning their necks to see, ran alongside; the men, perched on the log, fell off as it rocked from side to side, and then the young horse paused for breath—or to recover his strength.

Utter silence was over all. There was no jeering now. The second pull landed the log on the logway, and the amazed men broke into the wildest cheers ever heard at Chase's Mill.

Burnham continues the fictionalized story of the first Morgan horse. Justin Morgan the man becomes increasingly ill and is forced to sell Justin Morgan the horse. With his new owners he finds kind treatment, satisfying work, cheerful conversations with interesting horses, and, improbably, a role as an equine Paul Revere in the War of 1812. Except for a brief period late in life he lives out his years in comfort and honor. Burnham makes little mention of what really made Justin Morgan famous—the hundreds of offspring that created the Morgan breed.

39

Memoirs of a Fox-Hunting Man

By Siegfried Sassoon

This excerpt is from the book published in 1928, in which the author hoped to make readers connect with his love of horses and fox-hunting as it was known in England. Before the book's publication, Sassoon was known for his poetry, which was mostly written during and about World War I. Because of that reputation, Sassoon elected to publish the original manuscript as "anonymous." The depiction of his early years was presented in the form of an autographical novel, with false name given to the characters, including Sassoon himself. The ultimate success of the book and its reputation today can be traced to Sassoon's attention to detail. He says he was inspired by the work of Marcel Proust. "A few pages of Proust have made me wonder whether insignificant episodes aren't the most significant."

THE SUN WAS STILL SHINING WHEN I GOT TO THE COURSE; BUT IT WAS now less easy to believe that I had engaged myself to contribute to the entertainment which was attracting such a crowd of cheerful country folk. I felt extraneous and forlorn. Everyone else seemed intent on having as good a time as possible on such a lovely afternoon. I had come briskly out from Downfield on a two-horse char-a-banc which was waiting outside the station. The journey cost half a crown. Several of my fellow passengers were "bookies" and their clerks, with their name boards and giant umbrellas; their jocosities accentuated the crudity of the impact on my mind made by the realistic atmosphere of racing. I did my best to feel as much like a "gentleman rider" as I could, and to forget that I was making my first appearance in a race.

The air smelt of trodden turf as I lugged my bag (loaded with fourteen one-pound lead weights) into the dressing room, which was in a farm building under some elms on the crest of the rising ground which overlooked the sparsely flagged course. After dumping the bag in a corner of the dry-mud floored barn, I went out to look for Cockbird and Dixon. They were nowhere to be seen, so I returned to the dressing room, reminding myself that Dixon had said he wouldn't bring "our horse" out there any earlier than he was obliged to, since it would only excite him; I also realized that I should get "rattled" myself unless I kept quiet and reserved my energies for three o'clock.

The first race was run at two, and mine was the third event on the card, so I bought that absorbing document and perched myself on an old corn bin to peruse it. "Riders are requested to return their number-cloths to the Clerk of the Scales immediately after each race." I had forgotten that number-cloths existed, so that was news to me. "These Steeplechases are held subject to National Hunt Rules as to corrupt and fraudulent practices." A moment's reflection convinced me that I need not worry about that admonition; it was sufficiently obvious that I had a clean sheet under National Hunt Rules, though it flattered me to feel that I was at least within their jurisdiction.

After these preliminaries, I looked inside the card at the entries. Good heavens, there were fourteen in my race! Several of the names I didn't know: Captain Silcock's "Crumpet"; Mr. F. Duckwith's "Grasshopper"—those must be the soldiers who hunted from Downfield—Mr. G. Bagwell's "Kilgrubbin III." That might be—yes, of course, it was—the fat little man on the weedy chestnut, who was always refusing small timber out hunting. Not much danger from him as long as I kept well out of his way at the first fence, and probably he, and several of the others, wouldn't go to the post after all. My own name looked nice.

A blue-jowled man in a yellow waistcoat hurried in, exclaiming, "Can anybody lend me a weightcloth?"

I glanced at my bag and resolved that nothing would induce me to lend him mine (which had yet to receive its baptismal installment of sweat).

Several riders were now preparing for the first race, but no one took any notice of me until ginger-haired Roger Pomfret came in. He had been inspecting the fences, and he wiped his fleshy red face with his sleeve as he sat down and started rummaging in his bag. Tentatively, I asked him what he thought of the course. I was quite glad to see someone I knew, though I'd have preferred to see someone else. He chucked me a surly nod, which he supplemented with—"Course? I don't mind telling you, this something course would break the heart of a blank buffalo. It's nothing but twists and turns, and there isn't a something fence you could go fast at without risking your something neck, and a nice hope I've got on that blank sketchy jumper of Brandwick's!"

Before I could think of an answer his boon companion in blasphemy, Dill Jaggett, came in (embellished with a brown billycock hat and black and white check breeches). Jaggett began chaffing him about the something unhealthy ride he was going to have in the Heavy Weights. "I'll lay you a tenner to a fiver you don't get round without falling," he guffawed. Pomfret took the bet and called him a pimply faced bastard into the bargain.

I thought I might as well get dressed up; when I had pulled my boots on and was very deliberately tucking the straps in with the boot hook, Stephen strolled in; he was already wearing his faded pink cap, and the same elongated and anxious countenance which I had seen a year ago. No doubt my own face matched his. When we'd reassured one another about the superlative fitness of our horses he asked if I'd had any lunch, and as I hadn't he produced a bar of chocolate and an orange, which I was glad to get. Stephen was always thoughtful of other people.

The shouts of the bookies were now loudening outside in the sunlight, and when I'd slipped on my raincoat we went out to see what we could of the Light Weight Race.

The first two races were little more than the clamour and commotion of a passing procession. The Open Race was the main excitement of the afternoon, it was run "in colours," and there were about a dozen dashing competitors, several of them well-known winners in such events.

But everything connected with this contest reached me as though from a long way off, since I was half-stupefied by yawning nervousness.

They appeared to be accomplishing something incredible by galloping round the course. I had got to do it myself in half an hour; and what was worse, Dixon was relying on me to put up a creditable performance. He even expected me to give the others "a shaking up." Stephen had ceased to be any moral support at all: in spite of his success last year he was nearly as nervous as I was, and when the field for the Open Race had filed out of the hurdle-guarded enclosure, which did duty as the paddock, he disappeared in the direction of Jerry and I was left to face the future alone.

Also, as far as I knew, my horse hadn't yet arrived, and it was with a new species of alarm that I searched for him after I had seen the race start; the paddock and its environs now looked unfriendly and forsaken.

I discovered my confederates in a quiet corner under a hayrick. They seemed a discreet and unassuming pair, but Dixon greeted me with an invigorative grin. "I kept him away from the course as long as I could," he said confidentially. "He's quiet as a sheep, but he knows what he's here for; he's staled twice since we got here." He told me that Mr. Gaffikin was about and had been looking for me. "He says our horse stands a jolly good chance with the going as good as it is."

I said there was one place, in and out of a lane, where I'd have to be careful.

We then escorted Cockbird to the paddock; by the time we were there and I'd fetched my weight-cloth, the Open Race was over and the spectators were trooping back again. Among them was Mr. Gaffikin, who hailed me companionably with "Hullo, old chap; jolly sporting of you to be having a ride!" and thereafter took complete charge of me in a most considerate manner, going with me to the weighing tent with the weight-cloth over his arm, while I, of course, carried my saddle.

The winner of the Open Race was weighing in when we arrived, and I stepped diffidently onto the machine immediately after his glorified and perspiring vacation of the seat. Mr. Gaffikin doled out a few leads for me to slip into the leather pouches on the dark blue cloth until I tipped the scale at fourteen stone. The Clerk of the Scales, an unsmiling person with a large sallow face—he was a corn merchant—verified my name on the card and handed me my number-cloth and armlet; my number was seven; under less exacting conditions I might have wondered whether it was a lucky number, but I was pushed out of the way by Pomfret. Arthur Brandwick (in a grey bowler) was at his elbow, talking nineteen to the dozen; I caught a glimpse of Stephen's serious face; Colonel Hemson was with him, behaving exactly the same as last year, except that, having already "given the boy the horse," he could no longer say that he was going to do so if he won the race.

While Dixon was putting the last testing touches to Cockbird's straps and buckles, the little colonel came across to assure me that if Jerry didn't win there was no one he'd rather see first past the judge's waggon than me. He added that he'd taken a lot of trouble in choosing the cup—"very nice goblet shape—got it from Stegman & Wilks—excellent old firm in the city." But his eye wandered away from Cockbird; his sympathies were evidently strongly implicated in Jerry, who was as unperturbed as if he were being put into a brougham to fetch someone from the station.

Near him, Nigel Croplady was fussing round his horse, with quite a crowd round him.

The terrific "Boots" Brownrigg was puffing a cigarette with apparent unconcern; his black cap was well over his eyes and both hands were plunged in the pockets of a short blue overcoat; from one of the pockets protruded a short cutting whip. His boots were perfection. Spare-built and middle-sized, he looked absolutely undefeatable; and if he had any doubts about his own abilities he concealed them well.

Stifling another yawn, I did my best to imitate his demeanour. The bookies were bawling "Two to one bar one." Cockbird, stimulated by publicity, now began to give himself the airs of a real restive racehorse, chucking his head about, flattening his ears, and capering sideways in a manner which caused the onlookers to skip hastily out of range of his heels.

"I say, that's a classy looking quad!" exclaimed a youth who appeared to have purchased the paddock. He consulted his card, and I overheard his companion, as they turned away, saying something about "his jockey looking a bit green." "We'd better back Nigel's horse. They say he'll win for a cert."

For want of anything else to do at this critical moment I asked Dixon whether he'd put Homeward's half crown on. He said, "Yes, sir; Mr. Gaffikin's man has just done it for me, and I've got a bit on for myself. It's a good thing; they're laying five to one about him. Mr. Stephen's horse is at two's."

Mr. Gaffikin chimed in with "Mikado's a hot favourite. Two to one on, all along the line!" Mikado was Croplady's horse.

Mr. Gaffikin then tied the strings of my cap in a very tight bow; a bell jangled and a stentorian voice shouted, "Now, then, gentleman, I'm going down to the post." The blue sky suddenly went white; my heart bumped; I felt dazed and breathless. Then Mr. Gaffikin's remote voice said, "Let me give you a leg up, old chap." I grabbed hold of the reins, lifted an awkward foot, and was lifted airily onto the slippery saddle; Cockbird gave one prance and then stood still; Dixon was holding him firmly by the head. Pressing my knees into the saddle, I overheard Mr. Gaffikin's ultimate advice. "Don't go in front unless you can help it; but keep well with 'em." They both wished me luck and released me to my destiny.

I felt as if I'd never been on Cockbird's back before; everything around me appeared unreal and disconnected from all my previous experience. As I followed Stephen out of the paddock in a sort of equestrian trance I caught sight of his father's face, pale and fixed in its most strenuous expression; his eyes followed his son, on whose departure he was too intent to be able to take in anyone else. We filed through a gate under some trees: "Gentleman George" was standing by the gate; he stared up at me as I passed. "That's the 'oss for my money," was all that he said, but his measured tone somehow brought me to my senses, and I was able to look about me when we got down to the starting place.

But even then I was much more a passenger than a resolute rider with his wits about him to "pinch" a good start. There were seven others. I kept close to Stephen. We lined up uneasily. While the starter (on his dumpy grey cob) was instructing us to keep the red flags on the right and the white flags on the left (which we already knew) I noticed Pomfret (on a well-bred, excitable brown) and Brownrigg (Croplady's bright chestnut looking very compact) already stealing forward on the side furthest from him.

When he said "Go," I went with the others; albeit with no sense of initiative. The galloping hoofs sounded strange. But Cockbird felt strong under me and he flicked over the first fence with level and unbroken stride; he was such a big jumper and so quick over his fences that I had to pull him back after each one in order to keep level with Jerry, who was going his best pace all the way. One of the soldiers (in a tophat) was making the running with Brownrigg and Pomfret close behind him. At the awkward fifth fence (the one on a bank) Pomfret's horse jumped sideways and blundered as he landed, this caused Pomfret to address him in uncomplimentary language, and at the next obstacle (another awkward one) he ran out to the left, taking one of the soldiers with him. This, to my intense relief, was the last I saw of him. I took it at a place where a hole had been knocked in it in the previous races. The next thing I remember was the brook, which had seemed wide and intimidating when I was on foot and had now attracted a small gathering of spectators. But water jumps are deceptive things and Cockbird shot over this one beautifully. (Stephen had told me afterwards that he'd "never seen a horse throw such an enormous lep.") We went on up a long slope of firm pasture land, and I now became aware of my responsibility; my arms were aching and my fingers were numb and I found it increasingly difficult to avoid taking the lead, for after jumping a couple more fences and crossing a field of light ploughland we soared over a hedge with a big drop and began to go down the other side of the hill. Jerry was outpaced and I was level with Mikado and the cavalry soldier who had been cutting out the work. As Stephen dropped behind he said, "Go on, George; you've got 'em stone-cold."

We were now more than three parts of the way round, and there was a sharp turn left-handed where we entered on the last half-mile of the course. I lost several lengths here by taking a wide sweep round the white flag, which Brownrigg almost touched with his left boot. At the next fence the soldier went head over heels, so it was just as well for me that I was a few lengths behind him. He and his horse were still rolling about on the ground when I landed well clear of them. Brownrigg looked round and then went steadily on across a level and rather wet field which compelled me to take my last pull at Cockbird. Getting on to better ground, I remembered Mr. Gaffikin's advice, and let my horse go after him. When I had drawn up to him it was obvious that Cockbird and Mikado were the only ones left in it. I was alone with the formidable Brownrigg. The difference between us was that he was quite self-contained and I was palpitating with excitement.

We were side by side: approaching the fourth fence from the finish he hit his horse and went ahead. This caused Cockbird to quicken his pace and make his first mistake in the race by going too fast at the fence. He hit it hard and pecked badly, Brownrigg, of course, had steadied Mikado for the jump after the quite legitimate little piece of strategy which so nearly caused me to "come unstuck," nearly, but not quite. For after my arrival at Cockbird's ears his recovery tipped me halfway back again and he cantered on across the next field with me clinging round his neck. At one moment I was almost in front of his chest. I said to myself, "I won't fall off" as I gradually worked my way back into the saddle. My horse was honestly following Mikado, and my fate depended on whether I could get into the saddle before we arrived at the next fence. This I just succeeded in doing, and we got over somehow. I then regained my stirrups and set off in urgent pursuit.

After that really remarkable recovery of mine, life became lyrical, beatified, ecstatic, or anything else you care to call it. To put it tersely, I just galloped past Brownrigg, sailed over the last two fences, and won by ten lengths. Stephen came in a bad third. I also remember seeing Roger Pomfret ride up to Jaggett in the paddock and inform him in a most aggressive voice that he'd got to "something well pay up and look pleasant."

Needless to say that Dixon's was the first face I was aware of; his eager look and the way he said, "Well done," were beyond all doubt the quintessence of what my victory meant to me. All else was irrelevant at that moment, even Stephen's unselfish exultation and Mr. Gaffikin's loquacious enthusiasm. As for Cockbird, no words could ever express what we felt about him. He had become the equine equivalent of Divinity.

Excited as I was, an inward voice cautioned me to control my volubility. So when I had weighed in and returned with my saddle to find a cluster of knowing ones casting an eye over the winner, I just waited soberly until Dixon had rubbed him down, mounted, and ridden serenely out of sight. The colonel was on the spot to congratulate me on my "nailing good performance" and, better still, to give Dixon his due for having got Cockbird so fit. Those few lofty minutes when he was making so much of his horse were Dixon's reward for all the trouble he had taken since Cockbird had been in his charge. He had needed no such incentive, but he asked for nothing more. While he was on his way back to Downfield he may also have thought to himself how he had made me into a good enough rider to have got round the course without a catastrophe. (He had yet to hear full details of the race—including my peculiar acrobatics towards the end, which had been witnessed by no one except the rider of Mikado, who had been kind enough to tell Croplady that he never saw such a thing in his life, which was, I hoped, intended as a compliment.)

When I had watched Dixon's departure I found that public interest was being focused on the Yeomanry Team Race. I was glad to slip away by myself. A few fields out in the country I relaxed my legs on a five-barrel gate and contemplated my achievement with as much mental detachment as I could muster. Even in those days I had an instinct for getting the full flavour of an experience. Perhaps I was fortunate in not yet having become aware that the winner of the last race is forgotten as soon as the next one starts.

Forty minutes later I had claimed my cup (there was no ceremony of presentation). Having crammed the ebony pedestal into my kit bag I came out into the paddock with the cup in my other hand. It was convenient to carry, for it had handles to it.

Good-natured Arthur Brandwick came up and offered me a lift back to Downfield. While he was patting me on the back I caught sight of a figure which seemed somehow familiar. A loose-built ruddy-faced young sportsman was talking to a couple of jovial whiskered farmers; he sat on a shooting-stick with his thin neatly gaitered legs straightened; a brown felt hat was tipped well over his blunt nose, for the five o'clock sun was glaring full in his eyes. I wondered who it was he reminded me of. Brandwick answered my unspoken question.

"D'you twig who that is?" I shook my head. "Well, take another good look at him. It's our new master, and a hell of a good lad he is, from all I've heard. Up till a month ago everyone thought the country'd have to be hunted by a committee next season. There was something fishy about every one of the coves who'd applied for the mastership. And then this chap wrote and offered to hunt the hounds himself and put up fifteen thousand a year if we guaranteed him another two thousand. Hardly a soul knew about it till today. We're lucky to get him.

"He's been hunting a good rough country in Ireland the last two seasons and showing rare sport. He's run across for a couple of days to look at us." As we walked away the new master turned his head and favoured us with a slow and rather blank stare.

"What did you say his name was?" I asked, when we were out of earshot. Brandwick informed me that his name was Milden—Denis Milden—and I knew that I'd known it all the time, though I hadn't set eyes on him since I was eleven years old.

Aquamarine and celestial were the shoals of sunset as I hacked pensively home from Dumbridge. The Colonel's Cup clinked and joggled against my saddle. Time was irrelevant. But I was back at Butley by eight o'clock, and Cockbird, who had returned by an earlier train, was safe and sound; a little uneasily he wandered around his loose-box, rustling the deep straw, but always going back to the manger for another mouthful of clover hay. Dixon serenely digested triumph with his tea; presently he would go out to the "Rose and Crown" to hand Homeward his multiplied half crown and overawe the gossips with his glory.

Absolved and acquiescent was the twilight as I went quietly across the lawn and in at the garden door to the drawing room. Aunt Evelyn's armchair scrooped on the bees-waxed floor as she pushed it back and stood up with her bottle of smelling salts in her hand. For the first time since my success I really felt like a hero. And Miriam served the dinner with the tired face of a saint that seemed lit with foreknowledge of her ultimate reward. But at that time I didn't know what her goodness meant.

At the end of our evening, when they had gone upstairs with my highly coloured history of the day in their heads, I strolled out into the garden; for quite a long time I stared at the friendly lights that twinkled from the railway station and along the dark Weald. I had brought something home with me as well as the Cup. There was this new idea of Denis Milden as master. For I hadn't forgotten him, and my persistent studying of Horse and Hound and The Hunting Directory had kept me acquainted with his career as an amateur huntsman since he had left Oxford. A dog barked and a train went along the Weald . . . the last train to London, I thought. . . .

Going back to the drawing room, I lit a pair of candles which made their miniature gold reflections on the shining surface of the massive Cup. I couldn't keep my eyes away from it. I looked round the shadowed room on which all my childhood and adolescence had converged, but everything led back to the talisman; while I gazed and gazed on its luster I said to myself, aloud, "It can't be true that it's really there on the table!" The photograph of Watts's "Love and Death" was there on the wall, but it meant no more to me than the strangeness of the stars which I had seen without question, out in the quiet spring night. I was secure in a cozy little universe of my own, and it had rewarded me with the Colonel's Cup. My last thought before I fell asleep was, "Next season I'll come out in a pink coat."

40

The Man Who Hunts and Doesn't Like It

By Anthony Trollope

‹‹‹

From Anthony Trollope's Hunting Sketches *comes this selection that narrowly nosed out the hunting scene in his novel* The Eustace Diamonds. *The author's works provide an embarrassment of equestrian literary riches. That's because Mr. T. was a passionate foxhunter, and in ways that made him something of a folk hero in my eyes. According to his autobiography, he spent most of his literary career writing from five to eight in the morning before going off to his "day" job as a postal inspector . . . except for those mornings when he hunted. That is to say, anyone who would put his job on the back burner in favor of going riding certainly had his priorities straight!*

—STEVEN D. PRICE

‹‹‹

IT SEEMS TO BE ODD, AT FIRST SIGHT, THAT THERE SHOULD BE ANY SUCH men as these; but their name and number are legion. If we were to deduct from the hunting-crowd farmers, and others who hunt because hunting is brought to their door, of the remainder we should find that the "men who don't like it" have the preponderance. It is pretty much the same, I think, with all amusements. How many men go to balls, to races, to the theatre, how many women to concerts and races, simply because it is the thing to do? They have, perhaps, a vague idea that they may ultimately find some joy in the pastime; but, though they do the thing constantly, they never like it. Of all such men, the hunting men are perhaps the most to be pitied.

They are easily recognized by anyone who cares to scrutinize the men around him in the hunting field. It is not to be supposed that all those who, in common parlance, do not ride, are to be included among the number of hunting men who don't like it. Many a man who sticks constantly to the roads and lines of gates—who, from principle, never looks at a fence, is much attached to hunting. Some of those who have borne great names as Nimrods in our hunting annals would as life have led a forlorn hope as put a horse at a flight of hurdles. But they, too, are known; and though the nature of their delight is a mystery to straight-going men, it is manifest enough that they do like it. Their theory of hunting is at any rate plain. They have an acknowledged system, and know what they are doing. But the men who don't like it, have no system, and never know distinctly what is their own aim. During some portion of their career they commonly try to ride hard, and sometimes for a while they will succeed. In short spurts, while the cherry brandy prevails, they often have small successes; but even with the assistance of a spur in the head they never like it.

Dear old John Leech! What an eye he had for the man who hunts and doesn't like it! But for such, as a pictorial chronicler of the hunting field he would have had no fame. Briggs, I fancy, in his way did like it. Briggs was a full-blooded, up-apt, awkward, sanguine man, who was able to like anything, from gin and water upwards. But with how many a wretched companion of Briggs's are we not familiar? Men as to whom any girl of eighteen would swear from the form of his visage and the carriage of his legs as he sits on his horse that he was seeking honour where honour was not to be found, and looking for pleasure in places where no pleasure lay for him.

But the man who hunts and doesn't like it has his moments of gratification, and finds a source of pride in his penance. In the summer, hunting does much for him. He does not usually take much personal care of his horses, as he is probably a town man and his horses are summered by a keeper of hunting stables; but he talks of them. He talks of them freely, and the keeper of the hunting stables is occasionally forced to write to him. And he can run down to look at his nags, and spend a few hours eating bad mutton chops, walking about the yards and paddocks, and, bleeding half crowns through the nose. In all this there is a delight which offers some compensation for his winter misery to our friend who hunts and doesn't like it.

He finds it pleasant to talk of his horses especially to young women, with whom, perhaps, the ascertained fact of his winter employment does give him some credit. It is still something to be a hunting man even yet, though the multiplicity of railways and the existing plethora of money has so increased the number of sportsmen, that to keep a nag or two near some well-known station, is nearly as common as to die. But the delight of these martyrs is at the highest in the presence of their tailors; or, higher still, perhaps, in that of their bootmakers. The hunting man does receive some honour from him who makes his breeches; and, with a well-balanced sense of justice, the tailor's foreman is, I think, more patient, more admiring, more demonstrative in his assurances, more ready with his bit of chalk, when handling the knee of the man who doesn't like the work, than he ever is with the customer who comes to him simply because he wants some clothes fit for the saddle. The judicious conciliating trades-man knows that compensation should be given, and he helps to give it. But the visits to the bootmaker are better still. The tailor persists in telling his customer how his breeches should be made, and after what fashion they should be worn, but the bootmaker will take his orders meekly. If not ruffled by paltry objections as to the fit of the foot, he will accede to any amount of instructions as to the legs and tops. And then a new pair of top boots is a pretty toy; costly, perhaps, if needed only as a toy, but very pretty, and more decorative in a gentleman's dressing room than any other type of garment. And top boots, when multiplied in such a locality—when seen in a phalanx—tell such pleasant lies on their owner's behalf. While your breeches are as dumb in their retirement as though you had not paid for them, your conspicuous boots are eloquent with a thousand tongues! There is pleasure found, no doubt, in this.

As the season draws nigh the delights become vague, and still more vague; but, nevertheless, there are delights. Getting up at six o'clock in November to go down to Bletchley by an early train is not in itself pleasant, but on the opening morning—on the few first opening morn-ings—there is a promise about the thing which invigorates and encour-ages the early riser. He means to like it this year—if he can. He has still some undefined notion that his period of pleasure will now come. He has not, as yet, accepted the adverse verdict which his own nature has given against him. In this matter of hunting, and he gets into his early tub with acme glow of satisfaction. And afterwards it is nice to find himself bright with mahogany tops, buff-tinted breeches, and a pink coat. The ordinary habiliments of an English gentleman are so somber that his own eye is gratified, and he feels that he has placed himself in the vanguard of society by thus shining in his apparel. And he will ride this year! He is fixed to that purpose. He will ride straight—and, if possible, he will like it.

But the Ethiop cannot change his skin, nor can any man add a cubit to his stature. He doesn't like it, and all around him in the field know how it is with him. He himself knows how it is with others like himself, and he congregates with his brethren. The period of his penance has come upon him. He has to pay the price of those pleasant interviews with his tradesmen. He has to expiate the false boasts made to his female cousins. That row of boots cannot be made to shine in his chamber for nothing. The hounds have found, and the fox is away. Men are fastening on their flat-topped hats and feeling themselves in their stirrups. Horses are hot for the run, and the moment for liking it has come—if only it were possible!

But at moments such as these something has to be done. The man who doesn't like it, let him dislike it ever so much, cannot check his horse and simply ride back to the hunting stables. He understands that were he to do that, he must throw up his cap at once and resign. Nor can he trot easily along the roads with the fat old country gentleman who is out on his rough cob, and who, looking up to the wind and remembering the position of adjacent coverts, will give a good guess as to the direction in which the field will move. No, he must make an effort. The time of his penance has come, and the penance must be borne. There is a spark of pluck about him, though unfortunately he has brought it to bear in a wrong direction. The blood still runs at his heart, and he resolves that he will ride—if only he could tell which way.

The stout gentleman on the cob has taken the road to the left with a few companions, but our friend knows that the stout gentleman has a little game of his own which will not be suitable for one who intends to ride. Then the crowd in front has divided itself. Those to the right rush down a hill towards a brook with a ford. One or two men, whom he hates with an intensity of envy, have jumped the brook, and have settled to their work. Twenty or thirty others are hustling themselves through the water. The time for a judicious start on that side is already gone. But others—a crowd of others, are facing the big ploughed field immediately before them. That is the straightest riding, and with them he goes. Why has the scent lain so hot over the upturned heavy ground? Why do they go so fast at this, the very first blush of morning? Fortune is always against him, and the horse is pulling him through the mud as though the brute meant to drag his arm out of the socket. At the first fence, as he is steadying himself, a butcher passes him roughly in the jump and nearly takes away the side of his top boot. He is knocked half out of his saddle, and in that condition scrambles through. When he has regained his equilibrium he sees the happy butcher going into the field beyond. He means to curse the butcher when he catches him, but the butcher is safe. A field and a half before him he sees the tail hounds, and renews his effort. He has meant to like it today, and he will. So he rides at the next fence boldly, where the butcher has left his mark, and docs it pretty well—with a slight struggle. Why is it that he can never get over a ditch without some struggle in his saddle, some scramble with his horse? Why does he curse the poor animal so constantly—unless it be that he cannot catch the butcher? Now he rushes at a gate which others have opened for him, but be rushes too late and catches his leg. Mad with pain, he nearly gives it up, but the spark of pluck is still there, and with throbbing knee he perseveres. How he hates it! It is all detestable now. He cannot hold his horse because of his gloves, and he cannot get them off. The sympathetic beast knows that his master is unhappy, and makes himself unhappy and troublesome in consequence. Our friend is still going, riding wildly, but still keeping a grain of caution for his fences. He has not been down yet, but has barely saved himself more than once. The ploughs are very deep, and his horse, though still boring at him, pants heavily. Oh, that there might come a check, or that the brute of a fox might happily go to ground! But no! The ruck of the hunt is far away from him in front, and the game is running steadily straight for some well known though still distant protection. But the man who doesn't like it still sees a red coat before him, and perseveres in chasing the wearer of it. The solitary red coat becomes distant, and still more distant from him, but he goes on while he can yet keep the line in which the red coat has ridden. He must hurry himself, however, or he will be lost to humanity, and will be alone. He must hurry himself, but his horse now desires to hurry no more. So he puts the spurs to the brute savagely, and then at some little fence, some ignoble ditch, they come down together in the mud, and the question of any further effort is saved for the rider. When he arises the red coat is out of sight, and his own horse is half across the field before him. In such a position, is it possible that a man should like it?

About four o'clock in the afternoon, when the other men are coming in, he turns up at the hunting stables, and nobody asks him any questions. He may have been doing fairly well for what anybody knows, and, as he says nothing of himself, his disgrace is at any rate hidden. Why should he tell that he had been nearly an hour on foot trying to catch his horse, that he had sat himself down on a bank and almost cried, and that he had drained his flask to the last drop before one o'clock? No one need know the extent of his miseries. And no one does know how great is the misery endured by those who hunt regularly, and who do not like it.

41

Bones

By Helen Busher

This incredible tale is from Conversations with a Prince *by Helen Busher. It tells the story of Busher's developing bond with a difficult horse. Unlike in the past when horses were merely beasts of burden, today riders enjoy making an emotional connection with their horses. Busher's horse, Bones, was a flighty, opinionated mare that did not seem to have much interest in developing a relationship with her human companion. Over time, and using some fairly unorthodox methods, Busher is able to break through Bones's outer shell. The incredible truth that emerges is that humans and horses, two animals of completely different species are able to communicate and cooperate to an intense degree.*

WHEN WE TELL OUR STORIES ABOUT HORSES, THEY ANSWER BY TELLING us the truth, which can make for an unsettling transaction. Even though all animals are generically honest, they really do vary in how much they play along with the human urge to shape events into fiction. Dogs, for example, often accommodate us with great sensitivity, sometimes accepting a leading role in the family melodrama; most of us know of households where Fido is the object of endless and often quite uninteresting discussion. Even cats can contribute to the domestic narrative, though far more obliquely, but as we have seen these companion animals have a high level of indoorsy affectation that horses simply do not have. This isn't an equine moral posture, but a result of simply being horses. Of course horses can be wrong in their truthfulness—they may report a tiger in the laundry basket or a brace of dragons flying overhead—but this wrongness isn't deception. Horses do not lie. This leads to more problems than you'd think, mostly because we humans claim superior knowledge and access to the truth. To complicate matters, we are ourselves skilled and elaborate liars. It can be argued, cogently I think, that one of the big things that sets humans apart from other animals is our passion for dissembling. This passion goes by other, nicer names—metaphor, storytelling, mythmaking, poetics—but it often yanks us away from understanding plain animal utterances.

I learned this lesson the hard way from Bones. Because she fidgeted and had a lot of unwarranted opinions, I slid easily into the posture of the tolerant mother, which meant I often ignored any response I didn't approve of. This approach seemed humane and neutral and reflected well on me; it also meant, on some deeper and lazier level, that I had less static in my life, less information to process, and less to do. She would still sometimes twirl in the cross ties, bump me, rush ahead, lag behind, and make rude faces at me behind my back; once I got on, she was mostly obedient, but she always reserved the right to bounce up and down in one place and paw at the ground when I asked her to stand still. My planned ignoring of her outbursts was meant to be soothing and non-reinforcing, but it didn't work; she never got bored with her behavior, and it took me a long time to realize that there was something about it that was intrinsically gratifying. Every time she bumped me out of balance, every time I yielded, she was manufacturing her own reward. She would lift her head in triumph: I win.

But here's the thing: by this time she was winning, in at least two conflicting senses of the word, since during this same time she was also improving incrementally in her ring work, on the trails, and over fences. As I adapted, coaxed, ignored, and made allowances, I found I could now finesse her around a course of jumps at a local show and, because she was so talented, win a goodly share of prizes. I could even enter a hack class where, if there were no explosions, I could exploit her forwardness and her flashy style. Her coloring was decidedly unfashionable, but she was also impossible to miss among the bays and chestnuts. If a hack class has forty horses in it, it helps to be memorable.

This sounds like progress, and at the time it felt like progress, but it wasn't solid because it was partially grounded in deceit. By pretending that her attempts to dominate me didn't really matter, I was actually keeping the domination conversation alive. I wasn't really smart enough to know this, but, like the business with the bridle and the Necco wafer, I was smart enough to know when something bothered me, despite having other evidence—in this case, ribbons in various colors—that things were fine.

Then one spring I was allowed to move her temporarily to a local teaching barn where I could get more instruction and where, for the first time in her rather long life, she was expected to live in a box stall. She hated it, and deteriorated into pacing and sulking, and the obvious fix was to simply let her live outdoors again. She genuinely and absolutely preferred it—most horses do—and there happened to be a large turnout yard and shed behind the main barn where a dozen or so reliable school horses loafed and rolled and grimaced at each other in what appeared to be largely symbolic, recreational confrontations. So Bones, despite being a paying, box-stall boarder, was deposited into this good-natured, somewhat blue-collar neighborhood, which she organized with amazing speed and assurance into a tight, delinquent band of troublemakers. I was awestruck—she had always been the second-stringer at home, accepting instruction and correction from my sister's Standardbred, a horse blessed with deep reserves of poise and rectitude. Freed from Baby's tyranny, Bones became a thug. Within three days, she had all the horses taking cues from her, refusing to be caught, and moving as one across the half acre of grubby, broken ground. By the end of the week, she was in complete, undisputed charge of all hay piles, watering stations, and rules of proximity. No child could wander innocently into this equine Mafia to catch Spotty or Smoky or Bruce; no amount of gentle bribery could divide or conquer.

Bones's new criminal status was embarrassing and disruptive, but two good things came of it. First, I realized that my troubled mare was not the basket case I had always assumed her to be, and that I'd badly misjudged her. But second, I felt compelled to hang over the rail and watch as this herd went about its business, something I'd never had an opportunity to do before. Once I got accustomed to its swirly logic, I began to grasp that horse society is a profound matriarchy.

I hadn't understood this before—I had a bunch of squishy, rather sexist ideas, derived mostly from horse stories, that stallions were somehow in charge of things. If no stallion was in the offing, I went on to assume, unthinkingly, that the geldings would be in charge. Not true. I learned later that stallions are, quite literally, peripheral presences; a young girl's stud horse in the wild will wander alone or in a bachelor group until a band of mares and their young offspring consent to his presence, provided he behaves. This last point is important, since, when it comes to mares, their standards are high and their decisions are final. Jane Smiley, that consummate observer of equine behavior, describes this dynamic in her novel Horse Heaven. A recently gelded, unusually aggressive specimen named Epic Steam has discovered that he can jump out of his isolated pasture and engage in an extended meet-and-greet with other horses on the farm. Eventually he finds himself "just where he wanted to be for so very long, in a paddock with four mares. Something this exciting for the four mares hadn't happened in years, so they stood stock-still, ears pricked, tails up, staring at him."

He took this as encouragement, and lifted his own tail, arched his neck, and progressed in a beautiful passage around the perimeter of the pasture, picking his feet up as quick and high as if the ground were strewn with hot coals. All the horses in every other pasture looked on and occasionally whinnied encouragement. After displaying himself to his own satisfaction, Epic Steam lowered his head and snaked it toward one of the mares, a little bay. He approached her. She moved away, toward the other mares, and he paused, but then approached again. Manners do not come naturally to a young stallion, and did not come naturally to Epic Steam in any event. Her retreat aroused some of his inherent aggression, and he went after her. He thought he might bite her. Intent upon this thought, he did not pay attention to his position relative to the other mares, and so he did not realize until it was already happening that they were kicking the stuffing out of him.

The reader cheers—this particular horse has been in need of a come-uppance for some time now—but the deeper point is that this scene is a counternarrative to the established tale of the proud, wily stallion who dominates his mares and assumes the role of chief executive. This alternate version isn't feminism run amok; it actually happens to be true. An alpha mare is a formidable and profoundly social creature, and leaning over the fence watching Bones run everything I began to understand that her endless bumps and challenges, her squirminess, and her willingness to crowd me were something I should no longer deceive myself about or studiously ignore. She would not stop out of boredom, because it didn't bore her; instead it was primal and compelling. And hard to bring to closure—it took two skilled handlers most of an afternoon to settle the herd, siphon off the school horses, catch her, and then seduce her back into her old dominance pattern with me, which must have seemed pretty insipid after seven days of the real thing.

It was only after this encounter that I began to develop an enduring love for watching horses in groups at liberty, since this is when they wear their truthfulness—their wishes and decisions—on their metaphorical sleeves. At East Hill, where horses are turned out with an almost obsessive regularity, in all but the most horrible weather, the opportunities to do this are ongoing—horse society there is allowed to operate in clusters of twos and threes, and even the unredeemably rowdy ones, who really have to be kept by themselves, still have an opportunity to gossip over the fence. This is healthy, even though it means the animals are often dirty; I have visited and briefly worked in barns where the horses were almost never at liberty, and they spent most of their time spanking clean but going quietly (or not so quietly) insane.

All this fence hanging has taught me that what often matters to a horse is something as basic as whether he can get another horse to move. Like the talent for mapping, this is essentially a spatial behavior, and space, for horses, is packed with meaning. Where they are, where they stand in relationship to each other, what they do about it, and what happened when all were assembled here the last time are the important social verbs that drive what will happen now; now is the construct that horses pay attention to, and it sometimes seems that their prodigious and detailed memories do not really exist for learning or reflection, but for refining and animating now. As a group of horses moves out to grass, in for feeding, or from one place in the pasture to another, they act out complex little dramas about leading, following, clustering, and standing ground, and the results of these transactions are often surprising. The best horse in the barn—well schooled, fun to be around, responsive, and even-tempered— is hardly ever the best horse in equine society, which is perhaps more proof that horses and people do not really agree on what's important. With Bones back home in the pasture with Baby, I was able to see something that hadn't registered before. Baby, unlike my big spotted mare, was never thuggish or punishing—watching them together, all I could see was equilibrium. They grazed close together and spent huge amounts of time doing what looked like nothing at all. Horses can be spectacularly idle, and the two of them loafed, scratched, swished away flies, snoozed, watched the wildlife, and made leisurely strolls of the perimeter. Every now and again, they would buck and play. If we needed to rotate the two of them from one pasture to another—a very common exercise in my foster mother's grazing programwe would set the gates, pick up the water buckets, call to Baby, and the two of them would trot complacently up or down the long driveway, technically loose but completely under control. Baby came when she was called, and Bones followed Baby.

The vast difference between this arrangement and the quarreling I had witnessed at the other barn was more than a little confusing, and it took me a while to find a name for what I was seeing. This wasn't just the absence of discord; it seemed obvious that these two were friends. But friendship is a tricky term. Many of the people who study animals— including the primatologists who study our very closest relatives—sometimes call friendship the f-word, because it's been so folded and smudged by human fingers. It's hard to know, they say, what really goes on between two animals of the same species who hang around together. These creatures may not be, in the sense we mean, actual friends, although I have to add that this objection seems a little fussy, since there's no question that many animals form social bonds that have nothing to do with reproduction or kinship or advancing their DNA. Why should we assume that, when humans do it, it's somehow different and needs a distinctive name? It is also hard not to notice that these supposedly nonessential relationships are the very thing that makes both animals and people more interesting. Recreational bonds, whether we call them friendships or not, are well worth watching, and it was by watching that I learned that Baby was the undisputed alpha horse because she was completely sure of herself and utterly trustworthy, and Bones put faith in her in exactly the way I yearned for her to put faith in me. They were at peace together, a kind of equine binary star.

This trustworthiness, this final confidence, is what riders like Ruth have and I do not. My greatest flaw as a rider, then and now, is that I am not always sure I know what I want to have happen. I'm not talking here about navigational things—I can almost always get to the jump, around the barrel, through the gate, across the pasture, or up the hill. But there are other things, subtler things—dressage things and these are what really matter. There's a way to travel and a way not to, and the difference has to do with intangibles like style and forwardness and way of going—these terms refer to the horse's physical state and level of happiness with the proceedings, and mainly tell us that riding is more than the mere fact of arrival. These important intangibles have always eluded me. I know when things are going badly, but I have no clear picture in my mind of how I want them to go, and this has tended to make me tentative and blank and hopeful. This absence of mental aggression is what makes it hard for me to succeed with a horse like Railund, who relies absolutely on having a definite, controlling, rather bossy rider. But the upside to being vague is that horses with ideas—Abbott, Prince, Reba—would often fill up that blank space with their own material, and this gave me access to the very thing that attracted me to riding in the first place. I wanted to know, feel, and be able to think about horses in a firsthand way; I liked it when they did this, since it was a way for them to be present and truthful with me.

The trouble with the truth is that it can be unattractive and uncomfortable—there were times, on Bones, when I felt like I was on a trampoline, and other times when I felt caught in a blender. This wasn't just bad behavior, and I want to digress for a moment and say that the word just should be stricken forever from a rider's vocabulary: "He's just being a stinker," "He's just trying to scare me," "He's just not listening," are all sentences that dismiss the thing that matters with horses, which is now. By using this word, we lapse into telling ourselves a story that we hope will turn out differently tomorrow, which is a thing a horse never thinks about. One thing I continually appreciate about Kathie's teaching is that I never hear this word. She sometimes says a problem doesn't matter, but I think she means something different by this—when Prince drops unexpectedly out of his canter into a scrambling trot, or when Reba's backlog of awkwardness catches up with her, she uses this phrase to indicate that, now notwithstanding, it is not possible to do everything at once. The problem of now certainly applied to my dominance struggle with the spotted mare—after the episode with the school horses, I saw for the first time that her boorishness wasn't just bad behavior. She, like Epic Steam, could be a monumental troublemaker, and her need to win had more momentum than my need for a reasonable level of tranquillity. I also saw that if I entered into a direct war with her on the issue, she would love every minute of it, and she would also, most assuredly, defeat me—horses are very strong. All I really had on my side of the ledger was that she had already made many important concessions, that we had come to know and understand each other, and so something was at stake for both of us. Thinking about Baby, and about friendship, I concluded that it was my job to become not just a rider she mostly consented to carry, but a rider who was somehow trustworthy.

So I began riding her alone. This was fairly new for both of us except for the occasional schooling session in the ring, we tended, generally, to ride out in company of twos or threes, and sometimes as part of a congenial larger lump of other horses. Baby was almost always there, a soothing presence, and this happy serum also meant the humans could chatter, making it a social event for everyone. But I decided that, for me to become trustworthy, Bones and I had to spend more time out in the woods and fields together.

This decision made her horribly anxious, and when she was anxious she became noisy, shouting and weeping as she stomped through the woods, calling out endlessly for an acceptable companion. Her old reactiveness returned; there were tigers everywhere; when I finally turned her back toward the stable, she leaned into my hands, jigging and flailing in frustration that she couldn't go faster. I became so accustomed to the lift and shiver of the saddle as she whinnied that I hardly paid attention, although the decibel level did embarrass me—as we thrashed our way down the trails and dirt roads around town, people stepped out on their porches to see what all the noise was about and perhaps to check up on me. I don't blame them—it sounded as if I were extracting her teeth with rusty pliers. Bones would roll up into a tight, unhappy ball, bounce, squall, dribble, crimp her tail, and periodically vent her upset with a potent outburst of bucking. With her rolling eyes, her noise, and her splashy coloration, I think we made quite a spectacle, escapees from some demonic merry-go-round.

It wasn't much fun, but it sort of worked. With only me to fall back on, my mare discovered that her isolation really wasn't absolute: I spoke, I made decisions, I directed her as best I could, and she always managed to come home uneaten, despite the many tigers. She realized she wasn't going to die gradually, over the course of about a month—a difficult month, but one well worth getting through. She didn't like this forced acceptance very much, but still gradually toned down the racket and even, at times, seemed to acquiesce without resentment, cocking her ears back toward me as I chose the safe route around the unacceptable puddle. Like with the business with the halter, hup, and ho, the ground between us shifted again, and again to my slight advantage. But I found the state of things coercive and disagreeable.

Then my older brother, Allan, went to the pound and got a dog. This was a background, household sort of event, done on an impulse that didn't involve me, although I liked the dog. His name was Ranger—a good name for a dog-pound animal—and he looked like a cross between some sort of husky and some sort of generic, bigheaded hound. He had impenetrable fur that was layered and curiously short, a soaring and distinctive olla-olla call, and more skin than a dog his size was really entitled to. Despite his iffy, jailbird background, Ranger was free of any kennel neurosis and went at life with a healthy doggy vigor: he swam, hunted, womanized, and carried disgraceful and smelly things around in his mouth, but above all these things nothing made him happier than an expedition. This is how, within a week or two of his arrival, Ranger became the third leg of a weird and unplanned three-legged stool, since he would not let me go out for a ride without him.

Relations between species are hard to categorize, and it's important not to romanticize or misjudge what happens. This is especially the case when we talk about domestic animals, where our urge to make up a story can be almost irresistible. So I must be careful here, and simply tell what I think must be the truth, which is that Bones, at least some of the time, did not particularly care about Ranger, and Ranger, for his part, was probably more interested in horse excrement than he was in horses themselves. Yet there he was, a sudden presence in our daily doings, and his bumptious and smiling being radically transformed the proceedings.

Dogs like to go scouting. Nothing pleases them more than the sort of outing where they are free to circle forward, let you slide by, cross you to leeward, and appear magically in the lead again—and Ranger took scouting to heart. As far as he was concerned, the entire point of existence was to secure the moving perimeter and verify that the landscape was operating smoothly, and, in an unusual intersection of desires, this was a task that my mare desperately wanted performed. Whatever residual worries she had about my ability to protect her simply vanished, and there is no question that they vanished only when Ranger was there.

I agreed with Bones that Ranger was an excellent escort, and I got a huge amount of pleasure out of watching him do his job. While we stuck to the trail, he would break ground out ahead of us in a kind of huge fan, crossing and recrossing our line of travel, the white tip of his tail mostly visible above the scrubby undergrowth. He would then fall backward or off to the side to inspect holes, wet places, and evidence of animal life, and this sometimes involved the unexpected appearance of a rabbit or pheasant. Bones was interested in and sometimes startled by these animal materializations, but they didn't seem to actually frighten her. Ranger would then fall behind—sometimes far behind—and when this happened he would race to catch up, his tongue hanging sideways and his expression at once joyful and businesslike. He then began the entire scouting pattern all over again—he crashed ahead of us through the bushes, plunged into streams, and generally made an amazing racket, all of which my horse monitored with interest. Sometimes he would gallop right up on her heels—a fine excuse for an explosion—and she merely noted his return with satisfaction and composure. When we reached an open place—a cornfield or the local tree nursery with its potbellied arborvitae standing in unnatural rows—Ranger made a point of closing ranks and circling us rather tightly, and more than once he nearly tangled himself under the mare's hard, pumping feet. She hopped to avoid stepping on him, he scooted, and we all continued on as if nothing exciting had happened, which it obviously hadn't.

Ranger brought to these long rides the confidence and knowledge that I lacked, since he obviously understood that tigers were out there and was determined to find and vanquish them. The result was that Bones traveled happily on a long rein, swinging her neck and back, and was perfectly fine about standing still while I checked my bearings or drank some water. She went uphill and down, into thick places and dark places and narrow places and queer places; she even stepped daintily through the puddles she'd once assumed to be a mile deep and requiring a prolonged detour. Better still, she stopped bumping and crowding, and, for the first time, began showing me some signs of routine affection—she ran her wiggly nose over my chest and neck when I brushed her face and sighed with pleasure when I rubbed stinky, soothing liniment on her hardworking legs.

The transformation was quick, and quite impressive. I have a photograph of our triumvirate, Ranger in the foreground and horse and handler in the midground, that captures this odd arrangement. It must have been taken in either late fall or early spring, since I am cooling my horse with a rug thrown over her haunches and the front folded back and buckled over her withers so her chest is exposed. Her winter coat is either growing in or shedding out—it's impossible to tell which—and the trees along the driveway look chilled and bare. A trick of elevation—I am walking on the high mound in the middle of road, while Bones is walking on the low dip made by passing tires—makes me look even taller than I actually am; my horse looks curiously medium-sized, as opposed to the very substantial horse she really was. Horse, dog, and human are all tired, damp, and dirty; Bones walks next to me, her shoulder exactly level with mine, her head lowered and her ears tuned backward toward me. She curls her head and neck around me very slightly, interested in my agenda, but her weather eye is glued on Ranger, who, even so close to home, is still taking his job seriously and breaking trail. Everything about her body language signals contentment, willingness, submission; everything about mine conveys a disheveled, unthinking happiness. My braids are coming loose, my hands are in my pockets, and I do not see a lead rope anywhere. Yet we are deeply tethered, the three of us, by a common, treasured enterprise. When I look at this picture, which I do often because it sits on my desk, I understand it captures a moment of peace and equilibrium. In it, I seem to loom over the horse who once dominated me, and who now chooses to walk freely and respectfully in my orbit. For my part, I am built around a smile, and the message in that smile is plain: I win.

42

Dark Clouds, Then Tall Grass

By Will James

◇◇

We opened this collection with the opening chapter of Will James's outstanding book, Smoky the Cowhorse, *first published in 1926. Determined to close this huge book with a chapter upbeat and sustaining, my choice was the last chapter of* Smoky. *The first chapter of* Smoky *opened our book; the last chapter of* Smoky *closes it. I can think of no better way to end what has been one heck of a ride.*

—LAMAR UNDERWOOD

◇◇

THE MAN COLLECTING OLD WORE OUT AND CRIPPLED HORSES HAD COME along and led him away. He had a little salt-grass pasture a short distance out of town, and there's where he took the old horse. He turned him loose amongst a few more old horses, and would keep him there till the time come when some "chicken man" around town would need the carcass of one of the horses to feed to his chickens; then the horse what looked like it had the shortest to live would be killed and hauled away.

It didn't look like the end was very far for the mouse colored horse. All the work he'd done and the interest he'd had while under the names of Smoky and The Cougar, had stopped being accounted for, and sort of pinched out under the name of Cloudy; and now he had no name. He was just "chicken feed," and soon, if he stayed in that pasture, all what he'd been and done would be blotted out with the crack of a rifle shot.

But the old pony had no hint of that, and as it was he wasn't for quitting as yet. His old stiff legs was still able to carry him around some, the doctoring he'd got at the stable had helped him more than what had been hoped, and then getting out in a pasture where he could keep moving around as he wanted to was helping him some more. Besides, his old heart was still strong, quite a bit solid meat was covering his ribs, and with the salt and wire grass to graze on he could still make out and mighty well.

A few weeks went by when once in a while and every few days, one of the old horses he was pasturing with was caught, led out, a rifle shot was heard, and he'd never be seen no more. Other old horses was brought in and they'd pasture on with him till one by one they'd also disappear only to be replaced by more of 'em.

The old mouse colored horse must of looked like he was good to live for a long time yet; anyway, the "chicken horse" man had kept him, maybe for emergency, and so he wouldn't be out of horses if an order for one came; and that kind was hard to get.

Then one day, a man came, looked all the old horses over. And finally, like he'd decided, pointed a finger towards the horse that'd last been known as Cloudy. That pony was caught and led out the same way other horses had disappeared, but no rifle shot was heard. Instead, a lot of parleying went on.

Cloudy was led alongside of an old bony something that'd once been a horse. The old rack of bones was hooked onto a light wagon and seeming like hardly able to stand as the eyes of the two men went from him to Cloudy, to sort of figger out which of the two was worth the most, and how much the most.

Finally the dickering came to an end and seemed like agreeable to both parties. Three dollars to boot was handed, and the trade was made. The rack of bones was unhooked, the harness pulled off of him, and turned loose in the chicken horse pasture. Then Cloudy's old heart missed a few beats as that same harness was picked up again and throwed over his own back.

As true a saddle horse, and once hard to set on, as the mouse colored horse had been, the feel of that harness on his back was as much the same as if a shovel or a hayfork had been handed to a cow-puncher with the idea of his using 'em. The old horse felt it a plain disgrace, and snorted as it was buckled around him to stay; but the black whiskered hombre that buckled it on never seemed to notice or care that the horse had no liking for the collar and all the straps.

He kept on a fastening the harness, and when that was done, he jerked the old pony around and backed him into the shafts of the same old wagon that the rack of bones had been unhooked out of. Cloudy kept on a snorting and looked on one side and then the other as the shafts of the wagon was raised. If only he could act the way his heart wanted him to; but he didn't have the strength, the action to put in it, nor the energy no more. The most he could do was to snort, quiver, and shake his head.

But, as he was all hooked up and the man jumping in the wagon grabbed his whip, Old Cloudy done his best to try and get back to some of the life and tearing ability that'd once been his. He kicked a couple of times at the rattling thing on wheels and which he was fastened to, then he tried to buck some and finally wound up by wanting to run away; but the harness held and the rattling thing behind came right along wherever he went, and worse yet, he felt the stinging lash of the man's whip as he fought on and tried to clear himself. Then the jerking of the bit thru his mouth, and with all that to show how useless his fighting and wanting to get away really was, the old pony soon lost heart. He finally settled down to a choppy lope, then a trot that was just as choppy, and at last to a walk.

Another sting of the whip was felt on his flank, and at the same time, the line was jerked at the bit, and Cloudy, still pulling the wagon, was made to turn up a lane. At the end of the lane was a shack made of old pieces of boards and covered over with the tin of old oil-cans. To the right of that and a little ways further was another shack that looked like a mate to the first, only worse, and that one was going to be Cloudy's place of rest and shelter whenever work was over.

There he was pulled to a stop, unhooked, led to the manger, and tied. The stable door was closed with a bang, and after a while the old horse, still wanting to cling to life regardless of what came, stuck his nose in the manger to nibble on some of what was in it. He reached for a mouthful of what he'd naturally took for hay, and chewed for a spell, but he didn't chew on it long. There was a musty taste about the long dirty brown stems that didn't at all fit in with any hay he'd ever et. The kind that'd been put in the manger for him to eat was the same that the livery stableman had used to put in the stalls and bed the horses down with. It was straw, only this was musty straw and wouldn't even make good bedding for horses.

Cloudy felt hungry long before the next morning came, and often thru the night he'd nosed into the musty straw with the hopes of finding a few stems that'd do to fill an empty space, but there wasn't any to be found. The old rack of bones that'd been there before him had looked for some too, and with no better luck. Cloudy's new owner figgered it cheaper to swap horses with the "chicken man" and give him a few dollars to boot whenever any horse of his give out; he wasn't going to buy no high-priced hay for no horse. The straw was given to him for the getting and would keep any horse alive and working for at least six months, and then, or whenever the horse would be too weak to go any more, he'd trade him for another. Any kind of a horse, fat or thin, could always be used by the chicken man, and in trade, he'd always take one of the fattest to take the place of the one he'd just starved near to death. That way, year in year out, he'd keep a draining the last of the life of every horse he'd get his claws onto.

His property, and where he starved the horses into making a living for him, took in a couple of acres. Half of that land was rocks, mostly, and where he kept a few chickens. He bought, or stole a little grain for *them*; but they well repaid him. Every time he went to town there was a basket of eggs in his wagon and which he sold well. The other half of his land was cultivated, and where vegetables of all kinds had been made to grow. There's where the help of a horse was needed, to pull the cultivator or the plow, then the hauling of the vegetables to town, and once there, any odd job that could be got and which would bring a few dollars for the use of the horse and wagon.

It was bright and early the next morning when the work begin for Cloudy. The man showed his teeth in a grin as he looked in the manger while putting the harness on the horse, and noticing the straw in there hadn't hardly been touched, remarked: "You'll be eating some of that before you get thru."

Cloudy was made acquainted with many different kinds of implements and work that day. All was mighty strange and plum against the ways of working which he'd been broke to do. It was pull, and pull, one contraption and then another, back and forth thru furrows, turn at the end and then back again. If he slowed down, or hesitated, wondering what to do, there was the whip always on hand to make him decide and mighty quick.

His muscles, having developed under the saddle, used to pack weight, and set that way, wasn't for getting next to the change very easy. Looking thru a collar and pulling steady was so different to heading off and turning a wild-eyed critter. It wasn't at all like coming out of the chute in front of a grandstand and seeing how many jumps could be put into one; nor didn't compare even with packing equestrians around. He'd felt some free under the saddle, and even tho all of it had been real work, there'd always been something that fitted in and which made him feel natural.

But now, with all these straps a hanging onto him, there was a feeling that he was tied down—them straps even seemed to wrap around his heart at times and keep it from beating. And taking all, the strange hard work, the sting of the whiplash on his ribs, nothing fit to eat after he was tired out and the day was over, it was no wonder that the old pony's heart begin to shrivel up on him.

As the long days run into weeks and the work in the field and in the town got to bearing down on him, the old pony even got so he couldn't hate no more; abuse or kindness had both got to be the same, and one brought out no more results or show of interest than the other. He went to the jerk of the lines like without realizing; and when he was finally led into the stable when night come the feeling was the same. There he et the musty straw because it was under his nose. He didn't mind the taste of it, he didn't mind anything, any more.

Of the odd jobs that Cloudy's owner would get to do around town and whenever he could get away from his truck and chicken farm, there was one which he looked forward to the most, and which the thought of made him rub his hands together with pleasure. It was that of scattering the posters advertising The Annual Rodeo, and Celebration, that was pulled off in town and every early fall. But that wasn't all. There was many other things for him to do at that time for which he could charge without anybody ever finding out whether all he'd been paid to do really had been done.

That year as usual he was ready, and right on the dot, to take on some more of that kind of work. He'd hooked up the old mouse colored horse and taking a load of vegetables on the way in, stuck around town doing the different kinds of work the rodeo association had furnished him with. He'd be on the go all day and prodding the old horse into a trot, sometimes even if the wagon was loaded.

It'd be away into the night before he'd turn the tired horse towards home. Every day was a great day, *for the man*, there was so many people around to make the town lively; and being most of 'em was strangers, he could get to within talking distance of 'em easy enough, and a few would even stand to have him around for a few minutes at the time.

Them strangers had come to see the rodeo. Most of 'em was from other towns around, and mixed in the crowd once in a while could be seen the high-crowned hat of a cowboy who'd come to ride, rope, and bulldog. Then at the Casa Grande Hotel, and registered there, was many cattle buyers from the northern States.

They'd come to bid on the big herds of cattle that was being crowded acrost the border from Mexico; for Pancho Villa and the Yaquis was making it hard for the cattleman of that country. Villa took the cattle to feed his army, while the Yaquis run off whatever Villa overlooked; and the cowman that could, and had any stock left, soon seen where if he wanted to save anything of what he'd worked to accumulate, he'd have to rush whatever that was to the border and get it on American soil mighty quick.

That's how come that the stockyards of the border towns was filled with cattle and that the hotels along them same towns was filled with cattle buyers. The Casa Grande Hotel was the most filled on account that along with the business of buying cattle, a little pleasure could be got there afterwards. A rodeo was in that town, and night celebrations; and being that them cattle buyers was still as much cowboys as ever, a good bucking contest and the fun afterwards couldn't be overlooked, not if it could be helped. "Yep, the town was sure lively."

Two of the buyers was sitting in the lobby of the hotel one morning and a talking on the first day's event of the rodeo. A telegraph pole stuck up right before their vision and on the edge of the sidewalk, and nailed to that pole was a poster advertising the rodeo, and with a photograph of a bucking horse in action on it, told all about "the great bucking horse and outlaw The Grey Cougar, the only one that could compare, in wickedness and bucking ability, to The Cougar, that once famous man killing horse."

The two went on to talking about the rodeo, and naturally the talk drifted on about The Grey Cougar, and "*how* he could buck."

"The boys tell me," says one of the men, "that this Grey Cougar horse couldn't hold a candle to the real Cougar when it come to bucking and fighting. According to that, the other horse must of been *some* wicked."

The man was still talking on the subject, when an old mouse colored horse, pulling an old wagon loaded down with vegetables, came to a stiff legged stop, and right by the telegraph pole on which the poster telling all about The Grey Cougar was nailed. The man in the lobby grinned a little at the sight of the old horse a standing there like in comparison with the famous grey outlaw, and pointing a finger in his direction, he remarked: "There must be the Old Cougar right there, Clint. Anyway he's got the same color."

The man called Clint grinned some at the joke, but the grin soon faded away as he kept a looking at the old horse, and noticed the condition he was in. Then he seen the saddle-marks that was all over the pony's back, and he says: "You can never tell, that old pony might of been mighty hard to set at one time too—but the way he looks like now, them times are sure done past and gone."

"Yep," agreed the other man, "it's a miracle that pony can navigate at all—I wonder how it is that this Humane Society hombre that's sticking around the rodeo grounds don't happen to notice such as this. I'd like to help hang a feller for driving a horse like that around."

The conversation was held up for a spell as time two men watched the bewhiskered man come out of the hotel with an empty basket and climbed the wagon on which the old mouse colored horse was hooked. He grabbed the lines and the whip both at the same time and went to work a putting the horse into a trot.

Clint was for getting up as he seen the whip land on the old pony's hide, but the other man grabbed a hold of his arm and says:

"Never mind, old boy, most likely that Humane Society outfit'll fall on the bolshevik's neck before he gets very far."

The man called Clint set down again, but he was boiling up inside, and he didn't at all look pleasant as the conversation was resumed and noticed how his friend turned it to other things and away from the subject of old horses and such. He wasn't for answering very quick when that same friend went on to talking about that country to the north—how he'd heard rumors that the Rocking II might be selling out in another year or so. "I wonder why?" he asks.

Clint, turned to his friend and grinning at his idea of changing time subject that way, finally answered: "I guess it's because Old Tom feels the end a coming, besides he's getting crowded all around by small outfits, and his range ain't holding up like it used to."

"But what are you going to do when the Rocking R sells out? You left that country quite a few times the last few years, and I notice you always go back like there was no other that suited you."

"I've got that fixed," says Clint gradually taking more heart in the new subject, and there he tried to describe some; "You know about where that camp is where I used to break horses when I first started working for the Rocking R? It's where the outfit used to run their stock horses. Well, I bought that camp from Old Tom Jarvis—that is, I talked him into selling it to me, and four thousand acres of the fine range around to go with it.

"I'm thinking that this shipment I'm getting together now will be the last Old Tom'll ever buy, and by the time I get this trainload of Sonora Reds north and delivered to him, I'll have enough money to make the final payment on my place and still have enough left to buy a few head of cattle and start stocking it."

Clint often thought of his little place up in the heart of the cow country to the north. He could picture his own cattle ranging there and packing a brand of his on their slick hides. He'd a long time hoped for the likes, and at last he was getting it. A couple more days now, and he'd be heading north again, and there to stay, this time.

The last day of the rodeo had come, and Clint was to start with his trainload of stock that night. Him and his friend was sitting in the lobby of the hotel that evening a talking and wondering when they'd be seeing one another again, when outside and by the telegraph pole, came the same old mouse colored horse and stopped not an inch from where the two men had seen him a couple of days before.

Both was quick to spot him again this time, and right then, for some reason or other, the conversation died down. The first sight of that old pony hadn't been forgot, and when he showed up this second time, right before their eyes, he was like reminding 'em, and natural like, set the two men to thinking. That old shadow of a horse told some of the hard knocks of life, of things that was past and gone and which could of been bettered while the bettering could be done.

It was while the thinking was going on that way, that Clint sort of felt a faint, far away something a knocking and from down the bottom of his think tank. That something was trying hard to come back to life as that man's eyes kept a going over the pony's blazed face and bony frame, but it was buried so far underneath so many things that'd been stacked there that the knocking was pretty well muffled up. It'd have to be helped by some sort of a sudden jolt before it could come out on top.

The jolt came as the vegetable man got his seat on the wagon and as usual reached for the whip. Clint's friend a trying to keep him from running out and starting a rompus had tried to draw his interest by asking:

"What's become of that cowhorse *Smoky*, that used to—?"

But the question was left for *him* to wonder about, for Clint wasn't there to answer. Instead the hotel door slammed and only a glimpse of that same cowboy could be seen as he passed by the lobby window. In less than it takes to tell it, he was up on the wagon, took a bulldogging holt of the surprised vegetable man, and by his whiskers, drug him off his seat and down to earth.

The telephone on the desk of the sheriff's office rang till it near danced a jig, and when that feller lifted the receiver, a female voice was heard to holler:

"Somebody is killing somebody else with a whip, by the Casa Grande Hotel. *Hurry! Quick!*"

The sheriff appeared on the scene and took in the goings on at a glance. Like a man who knowed his business, his eyes went to looking for what might of caused the argument as he came. He looked at the old horse whose frame showed thru the hide, then the whip marks on that hide. He knowed horses as well as he did men; and when he noticed more marks of the same whip on the bewhiskered man's face, he stood his ground, watched, and then grinned.

"Say, cowboy," he finally says, "don't scatter that hombre's remains too much; you know we got to keep record of that kind the same as if it was a white man, and I don't want to be looking all over the streets to find out who he was."

Clint turned at the sound of the voice, and sizing up the grinning sheriff, went back to his victim and broke the butt end of the whip over his head; after which he wiped his hands, and proceeded to unhook the old horse off the wagon.

That evening was spent in "investigating." Clint and the sheriff went to the chicken-horse man and found out enough from him about the vegetable man and his way of treating horses to put that hombre in a cool place and keep him there for a spell.

"I'm glad to've caught on to that feller's doings," remarks the sheriff as him and Clint went to the livery stable, their next place of investigation.

There Clint listened mighty close as he learned a heap about the mouse colored horse when he was known as Cloudy. The stable man went on to tell as far as he knowed about the horse and the whole history of him, and when that pony was known thru the Southwest and many other places as *The Cougar*, the wickedest bucking horse and fighting outlaw the country had ever layed eyes on.

Clint was kinda proud in hearing that. He'd heard of The Cougar and that pony's bucking ability even up to the Canadian line and acrost it, and to himself he says: "That Smoky horse never did do things halfways." But he got to wondering, and then asked how come the pony had turned out to be that kind of a horse. That, the stable man didn't know. It was news to him that the horse had ever been anything else, and as he says:

"The first that was seen of that horse is when some cowboys found him in the desert, amongst a bunch of wild horses, and packing a saddle. Nobody had ever showed up to claim him, and as that pony had been more than inclined to buck and fight is how come he was sold as a bucking horse—and believe me, old timer," went on the stable man, a shaking his head, "he was *some* bucking horse."

"Well," says the sheriff, "that's another clue run to the ground with nothing left of, but the remains."

That night, the big engine was hooked on to the trainload of cattle as to per schedule and started puffing its way on to the north. In the last car, the one next to the caboose, and the least crowded, a space had been partitioned off. In that space was a bale of good hay, a barrel of water, and an old mouse colored horse.

The winter that came was very different to any the old mouse colored horse had ever put in. The first part of it went by with him like in a trance, not realizing and hardly seeing. His old heart had dwindled down till only a sputtering flame was left, and that threatened to go out with the first hint of any kind of breeze.

Clint had got the old horse in a warm box stall, filled the manger full of the best blue joint hay there was, and even bedded him down with more of the same; water was in that same stall and where it could be easy reached, and then that cowboy had bought many a dollar's worth of condition powders, and other preparations which would near coax life back even in a dead body.

Two months went by when all seemed kinda hopeless, but Clint worked on and kept a hoping. He'd brought the old horse in the house, and made him a bed by the stove if that would of helped; and far as that goes, he'd of done anything else, just so a spark of life showed in the old pony's eyes; but he'd done all he could do, and as he'd lay a hand on the old skinny neck and felt of the old hide, he'd cuss and wish for the chance of twisting out of shape who all had been responsible. Then his expression would change, and he'd near bust out crying as he'd think back and compare the old wreck with what that horse had been.

As much as Clint had liked Smoky, the old wreck of a shadow of that horse wasn't wanting for any of the same liking. It was still in the cowboy's heart a plenty, and if anything, more so on account that the old pony was now needing help, and a friend like he'd never needed before; and Clint was more on hand with the horse, now that he was worthless, than he'd been when Smoky was the four hundred dollar cowhorse and worth more.

Finally, and after many a day of care and worrying, Clint begin to notice with a glad smile that the pony's hide was loosening up. Then after a week or so more of shoving hay and grain, condition powders, and other things down the old pony's throat, a layer of meat begin to spread over them bones and under that hide. Then one day a spark showed in the pony's eye, soon after that he started taking interest in the things around.

As layer after layer of meat and then tallow accumulated and rounded the sharp corners of Smoky's frame, that pony was for noticing more and more till after a while his interest spread enough, and with a clearer vision, went as far as to take in the man, who kept a going and coming, once in a while touched him, and then talked.

Clint liked to had a fit one day, when talking to the horse and happened to say *Smoky*, he noticed that pony cock an ear.

The recuperating of the horse went pretty fast from then on; and as the winter days howled past and early spring drawed near, there was no more fear of Smoky's last stand being anywheres near. As the days growed longer and the sun got warmer, there was times when Clint would lead the horse out and turn him loose to walk around in the sunshine, and that way get the blood to circulating. Smoky would sometimes mosey along for hours around the place and then start out on some trail, but always when the sun went down, he was by the stable door again and then Clint would let him in.

Clint would watch him by the hour whenever the horse was out that way, and he'd wonder, as he kept his eye on him, if that pony remembered, if the knocks he'd got from different people in different countries, didn't forever make him forget his home range and all that went with it. Not many miles away was where he was born; the big mountains now covered with snow was the same he was raised on, and which he tore up with his hoofs as he played while a little colt, and by his mammy. The corrals by the stable and sheds was the ones he was first run into when branded, and in them, a few years later, broke to saddle; but what Clint would wonder the most, as he watched, is whether Smoky remembered him.

The cowboy had kept a hoping that sometime he'd be greeted with a nicker as he'd open the stable door in the morning. Clint felt if the horse remembered, he would nicker that way at the sight of him and like he used to; but morning after morning went by, and even tho Smoky seemed full of life and rounded out to near natural again, no nicker was ever heard.

"Somebody must of stretched that pony's heartstrings to the breaking point," he remarked one day, as he'd stopped, wondering as usual, and looked at the horse.

Finally spring came sure enough, and broke up the winter. Green grass-covered ridges took the place of snow banks, and the cottonwoods along the creeks was beginning to bud. It was during one of them fine spring days, when riding along and looking the country over, Clint run acrost a bunch of horses. In the bunch was a couple of colts just a few days old, and knowing that old ponies have such a strong interest and liking for the little fellers, the cowboy figgered the sight of 'em would help considerable in bringing Smoky's heart up a few notches, and maybe to remembering. He fell in behind the bunch and hazed 'em all towards the corrals, and as Smoky, turned loose that day, spotted the bunch, his head went up. Then he noticed the little fellers, and that old pony, gathering all the speed there was in him, headed straight for the bunch and amongst 'em.

Clint corralled him and all the rest together and setting on his horse at the gate, watched Smoky while that horse was having the time of his life getting acquainted. The pony dodged kicks and bites and went back and forth thru the bunch, and a spark showed in his eye which hadn't been there for many a day.

The cowboy could near see the horse smile at the little colts; and he was surprised at the show of action and interest the old pony had reserved, or gained. He was acting near like a two-year-old, and Clint grinned as he watched.

"Daggone his old hide," says the cowboy, "it looks to me like he's good to live and enjoy life for many summers yet"; then thinking strong, he went on, "and maybe in that time he might get to remembering me again—I wonder."

He watched Smoky a while longer and till he got acquainted some, and at last deciding it'd be for the best to let him go, he reined his horse out of the gate and let the bunch run by. The old pony seemed to hesitate some as the bunch filed out. He liked their company mighty well but something held him back; then a horse nickered, and even tho that nicker might not of been meant for him, it was enough to make him decide. He struck out on a high lope and towards the bunch. One of the little colts and full of play waited for him, and nipping the old horse in the flanks, run by his side till the bunch was caught up with—Smoky was *living* again.

Clint sat on his horse and watched the bunch lope out over a ridge and out of sight; and with a last glimpse at the mouse colored rump he grinned a little, but it was a sorry grin, and as he kept a looking the way Smoky had gone, he says: "I wonder if he ever will."

With the green grass growing near an inch a day, Clint wasn't worried much on how old Smoky was making it. He figgered a horse couldn't die if he wanted to, not on that range at that time of the year; but some day soon he was going to try and locate the old horse and find out for sure how he really was. Then a lot of work came on which kept the cowboy from going out soon as he wanted to, and then one morning, bright and early, as he stepped out to get a bucket of water, the morning sun throwed a shadow on the door; and as he stuck his head out a nicker was heard.

Clint dropped his bucket in surprise at what he heard and then seen. For, standing out a ways, slick and shiny, was the old mouse colored horse. The good care the cowboy had handed him, and afterwards, the ramblings over the old home range, had done its work. The heart of Smoky had come to life again, and full size.

Sources

"Memoirs of Conquistador," by Bernal Di' Az Del Castillo, translated by John Ingram Lockhart, 1844.

"The Dun Horse," from *Pawnee Hero Stories and Folk-Tales*, by George Bird Grinnell, 1890.

"The Woman Who Became a Horse," from *Traditions of the Skidi Pawnee: Memoirs of the American Folk-Lore Society*, vol. 8, by George A. Dorsey, 1904.

"The Comanches' Manner of Capturing Wild Horses," from *The Delahoydes: Boy Life on the Old Santa Fe Trail*, by Henry Inman, 1899.

"The Camp of the Wild Horse," from *A Tour on the Prairies*, by Washington Irving, 1832.

"Chu Chu," from *The Bell-Ringer of Angel's and Other Stories*, by Bret Harte, 1894.

"A Chestnut Pony," from *Out of Drowning Valley*, by S. Carleton Jones, 1910.

Wildfire, by Zane Grey, 1916.

"His Love for His Old Gray Horse," from *Ladies' Home Journal*, by Laura Spencer Portor and Charles Marshall Graves, January 1908.

"How Miss Lake's Circus Horses Were Restored," from *Horse Stories and Stories of Other Animals*, by Thomas Wallace Knox, 1890.

"A Ride with a Mad Horse in a Freight-Car," from *Atlantic Monthly*, by W. H. H. Murray, April 1869.

"How Comanche Came into Camp," from *The Master of the Strong Hearts: A Story of Custer's Last Rally*, by Elbridge Streeter Brooks, 1898.

"Soldier Boy—Privately to Himself," "Soldier Boy and the Mexican Plug," "Soldier Boy and Shekels," "Soldier Boy and Shekels Again," "Mongrel and the Other Horse," "Soldier Boy—To Himself," from *A Horse's Tale*, by Mark Twain, 1907.

"The American Cavalry Horse," from *Munsey's Magazine*, by Wilmot E. Ellis, April 1905.

"Anecdotes of American Horses," from *The Family Magazine or Monthly Abstract of General Knowledge*, unknown author, 1841.

"The Cumbersome Horse," from *More Short Sixes*, by H. C. Bunner, 1894.

"A Drummer's Horse," from *Our Dumb Animals*, by R. M. Lockhart, 1912.

Chapter 11 from *White Dandy: Master and I—A Horse's Story*, by Velma Caldwell Melville, 1898.

"The Great Match Race between Eclipse and Sir Henry," from the *American Sporting Magazine*, by "An Old Turfman" (Calwallader R. Colden), July 3, 1830.

"The Story of a Jockey," from *Stories for Boys*, by Richard Harding Davis, 1916.

"World Record Is Set by Man o' War," from the *New York Times*, June 13, 1920.

"How I Bought and Trained Captain," by W. A. Sigsbee, from *The Story of Captain: The Horse with a Human Brain*, by George Wharton James, 1917.

"In Which True Becomes Justin Morgan," from *Justin Morgan, Founder of his Race: The Romantic History of a Horse*, by Eleanor Waring Burnham, 1911.

"White Horse Winter," from *Atlantic Monthly*, by Wilbur Daniel Steele, April 1912.

"Smoky the Cowhorse," by Will James, from novel of the same title, Scribner's, 1926.

"Black Beauty's Early Home," by Anna Sewell, from *Black Beauty*, 1877.

"A Horse's Tale," by Mark Twain, from book of the same title, 1907.

"The Ben-Hur Chariot Race," by Lew Wallace, from the novel *Ben-Hur: A Tale of the Christ*, 1880.

"Old Bill," by Henry C. Wallace, from *Prairie Gold*, 1917.

"Sensations of a Cavalry Charge," by Winston Churchill.

"Philippa's Fox Hunt," by E. OE Somerville and Martin Ross, from *Some Experiences of an Irish R.M.*

"The Chimaera," by Nathaniel Hawthorne, from *Wonder Book for Girls and Boys*, 1851.

"Strider—the Story of a Horse," by Leo Tolstoy.

"Blue Murder," by William Daniel Steele.

"The Horse of Hurricane Reef," by Charles Tenney Jackson.

"The Round-Up," by Theodore Roosevelt, from *Ranch Life and the Hunting Trail*, 1888.

"Esmé," by Saki (H. H. Munro), from *The Chronicles of Clovis*, 1911.

"The Story of the Pony Express," by Glenn D. Bradley.

"Mark Twain's Pony Express Adventure," by Mark Twain, from *Roughing It*.

"The Pacing Mustang," by Ernest Thompson Seton, from *Wild Animals I Have Known*.

"The Maltese Cat," by Rudyard Kipling, from *A Day's Work*.

"Jerry Strann and the Gift Horse," by Max Brand, excerpted from *The Night Horseman*.

"How Blister Got His Name," by John Taintor Foote, from *Blister Jones*, Bobbs-Merrill, 1913.

"Horses," by Stephen Crane, from *The Open Boat and Other Stories*, 1898.

"Memoirs of a Fox-Hunting Man," by Siegfried Sassoon, 1928.

"The Man Who Hunts and Doesn't Like It," by Anthony Trollope, from *Hunting Sketches*.

"Bones," by Helen Busher, from *Conversations with a Prince*.

"Dark Clouds, Then Tall Grass," by Will James, from *Smoky the Cowhorse*, Scribner's, 1926.